FEDERAL RULES OF EVIDENCE

2018–2019
Statutory and Case Supplement

Includes:

Federal Rules of Evidence
Proposed Federal Rules of Evidence
Deleted and Superseded Federal Rules of Evidence
Proposed Amendments to the Rules
Case Notes on *Ohio v. Clark, Peña-Rodriguez v. Colorado,*
Salinas v. Texas, and *Warger v. Shauers*

For use with

Evidence

(Third Edition)

GEORGE FISHER
Judge John Crown Professor of Law
Stanford Law School

Compiled by
Gabriel Schlabach (Third Edition)
Binyamin Blum (Second Edition)
Frederic Bloom (First Edition)

© 2013 LEG, Inc. d/b/a West Academic Publishing
© 2014–2017 LEG, Inc. d/b/a West Academic
© 2018 LEG, Inc. d/b/a West Academic

    444 Cedar Street, Suite 700
    St. Paul, MN 55101
    1-877-888-1330

Printed in the United States of America

ISBN: 978-1-64020-939-8

INTRODUCTION[1]

This pamphlet consists of the Federal Rules of Evidence and materials designed to aid in understanding, construing, and applying them.

Chief Justice Warren in 1965 appointed an advisory committee to draft rules of evidence for the federal courts. The Committee's preliminary draft was published and circulated for comment in 1969. 46 F.R.D. 161. A revised draft was circulated in 1971. 51 F.R.D. 315. In 1972, the Supreme Court prescribed Federal Rules of Evidence, to be effective July 1, 1973. 56 F.R.D. 183. Justice Douglas dissented. Pursuant to the various enabling acts, Chief Justice Burger transmitted the rules to the Congress, which suspended the rules pending further study by Congress. Pub. L. No. 93-12. After extensive study, the Congress enacted the rules into law with various amendments, to become effective July 1, 1975. Pub. L. No. 93-595, 88 Stat. 1926 (Jan. 2, 1975). The occasional amendments and additions that have since been made are reflected in the rules as here presented.

Thus the Federal Rules of Evidence are the product of both the rulemaking process established by the Supreme Court and the legislative process of Congress. Of at least equal importance is the vast collection of common law precedents, with occasional statutes, that constituted the background against which the rules evolved. It can be seen that each of these sources must be taken into consideration in reaching understanding of the rules.

The rules are in the final analysis legislative in nature, and problems of their effect are problems of statutory interpretation. Questions whether interpretive inquiry should be directed to ascertaining the intent of the legislature or the meaning to its audience tend to be minimal, since the rules are directed to a skilled professional audience in the main, in contrast to, say, a criminal statute directed to the public generally. With the rules, intent and meaning tend to come together, with the same interpretive materials relevant to both. The basic relevant interpretive materials are the common law background and the legislative history, with the most significant aspects of the latter consisting of the Advisory Committee's Notes and various congressional reports and debates, briefly described below. To help a reader working sequentially through the legislative

---

[1] This introductory material was prepared by the late Professor Edward W. Cleary, Reporter to the Advisory Committee for the Federal Rules of Evidence. For a more detailed discussion, see Cleary, *Preliminary Notes on Reading the Rules of Evidence*, 57 NEB. L. REV. 908 (1978).

background of any given rule, if a rule was commented upon by reference to subdivisions within that rule, the Advisory Committee notes and reports of House/Senate Committees have been segmented and arranged to display those comments in descending order, by subdivision.

. . .

Rules Prescribed by the Supreme Court. These rules were transmitted by the Court to the Congress, carried the prestige of the Court, and were the Court's exercise of the rulemaking powers granted by the various enabling acts. They constitute the framework and to a large extent also the particulars of the rules enacted by the Congress. Whether and how a Court's rule was amended by the Congress is described in the *Note be Federal Judicial Center* following each rule in the pamphlet.

Advisory Committee's Notes. The notes supported and explained the rules, were circulated with them, and were transmitted to the Congress with the rules. The involved congressional committees and subcommittees were thoroughly familiar with the notes, and except where changes were made in the rules the notes should be taken as the equivalent of a congressional committee report as representing the thinking of the Congress. The pertinent note, or portion thereof, is set forth in the Pamphlet for each rule. Where the Congress returned to an earlier version of the rule, the note is the one that corresponds to that version. Portions no longer relevant because of congressional changes in the rule are omitted.

Congressional Materials. The House took the lead in congressional consideration of the rules. Accordingly, in the Pamphlet any pertinent portion of the *Report of the House Committee on the Judiciary* is the first of the congressional materials under each rule. Senate consideration of the rules chronologically followed that of the House, and as a result any pertinent portion of the *Report of the Senate Committee on the Judiciary* is located under each rule in the Pamphlet after that of the House committee. Where House and Senate passed differing versions of a rule, the difference was resolved by conference, and the *Conference Report* generally concludes the congressional materials. In some instances other congressional materials which are authoritative and helpful are, however, also included.

Some General Observations

Questions as to what a rule really means present probably the most basic problem of interpretation. The language of the rule itself should be taken as the prime source of meaning, read in the light of such context as may be relevant. The most relevant context will often be legislative history, which on occasion may even override an apparently plain and unmistakable meaning of the words of the rule.[2] The result may be startling, as when the Court of Appeals for the District of Columbia Circuit concluded that a conviction for attempted burglary used for impeachment under Rule 609(a) did not involve dishonesty as the language was used in the rule.[3] Yet the opposite conclusion would have been most difficult to reach in view of the legislative history of the rule.[4]

No common law of evidence in principle remains under the rules. "All relevant evidence is admissible except as otherwise provided . . . ."[5] In reality, of course, the common law remains as a source of guidance in identifying problems and suggesting solutions, within the confines of the rules.

A recurring question is that of the extent to which the application of the rules may be extended beyond their express provisions. Some explicit authorizations to courts to invent and create are found, as for example the provision of Rule 501 that privileges "shall be governed by the principles of the common law as they may be interpreted by the courts of the United States in light of reason and experience," and the provisions of Rules 803(24) and 804(b)(5) [now Rule 807] for the restricted admission of hearsay statements not falling within an enumerated exception. A somewhat tighter rein is kept on the judiciary by the rules that obviously contemplate a measure of invention but only within the confines of a stated principle, as in Rule 404(b) where illustrations are given of purposes for which evidence of other crimes may be admitted.

With regard to the more particularized rules, how should parallel situations be treated? Should the rule be regarded as occupying the field exclusively, or should it be extended by

---

[2] The manner of exercise of its legislative powers by the Congress as spelled out in the Constitution is the passing of bills and obtaining the President's approval or overriding his veto. U.S. CONST. art. I, § 7. While this may suggest the irrelevance of legislative history, in the British tradition, the American commitment is contrary, and it can scarcely be denied that the reasoning of those involved is a helpful source of illumination, without having the authority of law.

[3] United States v. Smith, 551 F.2d 348 (D.C. Cir. 1976).

[4] *Id.* at 362.

[5] FED. R. EVID. 402.

analogy to related situations? The answer lies in the purpose of the rule: if the additional situation presents the same problem as that with which the rule was designed to deal, application of the rule is appropriate. For example, under Rule 801(d)(1)(C) an out-of-court identification statement made after viewing a photograph has been held to be governed by the nonhearsay rule specifically applicable to statements made after viewing the accused in person.[6] Or again, the prohibition against testimony by the judge in the trial over which he is presiding, in Rule 605, was extended to preclude testimony by his clerk.[7]

Not to be confused with the foregoing is the judicial engrafting onto a rule of a requirement not set forth in the rule and not supported by legislative history or other relevant context. An example is the engrafting of a requirement that other crimes as proof of intent under Rule 404(b) be proved by clear and convincing evidence, although no such provision is found in the rule.[8]

Rule 102 provides:

These rules shall be construed to secure fairness in administration, elimination of unjustifiable expense and delay, and promotion of growth and development of the law of evidence to the end that the truth may be ascertained and proceedings justly determined.

Entitled "Purpose and Construction," the rule sets a high standard for approaching problems of application and meaning but furnishes small guidance to solving particular questions. The most important aspect of the rule may well be its implicit recognition that rules do not, and cannot, resolve in specific terms a very large proportion of evidentiary uncertainties that may arise, and that solutions must be reached through application of accepted principles of statutory construction.

---

[6] United States v. Lewis, 565 F.2d 1248 (2d Cir. 1977), *cert. denied*, 435 U.S. 973 (1978).

[7] Kennedy v. Great Atl. & Pac. Tea Co., 551 F.2d 593 (5th Cir. 1977), *reh'g denied*, 554 F.2d 475 (1977).

[8] United States v. Beechum, 555 F.2d 487 (5th Cir. 1977), *rev'd*, 582 F.2d 898 (5th Cir. 1978) (en banc), *cert. denied*, 440 U.S. 920 (1979).

TABLE OF CONTENTS

Introduction   i

FEDERAL RULES OF EVIDENCE
FOR UNITED STATES COURTS

ARTICLE I. GENERAL PROVISIONS

101	Scope; Definitions	1
102	Purpose	5
103	Rulings on Evidence	5
104	Preliminary Questions	11
105	Limiting Evidence That Is Not Admissible Against Other Parties or for Other Purposes	17
106	Remainder of or Related Writings or Recorded Statements	18

ARTICLE II. JUDICIAL NOTICE

201	Judicial Notice of Adjudicative Facts	19

ARTICLE III. PRESUMPTIONS IN CIVIL CASES

301	Presumptions in Civil Cases Generally	29
302	Applicability of State Law to Presumptions in Civil Cases	35

ARTICLE IV. RELEVANCE AND ITS LIMITS

401	Test for Relevant Evidence	37
402	General Admissibility of Relevant Evidence	39
403	Excluding Relevant Evidence for Prejudice, Confusion, Waste of Time, or Other Reasons	41
404	Character Evidence; Crimes or Other Acts	43
405	Methods of Proving Character	51
406	Habit; Routine Practice	53
407	Subsequent Remedial Measures	56
408	Compromise Offers and Negotiations	59

409	Offers to Pay Medical and Similar Expenses	67
410	Pleas, Plea Discussions, and Related Statements	68
411	Liability Insurance	78
412	Sex-Offense Cases: The Victim's Sexual Behavior or Predisposition	80
413	Similar Crimes in Sexual-Assault Cases	92
414	Similar Crimes in Child-Molestations Cases	93
415	Similar Acts in Civil Cases Involving Sexual Assault or Child Molestation	94

ARTICLE V. PRIVILEGES

501	Privilege in General	97
502	Attorney–Client Privilege and Work Product; Limitations on Waiver	102

ARTICLE VI. WITNESSES

601	Competency to Testify in General	113
602	Need for Personal Knowledge	115
603	Oath or Affirmation to Testify Truthfully	116
604	Interpreter	117
605	Judge's Competency as a Witness	117
606	Juror's Competency as a Witness	118
607	Who May Impeach a Witness	125
608	A Witness's Character for Truthfulness or Untruthfulness	126
609	Impeachment by Evidence of a Criminal Conviction	131
610	Religious Beliefs or Opinions	146
611	Mode and Order of Examining Witnesses and Presenting Evidence	147
612	Writing Used to Refresh a Witness's Memory	153
613	Witness's Prior Statement	156
614	Court's Calling or Examining a Witness	158
615	Excluding Witnesses	159

ARTICLE VII. OPINIONS AND EXPERT TESTIMONY

701	Opinion Testimony by Lay Witnesses	163
702	Testimony by Expert Witnesses	166
703	Bases for an Expert's Opinion Testimony	175

704	Opinion on an Ultimate Issues	179
705	Disclosing the Facts or Data Underlying an Expert's Opinion	182
706	Court-Appointed Expert Witnesses	184

ARTICLE VIII. HEARSAY

801	Definitions That Apply to This Article; Exclusions from Hearsay	194
802	The Rule Against Hearsay	210
803	Exceptions to the Rule Against Hearsay— Regardless of Whether the Declarant Is Available as a Witness	211
804	Exceptions to the Rule Against Hearsay— When the Declarant Is Unavailable as a Witness	263
805	Hearsay Within Hearsay	282
806	Attacking and Supporting the Declarant's Credibility	283
807	Residual Exception	287

ARTICLE IX. AUTHENTICATION AND IDENTIFICATION

901	Authenticating or Identifying Evidence	289
902	Evidence That Is Self-Authenticating	295
903	Subscribing Witness's Testimony	302

ARTICLE X. CONTENTS OF WRITINGS, RECORDINGS, AND PHOTOGRAPHS

1001	Definitions That Apply to This Article	303
1002	Requirement of the Original	305
1003	Admissibility of Duplicates	307
1004	Admissibility of Other Evidence of Content	308
1005	Copies of Public Records to Prove Content	310
1006	Summaries to Prove Content	311
1007	Testimony or Statement of a Party to Prove Content	311
1008	Functions of the Court and Jury	312

ARTICLE XI. MISCELLANEOUS RULES

1101	Applicability of the Rules	315
1102	Amendments	320
1103	Title	321

TABLE OF CONTENTS

DELETED AND SUPERSEDED MATERIALS

105	Summing Up and Comment by Judge [Not enacted.]	323
301	Presumptions in General [As prescribed by Supreme Court]	324
301	Presumptions in General [As passed by House of Representatives]	324
303	Presumptions in Criminal Cases [Not enacted.]	329
406	Habit; Routine Practice [Subdivision (b) not enacted.]	333
501	Privileges Recognized Only as Provided [Not enacted.]	334
502	Required Reports Privileged by Statute [Not enacted.]	339
503	Lawyer-Client Privilege [Not enacted.]	340
504	Psychotherapist-Patient Privilege [Not enacted.]	346
505	Husband-Wife Privilege [Not enacted.]	351
506	Communications to Clergymen [Not enacted.]	354
507	Political Vote [Not enacted.]	357
508	Trade Secrets [Not enacted.]	358
509	Secrets of State and Other Official Information [Not enacted.]	359
510	Identity of Informer [Not enacted.]	364
511	Waiver of Privilege by Voluntary Disclosure [Not enacted.]	368
512	Privileged Matter Disclosed Under Compulsion or Without Opportunity to Claim Privilege [Not enacted.]	369
513	Comment Upon or Inference From Claim of Privilege; Instruction [Not enacted.]	370
804	Hearsay Exceptions; Declarant Unavailable [Subdivision (b)(2) not enacted.]	372

EVIDENCE RULES RESTYLING PROJECT — 375

Unrestyled and Restyled Federal Rules of Evidence — 380

CASE SUPPLEMENT   499

Warger v. Shauers: Case Note   499

Peña-Rodriguez v. Colorado: Case Note   504

Tanner, Warger, & Peña-Rodriguez: Afterthoughts   510

Miranda and Silence (addressing *Salinas v. Texas*)   512

Ohio v. Clark: Case Note   523

ARTICLE I. GENERAL PROVISIONS

Rule 101.   SCOPE; DEFINITIONS

(a) Scope. These rules apply to proceedings in United States courts. The specific courts and proceedings to which the rules apply, along with exceptions, are set out in Rule 1101.

(b) Definitions. In these rules:

    (1) "civil case" means a civil action or proceeding;

    (2) "criminal case" includes a criminal proceeding;

    (3) "public office" includes a public agency;

    (4) "record" includes a memorandum, report, or data compilation;

    (5) a "rule prescribed by the Supreme Court" means a rule adopted by the Supreme Court under statutory authority; and

    (6) a reference to any kind of written material or any other medium includes electronically stored information.

(Enacted Jan. 2, 1975; as amended Mar. 2, 1987, eff. Oct. 1, 1987; Apr. 25, 1988, eff. Nov. 1, 1988; Apr. 22, 1993, eff. Dec. 1, 1993; as restyled Apr. 26, 2011, eff. Dec. 1, 2011.)

NOTE BY FEDERAL JUDICIAL CENTER

The rule enacted by the Congress is the rule prescribed by the Supreme Court without change.

ADVISORY COMMITTEE'S NOTE

Rule 1101 specifies in detail the courts, proceedings, questions, and stages of proceedings to which the rules apply in whole or in part.

<u>ADVISORY COMMITTEE'S NOTE TO 1993 AMENDMENT TO RULE 101</u>

This revision is made to conform the rule to changes made by the Judicial Improvements Act of 1990.

<u>ADVISORY COMMITTEE NOTE'S TO 2011 RESTYLING OF RULE 101</u>

The language of Rule 101 has been amended, and definitions have been added, as part of the general restyling of the Evidence Rules to make them more easily understood and to make style and terminology consistent throughout the rules. These changes are intended to be stylistic only. There is no intent to change any result in any ruling on evidence admissibility.[1]

The reference to electronically stored information is intended to track the language of Fed. R. Civ. P. 34.

The Style Project

The Evidence Rules are the fourth set of national procedural rules to be restyled. The restyled Rules of Appellate Procedure took effect in 1998. The restyled Rules of Criminal Procedure took effect in 2002. The restyled Rules of Civil Procedure took effect in 2007. The restyled Rules of Evidence apply the same general drafting guidelines and principles used in restyling the Appellate, Criminal, and Civil Rules.

1. General Guidelines.

Guidance in drafting, usage, and style was provided by BRYAN GARNER, GUIDELINES FOR DRAFTING AND EDITING COURT RULES (Admin. Office of the U.S. Courts 1996) and BRYAN GARNER, DICTIONARY OF MODERN LEGAL USAGE (2d ed. 1995). *See also* Joseph Kimble, *Guiding Principles for Restyling the Civil Rules, in* PRELIMINARY DRAFT OF PROPOSED STYLE REVISION OF THE FEDERAL RULES OF CIVIL PROCEDURE, at x (Feb. 2005) (available at

http://www.uscourts.gov/uscourts/RulesAndPolicies/rules/Prelim_draft_proposed_pt1.pdf);

---

[1] [A similar paragraph appears in the Advisory Committee's Note to each of the restyled rules. To avoid repetition, I have omitted this paragraph throughout the volume. Still, the Committee's injunction that it intended no substantive change in restyling the rules applies throughout. I have retained the balance of the Advisory Committee's notes, which address issues peculiar to one or a few of the restyled rules.—GF]

Joseph Kimble, *Lessons in Drafting from the New Federal Rules of Civil Procedure*, 12 SCRIBES J. LEGAL WRITING 25 (2008–2009). For specific commentary on the Evidence restyling project, see Joseph Kimble, *Drafting Examples from the Proposed New Federal Rules of Evidence*, 88 MICH. B.J. 52 (Aug. 2009); 88 MICH. B.J. 46 (Sept. 2009); 88 MICH. B.J. 54 (Oct. 2009); 88 MICH. B.J. 50 (Nov. 2009).

2. Formatting Changes.

Many of the changes in the restyled Evidence Rules result from using format to achieve clearer presentations. The rules are broken down into constituent parts, using progressively indented subparagraphs with headings and substituting vertical for horizontal lists. "Hanging indents" are used throughout. These formatting changes make the structure of the rules graphic and make the restyled rules easier to read and understand even when the words are not changed. Rules 103, 404(b), 606(b), and 612 illustrate the benefits of formatting changes.

3. Changes to Reduce Inconsistent, Ambiguous, Redundant, Repetitive, or Archaic Words.

The restyled rules reduce the use of inconsistent terms that say the same thing in different ways. Because different words are presumed to have different meanings, such inconsistencies can result in confusion. The restyled rules reduce inconsistencies by using the same words to express the same meaning. For example, consistent expression is achieved by not switching between "accused" and "defendant" or between "party opponent" and "opposing party" or between the various formulations of civil and criminal action/case/proceeding.

The restyled rules minimize the use of inherently ambiguous words. For example, the word "shall" can mean "must," "may," or something else, depending on context. The potential for confusion is exacerbated by the fact the word "shall" is no longer generally used in spoken or clearly written English. The restyled rules replace "shall" with "must," "may," or "should," depending on which one the context and established interpretation make correct in each rule.

The restyled rules minimize the use of redundant "intensifiers." These are expressions that attempt to add emphasis, but instead state the obvious and create negative implications for other rules. The absence of intensifiers in the restyled rules does not change their substantive meaning. *See, e.g.*, Rule 104(c) (omitting "in all cases"); Rule 602 (omitting "but need not"); Rule 611(b) (omitting "in the exercise of discretion").

The restyled rules also remove words and concepts that are outdated or redundant.

4. Rule Numbers.

The restyled rules keep the same numbers to minimize the effect on research. Subdivisions have been rearranged within some rules to achieve greater clarity and simplicity.

5. No Substantive Change.

The Committee made special efforts to reject any purported style improvement that might result in a substantive change in the application of a rule. The Committee considered a change to be "substantive" if any of the following conditions were met:

    a. Under the existing practice in any circuit, the change could lead to a different result on a question of admissibility (e.g., a change that requires a court to provide either a less or more stringent standard in evaluating the admissibility of particular evidence);

    b. Under the existing practice in any circuit, it could lead to a change in the procedure by which an admissibility decision is made (e.g., a change in the time in which an objection must be made, or a change in whether a court must hold a hearing on an admissibility question);

    c. The change would restructure a rule in a way that would alter the approach that courts and litigants have used to think about, and argue about, questions of admissibility (e.g., merging Rules 104(a) and 104(b) into a single subdivision); or

    d. The amendment would change a "sacred phrase"—one that has become so familiar in practice that to alter it would be unduly disruptive to practice and expectations. Examples in the Evidence Rules include "unfair prejudice" and "truth of the matter asserted."

Rule 102. PURPOSE

These rules should be construed so as to administer every proceeding fairly, eliminate unjustifiable expense and delay, and promote the development of evidence law, to the end of ascertaining the truth and securing a just determination.

(Enacted Jan. 2, 1975; as restyled Apr. 26, 2011, eff. Dec. 1, 2011.)

NOTE BY FEDERAL JUDICIAL CENTER

The rule enacted by the Congress is the rule prescribed by the Supreme Court without change.

ADVISORY COMMITTEE'S NOTE

For similar provisions see Rule 2 of the Federal Rules of Criminal Procedure, Rule 1 of the Federal Rules of Civil Procedure, California Evidence Code § 2, and New Jersey Evidence Rule 5 (repealed and replaced by New Jersey Rule of Evidence 102 (1993)).

Rule 103. RULINGS ON EVIDENCE

(a) Preserving a Claim of Error. A party may claim error in a ruling to admit or exclude evidence only if the error affects a substantial right of the party and:

(1) if the ruling admits evidence, a party, on the record:

(A) timely objects or moves to strike; and

(B) states the specific ground, unless it was apparent from the context; or

(2) if the ruling excludes evidence, a party informs the court of its substance by an offer of proof, unless the substance was apparent from the context.

(b) Not Needing to Renew an Objection or Offer of Proof. Once the court rules definitively on the record—either before or at trial—a party need not renew an objection or offer of proof to preserve a claim of error for appeal.

(c) Court's Statement About the Ruling; Directing an Offer of Proof. The court may make any statement about the character or form of the evidence, the objection made, and the ruling. The court may direct that an offer of proof be made in question-and-answer form.

(d) Preventing the Jury from Hearing Inadmissible Evidence. To the extent practicable, the court must conduct a jury trial so that inadmissible evidence is not suggested to the jury by any means.

(e) Taking Notice of Plain Error. A court may take notice of a plain error affecting a substantial right, even if the claim of error was not properly preserved.

(Enacted Jan. 2, 1975; as amended Apr. 17, 2000, eff. Dec. 1, 2000; as restyled Apr. 26, 2011, eff. Dec. 1, 2011.)

<u>NOTE BY FEDERAL JUDICIAL CENTER</u>

The rule enacted by the Congress is the rule prescribed by the Supreme Court, amended by substituting "court" in place of "judge," with appropriate pronominal change.

<u>ADVISORY COMMITTEE'S NOTE</u>

Subdivision (a) states the law as generally accepted today. Rulings on evidence cannot be assigned as error unless (1) a substantial right is affected, and (2) the nature of the error was called to the attention of the judge, so as to alert him to the proper course of action and enable opposing counsel to take proper corrective measures. The objection and the offer of proof are the techniques for accomplishing these objectives. For similar provisions see Uniform Rules 4 and 5; California Evidence Code §§ 353 and 354; Kansas Statutes Annotated §§ 60-404 and 60-405. The rule does not purport to change the law with respect to harmless error. *See* 28 U.S.C. § 2111; FED. R. CIV. P. 61; FED. R. CRIM. P. 52; and decisions construing them. The status of constitutional error as harmless or not is treated in *Chapman v. California*, 386 U.S. 18, *reh'g denied*, 386 U.S. 987 (1967).

[**Subdivision (c)**]. The first sentence is the third sentence of Rule 43(c) of the Federal Rules of Civil Procedure virtually verbatim. Its purpose is to reproduce for an appellate court, insofar as possible, a true reflection of what occurred in the trial court. The second sentence is in part derived from the final sentence of Rule 43(c).[2] It is designed to resolve doubts as to what testimony the witness would have in fact given, and, in nonjury cases, to provide the appellate court with material for a possible final disposition of the case in the event of reversal of a ruling which excluded evidence. *See* 5 MOORE'S FEDERAL PRACTICE § 43.11 (2d ed. 1968). Application is made discretionary in view of the practical impossibility of formulating a satisfactory rule in mandatory terms.

[**Subdivision (d)**]. This subdivision proceeds on the supposition that a ruling which excludes evidence in a jury case is likely to be a pointless procedure if the excluded evidence nevertheless comes to the attention of the jury. Bruton v. United States, 391 U.S. 123 (1968). Rule 43(c) of the Federal Rules of Civil Procedure[2] provides: "The court may require the offer to be made out of the hearing of the jury." *In re McConnell*, 370 U.S. 230 (1962), left some doubt whether questions on which an offer is based must first be asked in the presence of the jury. The subdivision answers in the negative. The judge can foreclose a particular line of testimony and counsel can protect his record without a series of questions before the jury, designed at best to waste time and at worst "to waft into the jury box" the very matter sought to be excluded.

[**Subdivision (e)**]. This wording of the plain error principle is from Rule 52(b) of the Federal Rules of Criminal Procedure. While judicial unwillingness to be constr[i]cted by mechanical breakdowns of the adversary system has been more pronounced in criminal cases, there is no scarcity of decisions to the same effect in civil cases. *See generally* Campbell, *Extent to Which Courts of Review Will Consider Questions Not Properly Raised and Preserved*, 7 WIS. L. REV. 91, 160 (1932); Vestal, *Sua Sponte Consideration in Appellate Review*, 27 FORDHAM L. REV. 477 (1958–1959); 64 HARV. L. REV. 652 (1951). In the nature of things the application of the plain error rule will be more likely with respect to the admission of evidence than to exclusion, since failure to comply with normal requirements of offers of proof is likely to produce a record which simply does not disclose the error.

---

[2] Rule 43(c) of the Federal Rules of Civil Procedure was deleted by order of the Supreme Court entered on November 20, 1972, 93 S. Ct. 3073, 3075–3077, which action was affirmed by the Congress in Pub. L. No. 93-595, § 3 (Jan. 2, 1975).

The amendment applies to all rulings on evidence whether they occur at or before trial, including so-called "in limine" rulings. One of the most difficult questions arising from in limine and other evidentiary rulings is whether a losing party must renew an objection or offer of proof when the evidence is or would be offered at trial, in order to preserve a claim of error on appeal. Courts have taken differing approaches to this question. Some courts have held that a renewal at the time the evidence is to be offered at trial is always required. *See, e.g.,* Collins v. Wayne Corp., 621 F.2d 777 (5th Cir. 1980). Some courts have taken a more flexible approach, holding that renewal is not required if the issue decided is one that (1) was fairly presented to the trial court for an initial ruling, (2) may be decided as a final matter before the evidence is actually offered, and (3) was ruled on definitively by the trial judge. *See, e.g.,* Rosenfeld v. Basquiat, 78 F.3d 84 (2d Cir. 1996) (admissibility of former testimony under the Dead Man's Statute; renewal not required). Other courts have distinguished between objections to evidence, which must be renewed when evidence is offered, and offers of proof, which need not be renewed after a definitive determination is made that the evidence is inadmissible. *See, e.g.,* Fusco v. General Motors Corp., 11 F.3d 259 (1st Cir. 1993). Another court, aware of this Committee's proposed amendment, has adopted its approach. Wilson v. Williams, 182 F.3d 562 (7th Cir. 1999) (en banc). Differing views on this question create uncertainty for litigants and unnecessary work for the appellate courts.

The amendment provides that a claim of error with respect to a definitive ruling is preserved for review when the party has otherwise satisfied the objection or offer of proof requirements of Rule 103(a). When the ruling is definitive, a renewed objection or offer of proof at the time the evidence is to be offered is more a formalism than a necessity. *See* FED. R. CIV. P. 46 (formal exceptions unnecessary); FED. R. CR. P. 51 (same); United States v. Mejia–Alarcon, 995 F.2d 982, 986 (10th Cir. 1993) ("Requiring a party to renew an objection when the district court has issued a definitive ruling on a matter that can be fairly decided before trial would be in the nature of a formal exception and therefore unnecessary."). On the other hand, when the trial court appears to have reserved its ruling or to have indicated that the ruling is provisional, it makes sense to require the party to bring the issue to the court's attention subsequently. *See, e.g.,* United States v. Vest, 116 F.3d 1179, 1188 (7th Cir. 1997) (where the trial court ruled in limine that testimony from defense witnesses could not be admitted, but allowed the defendant to seek leave at trial to call the witnesses should their testimony turn out to be relevant, the defendant's failure to seek such leave at trial meant that it was "too late to reopen the issue now on appeal"); United States v. Valenti, 60 F.3d 941 (2d Cir. 1995) (failure to proffer evidence at trial waives any claim of error where the trial judge had stated that he would reserve judgment on the in limine motion until he had heard the trial evidence).

The amendment imposes the obligation on counsel to clarify whether an in limine or other evidentiary ruling is definitive when there is doubt on that point. *See, e.g.,* Walden v. Georgia–Pacific Corp., 126 F.3d 506, 520 (3d Cir. 1997) (although "the district court told plaintiffs' counsel not to reargue every ruling, it did not countermand its clear opening statement that all of its rulings were tentative, and counsel never requested clarification, as he might have done").

Even where the court's ruling is definitive, nothing in the amendment prohibits the court from revisiting its decision when the evidence is to be offered. If the court changes its initial ruling, or if the opposing party violates the terms of the initial ruling, objection must be made when the evidence is offered to preserve the claim of error for appeal. The error, if any, in such a situation occurs only when the evidence is offered and admitted. U.S. Aviation Underwriters, Inc. v. Olympia Wings, Inc., 896 F.2d 949, 956 (5th Cir. 1990) ("objection is required to preserve error when an opponent, or the court itself, violates a motion in limine that was granted"); United States v. Roenigk, 810 F.2d 809 (8th Cir. 1987) (claim of error was not preserved where the defendant failed to object at trial to secure the benefit of a favorable advance ruling).

A definitive advance ruling is reviewed in light of the facts and circumstances before the trial court at the time of the ruling. If the relevant facts and circumstances change materially after the advance ruling has been made, those facts and circumstances cannot be relied upon on appeal unless they have been brought to the attention of the trial court by way of a renewed, and timely, objection, offer of proof, or motion to strike. *See* Old Chief v. United States, 519 U.S. 172, 182 n.6 (1997) ("It is important that a reviewing court evaluate the trial court's decision from its perspective when it had to rule and not indulge in review by hindsight."). Similarly, if the court decides in an advance ruling that proffered evidence is admissible subject to the eventual introduction by the proponent of a foundation for the evidence, and that foundation is never provided, the opponent cannot claim error based on the failure to establish the foundation unless the opponent calls that failure to the court's attention by a timely motion to strike or other suitable motion. *See* Huddleston v. United States, 485 U.S. 681, 690 n.7 (1988) ("It is, of course, not the responsibility of the judge *sua sponte* to ensure that the foundation evidence is offered; the objector must move to strike the evidence if at the close of the trial the offeror has failed to satisfy the condition.").

Nothing in the amendment is intended to affect the provisions of Federal Rule of Civil Procedure 72(a) or 28 U.S.C. § 636(b)(1) pertaining to nondispositive pretrial rulings by magistrate judges in proceedings that are not before a magistrate judge by consent of the parties. Federal Rule of Civil Procedure 72(a) provides that a party who fails to file a written objection to a magistrate judge's nondispositive order within ten days of receiving a copy "may not thereafter assign as error a defect" in the order. 28 U.S.C. § 636(b)(1) provides that any party "may serve and file written objections to such proposed findings and recommendations as provided by rules of court" within ten days of receiving a copy of the order. Several courts have held that a party must comply with this statutory provision in order to preserve a claim of error. *See, e.g.*, Wells v. Shriners Hosp., 109 F.3d 198, 200 (4th Cir. 1997) ("In this circuit, as in others, a party 'may' file objections within ten days or he may not, as he chooses, but he 'shall' do so if he wishes further consideration."). When Federal Rule of Civil Procedure 72(a) or 28 U.S.C. § 636(b)(1) is operative, its requirement must be satisfied in order for a party to preserve a claim of error on appeal, even where Evidence Rule [103(b)] would not require a subsequent objection or offer of proof.

Nothing in the amendment is intended to affect the rule set forth in *Luce v. United States,* 469 U.S. 38 (1984), and its progeny. The amendment provides that an objection or offer of proof need not be renewed to preserve a claim of error with respect to a definitive pretrial ruling. *Luce* answers affirmatively a separate question: whether a criminal defendant must testify at trial in order to preserve a claim of error predicated upon a trial court's decision to admit the defendant's prior convictions for impeachment. The *Luce* principle has been extended by many lower courts to other situations. *See* United States v. DiMatteo, 759 F.2d 831 (11th Cir. 1985) (applying *Luce* where the defendant's witness would be impeached with evidence offered under Rule 608); *see also* United States v. Goldman, 41 F.3d 785, 788 (1st Cir. 1994) ("Although *Luce* involved impeachment by conviction under Rule 609, the reasons given by the Supreme Court for requiring the defendant to testify apply with full force to the kind of Rule 403 and 404 objections that are advanced by Goldman in this case."); Palmieri v. DeFaria, 88 F.3d 136 (2d Cir. 1996) (where the plaintiff decided to take an adverse judgment rather than challenge an advance ruling by putting on evidence at trial, the in limine ruling would not be reviewed on appeal); United States v. Ortiz, 857 F.2d 900 (2d Cir. 1988) (where uncharged misconduct is ruled admissible if the defendant pursues a certain defense, the defendant must actually pursue that defense at trial in order to preserve a claim of error on appeal); United States v. Bond, 87 F.3d 695 (5th Cir. 1996) (where the trial court rules in limine that the defendant would waive his Fifth Amendment privilege were he to testify, the defendant must take the stand and testify in order to challenge that ruling on appeal).

The amendment does not purport to answer whether a party who objects to evidence that the court finds admissible in a definitive ruling, and who then offers the evidence to "remove the sting" of its anticipated prejudicial effect, thereby waives the right to appeal the trial court's ruling. *See, e.g.,* United States v. Fisher, 106 F.3d 622 (5th Cir. 1997) (where the trial judge ruled in limine that the government could use a prior conviction to impeach the defendant if he testified, the defendant did not waive his right to appeal by introducing the conviction on direct examination); Judd v. Rodman, 105 F.3d 1339 (11th Cir. 1997) (an objection made in limine is sufficient to preserve a claim of error when the movant, as a matter of trial strategy, presents the objectionable evidence herself on direct examination to minimize its prejudicial effect); Gill v. Thomas, 83 F.3d 537, 540 (1st Cir. 1996) ("[B]y offering the misdemeanor evidence himself, Gill waived his opportunity to object and thus did not preserve the issue for appeal."); United States v. Williams, 939 F.2d 721 (9th Cir. 1991) (objection to impeachment evidence was waived where the defendant was impeached on direct examination).

Rule 104.   PRELIMINARY QUESTIONS

(a) In General. The court must decide any preliminary question about whether a witness is qualified, a privilege exists, or evidence is admissible. In so deciding, the court is not bound by evidence rules, except those on privilege.

(b) Relevance That Depends on a Fact. When the relevance of evidence depends on whether a fact exists, proof must be introduced sufficient to support a finding that the fact does exist. The court may admit the proposed evidence on the condition that the proof be introduced later.

(c) Conducting a Hearing So That the Jury Cannot Hear It. The court must conduct any hearing on a preliminary question so that the jury cannot hear it if:

(1) the hearing involves the admissibility of a confession;

(2) a defendant in a criminal case is a witness and so requests; or

(3) justice so requires.

(d) Cross-Examining a Defendant in a Criminal Case. By testifying on a preliminary question, a defendant in a criminal case does not become subject to cross-examination on other issues in the case.

(e) Evidence Relevant to Weight and Credibility. This rule does not limit a party's right to introduce before the jury evidence that is relevant to the weight or credibility of other evidence.

(Enacted Jan. 2, 1975; as amended Mar. 2, 1987, eff. Oct. 1, 1987; as restyled Apr. 26, 2011, eff. Dec. 1, 2011.)

NOTE BY FEDERAL JUDICIAL CENTER

The rule enacted by the Congress is the rule prescribed by the Supreme Court, amended by substituting "court" in place of "judge," with appropriate pronominal change, and by adding to subdivision (c) the concluding phrase, "or when an accused is a witness, if he so requests."[3]

ADVISORY COMMITTEE'S NOTE TO RULE 104(a)–(c)

Subdivision (a). The applicability of a particular rule of evidence often depends upon the existence of a condition. Is the alleged expert a qualified physician? Is a witness whose former testimony is offered unavailable? Was a stranger present during a conversation between attorney and client? In each instance the admissibility of evidence will turn upon the answer to the question of the existence of the condition. Accepted practice, incorporated in the rule, places on the judge the responsibility for these determinations. MCCORMICK § 53; MORGAN, BASIC PROBLEMS OF EVIDENCE 45–50 (1962).

To the extent that these inquiries are factual, the judge acts as a trier of fact. Often, however, rulings on evidence call for an evaluation in terms of a legally set standard. Thus when a hearsay

---

[3] The effect of the amendment was to restore language included in the 1971 Revised Draft of the Proposed Rules but deleted before the rules were presented to and prescribed by the Supreme Court.

statement is offered as a declaration against interest, a decision must be made whether it possesses the required against-interest characteristics. These decisions, too, are made by the judge.

In view of these considerations, this subdivision refers to preliminary requirements generally by the broad term "questions," without attempt at specification.

This subdivision is of general application. It must, however, be read as subject to the special provisions for "conditional relevancy" in subdivision (b) and those for confessions in subdivision (c).

If the question is factual in nature, the judge will of necessity receive evidence pro and con on the issue. The rule provides that the rules of evidence in general do not apply to this process. MCCORMICK § 53, at 123 n.8, points out that the authorities are "scattered and inconclusive," and observes:

> Should the exclusionary law of evidence, "the child of the jury system" in Thayer's phrase, be applied to this hearing before the judge? Sound sense backs the view that it should not, and that the judge should be empowered to hear any relevant evidence, such as affidavits or other reliable hearsay.

This view is reinforced by practical necessity in certain situations. An item, offered and objected to, may itself be considered in ruling on admissibility, though not yet admitted in evidence. Thus the content of an asserted declaration against interest must be considered in ruling whether it is against interest. Again, common practice calls for considering the testimony of a witness, particularly a child, in determining competency. Another example is the requirement of Rule 602 dealing with personal knowledge. In the case of hearsay, it is enough, if the declarant "so far as appears [has] had an opportunity to observe the fact declared." MCCORMICK § 10, at 19.

If concern is felt over the use of affidavits by the judge in preliminary hearings on admissibility, attention is directed to the many important judicial determinations made on the basis of affidavits. Rule 47 of the Federal Rules of Criminal Procedure provides:

> An application to the court for an order shall be by motion . . . . It may be supported by affidavit.

The Rules of Civil Procedure are more detailed. Rule [43(c)], dealing with motions generally, provides:

When a motion is based on facts not appearing of record the court may hear the matter on affidavits presented by the respective parties, but the court may direct that the matter be heard wholly or partly on oral testimony or depositions.

Rule 4(*l*) provides for proof of service by affidavit. Rule 56 provides in detail for the entry of summary judgment based on affidavits. Affidavits may supply the foundation for temporary restraining orders under Rule 65(b).

The study made for the California Law Revision Commission recommended an amendment to Uniform Rule 2 as follows:

In the determination of the issue aforesaid [preliminary determination], exclusionary rules shall not apply, subject, however, to Rule 45 and any valid claim of privilege.

Tentative Recommendation and a Study Relating to the Uniform Rules of Evidence (Article VIII, Hearsay), *in* CAL. LAW REVISION COMM'N, REP., REC. & STUDIES 470 (1962). The proposal was not adopted in the California Evidence Code. The Uniform Rules are likewise silent on the subject. However, New Jersey Evidence Rule 8(1) (repealed and replaced by New Jersey Rule of Evidence 104(a) (1993)), dealing with preliminary inquiry by the judge, provides:

In his determination the rules of evidence shall not apply except for Rule 4 [exclusion on grounds of confusion, etc.] or a valid claim of privilege.

Subdivision (b). In some situations, the relevancy of an item of evidence, in the large sense, depends upon the existence of a particular preliminary fact. Thus when a spoken statement is relied upon to prove notice to X, it is without probative value unless X heard it. Or if a letter purporting to be from Y is relied upon to establish an admission by him, it has no probative value unless Y wrote or authorized it. Relevance in this sense has been labeled "conditional relevancy." MORGAN, BASIC PROBLEMS OF EVIDENCE 45–46 (1962). Problems arising in connection with it are to be distinguished from problems of logical relevancy, e.g., evidence in a murder case that accused on the day before purchased a weapon of the kind used in the killing, treated in Rule 401.

If preliminary questions of conditional relevancy were determined solely by the judge, as provided in subdivision (a), the functioning of the jury as a trier of fact would be greatly restricted and in some cases virtually destroyed. These are appropriate questions for juries. Accepted treatment, as provided in the rule, is consistent with that given fact questions generally. The judge makes a preliminary determination whether the foundation evidence is sufficient to support a finding of fulfillment of the condition. If so, the item is admitted. If after all the evidence on the issue is in, pro and con, the jury could reasonably conclude that fulfillment of the condition is not[4] established, the issue is for them. If the evidence is not such as to allow a finding, the judge withdraws the matter from their consideration. MORGAN, *supra*; CAL. EVID. CODE § 403; N.J. EVID. R. 8(2) (repealed and replaced by N.J. R. EVID. 104(b) (1993)); *see also* UNIF. R. EVID. 19 and 67.

The order of proof here, as generally, is subject to the control of the judge.

Subdivision (c). Preliminary hearings on the admissibility of confessions must be conducted outside the hearing of the jury. *See* Jackson v. Denno, 378 U.S. 368 (1964).[5] Otherwise, detailed treatment of when preliminary matters should be heard outside the hearing of the jury is not feasible. The procedure is time consuming. Not infrequently the same evidence which is relevant to the issue of establishment of fulfillment of a condition precedent to admissibility is also relevant to weight or credibility, and time is saved by taking foundation proof in the presence of the jury. Much evidence on preliminary questions, though not relevant to jury issues, may be heard by the jury with no adverse effect. A great deal must be left to the discretion of the judge who will act as the interests of justice require.

<u>REPORT OF THE HOUSE COMMITTEE ON THE JUDICIARY</u>

Rule 104(c) as submitted to the Congress provided that hearings on the admissibility of confessions shall be conducted outside the presence of the jury and hearings on all other preliminary matters should be so conducted when the interests of justice require. The Committee amended the rule to provide that where an accused is a witness as to a preliminary matter, he has the right, upon his request, to be heard outside the jury's presence. Although recognizing that in some cases duplication of evidence would occur and that the procedure could be subject to abuse, the Committee

---

[4] [As I suggest in the casebook in the Afterthoughts to *Cox v. State* at pages 41 to 42, this "not" is almost certainly an error. Try reading this sentence without it.—GF]

[5] At this point the Advisory Committee's Note to the 1971 Revised Draft contained the sentence, "Also, due regard for the right of an accused not to testify generally in the case requires that he be given an option to testify out of the presence of the jury upon preliminary matters." The statement was deleted in view of the deletion from the rule, mentioned in [footnote 3].

believed that a proper regard for the right of an accused not to testify generally in the case dictates that he be given an option to testify out of the presence of the jury on preliminary matters.

The Committee construes the second sentence of subdivision (c) as applying to civil actions and proceedings as well as to criminal cases, and on this assumption has left the sentence unamended.

ADVISORY COMMITTEE'S NOTE TO RULE 104(d)

Subdivision (d). The limitation upon cross-examination is designed to encourage participation by the accused in the determination of preliminary matters. He may testify concerning them without exposing himself to cross-examination generally. The provision is necessary because of the breadth of cross-examination [possible] under Rule 611(b).

The rule does not address itself to questions of the subsequent use of testimony given by an accused at a hearing on a preliminary matter. *See* Walder v. United States, 347 U.S. 62 (1954); Simmons v. United States, 390 U.S. 377 (1968); Harris v. New York, 401 U.S. 222 (1971).

REPORT OF THE SENATE COMMITTEE ON THE JUDICIARY

Under Rule 104(c) the hearing on a preliminary matter may at times be conducted in front of the jury. Should an accused testify in such a hearing, waiving his privilege against self-incrimination as to the preliminary issue, Rule 104(d) provides that he will not generally be subject to cross-examination as to any other issue. This rule is not, however, intended to immunize the accused from cross-examination where, in testifying about a preliminary issue, he injects other issues into the hearing. If he could not be cross-examined about any issues gratuitously raised by him beyond the scope of the preliminary matters, injustice might result. Accordingly, in order to prevent any such unjust result, the Committee intends the rule to be construed to provide that the accused may subject himself to cross-examination as to issues raised by his own testimony upon a preliminary matter before a jury.

ADVISORY COMMITTEE'S NOTE TO RULE 104(e)

Subdivision (e). For similar provisions see Uniform Rule 8; California Evidence Code § 406; Kansas Statutes Annotated § 60-408; New Jersey Evidence Rule 8(1) (repealed and replaced by New Jersey Rule of Evidence 104(e) (1993)).

Rule 105.   LIMITING EVIDENCE THAT IS NOT ADMISSIBLE AGAINST OTHER PARTIES OR FOR OTHER PURPOSES

If the court admits evidence that is admissible against a party or for a purpose—but not against another party or for another purpose—the court, on timely request, must restrict the evidence to its proper scope and instruct the jury accordingly.

(Enacted Jan. 2, 1975; as restyled Apr. 26, 2011, eff. Dec. 1, 2011.)

NOTE BY FEDERAL JUDICIAL CENTER

The rule enacted by the Congress is the rule prescribed by the Supreme Court as Rule 106, amended by substituting "court" in place of "judge." Rule 105 as prescribed by the Court, which was deleted from the rules enacted by the Congress, is set forth in the appendix hereto, together with a statement of the reasons for the deletion.

ADVISORY COMMITTEE'S NOTE

A close relationship exists between this rule and Rule 403 which . . . [provides for] exclusion when "probative value is substantially outweighed by the danger of unfair prejudice, confusion of the issues, or misleading the jury." The present rule recognizes the practice of admitting evidence for a limited purpose and instructing the jury accordingly. The availability and effectiveness of this practice must be taken into consideration in reaching a decision whether to exclude for unfair prejudice under Rule 403. In *Bruton v. United States*, 391 U.S. 123 (1968), the Court ruled that a limiting instruction did not effectively protect the accused against the prejudicial effect of admitting in evidence the confession of a codefendant which implicated him. The decision does not, however, bar the use of limited admissibility with an instruction where the risk of prejudice is less serious.

Similar provisions are found in Uniform Rule 6; California Evidence Code § 355; Kansas Statutes Annotated § 60-406; New Jersey Evidence Rule 6 (repealed and replaced by New Jersey Rule of Evidence 105 (1993)). The wording of the present rule differs, however, in repelling any implication that limiting or curative instructions are sufficient in all situations.

<u>REPORT OF THE HOUSE COMMITTEE ON THE JUDICIARY</u>

Rule 106 as submitted by the Supreme Court [now Rule 105] dealt with the subject of evidence which is admissible as to one party or for one purpose but is not admissible against another party or for another purpose. The Committee adopted this rule without change on the understanding that it does not affect the authority of a court to order a severance in a multi-defendant case.

Rule 106.   **REMAINDER OF OR RELATED WRITINGS OR RECORDED STATEMENTS**

If a party introduces all or part of a writing or recorded statement, an adverse party may require the introduction, at that time, of any other part—or any other writing or recorded statement—that in fairness ought to be considered at the same time.

(Enacted Jan. 2, 1975; as amended Mar. 2, 1987, eff. Oct. 1, 1987; as restyled Apr. 26, 2011, eff. Dec. 1, 2011.)

<u>NOTE BY FEDERAL JUDICIAL CENTER</u>

The rule enacted by the Congress is the rule prescribed by the Supreme Court as Rule 107 without change.

<u>ADVISORY COMMITTEE'S NOTE</u>

The rule is an expression of the rule of completeness. MCCORMICK § 56. It is manifested as to depositions in Rule 32(a)(4) of the Federal Rules of Civil Procedure, of which the proposed rule is substantially a restatement.

The rule is based on two considerations. The first is the misleading impression created by taking matters out of context. The second is the inadequacy of repair work when delayed to a point later in the trial. *See* MCCORMICK § 56; CAL. EVID. CODE § 356. The rule does not in any way circumscribe the right of the adversary to develop the matter on cross-examination or as part of his own case.

For practical reasons, the rule is limited to writings and recorded statements and does not apply to conversations.

ARTICLE II. JUDICIAL NOTICE

Rule 201.   JUDICIAL NOTICE OF ADJUDICATIVE FACTS

(a) Scope. This rule governs judicial notice of an adjudicative fact only, not a legislative fact.

(b) Kinds of Facts That May Be Judicially Noticed. The court may judicially notice a fact that is not subject to reasonable dispute because it:

(1) is generally known within the trial court's territorial jurisdiction; or

(2) can be accurately and readily determined from sources whose accuracy cannot reasonably be questioned.

(c) Taking Notice. The court:

(1) may take judicial notice on its own; or

(2) must take judicial notice if a party requests it and the court is supplied with the necessary information.

(d) Timing. The court may take judicial notice at any stage of the proceeding.

(e) Opportunity to Be Heard. On timely request, a party is entitled to be heard on the propriety of taking judicial notice and the nature of the fact to be noticed. If the court takes judicial notice before notifying a party, the party, on request, is still entitled to be heard.

(f) Instructing the Jury. In a civil case, the court must instruct the jury to accept the noticed fact as conclusive. In a criminal case, the court must instruct the jury that it may or may not accept the noticed fact as conclusive.

(Enacted Jan. 2, 1975; as restyled Apr. 26, 2011, eff. Dec. 1, 2011.)

<u>NOTE BY FEDERAL JUDICIAL CENTER</u>

The rule enacted by the Congress is the rule prescribed by the Supreme Court with the following changes:

In subdivisions (c) and (d) the words "judge or" before "court" were deleted.

[Subdivision (f)] as it is shown was substituted in place of, "The judge shall instruct the jury to accept as established any facts judicially noticed." The substituted language is from the 1969 Preliminary Draft. 46 F.R.D. 161, 195.

<u>ADVISORY COMMITTEE'S NOTE</u>

Subdivision (a). This is the only evidence rule on the subject of judicial notice. It deals only with judicial notice of "adjudicative" facts. No rule deals with judicial notice of "legislative" facts. Judicial notice of matters of foreign law is treated in Rule 44.1 of the Federal Rules of Civil Procedure and Rule 26.1 of the Federal Rules of Criminal Procedure.

The omission of any treatment of legislative facts results from fundamental differences between adjudicative facts and legislative facts. Adjudicative facts are simply the facts of the particular case. Legislative facts, on the other hand, are those which have relevance to legal reasoning and the lawmaking process, whether in the formulation of a legal principle or ruling by a judge or court or in the enactment of a legislative body. The terminology was coined by Professor Kenneth Davis in his article *An Approach to Problems of Evidence in the Administrative Process*, 55 HARV. L. REV. 364, 404–07 (1942). The following discussion draws extensively upon his writings. In addition, see the same author's *Judicial Notice*, 55 COLUM. L. REV. 945 (1955); ADMINISTRATIVE LAW TREATISE ch. 15 (1958); *A System of Judicial Notice Based on Fairness and Convenience, in* PERSPECTIVES OF LAW 69 (1964).

The usual method of establishing adjudicative facts is through the introduction of evidence, ordinarily consisting of the testimony of witnesses. If particular facts are outside the area of reasonable controversy, this process is dispensed with as unnecessary. A high degree of indisputability is the essential prerequisite.

Legislative facts are quite different. As Professor Davis says:

My opinion is that judge-made law would stop growing if judges, in thinking about questions of law and policy, were forbidden to take into account the facts they believe, as distinguished from facts which are "clearly ... within the domain of the indisputable." Facts most needed in thinking about difficult problems of law and policy have a way of being outside the domain of the clearly indisputable.

A System of Judicial Notice Based on Fairness and Convenience, supra, at 82.

An illustration is *Hawkins v. United States,* 358 U.S. 74 (1958), in which the Court refused to discard the common law rule that one spouse could not testify against the other, saying, "Adverse testimony given in criminal proceedings would, we think, be likely to destroy almost any marriage." This conclusion has a large intermixture of fact, but the factual aspect is scarcely "indisputable." *See* Hutchins & Slesinger, *Some Observations on the Law of Evidence—Family Relations,* 13 MINN. L. REV. 675 (1929). If the destructive effect of the giving of adverse testimony by a spouse is not indisputable, should the Court have refrained from considering it in the absence of supporting evidence?

If the Model Code or the Uniform Rules had been applicable, the Court would have been barred from thinking about the essential factual ingredient of the problems before it, and such a result would be obviously intolerable. What the law needs at its growing points is more, not less, judicial thinking about the factual ingredients of problems of what the law ought to be, and the needed facts are seldom "clearly" indisputable.

A System of Judicial Notice Based on Fairness and Convenience, supra, at 83.

Professor Morgan gave the following description of the methodology of determining domestic law:

In determining the content or applicability of a rule of domestic law, the judge is unrestricted in his investigation and conclusion. He may reject the propositions of either party or of both parties. He may consult the sources of pertinent data to which they refer, or he may refuse to do so. He may make an independent search for persuasive data or rest content with what he has or what the parties present. . . . [T]he parties do no more than to assist; they control no part of the process.

Morgan, *Judicial Notice,* 57 HARV. L. REV. 269, 270–71 (1944).

This is the view which should govern judicial access to legislative facts. It renders inappropriate any limitation in the form of indisputability, any formal requirements of notice other than those already inherent in affording opportunity to hear and be heard and exchanging briefs, and any requirement of formal findings at any level. It should, however, leave open the possibility of introducing evidence through regular channels in appropriate situations. See *Borden's Farm Products Co. v. Baldwin*, 293 U.S. 194 (1934), where the cause was remanded for the taking of evidence as to the economic conditions and trade practices underlying the New York Milk Control Law.

Similar considerations govern the judicial use of non-adjudicative facts in ways other than formulating laws and rules. Thayer described them as a part of the judicial reasoning process.

In conducting a process of judicial reasoning, as of other reasoning, not a step can be taken without assuming something which has not been proved; and the capacity to do this with competent judgment and efficiency, is imputed to judges and juries as part of their necessary mental outfit.

THAYER, PRELIMINARY TREATISE ON EVIDENCE 279–80 (1898).

As Professor Davis points out, *A System of Judicial Notice Based on Fairness and Convenience,* in PERSPECTIVES OF LAW 69, 73 (1964), every case involves the use of hundreds or thousands of non-evidence facts. When a witness in an automobile accident case says "car," everyone, judge and jury included, furnishes, from non-evidence sources within himself, the supplementing information that the "car" is an automobile, not a railroad car, that it is self-propelled, probably by an internal combustion engine, that it may be assumed to have four wheels with pneumatic rubber tires, and so on. The judicial process cannot construct every case from scratch, like Descartes creating a world based on the postulate *Cogito, ergo sum*. These items could not possibly be introduced into evidence, and no one suggests that they be. Nor are they appropriate subjects for any formalized treatment of judicial notice of facts. *See* Levin & Levy, *Persuading the Jury with Facts Not in Evidence: The Fiction–Science Spectrum*, 105 U. PA. L. REV. 139 (1956).

Another aspect of what Thayer had in mind is the use of non-evidence facts to appraise or assess the adjudicative facts of the case. Pairs of cases from two jurisdictions illustrate this use and also the difference between non-evidence facts thus used and adjudicative facts. In *People v. Strook*, 347 Ill. 460 (1932), venue in Cook County had been held not established by testimony that the crime was committed at 7956 South Chicago Avenue, since judicial notice would not be taken that the address was in Chicago. However, the same court subsequently ruled that venue in Cook County was established by testimony that a crime occurred at 8900 South Anthony Avenue, since notice would be taken of the common practice of omitting the name of the city when speaking of local addresses, and the witness was testifying in Chicago. People v. Pride, 16 Ill. 2d 82 (1959). And in *Hughes v. Vestal*, 264 N.C. 500 (1965), the Supreme Court of North Carolina disapproved the trial judge's admission in evidence of a state-published table of automobile stopping distances on the basis of judicial notice, though the court itself had referred to the same table in an earlier case in a "rhetorical and illustrative" way in determining that the defendant could not have stopped her car in time to avoid striking a child who suddenly appeared in the highway and that a nonsuit was properly granted. Ennis v. Dupree, 262 N.C. 224 (1964); *see also* Brown v. Hale, 263 N.C. 176 (1964); Clayton v. Rimmer, 262 N.C. 302 (1964). It is apparent that this use of non-evidence facts in evaluating the adjudicative facts of the case is not an appropriate subject for a formalized judicial notice treatment.

In view of these considerations, the regulation of judicial notice of facts by the present rule extends only to adjudicative facts.

What, then, are "adjudicative" facts? Davis refers to them as those "which relate to the parties," or more fully:

> When a court or an agency finds facts concerning the immediate parties—who did what, where, when, how, and with what motive or intent—the court or agency is performing an adjudicative function, and the facts are conveniently called adjudicative facts . . . .

> Stated in other terms, the adjudicative facts are those to which the law is applied in the process of adjudication. They are the facts that normally go to the jury in a jury case. They relate to the parties, their activities, their properties, their businesses.

2 ADMINISTRATIVE LAW TREATISE 353.

Subdivision (b). With respect to judicial notice of adjudicative facts, the tradition has been one of caution in requiring that the matter be beyond reasonable controversy. This tradition of circumspection appears to be soundly based, and no reason to depart from it is apparent. As Professor Davis says:

> The reason we use trial-type procedure, I think, is that we make the practical judgment, on the basis of experience, that

taking evidence, subject to cross-examination and rebuttal, is the best way to resolve controversies involving disputes of adjudicative facts, that is, facts pertaining to the parties. The reason we require a determination on the record is that we think fair procedure in resolving disputes of adjudicative facts calls for giving each party a chance to meet in the appropriate fashion the facts that come to the tribunal's attention, and the appropriate fashion for meeting disputed adjudicative facts includes rebuttal evidence, cross-examination, usually confrontation, and argument (either written or oral or both). The key to a fair trial is opportunity to use the appropriate weapons (rebuttal evidence, cross-examination, and argument) to meet adverse materials that come to the tribunal's attention.

A System of Judicial Notice Based on Fairness and Convenience, in PERSPECTIVES OF LAW 69, 93 (1964).

The rule proceeds upon the theory that these considerations call for dispensing with traditional methods of proof only in clear cases. Compare Professor Davis's conclusion that judicial notice should be a matter of convenience, subject to requirements of procedural fairness. *Id.* at 94.

This rule is consistent with Uniform Rule 9(1) and (2) which limit judicial notice of facts to those "so universally known that they cannot reasonably be the subject of dispute," those "so generally known or of such common notoriety within the territorial jurisdiction of the court that they cannot reasonably be the subject of dispute," and those "capable of immediate and accurate determination by resort to easily accessible sources of indisputable accuracy." The traditional textbook treatment has included these general categories (matters of common knowledge, facts capable of verification), MCCORMICK §§ 324, 325, and then has passed on into detailed treatment of such specific topics as facts relating to the personnel and records of the court, *id.* § 327, and other governmental facts, *id.* § 328. The California draftsmen, with a background of detailed statutory regulation of judicial notice, followed a somewhat similar pattern. CAL. EVID. CODE §§ 451, 452. The Uniform Rules, however, were drafted on the theory that these particular matters are included within the general categories and need no specific mention. This approach is followed in the present rule.

The phrase "propositions of generalized knowledge," found in Uniform Rule 9(1) and (2), is not included in the present rule. It was, it is believed, originally included in Model Code Rules 801 and 802 primarily in order to afford some minimum recognition to the right of the judge in his "legislative" capacity (not acting as the trier of fact) to take judicial notice of very limited categories of generalized knowledge. The limitations thus imposed have been discarded herein as undesirable, unworkable, and contrary to existing practice. What is left, then, to be considered, is the status of a "proposition of generalized knowledge" as an "adjudicative" fact to be noticed judicially and communicated by the judge to the jury. Thus viewed, it is considered to be lacking practical significance. While judges use judicial notice of "propositions of generalized knowledge" in a variety of situations: determining the validity and meaning of statutes, formulating common-law rules, deciding whether evidence should be admitted, assessing the sufficiency and effect of evidence, all are essentially nonadjudicative in nature. When judicial notice is seen as a significant vehicle for progress in the law, these are the areas involved, particularly in developing fields of scientific knowledge. *See* MCCORMICK 712. It is not believed that judges now instruct juries as to "propositions of generalized knowledge" derived from encyclopedias or other sources, or that they are likely to do so, or, indeed, that it is desirable that they do so. There is a vast difference between ruling on the basis of judicial notice that radar evidence of speed is admissible and explaining to the jury its principles and degree of accuracy, or between using a table of stopping distances of automobiles at various speeds in a judicial evaluation of testimony and telling the jury its precise application in the case. For cases raising doubt as to the propriety of the use of medical texts by lay triers of fact in passing on disability claims in administrative proceedings, see *Sayers v. Gardner*, 380 F.2d 940 (6th Cir. 1967); *Ross v. Gardner*, 365 F.2d 554 (6th Cir. 1966); *Sosna v. Celebrezze*, 234 F. Supp. 289 (E.D. Pa. 1964); *Glendenning v. Ribicoff*, 213 F. Supp. 301 (W.D. Mo. 1962).

[Subdivision (c)]. Under subdivision [(c)(1)] the judge has discretionary authority to take judicial notice, regardless of whether he is so requested by a party. The taking of judicial notice is mandatory, under subdivision [(c)(2)], only when a party requests it and the necessary information is supplied. This scheme is believed to reflect existing practice. It is simple and workable. It avoids troublesome distinctions in the many situations in which the process of taking judicial notice is not recognized as such.

Compare Uniform Rule 9 making judicial notice of facts universally known mandatory without request, and making judicial notice of facts generally known in the jurisdiction or capable of determination by resort to accurate sources discretionary in the absence of request but mandatory if request is made and the information furnished. But see Uniform Rule 10(3), which directs the judge to decline to take judicial notice if available information fails to convince him that the matter falls clearly within Uniform

Rule 9 or is insufficient to enable him to notice it judicially. Substantially the same approach is found in California Evidence Code §§ 451–453 and in New Jersey Evidence Rule 9 (repealed and replaced by New Jersey Rule of Evidence 201 (1993)). In contrast, the present rule treats alike all adjudicative facts which are subject to judicial notice.

[Subdivision (d)]. In accord with the usual view, judicial notice may be taken at any stage of the proceedings, whether in the trial court or on appeal. UNIF. R. EVID. 12; CAL. EVID. CODE § 459; KAN. STAT. ANN. § 60-412; N.J. EVID. R. 12 (repealed and replaced by N.J. R. EVID. 202 (1993)); MCCORMICK § 330, at 712.

Subdivision (e). Basic considerations of procedural fairness demand an opportunity to be heard on the propriety of taking judicial notice and the tenor of the matter noticed. The rule requires the granting of that opportunity upon request. No formal scheme of giving notice is provided. An adversely affected party may learn in advance that judicial notice is in contemplation, either by virtue of being served with a copy of a request by another party under subdivision [(c)(2)] that judicial notice be taken, or through an advance indication by the judge. Or he may have no advance notice at all. The likelihood of the latter is enhanced by the frequent failure to recognize judicial notice as such. And in the absence of advance notice, a request made after the fact could not in fairness be considered untimely. See the provision for hearing on timely request in the Administrative Procedure Act, 5 U.S.C. § 556(e). *See also* REVISED MODEL STATE ADMINISTRATIVE PROCEDURE ACT (1961), 9C U.L.A. § 10(4) (Supp. 1967).

[Subdivision (f)]. Much of the controversy about judicial notice has centered upon the question whether evidence should be admitted in disproof of facts of which judicial notice is taken.

The writers have been divided. Favoring admissibility are THAYER, PRELIMINARY TREATISE ON EVIDENCE 308 (1898); 9 WIGMORE § 2567; Davis, *A System of Judicial Notice Based on Fairness and Convenience, in* PERSPECTIVES OF LAW 69, 76–77 (1964). Opposing admissibility are Keeffe, Landis & Shaad, *Sense and Nonsense about Judicial Notice*, 2 STAN. L. REV. 664, 668 (1950); McNaughton, *Judicial Notice—Excerpts Relating to the Morgan–Whitmore Controversy*, 14 VAND. L. REV. 779 (1961); Morgan, *Judicial Notice*, 57 HARV. L. REV. 269, 279 (1944); MCCORMICK 710–11. The Model Code and the Uniform Rules are predicated upon indisputability of judicially noticed facts.

The proponents of admitting evidence in disproof have concentrated largely upon legislative facts. Since the present rule deals only with judicial notice of adjudicative facts, arguments directed to legislative facts lose their relevancy.

REPORT OF THE HOUSE COMMITTEE ON THE JUDICIARY

Rule [201(f)] as received from the Supreme Court provided that when judicial notice of a fact is taken, the court shall instruct the jury to accept that fact as established. Being of the view that mandatory instruction to a jury in a criminal case to accept as conclusive any fact judicially noticed is inappropriate because contrary to the spirit of the Sixth Amendment right to a jury trial, the Committee adopted the 1969 Advisory Committee draft of this subsection, allowing a mandatory instruction in civil actions and proceedings and a discretionary instruction in criminal cases.

ADVISORY COMMITTEE'S NOTE, 1969 PRELIMINARY DRAFT

Within its relatively narrow area of adjudicative facts, the rule contemplates there is to be no evidence before the jury in disproof in civil cases. The judge instructs the jury to take judicially noticed facts as conclusive. This position is justified by the undesirable effects of the opposite rule in limiting the rebutting party, though not his opponent, to admissible evidence, in defeating the reasons for judicial notice, and in affecting the substantive law to an extent and in ways largely unforeseeable. Ample protection and flexibility are afforded by the broad provision for opportunity to be heard on request, set forth in subdivision (e).

Criminal cases are treated somewhat differently in the rule. While matters falling within the common fund of information supposed to be possessed by jurors need not be proved, State v. Dunn, 221 Mo. 530 (1909), these are not, properly speaking, adjudicative facts but an aspect of legal reasoning. The considerations which underlie the general rule that a verdict cannot be directed against the accused in a criminal case seem to foreclose the judge's directing the jury on the basis of judicial notice to accept as conclusive any adjudicative facts in the case. State v. Main, 94 R.I. 338 (1962); State v. Lawrence, 120 Utah 323 (1951); *cf.* People v. Mayes, 113 Cal. 618 (1896); Ross v. United States, 374 F.2d 97 (8th Cir. 1967). However, this view presents no obstacle to the judge's advising the jury as to a matter judicially noticed, if he instructs them that it need not be taken as conclusive.

NOTE ON JUDICIAL NOTICE OF LAW (BY THE ADVISORY COMMITTEE)

By rules effective July 1, 1966, the method of invoking the law of a foreign country is covered elsewhere. FED. R. CIV. P. 44.1; FED. R. CR. P. 26.1. These two new admirably designed rules are founded upon the assumption that the manner in which law is fed into the judicial process is never a proper concern of the rules of evidence but rather of the rules of procedure. The Advisory Committee on Evidence, believing that this assumption is entirely correct, proposes no evidence rule with respect to judicial notice of law, and suggests that those matters of law which, in addition to foreign-country law, have traditionally been treated as requiring pleading and proof and more recently as the subject of judicial notice be left to the Rules of Civil and Criminal Procedure.

ARTICLE III. PRESUMPTIONS IN CIVIL CASES

Rule 301.   PRESUMPTIONS IN CIVIL CASES GENERALLY

In a civil case, unless a federal statute or these rules provide otherwise, the party against whom a presumption is directed has the burden of producing evidence to rebut the presumption. But this rule does not shift the burden of persuasion, which remains on the party who had it originally.

(Enacted Jan. 2, 1975; as restyled Apr. 26, 2011, eff. Dec. 1, 2011.)

NOTE BY FEDERAL JUDICIAL CENTER

The bill passed by the House substituted a substantially different rule in place of that prescribed by the Supreme Court. The Senate bill substituted yet a further version, which was accepted by the House, was enacted by the Congress, and is the rule shown above.

ADVISORY COMMITTEE'S NOTE

This rule governs presumptions generally. See Rule 302 for presumptions controlled by state law and Rule 303 [deleted] for those against an accused in a criminal case.

Presumptions governed by this rule are given the effect of placing upon the opposing party the burden of establishing the nonexistence of the presumed fact, once the party invoking the presumption establishes the basic facts giving rise to it. The same considerations of fairness, policy, and probability which dictate the allocation of the burden of the various elements of a case as between the prima facie case of a plaintiff and affirmative defenses also underlie the creation of presumptions. These considerations are not satisfied by giving a lesser effect to presumptions. Morgan & Maguire, *Looking Backward and Forward at Evidence*, 50 HARV. L. REV. 909, 913 (1937); Morgan, *Instructing the Jury upon Presumptions and Burden of Proof*, 47 HARV. L. REV. 59, 82 (1933); Cleary, *Presuming and Pleading: An Essay on Juristic Immaturity*, 12 STAN. L. REV. 5 (1959).

The so-called "bursting bubble" theory, under which a presumption vanishes upon the introduction of evidence which would support a finding of the nonexistence of the presumed fact, even though not believed, is rejected as according presumptions too "slight and evanescent" an effect. Morgan & Maguire, *supra*, at 913.

In the opinion of the Advisory Committee, no constitutional infirmity attends this view of presumptions. In *Mobile, Jackson & Kansas City Railroad Co. v. Turnipseed*, 219 U.S. 35 (1910), the Court upheld a Mississippi statute which provided that in actions against railroads proof of injury inflicted by the running of trains should be prima facie evidence of negligence by the railroad. The injury in the case had resulted from a derailment. The opinion made the points (1) that the only effect of the statute was to impose on the railroad the duty of producing some evidence to the contrary, (2) that an inference may be supplied by law if there is a rational connection between the fact proved and the fact presumed, as long as the opposite party is not precluded from presenting his evidence to the contrary, and (3) that considerations of public policy arising from the character of the business justified the application in question. Nineteen years later, in *Western & Atlantic Railroad Co. v. Henderson*, 279 U.S. 639 (1929), the Court overturned a Georgia statute making railroads liable for damages done by trains, unless the railroad made it appear that reasonable care had been used, the presumption being against the railroad. The declaration alleged the death of plaintiff's husband from a grade crossing collision, due to specified acts of negligence by defendant. The jury were instructed that proof of the injury raised a presumption of negligence; the burden shifted to the railroad to prove ordinary care; and unless it did so, they should find for plaintiff. The instruction was held erroneous in an opinion stating (1) that there was no rational connection between the mere fact of collision and negligence on the part of anyone, and (2) that the statute was different from that in *Turnipseed* in imposing a burden upon the railroad. The reader is left in a state of some confusion. Is the difference between a derailment and a grade crossing collision of no significance? Would the *Turnipseed* presumption have been bad if it had imposed a burden of persuasion on defendant, although that would in nowise have impaired its "rational connection"? If *Henderson* forbids imposing a burden of persuasion on defendants, what happens to affirmative defenses?

Two factors serve to explain *Henderson*. The first was that it was common ground that negligence was indispensable to liability. Plaintiff thought so, drafted her complaint accordingly, and relied upon the presumption. But how in logic could the same presumption establish her alternative grounds of negligence that the engineer was so blind he could not see decedent's truck and that he failed to stop after he saw it? Second, take away the basic assumption of no liability without fault, as *Turnipseed* intimated might be done ("considerations of public policy arising out of the character of the business"), and the structure of the decision in

Henderson fails. No question of logic would have arisen if the statute had simply said: a prima facie case of liability is made by proof of injury by a train; lack of negligence is an affirmative defense, to be pleaded and proved as other affirmative defenses. The problem would be one of economic due process only. While it seems likely that the Supreme Court of 1929 would have voted that due process was denied, that result today would be unlikely. See, for example, the shift in the direction of absolute liability in the consumer cases. Prosser, *The Assault upon the Citadel (Strict Liability to the Consumer)*, 69 YALE L.J. 1099 (1960).

Any doubt as to the constitutional permissibility of a presumption imposing a burden of persuasion of the nonexistence of the presumed fact in civil cases is laid at rest by *Dick v. New York Life Insurance Co.*, 359 U.S. 437 (1959). The Court unhesitatingly applied the North Dakota rule that the presumption against suicide imposed on defendant the burden of proving that the death of insured, under an accidental death clause, was due to suicide.

> Proof of coverage and of death by gunshot wound shifts the burden to the insurer to establish that the death of the insured was due to his suicide.

Id. at 443.

> In a case like this one, North Dakota presumes that death was accidental and places on the insurer the burden of proving that death resulted from suicide.

Id. at 446.

The rational connection requirement survives in criminal cases, Tot v. United States, 319 U.S. 463 (1943), because the Court has been unwilling to extend into that area the greater-includes-the-lesser theory of *Ferry v. Ramsey*, 277 U.S. 88 (1928). In that case the Court sustained a Kansas statute under which bank directors were personally liable for deposits made with their assent and with knowledge of insolvency, and the fact of insolvency was prima facie evidence of assent and knowledge of insolvency. Mr. Justice Holmes pointed out that the state legislature could have made the directors personally liable to depositors in every case. Since the statute imposed a less stringent liability, "the thing to be considered is the result reached, not the possibly inartificial or clumsy way of reaching it." *Id.* at 94. Mr. Justice Sutherland dissented: though the state could have created an absolute liability, it did not purport to do so; a rational connection was necessary, but lacking, between the liability created and the prima facie evidence of it; the result might be different if the basis of the presumption were being open for business.

The Sutherland view has prevailed in criminal cases by virtue of the higher standard of notice there required. The fiction that everyone is presumed to know the law is applied to the substantive law of crimes as an alternative to complete unenforceability. But the need does not extend to criminal evidence and procedure, and the fiction does not encompass them. "Rational connection" is not fictional or artificial, and so it is reasonable to suppose that Gainey should have known that his presence at the site of an illicit still could convict him of being connected with (carrying on) the business, United States v. Gainey, 380 U.S. 63 (1965), but not that Romano should have known that his presence at a still could convict him of possessing it, United States v. Romano, 382 U.S. 136 (1965).

In his dissent in *Gainey*, Mr. Justice Black put it more artistically:

It might be argued, although the Court does not so argue or hold, that Congress if it wished could make presence at a still a crime in itself, and so Congress should be free to create crimes which are called "possession" and "carrying on an illegal distillery business" but which are defined in such a way that unexplained presence is sufficient and indisputable evidence in all cases to support conviction for those offenses. *See* Ferry v. Ramsey, 277 U.S. 88 (1928). Assuming for the sake of argument that Congress could make unexplained presence a criminal act, and ignoring also the refusal of this Court in other cases to uphold a statutory presumption on such a theory, *see* Heiner v. Donnan, 285 U.S. 312 (1932), there is no indication here that Congress intended to adopt such a misleading method of draftsmanship, nor in my judgment could the statutory provisions if so construed escape condemnation for vagueness, under the principles applied in *Lanzetta v. New Jersey*, 306 U.S. 451 (1939), and many other cases.

380 U.S. at 84 n.12.

And the majority opinion in *Romano* agreed with him:

It may be, of course, that Congress has the power to make presence at an illegal still a punishable crime, but we find no clear indication that it intended to so exercise this power. The crime remains possession, not presence, and with all due deference to the judgment of Congress, the former may not constitutionally be inferred from the latter.

382 U.S. at 144.

The rule does not spell out the procedural aspects of its application. Questions as to when the evidence warrants submission of a presumption and what instructions are proper under varying states of fact are believed to present no particular difficulties.

REPORT OF THE SENATE COMMITTEE ON THE JUDICIARY

The rule governs presumptions in civil cases generally. Rule 302 provides for presumptions in cases controlled by state law.

As submitted by the Supreme Court, presumptions governed by this rule were given the effect of placing upon the opposing party the burden of establishing the nonexistence of the presumed fact, once the party invoking the presumption established the basic facts giving rise to it.

Instead of imposing a burden of persuasion on the party against whom the presumption is directed, the House adopted a provision which shifted the burden of going forward with the evidence. They further provided that "even though met with contradicting evidence, a presumption is sufficient evidence of the fact presumed, to be considered by the trier of fact." The effect of the amendment is that presumptions are to be treated as evidence.

The Committee feels the House amendment is ill-advised. As the joint committees (the Standing Committee on Practice and Procedure of the Judicial Conference and the Advisory Committee on the Rules of Evidence) stated: "Presumptions are not evidence, but ways of dealing with evidence." This treatment requires juries to perform the task of considering "as evidence" facts upon which they have no direct evidence and which may confuse them in performance of their duties. California had a rule much like that contained in the House amendment. It was sharply criticized by Justice Traynor in *Speck v. Sarver*[1] and was repealed after 93 troublesome years.[2]

Professor McCormick gives a concise and compelling critique of the presumption as evidence rule:

Another solution, formerly more popular than now, is to instruct the jury that the presumption is "evidence," to be weighed and considered with the testimony in the case. This avoids the danger that the jury may infer that the

---

[1] 20 Cal. 2d 585, 594 (1942).

[2] CAL. EVID. CODE § 600.

presumption is conclusive, but it probably means little to the jury and certainly runs counter to accepted theories of the nature of evidence.[3]

For these reasons the Committee has deleted that provision of the House-passed rule that treats presumptions as evidence. The effect of the rule as adopted by the Committee is to make clear that while evidence of facts giving rise to a presumption shifts the burden of coming forward with evidence to rebut or meet the presumption, it does not shift the burden of persuasion on the existence of the presumed facts. The burden or persuasion remains on the party to whom it is allocated under the rules governing the allocation in the first instance.

The court may instruct the jury that they may infer the existence of the presumed fact from proof of the basic facts giving rise to the presumption. However, it would be inappropriate under this rule to instruct the jury that the inference they are to draw is conclusive.

CONFERENCE REPORT

The House bill provides that a presumption in civil actions and proceedings shifts to the party against whom it is directed the burden of going forward with evidence to meet or rebut it. Even though evidence contradicting the presumption is offered, a presumption is considered sufficient evidence of the presumed fact to be considered by the jury. The Senate amendment provides that a presumption shifts to the party against whom it is directed the burden of going forward with evidence to meet or rebut the presumption, but it does not shift to that party the burden of persuasion on the existence of the presumed fact.

Under the Senate amendment, a presumption is sufficient to get a party past an adverse party's motion to dismiss made at the end of his case-in-chief. If the adverse party offers no evidence contradicting the presumed fact, the court will instruct the jury that if it finds the basic facts, it may presume the existence of the presumed fact. If the adverse party does offer evidence contradicting the presumed fact, the court cannot instruct the jury that it may *presume* the existence of the presumed fact from proof of the basic facts. The court may, however, instruct the jury that it may infer the existence of the presumed fact from proof of the basic facts.

The Conference adopts the Senate amendment.

---

[3] McCORMICK, EVIDENCE 669 (1954); *id*. at 825 (2d ed. 1972).

Rule 302.   APPLYING STATE LAW TO PRESUMPTIONS IN CIVIL CASES

In a civil case, state law governs the effect of a presumption regarding a claim or defense for which state law supplies the rule of decision.

(Enacted Jan. 2, 1975; as restyled Apr. 26, 2011, eff. Dec. 1, 2011.)

<u>NOTE BY FEDERAL JUDICIAL CENTER</u>

The rule enacted by the Congress is the rule prescribed by the Supreme Court, amended by adding "and proceedings" after "actions."

<u>ADVISORY COMMITTEE'S NOTE</u>

A series of Supreme Court decision in diversity cases leaves no doubt of the relevance of *Erie Railroad Co. v. Tompkins*, 304 U.S. 64 (1938), to questions of burden of proof. These decisions are *Cities Service Oil Co. v. Dunlap*, 308 U.S. 208 (1939), *Palmer v. Hoffman*, 318 U.S. 109 (1943), and *Dick v. New York Life Insurance Co.*, 359 U.S. 437 (1959). They involved burden of proof, respectively, as to status as bona fide purchaser, contributory negligence, and nonaccidental death (suicide) of an insured. In each instance the state rule was held to be applicable. It does not follow, however, that all presumptions in diversity cases are governed by state law. In each case cited, the burden of proof question had to do with a substantive element of the claim or defense. Application of the state law is called for only when the presumption operates upon such an element. Accordingly the rule does not apply state law when the presumption operates upon a lesser aspect of the case, i.e., "tactical" presumptions.

The situations in which the state law is applied have been tagged for convenience in the preceding discussion as "diversity cases." The designation is not a completely accurate one since *Erie* applies to any claim or issue having its source in state law, regardless of the basis of federal jurisdiction, and does not apply to a federal claim or issue, even though jurisdiction is based on diversity. Vestal, Erie R.R. v. Tompkins: *A Projection*, 48 IOWA L. REV. 248, 257 (1963); HART & WECHSLER, THE FEDERAL COURTS AND THE FEDERAL SYSTEM 697 (1953); 1A MOORE, FEDERAL PRACTICE ¶ 0.305[3] (2d ed. 1965); WRIGHT, FEDERAL COURTS 217–18 (1963). Hence the rule employs, as appropriately descriptive, the phrase "as to which state law supplies the rule of decision." *See* ALI STUDY of the Division of Jurisdiction Between State and Federal Courts § 2344(c), at 40 (Proposed Official Draft 1965).

Presumptions in Criminal Cases
Note by Federal Judicial Center

The rules prescribed by the Supreme Court included Rule 303, Presumptions in Criminal Cases. The rule was not included in the rules enacted by the Congress. . . .

ARTICLE IV. RELEVANCE AND ITS LIMITS

Rule 401.   TEST FOR RELEVANT EVIDENCE

Evidence is relevant if:

(a) it has any tendency to make a fact more or less probable than it would be without the evidence; and

(b) the fact is of consequence in determining the action.

(Enacted Jan. 2, 1975; as restyled Apr. 26, 2011, eff. Dec. 1, 2011.)

NOTE BY FEDERAL JUDICIAL CENTER

The rule enacted by the Congress is the rule prescribed by the Supreme Court without change.

ADVISORY COMMITTEE'S NOTE

Problems of relevancy call for an answer to the question whether an item of evidence, when tested by the processes of legal reasoning, possesses sufficient probative value to justify receiving it in evidence. Thus, assessment of the probative value of evidence that a person purchased a revolver shortly prior to a fatal shooting with which he is charged is a matter of analysis and reasoning.

The variety of relevancy problems is coextensive with the ingenuity of counsel in using circumstantial evidence as a means of proof. An enormous number of cases fall in no set pattern, and this rule is designed as a guide for handling them. On the other hand, some situations recur with sufficient frequency to create patterns susceptible of treatment by specific rules. Rule 404 and those following it are of that variety; they also serve as illustrations of the application of the present rule as limited by the exclusionary principles of Rule 403.

Passing mention should be made of so-called "conditional" relevancy. MORGAN, BASIC PROBLEMS OF EVIDENCE 45–46 (1962). In this situation, probative value depends not only upon satisfying the basic requirement of relevancy as described above but also upon the existence of some matter of fact. For example, if evidence of a spoken statement is relied upon to prove notice, probative value is lacking unless the person sought to be charged heard the statement.

The problem is one of fact, and the only rules needed are for the purpose of determining the respective functions of judge and jury. *See* Rules 104(b) and 901. The discussion which follows in the present note is concerned with relevancy generally, not with any particular problem of conditional relevancy.

Relevancy is not an inherent characteristic of any item of evidence but exists only as a relation between an item of evidence and a matter properly provable in the case. Does the item of evidence tend to prove the matter sought to be proved? Whether the relationship exists depends upon principles evolved by experience or science, applied logically to the situation at hand. James, *Relevancy, Probability and the Law*, 29 CALIF. L. REV. 689, 696 n.15 (1941), *in* SELECTED WRITINGS ON EVIDENCE AND TRIAL 610, 615 n.15 (Fryer ed., 1957). The rule summarizes this relationship as a "tendency to make the existence" of the fact to be proved "more probable or less probable." Compare Uniform Rule 1(2) which states the crux of relevancy as "a tendency in reason," thus perhaps emphasizing unduly the logical process and ignoring the need to draw upon experience or science to validate the general principle upon which relevancy in a particular situation depends.

The standard of probability under the rule is "more . . . probable than it would be without the evidence." Any more stringent requirement is unworkable and unrealistic. As McCORMICK § 152, at 317, says, "A brick is not a wall," or, as Falknor, *Extrinsic Policies Affecting Admissibility*, 10 RUTGERS L. REV. 574, 576 (1956), quotes Professor McBaine, "[I]t is not to be supposed that every witness can make a home run." Dealing with probability in the language of the rule has the added virtue of avoiding confusion between questions of admissibility and questions of the sufficiency of the evidence.

The rule uses the phrase "fact that is of consequence to the determination of the action" to describe the kind of fact to which proof may properly be directed. The language is that of California Evidence Code § 210; it has the advantage of avoiding the loosely used and ambiguous word "material." *Tentative Recommendation and a Study Relating to the Uniform Rules of Evidence* (Article I, General Provisions), *in* CAL. LAW REVISION COMM'N, REP., REC. & STUDIES 10–11 (1964). The fact to be proved may be ultimate, intermediate, or evidentiary; it matters not, so long as it is of consequence in the determination of the action. Compare Uniform Rule 1(2) which requires that the evidence relate to a "material" fact.

The fact to which the evidence is directed need not be in dispute. While situations will arise which call for the exclusion of evidence offered to prove a point conceded by the opponent, the ruling should be made on the basis of such considerations as waste of time and undue prejudice (see Rule 403), rather than under any general requirement that evidence is admissible only if directed to matters in dispute. Evidence which is essentially background in nature can scarcely be said to involve disputed matter, yet it is universally offered and admitted as an aid to understanding. Charts, photographs, views of real estate, murder weapons, and many other items of evidence fall in this category. A rule limiting admissibility to evidence directed to a controversial point would invite the exclusion of this helpful evidence, or at least the raising of endless questions over its admission. *Cf.* CAL. EVID. CODE § 210 (defining relevant evidence in terms of tendency to prove a disputed fact).

Rule 402.   GENERAL ADMISSIBILITY OF RELEVANT EVIDENCE

Relevant evidence is admissible unless any of the following provides otherwise:

- the United States Constitution;

- a federal statute;

- these rules; or

- other rules prescribed by the Supreme Court.

Irrelevant evidence is not admissible.

(Enacted Jan. 2, 1975; as restyled Apr. 26, 2011, eff. Dec. 1, 2011.)

NOTE BY FEDERAL JUDICIAL CENTER

The rule enacted by the Congress is the rule prescribed by the Supreme Court, with the first sentence amended by substituting "prescribed" in place of "adopted," and by adding at the end thereof the phrase "pursuant to statutory authority."

ADVISORY COMMITTEE'S NOTE

The provisions that all relevant evidence is admissible, with certain exceptions, and that evidence which is not relevant is not admissible are "a presupposition involved in the very conception of a rational system of evidence." THAYER, PRELIMINARY TREATISE ON EVIDENCE 264 (1898). They constitute the foundation upon which the structure of admission and exclusion rests. For similar provisions see California Evidence Code §§ 350, 351. Provisions that all relevant evidence is admissible are found in Uniform Rule 7(f); Kansas Statutes Annotated § 60-407(f); and New Jersey Evidence Rule 7(f) (repealed and replaced by New Jersey Rule of Evidence 402 (1993)); but the exclusion of evidence which is not relevant is left to implication.

Not all relevant evidence is admissible. The exclusion of relevant evidence occurs in a variety of situations and may be called for by these rules, by the Rules of Civil and Criminal Procedure, by Bankruptcy Rules, by Act of Congress, or by constitutional considerations.

Succeeding rules in the present article, in response to the demands of particular policies, require the exclusion of evidence despite its relevancy. In addition, Article V recognizes a number of privileges; Article VI imposes limitations upon witnesses and the manner of dealing with them; Article VII specifies requirements with respect to opinions and expert testimony; Article VIII excludes hearsay not falling within an exception; Article IX spells out the handling of authentication and identification; and Article X restricts the manner of proving the contents of writings and recordings.

The Rules of Civil and Criminal Procedure in some instances require the exclusion of relevant evidence. For example, Rules 30(b) and [32(a)(4)] of the Rules of Civil Procedure, by imposing requirements of notice and unavailability of the deponent, place limits on the use of relevant depositions. Similarly, Rule 15 of the Rules of Criminal Procedure restricts the use of depositions in criminal cases, even though relevant. And the effective enforcement of the command, originally statutory and now found in Rule 5(a) of the Rules of Criminal Procedure, that an arrested person be taken without unnecessary delay before a commissioner or other similar officer is held to require the exclusion of statements elicited during detention in violation thereof. Mallory v. United States, 354 U.S. 449 (1957); 18 U.S.C. § 3501(c).

While congressional enactments in the field of evidence have generally tended to expand admissibility beyond the scope of the common law rules, in some particular situations they have restricted the admissibility of relevant evidence. Most of this legislation has consisted of the formulation of a privilege or of a prohibition against disclosure. 8 U.S.C. § 1202(f) (records of refusal of visas or permits to enter United States confidential, subject to discretion of Secretary of State to make available to court upon certification of need); 10 U.S.C. § [1041] (replacement certificate of honorable discharge from Army not admissible in evidence); [*id.*] (same as to Air Force); 11 U.S.C. § 25(a)(10) (repealed 1978) (testimony given by bankrupt on his examination not admissible in criminal proceedings against him, except that given in hearing upon objection to discharge); 11 U.S.C. § 205(a) (railroad reorganization petition, if dismissed, not admissible in evidence); 11 U.S.C. § 403(a) (list of creditors filed with municipal composition plan not an admission); 13 U.S.C. § 9(a) (census information confidential, retained copies of reports privileged); 47 U.S.C. § 605 (interception and divulgence of wire or radio communications prohibited unless authorized by sender). These statutory provisions would remain undisturbed by the rules.

The rule recognizes but makes no attempt to spell out the constitutional considerations which impose basic limitations upon the admissibility of relevant evidence. Examples are evidence obtained by unlawful search and seizure, Weeks v. United States, 232 U.S. 383 (1914); Katz v. United States, 389 U.S. 347 (1967); incriminating statement elicited from an accused in violation of right to counsel, Massiah v. United States, 377 U.S. 201 (1964).

<u>REPORT OF THE HOUSE COMMITTEE ON THE JUDICIARY</u>

Rule 402 as submitted to the Congress contained the phrase "or by other rules adopted by the Supreme Court." To accommodate the view that the Congress should not appear to acquiesce in the Court's judgment that it has authority under the existing Rules Enabling Acts to promulgate Rules of Evidence, the Committee amended the above phrase to read "or by other rules prescribed by the Supreme Court pursuant to statutory authority" in this and other rules where the reference appears.

Rule 403. EXCLUDING RELEVANT EVIDENCE FOR PREJUDICE, CONFUSION, WASTE OF TIME, OR OTHER REASONS

The court may exclude relevant evidence if its probative value is substantially outweighed by a danger of one or more of the following: unfair prejudice, confusing the issues, misleading the jury, undue delay, wasting time, or needlessly presenting cumulative evidence.

(Enacted Jan. 2, 1975; as restyled Apr. 26, 2011, eff. Dec. 1, 2011.)

<u>NOTE BY FEDERAL JUDICIAL CENTER</u>

The rule enacted by the Congress is the rule prescribed by the Supreme Court without change.

<u>ADVISORY COMMITTEE'S NOTE</u>

The case law recognizes that certain circumstances call for the exclusion of evidence which is of unquestioned relevance. These circumstances entail risks which range all the way from inducing decision on a purely emotional basis, at one extreme, to nothing more harmful than merely wasting time, at the other extreme. Situations in this area call for balancing the probative value of and need for the evidence against the harm likely to result from its admission. Slough, *Relevancy Unraveled*, 5 U. KAN. L. REV. 1, 12–15 (1956); Trautman, *Logical or Legal Relevancy—A Conflict in Theory*, 5 VAND. L. REV. 385, 392 (1952); MCCORMICK § 152, at 319–21. The rules which follow in this Article are concrete applications evolved for particular situations. However, they reflect the policies underlying the present rule, which is designed as a guide for the handling of situations for which no specific rules have been formulated.

Exclusion for risk of unfair prejudice, confusion of issues, misleading the jury, or waste of time all find ample support in the authorities. "Unfair prejudice" within its context means an undue tendency to suggest decision on an improper basis, commonly, though not necessarily, an emotional one.

The rule does not enumerate surprise as a ground for exclusion, in this respect following Wigmore's view of the common law. 6 WIGMORE § 1849; *cf.* MCCORMICK § 152, at 320 n.29 (listing unfair surprise as a ground for exclusion but stating that it is usually "coupled with the danger of prejudice and confusion of issues."). While Uniform Rule 45 incorporates surprise as a ground and is followed in Kansas Statutes Annotated § 60-445, surprise is not included in California Evidence Code § 352 or New Jersey Evidence Rule 4 (repealed and replaced by New Jersey Rule of Evidence 403 (1993)), though both the latter otherwise substantially embody Uniform Rule 45. While it can scarcely be doubted that claims of unfair surprise may still be justified despite procedural requirements of notice and instrumentalities of discovery, the granting of a continuance is a more appropriate remedy than exclusion of the evidence. *Tentative Recommendation and a Study Relating to the Uniform Rules of Evidence* (Article VI, Extrinsic Policies Affecting Admissibility), *in* CAL. LAW REVISION COMM'N, REP., REC. & STUDIES 612 (1964). Moreover, the impact of a rule excluding evidence on the ground of surprise would be difficult to estimate.

In reaching a decision whether to exclude on grounds of unfair prejudice, consideration should be given to the probable effectiveness or lack of effectiveness of a limiting instruction. See Rule [105] and Advisory Committee's Note thereunder. The availability of other means of proof may also be an appropriate factor.

Rule 404. CHARACTER EVIDENCE; CRIMES OR OTHER ACTS

(a) Character Evidence.

(1) *Prohibited Uses.* Evidence of a person's character or character trait is not admissible to prove that on a particular occasion the person acted in accordance with the character or trait.

(2) *Exceptions for a Defendant or Victim in a Criminal Case.* The following exceptions apply in a criminal case:

(A) a defendant <u>may</u> offer evidence of the defendant's pertinent trait, and if the evidence is admitted, the prosecutor may offer evidence to rebut it;

(B) subject to the limitations in Rule 412, a <u>defendant</u> <u>may</u> offer evidence of an alleged <u>victim's</u> pertinent trait, and if the evidence is admitted, the prosecutor may:

(i) offer evidence to rebut it; and

(ii) offer evidence of the defendant's same trait; and   *rehabilitate*

(C) in a homicide case, the prosecutor <u>may</u> offer evidence of the alleged victim's trait of peacefulness to rebut evidence that the victim was <u>the first aggressor.</u>

(3) *Exceptions for a Witness.* Evidence of a witness's character may be admitted under Rules 607, 608, and 609.

(b) Crimes, Wrongs, or Other Acts.

(1) *Prohibited Uses.* Evidence of a crime, wrong, or other act is not admissible to prove a person's character in order to show that on a particular occasion the person acted in accordance with the character.

(2) *Permitted Uses; Notice in a Criminal Case.* This evidence may be admissible for another purpose, such as proving motive, opportunity, intent, preparation, plan, knowledge, identity, absence of mistake, or lack of accident. On request by a defendant in a criminal case, the prosecutor must:

(A) provide reasonable notice of the general nature of any such evidence that the prosecutor intends to offer at trial; and

(B) do so before trial—or during trial if the court, for good cause, excuses lack of pretrial notice.

(Enacted Jan. 2, 1975; as amended, Mar. 2, 1987, eff. Oct. 1, 1987; Apr. 30, 1991, eff. Dec. 1, 1991; Apr. 17, 2000, eff. Dec. 1, 2000; Apr. 12, 2006, eff. Dec. 1, 2006; as restyled Apr. 26, 2011, eff. Dec. 1, 2011.)

NOTE BY FEDERAL JUDICIAL CENTER

The rule enacted by the Congress is the rule prescribed by the Supreme Court, with the second sentence of subdivision (b) amended by substituting "It may, however, be admissible" in place of "This subdivision does not exclude the evidence when offered."

ADVISORY COMMITTEE'S NOTE

Subdivision (a). This subdivision deals with the basic question whether character evidence should be admitted. Once the admissibility of character evidence in some form is established under this rule, reference must then be made to Rule 405, which follows, in order to determine the appropriate method of proof. If the character is that of a witness, see Rules 608 and [609] for methods of proof.

Character questions arise in two fundamentally different ways. (1) Character may itself be an element of a crime, claim, or defense. A situation of this kind is commonly referred to as "character in issue." Illustrations are: the chastity of the victim under a statute specifying her chastity as an element of the crime of seduction, or the competency of the driver in an action for negligently entrusting a motor vehicle to an incompetent driver. No problem of the general relevancy of character evidence is involved, and the present rule therefore has no provision on the subject. The only question relates to allowable methods of proof, as to which see Rule 405, immediately following. (2) Character evidence is susceptible of being used for the purpose of suggesting an inference that the person acted on the occasion in question consistently with his character. This use of character is often described as "circumstantial." Illustrations are: evidence of a violent disposition to prove that the person was the aggressor in an affray, or evidence of honesty in disproof of a charge of theft. This circumstantial use of character evidence raises questions of relevancy as well as questions of allowable methods of proof.

In most jurisdictions today, the circumstantial use of character is rejected but with important exceptions: (1) an accused may introduce pertinent evidence of good character (often misleadingly described as "putting his character in issue"), in which event the prosecution may rebut with evidence of bad character; (2) an accused may introduce pertinent evidence of the character of the victim, as in support of a claim of self-defense to a charge of homicide or consent in a case of rape,[1] and the prosecution may introduce similar evidence in rebuttal of the character evidence, or, in a homicide case, to rebut a claim that deceased was the first aggressor, however proved; and (3) the character of a witness may be gone into as bearing on his credibility. MCCORMICK §§ 155–161. This pattern is incorporated in the rule. While its basis lies more in history and experience than in logic an underlying justification can fairly be found in terms of the relative presence and absence of prejudice in the various situations. Falknor, *Extrinsic Policies Affecting Admissibility*, 10 RUTGERS L. REV. 574, 584 (1956); MCCORMICK § 157. In any event, the criminal rule is so deeply imbedded in our jurisprudence as to assume almost constitutional proportions and to override doubts of the basic relevancy of the evidence.

The limitation to pertinent traits of character, rather than character generally, in [404(a)(2)(A)–(C)] is in accordance with the prevailing view. MCCORMICK § 158, at 334. A similar provision in Rule 608, to which reference is made in [404(a)(3)], limits character

---

[1] [Rule 412 (the rape shield law), which Congress added in 1978, now generally bars this application of Rule 404(a)(2)(B) in sex offense cases. The 2006 amendment to what is now Rule 404(a)(2)(B) added a proviso that evidence of a victim's character is "subject to the limitations imposed by Rule 412."—GF]

evidence respecting witnesses to the trait of truthfulness or untruthfulness.

The argument is made that circumstantial use of character ought to be allowed in civil cases to the same extent as in criminal cases, i.e., evidence of good (nonprejudicial) character would be admissible in the first instance, subject to rebuttal by evidence of bad character. Falknor, *Extrinsic Policies Affecting Admissibility*, 10 RUTGERS L. REV. 574, 581–83 (1956); *Tentative Recommendation and a Study Relating to the Uniform Rules of Evidence* (Article VI, Extrinsic Policies Affecting Admissibility), *in* CAL. LAW REVISION COMM'N, REP., REC. & STUDIES 657–58 (1964). Uniform Rule 47 goes farther, in that it assumes that character evidence in general satisfies the conditions of relevancy, except as provided in Uniform Rule 48. The difficulty with expanding the use of character evidence in civil cases is set forth by the California Law Revision Commission in its ultimate rejection of Uniform Rule 47, CAL. LAW REVISION COMM'N, *supra*, at 615:

> Character evidence is of slight probative value and may be very prejudicial. It tends to distract the trier of fact from the main question of what actually happened on the particular occasion. It subtly permits the trier of fact to reward the good man and to punish the bad man because of their respective characters despite what the evidence in the case shows actually happened.

Much of the force of the position of those favoring greater use of character evidence in civil cases is dissipated by their support of Uniform Rule 48 which excludes the evidence in negligence cases, where it could be expected to achieve its maximum usefulness. Moreover, expanding concepts of "character," which seem of necessity to extend into such areas as psychiatric evaluation and psychological testing, coupled with expanded admissibility, would open up such vistas of mental examinations as caused the Court concern in *Schlagenhauf v. Holder*, 379 U.S. 104 (1964). It is believed that those espousing change have not met the burden of persuasion.

Subdivision (b) deals with a specialized but important application of the general rule excluding circumstantial use of character evidence. Consistently with that rule, evidence of other crimes, wrongs, or acts is not admissible to prove character as a basis for suggesting the inference that conduct on a particular occasion was in conformity with it. However, the evidence may be offered for another purpose, such as proof of motive, opportunity, and so on, which does not fall within the prohibition. In this situation the rule does not require that the evidence be excluded.

No mechanical solution is offered. The determination must be made whether the danger of undue prejudice outweighs the probative value of the evidence in view of the availability of other means of proof and other factors appropriate for making decisions of this kind under Rule 403. Slough & Knightly, *Other Vices, Other Crimes*, 41 IOWA L. REV. 325 (1956).

REPORT OF THE HOUSE COMMITTEE ON THE JUDICIARY

The second sentence of Rule 404(b) as submitted to the Congress began with the words "This subdivision does not exclude the evidence when offered." The Committee amended this language to read "It may, however, be admissible," the words used in the 1971 Advisory Committee draft, on the ground that this formulation properly placed greater emphasis on admissibility than did the final Court version.

REPORT OF THE SENATE COMMITTEE ON THE JUDICIARY

This rule provides that evidence of other crimes, wrongs, or acts is not admissible to prove character but may be admissible for other specified purposes such as proof of motive.

Although your Committee sees no necessity in amending the rule itself, it anticipates that the use of the discretionary word "may" with respect to the admissibility of evidence of crimes, wrongs, or acts is not intended to confer any arbitrary discretion on the trial judge. Rather, it is anticipated that with respect to permissible uses for such evidence, the trial judge may exclude it only on the basis of those considerations set forth in Rule 403, i.e., prejudice, confusion, or waste of time.

ADVISORY COMMITTEE'S NOTE TO 1991 AMENDMENT TO RULE 404

Rule 404(b) has emerged as one of the most cited rules in the Rules of Evidence. And in many criminal cases evidence of an accused's extrinsic acts is viewed as an important asset in the prosecution's case against an accused. Although there are a few reported decisions on use of such evidence by the defense, *see, e.g.*, United States v. McClure, 546 F.2d 670 (5th Cir. 1977) (acts of informant offered in entrapment defense), the overwhelming number of cases involve introduction of that evidence by the prosecution.

The amendment to Rule 404(b) adds a pretrial notice requirement in criminal cases and is intended to reduce surprise and promote early resolution on the issue of admissibility. The notice requirement thus places Rule 404(b) in the mainstream with notice and disclosure provisions in other rules of evidence. *See, e.g.,* Rule 412 (written motion of intent to offer evidence under rule), Rule 609 (written notice of intent to offer conviction older than 10 years), Rule [807] (notice of intent to use residual hearsay exception).

The rule expects that counsel for both the defense and the prosecution will submit the necessary request and information in a reasonable and timely fashion. Other than requiring pretrial notice, no specific time limits are stated in recognition that what constitutes a reasonable request or disclosure will depend largely on the circumstances of each case. *Compare* FLA. STAT. ANN. § [90.404(2)(d)] (notice must be given at least ten days before trial) *with* TEX. R. EVID. 404(b) (no time limit).

Likewise, no specific form of notice is required. The Committee considered and rejected a requirement that the notice satisfy the particularity requirements normally required of language used in a charging instrument. *Cf.* FLA. STAT. ANN. § [90.404(2)(d)] (written disclosure must describe uncharged misconduct with particularity required of an indictment or information). Instead, the Committee opted for a generalized notice provision which requires the prosecution to apprise the defense of the general nature of the evidence of extrinsic acts. The Committee does not intend that the amendment will super[s]ede other rules of admissibility or disclosure, such as the Jencks Act, 18 U.S.C. § 3500, et seq., nor require the prosecution to disclose directly or indirectly the names and addresses of its witnesses, something it is currently not required to do under Federal Rule of Criminal Procedure 16.

The amendment requires the prosecution to provide notice, regardless of how it intends to use the extrinsic act evidence at trial, i.e., during its case-in-chief, for impeachment, or for possible rebuttal. The court in its discretion may, under the facts, decide that the particular request or notice was not reasonable, either because of the lack of timeliness or completeness. Because the notice requirement serves as [a] condition precedent to admissibility of 404(b) evidence, the offered evidence is inadmissible if the court decides that the notice requirement has not been met.

Nothing in the amendment precludes the court from requiring the government to provide it with an opportunity to rule in limine on 404(b) evidence before it is offered or even mentioned during trial. When ruling in limine, the court may require the government to disclose to it the specifics of such evidence which the court must consider in determining admissibility.

The amendment does not extend to evidence of acts which are "intrinsic" to the charged offense. *See* United States v. Williams, 900 F.2d 823 (5th Cir. 1990) (noting distinction between 404(b) evidence and intrinsic offense evidence). Nor is the amendment intended to redefine what evidence would otherwise be admissible under Rule 404(b). Finally, the Committee does not intend through the amendment to affect the role of the court and the jury in considering such evidence. *See* Huddleston v. United States, 485 U.S. 681 (1988).

ADVISORY COMMITTEE'S NOTE TO 2000 AMENDMENT TO RULE 404

Rule [404(a)(2)(B)(ii)] has been amended to provide that when the accused attacks the character of an alleged victim under subdivision [(a)(2)(B)] of this rule, the door is opened to an attack on the same character trait of the accused. Current law does not allow the government to introduce negative character evidence as to the accused unless the accused introduces evidence of good character. *See, e.g.*, United States v. Fountain, 768 F.2d 790 (7th Cir. 1985) (when the accused offers proof of self-defense, this permits proof of the alleged victim's character trait for peacefulness, but it does not permit proof of the accused's character trait for violence).

The amendment makes clear that the accused cannot attack the alleged victim's character and yet remain shielded from the disclosure of equally relevant evidence concerning the same character trait of the accused. For example, in a murder case with a claim of self-defense, the accused, to bolster this defense, might offer evidence of the alleged victim's violent disposition. If the government has evidence that the accused has a violent character, but is not allowed to offer this evidence as part of its rebuttal, the jury has only part of the information it needs for an informed assessment of the probabilities as to who was the initial aggressor. This may be the case even if evidence of the accused's prior violent acts is admitted under Rule 404(b), because such evidence can be admitted only for limited purposes and not to show action in conformity with the accused's character on a specific occasion. Thus, the amendment is designed to permit a more balanced presentation of character evidence when an accused chooses to attack the character of the alleged victim.

The amendment does not affect the admissibility of evidence of specific acts of uncharged misconduct offered for a purpose other than proving character under Rule 404(b). Nor does it affect the standards for proof of character by evidence of other sexual behavior or sexual offenses under Rules 412–415. By its placement in Rule [404(a)(2)(B)], the amendment covers only proof of character by way of reputation or opinion.

The amendment does not permit proof of the accused's character if the accused merely uses character evidence for a purpose other than to prove the alleged victim's propensity to act in a certain way. *See* United States v. Burks, 470 F.2d 432, 434–35 (D.C. Cir. 1972) (evidence of the alleged victim's violent character, when known by the accused, was admissible "on the issue of whether or not the defendant reasonably feared he was in danger of imminent great bodily harm"). Finally, the amendment does not permit proof of the accused's character when the accused attacks the alleged victim's character as a witness under Rule 608 or 609.

The term "alleged" is inserted before each reference to "victim" in the rule, in order to provide consistency with Evidence Rule 412.

ADVISORY COMMITTEE'S NOTE TO 2006 AMENDMENT TO RULE 404

The rule has been amended to clarify that in a civil case evidence of a person's character is never admissible to prove that the person acted in conformity with the character trait. The amendment resolves the dispute in the case law over whether the exceptions in subdivisions [(a)(2)(A) and (B)] permit the circumstantial use of character evidence in civil cases. *Compare* Carson v. Polley, 689 F.2d 562, 576 (5th Cir. 1982) ("[W]hen a central issue in a case is close to one of a criminal nature, the exceptions to the Rule 404(a) ban on character evidence may be invoked."), *with* SEC v. Towers Fin. Corp., 966 F. Supp. 203 (S.D.N.Y. 1997) (relying on the terms "accused" and "prosecution" in Rule 404(a) to conclude that the exceptions in subdivisions [(a)(2)(A) and (B)] are inapplicable in civil cases). The amendment is consistent with the original intent of the rule, which was to prohibit the circumstantial use of character evidence in civil cases, even where closely related to criminal charges. *See* Ginter v. Nw. Mut. Life Ins. Co., 576 F. Supp. 627, 629–30 (E.D. Ky. 1984) ("It seems beyond peradventure of doubt that the drafters of Fed. R. Evid. 404(a) explicitly intended that all character evidence, except where 'character is at issue' was to be excluded [in civil cases].").

The circumstantial use of character evidence is generally discouraged because it carries serious risks of prejudice, confusion, and delay. *See* Michelson v. United States, 335 U.S. 469, 476 (1948) ("The overriding policy of excluding such evidence, despite its admitted probative value, is the practical experience that its disallowance tends to prevent confusion of issues, unfair surprise and undue prejudice."). In criminal cases, the so-called "mercy rule" permits a criminal defendant to introduce evidence of pertinent character traits of the defendant and the victim. But that is because the accused, whose liberty is at stake, may need "a counterweight against the strong investigative and prosecutorial resources of the government." C. MUELLER & L. KIRKPATRICK, EVIDENCE: PRACTICE UNDER THE RULES 264–65 (2d ed. 1999); *see also* Richard Uviller, *Evidence of Character to Prove Conduct: Illusion, Illogic, and Injustice in the Courtroom*, 130 U. PA. L. REV. 845, 855 (1982) (the rule prohibiting circumstantial use of character evidence "was relaxed to allow the criminal defendant with so much at stake and so little available in the way of conventional proof to have special dispensation to tell the factfinder just what sort of person he really is"). Those concerns do not apply to parties in civil cases.

The amendment also clarifies that evidence otherwise admissible under Rule [404(a)(2)(B)] may nonetheless be excluded in a criminal case involving sexual misconduct. In such a case, the admissibility of evidence of the victim's sexual behavior and predisposition is governed by the more stringent provisions of Rule 412.

Nothing in the amendment is intended to affect the scope of Rule 404(b). While Rule 404(b) refers to the "accused," the "prosecution," and a "criminal case," it does so only in the context of a notice requirement. The admissibility standards of Rule 404(b) remain fully applicable to both civil and criminal cases.

PROPOSED AMENDMENT TO RULE 404(b)
(Approved by the Advisory Committee on Evidence Rules
in April 2018 and by the Standing Committee on
Rules of Practice and Procedure in June 2018;
released for public comment on August 1, 2018;
to take effect no earlier than December 1, 2020.)

EDITOR'S NOTE

In April 2018 the Advisory Committee on Evidence Rules approved and sent to the Standing Committee on Rules of Practice and Procedure a proposed amendment to Rule 404(b). The amendment would clarify and expand the prosecution's obligation in a criminal trial to disclose to the defense its intent to introduce evidence of other acts for a non-propensity purpose under Rule 404(b)(2). The proposed amendment would make three noteworthy changes to the prosecution's disclosure obligation:

• A defense request for disclosure no longer would be necessary to trigger the prosecution's obligation. The rule would require the prosecution in *all* criminal cases to disclose its intent to offer other-acts evidence under Rule 404(b)(2).

• The prosecution no longer could fulfill this obligation by disclosing "the general nature" of the other-acts evidence, but would have to identify the evidence and articulate the prosecution's purpose in offering that evidence.

•   The prosecution would have to make this disclosure not merely "before trial," as under the present rule, but "sufficiently ahead of trial to give the defendant a fair opportunity to meet the evidence" unless "the court, for good cause, excuses lack of pretrial notice."

Perhaps the most significant proposed change is stated only in passing. The amendment would require the prosecution to "articulate . . . the *non-propensity* purpose for which [it] intends to offer the [other-acts] evidence . . . ." (Emphasis added.) That is, the amendment would make explicit the crucial principle that when parties introduce other-acts evidence "for another purpose" under Rule 404(b)(2), that other purpose must not be the one banned by Rules 404(a)(1) and (b)(1): to prove character to show action in accordance with that character. As if to stress the importance of this principle, the Advisory Committee's Note to the proposed amendment refers three more times to the prosecution's duty to disclose the "non-propensity purpose" of its other-acts evidence.

The proposed amendment was approved by the Standing Committee on Rules of Practice and Procedure in June 2018 and released for public comment on August 1, 2018. The public-comment period closes on February 15, 2019. If the proposed amendment gains final approval from the Judicial Conference and Supreme Court and if Congress does not amend, delay, or disapprove it, the amendment will take effect no earlier than December 1, 2020.

Proposed Amendment to Rule 404(b)

Rule 404.   CHARACTER EVIDENCE; <u>OTHER</u> CRIMES<u>, WRONGS</u> OR <s>OTHER</s> ACTS

(b) <u>Other</u> Crimes, Wrongs, or <s>Other</s> Acts.

(1) *Prohibited Uses.* Evidence of <s>a</s> <u>any other</u> crime, wrong, or <s>other</s> act is not admissible to prove a person's character in order to show that on a particular occasion the person acted in accordance with the character.

(2) *Permitted Uses<s>; Notice in a Criminal Case</s>.* This evidence may be admissible for another purpose,

---

such as proving motive, opportunity, intent, preparation, plan, knowledge, identity, absence of mistake, or lack of accident. ~~On request by a defendant in a criminal case, the prosecutor must:~~

(3) ***Notice in a Criminal Case.*** In a criminal case, the prosecutor must:

    (A) provide reasonable notice ~~of the general nature~~ of any such evidence that the prosecutor intends to offer at trial; ~~and~~

    (B) articulate in the notice the non-propensity purpose for which the prosecutor intends to offer the evidence and the reasoning that supports the purpose; and

    (C) do so in writing ~~before trial~~ sufficiently ahead of trial to give the defendant a fair opportunity to meet the evidence—or in any form during trial if the court, for good cause, excuses lack of pretrial notice.

ADVISORY COMMITTEE'S NOTE TO PROPOSED AMENDMENT

Rule 404(b) has been amended principally to impose additional notice requirements on the prosecution in a criminal case. In addition, clarifications have been made to the text and headings.

The notice provision has been changed in a number of respects:

• The prosecution must not only identify the evidence that it intends to offer pursuant to the rule but also articulate a non-propensity purpose for which the evidence is offered and the basis for concluding that the evidence is relevant in light of this purpose. The earlier requirement that the prosecution provide notice of only the "general nature" of the evidence was understood by some courts to permit the government to satisfy the notice obligation without describing the specific act that the evidence would tend to prove, and without explaining the relevance of the evidence for a non-propensity purpose. This amendment makes clear what notice is required.

• The pretrial notice must be in writing—which requirement is satisfied by notice in electronic form. *See* Rule 101(b)(6). Requiring the notice to be in writing provides certainty and reduces arguments about whether notice was actually provided. In addition, notice must be provided before trial in such time as to allow the defendant a fair opportunity to meet the evidence, unless the court excuses that requirement upon a showing of good cause. *See* Rules 609(b), 807, and 902(11). Advance notice of Rule 404(b) evidence is important so that the parties and the court have adequate opportunity to assess the evidence, the purpose for which it is offered, and whether the requirements of Rule 403 have been satisfied, even in cases in which a final determination as to the admissibility of the evidence must await trial.

• The good cause exception applies not only to the timing of the notice as a whole but also to the obligations to articulate a non-propensity purpose and the reasoning supporting that purpose. A good cause exception for the articulation requirements is necessary because in some cases an additional permissible purpose for the evidence may not become clear until just before, or even during, trial.

• Finally, the amendment eliminates the requirement that the defendant must make a request before notice is provided. That requirement is not found in any other notice provision in the Federal Rules of Evidence. It has resulted mostly in boilerplate demands on the one hand, and a trap for the unwary on the other. Moreover, many local rules require the government to provide notice of Rule 404(b) material without regard to whether it has been requested. And in many cases, notice is provided when the government moves *in limine* for an advance ruling on the admissibility of Rule 404(b) evidence. The request requirement has thus outlived any usefulness it may once have had.

As to the textual clarifications, the word "other" is restored to the location it held before restyling in 2011, to confirm that Rule 404(b) applies to crimes, wrongs and acts "other" than those at issue in the case; and the headings are changed accordingly. No substantive change is intended.

[This space is intentionally blank.]

[This space is intentionally blank.]

$404(a) \rightarrow 405(a)$ crim only

Rule 405.   METHODS OF PROVING CHARACTER

(a) By Reputation or Opinion.   When evidence of a person's character or character trait is admissible, it may be proved by testimony about the person's reputation or by testimony in the form of an opinion. On cross-examination of the character witness, the court may allow an inquiry into relevant specific instances of the person's conduct.

(b) By Specific Instances of Conduct.   When a person's character or character trait is an essential element of a charge, claim, or defense, the character or trait may also be proved by relevant specific instances of the person's conduct.

(Enacted Jan. 2, 1975; as amended Mar. 2, 198_ restyled Apr. 26, 2011, eff. Dec. 1, 2011.)

In your opinion, s/ Defamation is have you had violent encounter an exception to a lif+only if essent. elem. change

NOTE BY FEDERAL JUDICIAL CENTER

The rule enacted by the Congress is the rule prescribed by the Supreme Court without change. The bill reported by the House Committee on the Judiciary deleted the provision in subdivision (a) for making proof by testimony in the form of an opinion, but the provision was reinstated on the floor of the House. *See* 120 CONG. REC. H546–49 (daily ed. Feb. 6, 1974).

ADVISORY COMMITTEE'S NOTE

The rule deals only with allowable methods of proving character, not with the admissibility of character evidence, which is covered in Rule 404.

Of the three methods of proving character provided by the rule, evidence of specific instances of conduct is the most convincing. At the same time it possesses the greatest capacity to arouse prejudice, to confuse, to surprise, and to consume time. Consequently the rule confines the use of evidence of this kind to cases in which character is, in the strict sense, in issue and hence deserving of a searching inquiry. When character is used circumstantially and hence occupies a lesser status in the case, proof may be only by reputation and opinion. These latter methods are also available when character is in issue. This treatment is, with respect to specific instances of conduct and reputation, conventional contemporary common law doctrine. MCCORMICK § 153.

In recognizing opinion as a means of proving character, the rule departs from usual contemporary practice in favor of that of an earlier day. *See* 7 WIGMORE § 1986, pointing out that the earlier practice permitted opinion and arguing strongly for evidence based on personal knowledge and belief as contrasted with "the secondhand, irresponsible product of multiplied guesses and gossip which we term 'reputation.'" It seems likely that the persistence of reputation evidence is due to its largely being opinion in disguise. Traditionally character has been regarded primarily in moral overtones of good and bad: chaste, peaceable, truthful, honest. Nevertheless, on occasion nonmoral considerations crop up, as in the case of the incompetent driver, and this seems bound to happen increasingly. If character is defined as the kind of person one is, then account must be taken of varying ways of arriving at the estimate. These may range from the opinion of the employer who has found the man honest to the opinion of the psychiatrist based upon examination and testing. No effective dividing line exists between character and mental capacity, and the latter traditionally has been provable by opinion.

According to the great majority of cases, on cross-examination inquiry is allowable as to whether the reputation witness has heard of particular instances of conduct pertinent to the trait in question. Michelson v. United States, 335 U.S. 469 (1948); Annotation, [13 A.L.R.4th 796]. The theory is that, since the reputation witness relates what he has heard, the inquiry tends to shed light on the accuracy of his hearing and reporting. Accordingly, the opinion witness would be asked whether he knew, as well as whether he had heard. The fact is, of course, that these distinctions are of slight if any practical significance, and the second sentence of subdivision (a) eliminates them as a factor in formulating questions. This recognition of the propriety of inquiring into specific instances of conduct does not circumscribe inquiry otherwise into the bases of opinion and reputation testimony.

The express allowance of inquiry into specific instances of conduct on cross-examination in subdivision (a) and the express allowance of it as part of a case in chief when character is actually in issue in subdivision (b) contemplate that testimony of specific instances is not generally permissible on the direct examination of an ordinary opinion witness to character. Similarly as to witnesses to the character of witnesses under Rule 608(b). Opinion testimony on direct in these situations ought in general to correspond to reputation testimony as now given, i.e., be confined to the nature and extent of observation and acquaintance upon which the opinion is based. *See* Rule 701.

Rule 406.   HABIT; ROUTINE PRACTICE

Evidence of a person's habit or an organization's routine practice may be admitted to prove that on a particular occasion the person or organization acted in accordance with the habit or routine practice. The court may admit this evidence regardless of whether it is corroborated or whether there was an eyewitness.

(Enacted Jan. 2, 1975; as restyled Apr. 26, 2011, eff. Dec. 1, 2011.)

NOTE BY FEDERAL JUDICIAL CENTER

The rule enacted by the Congress is subdivision (a) of the rule prescribed by the Supreme Court. Subdivision (b) of the Court's rule was deleted for reasons stated in the Report of the House Committee on the Judiciary set forth below.

ADVISORY COMMITTEE'S NOTE

An oft-quoted paragraph, MCCORMICK § 162, at 340, describes habit in terms effectively contrasting it with character:

Character and habit are close akin. Character is a generalized description of one's disposition, or of one's disposition in respect to a general trait, such as honesty, temperance, or peacefulness. "Habit," in modern usage, both lay and psychological, is more specific. It describes one's regular response to a repeated specific situation. If we speak of character for care, we think of the person's tendency to act prudently in all the varying situations of life, in business, family life, in handling automobiles, and in walking across the street. A habit, on the other hand, is the person's regular practice of meeting a particular kind of situation with a specific type of conduct, such as the habit of going down a particular stairway two stairs at a time, or of giving the hand-signal for a left turn, or of alighting from railway cars while they are moving. The doing of the habitual acts may become semi-automatic.

Equivalent behavior on the part of a group is designated "routine practice of an organization" in the rule.

Agreement is general that habit evidence is highly persuasive as proof of conduct on a particular occasion. Again quoting McCormick § 162, at 341:

Character may be thought of as the sum of one's habits though doubtless it is more than this. But unquestionably the uniformity of one's response to habit is far greater than the consistency with which one's conduct conforms to character or disposition. Even though character comes in only exceptionally as evidence of an act, surely any sensible man in investigating whether X did a particular act would be greatly helped in his inquiry by evidence as to whether he was in the habit of doing it.

When disagreement has appeared, its focus has been upon the question what constitutes habit, and the reason for this is readily apparent. The extent to which instances must be multiplied and consistency of behavior maintained in order to rise to the status of habit inevitably gives rise to differences of opinion. Lewan, *Rationale of Habit Evidence*, 16 SYRACUSE L. REV. 39, 49 (1964). While adequacy of sampling and uniformity of response are key factors, precise standards for measuring their sufficiency for evidence purposes cannot be formulated.

The rule is consistent with prevailing views. Much evidence is excluded simply because of failure to achieve the status of habit. Thus, evidence of intemperate "habits" is generally excluded when offered as proof of drunkenness in accident cases, Annotation, 46

A.L.R.2d 103, and evidence of other assaults is inadmissible to prove the instant one in a civil assault action, Annotation, 66 A.L.R.2d 806. In *Levin v. United States*, 338 F.2d 265 (D.C. Cir. 1964), testimony as to the religious "habits" of the accused, offered as tending to prove that he was at home observing the Sabbath rather than out obtaining money through larceny by trick, was held properly excluded:

> It seems apparent to us that an individual's religious practices would not be the type of activities which would lend themselves to the characterization of "invariable regularity."[2] Certainly the very volitional basis of the activity raises serious questions as to its invariable nature, and hence its probative value.

Id. at 272.

These rulings are not inconsistent with the trend towards admitting evidence of business transactions between one of the parties and a third person as tending to prove that he made the same bargain or proposal in the litigated situation. Slough, *Relevancy Unraveled*, 6 U. KAN. L. REV. 38–41 (1957). Nor are they inconsistent with such cases as *Whittemore v. Lockheed Aircraft Corp.*, 65 Cal. App. 2d 737, 151 P.2d 670 (1944), upholding the admission of evidence that plaintiff's intestate had on four other occasions flown planes from defendant's factory for delivery to his employer airline, offered to prove that he was piloting rather than a guest on a plane which crashed and killed all on board while en route for delivery.

A considerable body of authority has required that evidence of the routine practice of an organization be corroborated as a condition precedent to its admission in evidence. Slough, *Relevancy Unraveled*, 5 U. KAN. L. REV. 404, 449 (1957). This requirement is specifically rejected by the rule on the ground that it relates to the sufficiency of the evidence rather than admissibility. A similar position is taken in New Jersey Evidence Rule 49 (repealed and replaced by New Jersey Rule of Evidence 406 (1993)). The rule also rejects the requirement of the absence of eyewitnesses, sometimes encountered with respect to admitting habit evidence to prove freedom from contributory negligence in wrongful death cases. For comment critical of the requirements see Frank, J., in *Cereste v. New York, New Haven & Hartford Railroad Co.*, 231 F.2d 50 (2d Cir.), *cert. denied*, 351 U.S. 951 (1956); 10 VAND. L. REV. 447 (1957); MCCORMICK § 162, at 342. The omission of the requirement from

---

[2] 1 WIGMORE 520.

the California Evidence Code is said to have effected its elimination. *Comment*, CAL. EVID. CODE § 1105.

Rule 406 as submitted to Congress contained a subdivision (b) providing that the method of proof of habit or routine practice could be "in the form of an opinion or by specific instances of conduct sufficient in number to warrant a finding that the habit existed or that the practice was routine." The Committee deleted this subdivision believing that the method of proof of habit and routine practice should be left to the courts to deal with on a case-by-case basis. At the same time, the Committee does not intend that its action be construed as sanctioning a general authorization of opinion evidence in this area.

Rule 407.   SUBSEQUENT REMEDIAL MEASURES

When measures are taken that would have made an earlier injury or harm less likely to occur, evidence of the subsequent measures is not admissible to prove:

- negligence;

- culpable conduct;

- a defect in a product or its design; or

- a need for a warning or instruction.

But the court may admit this evidence for another purpose, such as impeachment or—if disputed—proving ownership, control, or the feasibility of precautionary measures.

(Enacted Jan. 2, 1975; as amended Apr. 11, 1997, eff. Dec. 1, 1997; as restyled Apr. 26, 2011, eff. Dec. 1, 2011.)

The rule enacted by the Congress is the rule prescribed by the Supreme Court without change.

ADVISORY COMMITTEE'S NOTE

The rule incorporates conventional doctrine which excludes evidence of subsequent remedial measures as proof of an admission of fault. The rule rests on two grounds. (1) The conduct is not in fact an admission, since the conduct is equally consistent with injury by mere accident or through contributory negligence. Or, as Baron Bramwell put it, the rule rejects the notion that "because the world gets wiser as it gets older, therefore it was foolish before." Hart v. Lancashire & Yorkshire Ry. Co., (1869) 21 L.T.R. N.S. 261 at 263. Under a liberal theory of relevancy this ground alone would not support exclusion as the inference is still a possible one. (2) The other, and more impressive, ground for exclusion rests on a social policy of encouraging people to take, or at least not discouraging them from taking, steps in furtherance of added safety. The courts have applied this principle to exclude evidence of subsequent repairs, installation of safety devices, changes in company rules, and discharge of employees, and the language of the present rule is broad enough to encompass all of them. *See* Falknor, *Extrinsic Policies Affecting Admissibility*, 10 RUTGERS L. REV. 574, 590 (1956).

The second sentence of the rule directs attention to the limitations of the rule. Exclusion is called for only when the evidence of subsequent remedial measures is offered as proof of negligence or culpable conduct. In effect it rejects the suggested inference that fault is admitted. Other purposes are, however, allowable, including ownership or control, existence of duty, and feasibility of precautionary measures, if controverted, and impeachment. 2 WIGMORE § 283; Annotation, [15 A.L.R.5th 119]. Two recent federal cases are illustrative. *Boeing Airplane Co. v. Brown*, 291 F.2d 310 (9th Cir. 1961), an action against an airplane manufacturer for using an allegedly defectively designed alternator shaft which caused a plane crash, upheld the admission of evidence of subsequent design modification for the purpose of showing that design changes and safeguards were feasible. And *Powers v. J.B. Michael & Co.*, 329 F.2d 674 (6th Cir. 1964), an action against a road contractor for negligent failure to put out warning signs, sustained the admission of evidence that defendant subsequently put out signs to show that the portion of the road in question was under defendant's control. The requirement that the other purpose be controverted calls for automatic exclusion unless a genuine issue be present and allows the opposing party to lay the groundwork for exclusion by making an admission. Otherwise the factors of undue prejudice, confusion of issues, misleading the jury, and waste of time remain for consideration under Rule 403.

For comparable rules, see Uniform Rule 51; California Evidence Code § 1151; Kansas Statutes Annotated § 60-451; New Jersey

Evidence Rule 51 (repealed and replaced by New Jersey Rule of Evidence 407 (1993)).

ADVISORY COMMITTEE'S NOTE TO 1997 AMENDMENT TO RULE 407

The amendment to Rule 407 makes two changes in the rule. First, the words "an injury or harm allegedly caused by" were added to clarify that the rule applies only to changes made after the occurrence that produced the damages giving rise to the action. Evidence of measures taken by the defendant prior to the "event" causing injury or harm do not fall within the exclusionary scope of Rule 407 even if they occurred after the manufacture or design of the product. *See* Chase v. General Motors Corp., 856 F.2d 17, 21–22 (4th Cir. 1988).

Second, Rule 407 has been amended to provide that evidence of subsequent remedial measures may not be used to prove "a defect in a product or its design, or that a warning or instruction should have accompanied a product." This amendment adopts the view of a majority of the circuits that have interpreted Rule 407 to apply to products liability actions. *See* Raymond v. Raymond Corp., 938 F.2d 1518, 1522 (1st Cir. 1991); *In re* Joint E. Dist. & S. Dist. Asbestos Litig., 995 F.2d 343, 345 (2d Cir. 1993); Cann v. Ford Motor Co., 658 F.2d 54, 60 (2d Cir. 1981), *cert. denied*, 456 U.S. 960 (1982); Kelley v. Crown Equip. Co., 970 F.2d 1273, 1275 (3d Cir. 1992); Werner v. Upjohn Co., 628 F.2d 848, 856 (4th Cir. 1980), *cert. denied*, 449 U.S. 1080 (1981); Gren. Steel Indus., Inc. v. Ala. Oxygen Co., 695 F.2d 883, 887 (5th Cir. 1983); Bauman v. Volkswagenwerk Aktiengesellschaft, 621 F.2d 230, 232 (6th Cir. 1980); Flaminio v. Honda Motor Co., 733 F.2d 463, 469 (7th Cir. 1984); Gauthier v. AMF, Inc., 788 F.2d 634, 636–37 (9th Cir. 1986).

Although this amendment adopts a uniform federal rule, it should be noted that evidence of subsequent remedial measures may be admissible pursuant to the second sentence of Rule 407. Evidence of subsequent measures that is not barred by Rule 407 may still be subject to exclusion on Rule 403 grounds when the dangers of prejudice or confusion substantially outweigh the probative value of the evidence.

ADVISORY COMMITTEE'S NOTE TO 2011 RESTYLING OF RULE 407

Rule 407 previously provided that evidence was not excluded if offered for a purpose not explicitly prohibited by the rule. To improve the language of the rule, it now provides that the court may admit evidence if offered for a permissible purpose. There is no intent to change the process for admitting evidence covered by the rule. It remains the case that if offered for an impermissible purpose, it must be excluded, and if offered for a purpose not barred by the rule, its admissibility remains governed by the general principles of Rules 402, 403, 801, etc.

Rule 408.   COMPROMISE OFFERS AND NEGOTIATIONS

(a) Prohibited Uses.   Evidence of the following is not admissible—on behalf of any party—either to prove or disprove the validity or amount of a disputed claim or to impeach by a prior inconsistent statement or a contradiction:

(1) furnishing, promising, or offering—or accepting, promising to accept, or offering to accept—a valuable consideration in compromising or attempting to compromise the claim; and

(2) conduct or a statement made during compromise negotiations about the claim—except when offered in a criminal case and when the negotiations related to a claim by a public office in the exercise of its regulatory, investigative, or enforcement authority.

(b) Exceptions.   The court may admit this evidence for another purpose, such as proving a witness's bias or prejudice, negating a contention of undue delay, or proving an effort to obstruct a criminal investigation or prosecution.

(Enacted Jan. 2, 1975; as amended Apr. 12, 2006, eff. Dec. 1, 2006; as restyled Apr. 26, 2011, eff. Dec. 1, 2011.)

NOTE BY FEDERAL JUDICIAL CENTER

The rule enacted by the Congress is the rule prescribed by the Supreme Court, amended by the insertion of the third sentence. Other amendments, proposed by the House bill, were not enacted for reasons stated in the Report of the Senate Committee on the Judiciary and in the Conference Report, set forth below.

ADVISORY COMMITTEE'S NOTE

As a matter of general agreement, evidence of an offer to compromise a claim is not receivable in evidence as an admission of, as the case may be, the validity or invalidity of the claim. As with evidence of subsequent remedial measures, dealt with in Rule

407, exclusion may be based on two grounds. (1) The evidence is irrelevant, since the offer may be motivated by a desire for peace rather than from any concession of weakness of position. The validity of this position will vary as the amount of the offer varies in relation to the size of the claim and may also be influenced by other circumstances. (2) A more consistently impressive ground is promotion of the public policy favoring the compromise and settlement of disputes. MCCORMICK §§ 76, 251. While the rule is ordinarily phrased in terms of offers of compromise, it is apparent that a similar attitude must be taken with respect to completed compromises when offered against a party thereto. This latter situation will not, of course, ordinarily occur except when a party to the present litigation has compromised with a third person.

The same policy underlies the provision of Rule 68 of the Federal Rules of Civil Procedure that evidence of an unaccepted offer of judgment is not admissible except in a proceeding to determine costs.

The practical value of the common law rule has been greatly diminished by its inapplicability to admissions of fact, even though made in the course of compromise negotiations, unless hypothetical, stated to be "without prejudice," or so connected with the offer as to be inseparable from it. MCCORMICK § 251, at 540–41. An inevitable effect is to inhibit freedom of communication with respect to compromise, even among lawyers. Another effect is the generation of controversy over whether a given statement falls within or without the protected area. These considerations account for the expansion of the rule herewith to include evidence of conduct or statements made in compromise negotiations, as well as the offer or completed compromise itself. For similar provisions see California Evidence Code §§ 1152, 1154.

The policy considerations which underlie the rule do not come into play when the effort is to induce a creditor to settle an admittedly due amount for a lesser sum. MCCORMICK § 251, at 540. Hence the rule requires that the claim be disputed as to either validity or amount.

The final sentence of the rule serves to point out some limitations upon its applicability. Since the rule excludes only when the purpose is proving the validity or invalidity of the claim or its amount, an offer for another purpose is not within the rule. The illustrative situations mentioned in the rule are supported by the authorities. As to proving bias or prejudice of a witness, see Annotation, 161 A.L.R. 395. *Contra* Fenberg v. Rosenthal, 348 Ill. App. 510 (1952); 4 WIGMORE § 1061 (negativing a contention of lack of due diligence in presenting a claim). An effort to "buy off" the prosecution or a prosecuting witness in a criminal case is not within the policy of the rule of exclusion. MCCORMICK § 251, at 542.

For other rules of similar import, see Uniform Rules 52 and 53; California Evidence Code §§ 1152, 1154; Kansas Statutes Annotated §§ 60-452, -453; New Jersey Evidence Rules 52 and 53 (repealed and replaced by New Jersey Rule of Evidence 408 (1993)).

REPORT OF THE HOUSE COMMITTEE ON THE JUDICIARY

Under existing federal law evidence of conduct and statements made in compromise negotiations is admissible in subsequent litigation between the parties. The second sentence of Rule 408 as submitted by the Supreme Court proposed to reverse that doctrine in the interest of further promoting non-judicial settlement of disputes. Some agencies of government expressed the view that the Court formulation was likely to impede rather than assist efforts to achieve settlement of disputes. For one thing, it is not always easy to tell when compromise negotiations begin, and informal dealings end. Also, parties dealing with government agencies would be reluctant to furnish factual information at preliminary meetings; they would wait until "compromise negotiations" began and thus hopefully effect an immunity for themselves with respect to the evidence supplied. In light of these considerations, the Committee recast the rule so that admissions of liability or opinions given during compromise negotiations continue [to be] inadmissible, but evidence of unqualified factual assertions is admissible. The latter aspect of the rule is drafted, however, so as to preserve other possible objections to the introduction of such evidence. The Committee intends no modification of current law whereby a party may protect himself from future use of his statements by couching them in hypothetical conditional form.

REPORT OF THE SENATE COMMITTEE ON THE JUDICIARY

This rule as reported makes evidence of settlement or attempted settlement of a disputed claim inadmissible when offered as an admission of liability or the amount of liability. The purpose of this rule is to encourage settlements which would be discouraged if such evidence were admissible.

Under present law, in most jurisdictions, statements of fact made during settlement negotiations, however, are excepted from this ban and are admissible. The only escape from admissibility of statements of fact made in a settlement negotiation is if the declarant or his representative expressly states that the statement is hypothetical in nature or is made without prejudice. Rule 408 as submitted by the Court reversed the traditional rule. It would have brought statements of fact within the ban and made them, as well as an offer of settlement, inadmissible.

The House amended the rule and would continue to make evidence of facts disclosed during compromise negotiations admissible. It thus reverted to the traditional rule. The House Committee report states that the Committee intends to preserve current law under which a party may protect himself by couching his statements in hypothetical form.[3] The real impact of this amendment, however, is to deprive the rule of much of its salutary effect. The exception for factual admissions was believed by the Advisory Committee to hamper free communication between parties and thus to constitute an unjustifiable restraint upon efforts to negotiate settlements—the encouragement of which is the purpose of the rule. Further, by protecting hypothetically phrased statements, it constituted a preference for the sophisticated, and a trap for the unwary.

Three states which had adopted rules of evidence patterned after the proposed rules prescribed by the Supreme Court opted for versions of Rule 408 identical with the Supreme Court draft with respect to the inadmissibility of conduct or statements made in compromise negotiations.[4]

For these reasons, the Committee has deleted the House amendment and restored the rule to the version submitted by the Supreme Court with one additional amendment. This amendment adds a sentence to insure that evidence, such as documents, is not rendered inadmissible merely because it is presented in the course of compromise negotiations if the evidence is otherwise discoverable. A party should not be able to immunize from admissibility documents otherwise discoverable merely by offering them in a compromise negotiation.[5]

---

[3] *See* H.R. REP. NO. 93-650, dated November 15, 1973.

[4] NEV. REV. STAT. § 48.105; N.M. STAT. ANN. § 20-4-408 (Supp. 1973) (current version at N.M. R. EVID. 11-408); WIS. STAT. ANN. § 904.08 (Supp. 1973).

[5] [The 2006 amendment to FRE 408 eliminated this provision, which is also mentioned in the original Conference Report. The Advisory Committee's Note to the 2006 amendment states in its closing paragraph that "[t]he sentence of the Rule referring to evidence 'otherwise discoverable' has been deleted as superfluous."—GF]

CONFERENCE REPORT

The House bill provides that evidence of admissions of liability or opinions given during compromise negotiations is not admissible, but that evidence of facts disclosed during compromise negotiations is not inadmissible by virtue of having been first disclosed in the compromise negotiations. The Senate amendment provides that evidence of conduct or statements made in compromise negotiations is not admissible. The Senate amendment also provides that the rule does not require the exclusion of any evidence otherwise discoverable merely because it is presented in the course of compromise negotiations.

The House bill was drafted to meet the objection of executive agencies that under the rule as proposed by the Supreme Court, a party could present a fact during compromise negotiations and thereby prevent an opposing party from offering evidence of that fact at trial even though such evidence was obtained from independent sources. The Senate amendment expressly precludes this result.

The Conference adopts the Senate amendment.

ADVISORY COMMITTEE'S NOTE TO 2006 AMENDMENT TO RULE 408

Rule 408 has been amended to settle some questions in the courts about the scope of the rule, and to make it easier to read. First, the amendment provides that Rule 408 does not prohibit the introduction in a criminal case of statements or conduct during compromise negotiations regarding a civil dispute by a government regulatory, investigative, or enforcement agency. *See, e.g.,* United States v. Prewitt, 34 F.3d 436, 439 (7th Cir. 1994) (admissions of fault made in compromise of a civil securities enforcement action were admissible against the accused in a subsequent criminal action for mail fraud). Where an individual makes a statement in the presence of government agents, its subsequent admission in a criminal case should not be unexpected. The individual can seek to protect against subsequent disclosure through negotiation and agreement with the civil regulator or an attorney for the government.

Statements made in compromise negotiations of a claim by a government agency may be excluded in criminal cases where the circumstances so warrant under Rule 403. For example, if an individual was unrepresented at the time the statement was made in a civil enforcement proceeding, its probative value in a subsequent criminal case may be minimal. But there is no absolute exclusion imposed by Rule 408.

In contrast, statements made during compromise negotiations of other disputed claims are not admissible in subsequent criminal litigation, when offered to prove liability for, invalidity of, or amount of those claims. When private parties enter into compromise negotiations they cannot protect against the subsequent use of statements in criminal cases by way of private ordering. The inability to guarantee protection against subsequent use could lead to parties refusing to admit fault, even if by doing so they could favorably settle the private matter. Such a chill on settlement negotiations would be contrary to the policy of Rule 408.

The amendment distinguishes statements and conduct (such as a direct admission of fault) made in compromise negotiations of a civil claim by a government agency from an offer or acceptance of a compromise of such a claim. An offer or acceptance of a compromise of any civil claim is excluded under the rule if offered against the defendant as an admission of fault. In that case, the predicate for the evidence would be that the defendant, by compromising with the government agency, has admitted the validity and amount of the civil claim, and that this admission has sufficient probative value to be considered as evidence of guilt. But unlike a direct statement of fault, an offer or acceptance of a compromise is not very probative of the defendant's guilt. Moreover, admitting such an offer or acceptance could deter a defendant from settling a civil regulatory action, for fear of evidentiary use in a subsequent criminal action. *See, e.g.*, FISHMAN, JONES ON EVIDENCE, CIVIL AND CRIMINAL § 22:16, at 199 n.83 (7th ed. 2000) ("A target of a potential criminal investigation may be unwilling to settle civil claims against him if by doing so he increases the risk of prosecution and conviction.").

The amendment retains the language of the original rule that bars compromise evidence only when offered as evidence of the "validity," "invalidity," or "amount" of the disputed claim. The intent is to retain the extensive case law finding Rule 408 inapplicable when compromise evidence is offered for a purpose other than to prove the validity, invalidity, or amount of a disputed claim. *See, e.g.*, Athey v. Farmers Ins. Exch., 234 F.3d 357 (8th Cir. 2000) (evidence of settlement offer by insurer was properly admitted to prove insurer's bad faith); Coakley & Williams Const., Inc. v. Structural Concrete Equip., Inc., 973 F.2d 349 (4th Cir. 1992) (evidence of settlement is not precluded by Rule 408 where offered to prove a party's intent with respect to the scope of a release); Cates v. Morgan Portable Bldg. Corp., 708 F.2d 683 (7th Cir. 1985) (Rule 408 does not bar evidence of a settlement when offered to prove a breach of the settlement agreement, as the purpose of the evidence is to prove the fact of settlement as opposed to the validity or amount of the underlying claim); Uforma/Shelby Bus. Forms, Inc. v. NLRB, 111 F.3d 1284 (6th Cir. 1997) (threats made in settlement negotiations were admissible; Rule 408 is inapplicable when the claim is based upon a wrong that is committed during the course of settlement negotiations). So for example, Rule 408 is inapplicable if offered to show that a party made fraudulent statements in order to settle a litigation.

The amendment does not affect the case law providing that Rule 408 is inapplicable when evidence of the compromise is offered to prove notice. *See, e.g.,* United States v. Austin, 54 F.3d 394 (7th Cir. 1995) (no error to admit evidence of the defendant's settlement with the FTC, because it was offered to prove that the defendant was on notice that subsequent similar conduct was wrongful); Spell v. McDaniel, 824 F.2d 1380 (4th Cir. 1987) (in a civil rights action alleging that an officer used excessive force, a prior settlement by the City of another brutality claim was properly admitted to prove that the City was on notice of aggressive behavior by police officers).

The amendment prohibits the use of statements made in settlement negotiations when offered to impeach by prior inconsistent statement or through contradiction. Such broad impeachment would tend to swallow the exclusionary rule and would impair the public policy of promoting settlements. *See* MCCORMICK ON EVIDENCE 186 (5th ed. 1999) ("Use of statements made in compromise negotiations to impeach the testimony of a party, which is not specifically treated in Rule 408, is fraught with danger of misuse of the statements to prove liability, threatens frank interchange of information during negotiations, and generally should not be permitted."); *see also* EEOC v. Gear Petroleum, Inc., 948 F.2d 1542 (10th Cir. 1991) (letter sent as part of settlement negotiation cannot be used to impeach defense witnesses by way of contradiction or prior inconsistent statement; such broad impeachment would undermine the policy of encouraging uninhibited settlement negotiations).

The amendment makes clear that Rule 408 excludes compromise evidence even when a party seeks to admit its own settlement offer or statements made in settlement negotiations. If a party were to reveal its own statement or offer, this could itself reveal the fact that the adversary entered into settlement negotiations. The protections of Rule 408 cannot be waived unilaterally because the rule, by definition, protects both parties from having the fact of negotiation disclosed to the jury. Moreover, proof of statements and offers made in settlement would often have to be made through the testimony of attorneys, leading to the risks and costs of disqualification. *See generally* Pierce v. F.R. Tripler & Co., 955 F.2d 820, 828 (2d Cir. 1992) (settlement offers are excluded under Rule 408 even if it is the offeror who seeks to admit them;

noting that the "widespread admissibility of the substance of settlement offers could bring with it a rash of motions for disqualification of a party's chosen counsel who would likely become a witness at trial").

The sentence of the rule referring to evidence "otherwise discoverable" has been deleted as superfluous. *See, e.g.,* Advisory Committee Note to Maine Rule of Evidence 408 (refusing to include the sentence in the Maine version of Rule 408 and noting that the sentence "seems to state what the law would be if it were omitted"); Advisory Committee Note to Wyoming Rule of Evidence 408 (refusing to include the sentence in Wyoming Rule 408 on the ground that it was "superfluous"). The intent of the sentence was to prevent a party from trying to immunize admissible information, such as a pre-existing document, through the pretense of disclosing it during compromise negotiations. *See* Ramada Dev. Co. v. Rauch, 644 F.2d 1097 (5th Cir. 1981). But even without the sentence, the rule cannot be read to protect pre-existing information simply because it was presented to the adversary in compromise negotiations.

ADVISORY COMMITTEE'S NOTE TO 2011 RESTYLING OF RULE 408

Rule 408 previously provided that evidence was not excluded if offered for a purpose not explicitly prohibited by the rule. To improve the language of the rule, it now provides that the court may admit evidence if offered for a permissible purpose. There is no intent to change the process for admitting evidence covered by the rule. It remains the case that if offered for an impermissible purpose, it must be excluded, and if offered for a purpose not barred by the rule, its admissibility remains governed by the general principles of Rules 402, 403, 801, etc.

The Committee deleted the reference to "liability" on the ground that the deletion makes the rule flow better and easier to read, and because "liability" is covered by the broader term "validity." Courts have not made substantive decisions on the basis of any distinction between validity and liability. No change in current practice or in the coverage of the rule is intended.

Rule 409.   OFFERS TO PAY MEDICAL AND SIMILAR EXPENSES

Evidence of furnishing, promising to pay, or offering to pay medical, hospital, or similar expenses resulting from an injury is not admissible to prove liability for the injury.

(Enacted Jan. 2, 1975; as restyled Apr. 26, 2011, eff. Dec. 1, 2011.)

NOTE BY FEDERAL JUDICIAL CENTER

The rule enacted by the Congress is the rule prescribed by the Supreme Court without change.

ADVISORY COMMITTEE'S NOTE

The considerations underlying this rule parallel those underlying Rules 407 and 408, which deal respectively with subsequent remedial measures and offers of compromise. As stated in Annotation, 20 A.L.R.2d 291, 293 (superseded by 65 A.L.R.3d 932):

> [G]enerally, evidence of payment of medical, hospital, or similar expenses of an injured party by the opposing party, is not admissible, the reason often given being that such payment or offer is usually made from humane impulses and not from an admission of liability, and that to hold otherwise would tend to discourage assistance to the injured person.

Contrary to Rule 408, dealing with offers of compromise, the present rule does not extend to conduct or statements not a part of the act of furnishing or offering or promising to pay. This difference in treatment arises from fundamental differences in nature. Communication is essential if compromises are to be effected, and consequently broad protection of statements is needed. This is not so in cases of payments or offers or promises to pay medical expenses, where factual statements may be expected to be incidental in nature.

For rules on the same subject, but phrased in terms of "humanitarian motives," see Uniform Rule 52; California Evidence Code § 1152; Kansas Statutes Annotated § 60-452; New Jersey Evidence Rule 52 (repealed and replaced by New Jersey Rule of Evidence 409 (1993)).

Rule 410. PLEAS, PLEA DISCUSSIONS, AND RELATED STATEMENTS

(a) Prohibited Uses. In a civil or criminal case, evidence of the following is not admissible against the defendant who made the plea or participated in the plea discussions:

> **(1)** a guilty plea that was later withdrawn;

> **(2)** a nolo contendere plea;

> **(3)** a statement made during a proceeding on either of those pleas under Federal Rule of Criminal Procedure 11 or a comparable state procedure; or

> **(4)** a statement made during plea discussions with an attorney for the prosecuting authority if the discussions did not result in a guilty plea or they resulted in a later-withdrawn guilty plea.

(b) Exceptions. The court may admit a statement described in Rule 410(a)(3) or (4):

> **(1)** in any proceeding in which another statement made during the same plea or plea discussions has been introduced, if in fairness the statements ought to be considered together; or

> **(2)** in a criminal proceeding for perjury or false statement, if the defendant made the statement under oath, on the record, and with counsel present.

(Enacted Jan. 2, 1975; as amended Dec. 12, 1975; Apr. 30, 1979, eff. Dec. 1, 1980; as restyled Apr. 26, 2011, eff. Dec. 1, 2011.)

RULE 410 AS ORIGINALLY ENACTED

When first enacted, Rule 410 read as follows:

Except as otherwise provided by Act of Congress, evidence of a plea of guilty, later withdrawn, or a plea of nolo contendere, or of an offer to plead guilty or nolo contendere to the crime charged or any other crime, or of statements made in connection with any of the foregoing pleas or offers, is not admissible in any civil or criminal action, case, or proceeding against the person who made the plea or offer. This rule shall not apply to the introduction of voluntary and reliable statements made in court on the record in connection with any of the foregoing pleas or offers where offered for impeachment purposes or in a subsequent prosecution of the declarant for perjury or false statement.

This rule shall not take effect until August 1, 1975, and shall be superseded by any amendment to the Federal Rules of Criminal Procedure which is inconsistent with this rule, and which takes effect after the date of the enactment of the Act establishing these Federal Rules of Evidence.

As approved by the Supreme Court, Rule 410 consisted only of the first sentence, without the clause, "Except as otherwise provided by Act of Congress . . . ." Congress added that clause and the remaining language by amendment. The Advisory Committee note below explains the rationale of the original rule, and the following congressional reports set forth the reasons for Congress's amendment.

ADVISORY COMMITTEE'S NOTE

Withdrawn pleas of guilty were held inadmissible in federal prosecutions in *Kercheval v. United States*, 274 U.S. 220 (1927). The Court pointed out that to admit the withdrawn plea would effectively set at naught the allowance of withdrawal and place the accused in a dilemma utterly inconsistent with the decision to award him a trial. The New York Court of Appeals, in *People v. Spitaleri*, 9 N.Y.2d 168 (1961), reexamined and overturned its earlier decisions which had allowed admission. In addition to the reasons set forth in *Kercheval*, which was quoted at length, the court pointed out that the effect of admitting the plea was to compel defendant to take the stand by way of explanation and to open the way for the prosecution to call the lawyer who had represented him at the time of entering the plea. State court decisions for and against admissibility are collected in Annotation, 86 A.L.R.2d 326.

Pleas of nolo contendere are recognized by Rule 11 of the Rules of Criminal Procedure, although the law of numerous states is to the contrary. The present rule gives effect to the principal traditional characteristic of the nolo plea, i.e., avoiding the admission of guilt which is inherent in pleas of guilty. This position is consistent with the construction of section 5 of the Clayton Act, 15 U.S.C. § 16(a), recognizing the inconclusive and compromise nature of judgments based on nolo pleas. Gen. Elec. Co. v. City of San Antonio, 334 F.2d 480 (5th Cir. 1964); Commonwealth Edison Co. v. Allis–Chalmers Mfg. Co., 323 F.2d 412 (7th Cir. 1963), *cert. denied*, 376 U.S. 939 (1964); Armco Steel Corp. v. North Dakota *ex rel.* State Highway Fund, 376 F.2d 206 (8th Cir. 1967); City of Burbank v. Gen. Elec. Co., 329 F.2d 825 (9th Cir. 1964). See also state court decisions in Annotation, 18 A.L.R.2d 1287, 1314.

Exclusion of offers to plead guilty or nolo has as its purpose the promotion of disposition of criminal cases by compromise. As pointed out in McCormick § 251, at 543:

> Effective criminal law administration in many localities would hardly be possible if a large proportion of the charges were not disposed of by such compromises.

See also People v. Hamilton, 60 Cal.2d 105 (1963) (discussing legislation designed to achieve this result). As with compromise offers generally, Rule 408, free communication is needed, and security against having an offer of compromise or related statement admitted in evidence effectively encourages it.

Limiting the exclusionary rule to use against the accused is consistent with the purpose of the rule, since the possibility of use for or against other persons will not impair the effectiveness of withdrawing pleas or the freedom of discussion which the rule is designed to foster. *See* ABA STANDARDS RELATING TO PLEAS OF GUILTY § 2.2 (1968). See also the narrower provisions of New Jersey Evidence Rule 52(2) (repealed and replaced by New Jersey Rule of Evidence 410 (1993)) and the unlimited exclusion provided in California Evidence Code § 1153.

REPORT OF THE HOUSE COMMITTEE ON THE JUDICIARY

The Committee added the phrase "Except as otherwise provided by Act of Congress" to Rule 410 as submitted by the Court in order to preserve particular congressional policy judgments as to the effect of a plea of guilty or of nolo contendere. *See* 15 U.S.C. § 16(a). The Committee intends that its amendment refers to both present statutes and statutes subsequently enacted.

REPORT OF THE SENATE COMMITTEE ON THE JUDICIARY

As adopted by the House, Rule 410 would make inadmissible pleas of guilty or nolo contendere subsequently withdrawn as well as offers to make such pleas. Such a rule is clearly justified as a means of encouraging pleading. However, the House rule would then go on to render inadmissible for any purpose statements made in connection with these pleas or offers as well.

The Committee finds this aspect of the House rule unjustified. Of course, in certain circumstances such statements should be excluded. If, for example, a plea is vitiated because of coercion, statements made in connection with the plea may also have been coerced and should be inadmissible on that basis. In other cases, however, voluntary statements of an accused made in court on the record, in connection with a plea, and determined by a court to be reliable should be admissible even though the plea is subsequently withdrawn. This is particularly true in those cases where, if the House rule were in effect, a defendant would be able to contradict his previous statements and thereby lie with impunity.[6] To prevent such an injustice, the rule has been modified to permit the use of such statements for the limited purposes of impeachment and in subsequent perjury or false statement prosecutions.

CONFERENCE REPORT

The House bill provides that evidence of a guilty or nolo contendere plea, of an offer of either plea, or of statements made in connection with such pleas or offers of such pleas, is inadmissible in any civil or criminal action, case, or proceeding against the person making such plea or offer. The Senate amendment makes the rule inapplicable to a voluntary and reliable statement made in court on the record where the statement is offered in a subsequent prosecution of the declarant for perjury or false statement.

The issues raised by Rule 410 are also raised by proposed Rule 11(e)(6) of the Federal Rules of Criminal Procedure presently pending before Congress.[7] This proposed rule, which deals with the admissibility of pleas of guilty or nolo contendere, offers to make such pleas, and statements made in connection with such pleas, was promulgated by the Supreme Court on April 22, 1974, and in the absence of congressional action will become effective on August 1, 1975. The Conferees intend to make no change in the presently-existing case law until that date, leaving the courts free to develop rules in this area on a case-by-case basis.

---

[6] *See* Harris v. New York, 401 U.S. 222 (1971).

[7] [Rule 11(e)(6) of the Federal Rules of Criminal Procedure used to be almost identical to Rule 410 of the Federal Rules of Evidence. Today Federal Rule of Criminal Procedure 11(f) simply incorporates by reference Federal Rule of Evidence 410.—GF]

The Conferees further determined that the issues presented by the use of guilty and nolo contendere pleas, offers of such pleas, and statements made in connection with such pleas or offers, can be explored in greater detail during Congressional consideration of Rule 11(e)(6) of the Federal Rules of Criminal Procedure. The Conferees believe, therefore, that it is best to defer its effective date until August 1, 1975. The Conferees intend that Rule 410 would be superseded by any subsequent Federal Rule of Criminal Procedure or Act of Congress with which it is inconsistent, if the Federal Rule of Criminal Procedure or Act of Congress takes effect or becomes law after the date of the enactment of the act establishing the rules of evidence.

The Conference adopts the Senate amendment with an amendment that expresses the above intentions.

<u>EDITOR'S NOTE: 1975 AMENDMENT TO RULE 410</u>

Congress amended Rule 11(e)(6) of the Federal Rules of Criminal Procedure in 1975, Pub. L. No. 94-64, 89 Stat. 371 (July 31, 1975), and then amended Rule 410 to keep the rules in parity. As amended, Rule 410 read:

> Except as otherwise provided in this rule, evidence of a plea of guilty, later withdrawn, or a plea of nolo contendere, or of an offer to plead guilty or nolo contendere to the crime charged or any other crime, or of statements made in connection with, and relevant to, any of the foregoing pleas or offers, is not admissible in any civil or criminal proceeding against the person who made the plea or offer. However, evidence of a statement made in connection with, and relevant to, a plea of guilty, later withdrawn, a plea of nolo contendere, or an offer to plead guilty or nolo contendere to the crime charged or any other crime, is admissible in a criminal proceeding for perjury or false statement if the statement was made by the defendant under oath, on the record, and in the presence of counsel.

<u>REPORT OF THE HOUSE COMMITTEE ON THE JUDICIARY</u>

The Committee added an exception to [Federal Rule of Criminal Procedure 11(e)(6)]. That subdivision provides:[8]

> Evidence of a plea of guilty, later withdrawn, or a plea of nolo contendere, or of an offer to plead guilty or nolo contendere to the crime charged or any other crime, or of

---

[8] As prescribed by the Supreme Court and transmitted to Congress.

statements made in connection with any of the foregoing pleas or offers, is not admissible in any civil or criminal proceeding against the person who made the plea or offer.

The Committee's exception permits the use of such evidence in a perjury or false statement prosecution where the plea, offer, or related statement was made by the defendant on the record, under oath and in the presence of counsel. The Committee recognizes that even this limited exception may discourage defendants from being completely candid and open during plea negotiations and may even result in discouraging the reaching of plea agreements. However, the Committee believes that, on balance, it is more important to protect the integrity of the judicial process from willful deceit and untruthfulness.[9] The Committee recast the language of [11(b)], which deals with the advice given to a defendant before the court can accept his plea of guilty or nolo contendere. The Committee acted in part because it believed that the warnings given to the defendant ought to include those that *Boykin v. Alabama*, 395 U.S. 238 (1969), said were constitutionally required. In addition, and as a result of its change in subdivision (e)(6), the Committee thought it only fair that the defendant be warned that his plea of guilty (later withdrawn) or nolo contendere, or his offer of either plea, or his statements made in connection with such pleas or offers, could later be used against him in a perjury trial if made under oath, on the record, and in the presence of counsel.

CONFERENCE REPORT

Rule 11(e)(6) [of the Federal Rules of Criminal Procedure] deals with the use of statements made in connection with plea agreements. The House version permits a limited use of pleas of guilty, later withdrawn, or nolo contendere, offers of such pleas, and statements made in connection with such pleas or offers. Such evidence can be used in a perjury or false statement prosecution if the plea, offer, or related statement was made under oath, on the record, and in the presence of counsel. The Senate version permits evidence of voluntary and reliable statements made in court on the record to be used for the purpose of impeaching the credibility of the declarant or in a perjury or false statement prosecution.

The Conference adopts the House version with changes. The Conference agrees that neither a plea nor the offer of a plea ought to be admissible for any purpose. The Conference-adopted provision,

---

[9] The Committee does not intend its language to be construed as mandating or encouraging the swearing-in of the defendant during proceedings in connection with the disclosure and acceptance or rejection of a plea agreement.

therefore, like the Senate provision, permits only the use of statements made in connection with a plea of guilty, later withdrawn, or a plea of nolo contendere, or in connection with an offer of a guilty or nolo contendere plea.

ADVISORY COMMITTEE'S NOTE TO 1980 AMENDMENT TO RULE 410

The major objective of the amendment to Rule 11(e)(6) [of the Federal Rules of Criminal Procedure] is to describe more precisely, consistent with the original purpose of the provision, what evidence relating to pleas or plea discussions is inadmissible. The present language is susceptible to interpretation which would make it applicable to a wide variety of statements made under various circumstances other than within the context of those plea discussions authorized by Rule 11(e) and intended to be protected by subdivision (e)(6) of the rule. See *United States v. Herman*, 544 F.2d 791 (5th Cir. 1977), discussed herein.

Federal Rule of Evidence 410, as originally adopted by Public Law 93-595, provided in part that "evidence of a plea of guilty, later withdrawn, or a plea of nolo contendere, or of an offer to plead guilty or nolo contendere to the crime charged or any other crime, or of statements made in connection with any of the foregoing pleas or offers, is not admissible in any civil or criminal action, case, or proceeding against the person who made the plea or offer." (This rule was adopted with the proviso that it "shall be superseded by any amendment to the Federal Rules of Criminal Procedure which is inconsistent with this rule.") As the Advisory Committee note explained: "Exclusion of offers to plead guilty or nolo has as its purpose the promotion of disposition of criminal cases by compromise." The amendment of Federal Rule of Criminal Procedure 11, transmitted to Congress by the Supreme Court in April 1974, contained a subdivision (e)(6) essentially identical to the Rule 410 language quoted above, as a part of a substantial revision of Rule 11. The most significant feature of this revision was the express recognition given to the fact that the "attorney for the government and the attorney for the defendant or the defendant when acting pro se may engage in discussions with a view toward reaching" a plea agreement. Subdivision (e)(6) was intended to encourage such discussions. As noted in H.R. REP. NO. 94-247, 94th Cong., 1st Sess., at 7 (1975), the purpose of subdivision (e)(6) is to not "discourage defendants from being completely candid and open during plea negotiations." Similarly, H.R. REP. NO. 94-414, 94th Cong., 1st Sess., at 10 (1975), states that "Rule 11(e)(6) deals with the use of statements made in connection with plea agreements." (Rule 11(e)(6) was thereafter enacted, with the addition of the proviso allowing use of statements for purposes of impeachment and in a prosecution for perjury, and with the qualification that the inadmissible statements must also be "relevant to" the inadmissible pleas or offers. Pub. L. No. 94-64. Federal Rule of Evidence 410 was then amended to conform. Pub. L. No. 94-149.)

While this history shows that the purpose of Federal Rule of Evidence 410 and Federal Rule of Criminal Procedure 11(e)(6) is to permit the unrestrained candor which produces effective plea discussions between the "attorney for the government and the attorney for the defendant or the defendant when acting pro se," given visibility and sanction in Rule 11(e), a literal reading of the language of these two rules could reasonably lead to the conclusion that a broader rule of inadmissibility obtains. That is, because "statements" are generally inadmissible if "made in connection with, and relevant to" an "offer to plead guilty," it might be thought that an otherwise voluntary admission to law enforcement officials is rendered inadmissible merely because it was made in the hope of obtaining leniency by a plea. Some decisions interpreting Rule 11(e)(6) point in this direction. *See* United States v. Herman, 544 F.2d 791 (5th Cir. 1977) (defendant in custody of two postal inspectors during continuance of removal hearing instigated conversation with them and at some point said he would plead guilty to armed robbery if the murder charge was dropped; one inspector stated they were not "in position" to make any deals in this regard; held, defendant's statement inadmissible under Rule 11(e)(6) because the defendant "made the statements during the course of a conversation in which he sought concessions from the government in return for a guilty plea"); United States v. Brooks, 536 F.2d 1137 (6th Cir. 1976) (defendant telephoned postal inspector and offered to plead guilty if he got 2-year maximum; statement inadmissible).

The amendment makes inadmissible statements made "in the course of any proceedings under this rule regarding" either a plea of guilty later withdrawn or a plea of nolo contendere, and also statements "made in the course of plea discussions with an attorney for the government which do not result in a plea of guilty or which result in a plea of guilty later withdrawn." It is not limited to statements by the defendant himself, and thus would cover statements by defense counsel regarding defendant's incriminating admissions to him. It thus fully protects the plea discussion process authorized by Rule 11 without attempting to deal with confrontations between suspects and law enforcement agents, which involve problems of quite different dimensions. *See, e.g.,* ALI MODEL CODE OF PRE-ARRAIGNMENT PROCEDURE art. 140 and § 150.2(8) (Proposed Official Draft 1975) (latter section requires exclusion if "a law enforcement officer induces any person to make a statement by promising leniency"). This change, it must be emphasized, does not compel the conclusion that statements made to law enforcement agents, especially when the agents purport to have authority to bargain, are inevitably admissible. Rather, the point is that such cases are not covered by the per se rule of 11(e)(6) and thus must be resolved by that body of law dealing with police interrogations.

If there has been a plea of guilty later withdrawn or a plea of nolo contendere, subdivision (e)(6)(C) makes inadmissible statements made "in the course of any proceedings under this rule" regarding such pleas. This includes, for example, admissions by the defendant when he makes his plea in court pursuant to Rule 11 and also admissions made to provide the factual basis pursuant to subdivision [(b)(3)]. However, subdivision (e)(6)(C) is not limited to statements made in court. If the court were to defer its decision on a plea agreement pending examination of the presentence report, as authorized by subdivision (e)(2), statements made to the probation officer in connection with the preparation of that report would come within this provision.

This amendment is fully consistent with all recent and major law reform efforts on this subject. ALI MODEL CODE OF PRE-ARRAIGNMENT PROCEDURE § 350.7 (Proposed Official Draft, 1975), and ABA STANDARDS RELATING TO PLEAS OF GUILTY § 3.4 (Approved Draft, 1968) both provide:

> Unless the defendant subsequently enters a plea of guilty or nolo contendere which is not withdrawn, the fact that the defendant or his counsel and the prosecuting attorney engaged in plea discussions or made a plea agreement should not be received in evidence against or in favor of the defendant in any criminal or civil action or administrative proceedings.

The Commentary to the latter states:

> The above standard is limited to discussions and agreements with the prosecuting attorney. Sometimes defendants will indicate to the police their willingness to bargain, and in such instances these statements are sometimes admitted in court against the defendant. State v. Christian, 245 S.W.2d 895 (Mo. 1952). If the police initiate this kind of discussion, this may have some bearing on the admissibility of the defendant's statement. However, the policy considerations relevant to this issue are better dealt with in the context of standards governing in-custody interrogation by the police.

Similarly, Uniform Rule of Criminal Procedure 441(d) (Approved Draft 1974) provides that except under limited circumstances "no discussion between the parties or statement by the defendant or his lawyer under this rule," i.e., the rule providing "the parties may meet to discuss the possibility of pretrial diversion . . . or of a plea agreement," are admissible. The amendment is likewise consistent with the typical state provision on this subject. *See, e.g.,* ILL. SUP. CT. R. 402(f).

The language of the amendment identifies with more precision than the present language the necessary relationship between the statements and the plea or discussion. See the dispute between the majority and concurring opinion in *United States v. Herman,* 544 F.2d 791 (5th Cir. 1977), concerning the meanings and effect of the phrases "connection to" and "relevant to" in the present rule. Moreover, by relating the statements to "plea discussions" rather than "an offer to plead," the amendment ensures "that even an attempt to open plea bargaining [is] covered under the same rule of inadmissibility." United States v. Brooks, 536 F.2d 1137 (6th Cir. 1976).

The last sentence of Rule 11(e)(6) is amended to provide a second exception to the general rule of nonadmissibility of the described statements. Under the amendment, such a statement is also admissible "in any proceeding wherein another statement made in the course of the same plea or plea discussions has been introduced and the statement ought in fairness be considered contemporaneously with it." This change is necessary so that, when evidence of statements made in the course of or as a consequence of a certain plea or plea discussions are introduced under circumstances not prohibited by this rule (e.g., not "against" the person who made the plea), other statements relating to the same plea or plea discussions may also be admitted when relevant to the matter at issue. For example, if a defendant upon a motion to dismiss a prosecution on some ground were able to admit certain statements made in aborted plea discussions in his favor, then other relevant statements made in the same plea discussions should be admissible against the defendant in the interest of determining the truth of the matter at issue. The language of the amendment follows closely that in Federal Rule of Evidence 106, as the considerations involved are very similar.

The phrase "in any civil or criminal proceeding" has been moved from its present position, following the word "against," for purposes of clarity. An ambiguity presently exists because the word "against" may be read as referring either to the kind of proceeding in which the evidence is offered or the purpose for which it is offered. The change makes it clear that the latter construction is correct. No change is intended with respect to provisions making evidence rules inapplicable in certain situations. *See, e.g.,* FED. R. EVID. 104(a), 1101(d).

Unlike ABA STANDARDS RELATING TO PLEAS OF GUILTY § 3.4 (Approved Draft 1968), and ALI MODEL CODE OF PRE-ARRAIGNMENT PROCEDURE § 350.7 (Proposed Official Draft 1975), Rule 11(e)(6) does not also provide that the described evidence is inadmissible "in favor of" the defendant. This is not intended to suggest, however, that such evidence will inevitably be admissible in the defendant's favor. Specifically, no disapproval is intended of such decisions as *United States v. Verdoorn,* 528 F.2d 103 (8th Cir. 1976), holding that the trial judge properly refused to permit the defendants to put into evidence at their trial the fact the prosecution had attempted to plea bargain with them, as "meaningful dialogue between the parties would, as a practical matter, be impossible if either party had to assume the risk that plea offers would be admissible in evidence."

Rule 411. LIABILITY INSURANCE

Evidence that a person was or was not insured against liability is not admissible to prove whether the person acted negligently or otherwise wrongfully. But the court may admit this evidence for another purpose, such as proving a witness's bias or prejudice or proving agency, ownership, or control.

(Enacted Jan. 2, 1975; as amended Mar. 2, 1987, eff. Oct. 1, 1987; as restyled Apr. 26, 2011, eff. Dec. 1, 2011.)

<u>NOTE BY FEDERAL JUDICIAL CENTER</u>

The rule enacted by the Congress is the rule prescribed by the Supreme Court without change.

<u>ADVISORY COMMITTEE'S NOTE</u>

The courts have with substantial unanimity rejected evidence of liability insurance for the purpose of proving fault, and absence of liability insurance as proof of lack of fault. At best the inference of fault from the fact of insurance coverage is a tenuous one, as is its converse. More important, no doubt, has been the feeling that knowledge of the presence or absence of liability insurance would induce juries to decide cases on improper grounds. MCCORMICK § 168; Annotation, 4 A.L.R.2d 761. The rule is drafted in broad terms so as to include contributory negligence or other fault of a plaintiff as well as fault of a defendant.

The second sentence points out the limits of the rule, using well established illustrations. *Id.*

For similar rules see Uniform Rule 54; California Evidence Code § 1155; Kansas Statutes Annotated § 60-454; New Jersey Evidence Rule 54 (repealed and replaced by New Jersey Rule of Evidence 411 (1993)).

Advisory Committee's Note to 2011 Restyling of Rule 411

Rule 411 previously provided that evidence was not excluded if offered for a purpose not explicitly prohibited by the rule. To improve the language of the rule, it now provides that the court may admit evidence if offered for a permissible purpose. There is no intent to change the process for admitting evidence covered by the rule. It remains the case that if offered for an impermissible purpose, it must be excluded, and if offered for a purpose not barred by the rule, its admissibility remains governed by the general principles of Rules 402, 403, 801, etc.

Rule 412.   SEX-OFFENSE   CASES: THE   VICTIM'S   SEXUAL BEHAVIOR OR PREDISPOSITION

(a) Prohibited Uses.   The following evidence is not admissible in a civil or criminal proceeding involving alleged sexual misconduct:

(1) evidence offered to prove that a victim engaged in other sexual behavior; or

(2) evidence offered to prove a victim's sexual predisposition.

(b) Exceptions.

(1) *Criminal Cases.*   The court may admit the following evidence in a criminal case:

(A) evidence of specific instances of a victim's sexual behavior, if offered to prove that someone other than the defendant was the source of semen, injury, or other physical evidence;

(B) evidence of specific instances of a victim's sexual behavior with respect to the person accused of the sexual misconduct, if offered by the defendant to prove consent or if offered by the prosecutor; and

(C) evidence whose exclusion would violate the defendant's constitutional rights.

(2) Civil Cases. In a civil case, the court may admit evidence offered to prove a victim's sexual behavior or sexual predisposition if its probative value substantially outweighs the danger of harm to any victim and of unfair prejudice to any party. The court may admit evidence of a victim's reputation only if the victim has placed it in controversy.

(c) Procedure to Determine Admissibility.

(1) *Motion.* If a party intends to offer evidence under Rule 412(b), the party must:

(A) file a motion that specifically describes the evidence and states the purpose for which it is to be offered;

(B) do so at least 14 days before trial unless the court, for good cause, sets a different time;

(C) serve the motion on all parties; and

(D) notify the victim or, when appropriate, the victim's guardian or representative.

(2) *Hearing.* Before admitting evidence under this rule, the court must conduct an in camera hearing and give the victim and parties a right to attend and be heard. Unless the court orders otherwise, the motion, related materials, and the record of the hearing must be and remain sealed.

(d) Definition of "Victim." In this rule, "victim" includes an alleged victim.

(Enacted Oct. 28, 1978; as amended Nov. 18, 1988; Apr. 29, 1994, eff. Dec. 1, 1994; Sept. 13, 1994; as restyled Apr. 26, 2011, eff. Dec. 1, 2011.)

ADVISORY COMMITTEE'S NOTE TO 1994 AMENDMENT TO RULE 412

Rule 412 has been revised to diminish some of the confusion engendered by the original rule and to expand the protection afforded alleged victims of sexual misconduct. Rule 412 applies to both civil and criminal proceedings. The rule aims to safeguard the alleged victim against the invasion of privacy, potential embarrassment, and sexual stereotyping that is associated with public disclosure of intimate sexual details and the infusion of sexual innuendo into the factfinding process. By affording victims protection in most instances, the rule also encourages victims of sexual misconduct to institute and to participate in legal proceedings against alleged offenders.

Rule 412 seeks to achieve these objectives by barring evidence relating to the alleged victim's sexual behavior or alleged sexual predisposition, whether offered as substantive evidence or for impeachment, except in designated circumstances in which the probative value of the evidence significantly outweighs possible harm to the victim.

The revised rule applies in all cases involving sexual misconduct without regard to whether the alleged victim or person accused is a party to the litigation. Rule 412 extends to "pattern" witnesses in both criminal and civil cases whose testimony about other instances of sexual misconduct by the person accused is otherwise admissible. When the case does not involve alleged sexual misconduct, evidence relating to a third-party witness's alleged sexual activities is not within the ambit of Rule 412. The witness will, however, be protected by other rules such as Rules 404 and 608, as well as Rule 403.

The terminology "alleged victim" is used because there will frequently be a factual dispute as to whether sexual misconduct occurred. It does not connote any requirement that the misconduct be alleged in the pleadings. Rule 412 does not, however, apply unless the person against whom the evidence is offered can reasonably be characterized as a "victim of alleged sexual misconduct." When this is not the case, as for instance in a defamation action involving statements concerning sexual misconduct in which the evidence is offered to show that the alleged defamatory statements were true or did not damage the plaintiff's reputation, neither Rule 404 nor this rule will operate to bar the evidence; Rule[s] 401 and 403 will continue to control. Rule 412 will, however, apply in a Title VII action in which the plaintiff has alleged sexual harassment.

The reference to a person "accused" is also used in a non-technical sense. There is no requirement that there be a criminal charge pending against the person or even that the misconduct would constitute a criminal offense. Evidence offered to prove allegedly false prior claims by the victim is not barred by Rule 412. However, the evidence is subject to the requirements of Rule 404.

Subdivision (a). As amended, Rule 412 bars evidence offered to prove the victim's sexual behavior and alleged sexual predisposition. Evidence, which might otherwise be admissible under Rules 402, 404(b), 405, 607, 608, 609 or some other evidence rule, must be excluded if Rule 412 so requires. The word "other" is used to suggest some flexibility in admitting evidence "intrinsic" to the alleged sexual misconduct. *Cf.* Advisory Committee's Note to 1991 amendment to Rule 404(b).

Past sexual behavior connotes all activities that involve actual physical conduct, i.e., sexual intercourse or sexual contact, or that imply sexual intercourse or sexual contact. *See, e.g.,* United States v. Galloway, 937 F.2d 542 (10th Cir. 1991) (use of contraceptives inadmissible since use implies sexual activity), *cert. denied,* 506 U.S. 957 (1992); United States v. One Feather, 702 F.2d 736 (8th Cir. 1983) (birth or an illegitimate child inadmissible); State v. Carmichael, 240 Kan. 149 (1986) (evidence of venereal disease inadmissible). In addition, the word "behavior" should be construed to include activities of the mind, such as fantasies or dreams. *See* 23 C. WRIGHT & K. GRAHAM, JR., FEDERAL PRACTICE AND PROCEDURE § 5384, at 548 (1980) ("While there may be some doubt under statutes that require 'conduct,' it would seem that the language of Rule 412 is broad enough to encompass the behavior of the mind.").

The rule has been amended to also exclude all other evidence relating to an alleged victim of sexual misconduct that is offered to prove a sexual predisposition. This amendment is designed to exclude evidence that does not directly refer to sexual activities or thoughts but that the proponent believes may have a sexual connotation for the factfinder. Admission of such evidence would contravene Rule 412's objectives of shielding the alleged victim from potential embarrassment and safeguarding the victim against stereotypical thinking. Consequently, unless the (b)(2) exception is satisfied, evidence such as that relating to the alleged victim's mode of dress, speech, or life-style will not be admissible.

The introductory phrase in subdivision (a) was deleted because it lacked clarity and contained no explicit reference to the other provisions of the law that were intended to be overridden. The conditional clause, "except as provided in subdivisions (b) and (c)" is intended to make clear that evidence of the types described in subdivision (a) is admissible only under the strictures of those sections.

The reason for extending the rule to all criminal cases is obvious. The strong social policy of protecting a victim's privacy and encouraging victims to come forward to report criminal acts is not confined to cases that involve a charge of sexual assault. The need to protect the victim is equally great when a defendant is charged with kidnapping, and evidence is offered, either to prove motive or as background, that the defendant sexually assaulted the victim.

The reason for extending Rule 412 to civil cases is equally obvious. The need to protect alleged victims against invasions of privacy, potential embarrassment, and unwarranted sexual stereotyping, and the wish to encourage victims to come forward when they have been sexually molested do not disappear because the context has shifted from a criminal prosecution to a claim for damages or injunctive relief. There is a strong social policy in not only punishing those who engage in sexual misconduct, but in also providing relief to the victim. Thus, Rule 412 applies in any civil case in which a person claims to be the victim of sexual misconduct, such as actions for sexual battery or sexual harassment.

Subdivision (b). Subdivision (b) spells out the specific circumstances in which some evidence may be admissible that would otherwise be barred by the general rule expressed in subdivision (a). As amended, Rule 412 will be virtually unchanged in criminal cases, but will provide protection to any person alleged to be a victim of sexual misconduct regardless of the charge actually brought against an accused. A new exception has been added for civil cases.

In a criminal case, evidence may be admitted under subdivision (b)(1) pursuant to three possible exceptions, provided the evidence also satisfies other requirements for admissibility specified in the Federal Rules of Evidence, including Rule 403. Subdivisions (b)(1)(A) and (b)(1)(B) require proof in the form of specific instances of sexual behavior in recognition of the limited probative value and dubious reliability of evidence of reputation or evidence in the form of an opinion.

Under subdivision (b)(1)(A), evidence of specific instances of sexual behavior with persons other than the person whose sexual misconduct is alleged may be admissible if it is offered to prove that another person was the source of semen, injury, or other physical evidence. Where the prosecution has directly or indirectly asserted that the physical evidence originated with the accused, the defendant must be afforded an opportunity to prove that another person was responsible. *See* United States v. Begay, 937 F.2d 515, 523 n.10 (10th Cir. 1991). Evidence offered for the specific purpose identified in this subdivision may still be excluded if it does not satisfy Rules 401 or 403. *See, e.g.,* United States v. Azure, 845 F.2d 1503, 1505–06 (8th Cir. 1988) (10 year old victim's injuries indicated recent use of force; court excluded evidence of consensual sexual activities with witness who testified at in camera hearing that he had never hurt victim and failed to establish recent activities).

Under the exception in subdivision (b)(1)(B), evidence of specific instances of sexual behavior with respect to the person whose sexual misconduct is alleged is admissible if offered to prove consent or offered by the prosecution. Admissible pursuant to this exception might be evidence of prior instances of sexual activities between the alleged victim and the accused, as well as statements in which the alleged victim expresses an intent to engage in sexual intercourse with the accused, or voiced sexual fantasies involving that specific accused. In a prosecution for child sexual abuse, for example, evidence of uncharged sexual activity between the accused and the alleged victim offered by the prosecution may be admissible pursuant to Rule 404(b) to show a pattern of behavior. Evidence relating to the victim's alleged sexual predisposition is not admissible pursuant to this exception.

Under subdivision (b)(1)(C), evidence of specific instances of conduct may not be excluded if the result would be to deny a criminal defendant the protections afforded by the Constitution. For example, statements in which the victim has expressed an intent to have sex with the first person encountered on a particular occasion might not be excluded without violating the due process right of a rape defendant seeking to prove consent. Recognition of this basic principle was expressed in subdivision (b)(1) of the original rule. The United States Supreme Court has recognized that in various circumstances a defendant may have a right to introduce evidence otherwise precluded by an evidence rule under the Confrontation Clause. *See, e.g.*, Olden v. Kentucky, 488 U.S. 227 (1988) (defendant in rape cases had right to inquire into alleged victim's cohabitation with another man to show bias).

Subdivision (b)(2) governs the admissibility of otherwise proscribed evidence in civil cases. It employs a balancing test rather than the specific exceptions stated in subdivision (b)(1) in recognition of the difficulty of foreseeing future developments in the law. Greater flexibility is needed to accommodate evolving causes of action such as claims for sexual harassment.

The balancing test requires the proponent of the evidence, whether plaintiff or defendant, to convince the court that the probative value of the proffered evidence "substantially outweighs the danger of harm to any victim and of unfair prejudice to any party." This test for admitting evidence offered to prove sexual behavior or sexual propensity in civil cases differs in three respects from the general rule governing admissibility set forth in Rule 403. First, it reverses the usual procedure spelled out in Rule 403 by shifting the burden to the proponent to demonstrate admissibility rather than making the opponent justify exclusion of the evidence. Second, the standard expressed in subdivision (b)(2) is more stringent than in the original rule; it raises the threshold for admission by requiring that the probative value of the evidence substantially outweigh the specified dangers. Finally, the Rule 412 test puts "harm to the victim" on the scale in addition to prejudice to the parties.

Evidence of reputation may be received in a civil case only if the alleged victim has put his or her reputation into controversy. The victim may do so without making a specific allegation in a pleading. *Cf.* FED. R. CIV. P. 35(a).

Subdivision (c). Amended subdivision (c) is more concise and understandable than the subdivision it replaces. The requirement of a motion before trial is continued in the amended rule, as is the provision that a late motion may be permitted for good cause shown. In deciding whether to permit late filing, the court may take into account the conditions previously included in the rule: namely whether the evidence is newly discovered and could not have been obtained earlier through the existence of due diligence, and whether the issue to which such evidence relates has newly arisen in the case. The rule recognizes that in some instances the circumstances that justify an application to introduce evidence otherwise barred by Rule 412 will not become apparent until trial.

The amended rule provides that before admitting evidence that falls within the prohibition of Rule 412(a), the court must hold a hearing in camera at which the alleged victim and any party must be afforded the right to be present and an opportunity to be heard. All papers connected with the motion and any record of a hearing on the motion must be kept and remain under seal during the course of trial and appellate proceedings unless otherwise ordered. This is to assure that the privacy of the alleged victim is preserved in all cases in which the court rules that proffered evidence is not admissible, and in which the hearing refers to matters that are not received, or are received in another form.

The procedures set forth in subdivision (c) do not apply to discovery of a victim's past sexual conduct or predisposition in civil cases, which will be continued to be governed by Federal Rule of Civil Procedure 26. In order not to undermine the rationale of Rule 412, however, courts should enter appropriate orders pursuant to Federal Rule of Civil Procedure 26(c) to protect the victim against unwarranted inquiries and to ensure confidentiality. Courts should presumptively issue protective orders barring discovery unless the party seeking discovery makes a showing that the evidence sought to be discovered would be relevant under the facts and theories of the particular case, and cannot be obtained except through discovery. In an action for sexual harassment, for instance, while some evidence of the alleged victim's sexual behavior and/or predisposition in the workplace may perhaps be relevant, non-work place conduct will usually be irrelevant. *Cf.* Burns v. McGregor Elec. Indus., Inc., 989 F.2d 959, 962–63 (8th Cir. 1993) (posing for a nude magazine outside work hours is irrelevant to issue of unwelcomeness of sexual advances at work). Confidentiality orders should be presumptively granted as well.

One substantive change made in subdivision (c) is the elimination of the following sentence: "Notwithstanding subdivision (b) of Rule 104, if the relevancy of the evidence which the accused seeks to offer in the trial depends upon the fulfillment of a condition of fact, the court, at the hearing in chambers or at a subsequent hearing in chambers scheduled for such purpose, shall accept evidence on the issue of whether such condition of fact is fulfilled and shall determine such issue." On its face, this language would appear to authorize a trial judge to exclude evidence of past sexual conduct between alleged victim and an accused or a defendant in a civil case based upon the judge's belief that such past acts did not occur. Such an authorization raises questions of invasion of the right to a jury trial under the Sixth and Seventh Amendments. *See* 1 S. SALTZBURG & M. MARTIN, FEDERAL RULES OF EVIDENCE MANUAL 396–97 (5th ed. 1990).

The Advisory Committee concluded that the amended rule provided adequate protection for all persons claiming to be the victims of sexual misconduct, and that it was inadvisable to continue to include a provision in the rule that has been confusing and that raises substantial constitutional issues.

<u>CONGRESSIONAL DISCUSSION</u>

The following discussion in the House of Representatives preceded passage of H.R. 4727, the Resolution enacting Rule 412. The complete discussion can be found in 124 Cong. Rec. H11944 (daily ed. Oct. 10, 1978).

> Mr. MANN. Mr. Speaker, for many years in this country, evidentiary rules have permitted the introduction of evidence about a rape victim's prior sexual conduct. Defense lawyers were permitted great latitude in bringing out intimate details about a rape victim's life. Such evidence quite often serves no real purpose and only results in embarrassment to the rape victim and unwarranted public intrusion into her private life.
>
> The evidentiary rules that permit such inquiry have in recent years come under question; and the states have taken the lead to change and modernize their evidentiary rules about evidence of a rape victim's prior sexual behavior. The bill before us similarly seeks to modernize the federal evidentiary rules.

The present Federal Rules of Evidence reflect the traditional approach. If a defendant in a rape case raises the defense of consent, that defendant may then offer evidence about the victim's prior sexual behavior. Such evidence may be in the form of opinion evidence, evidence of reputation, or evidence of specific instances of behavior. Rule [404(a)(2)(B)] of the Federal Rules of Evidence permits the introduction of evidence of a "pertinent character trait." The Advisory Committee note to that rule cites, as an example of what the rule covers, the character of a rape victim when the issue is consent. Rule 405 of the Federal Rules of Evidence permits the use of opinion or reputation evidence or the use of evidence of specific behavior to show a character trait.

Thus, federal evidentiary rules permit a wide ranging inquiry into the private conduct of a rape victim, even though that conduct may have at best a tenuous connection to the offense for which the defendant is being tried. H.R. 4727 amends the Federal Rules of Evidence to add a new rule, applicable only in criminal cases, to spell out when, and under what conditions, evidence of a rape victim's prior sexual behavior can be admitted. The new rule provides that reputation or opinion evidence about a rape victim's prior sexual behavior is not admissible. The new rule also provides that a court cannot admit evidence of specific instances of a rape victim's prior sexual conduct except in three circumstances.

The first circumstance is where the Constitution requires that the evidence be admitted. This exception is intended to cover those infrequent instances where, because of an unusual chain of circumstances, the general rule of inadmissibility, if followed, would result in denying the defendant a constitutional right.

The second circumstance in which the defendant can offer evidence of specific instances of a rape victim's prior sexual behavior is where the defendant raises the issue of consent and the evidence is of sexual behavior with the defendant. To admit such evidence, however, the court must find that the evidence is relevant and that its probative value outweighs the danger of unfair prejudice.

The third circumstance in which a court can admit evidence of specific instances of a rape victim's prior sexual behavior is where the evidence is of behavior with someone other than the defendant and is offered by the defendant on the issue of whether or not he was the source of semen or injury. Again, such evidence will be admitted only if the court finds that the evidence is relevant and that its probative value outweighs the danger of unfair prejudice.

The new rule further provides that before evidence is admitted under any of these exceptions, there must be an in camera hearing—that is, a proceeding that takes place in the judge's chambers out of the presence of the jury and the general public. At this hearing, the defendant will present the evidence he intends to offer and be able to argue why it should be admitted. The prosecution, of course, will be able to argue against that evidence being admitted.

The purpose of the in camera hearing is twofold. It gives the defendant an opportunity to demonstrate to the court why certain evidence is admissible and ought to be presented to the jury. At the same time, it protects the privacy of the rape victim in those instances when the court finds that evidence is inadmissible. Of course, if the court finds the evidence to be admissible, the evidence will be presented to the jury in open court.

The effect of this legislation, therefore, is to preclude the routine use of evidence of specific instances of a rape victim's prior sexual behavior. Such evidence will be admitted only in clearly and narrowly defined circumstances and only after an in camera hearing. In determining the admissibility of such evidence, the court will consider all of the facts and circumstances surrounding the evidence, such as the amount of time that lapsed between the alleged prior act and the rape charged in the prosecution. The greater the lapse of time, of course, the less likely it is that such evidence will be admitted.

Mr. Speaker, the principal purpose of this legislation is to protect rape victims from the degrading and embarrassing disclosure of intimate details about their private lives. It does so by narrowly circumscribing when such evidence may be admitted. It does not do so, however, by sacrificing any constitutional right possessed by the defendant. The bill before us fairly balances the interests involved—the rape victim's interest in protecting her private life from unwarranted public exposure; the defendant's interest in being able adequately to present a defense by offering relevant and probative evidence; and society's interest in a fair trial, one where unduly prejudicial evidence is not permitted to becloud the issues before the jury.

. . .

Mr. WIGGINS. Mr. Speaker, this legislation addresses itself to a subject that is certainly a proper one for our consideration. Many of us have been troubled for years about the indiscriminate and prejudicial use of testimony with respect to a victim's prior sexual behavior in rape and similar cases. This bill deals with that problem. It is not, in my opinion, Mr. Speaker, a perfect bill in the manner in which it deals with the problem, but my objections are not so fundamental as would lead me to oppose the bill.

I think, Mr. Speaker, that it is unwise to adopt a per se rule absolutely excluding evidence of reputation and opinion with respect to the victim—and this bill does that—but it is difficult for me to foresee the specific case in which such evidence might be admissible. The trouble is this, Mr. Speaker: None of us can foresee perfectly all of the various circumstances under which the propriety of evidence might be before the court. If this bill has a defect, in my view it is because it adopts a per se rule with respect to opinion and reputation evidence. Alternatively we might have permitted that evidence to be considered in camera as we do other evidence under the bill.

I should note, however, in fairness, having expressed minor reservations, that the bill before the House at this time does improve significantly upon the bill which was presented to our Committee.

I will not detail all of those improvements but simply observe that the bill upon which we shall soon vote is a superior product to that which was initially considered by our Subcommittee.

. . .

Mr. MANN. Mr. Speaker, this legislation has more than 100 cosponsors, but its principal sponsor, as well as its architect is the gentlewoman from New York (Ms. Holtzman). As the drafter of the legislation she will be able to provide additional information about the probable scope and effect of the legislation.

. . .

Ms. HOLTZMAN. Too often in this country victims of rape are humiliated and harassed when they report and prosecute the rape. Bullied and cross-examined about their prior sexual experiences, many find the trial almost as degrading as the rape itself. Since rape trials become inquisitions into the victim's morality, not trials of the defendant's innocence or guilt, it is not surprising that it is the least reported crime. It is estimated that as few as one in ten rapes is ever reported.

Mr. Speaker, over 30 states have taken some action to limit the vulnerability of rape victims to such humiliating cross-examination of their past sexual experiences and intimate personal histories. In federal courts, however, it is permissible still to subject rape victims to brutal cross-examination about their past sexual histories. H.R. 4727 would rectify this problem in federal courts and, I hope, also serve as a model to suggest to the remaining states that reform of existing rape laws is important to the equity of our criminal justice system.

H.R. 4727 applies only to criminal rape cases in federal courts. The bill provides that neither the prosecution nor the defense can introduce any reputation or opinion evidence about the victim's past sexual conduct. It does permit, however, the introduction of specific evidence about the victim's past sexual conduct in three very limited circumstances.

First, this evidence can be introduced if it deals with the victim's past sexual relations with the defendant and is relevant to the issue of whether she consented. Second, when the defendant claims he had no relations with the victim, he can use evidence of the victim's past sexual relations with others if the evidence rebuts the victim's claim that the rape caused certain physical consequences, such as semen or injury. Finally, the evidence can be introduced if it is constitutionally required. This last exception, added in subcommittee, will insure that the defendant's constitutional rights are protected.

Before any such evidence can be introduced, however, the court must determine at a hearing in chambers that the evidence falls within one of the exceptions.

Furthermore, unless constitutionally required, the evidence of specific instances of prior sexual conduct cannot be introduced at all if it would be more prejudicial and inflammatory than probative.

124 CONG. REC. H11,944–45 (daily ed. Oct. 10, 1978).

Rule 413.   SIMILAR CRIMES IN SEXUAL-ASSAULT CASES

(a) Permitted Uses.   In a criminal case in which a defendant is accused of a sexual assault, the court may admit evidence that the defendant committed any other sexual assault. The evidence _may_ be considered on any matter to which it is relevant.

(b) Disclosure to the Defendant.   If the prosecutor intends to offer this evidence, the prosecutor must disclose it to the defendant, including witnesses' statements or a summary of the expected testimony. The prosecutor must do so at least 15 days before trial or at a later time that the court allows for good cause.

(c) Effect on Other Rules.   This rule does not limit the admission or consideration of evidence under any other rule.

(d) Definition of "Sexual Assault."   In this rule and Rule 415, "sexual assault" means a crime under federal law or under state law (as "state" is defined in 18 U.S.C. § 513) involving:

> **(1)** any conduct prohibited by 18 U.S.C. chapter 109A;

> **(2)** contact, without consent, between any part of the defendant's body—or an object—and another person's genitals or anus;

> **(3)** contact, without consent, between the defendant's genitals or anus and any part of another person's body;

> **(4)** deriving sexual pleasure or gratification from inflicting death, bodily injury, or physical pain on another person; or

> **(5)** an attempt or conspiracy to engage in conduct described in subparagraphs (1)–(4).

(Enacted Sept. 13, 1994, eff. July 9, 1995; as restyled Apr. 26, 2011, eff. Dec. 1, 2011.)

See Editor's Note following Rule 415.

Rule 414.   SIMILAR CRIMES IN CHILD-MOLESTATION CASES

(a) Permitted Uses.   In a criminal case in which a defendant is accused of child molestation, the court may admit evidence that the defendant committed any other child molestation. The evidence may be considered on any matter to which it is relevant.

(b) Disclosure to the Defendant.   If the prosecutor intends to offer this evidence, the prosecutor must disclose it to the defendant, including witnesses' statements or a summary of the expected testimony. The prosecutor must do so at least 15 days before trial or at a later time that the court allows for good cause.

(c) Effect on Other Rules.   This rule does not limit the admission or consideration of evidence under any other rule.

(d) Definition of "Child" and "Child Molestation."   In this rule and Rule 415:

(1) "child" means a person below the age of 14; and

(2) "child molestation" means a crime under federal law or under state law (as "state" is defined in 18 U.S.C. § 513) involving:

(A) any conduct prohibited by 18 U.S.C. chapter 109A and committed with a child;

(B) any conduct prohibited by 18 U.S.C. chapter 110;

(C) contact between any part of the defendant's body—or an object—and a child's genitals or anus;

(D) contact between the defendant's genitals or anus and any part of a child's body;

(E) deriving sexual pleasure or gratification from inflicting death, bodily injury, or physical pain on a child; or

(F) an attempt or conspiracy to engage in conduct described in subparagraphs (A)–(E).

(Enacted Sept. 13, 1994, eff. July 9, 1995; as restyled Apr. 26, 2011, eff. Dec. 1, 2011.)

EDITOR'S NOTE

See Editor's Note following Rule 415.

Rule 415. SIMILAR ACTS IN CIVIL CASES INVOLVING SEXUAL ASSAULT OR CHILD MOLESTATION

(a) Permitted Uses. In a civil case involving a claim for relief based on a party's alleged sexual assault or child molestation, the court may admit evidence that the party committed any other sexual assault or child molestation. The evidence may be considered as provided in Rules 413 and 414.

(b) Disclosure to the Opponent. If a party intends to offer this evidence, the party must disclose it to the party against whom it will be offered, including witnesses' statements or a summary of the expected testimony. The party must do so at least 15 days before trial or at a later time that the court allows for good cause.

(c) Effect on Other Rules. This rule does not limit the admission or consideration of evidence under any other rule.

(Enacted Sept. 13, 1994, eff. July 9, 1995; as restyled Apr. 26, 2011, eff. Dec. 1, 2011.)

EDITOR'S NOTE

Congress enacted Rules 413, 414, and 415 as part of the Violent Crime Control and Law Enforcement Act of 1994. *See* Pub. L. No. 103-322 (Sept. 13, 1994). The Act invited the Judicial Conference of the United States to submit alternative recommendations within

150 days. After reviewing extensive public comment, the Judicial Conference opposed the new rules and recommended that Congress either abandon or redraft them. Congress took no further action, and the rules took effect on July 9, 1995. I have included excerpts from the floor statement of Representative Susan Molinari, the principal House sponsor of the new rules, as well as from the Judicial Conference's report in the casebook at pages 219 to 222.
—GF

ARTICLE V. PRIVILEGES

Rule 501.   PRIVILEGE IN GENERAL

The common law—as interpreted by United States courts in the light of reason and experience—governs a claim of privilege unless any of the following provides otherwise:

- the United States Constitution;

- a federal statute; or

- rules prescribed by the Supreme Court.

But in a civil case, state law governs privilege regarding a claim or defense for which state law supplies the rule of decision.

(Enacted Jan. 2, 1975; as restyled Apr. 26, 2011, eff. Dec. 1, 2011.)

NOTE BY FEDERAL JUDICIAL CENTER

The rules enacted by the Congress substituted the single Rule 501 in place of the thirteen rules dealing with privilege prescribed by the Supreme Court as Article V. . . . The reasons given in support of the congressional action are stated in the Report of the House Committee on the Judiciary, the Report of the Senate Committee on the Judiciary, and Conference Report, set forth below.

REPORT OF THE HOUSE COMMITTEE ON THE JUDICIARY

Article V as submitted to Congress contained thirteen rules. Nine of those rules defined specific nonconstitutional privileges which the federal courts must recognize (i.e., required reports, lawyer–client, psychotherapist–patient, husband–wife, communications to clergymen, political vote, trade secrets, secrets of state and other official information, and identity of informer). Another rule provided that only those privileges set forth in Article V or in some other Act of Congress could be recognized by the federal courts. The three remaining rules addressed collateral problems as to waiver of privilege by voluntary disclosure, privileged matter disclosed under compulsion or without opportunity to claim privilege, comment upon or inference from a claim of privilege, and jury instruction with regard thereto.

The Committee amended Article V to eliminate all of the Court's specific rules on privileges. Instead, the Committee, through a single rule, 501, left the law of privileges in its present state and further provided that privileges shall continue to be developed by the courts of the United States under a uniform standard applicable both in civil and criminal cases. That standard, derived from Rule 26 of the Federal Rules of Criminal Procedure, mandates the application of the principles of the common law as interpreted by the Courts of the United States in the light of reason and experience. The words "person, government, State, or political subdivision thereof" were added by the Committee to the lone term "witness" used in Rule 26 to make clear that, as under present law, not only witnesses may have privileges. The Committee also included in its amendment a proviso modeled after Rule 302 and similar to language added by the Committee to Rule 601 relating to the competency of witnesses. The proviso is designed to require the application of state privilege law in civil actions and proceedings governed by *Erie Railroad Co. v. Tompkins*, 304 U.S. 64 (1938), a result in accord with current federal court decisions. *See* Republic Gear Co. v. Borg–Warner Corp., 381 F.2d 551, 555 n.2 (2d Cir. 1967). The Committee deemed the proviso to be necessary in the light of the Advisory Committee's view (see its note to Court [proposed] Rule 501) that this result is not mandated under *Erie*.

The rationale underlying the proviso is that federal law should not supersede that of the states in substantive areas such as privilege absent a compelling reason. The Committee believes that in civil cases in the federal courts where an element of a claim or defense is not grounded upon a federal question, there is no federal interest strong enough to justify departure from state policy. In addition, the Committee considered that the Court's proposed Article V would have promoted forum shopping in some civil actions, depending upon differences in the privilege law applied as among the state and federal courts. The Committee's proviso, on the other hand, under which the federal courts are bound to apply the state's privilege law in actions founded upon a state-created right or defense, removes the incentive to "shop."

REPORT OF THE SENATE COMMITTEE ON THE JUDICIARY

Article V as submitted to Congress contained thirteen rules. Nine of those rules defined specific nonconstitutional privileges which the federal courts must recognize (i.e., required reports, lawyer–client, psychotherapist–patient, husband–wife, communications to clergymen, political vote, trade secrets, secrets of state and other official information, and identity of informer). Many of these rules contained controversial modifications or restrictions upon common law privileges. As noted *supra*, the House amended Article V to eliminate all of the Court's specific rules on privileges. Through a single rule, 501, the House provided that privileges shall be governed by the principles of the common law as interpreted by the courts of the United States in the light of reason and experience (a standard derived from Rule 26 of the Federal Rules of Criminal Procedure) except in the case of an element of a civil claim or defense as to which state law supplies the rule of decision, in which event state privilege law was to govern.

The Committee agrees with the main thrust of the House amendment: that a federally developed common law based on modern reason and experience shall apply except where the state nature of the issues renders deference to state privilege law the wiser course, as in the usual diversity case. The Committee understands that thrust of the House amendment to require that state privilege law be applied in "diversity" cases (actions on questions of state law between citizens of different states arising under 28 U.S.C. § 1332). The language of the House amendment, however, goes beyond this in some respects, and falls short of it in others; state privilege law applies even in nondiversity. Federal question civil cases, where an issue governed by state substantive law is the object of the evidence (such issues do sometimes arise in such cases); and, in all instances where state privilege law is to be applied, e.g., on proof of a state issue in a diversity case, a close reading reveals that state privilege law is not to be applied unless the matter to be proved is an element of that state claim or defense, as distinguished from a step along the way in the proof of it.

The Committee is concerned that the language used in the House amendment could be difficult to apply. It provides that "in civil actions . . . with respect to an element of a claim or defense as to which state law supplies the rule of decision," state law on privilege applies. The question of what is an element of a claim or defense is likely to engender considerable litigation. If the matter in question constitutes an element of a claim, state law supplies the privilege rule; whereas if it is a mere item of proof with respect to a claim, then, even though state law might supply the rule of decision, federal law on the privilege would apply. Further, disputes will arise as to how the rule should be applied in an antitrust action or in a tax case where the federal statute is silent as to a particular aspect of the substantive law in question, but federal cases had incorporated state law by reference to state law.[1] Is a

---

[1] For a discussion of reference to state substantive law, see HART & WECHSLER, *Note on Federal Incorporation by Reference of State Law*, *in* THE FEDERAL COURTS AND THE FEDERAL SYSTEM 491–94 (2d ed. 1973).

claim (or defense) based on such a reference a claim or defense as to which federal or state law supplies the rule of decision?

Another problem not entirely avoidable is the complexity or difficulty the rule introduces into the trial of a federal case containing a combination of federal and state claims and defenses, e.g., an action involving federal antitrust and state unfair competition claims. Two different bodies of privilege law would need to be consulted. It may even develop that the same witness-testimony might be relevant on both counts and privileged as to one but not the other.[2]

The formulation adopted by the House is pregnant with litigious mischief. The Committee has, therefore, adopted what we believe will be a clearer and more practical guideline for determining when courts should respect state rules of privilege. Basically, it provides that in criminal and federal question civil cases, federally evolved rules on privilege should apply since it is federal policy which is being enforced.[3] Conversely, in diversity cases where the litigation in question turns on a substantive question of state law, and is brought in the federal courts because the parties reside in different states, the Committee believes it is clear that state rules of privilege should apply unless the proof is directed at a claim or defense for which federal law supplies the rule of decision (a situation which would not commonly arise).[4] It is intended that the state rules of privilege should apply equally in

---

[2] The problems with the House formulation are discussed in Rothstein, *The Proposed Amendments to the Federal Rules of Evidence*, 62 GEO L.J. 125, 130 & nn.25–26, 138–39 & nn.70–74 (1973).

[3] It is also intended that the federal law of privileges should be applied with respect to pendant state law claims when they arise in a federal question case.

[4] While such a situation might require use of two bodies of privilege law, federal and state, in the same case, nevertheless the occasions on which this would be required are considerably reduced as compared with the House version, and confined to situations where the federal and state interests are such as to justify application of neither privilege law to the case as a whole. If the rule proposed here results in two conflicting bodies of privilege law applying to the same piece of evidence in the same case, it is contemplated that the rule favoring reception of the evidence should be applied. This policy is based on the present Rule 43(a) of the Federal Rules of Civil Procedure which provides: "In any case, the statute or rule which favors the reception of the evidence governs and the evidence shall be presented according to the most convenient method prescribed in any of the statutes or rules to which reference is herein made."

original diversity actions and diversity actions removed under 28 U.S.C. § 1441(b).

Two other comments on the privilege rule should be made. The Committee has received a considerable volume of correspondence from psychiatric organizations and psychiatrists concerning the deletion of Rule 504 of the rule submitted by the Supreme Court. It should be clearly understood that, in approving this general rule as to privileges, the action of Congress should not be understood as disapproving any recognition of a psychiatrist–patient, or husband–wife, or any other of the enumerated privileges contained in the Supreme Court rules. Rather, our action should be understood as reflecting the view that the recognition of a privilege based on a confidential relationship and other privileges should be determined on a case-by-case basis.

Further, we would understand that the prohibition against spouses testifying against each other is considered a rule of privilege and covered by this rule and not by Rule 601 of the competency of witnesses.

<u>CONFERENCE REPORT</u>

Rule 501 deals with the privilege of a witness not to testify. Both the House and Senate bills provide that federal privilege law applies in criminal cases. In civil actions and proceedings, the House bill provides that state privilege law applies "to an element of a claim or defense as to which state law supplies the rule of decision." The Senate bill provides that "in civil actions and proceedings arising under 28 U.S.C. § 1332 or 28 U.S.C. § 1335, or between citizens of different states and removed under 28 U.S.C. § 1441(b) the privilege of a witness, person, government, state, or political subdivision thereof is determined in accordance with state law, unless with respect to the particular claim or defense, federal law supplies the rule of decision."

The wording of the House and Senate bills differ in the treatment of civil actions and proceedings. The rule in the House bill applies to evidence that relates to "an element of a claim or defense." If an item of proof tends to support or defeat a claim or defense, or an element of a claim or defense, and if state law supplies the rule of decision for that claim or defense, then state privilege law applies to that item of proof.

Under the provision in the House bill, therefore, state privilege law will usually apply in diversity cases. There may be diversity cases, however, where a claim or defense is based upon federal law. In such instances, federal privilege law will apply to evidence relevant to the federal claim or defense. *See* Sola Elec. Co. v. Jefferson Elec. Co., 317 U.S. 173 (1942).

In nondiversity jurisdiction civil cases, federal privilege law will generally apply. In those situations where a federal court adopts or incorporates state law to fill interstices or gaps in federal statutory phrases, the court generally will apply federal privilege law. As Justice Jackson has said:

> A federal court sitting in a non-diversity case such as this does not sit as a local tribunal. In some cases it may see fit for special reasons to give the law of a particular state highly persuasive or even controlling effect, but in the last analysis its decision turns upon the law of the United States, not that of any state.

D'Oench, Duhme & Co. v. FDIC, 315 U.S. 447, 471 (1942) (Jackson, J., concurring). When a federal court chooses to absorb state law, it is applying the state law as a matter of federal common law. Thus, state law does not supply the rule of decision (even though the federal court may apply a rule derived from state decisions), and state privilege law would not apply. *See* C.A. WRIGHT, FEDERAL COURTS 251–52 (2d ed. 1970); Holmberg v. Armbrecht, 327 U.S. 392 (1946); DeSylva v. Ballentine, 351 U.S. 570, 581 (1956); 9 WRIGHT & MILLER, FEDERAL RULES AND PROCEDURE § 2408.

In civil actions and proceedings, where the rule of decision as to a claim or defense or as to an element of a claim or defense is supplied by state law, the House provision requires that state privilege law apply.

The Conference adopts the House provision.

Rule 502.   ATTORNEY–CLIENT   PRIVILEGE   AND   WORK PRODUCT; LIMITATIONS ON WAIVER

The following provisions apply, in the circumstances set out, to disclosure of a communication or information covered by the attorney–client privilege or work-product protection.

(a) Disclosure Made in a Federal Proceeding or to a Federal Office or Agency; Scope of a Waiver. When the disclosure is made in a federal proceeding or to a federal office or agency and waives the attorney–client privilege or work-product protection, the waiver extends to an undisclosed communication or information in a federal or state proceeding only if:

(1) the waiver is intentional;

(2) the disclosed and undisclosed communications or information concern the same subject matter; and

(3) they ought in fairness to be considered together.

(b) **Inadvertent Disclosure.** When made in a federal proceeding or to a federal office or agency, the disclosure does not operate as a waiver in a federal or state proceeding if:

(1) the disclosure is inadvertent;

(2) the holder of the privilege or protection took reasonable steps to prevent disclosure; and

(3) the holder promptly took reasonable steps to rectify the error, including (if applicable) following Federal Rule of Civil Procedure 26(b)(5)(B).

(c) **Disclosure Made in a State Proceeding.** When the disclosure is made in a state proceeding and is not the subject of a state-court order concerning waiver, the disclosure does not operate as a waiver in a federal proceeding if the disclosure:

(1) would not be a waiver under this rule if it had been made in a federal proceeding; or

(2) is not a waiver under the law of the state where the disclosure occurred.

(d) **Controlling Effect of a Court Order.** A federal court may order that the privilege or protection is not waived by disclosure connected with the litigation pending before the court—in which event the disclosure is also not a waiver in any other federal or state proceeding.

(e) **Controlling Effect of a Party Agreement.** An agreement on the effect of disclosure in a federal proceeding is binding only on the parties to the agreement, unless it is incorporated into a court order.

(f) Controlling Effect of this Rule. Notwithstanding Rules 101 and 1101, this rule applies to state proceedings and to federal court-annexed and federal court-mandated arbitration proceedings, in the circumstances set out in the rule. And notwithstanding Rule 501, this rule applies even if state law provides the rule of decision.

(g) Definitions. In this rule:

(1) "attorney–client privilege" means the protection that applicable law provides for confidential attorney–client communications; and

(2) "work-product protection" means the protection that applicable law provides for tangible material (or its intangible equivalent) prepared in anticipation of litigation or for trial.

(Enacted Sept. 19, 2008, eff. Sept. 19, 2008; as restyled Apr. 26, 2011, eff. Dec. 1, 2011.)

<u>ADVISORY COMMITTEE'S NOTE TO RULE 502</u>

This new rule has two major purposes:

1) It resolves some longstanding disputes in the courts about the effect of certain disclosures of communications or information protected by the attorney–client privilege or as work product— specifically those disputes involving inadvertent disclosure and subject matter waiver.

2) It responds to the widespread complaint that litigation costs necessary to protect against waiver of attorney–client privilege or work product have become prohibitive due to the concern that any disclosure (however innocent or minimal) will operate as a subject matter waiver of all protected communications or information. This concern is especially troubling in cases involving electronic discovery. *See, e.g.*, Hopson v. Mayor of Balt., 232 F.R.D. 228, 244 (D. Md. 2005) (electronic discovery may encompass "millions of documents" and to insist upon "record-by-record pre-production privilege review, on pain of subject matter waiver, would impose

upon parties costs of production that bear no proportionality to what is at stake in the litigation").

The rule seeks to provide a predictable, uniform set of standards under which parties can determine the consequences of a disclosure of a communication or information covered by the attorney–client privilege or work product protection. Parties to litigation need to know, for example, that if they exchange privileged information pursuant to a confidentiality order, the court's order will be enforceable. Moreover, if a federal court's confidentiality order is not enforceable in a state court then the burdensome costs of privilege review and retention are unlikely to be reduced.

The rule makes no attempt to alter federal or state law on whether a communication or information is protected under the attorney–client privilege or work product immunity as an initial matter. Moreover, while establishing some exceptions to waiver, the rule does not purport to supplant applicable waiver doctrine generally.

The rule governs only certain waivers by disclosure. Other common-law waiver doctrines may result in a finding of waiver even where there is no disclosure of privileged information or work product. *See, e.g.*, Nguyen v. Excel Corp., 197 F.3d 200 (5th Cir. 1999) (reliance on an advice of counsel defense waives the privilege with respect to attorney–client communications pertinent to that defense); Byers v. Burleson, 100 F.R.D. 436 (D.D.C. 1983) (allegation of lawyer malpractice constituted a waiver of confidential communications under the circumstances). The rule is not intended to displace or modify federal common law concerning waiver of privilege or work product where no disclosure has been made.

HOUSE OF REPRESENTATIVES

(Statement Offered by Representative Jackson Lee)
(Sept. 8, 2008)

Statement of Congressional Intent Regarding Rule 502 of the Federal Rules of Evidence

During consideration of this rule in Congress, a number of questions were raised about the scope and contours of the effect of the proposed rule on current law regarding attorney–client privilege and work-product protection. These questions were ultimately answered satisfactorily, without need to revise the text of the rule as submitted to Congress by the Judicial Conference.

In general, these questions are answered by keeping in mind the limited though important purpose and focus of the rule. The rule addresses only the effect of disclosure, under specified circumstances, of a communication that is otherwise protected by attorney–client privilege, or of information that is protected by work-product protection, on whether the disclosure itself operates as a waiver of the privilege or protection for purposes of admissibility of evidence in a federal or state judicial or administrative proceeding.

The rule does not alter the substantive law regarding attorney–client privilege or work-product protection in any other respect, including the burden on the party invoking the privilege (or protection) to prove that the particular information (or communication) qualifies for it. And it is not intended to alter the rules and practices governing use of information outside this evidentiary context. . . .

<u>REPORT OF THE SENATE COMMITTEE ON THE JUDICIARY</u>

B. *Purpose of the Bill*

. . . The bill provides a new rule to ensure that parties will take advantage of its protections by remaining enforceable in subsequent proceedings. If a federal court enters an order finding that an inadvertent disclosure of privileged information does not constitute a waiver, that order will be enforceable against persons in federal or state proceedings. This protects the rule's ability to limit discovery costs by ensuring that parties in any given case will know they can rely on the new waiver rules in subsequent proceedings.

Importantly, the bill respects federal–state comity. The bill will ensure that if there is a disclosure of privileged information at the federal level then courts must honor Rule 502 in any subsequent state proceedings. If there is a disclosure in a state proceeding, then admissibility in any subsequent federal proceeding will be determined by the law that is most protective against waiver. However, it does not apply to any disclosure made in a state proceeding that is later introduced in a subsequent state proceeding.

Litigants recognize the need to adopt a new waiver doctrine to adapt to the effects of changing technology in the business environment. The bill has attracted widespread support from major legal organizations representing stakeholders on all sides of modern litigation. Among those groups voicing support for the measure are the American Bar Association, American College of

Trial Lawyers, U.S. Chamber of Commerce, former Chairs of the Section of Litigation of the American Bar Association, Lawyers for Civil Justice, and several private law firms.

<u>ADVISORY COMMITTEE'S NOTE TO RULE 502(a)–(b)</u>

Subdivision (a). The rule provides that a voluntary disclosure in a federal proceeding or to a federal office or agency, if a waiver, generally results in a waiver only of the communication or information disclosed; a subject matter waiver (of either privilege or work product) is reserved for those unusual situations in which fairness requires a further disclosure of related, protected information, in order to prevent a selective and misleading presentation of evidence to the disadvantage of the adversary. *See, e.g., In re* United Mine Workers of Am. Emp. Benefit Plans Litig., 159 F.R.D. 307, 312 (D.D.C. 1994) (waiver of work product limited to materials actually disclosed, because the party did not deliberately disclose documents in an attempt to gain a tactical advantage). Thus, subject matter waiver is limited to situations in which a party intentionally puts protected information into the litigation in a selective, misleading, and unfair manner. It follows that an inadvertent disclosure of protected information can never result in a subject matter waiver. *See* Rule 502(b). The rule rejects the result in *In re Sealed Case*, 877 F.2d 976 (D.C. Cir. 1989), which held that inadvertent disclosure of documents during discovery automatically constituted a subject matter waiver.

The language concerning subject matter waiver—"ought in fairness"—is taken from Rule 106, because the animating principle is the same. Under both rules, a party that makes a selective, misleading presentation that is unfair to the adversary opens itself to a more complete and accurate presentation.

To assure protection and predictability, the rule provides that if a disclosure is made at the federal level, the federal rule on subject matter waiver governs subsequent state court determinations on the scope of the waiver by that disclosure.

Subdivision (b). Courts are in conflict over whether an inadvertent disclosure of a communication or information protected as privileged or work product constitutes a waiver. A few courts find that a disclosure must be intentional to be a waiver. Most courts find a waiver only if the disclosing party acted carelessly in disclosing the communication or information and failed to request its return in a timely manner. And a few courts hold that any inadvertent disclosure of a communication or information protected under the attorney–client privilege or as work product constitutes a waiver without regard to the protections taken to avoid such a disclosure. See generally *Hopson v. Mayor of Baltimore*, 232 F.R.D. 228 (D. Md. 2005), for a discussion of this case law.

The rule opts for the middle ground: inadvertent disclosure of protected communications or information in connection with a federal proceeding or to a federal office or agency does not constitute a waiver if the holder took reasonable steps to prevent disclosure and also promptly took reasonable steps to rectify the error. This position is in accord with the majority view on whether inadvertent disclosure is a waiver.

Cases such as *Lois Sportswear, U.S.A., Inc. v. Levi Strauss & Co.*, 104 F.R.D. 103, 105 (S.D.N.Y. 1985), and *Hartford Fire Insurance Co. v. Garvey*, 109 F.R.D. 323, 332 (N.D. Cal. 1985), set out a multi-factor test for determining whether inadvertent disclosure is a waiver. The stated factors (none of which is dispositive) are the reasonableness of precautions taken, the time taken to rectify the error, the scope of discovery, the extent of disclosure, and the overriding issue of fairness. The rule does not explicitly codify that test, because it is really a set of non-determinative guidelines that vary from case to case. The rule is flexible enough to accommodate any of those listed factors. Other considerations bearing on the reasonableness of a producing party's efforts include the number of documents to be reviewed and the time constraints for production. Depending on the circumstances, a party that uses advanced analytical software applications and linguistic tools in screening for privilege and work product may be found to have taken "reasonable steps" to prevent inadvertent disclosure. The implementation of an efficient system of records management before litigation may also be relevant.

The rule does not require the producing party to engage in a post-production review to determine whether any protected communication or information has been produced by mistake. But the rule does require the producing party to follow up on any obvious indications that a protected communication or information has been produced inadvertently.

The rule applies to inadvertent disclosures made to a federal office or agency, including but not limited to an office or agency that is acting in the course of its regulatory, investigative, or enforcement authority. The consequences of waiver, and the concomitant costs of pre-production privilege review, can be as great with respect to disclosures to offices and agencies as they are in litigation.

(Statement Offered by Representative Jackson Lee)
(Sept. 8, 2008)

Subdivision (b)—Fairness Considerations. The standard set
forth in this subdivision for determining whether a disclosure
operates as a waiver of the privilege or protection is, as explained
elsewhere in this note, the majority rule in the federal courts. The
majority rule has simply been distilled here into a standard
designed to be predictable in its application. This distillation is not
intended to foreclose notions of fairness from continuing to inform
application of the standard in all aspects as appropriate in the
particular cases—for example, as to whether the steps taken to
rectify an erroneous inadvertent disclosure were sufficiently
prompt under subdivision (b)(3) where the receiving party has
relied on the information disclosed.

ADVISORY COMMITTEE'S NOTE TO RULE 502(c)–(g)

Subdivision (c). Difficult questions can arise when 1) a
disclosure of a communication or information protected by the
attorney–client privilege or as work product is made in a state
proceeding, 2) the communication or information is offered in a
subsequent federal proceeding on the ground that the disclosure
waived the privilege or protection, and 3) the state and federal laws
are in conflict on the question of waiver. The Committee
determined that the proper solution for the federal court is to apply
the law that is most protective of privilege and work product. If the
state law is more protective (such as where the state law is that an
inadvertent disclosure can never be a waiver), the holder of the
privilege or protection may well have relied on that law when
making the disclosure in the state proceeding. Moreover, applying
a more restrictive federal law of waiver could impair the state
objective of preserving the privilege or work-product protection for
disclosures made in state proceedings. On the other hand, if the
federal law is more protective, applying the state law of waiver to
determine admissibility in federal court is likely to undermine the
federal objective of limiting the costs of production.

The rule does not address the enforceability of a state court
confidentiality order in a federal proceeding, as that question is
covered both by statutory law and principles of federalism and
comity. *See* 28 U.S.C. § 1738 (providing that state judicial
proceedings "shall have the same full faith and credit in every court
within the United States . . . as they have by law or usage in the
courts of such State . . . from which they are taken"); *see also* Tucker
v. Ohtsu Tire & Rubber Co., 191 F.R.D. 495, 499 (D. Md. 2000)

(noting that a federal court considering the enforceability of a state confidentiality order is "constrained by principles of comity, courtesy, and . . . federalism"). Thus, a state court order finding no waiver in connection with a disclosure made in a state court proceeding is enforceable under existing law in subsequent federal proceedings.

Subdivision (d). Confidentiality orders are becoming increasingly important in limiting the costs of privilege review and retention, especially in cases involving electronic discovery. But the utility of a confidentiality order in reducing discovery costs is substantially diminished if it provides no protection outside the particular litigation in which the order is entered. Parties are unlikely to be able to reduce the costs of pre-production review for privilege and work product if the consequence of disclosure is that the communications or information could be used by non-parties to the litigation.

There is some dispute on whether a confidentiality order entered in one case is enforceable in other proceedings. See generally *Hopson v. Mayor of Baltimore*, 232 F.R.D. 228 (D. Md. 2005), for a discussion of this case law. The rule provides that when a confidentiality order governing the consequences of disclosure in that case is entered in a federal proceeding, its terms are enforceable against non-parties in any federal or state proceeding. For example, the court order may provide for return of documents without waiver irrespective of the care taken by the disclosing party; the rule contemplates enforcement of "claw-back" and "quick peek" arrangements as a way to avoid the excessive costs of pre-production review for privilege and work product. *See* Zubulake v. UBS Warburg LLC, 216 F.R.D. 280, 290 (S.D.N.Y. 2003) (noting that parties may enter into "so-called 'claw-back' agreements that allow the parties to forego privilege review altogether in favor of an agreement to return inadvertently produced privilege documents"). The rule provides a party with a predictable protection from a court order—predictability that is needed to allow the party to plan in advance to limit the prohibitive costs of privilege and work product review and retention.

Under the rule, a confidentiality order is enforceable whether or not it memorializes an agreement among the parties to the litigation. Party agreement should not be a condition of enforceability of a federal court's order.

Under subdivision (d), a federal court may order that disclosure of privileged or protected information "in connection with" a federal proceeding does not result in waiver. But subdivision (d) does not allow the federal court to enter an order determining the waiver effects of a separate disclosure of the same information in other proceedings, state or federal. If a disclosure has been made in a state proceeding (and is not the subject of a state-court order on waiver), then subdivision (d) is inapplicable. Subdivision (c) would govern the federal court's determination whether the state-court disclosure waived the privilege or protection in the federal proceeding.

Subdivision (e). Subdivision (e) codifies the well-established proposition that parties can enter an agreement to limit the effect of waiver by disclosure between or among them. Of course such an agreement can bind only the parties to the agreement. The rule makes clear that if parties want protection against non-parties from a finding of waiver by disclosure, the agreement must be made part of a court order.

Subdivision (f). The protections against waiver provided by Rule 502 must be applicable when protected communications or information disclosed in federal proceedings are subsequently offered in state proceedings. Otherwise the holders of protected communications and information, and their lawyers, could not rely on the protections provided by the rule, and the goal of limiting costs in discovery would be substantially undermined. Rule 502(f) is intended to resolve any potential tension between the provisions of Rule 502 that apply to state proceedings and the possible limitations on the applicability of the Federal Rules of Evidence otherwise provided by Rules 101 and 1101.

The rule is intended to apply in all federal court proceedings, including court-annexed and court-ordered arbitrations, without regard to any possible limitations of Rules 101 and 1101. This provision is not intended to raise an inference about the applicability of any other rule of evidence in arbitration proceedings more generally.

The costs of discovery can be equally high for state and federal causes of action, and the rule seeks to limit those costs in all federal proceedings, regardless of whether the claim arises under state or federal law. Accordingly, the rule applies to state law causes of action brought in federal court.

Subdivision (g). The rule's coverage is limited to attorney– client privilege and work product. The operation of waiver by disclosure, as applied to other evidentiary privileges, remains a question of federal common law. Nor does the rule purport to apply to the Fifth Amendment privilege against compelled self- incrimination.

The definition of work product "materials" is intended to include both tangible and intangible information. *See In re* Cendant Corp. Sec. Litig., 343 F.3d 658, 662 (3d Cir. 2003) ("[W]ork product protection extends to both tangible and intangible work product.").

ARTICLE VI. WITNESSES

Rule 601.   COMPETENCY TO TESTIFY IN GENERAL

Every person is competent to be a witness unless these rules provide otherwise. But in a civil case, state law governs the witness's competency regarding a claim or defense for which state law supplies the rule of decision.

(Enacted Jan. 2, 1975; as restyled Apr. 26, 2011, eff. Dec. 1, 2011.)

NOTE BY FEDERAL JUDICIAL CENTER

The first sentence of the rule enacted by the Congress is the entire rule prescribed by the Supreme Court without change. The second sentence was added by congressional action.

ADVISORY COMMITTEE'S NOTE

This general ground-clearing eliminates all grounds of incompetency not specifically recognized in the succeeding rules of this article. Included among the grounds thus abolished are religious belief, conviction of crime, and connection with the litigation as a party or interested person or spouse of a party or interested person. With the exception of the so-called Dead Man's Acts, American jurisdictions generally have ceased to recognize these grounds.

The Dead Man's Acts are surviving traces of the common law disqualification of parties and interested persons. They exist in variety too great to convey conviction of their wisdom and effectiveness. These rules contain no provision of this kind. . . .

No mental or moral qualifications for testifying as a witness are specified. Standards of mental capacity have proved elusive in actual application. A leading commentator observes that few witnesses are disqualified on that ground. Weihofen, *Testimonial Competence and Credibility*, 34 GEO. WASH. L. REV. 53 (1965). Discretion is regularly exercised in favor of allowing the testimony. A witness wholly without capacity is difficult to imagine. The question is one particularly suited to the jury as one of weight and credibility, subject to judicial authority to review the sufficiency of the evidence. 2 WIGMORE §§ 501, 509. Standards of moral qualification in practice consist essentially of evaluating a person's truthfulness in terms of his own answers about it. Their principal utility is in affording an opportunity on voir dire examination to impress upon the witness his moral duty. This result may, however, be accomplished more directly, and without haggling in terms of legal standards, by the manner of administering the oath or affirmation under Rule 603.

Admissibility of religious belief as a ground of impeachment is treated in Rule 610. Conviction of crime as a ground of impeachment is the subject of Rule 609. Marital relationship is the basis for privilege under Rule 505.[1] Interest in the outcome of litigation and mental capacity are, of course, highly relevant to credibility and require no special treatment to render them admissible along with other matters bearing upon the perception, memory, and narration of witnesses.

REPORT OF THE HOUSE COMMITTEE ON THE JUDICIARY

Rule 601 as submitted to the Congress provided that "Every person is competent to be a witness except as otherwise provided in these rules." One effect of the rule as proposed would have been to abolish age, mental capacity, and other grounds recognized in some state jurisdictions as making a person incompetent as a witness. The greatest controversy centered around the rule's rendering inapplicable in the federal courts the so-called Dead Man's Statutes which exist in some states. Acknowledging that there is substantial disagreement as to the merit of Dead Man's Statutes, the Committee nevertheless believed that where such statutes have been enacted they represent state policy which should not be overturned in the absence of a compelling federal interest. The Committee therefore amended the rule to make competency in civil actions determinable in accordance with state law with respect to elements of claims or defenses as to which state law supplies the rule of decision. *Cf.* Courtland v. Walston & Co., 340 F. Supp. 1076, 1087–92 (S.D.N.Y. 1972).

REPORT OF THE SENATE COMMITTEE ON THE JUDICIARY

The amendment to Rule 601 parallels the treatment accorded Rule 501 discussed immediately above.

---

[1] [Rule 505 was among the many privilege rules proposed by the Advisory Committee but rejected by Congress. See pages 930 to 934 of the casebook.—GF]

Rule 601 deals with competency of witnesses. Both the House and Senate bills provide that federal competency law applies in criminal cases. In civil actions and proceedings, the House bill provides that state competency law applies "to an element of a claim or defense as to which state law supplies the rule of decision." The Senate bill provides that "in civil actions and proceedings arising under 28 U.S.C. § 1332 or 28 U.S.C. § 1335, or between citizens of different states and removed under 28 U.S.C. § 1441(b) the competency of a witness, person, government, state, or political subdivision thereof is determined in accordance with state law unless, with respect to the particular claim or defense, federal law supplies the rule of decision."

The wording of the House and Senate bills differs in the treatment of civil actions and proceedings. The rule in the House bill applies to evidence that relates to "an element of a claim or defense." If an item of proof tends to support or defeat a claim or defense, or an element of a claim or defense, and if state law supplies the rule of decision for that claim or defense, then state competency law applies to that item of proof.

For reasons similar to those underlying its action on Rule 501, the Conference adopts the House provision.

Rule 602.   NEED FOR PERSONAL KNOWLEDGE

A witness <u>may</u> testify to a matter only if evidence is introduced sufficient to support a finding that the witness has personal knowledge of the matter. Evidence to prove personal knowledge may consist of the witness's own testimony. This rule does not apply to a witness's expert testimony under Rule 703.

(Enacted Jan. 2, 1975; as amended Mar. 2, 1987, eff. Oct. 1, 1987; Apr. 25, 1988, eff. Nov. 1, 1988; as restyled Apr. 26, 2011, eff. Dec. 1, 2011.)

NOTE BY FEDERAL JUDICIAL CENTER

The rule enacted by the Congress is the rule prescribed by the Supreme Court without change.

"[T]he rule requiring that a witness who testifies to a fact which can be perceived by the senses must have had an opportunity to observe, and must have actually observed the fact" is a "most pervasive manifestation" of the common law insistence upon "the most reliable sources of information." MCCORMICK § 10, at 19. These foundation requirements may, of course, be furnished by the testimony of the witness himself; hence personal knowledge is not an absolute but may consist of what the witness thinks he knows from personal perception. 2 WIGMORE § 650. It will be observed that the rule is in fact a specialized application of the provisions of Rule 104(b) on conditional relevancy.

This rule does not govern the situation of a witness who testifies to a hearsay statement as such, if he has personal knowledge of the making of the statement. Rules 801 and 805 would be applicable. This rule would, however, prevent him from testifying to the subject matter of the hearsay statement, as he has no personal knowledge of it.

The reference to Rule 703 is designed to avoid any question of conflict between the present rule and the provisions of that rule allowing an expert to express opinions based on facts of which he does not have personal knowledge.

Rule 603.   OATH OR AFFIRMATION TO TESTIFY TRUTHFULLY

Before testifying, a witness must give an oath or affirmation to testify truthfully. It must be in a form designed to impress that duty on the witness's conscience.

(Enacted Jan. 2, 1975; as amended Mar. 2, 1987, eff. Oct. 1, 1987; as restyled Apr. 26, 2011, eff. Dec. 1, 2011.)

NOTE BY FEDERAL JUDICIAL CENTER

The rule enacted by the Congress is the rule prescribed by the Supreme Court without change.

ADVISORY COMMITTEE'S NOTE

The rule is designed to afford the flexibility required in dealing with religious adults, atheists, conscientious objectors, mental defectives, and children. Affirmation is simply a solemn undertaking to tell the truth; no special verbal formula is required. As is true generally, affirmation is recognized by federal law. "Oath" includes affirmation, 1 U.S.C. § 1; judges and clerks may administer oaths and affirmations, 28 U.S.C. §§ 459, 953; and affirmations are acceptable in lieu of oaths under Rule [43(b)] of the Federal Rules of Civil Procedure. Perjury by a witness is a crime, 18 U.S.C. § 1621.

Rule 604.   INTERPRETER

An interpreter must be qualified and must give an oath or affirmation to make a true translation.

(Enacted Jan. 2, 1975; as amended Mar. 2, 1987, eff. Oct. 1, 1987; as restyled Apr. 26, 2011, eff. Dec. 1, 2011.)

NOTE BY FEDERAL JUDICIAL CENTER

The rule enacted by the Congress is the rule prescribed by the Supreme Court without change.

ADVISORY COMMITTEE'S NOTE

The rule implements Rule [43(d)] of the Federal Rules of Civil Procedure and Rule [28] of the Federal Rules of Criminal Procedure, both of which contain provisions for the appointment and compensation of interpreters.

Rule 605.   JUDGE'S COMPETENCY AS A WITNESS

The presiding judge may not testify as a witness at the trial. A party need not object to preserve the issue.

(Enacted Jan. 2, 1975; as amended Apr. 26, 2011, eff. Dec. 1, 2011.)

NOTE BY FEDERAL JUDICIAL CENTER

The rule enacted by the Congress is the rule prescribed by the Supreme Court without change.

ADVISORY COMMITTEE'S NOTE

In view of the mandate of 28 U.S.C. § 455 that a judge disqualify himself in "any case in which he . . . is or has been a material witness," the likelihood that the presiding judge in a federal court might be called to testify in the trial over which he is presiding is slight. Nevertheless the possibility is not totally eliminated.

The solution here presented is a broad rule of incompetency, rather than such alternatives as incompetency only as to material matters, leaving the matter to the discretion of the judge, or recognizing no incompetency. The choice is the result of inability to evolve satisfactory answers to questions which arise when the judge abandons the bench for the witness stand. Who rules on objections? Who compels him to answer? Can he rule impartially on the weight and admissibility of his own testimony? Can he be impeached or cross-examined effectively? Can he, in a jury trial, avoid conferring his seal of approval on one side in the eyes of the jury? Can he, in a bench trial, avoid an involvement destructive of impartiality? The rule of general incompetency has substantial support. *See Report of the Special Committee on the Propriety of Judges Appearing as Witnesses*, 36 A.B.A.J. 630 (1950); cases collected in Annotation, 157 A.L.R. 315; MCCORMICK § 68, at 147; UNIF. R. EVID. 42; CAL. EVID. CODE § 703; KAN. STAT. ANN. § 60-442; N.J. EVID. R. 42 (repealed and replaced by N.J. R. EVID. 605 (1993)). Compare 6 WIGMORE § 1909, which advocates leaving the matter to the discretion of the judge, and statutes to that effect collected in Annotation, 157 A.L.R. 315.

The rule provides an "automatic" objection. To require an actual objection would confront the opponent with a choice between not objecting, with the result of allowing the testimony, and objecting, with the probable result of excluding the testimony but at the price of continuing the trial before a judge likely to feel that his integrity had been attacked by the objector.

Rule 606. JUROR'S COMPETENCY AS A WITNESS

(a) At the Trial. A juror may not testify as a witness before the other jurors at the trial. If a juror is called to testify, the court must give a party an opportunity to object outside the jury's presence.

(b) During an Inquiry Into the Validity of a Verdict or Indictment.

---

(1) *Prohibited Testimony or Other Evidence.* During an inquiry into the validity of a verdict or indictment, a juror may not testify about any statement made or incident that occurred during the jury's deliberations; the effect of anything on that juror's or another juror's vote; or any juror's mental processes concerning the verdict or indictment. The court may not receive a juror's affidavit or evidence of a juror's statement on these matters.

(2) *Exceptions.* A juror may testify about whether:

(A) extraneous prejudicial information was improperly brought to the jury's attention;

(B) an outside influence was improperly brought to bear on any juror; or

(C) a mistake was made in entering the verdict on the verdict form.

(Enacted Jan. 2, 1975; as amended Dec. 12, 1975; Mar. 2, 1987, eff. Oct. 1, 1987; Apr. 12, 2006, eff. Dec. 1, 2006; as restyled Apr. 26, 2011, eff. Dec. 1, 2011.)

<u>NOTE BY FEDERAL JUDICIAL CENTER</u>

The rule enacted by the Congress is the rule prescribed by the Supreme Court, amended only by the addition of the concluding phrase "for these purposes." The bill originally passed by the House did not contain in the first sentence the prohibition as to matters or statements during the deliberations or the clause beginning "except."

<u>ADVISORY COMMITTEE'S NOTE</u>

Subdivision (a). The considerations which bear upon the permissibility of testimony by a juror in the trial in which he is sitting as juror bear an obvious similarity to those evoked when the judge is called as a witness. *See* Advisory Committee's Note to Rule 605. The judge is not, however, in this instance so involved as to call for departure from usual principles requiring objection to be made; hence the only provision on objection is that opportunity be afforded for its making out of the presence of the jury. *Cf.* Rule 605.

Subdivision (b). Whether testimony, affidavits, or statements of jurors should be received for the purpose of invalidating or supporting a verdict or indictment, and if so, under what circumstances, has given rise to substantial differences of opinion. The familiar rubric that a juror may not impeach his own verdict, dating from Lord Mansfield's time, is a gross oversimplification. The values sought to be promoted by excluding the evidence include freedom of deliberation, stability and finality of verdicts, and protection of jurors against annoyance and embarrassment. McDonald v. Pless, 238 U.S. 264 (1915). On the other hand, simply putting verdicts beyond effective reach can only promote irregularity and injustice. The rule offers an accommodation between these competing considerations.

The mental operations and emotional reactions of jurors in arriving at a given result would, if allowed as a subject of inquiry, place every verdict at the mercy of jurors and invite tampering and harassment. *See* Grenz v. Werre, 129 N.W.2d 681 (N.D. 1964). The authorities are in virtually complete accord in excluding the evidence. Fryer, *Note on Disqualification of Witnesses, in* SELECTED WRITINGS ON EVIDENCE AND TRIAL 345, 347 (Fryer ed., 1957); MAGUIRE, WEINSTEIN, ET AL., CASES ON EVIDENCE 887 (5th ed. 1965); 8 WIGMORE § 2349 (McNaughton rev. 1961). As to matters other than mental operations and emotional reactions of jurors, substantial authority refuses to allow a juror to disclose irregularities which occur in the jury room, but allows his testimony as to irregularities occurring outside and allows outsiders to testify as to occurrences both inside and out. 8 WIGMORE § 2354 (McNaughton rev. 1961). However, the door of the jury room is not necessarily a satisfactory dividing point, and the Supreme Court has refused to accept it for every situation. Mattox v. United States, 146 U.S. 140 (1892).

Under the federal decisions the central focus has been upon insulation of the manner in which the jury reached its verdict, and this protection extends to each of the components of deliberation, including arguments, statements, discussions, mental and emotional reactions, votes, and any other feature of the process. Thus testimony or affidavits of jurors have been held incompetent to show a compromise verdict, Hyde v. United States, 225 U.S. 347, 382 (1912); a quotient verdict, McDonald v. Pless, 238 U.S. 264 (1915); speculation as to insurance coverage, Holden v. Porter, 405 F.2d 878 (10th Cir. 1969), Farmers Coop. Elevator Ass'n v. Strand, 382 F.2d 224, 230 (8th Cir.), *cert. denied*, 389 U.S. 1014 (1967); misinterpretation of instructions, *id.*; mistake in returning verdict, United States v. Chereton, 309 F.2d 197 (6th Cir. 1962); interpretation of guilty plea by one defendant as implicating others, United States v. Crosby, 294 F.2d 928, 949 (2d Cir. 1961). The policy does not, however, foreclose testimony by jurors as to prejudicial extraneous information or influences injected into or brought to bear upon the deliberative process. Thus a juror is recognized as competent to testify to statements by the bailiff or the introduction of a prejudicial newspaper account into the jury room. Mattox v. United States, 146 U.S. 140 (1892); *see also* Parker v. Gladden, 385 U.S. 363 (1966).

This rule does not purport to specify the substantive grounds for setting aside verdicts for irregularity; it deals only with the competency of jurors to testify concerning those grounds.

See also Rule 6(e) of the Federal Rules of Criminal Procedure and 18 U.S.C. § 3500, governing the secrecy of grand jury proceedings. The present rule does not relate to secrecy and disclosure but to the competency of certain witnesses and evidence.

REPORT OF THE HOUSE COMMITTEE ON THE JUDICIARY

As proposed by the Court, Rule 606(b) limited testimony by a juror in the course of an inquiry into the validity of a verdict or indictment. He could testify as to the influence of extraneous prejudicial information brought to the jury's attention (e.g., a radio newscast or a newspaper account) or an outside influence which improperly had been brought to bear upon a juror (e.g., a threat to the safety of a member of his family), but he could not testify as to other irregularities which occurred in the jury room. Under this formulation a quotient verdict could not be attacked through the testimony of a juror, nor could a juror testify to the drunken condition of a fellow juror which so disabled him that he could not participate in the jury's deliberations.

The 1969 and 1971 Advisory Committee drafts would have permitted a member of the jury to testify concerning these kinds of irregularities in the jury room. The Advisory Committee note in the 1971 draft stated that "the door of the jury room is not a satisfactory dividing point, and the Supreme Court has refused to accept it." The Advisory Committee further commented that—

> The trend has been to draw the dividing line between testimony as to mental processes, on the one hand, and as to the existence of conditions or occurrences of events calculated improperly to influence the verdict, on the other hand, without regard to whether the happening is within or without the jury room. . . . The jurors are the persons who know what really happened. Allowing them to testify as to matters other than their own reactions involves no particular hazard to the values sought to be protected. The rule is based upon this conclusion. It makes no attempt to

specify the substantive grounds for setting aside verdicts for irregularity.

Objective jury misconduct may be testified to in California, Florida, Iowa, Kansas, Nebraska, New Jersey, North Dakota, Ohio, Oregon, Tennessee, Texas, and Washington.

Persuaded that the better practice is that provided for in the earlier drafts, the Committee amended subdivision (b) to read in the text of those drafts.

REPORT OF THE SENATE COMMITTEE ON THE JUDICIARY

As adopted by the House, this rule would permit the impeachment of verdicts by inquiry into, not the mental processes of the jurors, but what happened in terms of conduct in the jury room. This extension of the ability to impeach a verdict is felt to be unwarranted and ill-advised.

The rule passed by the House embodies a suggestion by the Advisory Committee of the Judicial Conference that is considerably broader than the final version adopted by the Supreme Court, which embodies long-accepted federal law. Although forbidding the impeachment of verdicts by inquiry into the jurors' mental processes, it deletes from the Supreme Court version the proscription against testimony "as to any matter or statement occurring during the course of the jury's deliberations." This deletion would have the effect of opening verdicts up to challenge on the basis of what happened during the jury's internal deliberations, for example, where a juror alleged that the jury refused to follow the trial judge's instructions or that some of the jurors did not take part in deliberations.

Permitting an individual to attack a jury verdict based upon the jury's internal deliberations has long been recognized as unwise by the Supreme Court. In *McDonald v. Pless*, the Court stated:

[L]et it once be established that verdicts solemnly made and publicly returned into court can be attacked and set aside on the testimony of those who took part in their publication and all verdicts could be, and many would be, followed by an inquiry in the hope of discovering something which might invalidate the finding. Jurors would be harassed and beset by the defeated party in an effort to secure from them evidence of facts which might establish misconduct sufficient to set aside a verdict. If evidence thus secured could be thus used, the result would be to make what was intended to be a private deliberation, the constant subject of public investigation—to the destruction of all frankness and freedom of discussion and conference.

238 U.S. 264, 267 (1915).

As it stands, then, the rule would permit the harassment of former jurors by losing parties as well as the possible exploitation of disgruntled or otherwise badly motivated ex-jurors.

Public policy requires a finality to litigation. And common fairness requires that absolute privacy be preserved for jurors to engage in the full and free debate necessary to the attainment of just verdicts. Jurors will not be able to function effectively if their deliberations are to be scrutinized in post-trial litigation. In the interest of protecting the jury system and the citizens who make it work, Rule 606 should not permit any inquiry into the internal deliberations of the jurors.

CONFERENCE REPORT

Rule 606(b) deals with juror testimony in an inquiry into the validity of a verdict or indictment. The House bill provides that a juror cannot testify about his mental processes or about the effect of anything upon his or another juror's mind as influencing him to assent to or dissent from a verdict or indictment. Thus, the House bill allows a juror to testify about objective matters occurring during the jury's deliberation, such as the misconduct of another juror or the reaching of a quotient verdict. The Senate bill does not permit juror testimony about any matter or statement occurring during the course of the jury's deliberations. The Senate bill does provide, however, that a juror may testify on the question whether extraneous prejudicial information was improperly brought to the jury's attention and on the question whether any outside influence was improperly brought to bear on any juror.

The Conference adopts the Senate amendment. The Conferees believe that jurors should be encouraged to be conscientious in promptly reporting to the court misconduct that occurs during jury deliberations.

ADVISORY COMMITTEE'S NOTE TO 2006 AMENDMENT TO RULE 606

Rule 606(b) has been amended to provide that juror testimony may be used to prove that the verdict reported was the result of a mistake in entering the verdict on the verdict form. The amendment responds to a divergence between the text of the rule and the case law that has established an exception for proof of clerical errors. *See, e.g.,* Plummer v. Springfield Terminal Ry. Co., 5 F.3d 1, 3 (1st Cir.

1993) ("A number of circuits hold, and we agree, that juror testimony regarding an alleged clerical error, such as announcing a verdict different than that agreed upon, does not challenge the validity of the verdict or the deliberation of mental processes, and therefore is not subject to Rule 606(b)."); Teevee Toons, Inc., v. MP3.Com, Inc., 148 F.Supp.2d 276, 278 (S.D.N.Y. 2001) (noting that Rule 606(b) has been silent regarding inquiries designed to confirm the accuracy of a verdict).

In adopting the exception for proof of mistakes in entering the verdict on the verdict form, the amendment specifically rejects the broader exception, adopted by some courts, permitting the use of juror testimony to prove that the jurors were operating under a misunderstanding about the consequences of the result that they agreed upon. See, e.g., Attridge v. Cencorp Div. of Dover Techs. Int'l, Inc., 836 F.2d 113, 116 (2d Cir. 1987); Eastridge Dev. Co., v. Halpert Assocs., Inc., 853 F.2d 772 (10th Cir. 1988). The broader exception is rejected because an inquiry into whether the jury misunderstood or misapplied an instruction goes to the jurors' mental processes underlying the verdict, rather than the verdict's accuracy in capturing what the jurors had agreed upon. See, e.g., Karl v. Burlington N.R.R. Co., 880 F.2d 68, 74 (8th Cir. 1989) (error to receive juror testimony on whether verdict was the result of jurors' misunderstanding of instructions: "The jurors did not state that the figure written by the foreman was different from that which they agreed upon, but indicated that the figure the foreman wrote down was intended to be a net figure, not a gross figure. Receiving such statements violates Rule 606(b) because the testimony relates to how the jury interpreted the court's instructions, and concerns the jurors' 'mental processes,' which is forbidden by the rule."); Robles v. Exxon Corp., 862 F.2d 1201, 1208 (5th Cir. 1989) ("[T]he alleged error here goes to the substance of what the jury was asked to decide, necessarily implicating the jury's mental processes insofar as it questions the jury's understanding of the court's instructions and application of those instructions to the facts of the case."). Thus, the exception established by the amendment is limited to cases such as "where the jury foreperson wrote down, in response to an interrogatory, a number different from that agreed upon by the jury, or mistakenly stated that the defendant was 'guilty' when the jury had actually agreed that the defendant was not guilty." Id.

It should be noted that the possibility of errors in the verdict form will be reduced substantially by polling the jury. Rule 606(b) does not, of course, prevent this precaution. See 8 C. WIGMORE, EVIDENCE § 2350, at 691 (McNaughton rev. 1961) (noting that the reasons for the rule barring juror testimony, "namely, the dangers of uncertainty and of tampering with the jurors to procure testimony, disappear in large part if such investigation as may be desired is *made by the judge* and takes place *before the jurors' discharge and separation*") (emphasis in original). Errors that come to light after polling the jury "may be corrected on the spot, or the jury may be sent out to continue deliberations, or, if necessary, a new trial may be ordered." C. MUELLER & L. KIRKPATRICK, EVIDENCE UNDER THE RULES 671 (2d ed. 1999) (citing Sincox v. United States, 571 F.2d 876, 878–79 (5th Cir. 1978)).

Rule 607.   WHO MAY IMPEACH A WITNESS

Any party, including the party that called the witness, may attack the witness's credibility.

(Enacted Jan. 2, 1975; as amended Mar. 2, 1987, eff. Oct. 1, 1987; as restyled Apr. 26, 2011, eff. Dec. 1, 2011.)

<u>NOTE BY FEDERAL JUDICIAL CENTER</u>

The rule enacted by the Congress is the rule prescribed by the Supreme Court without change.

<u>ADVISORY COMMITTEE'S NOTE</u>

The traditional rule against impeaching one's own witness is abandoned as based on false premises. A party does not hold out his witnesses as worthy of belief, since he rarely has a free choice in selecting them. Denial of the right leaves the party at the mercy of the witness and the adversary. If the impeachment is by a prior statement, it is free from hearsay dangers and is excluded from the category of hearsay under Rule 801(d)(1). Ladd, *Impeachment of One's Own Witness—New Developments*, 4 U. CHI. L. REV. 69 (1936); MCCORMICK § 38; 3 WIGMORE §§ 896–918. The substantial inroads into the old rule made over the years by decisions, rules, and statutes are evidence of doubts as to its basic soundness and workability. Cases are collected in 3 WIGMORE § 905. Revised Rule [32(a)(2)] of the Federal Rules of Civil Procedure allows any party to impeach a witness by means of his deposition, and Rule 43(b) (repealed 1972) has allowed the calling and impeachment of an adverse party or person identified with him. Illustrative statutes allowing a party to impeach his own witness under varying circumstances are Illinois Revised Statutes 1967, ch. 110, § 60 (repealed and replaced by 735 Illinois Compiled Statutes 5/2-1102); Massachusetts General Laws ch. 233, § 23 (1959); 20 New Mexico Statutes Annotated § 20-2-4 (1953) (repealed and replaced by New Mexico Rule of Evidence 11-607); New York Civil Practice Law and Rules 4514 (McKinney 1963); 12 Vermont Statutes Annotated

§§ 1641a (repealed), 1642 (1959). Complete judicial rejection of the old rule is found in *United States v. Freeman*, 302 F.2d 347 (2d Cir. 1962). The same result is reached in Uniform Rule 20; California Evidence Code § 785; Kansas Statutes Annotated § 60-420. *See also* N.J. EVID. R. 20 (repealed and replaced by N.J. R. EVID. 607 (1993)).

Rule 608.   A WITNESS'S CHARACTER FOR TRUTHFULNESS OR UNTRUTHFULNESS.

(a) Reputation or Opinion Evidence.   A witness's credibility may be attacked or supported by testimony about the witness's reputation for having a character for truthfulness or untruthfulness, or by testimony in the form of an opinion about that character. But evidence of truthful character is admissible only after the witness's character for truthfulness has been attacked.

(b) Specific Instances of Conduct.   Except for a criminal conviction under Rule 609, extrinsic evidence is not admissible to prove specific instances of a witness's conduct in order to attack or support the witness's character for truthfulness. But the court may, on cross-examination, allow them to be inquired into if they are probative of the character for truthfulness or untruthfulness of:

    (1) the witness; or

    (2) another witness whose character the witness being cross-examined has testified about.

By testifying on another matter, a witness does not waive any privilege against self-incrimination for testimony that relates only to the witness's character for truthfulness.

(Enacted Jan. 2, 1975; as amended Mar. 2, 1987, eff. Oct. 1, 1987; Apr. 25, 1988, eff. Nov. 1, 1988; Mar. 27, 2003, eff. Dec. 1, 2003; as restyled Apr. 26, 2011, eff. Dec. 1, 2011.)

NOTE BY FEDERAL JUDICIAL CENTER

The rule enacted by the Congress is the rule prescribed by the Supreme Court, changed only by amending the second sentence of subdivision (b). The sentence as prescribed by the Court read:

They may, however, if probative of truthfulness or untruthfulness and not remote in time, be inquired into on cross-examination of the witness himself or on cross-examination of a witness who testifies to his character for truthfulness or untruthfulness.

The effect of the amendments was to delete the phrase "and not remote in time," to add the phrase "in the discretion of the court," and otherwise only to clarify the meaning of the sentence. The reasons for the amendments are stated in the Report of the House Committee on the Judiciary, set forth below. *See also* Note to Rule 405(a) by Federal Judicial Center, *supra*.

ADVISORY COMMITTEE'S NOTE

Subdivision (a). In Rule 404(a) the general position is taken that character evidence is not admissible for the purpose of proving that the person acted in conformity therewith, subject, however, to several exceptions, one of which is character evidence of a witness as bearing upon his credibility. The present rule develops that exception.

In accordance with the bulk of judicial authority, the inquiry is strictly limited to character for veracity, rather than allowing evidence as to character generally. The result is to sharpen relevancy, to reduce surprise, waste of time, and confusion, and to make the lot of the witness somewhat less unattractive. MCCORMICK § 44.

The use of opinion and reputation evidence as means of proving the character of witnesses is consistent with Rule 405(a). While the modern practice has purported to exclude opinion, witnesses who testify to reputation seem in fact often to be giving their opinions, disguised somewhat misleadingly as reputation. *See* MCCORMICK § 44. And even under the modern practice, a common relaxation has allowed inquiry as to whether the witnesses would believe the principal witness under oath. United States v. Walker, 313 F.2d 236 (6th Cir. 1963), and cases cited therein; MCCORMICK § 44, at 94 n.3.

Character evidence in support of credibility is admissible under the rule only after the witness's character has first been attacked, as has been the case at common law. MAGUIRE, WEINSTEIN, ET AL., CASES ON EVIDENCE 295 (5th ed. 1965); MCCORMICK § 49, at 105; 4 WIGMORE § 1104. The enormous needless consumption of time which a contrary practice would entail justifies the limitation. Opinion or reputation that the witness is untruthful specifically qualifies as an attack under the rule, and evidence of misconduct, including conviction of crime, and of corruption also fall within this category. Evidence of bias or interest does not. McCormick § 49; 4 Wigmore §§ 1106, 1107. Whether evidence in the form of contradiction is an attack upon the character of the witness must depend upon the circumstances. McCormick § 49; *cf.* 4 Wigmore §§ 1108–1109.

As to the use of specific instances on direct by an opinion witness, see the Advisory Committee's Note to Rule 405, *supra*.

Subdivision (b). In conformity with Rule 405, which forecloses use of evidence of specific incidents as proof in chief of character unless character is an issue in the case, the present rule generally bars evidence of specific instances of conduct of a witness for the purpose of attacking or supporting his credibility. There are, however, two exceptions: (1) specific instances are provable when they have been the subject of criminal conviction, and (2) specific instances may be inquired into on cross-examination of the principal witness or of a witness giving an opinion of his character for truthfulness.

(1) Conviction of crime as a technique of impeachment is treated in detail in Rule 609, and here is merely recognized as an exception to the general rule excluding evidence of specific incidents for impeachment purposes.

(2) Particular instances of conduct, though not the subject of criminal conviction, may be inquired into on cross-examination of the principal witness himself or of a witness who testifies concerning his character for truthfulness. Effective cross-examination demands that some allowance be made for going into matters of this kind, but the possibilities of abuse are substantial. Consequently safeguards are erected in the form of specific requirements that the instances inquired into be probative of truthfulness or its opposite .... Also, the overriding protection of Rule 403 requires that probative value not be outweighed by danger of unfair prejudice, confusion of issues, or misleading the jury, and that of Rule 611 bars harassment and undue embarrassment.

The final sentence constitutes a rejection of the doctrine of such cases as *People v. Sorge*, 301 N.Y. 198 (1950), that any past criminal act relevant to credibility may be inquired into on cross-examination, in apparent disregard of the privilege against self-incrimination. While it is clear that an ordinary witness cannot make a partial disclosure of incriminating matter and then invoke the privilege on cross-examination, no tenable contention can be made that merely by testifying he waives his right to foreclose inquiry on cross-examination into criminal activities for the purpose of attacking his credibility. So to hold would reduce the privilege to a nullity. While it is true that an accused, unlike an ordinary witness, has an option whether to testify, if the option can be exercised only at the price of opening up inquiry as to any and all criminal acts committed during his lifetime, the right to testify could scarcely be said to possess much vitality. In *Griffin v. California*, 380 U.S. 609 (1965), the Court held that allowing comment on the election of an accused not to testify exacted a constitutionally impermissible price, and so here. While no specific provision in terms confers constitutional status on the right of an accused to take the stand in his own defense, the existence of the right is so completely recognized that a denial of it or substantial infringement upon it would surely be of due process dimensions. *See* Ferguson v. Georgia, 365 U.S. 570 (1961); McCORMICK § 131; 8 WIGMORE § 2276 (McNaughton rev. 1961). In any event, wholly aside from constitutional considerations, the provision represents a sound policy.

REPORT OF THE HOUSE COMMITTEE ON THE JUDICIARY

. . .

The second sentence of Rule 608(b) as submitted by the Court permitted specific instances of misconduct of a witness to be inquired into on cross-examination for the purpose of attacking his credibility, if probative of truthfulness or untruthfulness, "and not remote in time." Such cross-examination could be of the witness himself or of another witness who testifies as to "his" character for truthfulness or untruthfulness.

The Committee amended the rule to emphasize the discretionary power of the court in permitting such testimony and deleted the reference to remoteness in time as being unnecessary and confusing (remoteness from time of trial or remoteness from the incident involved?). As recast, the Committee amendment also makes clear the antecedent of "his" in the original Court proposal.

ADVISORY COMMITTEE'S NOTE TO 2003 AMENDMENT TO RULE 608

The rule has been amended to clarify that the absolute prohibition on extrinsic evidence applies only when the sole reason for proffering that evidence is to attack or support the witness's character for truthfulness. *See* United States v. Abel, 469 U.S. 45 (1984); United States v. Fusco, 748 F.2d 996 (5th Cir. 1984) (Rule 608(b) limits the use of evidence "designed to show that the witness has done things, unrelated to the suit being tried, that make him more or less believable per se"); OHIO EVID. R. 608(b). On occasion the rule's use of the overbroad term "credibility" has been read "to bar extrinsic evidence for bias, competency, and contradiction impeachment since they too deal with credibility." AM. BAR ASS'N SECTION OF LITIG., EMERGING PROBLEMS UNDER THE FEDERAL RULES OF EVIDENCE 161 (3d ed. 1998). The amendment conforms to the language of the rule to its original intent, which was to impose an absolute bar on extrinsic evidence only if the sole purpose for offering the evidence was to prove the witness's character for veracity. *See* Advisory Committee's Note to Rule 608(b) (stating that the rule is "[i]n conformity with Rule 405, which forecloses use of evidence of specific incidents as proof in chief of character unless character is in issue in the case").

By limiting the application of the rule to proof of a witness's character for truthfulness, the amendment leaves the admissibility of extrinsic evidence offered for other grounds of impeachment (such as contradiction, prior inconsistent statement, bias, and mental capacity) to Rules 402 and 403. *See, e.g.,* United States v. Winchenbach, 197 F.3d 548 (1st Cir. 1999) (admissibility of a prior inconsistent statement offered for impeachment is governed by Rules 402 and 403, not Rule 608(b)); United States v. Tarantino, 846 F.2d 1384 (D.C. Cir. 1988) (admissibility of extrinsic evidence offered to contradict a witness is governed by Rule 402 and 403); United States v. Lindemann, 85 F.3d 1232 (7th Cir. 1996) (admissibility of extrinsic evidence of bias is governed by Rules 402 and 403). [Rules 402 and 403 displace the common-law rules prohibiting impeachment on "collateral" matters. *See* 4 WEINSTEIN'S EVIDENCE § 607.06[3][b][ii] (2d ed. 2000) (advocating that courts substitute "the discretion approach of Rule 403 for the collateral test advocated by case law").][2]

It should be noted that the extrinsic evidence prohibition of Rule 608(b) bars any reference to the consequences that a witness might have suffered as a result of an alleged bad act. For example, Rule 608(b) prohibits counsel from mentioning that a witness was suspended or disciplined for the conduct that is the subject of impeachment, when that conduct is offered only to prove the character of the witness. *See* United States v. Davis, 183 F.3d 231, 257 n.12 (3d Cir. 1999) (emphasizing that in attacking the defendant's character for truthfulness "the government cannot make reference to Davis's forty-four day suspension or that Internal Affairs found that he lied about" an incident because "[s]uch evidence would not only be hearsay to the extent it contains an assertion of fact, it would be inadmissible extrinsic evidence under Rule 608(b)"); *see also* Stephen A. Saltzburg, *Impeaching the Witness: Prior Bad Acts and Extrinsic Evidence*, CRIM. JUST., Winter 1993, at 28,

---

[2] [The bracketed material was deleted from the final version of the Advisory Committee's Note.—GF]

31 ("[C]ounsel should not be permitted to circumvent the no-extrinsic-evidence provision by tucking a third person's opinion about prior acts into a question asked of the witness who has denied the act.").

For purposes of consistency the term "credibility" has been replaced by the term "character for truthfulness" in the last sentence of subdivision (b). The term "credibility" is also used in subdivision (a). But the Committee found it unnecessary to substitute "character for truthfulness" for "credibility" in Rule 608(a), because subdivision [(a)] already serves to limit impeachment to proof of such character.

Rules [609] and 610 also use the term "credibility" when the intent of those Rules is to regulate impeachment of a witness's character for truthfulness. No inference should be derived from the fact that the Committee proposed an amendment to Rule 608(b) but not to Rules 609 and 610.

<u>ADVISORY COMMITTEE'S NOTE TO 2011 RESTYLING OF RULE 608</u>

The Committee is aware that the rule's limitation of bad-act impeachment to "cross-examination" is trumped by Rule 607, which allows a party to impeach witnesses on direct examination. Courts have not relied on the term "on cross-examination" to limit impeachment that would otherwise be permissible under Rules 607 and 608. The Committee therefore concluded that no change to the language of the rule was necessary in the context of a restyling project.

Rule 609.   IMPEACHMENT BY EVIDENCE OF A CRIMINAL CONVICTION

(a) In General. The following rules apply to attacking a witness's character for truthfulness by evidence of a criminal conviction:

(1) for a crime that, in the convicting jurisdiction, was punishable by death or by imprisonment for more than one year, the evidence:

(A) must be admitted, subject to Rule 403, in a civil case or in a criminal case in which the witness is not a defendant; and

(B) must be admitted in a criminal case in which the witness is a defendant, if the probative value of the evidence outweighs its prejudicial effect to that defendant; and

(2) for any crime regardless of the punishment, the evidence must be admitted if the court can readily determine that establishing the elements of the crime required proving—or the witness's admitting—a dishonest act or false statement.

(b) Limit on Using the Evidence After 10 Years. This subdivision (b) applies if more than 10 years have passed since the witness's conviction or release from confinement for it, whichever is later. Evidence of the conviction is admissible only if:

(1) its probative value, supported by specific facts and circumstances, substantially outweighs its prejudicial effect; and

(2) the proponent gives an adverse party reasonable written notice of the intent to use it so that the party has a fair opportunity to contest its use.

(c) Effect of a Pardon, Annulment, or Certificate of Rehabilitation. Evidence of a conviction is not admissible if:

(1) the conviction has been the subject of a pardon, annulment, certificate of rehabilitation, or other equivalent procedure based on a finding that the person has been rehabilitated, and the person has not been convicted of a later crime punishable by death or by imprisonment for more than one year; or

(2) the conviction has been the subject of a pardon, annulment, or other equivalent procedure based on a finding of innocence.

(d) Juvenile Adjudications. Evidence of a juvenile adjudication is admissible under this rule only if:

(1) it is offered in a criminal case;

(2) the adjudication was of a witness other than the defendant;

(3) an adult's conviction for that offense would be admissible to attack the adult's credibility; and

(4) admitting the evidence is necessary to fairly determine guilt or innocence.

(e) Pendency of an Appeal. A conviction that satisfies this rule is admissible even if an appeal is pending. Evidence of the pendency is also admissible.

(Enacted Jan. 2, 1975; as amended Mar. 2, 1987, eff. Oct. 1, 1987; Jan. 26, 1990, eff. Dec. 1, 1990; Apr. 12, 2006, eff. Dec. 1, 2006; as restyled Apr. 26, 2011, eff. Dec. 1, 2011.)

NOTE BY FEDERAL JUDICIAL CENTER

Subdivision (a) of the rule prescribed by the Supreme Court was revised successively in the House, in the Senate, and in the Conference. The nature of the rule prescribed by the Court, the various amendments, and the reasons therefor are stated in the Report of the House Committee on the Judiciary, the Report of the Senate Committee on the Judiciary, and the Conference Report, set forth below.

Subdivision (b) of the rule prescribed by the Supreme Court was also revised successively in the House, in the Senate, and in the Conference. The nature of the rule prescribed by the Court, the various amendments, and the reasons therefor are likewise stated in the Report of the House Committee on the Judiciary, the Report of the Senate Committee on the Judiciary, and the Conference Report, set forth below.

Subdivision (c) enacted by the Congress is the subdivision prescribed by the Supreme Court, with amendments and reasons therefor stated in the Report of the House Committee on the Judiciary, set forth below.

Subdivision (d) enacted by the Congress is the subdivision prescribed by the Supreme Court, amended in the second sentence by substituting "court" in place of "judge" and by adding the phrase "in a criminal case."

Subdivision (e) enacted by the Congress is the subdivision prescribed by the Supreme Court without change.

<u>ADVISORY COMMITTEE'S NOTE TO RULE 609(a)</u>

As a means of impeachment, evidence of conviction of crime is significant only because it stands as proof of the commission of the underlying criminal act. There is little dissent from the general proposition that at least some crimes are relevant to credibility but much disagreement among the cases and commentators about which crimes are usable for this purpose. *See* McCormick § 43; 2 Wright, Federal Practice and Procedure: Criminal § 416 (1969). The weight of traditional authority has been to allow use of felonies generally, without regard to the nature of the particular offense, and of *crimen falsi* without regard to the grade of the offense. This is the view accepted by Congress in the 1970 amendment of § 14-305 of the District of Columbia Code, Pub. L. No. 91-358, 84 Stat. 473. Uniform Rule 21 and Model Code Rule 106 permit only crimes involving "dishonesty or false statement." Others have thought that the trial judge should have discretion to exclude convictions if the probative value of the evidence of the crime is substantially outweighed by the danger of unfair prejudice. Luck v. United States, 348 F.2d 763 (D.C. Cir. 1965); McGowan, *Impeachment of Criminal Defendants by Prior Convictions*, 1970 Law & Soc. Ord. 1. . . .

The proposed rule incorporates certain basic safeguards, in terms applicable to all witnesses but of particular significance to an accused who elects to testify. These protections include the imposition of definite time limitations, giving effect to demonstrated rehabilitation, and generally excluding juvenile adjudications.

Subdivision (a). For purposes of impeachment, crimes are divided into two categories by the rule: (1) those of what is generally regarded as felony grade, without particular regard to the nature of the offense, and (2) those involving dishonesty or false statement, without regard to the grade of the offense. Provable convictions are not limited to violations of federal law. By reason of our constitutional structure, the federal catalog of crimes is far from being a complete one, and resort must be had to the laws of the states for the specification of many crimes. For example, simple theft as compared with theft from interstate commerce. Other instances of borrowing are the Assimilative Crimes Act, making the state law of crimes applicable to the special territorial and maritime jurisdiction of the United States, 18 U.S.C. § 13, and the provision of the Judicial Code disqualifying persons as jurors on the grounds of state as well as federal convictions, 28 U.S.C. § 1865. For evaluation of the crime in terms of seriousness, reference is made to the congressional measurement of felony (subject to imprisonment in excess of one year) rather than adopting state definitions which vary considerably. *See* 28 U.S.C. § 1865, *supra* (disqualifying jurors for conviction in state or federal court of crime punishable by imprisonment for more than one year).

REPORT OF THE HOUSE COMMITTEE ON THE JUDICIARY

Rule 609(a) as submitted by the Court was modeled after section 133(a) of Public Law 91-358, D.C. Code § 14-305(b)(1), enacted in 1970. The rule provided that:

> For the purpose of attacking the credibility of a witness, evidence that he has been convicted of a crime is admissible but only if the crime (1) was punishable by death or imprisonment in excess of one year under the law under which he was convicted or (2) involved dishonesty or false statement regardless of the punishment.

As reported to the Committee by the Subcommittee, Rule 609(a) was amended to read as follows:

> For the purpose of attacking the credibility of a witness, evidence that he has been convicted of a crime is admissible only if the crime (1) was punishable by death or imprisonment in excess of one year, unless the court determines that the danger of unfair prejudice outweighs the probative value of the evidence of the conviction, or (2) involved dishonesty or false statement.

In full committee, the provision was amended to permit attack upon the credibility of a witness by prior conviction only if the prior crime involved dishonesty or false statement. While recognizing that the prevailing doctrine in the federal courts and in most states allows a witness to be impeached by evidence of prior felony convictions without restriction as to type, the Committee was of the view that, because of the danger of unfair prejudice in such practice and the deterrent effect upon an accused who might wish to testify, and even upon a witness who was not the accused, cross-examination by evidence of prior conviction should be limited to those kinds of convictions bearing directly on credibility, i.e., crimes involving dishonesty or false statement.

REPORT OF THE SENATE COMMITTEE ON THE JUDICIARY

As proposed by the Supreme Court, the rule would allow the use of prior convictions to impeach if the crime was a felony or a misdemeanor if the misdemeanor involved dishonesty or false statement. As modified by the House, the rule would admit prior convictions for impeachment purposes only if the offense, whether felony or misdemeanor, involved dishonesty or false statement.

The Committee has adopted a modified version of the House-passed rule. In your Committee's view, the danger of unfair prejudice is far greater when the accused, as opposed to other witnesses, testifies, because the jury may be prejudiced not merely on the question of credibility but also on the ultimate question of guilt or innocence. Therefore, with respect to defendants, the Committee agreed with the House limitation that only offenses involving false statement or dishonesty may be used. By that phrase, the Committee means crimes such as perjury or subornation of perjury, false statement, criminal fraud, embezzlement, or false pretense, or any other offense, in the nature of *crimen falsi* the commission of which involves some element of untruthfulness, deceit or falsification bearing on the accused's propensity to testify truthfully.

With respect to other witnesses, in addition to any prior conviction involving false statement or dishonesty, any other felony may be used to impeach if, and only if, the court finds that the probative value of such evidence outweighs its prejudicial effect against the party offering that witness.

Notwithstanding this provision, proof of any prior offense otherwise admissible under Rule 404 could still be offered for the purposes sanctioned by that rule. Furthermore, the Committee intends that notwithstanding this rule, a defendant's misrepresentation regarding the existence or nature of prior convictions may be met by rebuttal evidence, including the record of such prior convictions. Similarly, such records may be offered to rebut representations made by the defendant regarding his attitude toward or willingness to commit a general category of offense, although denials or other representations by the defendant regarding the specific conduct which forms the basis of the charge against him shall not make prior convictions admissible to rebut such statement.

In regard to either type of representation, of course, prior convictions may be offered in rebuttal only if the defendant's statement is made in response to defense counsel's questions or is made gratuitously in the course of cross-examination. Prior convictions may not be offered as rebuttal evidence if the prosecution has sought to circumvent the purpose of this rule by asking questions which elicit such representations from the defendant.

One other clarifying amendment has been added to this subsection, that is, to provide that the admissibility of evidence of a prior conviction is permitted only upon cross-examination of a witness. It is not admissible if a person does not testify. It is to be understood, however, that a court record of a prior conviction is admissible to prove that conviction if the witness has forgotten or denies its existence.

CONFERENCE REPORT

The House bill provides that the credibility of a witness can be attacked by proof of prior conviction of a crime only if the crime involves dishonesty or false statement. The Senate amendment provides that a witness's credibility may be attacked if the crime (1) was punishable by death or imprisonment in excess of one year under the law under which he was convicted or (2) involves dishonesty or false statement, regardless of the punishment.

The Conference adopts the Senate amendment with an amendment. The Conference amendment provides that the credibility of a witness, whether a defendant or someone else, may be attacked by proof of a prior conviction but only if the crime: (1) was punishable by death or imprisonment in excess of one year under the law under which he was convicted and the court determines that the probative value of the conviction outweighs its prejudicial effect to the defendant; or (2) involved dishonesty or false statement regardless of the punishment.

By the phrase "dishonesty and false statement" the Conference means crimes such as perjury or subornation of perjury, false statement, criminal fraud, embezzlement, or false pretense, or any other offense in the nature of *crimen falsi*, the commission of which involves some element of deceit, untruthfulness, or falsification bearing on the accused's propensity to testify truthfully.

The admission of prior convictions involving dishonesty and false statement is not within the discretion of the Court. Such convictions are peculiarly probative of credibility and, under this rule, are always to be admitted. Thus, judicial discretion granted with respect to the admissibility of other prior convictions is not applicable to those involving dishonesty or false statement.

With regard to the discretionary standard established by [Rule 609(a)(1)], the Conference determined that the prejudicial effect to be weighed against the probative value of the conviction is specifically the prejudicial effect *to the defendant*. The danger of prejudice to a witness other than the defendant (such as injury to the witness's reputation in his community) was considered and rejected by the Conference as an element to be weighed in determining admissibility. It was the judgment of the Conference that the danger of prejudice to a nondefendant witness is outweighed by the need for the trier of fact to have as much relevant evidence on the issue of credibility as possible. Such evidence should only be excluded where it presents a danger of improperly influencing the outcome of the trial by persuading the trier of fact to convict the defendant on the basis of his prior criminal record.

ADVISORY COMMITTEE'S NOTE TO RULE 609(b)

Subdivision (b). Few statutes recognize a time limit on impeachment by evidence of conviction. However, practical considerations of fairness and relevancy demand that some boundary be recognized. *See* Ladd, *Credibility Tests—Current Trends*, 89 U. PA. L. REV. 166, 176–77 (1940). This portion of the rule is derived from the proposal advanced in CAL. LAW REVISION COMM'N, RECOMMENDATION PROPOSING AN EVIDENCE CODE § 788(5), at 142 (1965), though not adopted. *See* CAL. EVID. CODE § 788.

REPORT OF THE HOUSE COMMITTEE ON THE JUDICIARY

Rule 609(b) as submitted by the Court was modeled after Section 133(a) of Public Law 91-358, D.C. Code § 14-305(b)(2)(B), enacted in 1970. The rule provided:

> Evidence of a conviction under this rule is not admissible if a period of more than ten years has elapsed since the date of the release of the witness from confinement imposed for his most recent conviction, or the expiration of the period of his parole, probation, or sentence granted or imposed with respect to his most recent conviction, whichever is the later date.

Under this formulation, a witness's entire past record of criminal convictions could be used for impeachment (provided the conviction met the standard of subdivision (a)), if the witness had been most recently released from confinement, or the period of his parole or probation had expired, within ten years of the conviction.

The Committee amended the rule to read in the text of the 1971 Advisory Committee version to provide that upon the expiration of ten years from the date of a conviction of a witness, or of his release from confinement for that offense, that conviction may no longer be used for impeachment. The Committee was of the view that after ten years following a person's release from confinement (or from the date of his conviction) the probative value of the conviction with respect to that person's credibility diminished to a point where it should no longer be admissible.

REPORT OF THE SENATE COMMITTEE ON THE JUDICIARY

Although convictions over ten years old generally do not have much probative value, there may be exceptional circumstances under which the conviction substantially bears on the credibility of the witness. Rather than exclude all convictions over ten years old, the Committee adopted an amendment in the form of a final clause to the section granting the court discretion to admit convictions over ten years old, but only upon a determination by the court that the probative value of the conviction, supported by specific facts and circumstances, substantially outweighs its prejudicial effect.

It is intended that convictions over ten years old will be admitted very rarely and only in exceptional circumstances. The rules provide that the decision be supported by specific facts and circumstances thus requiring the court to make specific findings on the record as to the particular facts and circumstances it has considered in determining that the probative value of the conviction substantially outweighs its prejudicial impact. It is expected that, in fairness, the court will give the party against whom the conviction is introduced a full and adequate opportunity to contest its admission.

CONFERENCE REPORT

The House bill provides in subsection (b) that evidence of conviction of a crime may not be used for impeachment purposes under subsection (a) if more than ten years have elapsed since the date of the conviction or the date the witness was released from confinement imposed for the conviction, whichever is later. The Senate amendment permits the use of convictions older than ten years, if the court determines, in the interests of justice, that the probative value of the conviction, supported by specific facts and circumstances, substantially outweighs its prejudicial effect.

The Conference adopts the Senate amendment with an amendment requiring notice by a party that he intends to request that the court allow him to use a conviction older than ten years. The Conferees anticipate that a written notice, in order to give the adversary a fair opportunity to contest the use of the evidence, will ordinarily include such information as the date of the conviction, the jurisdiction, and the offense or statute involved. In order to eliminate the possibility that the flexibility of this provision may impair the ability of a party-opponent to prepare for trial, the

Conferees intend that the notice provision operate to avoid surprise.

<u>ADVISORY COMMITTEE'S NOTE TO RULE 609(c)</u>

Subdivision (c). A pardon or its equivalent granted solely for the purpose of restoring civil rights lost by virtue of a conviction has no relevance to an inquiry into character. If, however, the pardon or other proceeding is hinged upon a showing of rehabilitation the situation is otherwise. The result under the rule is to render the conviction inadmissible. The alternative of allowing in evidence both the conviction and the rehabilitation has not been adopted for reasons of policy, economy of time, and difficulties of evaluation.

A similar provision is contained in California Evidence Code § 788. *Cf.* MODEL PENAL CODE § 306.6(3)(e) (Proposed Official Draft 1962), and discussion in ALI PROCEEDINGS 310 (1961).

Pardons based on innocence have the effect, of course, of nullifying the conviction ab initio.

<u>REPORT OF THE HOUSE COMMITTEE ON THE JUDICIARY</u>

Rule 609(c) as submitted by the Court provided in part that evidence of a witness's prior conviction is not admissible to attack his credibility if the conviction was the subject of a pardon, annulment, or other equivalent procedure, based on a showing of rehabilitation, and the witness has not been convicted of a subsequent crime. The Committee amended the rule to provide that the "subsequent crime" must have been "punishable by death or imprisonment in excess of one year," on the ground that a subsequent conviction of an offense not a felony is insufficient to rebut the finding that the witness has been rehabilitated. The Committee also intends that the words "based on a finding of the rehabilitation of the person convicted" apply not only to "certificate of rehabilitation, or other equivalent procedure," but also to "pardon" and "annulment."

<u>ADVISORY COMMITTEE'S NOTE TO RULE 609(d)–(e)</u>

Subdivision (d). The prevailing view has been that a juvenile adjudication is not usable for impeachment. Thomas v. United States, 74 App. D.C. 167 (1941); Cotton v. United States, 355 F.2d 480 (10th Cir. 1966). This conclusion was based upon a variety of circumstances. By virtue of its informality, frequently diminished quantum of required proof, and other departures from accepted standards for criminal trials under the theory of parens patriae, the juvenile adjudication was considered to lack the precision and general probative value of the criminal conviction. While *In re Gault*, 387 U.S. 1 (1967), no doubt eliminates these characteristics insofar as objectionable, other obstacles remain. Practical problems of administration are raised by the common provisions in juvenile legislation that records be kept confidential and that they be destroyed after a short time. While *Gault* was skeptical as to the realities of confidentiality of juvenile records, it also saw no constitutional obstacles to improvement. 387 U.S. at 25; *see also* Note, *Rights and Rehabilitation in the Juvenile Courts*, 67 COLUM. L. REV. 281, 289 (1967). In addition, policy considerations much akin to those which dictate exclusion of adult convictions after rehabilitation has been established strongly suggest a rule of excluding juvenile adjudications. Admittedly, however, the rehabilitative process may in a given case be a demonstrated failure, or the strategic importance of a given witness may be so great as to require the overriding of general policy in the interests of particular justice. *See* Giles v. Maryland, 386 U.S. 66 (1967). Wigmore was outspoken in his condemnation of the disallowance of juvenile adjudications to impeach, especially when the witness is the complainant in a case of molesting a minor. 1 WIGMORE § 196; 3 *id.* §§ 924a, 980. The rule recognizes discretion in the judge to effect an accommodation among these various factors by departing from the general principle of exclusion. In deference to the general pattern and policy of juvenile statutes, however, no discretion is accorded when the witness is the accused in a criminal case.

Subdivision (e). The presumption of correctness which ought to attend judicial proceedings supports the position that pendency of an appeal does not preclude use of a conviction for impeachment. United States v. Empire Packing Co., 174 F.2d 16 (7th Cir.), *cert. denied*, 337 U.S. 959 (1949); Bloch v. United States, 226 F.2d 185 (9th Cir. 1955), *cert. denied*, 350 U.S. 948 (1956) and 353 U.S. 959 (1957); *see also* Newman v. United States, 331 F.2d 968 (8th Cir. 1964). *Contra* Campbell v. United States, 176 F.2d 45 (D.C. Cir. 1949). The pendency of an appeal is, however, a qualifying circumstance properly considerable.

ADVISORY COMMITTEE'S NOTE TO 1990 AMENDMENT TO RULE 609

The amendment to Rule 609(a) makes two changes in the rule. The first change removes from the rule the limitation that the conviction may only be elicited during cross-examination, a limitation that virtually every circuit has found to be inapplicable. It is common for witnesses to reveal on direct examination their convictions to "remove the sting" of the impeachment. *See, e.g.,* United States v. Bad Cob, 560 F.2d 877 (8th Cir. 1977). The amendment does not contemplate that a court will necessarily permit proof of prior convictions through testimony, which might be time-consuming and more prejudicial than proof through a written record. Rules 403 and 611(a) provide sufficient authority for the court to protect against unfair or disruptive methods of proof.

The second change effected by the amendment resolves an ambiguity as to the relationship of Rules 609 and 403 with respect to impeachment of witnesses other than the criminal defendant. *See* Green v. Bock Laundry Mach. Co., 490 U.S. 504 (1989). The amendment does not disturb the special balancing test for the criminal defendant who chooses to testify. Thus, the rule recognizes that, in virtually every case in which prior convictions are used to impeach the testifying defendant, the defendant faces a unique risk of prejudice—i.e., the danger that convictions that would be excluded under Federal Rule of Evidence 404 will be misused by a jury as propensity evidence despite their introduction solely for impeachment purposes. Although the rule does not forbid all use of convictions to impeach a defendant, it requires that the government show that the probative value of convictions as impeachment evidence outweighs their prejudicial effect.

Prior to the amendment, the rule appeared to give the defendant the benefit of the special balancing test when defense witnesses other than the defendant were called to testify. In practice, however, the concern about unfairness to the defendant is most acute when the defendant's own convictions are offered as evidence. Almost all of the decided cases concern this type of impeachment, and the amendment does not deprive the defendant of any meaningful protection, since Rule 403 now clearly protects against unfair impeachment of any defense witness other than the defendant. There are cases in which a defendant might be prejudiced when a defense witness is impeached. Such cases may arise, for example, when the witness bears a special relationship to the defendant such that the defendant is likely to suffer some spill-over effect from impeachment of the witness.

The amendment also protects other litigants from unfair impeachment of their witnesses. The danger of prejudice from the use of prior convictions is not confined to criminal defendants. Although the danger that prior convictions will be misused as character evidence is particularly acute when the defendant is impeached, the danger exists in other situations as well. The amendment reflects the view that it is desirable to protect all litigants from the unfair use of prior convictions, and that the ordinary balancing test of Rule 403, which provides that evidence shall not be excluded unless its prejudicial effect substantially outweighs its probative value, is appropriate for assessing the admissibility of prior convictions for impeachment of any witness other than a criminal defendant.

The amendment reflects a judgment that decisions interpreting Rule 609(a) as requiring a trial court to admit convictions in civil cases that have little, if anything, to do with credibility reach undesirable results. *See, e.g.,* Diggs v. Lyons, 741 F.2d 577 (3d Cir. 1984), *cert. denied,* 471 U.S. 1078 (1985). The amendment provides the same protection against unfair prejudice arising from prior convictions used for impeachment purposes as the rules provide for other evidence. The amendment finds support in decided cases. *See, e.g.,* Petty v. Ideco, 761 F.2d 1146 (5th Cir. 1985); Czajka v. Hickman, 703 F.2d 317 (8th Cir. 1983).

Fewer decided cases address the question whether Rule 609(a) provides any protection against unduly prejudicial prior convictions used to impeach government witnesses. Some courts have read Rule 609(a) as giving the government no protection for its witnesses. *See, e.g.,* United States v. Thorne, 547 F.2d 56 (8th Cir. 1976); United States v. Nevitt, 563 F.2d 406 (9th Cir. 1977), *cert. denied,* 444 U.S. 847 (1979). This approach also is rejected by the amendment. There are cases in which impeachment of government witnesses with prior convictions that have little, if anything, to do with credibility may result in unfair prejudice to the government's interest in a fair trial and unnecessary embarrassment to a witness. Federal Rule of Evidence 412 already recognizes this and excluded certain evidence of past sexual behavior in the context of prosecutions for sexual assaults.

The amendment applies the general balancing test of Rule 403 to protect all litigants against unfair impeachment of witnesses. The balancing test protects civil litigants, the government in criminal cases, and the defendant in a criminal case who calls other witnesses. The amendment addresses prior convictions offered under Rule 609, not for other purposes, and does not run afoul, therefore, of *Davis v. Alaska,* 415 U.S. 308 (1974). Davis involved the use of a prior juvenile adjudication not to prove a past law violation, but to prove bias. The defendant in a criminal case has the right to demonstrate the bias of a witness and to be assured a fair trial, but not to unduly prejudice a trier of fact. *See generally* Rule 412. In any case in which the trial court believes that confrontation rights require admission of impeachment evidence, obviously the Constitution would take precedence over the rule.

The probability that prior convictions of an ordinary government witness will be unduly prejudicial is low in most criminal cases. Since the behavior of the witness is not the issue in dispute in most cases, there is little chance that the trier of fact will misuse the convictions offered as impeachment evidence as propensity evidence. Thus, trial courts will be skeptical when the government objects to impeachment of its witnesses with prior convictions. Only when the government is able to point to a real danger of prejudice that is sufficient to outweigh substantially the probative value of the conviction for impeachment purposes will the conviction be excluded.

The amendment continues to divide subdivision (a) into subsections (1) and (2) thus facilitating retrieval under current computerized research programs which distinguish the two provisions. The Committee recommended no substantive change in subdivision (a)(2), even though some cases raise a concern about the proper interpretation of the words "dishonesty or false statement." These words were used but not explained in the original Advisory Committee note accompanying Rule 609. Congress extensively debated the rule, and the Report of the House and Senate Conference Committee states that "[b]y the phrase 'dishonesty and false statement,' the Conference means crimes such as perjury, subordination of perjury, false statement, criminal fraud, embezzlement, or false pretense, or any other offense in the nature of *crimen falsi*, commission of which involves some element of deceit, untruthfulness, or falsification bearing on the accused's propensity to testify truthfully." The Advisory Committee concluded that the Conference Report provides sufficient guidance to trial courts and that no amendment is necessary, notwithstanding some decisions that take an unduly broad view of "dishonesty," admitting convictions such as for bank robbery or bank larceny. Subsection (a)(2) continues to apply to any witness, including a criminal defendant.

Finally, the Committee determined that it was unnecessary to add to the rule language stating that, when a prior conviction is offered under Rule 609, the trial court is to consider the probative value of the prior conviction for impeachment, not for other purposes. The Committee concluded that the title of the rule, its first sentence, and its placement among the impeachment rules clearly establish that evidence offered under Rule 609 is offered only for purposes of impeachment.

ADVISORY COMMITTEE'S NOTE TO 2006 AMENDMENT TO RULE 609

The amendment provides that Rule 609(a)(2) mandates the admission of evidence of a conviction only when the conviction required the proof of (or in the case of a guilty plea, the admission of) an act of dishonesty or false statement. Evidence of all other convictions is inadmissible under this subsection, irrespective of whether the witness exhibited dishonesty or made a false statement in the process of the commission of the crime of conviction. Thus, evidence that a witness was convicted for a crime of violence, such as murder, is not admissible under Rule 609(a)(2), even if the witness acted deceitfully in the course of committing the crime.

The amendment is meant to give effect to the legislative intent to limit the convictions that are to be automatically admitted under subdivision (a)(2). The Conference Committee provided that by "dishonesty and false statement" it meant "crimes such as perjury, subornation of perjury, false statement, criminal fraud, embezzlement, or false pretense, or any other offense in the nature of *crimen falsi*, the commission of which involves some element of deceit, untruthfulness, or falsification bearing on the [witness's] propensity to testify truthfully." Historically, offenses classified as *crimina falsi* have included only those crimes in which the ultimate criminal act was itself an act of deceit. *See* Green, *Deceit and the Classification of Crimes: Federal Rule of Evidence 609(a)(2) and the Origins of* Crimen Falsi, 90 J. CRIM. L. & CRIMINOLOGY 1087 (2000).

Evidence of crimes in the nature of *crimina falsi* must be admitted under Rule 609(a)(2), regardless of how such crimes are specifically charged. For example, evidence that a witness was convicted of making a false claim to a federal agent is admissible under this subdivision regardless of whether the crime was charged under a section that expressly references deceit (e.g., 18 U.S.C. § 1001, Material Misrepresentation to the Federal Government) or a section that does not (e.g., 18 U.S.C. § 1503, Obstruction of Justice).

The amendment requires that the proponent have ready proof that the conviction required the factfinder to find, or the defendant to admit, an act of dishonesty or false statement. Ordinarily, the statutory elements of the crime will indicate whether it is one of dishonesty or false statement. Where the deceitful nature of the crime is not apparent from the statute and the face of the judgment—as, for example, where the conviction simply records a finding of guilt for a statutory offense that does not reference deceit expressly—a proponent may offer information such as an indictment, a statement of admitted facts, or jury instructions to show that the factfinder had to find, or the defendant had to admit, an act of dishonesty or false statement in order for the witness to have been convicted. *Cf.* Taylor v. United States, 495 U.S. 575, 602 (1990) (providing that a trial court may look to a charging instrument or jury instructions to ascertain the nature of a prior offense where the statute is insufficiently clear on its face); Shepard v. United States, 544 U.S. 13 (2005) (the inquiry to determine whether a guilty plea to a crime defined by a nongeneric statute necessarily admitted elements of the generic offense was limited to the charging document's terms, the terms of a plea agreement or transcript of colloquy between judge and defendant in which the factual basis for the plea was confirmed by the defendant, or a comparable judicial record). But the amendment does not contemplate a "mini-trial" in which the court plumbs the record of the previous proceeding to determine whether the crime was in the nature of *crimen falsi*.

The amendment also substitutes the term "character for truthfulness" for the term "credibility" in the first sentence of the rule. The limitations of Rule 609 are not applicable if a conviction is admitted for a purpose other than to prove the witness's character for untruthfulness. *See, e.g.*, United States v. Lopez, 979 F.2d 1024 (5th Cir. 1992) (Rule 609 was not applicable where the conviction was offered for purposes of contradiction). The use of the term "credibility" in subdivision (d) is retained, however, as that subdivision is intended to govern the use of a juvenile adjudication for any type of impeachment.

Rule 610.   RELIGIOUS BELIEFS OR OPINIONS

Evidence of a witness's religious beliefs or opinions is not admissible to attack or support the witness's credibility.

(Enacted Jan. 2, 1975; as amended Mar. 2, 1987, eff. Oct. 1, 1987; as restyled Apr. 26, 2011, eff. Dec. 1, 2011.)

NOTE BY FEDERAL JUDICIAL CENTER

The rule enacted by the Congress is the rule prescribed by the Supreme Court without change.

ADVISORY COMMITTEE'S NOTE

While the rule forecloses inquiry into the religious beliefs or opinions of a witness for the purpose of showing that his character for truthfulness is affected by their nature, an inquiry for the purpose of showing interest or bias because of them is not within the prohibition. Thus disclosure of affiliation with a church which is a party to the litigation would be allowable under the rule. *Cf.* Tucker v. Reil, 51 Ariz. 357 (1938). To the same effect, though less specifically worded, is California Evidence Code § 789. *See* 3 WIGMORE § 936.

Rule 611.   MODE AND ORDER OF EXAMINING WITNESSES AND PRESENTING EVIDENCE

(a) Control by the Court; Purposes. The court should exercise reasonable control over the mode and order of examining witnesses and presenting evidence so as to:

(1) make those procedures effective for determining the truth;

(2) avoid wasting time; and

(3) protect witnesses from harassment or undue embarrassment.

(b) Scope of Cross-Examination.   Cross-examination should not go beyond the subject matter of the direct examination and matters affecting the witness's credibility. The court may allow inquiry into additional matters as if on direct examination.

(c) Leading Questions. Leading questions should not be used on direct examination except as necessary to develop the witness's testimony. Ordinarily, the court should allow leading questions:

(1) on cross-examination; and

(2) when a party calls a hostile witness, an adverse party, or a witness identified with an adverse party.

(Enacted Jan. 2, 1975; as amended Mar. 2, 1987, eff. Oct. 1, 1987; as restyled Apr. 26, 2011, eff. Dec. 1, 2011.)

<u>NOTE BY FEDERAL JUDICIAL CENTER</u>

Subdivision (a) of the rule enacted by the Congress is the subdivision prescribed by the Supreme Court, amended only by substituting "court" in place of "judge."

Subdivision (b) of the rule enacted by the Congress is substantially different from the subdivision prescribed by the Supreme Court. The nature of the changes and the reasons therefor are stated in the Report of the House Committee on the Judiciary, set forth below.

The first two sentences of subdivision (c) of the rule enacted by the Congress are the same as prescribed by the Supreme Court. The third sentence has been amended in the manner and for the reasons stated in the Report of the House Committee on the Judiciary, set forth below.

<u>Advisory Committee's Note to Rule 611(a)–(b)</u>

Subdivision (a). Spelling out detailed rules to govern the mode and order of interrogating witnesses and presenting evidence is neither desirable nor feasible. The ultimate responsibility for the effective working of the adversary system rests with the judge. The rule sets forth the objectives which he should seek to attain.

Item (1) restates in broad terms the power and obligation of the judge as developed under common law principles. It covers such concerns as whether testimony shall be in the form of a free narrative or responses to specific questions, McCormick § 5, the order of calling witnesses and presenting evidence, 6 Wigmore § 1867, the use of demonstrative evidence, McCormick § 179, and the many other questions arising during the course of a trial which can be solved only by the judge's common sense and fairness in view of the particular circumstances.

Item (2) is addressed to avoidance of needless consumption of time, a matter of daily concern in the disposition of cases. A companion piece is found in the discretion vested in the judge to exclude evidence as a waste of time in Rule [403].

Item (3) calls for a judgment under the particular circumstances whether interrogation tactics entail harassment or undue embarrassment. Pertinent circumstances include the importance of the testimony, the nature of the inquiry, its relevance to credibility, waste of time, and confusion. McCormick § 42. In *Alford v. United States*, 282 U.S. 687, 694 (1931), the Court pointed out that, while the trial judge should protect the witness from questions which "go beyond the bounds of proper cross-examination merely to harass, annoy, or humiliate," this protection by no means forecloses efforts to discredit the witness. Reference to the transcript of the prosecutor's cross-examination in *Berger v. United States*, 295 U.S. 78 (1935), serves to lay at rest any doubts as to the need for judicial control in this area.

The inquiry into specific instances of conduct of a witness allowed under Rule 608(b) is, of course, subject to this rule.

Subdivision (b).[3] The tradition in the federal courts and in numerous state courts has been to limit the scope of cross-examination to matters testified to on direct, plus matters bearing upon the credibility of the witness. Various reasons have been advanced to justify the rule of limited cross-examination. (1) A party vouches for his own witness but only to the extent of matters elicited on direct. Resurrection Gold Mining Co. v. Fortune Gold Mining Co., 129 Fed. 668, 675 (8th Cir. 1904), *quoted in* MAGUIRE, WEINSTEIN, ET AL., CASES ON EVIDENCE 277 n.38 (5th ed. 1965). But the concept of vouching is discredited, and Rule [607] rejects it. (2) A party cannot ask his own witness leading questions. This is a problem properly solved in terms of what is necessary for a proper development of the testimony rather than by a mechanistic formula similar to the vouching concept. *See* discussion under subdivision (c). (3) A practice of limited cross-examination promotes orderly presentation of the case. Finch v. Weiner, 109 Conn. 616 (1929). In the opinion of the Advisory Committee this latter reason has merit. It is apparent, however, that the rule of limited cross-examination thus viewed becomes an aspect of the judge's general control over the mode and order of interrogating witnesses and presenting evidence, to be administered as such. The matter is not one in which involvement at the appellate level is likely to prove fruitful. *See, e.g.*, Moyer v. Aetna Life Ins. Co., 126 F.2d 141 (3d Cir. 1942); Butler v. N.Y. Cent. R.R. Co., 253 F.2d 281 (7th Cir. 1958); United States v. Johnson, 285 F.2d 35 (9th Cir. 1960); Union Auto. Indem. Ass'n v. Capitol Indem. Ins. Co., 310 F.2d 318 (7th Cir. 1962). In view of these considerations, the rule is phrased in terms of a suggestion rather than a mandate to the trial judge.

The qualification "as if on direct examination," applicable when inquiry into additional matters is allowed is designed to terminate at that point the asking of leading questions as a matter of right and to bring into operation subdivision (c) of the rule.

The rule does not purport to determine the extent to which an accused who elects to testify thereby waives his privilege against self-incrimination. The question is a constitutional one, rather than a mere matter of administering the trial. Under *Simmons v. United States*, 390 U.S. 377 (1968), no general waiver occurs when the accused testifies on such preliminary matters as the validity of a search and seizure or the admissibility of a confession. Rule [104(d)], *supra*. When he testifies on the merits, however, can he foreclose inquiry into an aspect or element of the crime by avoiding it on direct? The affirmative answer given in *Tucker v. United States*, 5 F.2d 818 (8th Cir. 1925), is inconsistent with the description of the waiver as extending to "all other relevant facts" in *Johnson v. United*

---

[3] The Advisory Committee's Note to subdivision (b) is from the 1969 Preliminary Draft. 46 F.R.D. 161, 304.—Federal Judicial Center

States, 318 U.S. 189, 195 (1943). *See also* Brown v. United States, 356 U.S. 148 (1958). The situation of an accused who desires to testify on some but not all counts of a multiple-count indictment is one to be approached, in the first instance at least, as a problem of severance under Rule 14 of the Federal Rules of Criminal Procedure. Cross v. United States, 335 F.2d 987 (D.C. Cir. 1964); *cf.* United States v. Baker, 262 F. Supp. 657, 686 (D.D.C. 1966). In all events, the extent of the waiver of the privilege against self-incrimination ought not to be determined as a by-product of a rule on scope of cross-examination.

REPORT OF HOUSE COMMITTEE ON THE JUDICIARY

As submitted by the Court, Rule 611(b) provided:

A witness may be cross-examined on any matter relevant to any issue in the case, including credibility. In the interests of justice, the judge may limit cross-examination with respect to matters not testified to on direct examination.

The Committee amended this provision to return to the rule which prevails in the federal courts and thirty-nine state jurisdictions. As amended, the rule is in the text of the 1969 Advisory Committee draft. It limits cross-examination to credibility and to matters testified to on direct examination, unless the judge permits more, in which event the cross-examiner must proceed as if on direct examination. This traditional rule facilitates orderly presentation by each party at trial. Further, in light of existing discovery procedures, there appears to be no need to abandon the traditional rule.

REPORT OF SENATE COMMITTEE ON THE JUDICIARY

Rule 611(b) as submitted by the Supreme Court permitted a broad scope of cross-examination: "cross-examination on any matter relevant to any issue in the case" unless the judge, in the interests of justice, limited the scope of cross-examination.

The House narrowed the rule to the more traditional practice of limiting cross-examination to the subject matter of direct examination (and credibility), but with discretion in the judge to permit inquiry into additional matters in situations where that would aid in the development of the evidence or otherwise facilitate the conduct of the trial.

The Committee agrees with the House amendment. Although there are good arguments in support of broad cross-examination from perspectives of developing all relevant evidence, we believe the factors of insuring an orderly and predictable development of the evidence weigh in favor of the narrower rule, especially when discretion is given to the trial judge to permit inquiry into additional matters. The Committee expressly approves this discretion and believes it will permit sufficient flexibility allowing a broader scope of cross-examination whenever appropriate.

The House amendment providing broader discretionary cross-examination permitted inquiry into additional matters only as if on direct examination. As a general rule, we concur with this limitation, however, we would understand that this limitation would not preclude the utilization of leading questions if the conditions of subsection (c) of this rule were met, bearing in mind the judge's discretion in any case to limit the scope of cross-examination.[4]

Further, the Committee has received correspondence from federal judges commenting on the applicability of this rule to [28 U.S.C. § 1407]. It is the Committee's judgment that this rule as reported by the House is flexible enough to provide sufficiently broad cross-examination in appropriate situations in multidistrict litigation.

ADVISORY COMMITTEE'S NOTE FOR RULE 611(c)

Subdivision (c). The rule continues the traditional view that the suggestive powers of the leading question are as a general proposition undesirable. Within this tradition, however, numerous exceptions have achieved recognition: The witness who is hostile, unwilling, or biased; the child witness or the adult with communication problems; the witness whose recollection is exhausted; and undisputed preliminary matters. 3 WIGMORE §§ 774–778. An almost total unwillingness to reverse for infractions has been manifested by appellate courts. *See* cases cited in 3 WIGMORE § 770. The matter clearly falls within the area of control by the judge over the mode and order of interrogation and presentation and accordingly is phrased in words of suggestion rather than command.

The rule also conforms to tradition in making the use of leading questions on cross-examination a matter of right. The purpose of the qualification "ordinarily" is to furnish a basis for denying the use of leading questions when the cross-examination is cross-examination in form only and not in fact, as for example the "cross-examination" of a party by his own counsel after being called by

---

[4] *See* MCCORMICK ON EVIDENCE, §§ 24–26 (especially § 24) (2d ed. 1972).

the opponent (savoring more of re-direct) or of an insured defendant who proves to be friendly to the plaintiff.

The final sentence deals with categories of witnesses automatically regarded and treated as hostile. Rule 43(b) of the Federal Rules of Civil Procedure has included only "an adverse party or an officer, director, or managing agent of a public or private corporation or of a partnership or association which is an adverse party." This limitation virtually to persons whose statements would stand as admissions is believed to be an unduly narrow concept of those who may safely be regarded as hostile without further demonstration. See, for example, *Maryland Casualty Co. v. Kador*, 225 F.2d 120 (5th Cir. 1955), and *Degelos v. Fidelity & Casualty Co.*, 313 F.2d 809 (5th Cir. 1963), holding despite the language of Rule 43(b) that an insured fell within it, though not a party in an action under the Louisiana direct action statute. The phrase of the rule, "witness identified with" an adverse party, is designed to enlarge the category of persons thus callable.

REPORT OF HOUSE COMMITTEE ON THE JUDICIARY

The third sentence of Rule 611(c) as submitted by the Court provided that:

In civil cases, a party is entitled to call an adverse party or witness identified with him and interrogate by leading questions.

The Committee amended this rule to permit leading questions to be used with respect to any hostile witness, not only an adverse party or person identified with such adverse party. The Committee also substituted the word "When" for the phrase "In civil cases" to reflect the possibility that in criminal cases a defendant may be entitled to call witnesses identified with the government, in which event the Committee believed the defendant should be permitted to inquire with leading questions.

REPORT OF THE SENATE COMMITTEE ON THE JUDICIARY

As submitted by the Supreme Court, the rule provided: "In civil cases, a party is entitled to call an adverse party or witness identified with him and interrogate by leading questions."

The final sentence of subsection (c) was amended by the House for the purpose of clarifying the fact that a "hostile witness"—that is a witness who is hostile in fact—could be subject to interrogation by leading questions. The rule as submitted by the Supreme Court declared certain witnesses hostile as a matter of law and thus subject to interrogation by leading questions without any showing of hostility in fact. These were adverse parties or witnesses identified with adverse parties. However, the wording of the first sentence of subsection (c), while generally prohibiting the use of leading questions on direct examination, also provides "except as may be necessary to develop his testimony." Further, the first paragraph of the Advisory Committee note explaining the subsection makes clear that they intended that leading questions could be asked of a hostile witness or a witness who was unwilling or biased and even though that witness was not associated with an adverse party. Thus, we question whether the House amendment was necessary.

However, concluding that it was not intended to affect the meaning of the first sentence of the subsection and was intended solely to clarify the fact that leading questions are permissible in the interrogation of a witness, who is hostile in fact, the Committee accepts that House amendment.

The final sentence of this subsection was also amended by the House to cover criminal as well as civil cases. The Committee accepts this amendment, but notes that it may be difficult in criminal cases to determine when a witness is "identified with an adverse party," and thus the rule should be applied with caution.

Rule 612.   WRITING USED TO REFRESH A WITNESS'S MEMORY

(a) **Scope.** This rule gives an adverse party certain options when a witness uses a writing to refresh memory:

(1) while testifying; or

(2) before testifying, if the court decides that justice requires the party to have those options.

(b) **Adverse Party's Options; Deleting Unrelated Matter.** Unless 18 U.S.C. § 3500 provides otherwise in a criminal case, an adverse party is entitled to have the writing produced at the hearing, to inspect it, to cross-examine the witness about it, and to introduce in evidence any portion that relates to the witness's testimony. If the producing party claims that the writing includes unrelated matter, the court must examine the writing in camera, delete any unrelated portion, and order that the rest be delivered to the adverse party. Any portion deleted over objection must be preserved for the record.

(c) Failure to Produce or Deliver the Writing. If a writing is not produced or is not delivered as ordered, the court may issue any appropriate order. But if the prosecution does not comply in a criminal case, the court must strike the witness's testimony or—if justice so requires—declare a mistrial.

(Enacted Jan. 2, 1975; as amended Mar. 2, 1987, eff. Oct. 1, 1987; as restyled Apr. 26, 2011, eff. Dec. 1, 2011.)

NOTE BY FEDERAL JUDICIAL CENTER

The rule enacted by the Congress is the rule prescribed by the Supreme Court, amended by substituting "court" in place of "judge," with appropriate pronominal change, and in the first sentence, by substituting "the writing" in place of "it" before "produced," and by substituting the phrase" (1) while testifying, or (2) before testifying if the court in its discretion determines it is necessary in the interests of justice" in place of "before or while testifying." The reasons for the latter amendment are stated in the Report of the House Committee on the Judiciary, set forth below.

ADVISORY COMMITTEE'S NOTE

The treatment of writings used to refresh recollection while on the stand is in accord with settled doctrine. MCCORMICK § 9, at 15. The bulk of the case law has, however, denied the existence of any right to access by the opponent when the writing is used prior to taking the stand, though the judge may have discretion in the matter. Goldman v. United States, 316 U.S. 129 (1942); Needelman v. United States, 261 F.2d 802 (5th Cir. 1958), *cert. dismissed*, 362 U.S. 600, *reh'g denied*, 363 U.S. 858 (1960). An increasing group of cases has repudiated the distinction, People v. Scott, 29 Ill.2d 97 (1963); State v. Mucci, 25 N.J. 423 (1957); State v. Hunt, 25 N.J. 514 (1958); State v. Deslovers, 40 R.I. 89 (1917), and this position is believed to be correct. As Wigmore put it, "the risk of imposition and the need of safeguard is just as great" in both situations. 3 WIGMORE § 762, at 111. To the same effect is MCCORMICK § 9, at 17.

The purpose of the phrase "for the purpose of testifying" is to safeguard against using the rule as a pretext for wholesale exploration of an opposing party's files and to insure that access is limited only to those writings which may fairly be said in fact to have an impact upon the testimony of the witness.

The purpose of the rule is the same as that of the Jencks statute, 18 U.S.C. § 3500: to promote the search of credibility and memory.

The same sensitivity to disclosure of government files may be involved; hence the rule is expressly made subject to the statute, subdivision (a) of which provides: "In any criminal prosecution brought by the United States, no statement or report in the possession of the United States which was made by a Government witness or prospective Government witness (other than the defendant) shall be the subject of subpoena, discovery, or inspection until said witness has testified on direct examination in the trial of the case." Items falling within the purview of the statute are producible only as provided by its terms, Palermo v. United States, 360 U.S. 343, 351 (1959), and disclosure under the rule is limited similarly by the statutory conditions. With this limitation in mind, some differences of application may be noted. The Jencks statute applies only to statements of witnesses; the rule is not so limited. The statute applies only to criminal cases; the rule applies to all cases. The statute applies only to government witnesses; the rule applies to all witnesses. The statute contains no requirement that the statement be consulted for purposes of refreshment before or while testifying; the rule so requires. Since many writings would qualify under either statute or rule, a substantial overlap exists, but the identity of procedures makes this of no importance.

The consequences of nonproduction by the government in a criminal case are those of the Jencks statute, striking the testimony or in exceptional cases a mistrial. 18 U.S.C. § 3500(d). In other cases these alternatives are unduly limited, and such possibilities as contempt, dismissal, finding issues against the offender, and the like are available. *See* Rule [16(d)] of the Federal Rules of Criminal Procedure and Rule 37(b) of the Federal Rules of Civil Procedure for appropriate sanctions.

REPORT OF THE HOUSE COMMITTEE ON THE JUDICIARY

As submitted to Congress, Rule 612 provided that except as set forth in 18 U.S.C. § 3500, if a witness uses a writing to refresh his memory for the purpose of testifying, "either before or while testifying," an adverse party is entitled to have the writing produced at the hearing, to inspect it, to cross-examine the witness on it, and to introduce in evidence those portions relating to the witness's testimony. The Committee amended the rule so as still to require the production of writings used by a witness while testifying, but to render the production of writings used by a witness to refresh his memory before testifying discretionary with the court in the interests of justice, as is the case under existing federal law. *See* Goldman v. United States, 316 U.S. 129 (1942). The Committee considered that permitting an adverse party to require the production of writings used before testifying could result in fishing expeditions among a multitude of papers which a witness may have used in preparing for trial.

The Committee intends that nothing in the rule be construed as barring the assertion of a privilege with respect to writings used by a witness to refresh his memory.

Rule 613.   WITNESS'S PRIOR STATEMENT

(a) Showing or Disclosing the Statement During Examination. When examining a witness about the witness's prior statement, a party need not show it or disclose its contents to the witness. But the party must, on request, show it or disclose its contents to an adverse party's attorney.

(b) Extrinsic Evidence of a Prior Inconsistent Statement. Extrinsic evidence of a witness's prior inconsistent statement is admissible only if the witness is given an opportunity to explain or deny the statement and an adverse party is given an opportunity to examine the witness about it, or if justice so requires. This subdivision (b) does not apply to an opposing party's statement under Rule 801(d)(2).

(Enacted Jan. 2, 1975; as amended Mar. 2, 1987, eff. Oct. 1, 1987; Apr. 25, 1988, eff. Nov. 1, 1988; as restyled Apr. 26, 2011, eff. Dec. 1, 2011.)

<u>NOTE BY FEDERAL JUDICIAL CENTER</u>

The rule enacted by the Congress is the rule prescribed by the Supreme Court, amended only by substituting "nor" in place of "or" in subdivision (a).

<u>ADVISORY COMMITTEE'S NOTE</u>

Subdivision (a). *The Queen's Case*, (1820) 129 Eng. Rep. 976; 2 Br. & B. 284., laid down the requirement that a cross-examiner, prior to questioning the witness about his own prior statement in writing, must first show it to the witness. Abolished by statute in the country of its origin, the requirement nevertheless gained currency in the United States. The rule abolishes this useless impediment to cross-examination. Ladd, *Some Observations on Credibility: Impeachment of Witnesses*, 52 CORNELL L.Q. 239, 246–47 (1967); MCCORMICK § 28; 4 WIGMORE §§ 1259–1260. Both oral and written statements are included.

The provision for disclosure to counsel is designed to protect against unwarranted insinuations that a statement has been made when the fact is to the contrary.

The rule does not defeat the application of Rule 1002 relating to production of the original when the contents of a writing are sought to be proved. Nor does it defeat the application of Rule 26(b)(3) of the Rules of Civil Procedure, as revised, entitling a person on request to a copy of his own statement, though the operation of the latter may be suspended temporarily.

Subdivision (b). The familiar foundation requirement that an impeaching statement first be shown to the witness before it can be proved by extrinsic evidence is preserved but with some modifications. *See* Ladd, *Some Observations on Credibility: Impeachment of Witnesses*, 52 CORNELL L.Q. 239, 247 (1967). The traditional insistence that the attention of the witness be directed to the statement on cross-examination is relaxed in favor of simply providing the witness an opportunity to explain and the opposite party an opportunity to examine on the statement, with no specification of any particular time or sequence. Under this procedure, several collusive witnesses can be examined before disclosure of a joint prior inconsistent statement. *See Comment*, CAL. EVID. CODE § 770. Also, dangers of oversight are reduced. *See* MCCORMICK § 37, at 68.

In order to allow for such eventualities as the witness becoming unavailable by the time the statement is discovered, a measure of discretion is conferred upon the judge. Similar provisions are found in California Evidence Code § 770 and New Jersey Evidence Rule 22(b) (repealed and replaced by New Jersey Rule of Evidence 613(b) (1993)).

Under principles of *expressio unius* the rule does not apply to impeachment by evidence of prior inconsistent conduct. The use of inconsistent statements to impeach a hearsay declaration is treated in Rule 806.

Rule 614.   COURT'S CALLING OR EXAMINING A WITNESS

(a) Calling. The court may call a witness on its own or at a party's request. Each party is entitled to cross-examine the witness.

(b) Examining. The court may examine a witness regardless of who calls the witness.

(c) Objections. A party may object to the court's calling or examining a witness either at that time or at the next opportunity when the jury is not present.

(Enacted Jan. 2, 1975; as restyled Apr. 26, 2011, eff. Dec. 1, 2011.)

<u>NOTE BY FEDERAL JUDICIAL CENTER</u>

The rule enacted by the Congress is the rule prescribed by the Supreme Court, amended only by substituting "court" in place of "judge," with conforming pronominal changes.

<u>ADVISORY COMMITTEE'S NOTE</u>

Subdivision (a). While exercised more frequently in criminal than in civil cases, the authority of the judge to call witnesses is well established. MCCORMICK § 8, at 14; MAGUIRE, WEINSTEIN, ET AL., CASES ON EVIDENCE 303–04 (5th ed. 1965); 9 WIGMORE § 2484. One reason for the practice, the old rule against impeaching one's own witness, no longer exists by virtue of Rule 607, *supra*. Other reasons remain, however, to justify the continuation of the practice of calling court's witnesses. The right to cross-examine, with all it implies, is assured. The tendency of juries to associate a witness with the party calling him, regardless of technical aspects of vouching, is avoided. And the judge is not imprisoned within the case as made by the parties.

Subdivision (b). The authority of the judge to question witnesses is also well established. MCCORMICK § 8, at 12–13; MAGUIRE, WEINSTEIN, ET AL., CASES ON EVIDENCE 737–39 (5th ed. 1965); 3 WIGMORE § 784. The authority is, of course, abused when the judge abandons his proper role and assumes that of advocate, but the manner in which interrogation should be conducted and the proper extent of its exercise are not susceptible of formulation in a rule. The omission in no sense precludes courts of review from continuing to reverse for abuse.

Subdivision (c). The provision relating to objections is designed to relieve counsel of the embarrassment attendant upon objecting to questions by the judge in the presence of the jury, while at the same time assuring that objections are made in apt time to afford the opportunity to take possible corrective measures. Compare the "automatic" objection feature of Rule 605 when the judge is called as a witness.

Rule 615.   EXCLUDING WITNESSES

At a party's request, the court must order witnesses excluded so that they cannot hear other witnesses' testimony. Or the court may do so on its own. But this rule does not authorize excluding:

(a) a party who is a natural person;

(b) an officer or employee of a party that is not a natural person, after being designated as the party's representative by its attorney;

(c) a person whose presence a party shows to be essential to presenting the party's claim or defense; or

(d) a person authorized by statute to be present.

(Enacted Jan. 2, 1975; as amended Mar. 2, 1987, eff. Oct. 1, 1987; Apr. 25, 1988, eff. Nov. 1, 1988; Nov. 18, 1988; Apr. 24, 1998, eff. Dec. 1, 1998; as restyled Apr. 26, 2011, eff. Dec. 1, 2011.)

<u>NOTE BY FEDERAL JUDICIAL CENTER</u>

The rule enacted by the Congress is the rule prescribed by the Supreme Court, amended only by substituting "court," in place of "judge," with conforming pronominal changes.

<u>ADVISORY COMMITTEE'S NOTE</u>

The efficacy of excluding or sequestering witnesses has long been recognized as a means of discouraging and exposing fabrication, inaccuracy, and collusion. 6 WIGMORE §§ 1837–1838. The authority of the judge is admitted, the only question being whether the matter is committed to his discretion or one of right.

The rule takes the latter position. No time is specified for making the request.

Several categories of persons are excepted. (1) Exclusion of persons who are parties would raise serious problems of confrontation and due process. Under accepted practice they are not subject to exclusion. 6 WIGMORE § 1841. (2) As the equivalent of the right of a natural-person party to be present, a party which is not a natural person is entitled to have a representative present. Most of the cases have involved allowing a police officer who has been in charge of an investigation to remain in court despite the fact that he will be a witness. United States v. Infanzon, 235 F.2d 318 (2d Cir. 1956); Portomene v. United States, 221 F.2d 582 (5th Cir. 1955); Powell v. United States, 208 F.2d 618 (6th Cir. 1953); Jones v. United States, 252 F. Supp. 781 (W.D. Okla. 1966). Designation of the representative by the attorney rather than by the client may at first glance appear to be an inversion of the attorney–client relationship, but it may be assumed that the attorney will follow the wishes of the client, and the solution is simple and workable. *See* CAL. EVID. CODE § 777. (3) The category contemplates such persons as an agent who handled the transaction being litigated or an expert needed to advise counsel in the management of the litigation. *See* 6 WIGMORE § 1841 n.4.

REPORT OF THE SENATE COMMITTEE ON THE JUDICIARY

Many district courts permit government counsel to have an investigative agent at counsel table throughout the trial although the agent is or may be a witness. The practice is permitted as an exception to the rule of exclusion and compares with the situation defense counsel finds himself in—he always has the client with him to consult during the trial. The investigative agent's presence may be extremely important to government counsel, especially when the case is complex or involves some specialized subject matter. The agent, too, having lived with the case for a long time, may be able to assist in meeting trial surprises where the best-prepared counsel would otherwise have difficulty. Yet, it would not seem the Government could often meet the burden under Rule 615 of showing that the agent's presence is essential. Furthermore, it could be dangerous to use the agent as a witness as early in the case as possible, so that he might then help counsel as a nonwitness, since the agent's testimony could be needed in rebuttal. Using another, nonwitness agent from the same investigative agency would not generally meet government counsel's needs.

This problem is solved if it is clear that investigative agents are within the group specified under the second exception made in the rule, for "an officer or employee of a party which is not a natural person designated as its representative by its attorney." It is our understanding that this was the intention of the House Committee. It is certainly this Committee's construction of the rule.

ARTICLE VII. OPINIONS AND EXPERT TESTIMONY

Rule 701.   OPINION TESTIMONY BY LAY WITNESSES

If a witness is not testifying as an expert, testimony in the form of an opinion is limited to one that is:

(a) rationally based on the witness's perception;

(b) helpful to clearly understanding the witness's testimony or to determining a fact in issue; and

(c) not based on scientific, technical, or other specialized knowledge within the scope of Rule 702.

(Enacted Jan. 2, 1975; as amended Mar. 2, 1987, eff. Oct. 1, 1987; Apr. 17, 2000, eff. Dec. 1, 2000; as restyled Apr. 26, 2011, eff. Dec. 1, 2011.)

NOTE BY FEDERAL JUDICIAL CENTER

The rule enacted by the Congress is the rule prescribed by the Supreme Court without change.

ADVISORY COMMITTEE'S NOTE

The rule retains the traditional objective of putting the trier of fact in possession of an accurate reproduction of the event.

Limitation (a) is the familiar requirement of first-hand knowledge or observation.

Limitation (b) is phrased in terms of requiring testimony to be helpful in resolving issues. Witnesses often find difficulty in expressing themselves in language which is not that of an opinion or conclusion. While the courts have made concessions in certain recurring situations, necessity as a standard for permitting opinions and conclusions has proved too elusive and too unadaptable to particular situations for purposes of satisfactory judicial administration. MCCORMICK § 11. Moreover, the practical impossibility of determining by rule what is a "fact," demonstrated by a century of litigation of the question of what is a fact for purposes of pleading under the Field Code, extends into evidence also. 7 WIGMORE § 1919. The rule assumes that the natural characteristics of the adversary system will generally lead to an acceptable result, since the detailed account carries more conviction than the broad assertion, and a lawyer can be expected to display his witness to the best advantage. If he fails to do so, cross-examination and argument will point up the weakness. *See* Ladd, *Expert Testimony*, 5 VAND. L. REV. 414, 415–17 (1952). If, despite these considerations, attempts are made to introduce meaningless assertions which amount to little more than choosing up sides, exclusion for lack of helpfulness is called for by the rule.

The language of the rule is substantially that of Uniform Rule 56(1). Similar provisions are California Evidence Code § 800; Kansas Statutes Annotated § 60-456(a); New Jersey Evidence Rule 56(1) (repealed and replaced by New Jersey Rule of Evidence 701 (1993)).

ADVISORY COMMITTEE'S NOTE TO 2000 AMENDMENT TO RULE 701

Rule 701 has been amended to eliminate the risk that the reliability requirements set forth in Rule 702 will be evaded through the simple expedient of proffering an expert in lay witness clothing. Under the amendment, a witness's testimony must be scrutinized under the rules regulating expert opinion to the extent that the witness is providing testimony based on scientific, technical, or other specialized knowledge within the scope of Rule 702. *See generally* Asplundh Mfg. Div. v. Benton Harbor Eng'g, 57 F.3d 1190 (3d Cir. 1995). By channeling testimony that is actually expert testimony to Rule 702, the amendment also ensures that a party will not evade the expert witness disclosure requirements set forth in Federal Rule of Civil Procedure 26 and Federal Rule of Criminal Procedure 16 by simply calling an expert witness in the guise of a layperson. *See* Joseph, *Emerging Expert Issues Under the 1993 Disclosure Amendments to the Federal Rules of Civil Procedure*, 164 F.R.D. 97, 108 (1996) (noting that "there is no good reason to allow what is essentially surprise expert testimony," and that "the Court should be vigilant to preclude manipulative conduct designed to thwart the expert disclosure and discovery process"); *see also* United States v. Figueroa–Lopez, 125 F.3d 1241, 1246 (9th Cir. 1997) (law enforcement agents testifying that the defendant's conduct was consistent with that of a drug trafficker could not testify as lay witnesses; to permit such testimony under Rule 701 "subverts the requirements of Federal Rule of Criminal Procedure [16(a)(1)(G)]").

The amendment does not distinguish between expert and lay *witnesses*, but rather between expert and lay *testimony*. Certainly it is possible for the same witness to provide both lay and expert testimony in a single case. *See, e.g.,* United States v. Figueroa–

Lopez, 125 F.3d 1241, 1246 (9th Cir. 1997) (law enforcement agents could testify that the defendant was acting suspiciously, without being qualified as experts; however, the rules on experts were applicable where the agents testified on the basis of extensive experience that the defendant was using code words to refer to drug quantities and prices). The amendment makes clear that any part of a witness's testimony that is based upon scientific, technical, or other specialized knowledge within the scope of Rule 702 is governed by the standards of Rule 702 and the corresponding disclosure requirements of the Civil and Criminal Rules.

The amendment is not intended to affect the "prototypical example[s] of the type of evidence contemplated by the adoption of Rule 701 relat[ing] to the appearance of persons or things, identity, the manner of conduct, competency of a person, degrees of light or darkness, sound, size, weight, distance, and an endless number of items that cannot be described factually in words apart from inferences." Asplundh Mfg. Div. v. Benton Harbor Eng'g, 57 F.3d 1190, 1196 (3d Cir. 1995).

For example, most courts have permitted the owner or officer of a business to testify to the value or projected profits of the business, without the necessity of qualifying the witness as an accountant, appraiser, or similar expert. *See, e.g.,* Lightning Lube, Inc. v. Witco Corp., 4 F.3d 1153 (3d Cir. 1993) (no abuse of discretion in permitting the plaintiff's owner to give lay opinion testimony as to damages, as it was based on his knowledge and participation in the day-to-day affairs of the business). Such opinion testimony is admitted not because of experience, training, or specialized knowledge within the realm of an expert, but because of the particularized knowledge that the witness has by virtue of his or her position in the business. The amendment does not purport to change this analysis. Similarly, courts have permitted lay witnesses to testify that a substance appeared to be a narcotic, so long as a foundation of familiarity with the substance is established. *See, e.g.,* United States v. Westbrook, 896 F.2d 330 (8th Cir. 1990) (two lay witnesses who were heavy amphetamine users were properly permitted to testify that a substance was amphetamine; but it was error to permit another witness to make such an identification where she had no experience with amphetamines). Such testimony is not based on specialized knowledge within the scope of Rule 702, but rather is based upon a layperson's personal knowledge. If, however, that witness were to describe how a narcotic was manufactured, or to describe the intricate workings of a narcotic distribution network, then the witness would have to qualify as an expert under Rule 702. *Figueroa–Lopez,* 125 F.3d at 1246.

The amendment incorporates the distinctions set forth in *State v. Brown*, 836 S.W.2d 530, 549 (Tenn. 1992), a case involving former Tennessee Rule of Evidence 701, a rule that precluded lay witness testimony based on "special knowledge." In *Brown*, the court declared that the distinction between lay and expert witness testimony is that lay testimony "results from a process of reasoning familiar in everyday life," while expert testimony "results from a process of reasoning which can be mastered only by specialists in the field." The court in *Brown* noted that a lay witness with experience could testify that a substance appeared to be blood, but that a witness would have to qualify as an expert before he could testify that bruising around the eyes is indicative of skull trauma. That is the kind of distinction made by the amendment to this rule.

ADVISORY COMMITTEE'S NOTE TO 2011 RESTYLING OF RULE 701

The Committee deleted all reference to an "inference" on the grounds that the deletion made the rule flow better and easier to read, and because any "inference" is covered by the broader term "opinion." Courts have not made substantive decisions on the basis of any distinction between an opinion and an inference. No change in current practice is intended.

Rule 702.   TESTIMONY BY EXPERT WITNESSES

A witness who is qualified as an expert by knowledge, skill, experience, training, or education may testify in the form of an opinion or otherwise if:

(a) the expert's scientific, technical, or other specialized knowledge will help the trier of fact to understand the evidence or to determine a fact in issue;

(b) the testimony is based on sufficient facts or data;

(c) the testimony is the product of reliable principles and methods; and

(d) the expert has reliably applied the principles and methods to the facts of the case.

(Enacted Jan. 2, 1975; as amended Apr. 17, 2000, eff. Dec. 1, 2000; as restyled Apr. 26, 2011, eff. Dec. 1, 2011.)

NOTE BY FEDERAL JUDICIAL CENTER

The rule enacted by the Congress is the rule prescribed by the Supreme Court without change.

ADVISORY COMMITTEE'S NOTE

An intelligent evaluation of facts is often difficult or impossible without the application of some scientific, technical, or other specialized knowledge. The most common source of this knowledge is the expert witness, although there are other techniques for supplying it.

Most of the literature assumes that experts testify only in the form of opinions. The assumption is logically unfounded. The rule accordingly recognizes that an expert on the stand may give a dissertation or exposition of scientific or other principles relevant to the case, leaving the trier of fact to apply them to the facts. Since much of the criticism of expert testimony has centered upon the hypothetical question, it seems wise to recognize that opinions are not indispensable and to encourage the use of expert testimony in nonopinion form when counsel believes the trier can itself draw the requisite inference. The use of opinions is not abolished by the rule, however. It will continue to be permissible for the expert to take the further step of suggesting the inference which should be drawn from applying the specialized knowledge to the facts. *See* Rules 703 to 705.

Whether the situation is a proper one for the use of expert testimony is to be determined on the basis of assisting the trier. "There is no more certain test for determining when experts may be used than the common sense inquiry whether the untrained layman would be qualified to determine intelligently and to the best possible degree the particular issue without enlightenment from those having a specialized understanding of the subject involved in the dispute." Ladd, *Expert Testimony*, 5 VAND. L. REV. 414, 418 (1952). When opinions are excluded, it is because they are unhelpful and therefore superfluous and a waste of time. 7 WIGMORE § 1918.

The rule is broadly phrased. The fields of knowledge which may be drawn upon are not limited merely to the "scientific" and "technical" but extend to all "specialized" knowledge. Similarly, the expert is viewed, not in a narrow sense, but as a person qualified by "knowledge, skill, experience, training, or education." Thus within the scope of the rule are not only experts in the strictest sense of the word, e.g., physicians, physicists, and architects, but also the large group sometimes called "skilled" witnesses, such as bankers or landowners testifying to land values.

Rule 702 has been amended in response to *Daubert v. Merrell Dow Pharmaceuticals, Inc.*, 509 U.S. 579 (1993), and to the many cases applying *Daubert*, including *Kumho Tire Co. v. Carmichael*, 526 U.S. 137 (1999). In *Daubert* the Court charged trial judges with the responsibility of acting as gatekeepers to exclude unreliable expert testimony, and the Court in *Kumho* clarified that this gatekeeper function applies to all expert testimony, not just testimony based in science. *See also Kumho*, 526 U.S. at 156–57 (citing the Committee note to the proposed amendment to Rule 702, which had been released for public comment before the date of the *Kumho* decision). The amendment affirms the trial court's role as gatekeeper and provides some general standards that the trial court must use to assess the reliability and helpfulness of proffered expert testimony. Consistently with *Kumho*, the rule as amended provides that all types of expert testimony present questions of admissibility for the trial court in deciding whether the evidence is reliable and helpful. Consequently, the admissibility of all expert testimony is governed by the principles of Rule 104(a). Under that rule, the proponent has the burden of establishing that the pertinent admissibility requirements are met by a preponderance of the evidence. *See* Bourjaily v. United States, 483 U.S. 171 (1987).

Daubert set forth a non-exclusive checklist for trial courts to use in assessing the reliability of scientific expert testimony. The specific factors explicated by the *Daubert* Court are (1) whether the expert's technique or theory can be or has been tested—that is, whether the expert's theory can be challenged in some objective sense, or whether it is instead simply a subjective, conclusory approach that cannot reasonably be assessed for reliability; (2) whether the technique or theory has been subject to peer review and publication; (3) the known or potential rate of error of the technique or theory when applied; (4) the existence and maintenance of standards and controls; and (5) whether the technique or theory has been generally accepted in the scientific community. The Court in *Kumho* held that these factors might also be applicable in assessing the reliability of non-scientific expert testimony, depending upon "the particular circumstances of the particular case at issue." 526 U.S. at 150.

No attempt has been made to "codify" these specific factors. *Daubert* itself emphasized that the factors were neither exclusive nor dispositive. Other cases have recognized that not all of the specific *Daubert* factors can apply to every type of expert testimony.

In addition to *Kumho*, 526 U.S. at 151, see *Tyus v. Urban Search Management*, 102 F.3d 256 (7th Cir. 1996) (noting that the factors mentioned by the Court in *Daubert* do not neatly apply to expert testimony from a sociologist). *See also* Kannankeril v. Terminix Int'l, Inc., 128 F.3d 802, 809 (3d Cir. 1997) (holding that lack of peer review or publication was not dispositive where the expert's opinion was supported by "widely accepted scientific knowledge"). The standards set forth in the amendment are broad enough to require consideration of any or all of the specific *Daubert* factors where appropriate.

Courts both before and after *Daubert* have found other factors relevant in determining whether expert testimony is sufficiently reliable to be considered by the trier of fact. These factors include:

(1) Whether experts are "proposing to testify about matters growing naturally and directly out of research they have conducted independent of the litigation, or whether they have developed their opinions expressly for purposes of testifying." Daubert v. Merrell Dow Pharm., Inc., 43 F.3d 1311, 1317 (9th Cir. 1995).

(2) Whether the expert has unjustifiably extrapolated from an accepted premise to an unfounded conclusion. *See* Gen. Elec. Co. v. Joiner, 522 U.S. 136, 146 (1997) (noting that in some cases a trial court "may conclude that there is simply too great an analytical gap between the data and the opinion proffered").

(3) Whether the expert has adequately accounted for obvious alternative explanations. *See* Claar v. Burlington N.R.R. Co., 29 F.3d 499 (9th Cir. 1994) (testimony excluded where the expert failed to consider other obvious causes for the plaintiff's condition); *cf.* Ambrosini v. Labarraque, 101 F.3d 129 (D.C. Cir. 1996) (the possibility of some uneliminated causes presents a question of weight, so long as the most obvious causes have been considered and reasonably ruled out by the expert).

(4) Whether the expert "is being as careful as he would be in his regular professional work outside his paid litigation consulting." Sheehan v. Daily Racing Form, Inc., 104 F.3d 940, 942 (7th Cir. 1997); *see* Kumho Tire Co. v. Carmichael, 526 U.S. 137, 152 (1999) (*Daubert* requires the trial court to assure itself that the expert "employs in the courtroom the same level of intellectual rigor that characterizes the practice of an expert in the relevant field").

(5) Whether the field of expertise claimed by the expert is known to reach reliable results for the type of opinion the

expert would give. *See* Kumho Tire Co. v. Carmichael, 526 U.S. 137, 151 (1999) (*Daubert*'s general acceptance factor does not "help show that an expert's testimony is reliable where the discipline itself lacks reliability, as, for example, do theories grounded in any so-called generally accepted principles of astrology or necromancy"); Moore v. Ashland Chem., Inc., 151 F.3d 269 (5th Cir. 1998) (en banc) (clinical doctor was properly precluded from testifying to the toxicological cause of the plaintiff's respiratory problem, where the opinion was not sufficiently grounded in scientific methodology); Sterling v. Velsicol Chem. Corp., 855 F.2d 1188 (6th Cir. 1988) (rejecting testimony based on "clinical ecology" as unfounded and unreliable).

All of these factors remain relevant to the determination of the reliability of expert testimony under the rule as amended. Other factors may also be relevant. *See Kumho*, 526 U.S. at 152 ("[W]e conclude that the trial judge must have considerable leeway in deciding in a particular case how to go about determining whether particular expert testimony is reliable."). Yet no single factor is necessarily dispositive of the reliability of a particular expert's testimony. *See, e.g.*, Heller v. Shaw Indus., Inc., 167 F.3d 146, 155 (3d Cir. 1999) ("[N]ot only must each stage of the expert's testimony be reliable, but each stage must be evaluated practically and flexibly without bright-line exclusionary (or inclusionary) rules."); Daubert v. Merrell Dow Pharm., Inc., 43 F.3d 1311, 1317 n.5 (9th Cir. 1995) (noting that some expert disciplines "have the courtroom as a principal theatre of operations" and as to these disciplines "the fact that the expert has developed an expertise principally for purposes of litigation will obviously not be a substantial consideration").

A review of the caselaw after *Daubert* shows that the rejection of expert testimony is the exception rather than the rule. *Daubert* did not work a "seachange over federal evidence law," and "the trial court's role as gatekeeper is not intended to serve as a replacement for the adversary system." United States v. 14.38 Acres of Land, 80 F.3d 1074, 1078 (5th Cir. 1996). As the Court in *Daubert* stated: "Vigorous cross-examination, presentation of contrary evidence, and careful instruction on the burden of proof are the traditional and appropriate means of attacking shaky but admissible evidence." 509 U.S. at 595. Likewise, this amendment is not intended to provide an excuse for an automatic challenge to the testimony of every expert. *See* Kumho Tire Co. v. Carmichael, 526 U.S. 137, 152 (1999) (noting that the trial judge has the discretion "both to avoid unnecessary 'reliability' proceedings in ordinary cases where the reliability of an expert's methods is properly taken for granted, and to require appropriate proceedings in the less usual or more complex cases where cause for questioning the expert's reliability arises").

When a trial court, applying this amendment, rules that an expert's testimony is reliable, this does not necessarily mean that contradictory expert testimony is unreliable. The amendment is broad enough to permit testimony that is the product of competing principles or methods in the same field of expertise. *See, e.g.,* Heller v. Shaw Indus., Inc., 167 F.3d 146, 160 (3d Cir. 1999) (expert testimony cannot be excluded simply because the expert uses one test rather than another, when both tests are accepted in the field and both reach reliable results). As the court stated in *In re Paoli Railroad Yard PCB Litigation,* 35 F.3d 717, 744 (3d Cir. 1994), proponents "do not have to demonstrate to the judge by a preponderance of the evidence that the assessments of their experts are correct, they only have to demonstrate by a preponderance of evidence that their opinions are reliable.... The evidentiary requirement of reliability is lower than the merits standard of correctness." *See also* Daubert v. Merrell Dow Pharm., Inc., 43 F.3d 1311, 1318 (9th Cir. 1995) (scientific experts might be permitted to testify if they could show that the methods they used were also employed by "a recognized minority of scientists in their field"); Ruiz–Troche v. Pepsi Cola of P.R. Bottling Co., 161 F.3d 77, 85 (1st Cir. 1998) ("*Daubert* neither requires nor empowers trial courts to determine which of several competing scientific theories has the best provenance.").

The Court in *Daubert* declared that the "focus, of course, must be solely on principles and methodology, not on the conclusions they generate." 509 U.S. at 595. Yet as the Court later recognized, "conclusions and methodology are not entirely distinct from one another." Gen. Elec. Co. v. Joiner, 522 U.S. 136, 146 (1997). Under the amendment, as under *Daubert,* when an expert purports to apply principles and methods in accordance with professional standards, and yet reaches a conclusion that other experts in the field would not reach, the trial court may fairly suspect that the principles and methods have not been faithfully applied. *See* Lust v. Merrell Dow Pharm., Inc., 89 F.3d 594, 598 (9th Cir. 1996). The amendment specifically provides that the trial court must scrutinize not only the principles and methods used by the expert, but also whether those principles and methods have been properly applied to the facts of the case. As the court noted in *In re Paoli Railroad Yard PCB Litigation,* 35 F.3d 717, 745 (3d Cir. 1994), "*any* step that renders the analysis unreliable ... renders the expert's testimony inadmissible. *This is true whether the step completely changes a reliable methodology or merely misapplies that methodology.*"

If the expert purports to apply principles and methods to the facts of the case, it is important that this application be conducted reliably. Yet it might also be important in some cases for an expert to educate the factfinder about general principles, without ever attempting to apply these principles to the specific facts of the case.

For example, experts might instruct the factfinder on the principles of thermodynamics, or bloodclotting, or on how financial markets respond to corporate reports, without ever knowing about or trying to tie their testimony into the facts of the case. The amendment does not alter the venerable practice of using expert testimony to educate the factfinder on general principles. For this kind of generalized testimony, Rule 702 simply requires that: (1) the expert be qualified; (2) the testimony address a subject matter on which the factfinder can be assisted by an expert; (3) the testimony be reliable; and (4) the testimony "fit" the facts of the case.

As stated earlier, the amendment does not distinguish between scientific and other forms of expert testimony. The trial court's gatekeeping function applies to testimony by any expert. *See* Kumho Tire Co. v. Carmichael, 526 U.S. 137, 141 (1999) ("We conclude that *Daubert*'s general holding—setting forth the trial judge's general 'gatekeeping' obligation—applies not only to testimony based on 'scientific' knowledge, but also to testimony based on 'technical' and 'other specialized' knowledge."). While the relevant factors for determining reliability will vary from expertise to expertise, the amendment rejects the premise that an expert's testimony should be treated more permissively simply because it is outside the realm of science. An opinion from an expert who is not a scientist should receive the same degree of scrutiny for reliability as an opinion from an expert who purports to be a scientist. *See* Watkins v. Telsmith, Inc., 121 F.3d 984, 991 (5th Cir. 1997) ("[I]t seems exactly backwards that experts who purport to rely on general engineering principles and practical experience might escape screening by the district court simply by stating that their conclusions were not reached by any particular method or technique."). Some types of expert testimony will be more objectively verifiable, and subject to the expectations of falsifiability, peer review, and publication, than others. Some types of expert testimony will not rely on anything like a scientific method, and so will have to be evaluated by reference to other standard principles attendant to the particular area of expertise. The trial judge in all cases of proffered expert testimony must find that it is properly grounded, well-reasoned, and not speculative before it can be admitted. The expert's testimony must be grounded in an accepted body of learning or experience in the expert's field, and the expert must explain how the conclusion is so grounded. *See, e.g.,* American College of Trial Lawyers, *Standards and Procedures for Determining the Admissibility of Expert Testimony after* Daubert, 157 F.R.D. 571, 579 (1994) ("[W]hether the testimony concerns economic principles, accounting standards, property valuation, or other non-scientific subjects, it should be evaluated by reference to the 'knowledge and experience' of that particular field.").

The amendment requires that the testimony must be the product of reliable principles and methods that are reliably applied to the facts of the case. While the terms "principles" and "methods" may convey a certain impression when applied to scientific knowledge, they remain relevant when applied to testimony based on technical or other specialized knowledge. For example, when a law enforcement agent testifies regarding the use of code words in a drug transaction, the principle used by the agent is that participants in such transactions regularly use code words to conceal the nature of their activities. The method used by the agent is the application of extensive experience to analyze the meaning of the conversations. So long as the principles and methods are reliable and applied reliably to the facts of the case, this type of testimony should be admitted.

Nothing in this amendment is intended to suggest that experience alone—or experience in conjunction with other knowledge, skill, training, or education—may not provide a sufficient foundation for expert testimony. To the contrary, the text of Rule 702 expressly contemplates that an expert may be qualified on the basis of experience. In certain fields, experience is the predominant, if not sole, basis for a great deal of reliable expert testimony. *See, e.g.*, United States v. Jones, 107 F.3d 1147 (6th Cir. 1997) (no abuse of discretion in admitting the testimony of a handwriting examiner who had years of practical experience and extensive training, and who explained his methodology in detail); Tassin v. Sears, Roebuck & Co., 946 F. Supp. 1241, 1248 (M.D. La. 1996) (design engineer's testimony can be admissible when the expert's opinions "are based on facts, a reasonable investigation, and traditional technical/mechanical expertise, and he provides a reasonable link between the information and procedures he uses and the conclusions he reaches"); *see also* Kumho Tire Co. v. Carmichael, 526 U.S. 137, 156 (1999) ("[N]o one denies that an expert might draw a conclusion from a set of observations based on extensive and specialized experience.").

If the witness is relying solely or primarily on experience, then the witness must explain how that experience leads to the conclusion reached, why that experience is a sufficient basis for the opinion, and how that experience is reliably applied to the facts. The trial court's gatekeeping function requires more than simply "taking the expert's word for it." *See* Daubert v. Merrell Dow Pharm., Inc., 43 F.3d 1311, 1319 (9th Cir. 1995) ("We've been presented with only the experts' qualifications, their conclusions and their assurances of reliability. Under *Daubert*, that's not enough."). The more subjective and controversial the expert's inquiry, the more likely the testimony should be excluded as unreliable. *See* O'Conner v. Commonwealth Edison Co., 13 F.3d 1090 (7th Cir. 1994) (expert testimony based on a completely subjective methodology held properly excluded); *see also* Kumho Tire Co. v. Carmichael, 526 U.S. 137, 151 (1999) ("[I]t will at times be useful to ask even of a witness whose expertise is based purely on experience, say, a perfume tester able to distinguish among 140 odors at a sniff, whether his preparation is of a kind that others in the field would recognize as acceptable.").

[Subdivision (b)] of Rule 702 calls for a quantitative rather than qualitative analysis. The amendment requires that expert testimony be based on sufficient underlying "facts or data." The term "data" is intended to encompass the reliable opinions of other experts. *See* the original Advisory Committee note to Rule 703. The language "facts or data" is broad enough to allow an expert to rely on hypothetical facts that are supported by the evidence. *Id*.

When facts are in dispute, experts sometimes reach different conclusions based on competing versions of the facts. The emphasis in the amendment on "sufficient facts or data" is not intended to authorize a trial court to exclude an expert's testimony on the ground that the court believes one version of the facts and not the other.

There has been some confusion over the relationship between Rules 702 and 703. The amendment makes clear that the sufficiency of the basis of an expert's testimony is to be decided under Rule 702. Rule 702 sets forth the overarching requirement of reliability, and an analysis of the sufficiency of the expert's basis cannot be divorced from the ultimate reliability of the expert's opinion. In contrast, the "reasonable reliance" requirement of Rule 703 is a relatively narrow inquiry. When an expert relies on inadmissible information, Rule 703 requires the trial court to determine whether that information is of a type reasonably relied on by other experts in the field. If so, the expert can rely on the information in reaching an opinion. However, the question whether the expert is relying on a *sufficient* basis of information—whether admissible information or not—is governed by the requirements of Rule 702.

The amendment makes no attempt to set forth procedural requirements for exercising the trial court's gatekeeping function over expert testimony. *See* Daniel J. Capra, *The* Daubert *Puzzle*, 38 GA. L. REV. 699, 766 (1998) ("Trial courts should be allowed substantial discretion in dealing with *Daubert* questions; any attempt to codify procedures will likely give rise to unnecessary changes in practice and create difficult questions for appellate review."). Courts have shown considerable ingenuity and flexibility in considering challenges to expert testimony under *Daubert*, and it is contemplated that this will continue under the amended rule. *See, e.g.*, Cortes–Irizarry v. Corporacion Insular de Seguros, 111 F.3d 184

(1st Cir. 1997) (discussing the application of *Daubert* in ruling on a motion for summary judgment); *In re* Paoli R.R. Yard PCB Litig., 35 F.3d 717, 736, 739 (3d Cir. 1994) (discussing the use of in limine hearings); Claar v. Burlington N.R.R. Co., 29 F.3d 499, 502–05 (9th Cir. 1994) (discussing the trial court's technique of ordering experts to submit serial affidavits explaining the reasoning and methods underlying their conclusions).

The amendment continues the practice of the original rule in referring to a qualified witness as an "expert." This was done to provide continuity and to minimize change. The use of the term "expert" in the rule does not, however, mean that a jury should actually be informed that a qualified witness is testifying as an "expert." Indeed, there is much to be said for a practice that prohibits the use of the term "expert" by both the parties and the court at trial. Such a practice "ensures that trial courts do not inadvertently put their stamp of authority" on a witness's opinion, and protects against the jury's being "overwhelmed by the so-called 'experts.'" Hon. Charles Richey, *Proposals to Eliminate the Prejudicial Effect of the Use of the Word "Expert" Under the Federal Rules of Evidence in Criminal and Civil Jury Trials*, 154 F.R.D. 537, 559 (1994) (setting forth limiting instructions and a standing order employed to prohibit the use of the term "expert" in jury trials).

Rule 703.   BASES OF AN EXPERT'S OPINION TESTIMONY

An expert may base an opinion on facts or data in the case that the expert has been made aware of or personally observed. If experts in the particular field would reasonably rely on those kinds of facts or data in forming an opinion on the subject, they need not be admissible for the opinion to be admitted. But if the facts or data would otherwise be inadmissible, the proponent of the opinion may disclose them to the jury only if their probative value in helping the jury evaluate the opinion substantially outweighs their prejudicial effect.

(Enacted Jan. 2, 1975; as amended Mar. 2, 1987, eff. Oct. 1, 1987; Apr. 17, 2000, eff. Dec. 1, 2000; as restyled Apr. 26, 2011, eff. Dec. 1, 2011.)

NOTE BY FEDERAL JUDICIAL CENTER

The rule enacted by the Congress is the rule prescribed by the Supreme Court without change.

<u>ADVISORY COMMITTEE'S NOTE</u>

Facts or data upon which expert opinions are based may, under the rule, be derived from three possible sources. The first is the firsthand observation of the witness, with opinions based thereon traditionally allowed. A treating physician affords an example. Rheingold, *The Basis of Medical Testimony*, 15 VAND. L. REV. 473, 489 (1962). Whether he must first relate his observations is treated in Rule 705. The second source, presentation at the trial, also reflects existing practice. The technique may be the familiar hypothetical question or having the expert attend the trial and hear the testimony establishing the facts. Problems of determining what testimony the expert relied upon, when the latter technique is employed and the testimony is in conflict, may be resolved by resort to Rule 705. The third source contemplated by the rule consists of presentation of data to the expert outside of court and other than by his own perception. In this respect the rule is designed to broaden the basis for expert opinions beyond that current in many jurisdictions and to bring the judicial practice into line with the practice of the experts themselves when not in court. Thus a physician in his own practice bases his diagnosis on information from numerous sources and of considerable variety, including statements by patients and relatives, reports and opinions from nurses, technicians, and other doctors, hospital records, and X rays. Most of them are admissible in evidence, but only with the expenditure of substantial time in producing and examining various authenticating witnesses. The physician makes life-and-death decisions in reliance upon them. His validation, expertly performed and subject to cross-examination, ought to suffice for judicial purposes. Rheingold, *supra*, at 531; MCCORMICK § 15. A similar provision is California Evidence Code § 801(b).

The rule also offers a more satisfactory basis for ruling upon the admissibility of public opinion poll evidence. Attention is directed to the validity of the techniques employed rather than to relatively fruitless inquiries whether hearsay is involved. See Judge Feinberg's careful analysis in *Zippo Manufacturing Co. v. Rogers Imports, Inc.*, 216 F. Supp. 670 (S.D.N.Y. 1963). *See also* Blum et al., *The Art of Opinion Research: A Lawyer's Appraisal of an Emerging Service*, 24 U. CHI. L. REV. 1 (1956); Bonynge, *Trademark Surveys and Techniques and Their Use in Litigation*, 48 A.B.A.J. 329 (1962); Zeisel, *The Uniqueness of Survey Evidence*, 45 CORNELL L.Q. 322 (1960); Annotation, 76 A.L.R.2d 619.

If it be feared that enlargement of permissible data may tend to break down the rules of exclusion unduly, notice should be taken that the rule requires that the facts or data "be of a type reasonably relied upon by experts in the particular field." The language would not warrant admitting in evidence the opinion of an "accidentologist" as to the point of impact in an automobile collision based on statements of bystanders, since this requirement is not satisfied. *See Comment*, CAL. LAW REV. COMM'N, RECOMMENDATION PROPOSING AN EVIDENCE CODE 148–50 (1965).

ADVISORY COMMITTEE'S NOTE TO 2000 AMENDMENT TO RULE 703

Rule 703 has been amended to emphasize that when an expert reasonably relies on inadmissible information to form an opinion or inference, the underlying information is not admissible simply because the opinion or inference is admitted. Courts have reached different results on how to treat inadmissible information when it is reasonably relied upon by an expert in forming an opinion or drawing an inference. *Compare* United States v. Rollins, 862 F.2d 1282 (7th Cir. 1988) (admitting, as part of the basis of an FBI agent's expert opinion on the meaning of code language, the hearsay statements of an informant), *with* United States v. 0.59 Acres of Land, 109 F.3d 1493 (9th Cir. 1997) (error to admit hearsay offered as the basis of an expert opinion, without a limiting instruction). Commentators have also taken differing views. *See, e.g.*, Ronald Carlson, *Policing the Bases of Modern Expert Testimony*, 39 VAND. L. REV. 577 (1986) (advocating limits on the jury's consideration of otherwise inadmissible evidence used as the basis for an expert opinion); Paul Rice, *Inadmissible Evidence as a Basis for Expert Testimony: A Response to Professor Carlson*, 40 VAND. L. REV. 583 (1987) (advocating unrestricted use of information reasonably relied upon by an expert).

When information is reasonably relied upon by an expert and yet is admissible only for the purpose of assisting the jury in evaluating an expert's opinion, a trial court applying this rule must consider the information's probative value in assisting the jury to weigh the expert's opinion on the one hand, and the risk of prejudice resulting from the jury's potential misuse of the information for substantive purposes on the other. The information may be disclosed to the jury, upon objection, only if the trial court finds that the probative value of the information in assisting the jury to evaluate the expert's opinion substantially outweighs its prejudicial effect. If the otherwise inadmissible information is admitted under this balancing test, the trial judge must give a limiting instruction upon request, informing the jury that the underlying information must not be used for substantive purposes. *See* Rule 105. In determining the appropriate course, the trial court should consider the probable effectiveness or lack of effectiveness of a limiting instruction under the particular circumstances.

The amendment governs only the disclosure to the jury of information that is reasonably relied on by an expert, when that information is not admissible for substantive purposes. It is not intended to affect the admissibility of an expert's testimony. Nor does the amendment prevent an expert from relying on information that is inadmissible for substantive purposes.

Nothing in this rule restricts the presentation of underlying expert facts or data when offered by an adverse party. *See* Rule 705. Of course, an adversary's attack on an expert's basis will often open the door to a proponent's rebuttal with information that was reasonably relied upon by the expert, even if that information would not have been discloseable initially under the balancing test provided by this amendment. Moreover, in some circumstances the proponent might wish to disclose information that is relied upon by the expert in order to "remove the sting" from the opponent's anticipated attack, and thereby prevent the jury from drawing an unfair negative inference. The trial court should take this consideration into account in applying the balancing test provided by this amendment.

This amendment covers facts or data that cannot be admitted for any purpose other than to assist the jury to evaluate the expert's opinion. The balancing test provided in this amendment is not applicable to facts or data that are admissible for any other purpose but have not yet been offered for such a purpose at the time the expert testifies.

The amendment provides a presumption against disclosure to the jury of information used as the basis of an expert's opinion and not admissible for any substantive purpose, when that information is offered by the proponent of the expert. In a multi-party case, where one party proffers an expert whose testimony is also beneficial to other parties, each such party should be deemed a "proponent" within the meaning of the amendment.

Advisory Committee's Note to 2011 Restyling of Rule 703

The Committee deleted all reference to an "inference" on the grounds that the deletion made the rule flow better and easier to read, and because any "inference" is covered by the broader term "opinion." Courts have not made substantive decisions on the basis of any distinction between an opinion and an inference. No change in current practice is intended.

Rule 704.   OPINION ON AN ULTIMATE ISSUE

(a) In General—Not Automatically Objectionable.   An opinion is not objectionable just because it embraces an ultimate issue.

(b) Exception.   In a criminal case, an expert witness must not state an opinion about whether the defendant did or did not have a mental state or condition that constitutes an element of the crime charged or of a defense. Those matters are for the trier of fact alone.

(Enacted Jan. 2, 1975; as amended Oct. 12, 1984; as restyled Apr. 26, 2011, eff. Dec. 1, 2011.)

<u>EDITOR'S NOTE</u>

Subdivision (a) is the rule as originally approved by the Supreme Court and enacted by Congress in 1974, minus the reference to subdivision (b) in the opening clause. Congress added the first clause of subdivision (a) and all of subdivision (b) in 1984 as part of the Insanity Defense Reform Act, Pub. L. No. 98-473, tit. II, ch. IV, § 406.

<u>ADVISORY COMMITTEE'S NOTE</u>

The basic approach to opinions, lay and expert, in these rules is to admit them when helpful to the trier of fact. In order to render this approach fully effective and to allay any doubt on the subject, the so-called "ultimate issue" rule is specifically abolished by the instant rule.

The older cases often contained strictures against allowing witnesses to express opinions upon ultimate issues, as a particular aspect of the rule against opinions. The rule was unduly restrictive, difficult of application, and generally served only to deprive the trier of fact of useful information. 7 WIGMORE §§ 1920–1921; MCCORMICK § 12. The basis usually assigned for the rule, to prevent the witness from "usurping the province of the jury," is aptly characterized as "empty rhetoric." 7 WIGMORE § 1920, at 17. Efforts to meet the felt needs of particular situations led to odd verbal circumlocutions which were said not to violate the rule. Thus a witness could express his estimate of the criminal responsibility of an accused in terms of sanity or insanity, but not in terms of ability to tell right from wrong or other more modern standard. And in cases of medical causation, witnesses were sometimes required to couch their opinions in cautious phrases of "might or could," rather than "did," though the result was to deprive many opinions of the positiveness to which they were entitled, accompanied by the hazard of a ruling of insufficiency to support a verdict. In other instances the rule was simply disregarded, and, as concessions to need, opinions were allowed upon such matters as intoxication, speed, handwriting, and value, although more precise coincidence with an ultimate issue would scarcely be possible.

Many modern decisions illustrate the trend to abandon the rule completely. People v. Wilson, 25 Cal. 2d 341 (1944) (whether abortion necessary to save life of patient); Clifford–Jacobs Forging Co. v. Indus. Comm'n, 19 Ill. 2d 236 (1960) (medical causation); Dowling v. L.H. Shattuck, Inc., 91 N.H. 234 (1941) (proper method of shoring ditch); Schweiger v. Solbeck, 191 Or. 454 (1951) (cause of landslide). In each instance the opinion was allowed.

The abolition of the ultimate issue rule does not lower the bars so as to admit all opinions. Under Rules 701 and 702, opinions must be helpful to the trier of fact, and Rule 403 provides for exclusion of evidence which wastes time. These provisions afford ample assurances against the admission of opinions which would merely tell the jury what result to reach, somewhat in the manner of the oath-helpers of an earlier day. They also stand ready to exclude opinions phrased in terms of inadequately explored legal criteria. Thus the question, "Did T have capacity to make a will?" would be excluded, while the question, "Did T have sufficient mental capacity to know the nature and extent of his property and the natural objects of his bounty and to formulate a rational scheme of distribution?" would be allowed. MCCORMICK § 12.

For similar provisions see Uniform Rule 56(4); California Evidence Code § 805; Kansas Statutes Annotated § 60-456(d); New Jersey Evidence Rule 56(3) (repealed and replaced by New Jersey Rule of Evidence 704 (1993)).

SENATE JUDICIARY COMMITTEE REPORT, 1984 AMENDMENT TO RULE 704

The purpose of this amendment is to eliminate the confusing spectacle of competing expert witnesses testifying to directly contradictory conclusions as to the ultimate legal issue to be found by the trier of fact. Under this proposal, expert psychiatric testimony would be limited to presenting and explaining their diagnoses, such as whether the defendant had a severe mental disease or defect and what the characteristics of such a disease or defect, if any, may have been. The basis for this limitation on expert testimony in insanity cases is ably stated by the American Psychiatric Association:

> [I]t is clear that psychiatrists are experts in medicine, not the law. As such, it is clear that the psychiatrist's first obligation and expertise in the courtroom is to "do psychiatry," i.e., to present medical information and opinion about the defendant's mental state and motivation and to explain in detail the reason for his medical-psychiatric conclusions. When, however, "ultimate issue" questions are formulated by the law and put to the expert witness who must then say "yea" and "nay," then the expert witness is required to make a leap in logic. He no longer addresses himself to medical concepts but instead must infer or intuit what is in fact unspeakable, namely, the probable relationship between medical concepts and legal or moral constructs such as free will. These impermissible leaps in logic made by expert witnesses confuse the jury. [Footnote omitted.] Juries thus find themselves listening to conclusory and seemingly contradictory psychiatric testimony that defendants are either "sane" or "insane" or that they do or do not meet the relevant legal test for insanity. This state of affairs does considerable injustice to psychiatry and, we believe, possibly to criminal defendants. In fact, in many criminal insanity trials both prosecution and defense psychiatrists do agree about the nature and even the extent of mental disorder exhibited by the defendant at the time of the act.

> Psychiatrists, of course, must be permitted to testify fully about the defendant's diagnosis, mental state and motivation (in clinical and commonsense terms) at the time of the alleged act so as to permit the jury or judge to reach the ultimate conclusion about which they and only they are expert. Determining whether a criminal defendant was legally insane is a matter for legal fact-finders, not for experts.

Moreover, the rationale for precluding ultimate opinion psychiatric testimony extends beyond the insanity defense to any ultimate mental state of the defendant that is relevant to the legal conclusion sought to be proven. The Committee has fashioned its Rule 704 provision to reach all such "ultimate" issues, e.g., premeditation in a homicide case or lack of predisposition in entrapment.

ADVISORY COMMITTEE'S NOTE TO 2011 RESTYLING OF RULE 704

The Committee deleted all reference to an "inference" on the grounds that the deletion made the rule flow better and easier to read, and because any "inference" is covered by the broader term "opinion." Courts have not made substantive decisions on the basis of any distinction between an opinion and an inference. No change in current practice is intended.

Rule 705.   DISCLOSING THE FACTS OR DATA UNDERLYING AN EXPERT'S OPINION

Unless the court orders otherwise, an expert may state an opinion—and give the reasons for it—without first testifying to the underlying facts or data. But the expert may be required to disclose those facts or data on cross-examination.

(Enacted Jan. 2, 1975; as amended Mar. 2, 1987, eff. Oct. 1, 1987; Apr. 22, 1993, eff. Dec. 1, 1993; as restyled Apr. 26, 2011, eff. Dec. 1, 2011.)

NOTE BY FEDERAL JUDICIAL CENTER

The rule enacted by the Congress is the rule prescribed by the Supreme Court, amended only by substituting "court" in place of "judge."

ADVISORY COMMITTEE'S NOTE

The hypothetical question has been the target of a great deal of criticism as encouraging partisan bias, affording an opportunity for summing up in the middle of the case, and as complex and time consuming. Ladd, *Expert Testimony*, 5 VAND. L. REV. 414, 426–27 (1952). While the rule allows counsel to make disclosure of the underlying facts or data as a preliminary to the giving of an expert opinion, if he chooses, the instances in which he is required to do so are reduced. This is true whether the expert bases his opinion on data furnished him at secondhand or observed by him at firsthand.

The elimination of the requirement of preliminary disclosure at the trial of underlying facts or data has a long background of support. In 1937 the Commissioners on Uniform State Laws incorporated a provision to this effect in their Model Expert Testimony Act, which furnished the basis for Uniform Rules 57 and

58. [New York Civil Practice Law and Rules 4515] (McKinney 1963), provides:

> Unless the court orders otherwise, questions calling for the opinion of an expert witness need not be hypothetical in form, and the witness may state his opinion and reasons without first specifying the data upon which it is based. Upon cross-examination, he may be required to specify the data . . . .

See also CAL. EVID. CODE § 802; KAN. STAT. ANN. §§ 60-456, -457; N.J. EVID. R. 57, 58 (repealed and replaced by N.J. R. EVID. 705 (1993)).

If the objection is made that leaving it to the cross-examiner to bring out the supporting data is essentially unfair, the answer is that he is under no compulsion to bring out any facts or data except those unfavorable to the opinion. The answer assumes that the cross-examiner has the advance knowledge which is essential for effective cross-examination. This advance knowledge has been afforded, though imperfectly, by the traditional foundation requirement. Rule 26(b)(4) of the Rules of Civil Procedure, as revised, provides for substantial discovery in this area, obviating in large measure the obstacles which have been raised in some instances to discovery of findings, underlying data, and even the identity of the experts. Friedenthal, *Discovery and Use of an Adverse Party's Expert Information*, 14 STAN. L. REV. 455 (1962).

These safeguards are reinforced by the discretionary power of the judge to require preliminary disclosure in any event.

ADVISORY COMMITTEE'S NOTES TO 1993 AMENDMENT TO RULE 705

This rule, which relates to the manner of presenting testimony at trial, is revised to avoid an arguable conflict with revised Rules 26(a)(2)(B) and [26(e)(2)] of the Federal Rules of Civil Procedure or with revised Rule 16 of the Federal Rules of Criminal Procedure, which require disclosure in advance of trial of the basis and reasons for an expert's opinions.

If a serious question is raised under Rule 702 or 703 as to the admissibility of expert testimony, disclosure of the underlying facts or data on which opinions are based may, of course, be needed by the court before deciding whether, and to what extent, the person should be allowed to testify. This rule does not preclude such an inquiry.

The Committee deleted all reference to an "inference" on the grounds that the deletion made the rule flow better and easier to read, and because any "inference" is covered by the broader term "opinion." Courts have not made substantive decisions on the basis of any distinction between an opinion and an inference. No change in current practice is intended.

Rule 706.   COURT-APPOINTED EXPERT WITNESSES

(a) Appointment Process. On a party's motion or on its own, the court may order the parties to show cause why expert witnesses should not be appointed and may ask the parties to submit nominations. The court may appoint any expert that the parties agree on and any of its own choosing. But the court may only appoint someone who consents to act.

(b) Expert's Role. The court must inform the expert of the expert's duties. The court may do so in writing and have a copy filed with the clerk or may do so orally at a conference in which the parties have an opportunity to participate. The expert:

    (1) must advise the parties of any findings the expert makes;

    (2) may be deposed by any party;

    (3) may be called to testify by the court or any party; and

    (4) may be cross-examined by any party, including the party that called the expert.

(c) Compensation. The expert is entitled to a reasonable compensation, as set by the court. The compensation is payable as follows:

    (1) in a criminal case or in a civil case involving just compensation under the Fifth Amendment, from any funds that are provided by law; and

(2) in any other civil case, by the parties in the proportion and at the time that the court directs—and the compensation is then charged like other costs.

(d) Disclosing the Appointment to the Jury. The court may authorize disclosure to the jury that the court appointed the expert.

(e) Parties' Choice of Their Own Experts. This rule does not limit a party in calling its own experts.

(Enacted Jan. 2, 1975; as amended Mar. 2, 1987, eff. Oct. 1, 1987; as restyled Apr. 26, 2011, eff. Dec. 1, 2011.)

NOTE BY FEDERAL JUDICIAL CENTER

The rule enacted by the Congress is the rule prescribed by the Supreme Court, amended by substituting "court" in place of "judge," with conforming pronominal changes, and, in subdivision [(c)], by substituting the phrase "and civil actions and proceedings" in place of "and cases" before "involving" in the second sentence.[1]

ADVISORY COMMITTEE'S NOTE

The practice of shopping for experts, the venality of some experts, and the reluctance of many reputable experts to involve themselves in litigation, have been matters of deep concern. Though the contention is made that court-appointed experts acquire an aura of infallibility to which they are not entitled, Levy, *Impartial Medical Testimony—Revisited*, 34 TEMPLE L.Q. 416 (1961), the trend is increasingly to provide for their use. While experience indicates that actual appointment is a relatively infrequent occurrence, the assumption may be made that the availability of the procedure in itself decreases the need for resorting to it. The ever-present possibility that the judge may appoint an expert in a given case must inevitably exert a sobering effect on the expert witness of a party and upon the person utilizing his services.

The inherent power of a trial judge to appoint an expert of his own choosing is virtually unquestioned. Scott v. Spanjer Bros., Inc., 298 F.2d 928 (2d Cir. 1962); Danville Tobacco Assn. v. Bryant–Buckner Assocs., Inc., 333 F.2d 202 (4th Cir. 1964); Sink, *The Unused*

---

[1] [The restyled Federal Rules of Evidence, made law in December 2011, substitute the phrase "or in a civil case" for "and civil actions and proceedings."—GF]

Power of a Federal Judge to Call His Own Expert Witnesses, 29 S. CAL. L. REV. 195 (1956); 2 WIGMORE § 563; 9 *id.* § 2484; Annotation, 95 A.L.R.2d 383. Hence the problem becomes largely one of detail.

The New York plan is well known and is described in REPORT BY SPECIAL COMMITTEE OF THE ASSOCIATION OF THE BAR OF THE CITY OF NEW YORK: IMPARTIAL MEDICAL TESTIMONY (1956). On recommendation of the Section of Judicial Administration, local adoption of an impartial medical plan was endorsed by the American Bar Association. 82 A.B.A. Rep. 184–85 (1957). Descriptions and analyses of plans in effect in various parts of the country are found in Van Dusen, *A United States District Judge's View of the Impartial Medical Expert System*, 32 F.R.D. 498 (1963); Wick & Kightlinger, *Impartial Medical Testimony Under the Federal Civil Rules: A Tale of Three Doctors*, 34 INS. COUNS. J. 115 (1967); and numerous articles collected in KLEIN, JUDICIAL ADMINISTRATION AND THE LEGAL PROFESSION 393 (1963). Statutes and rules include California Evidence Code §§ 730–733; Illinois Supreme Court Rule 215(d); Burns Indiana Statutes 1956, § 9-1702 (repealed and replaced by Indiana Code § 35-36-2-2 (1981)); Wisconsin Statutes Annotated 1958, § 957.27 (repealed and replaced by Wisconsin Statutes Annotated § 971.16 (1969)).

In the federal practice, a comprehensive scheme for court-appointed experts was initiated with the adoption of Rule 28 of the Federal Rules of Criminal Procedure in 1946. The Judicial Conference of the United States in 1953 considered court-appointed experts in civil cases, but only with respect to whether they should be compensated from public funds, a proposal which was rejected. REPORT OF THE JUDICIAL CONFERENCE OF THE UNITED STATES 23 (1953). The present rule expands the practice to include civil cases.

[Subdivisions (a) and (b) are] based on Rule 28 of the Federal Rules of Criminal Procedure, with a few changes, mainly in the interest of clarity. Language has been added to provide specifically for the appointment either on motion of a party or on the judge's own motion. A provision subjecting the court-appointed expert to deposition procedures has been incorporated. The rule has been revised to make definite the right of any party, including the party calling him, to cross-examine.

[Subdivision (c)] combines the present provision for compensation in criminal cases with what seems to be a fair and feasible handling of civil cases, originally found in the Model Act and carried from there into Uniform Rule 60. *See also* CAL. EVID. CODE §§ 730–731. The special provision for Fifth Amendment compensation cases is designed to guard against reducing constitutionally guaranteed just compensation by requiring the recipient to pay costs. *See* FED. R. CIV. P. 71.1(*l*).

[**Subdivision (d)**] seems to be essential if the use of court-appointed experts is to be fully effective. Uniform Rule 61 so provides.

[**Subdivision (e)**] is in essence the last sentence of Rule 28(a) of the Federal Rules of Criminal Procedure.

ARTICLE VIII. HEARSAY

ADVISORY COMMITTEE'S NOTE

Introductory Note: The Hearsay Problem

The factors to be considered in evaluating the testimony of a witness are perception, memory, and narration. Morgan, *Hearsay Dangers and the Application of the Hearsay Concept*, 62 HARV. L. REV. 177 (1948), *reprinted in* SELECTED WRITINGS ON EVIDENCE AND TRIAL 764–65 (Fryer ed., 1957); Shientag, *Cross-Examination — A Judge's Viewpoint*, 3 RECORD 12 (1948); Strahorn, *A Reconsideration of the Hearsay Rule and Admissions*, 85 U. PA. L. REV. 484, 485 (1937), *reprinted in* SELECTED WRITINGS ON EVIDENCE AND TRIAL, *supra*, at 756–57; Weinstein, *Probative Force of Hearsay*, 46 IOWA L. REV. 331 (1961). Sometimes a fourth is added, sincerity, but in fact it seems merely to be an aspect of the three already mentioned.

In order to encourage the witness to do his best with respect to each of these factors, and to expose any inaccuracies which may enter in, the Anglo–American tradition has evolved three conditions under which witnesses will ideally be required to testify: (1) under oath, (2) in the personal presence of the trier of fact, (3) subject to cross-examination.

(1) Standard procedure calls for the swearing of witnesses. While the practice is perhaps less effective than in an earlier time, no disposition to relax the requirement is apparent, other than to allow affirmation by persons with scruples against taking oaths.

(2) The demeanor of the witness traditionally has been believed to furnish trier and opponent with valuable clues. Universal Camera Corp. v. NLRB, 340 U.S. 474, 495–96 (1951); Sahm, *Demeanor Evidence: Elusive and Intangible Imponderables*, 47 A.B.A.J. 580 (1961), quoting numerous authorities. The witness himself will probably be impressed with the solemnity of the occasion and the possibility of public disgrace. Willingness to falsify may reasonably become more difficult in the presence of the person against whom directed. Rules 26 and 43(a) of the Federal Rules of Criminal and Civil Procedure, respectively, include the general requirement that testimony be taken orally in open court. The Sixth Amendment right of confrontation is a manifestation of these beliefs and attitudes.

(3) Emphasis on the basis of the hearsay rule today tends to center upon the condition of cross-examination. All may not agree with Wigmore that cross-examination is "beyond doubt the greatest

legal engine ever invented for the discovery of truth," but all will agree with his statement that it has become a "vital feature" of the Anglo–American system. 5 WIGMORE § 1367, at 29. The belief, or perhaps hope, that cross-examination is effective in exposing imperfections of perception, memory, and narration is fundamental. Morgan, *Foreword* to MODEL CODE OF EVIDENCE 1, 37 (1942).

The logic of the preceding discussion might suggest that no testimony be received unless in full compliance with the three ideal conditions. No one advocates this position. Common sense tells that much evidence which is not given under the three conditions may be inherently superior to much that is. Moreover, when the choice is between evidence which is less than best and no evidence at all, only clear folly would dictate an across-the-board policy of doing without. The problem thus resolves itself into effecting a sensible accommodation between these considerations and the desirability of giving testimony under the ideal conditions.

The solution evolved by the common law has been a general rule excluding hearsay but subject to numerous exceptions under circumstances supposed to furnish guarantees of trustworthiness. Criticisms of this scheme are that it is bulky and complex, fails to screen good from bad hearsay realistically, and inhibits the growth of the law of evidence.

Since no one advocates excluding all hearsay, three possible solutions may be considered: (1) abolish the rule against hearsay and admit all hearsay; (2) admit hearsay possessing sufficient probative force, but with procedural safeguards; (3) revise the present system of class exceptions.

(1) Abolition of the hearsay rule would be the simplest solution. The effect would not be automatically to abolish the giving of testimony under ideal conditions. If the declarant were available, compliance with the ideal conditions would be optional with either party. Thus the proponent could call the declarant as a witness as a form of presentation more impressive than his hearsay statement. Or the opponent could call the declarant to be cross-examined upon his statement. This is the tenor of Uniform Rule 63(1), admitting the hearsay declaration of a person "who is present at the hearing and available for cross-examination." Compare the treatment of declarations of available declarants in Rule 801(d)(1) of the instant rules. If the declarant were unavailable, a rule of free admissibility would make no distinctions in terms of degrees of noncompliance with the ideal conditions and would exact no quid pro quo in the form of assurances of trustworthiness. Rule 503 of the Model Code did exactly that, providing for the admissibility of any hearsay

declaration by an unavailable declarant, finding support in the
Massachusetts act of 1898, enacted at the instance of Thayer, MASS.
GEN. LAWS ch. 233, § 65 (1932), and in the English act of 1938,
Evidence Act, 1938, 1 & 2 Geo. 6, c. 28 (Eng.). Both are limited to
civil cases. The draftsmen of the Uniform Rules chose a less
advanced and more conventional position. *Comment*, UNIF. R. EVID.
63. The present Advisory Committee has been unconvinced of the
wisdom of abandoning the traditional requirement of some
particular assurance of credibility as a condition precedent to
admitting the hearsay declaration of an unavailable declarant.

In criminal cases, the Sixth Amendment requirement of
confrontation would no doubt move into a large part of the area
presently occupied by the hearsay rule in the event of the abolition
of the latter. The resultant split between civil and criminal evidence
is regarded as an undesirable development.

(2) Abandonment of the system of class exceptions in favor of
individual treatment in the setting of the particular case,
accompanied by procedural safeguards, has been impressively
advocated. Weinstein, *The Probative Force of Hearsay*, 46 IOWA L.
REV. 331 (1961). Admissibility would be determined by weighing
the probative force of the evidence against the possibility of
prejudice, waste of time, and the availability of more satisfactory
evidence. The bases of the traditional hearsay exceptions would be
helpful in assessing probative force. Ladd, *The Relationship of the
Principles of Exclusionary Rules of Evidence to the Problem of Proof*, 18
MINN. L. REV. 506 (1934). Procedural safeguards would consist of
notice of intention to use hearsay, free comment by the judge on the
weight of the evidence, and a greater measure of authority in both
trial and appellate judges to deal with evidence on the basis of
weight. The Advisory Committee has rejected this approach to
hearsay as involving too great a measure of judicial discretion,
minimizing the predictability of rulings, enhancing the difficulties
of preparation for trial, adding a further element to the already
over-complicated congeries of pretrial procedures, and requiring
substantially different rules for civil and criminal cases. The only
way in which the probative force of hearsay differs from the
probative force of other testimony is in the absence of oath,
demeanor, and cross-examination as aids in determining
credibility. For a judge to exclude evidence because he does not
believe it has been described as "altogether atypical,
extraordinary." Chadbourn, *Bentham and the Hearsay Rule—A
Benthamic View of Rule 63(4)(c) of the Uniform Rules of Evidence*, 75
HARV. L. REV. 932, 947 (1962).

(3) The approach to hearsay in these rules is that of the common
law, i.e., a general rule excluding hearsay, with exceptions under

which evidence is not required to be excluded even though hearsay. The traditional hearsay exceptions are drawn upon for the exceptions, collected under two rules, one dealing with situations where availability of the declarant is regarded as immaterial and the other with those where unavailability is made a condition to the admission of the hearsay statement. Each of the two rules concludes with a provision for hearsay statements not within one of the specified exceptions "but having comparable [equivalent] circumstantial guarantees of trustworthiness." Rules 803(24) and [804(b)(5)].[1] This plan is submitted as calculated to encourage growth and development in this area of the law, while conserving the values and experience of the past as a guide to the future.

Confrontation and Due Process[2]

Until very recently, decisions invoking the Confrontation Clause of the Sixth Amendment were surprisingly few, a fact probably explainable by the former inapplicability of the clause to the states and by the hearsay rule's occupancy of much the same ground. The pattern which emerges from the earlier cases invoking the clause is substantially that of the hearsay rule, applied to criminal cases: an accused is entitled to have the witnesses against him testify under oath, in the presence of himself and trier, subject to cross-examination; yet considerations of public policy and necessity require the recognition of such exceptions as dying declarations and former testimony of unavailable witnesses. Mattox v. United States, 156 U.S. 237 (1895); Motes v. United States, 178 U.S. 458 (1900); Delaney v. United States, 263 U.S. 586 (1924). Beginning with *Snyder v. Massachusetts*, 291 U.S. 97 (1934), the Court began to speak of confrontation as an aspect of procedural due process, thus extending its applicability to state cases and to federal cases other than criminal. The language of *Snyder* was that of an elastic concept of hearsay. The deportation case of *Bridges v. Wixon*, 326 U.S. 135 (1945), may be read broadly as imposing a strictly construed right of confrontation in all kinds of cases or narrowly as the product of a failure of the Immigration and Naturalization Service to follow its own rules. *In re Oliver*, 333 U.S. 257 (1948), ruled that cross-examination was essential to due process in a state contempt proceeding, but in *United States v. Nugent*, 346 U.S. 1 (1953), the Court held that it was not an essential aspect of a

---

[1] [As originally enacted in 1975, the Federal Rules included two catchall hearsay exceptions, one that did not require the declarant's unavailability (FRE 803(24)) and one that did (FRE 804(b)(5)). Rule 807, enacted in 1997, consolidated and displaced both rules.—GF]

[2] [The constitutional guarantee of confrontation has evolved a good deal since the Advisory Committee wrote this material. Please see Chapter 8 of the casebook.—GF]

"hearing" for a conscientious objector under the Selective Service Act. *Stein v. New York*, 346 U.S. 156 (1953), disclaimed any purpose to read the hearsay rule into the Fourteenth Amendment, but in *Greene v. McElroy*, 360 U.S. 474 (1959), revocation of security clearance without confrontation and cross-examination was held unauthorized, and a similar result was reached in *Willner v. Committee on Character & Fitness*, 373 U.S. 96 (1963). Ascertaining the constitutional dimensions of the confrontation–hearsay aggregate against the background of these cases is a matter of some difficulty, yet the general pattern is at least not inconsistent with that of the hearsay rule.

In 1965 the Confrontation Clause was held applicable to the states. Pointer v. Texas, 380 U.S. 400 (1965). Prosecution use of former testimony given at a preliminary hearing where petitioner was not represented by counsel was a violation of the clause. The same result would have followed under conventional hearsay doctrine read in the light of a constitutional right to counsel, and nothing in the opinion suggests any difference in essential outline between the hearsay rule and the right of confrontation. In the companion case of *Douglas v. Alabama*, 380 U.S. 415 (1965), however, the result reached by applying the Confrontation Clause is one reached less readily via the hearsay rule. A confession implicating petitioner was put before the jury by reading it to the witness in portions and asking if he made that statement. The witness refused to answer on grounds of self-incrimination. The result, said the Court, was to deny cross-examination, and hence confrontation. True, it could broadly be said that the confession was a hearsay statement which for all practical purposes was put in evidence. Yet a more easily accepted explanation of the opinion is that its real thrust was in the direction of curbing undesirable prosecutorial behavior, rather than merely applying rules of exclusion, and that the Confrontation Clause was the means selected to achieve this end. Comparable facts and a like result appeared in *Brookhart v. Janis*, 384 U.S. 1 (1966).

The pattern suggested in *Douglas* was developed further and more distinctly in a pair of cases at the end of the 1966 term. *United States v. Wade*, 388 U.S. 218 (1967), and *Gilbert v. California*, 388 U.S. 263 (1967), hinged upon practices followed in identifying accused persons before trial. This pretrial identification was said to be so decisive an aspect of the case that accused was entitled to have counsel present; a pretrial identification made in the absence of counsel was not itself receivable in evidence and, in addition, might fatally infect a courtroom identification. The presence of counsel at the earlier identification was described as a necessary prerequisite for "a meaningful confrontation at trial." *Wade*, 388 U.S. at 236. *Wade* involved no evidence of the fact of a prior identification and hence was not susceptible of being decided on hearsay grounds. In

Gilbert, witnesses did testify to an earlier identification, readily classifiable as hearsay under a fairly strict view of what constitutes hearsay. The Court, however, carefully avoided basing the decision on the hearsay ground, choosing confrontation instead. *Gilbert,* 388 U.S. at 272 n.3; *see also* Parker v. Gladden, 385 U.S. 363 (1966) (holding that the right of confrontation was violated when the bailiff made prejudicial statements to jurors); *Note,* 75 YALE L.J. 1434 (1966).

Under the earlier cases, the Confrontation Clause may have been little more than a constitutional embodiment of the hearsay rule, even including traditional exceptions but with some room for expanding them along similar lines. But under the recent cases the impact of the Clause clearly extends beyond the confines of the hearsay rule. These considerations have led the Advisory Committee to conclude that a hearsay rule can function usefully as an adjunct to the confrontation right in constitutional areas and independently in nonconstitutional areas. In recognition of the separateness of the Confrontation Clause and the hearsay rule, and to avoid inviting collisions between them or between the hearsay rule and other exclusionary principles, the exceptions set forth in Rules 803 and 804 are stated in terms of exemption from the general exclusionary mandate of the hearsay rule, rather than in positive terms of admissibility. *See* UNIF. R. EVID. 63(1)–(31) and CAL. EVID. CODE §§ 1200–1340.

Rule 801.   DEFINITIONS THAT APPLY TO THIS ARTICLE; EXCLUSIONS FROM HEARSAY

(a) Statement.   "Statement" means a person's oral assertion, written assertion, or nonverbal conduct, if the person intended it as an assertion.

(b) Declarant. "Declarant" means the person who made the statement.

(c) Hearsay. "Hearsay" means a statement that:

(1) the declarant does not make while testifying at the current trial or hearing; and

(2) a party offers in evidence to prove the truth of the matter asserted in the statement.

(d) Statements That Are Not Hearsay. A statement that meets the following conditions is not hearsay:

(1) *A Declarant-Witness's Prior Statement.* The declarant testifies and is subject to cross-examination about a prior statement, and the statement:

(A) is inconsistent with the declarant's testimony and was given under penalty of perjury at a trial, hearing, or other proceeding or in a deposition;

(B) is consistent with the declarant's testimony and is offered:

(i) to rebut an express or implied charge that the declarant recently fabricated it or acted from a recent improper influence or motive in so testifying; or

(ii) to rehabilitate the declarant's credibility as a witness when attacked on another ground; or

(C) identifies a person as someone the declarant perceived earlier.

(2) *An Opposing Party's Statement.* The statement is offered against an opposing party and:

(A) was made by the party in an individual or representative capacity;

(B) is one the party manifested that it adopted or believed to be true;

(C) was made by a person whom the party authorized to make a statement on the subject;

(D) was made by the party's agent or employee on a matter within the scope of that relationship and while it existed; or

(E) was made by the party's coconspirator during and in furtherance of the conspiracy.

The statement must be considered but does not by itself establish the declarant's authority under (C); the existence or scope of the relationship under (D); or the existence of the conspiracy or participation in it under (E).

(Enacted Jan. 2, 1975; as amended Oct. 16, 1975; Mar. 2, 1987, eff. Oct. 1, 1987; April 11, 1997, eff. Dec. 1, 1997; as restyled Apr. 26, 2011, eff. Dec. 1, 2011; as amended Dec. 1, 2014.)

NOTE BY FEDERAL JUDICIAL CENTER

The rule enacted by the Congress is the rule prescribed by the Supreme Court, with two amendments to subdivision (d)(1). The first of these amendments inserted in item (A), after "testimony," the phrase "and was given under oath subject to the penalty of perjury at a trial, hearing, or other proceeding, or in a deposition." The other amendment consisted of the deletion of item (C), which dealt with prior statements of identification. The reasons for these amendments are stated in the Report of the House Committee on the Judiciary, the Report of the Senate Committee on the Judiciary, and the Conference Report, set forth below.

ADVISORY COMMITTEE'S NOTE TO RULE 801(a)–(d)(1)(A)

Subdivision (a). The definition of "statement" assumes importance because the term is used in the definition of hearsay in subdivision (c). The effect of the definition of "statement" is to exclude from the operation of the hearsay rule all evidence of conduct, verbal or nonverbal, not intended as an assertion. The key to the definition is that nothing is an assertion unless intended to be one.

It can scarcely be doubted that an assertion made in words is intended by the declarant to be an assertion. Hence verbal assertions readily fall into the category of "statement." Whether nonverbal conduct should be regarded as a statement for purposes of defining hearsay requires further consideration. Some nonverbal conduct, such as the act of pointing to identify a suspect in a lineup, is clearly the equivalent of words, assertive in nature, and to be regarded as a statement. Other nonverbal conduct, however, may be offered as evidence that the person acted as he did because of his belief in the existence of the condition sought to be proved, from which belief the existence of the condition may be inferred. This sequence is, arguably, in effect an assertion of the existence of the condition and hence properly includable within the hearsay concept. See Morgan, *Hearsay Dangers and the Application of the Hearsay Concept*, 62 HARV. L. REV. 177, 214, 217 (1948), and the elaboration in Finman, *Implied Assertions as Hearsay: Some Criticisms of the Uniform Rules of Evidence*, 14 STAN. L. REV. 682 (1962). Admittedly evidence of this character is untested with respect to the perception, memory, and narration (or their equivalents) of the actor, but the Advisory Committee is of the view that these dangers are minimal in the absence of an intent to assert and do not justify the loss of the evidence on hearsay grounds. No class of evidence is free of the possibility of fabrication, but the likelihood is less with nonverbal than with assertive verbal conduct. The situations giving rise to the nonverbal conduct are such as virtually to eliminate questions of sincerity. Motivation, the nature of the conduct, and the presence or absence of reliance will bear heavily upon the weight to be given the evidence. Falknor, *The "Hear–Say" Rule as a "See–Do" Rule: Evidence of Conduct*, 33 ROCKY MTN. L. REV. 133 (1961). Similar considerations govern nonassertive verbal conduct and verbal conduct which is assertive but offered as a basis for inferring something other than the matter asserted, also excluded from the definition of hearsay by the language of subdivision (c).

When evidence of conduct is offered on the theory that it is not a statement, and hence not hearsay, a preliminary determination will be required to determine whether an assertion is intended. The rule is so worded as to place the burden upon the party claiming that the intention existed; ambiguous and doubtful cases will be resolved against him and in favor of admissibility. The determination involves no greater difficulty than many other preliminary questions of fact. Maguire, *The Hearsay System: Around and Through the Thicket*, 14 VAND. L. REV. 741, 765–67 (1961).

For similar approaches, see Uniform Rule 62(1); California Evidence Code §§ 225, 1200; Kansas Statutes Annotated § 60-459(a); New Jersey Evidence Rule 62(1) (repealed and replaced by New Jersey Rule of Evidence 801(a) (1993)).

Subdivision (c). The definition follows along familiar lines in including only statements offered to prove the truth of the matter asserted. MCCORMICK § 225; 5 WIGMORE § 1361, 6 *id.* § 1766. If the significance of an offered statement lies solely in the fact that it was made, no issue is raised as to the truth of anything asserted, and the statement is not hearsay. Emich Motors Corp. v. Gen. Motors Corp., 181 F.2d 70 (7th Cir. 1950) (letters of complaint from customers offered as a reason for cancellation of dealer's franchise, to rebut contention that franchise was revoked for refusal to finance sales through affiliated finance company), *rev'd on other grounds*, 340 U.S. 558 (1951),. The effect is to exclude from hearsay the entire category of "verbal acts" and "verbal parts of an act," in which the statement itself affects the legal rights of the parties or is a circumstance bearing on conduct affecting their rights.

The definition of hearsay must, of course, be read with reference to the definition of statement set forth in subdivision (a).

Testimony given by a witness in the course of court proceedings is excluded since there is compliance with all the ideal conditions for testifying.

Subdivision (d). Several types of statements which would otherwise literally fall within the definition are expressly excluded from it:

(1) *Prior statement by witness.* Considerable controversy has attended the question whether a prior out-of-court statement by a person now available for cross-examination concerning it, under oath and in the presence of the trier of fact, should be classed as hearsay. If the witness admits on the stand that he made the statement and that it was true, he adopts the statement and there is no hearsay problem. The hearsay problem arises when the witness on the stand denies having made the statement or admits having made it but denies its truth. The argument in favor of treating these latter statements as hearsay is based upon the ground that the conditions of oath, cross-examination, and demeanor observation did not prevail at the time the statement was made and cannot adequately be supplied by the later examination. The logic of the situation is troublesome. So far as concerns the oath, its mere presence has never been regarded as sufficient to remove a statement from the hearsay category, and it receives much less emphasis than cross-examination as a truth-compelling device. While strong expressions are found to the effect that no conviction can be had or important right taken away on the basis of statements not made under fear of prosecution for perjury, Bridges v. Wixon, 326 U.S. 135 (1945), the fact is that, of the many common law exceptions to the hearsay rule, only that for reported testimony has required the statement to have been made under oath.[3] Nor is it satisfactorily explained why cross-examination cannot be conducted subsequently with success. The decisions contending most vigorously for its inadequacy in fact demonstrate quite thorough exploration of the weaknesses and doubts attending the earlier statement. State v. Saporen, 205 Minn. 358 (1939); Ruhala v. Roby, 379 Mich. 102 (1967); People v. Johnson, 68 Cal. 2d 646 (1968). In respect to demeanor, as Judge Learned Hand observed in *Di Carlo v. United States*, 6 F.2d 364 (2d Cir. 1925), when the jury decides that the truth is not what the witness says now, but what he said before, they are still deciding from what they see and hear in court. The bulk of the case law nevertheless has been against allowing prior statements of witnesses to be used generally as substantive evidence. Most of the writers and Uniform Rule 63(1) have taken the opposite position.

The position taken by the Advisory Committee in formulating this part of the rule is founded upon an unwillingness to countenance the general use of prior prepared statements as substantive evidence, but with a recognition that particular circumstances call for a contrary result. The judgment is one more of experience than of logic. The rule requires in each instance, as a general safeguard, that the declarant actually testify as a witness, and it then enumerates three situations in which the statement is excepted from the category of hearsay. Compare Uniform Rule of Evidence 63(1), which allows any out-of-

---

[3] [As enacted, Rule 801(d)(1)(A) requires that a past inconsistent statement also have been made under oath.—GF]

court statement of a declarant who is present at the trial and available for cross-examination.

Subdivision (d)(1)(A). Prior inconsistent statements traditionally have been admissible to impeach but not as substantive evidence. Under the rule they are substantive evidence. As has been said by the California Law Revision Commission with respect to a similar provision:

> Section 1235 admits inconsistent statements of witnesses because the dangers against which the hearsay rule is designed to protect are largely nonexistent. The declarant is in court and may be examined and cross-examined in regard to his statements and their subject matter. In many cases, the inconsistent statement is more likely to be true than the testimony of the witness at the trial because it was made nearer in time to the matter to which it relates and is less likely to be influenced by the controversy that gave rise to the litigation. The trier of fact has the declarant before it and can observe his demeanor and the nature of his testimony as he denies or tries to explain away the inconsistency. Hence, it is in as good a position to determine the truth or falsity of the prior statement as it is to determine the truth or falsity of the inconsistent testimony given in court.[4] Moreover, Section 1235 will provide a party with desirable protection against the "turncoat" witness who changes his story on the stand and deprives the party calling him of evidence essential to his case.

Comment, CAL. EVID. CODE § 1235; *see also* McCORMICK § 39. The Advisory Committee finds these views more convincing than those expressed in *People v. Johnson*, 68 Cal. 2d 646 (1968). The constitutionality of the Advisory Committee's view was upheld in *California v. Green*, 399 U.S. 149 (1970). Moreover, the requirement that the statement be inconsistent with the testimony given assures a thorough exploration of both versions while the witness is on the stand and bars any general and indiscriminate use of previously prepared statements.

<u>REPORT OF THE HOUSE COMMITTEE ON THE JUDICIARY</u>

Present federal law, except in the Second Circuit, permits the use of prior inconsistent statements of a witness for impeachment only. Rule 801(d)(1) as proposed by the Court would have permitted all such statements to be admissible as substantive evidence, an approach followed by a small but growing number of state

---

[4] [As enacted, Rule 801(d)(1)(A) requires as additional assurances of reliability that the past inconsistent statement have been made under oath and that it have been made at a proceeding or in a deposition—GF.]

jurisdictions and recently held constitutional in *California v. Green*, 399 U.S. 149 (1970). Although there was some support expressed for the Court rule, based largely on the need to counteract the effect of witness intimidation in criminal cases, the Committee decided to adopt a compromise version of the rule similar to the position of the Second Circuit. The rule as amended draws a distinction between types of prior inconsistent statements (other than statements of identification of a person made after perceiving him which are currently admissible, *see* United States v. Anderson, 406 F.2d 719, 720 (4th Cir.), *cert. denied*, 395 U.S. 967 (1969), and allows only those made while the declarant was subject to cross-examination at a trial or hearing or in a deposition, to be admissible for their truth. *Cf.* United States v. De Sisto, 329 F.2d 929 (2d Cir.), *cert. denied*, 377 U.S. 979 (1964); United States v. Cunningham, 446 F.2d 194 (2d Cir. 1971) (restricting the admissibility of prior inconsistent statements as substantive evidence to those made under oath in a formal proceeding, but not requiring that there have been an opportunity for cross-examination). The rationale for the Committee's decision is that (1) unlike in most other situations involving unsworn or oral statements, there can be no dispute as to whether the prior statement was made; and (2) the context of a formal proceeding, an oath, and the opportunity for cross-examination provide firm additional assurances of the reliability of the prior statement.

REPORT OF THE SENATE COMMITTEE ON THE JUDICIARY

Rule 801 defines what is and what is not hearsay for the purpose of admitting a prior statement as substantive evidence. A prior statement of a witness at a trial or hearing which is inconsistent with his testimony is, of course, always admissible for the purpose of impeaching the witness's credibility.

As submitted by the Supreme Court, subdivision (d)(1)(A) made admissible as substantive evidence the prior statement of a witness inconsistent with his present testimony.

The House severely limited the admissibility of prior inconsistent statements by adding a requirement that the prior statement must have been subject to cross-examination, thus precluding even the use of grand jury statements. The requirement that the prior statement must have been subject to cross-examination appears unnecessary since this rule comes into play only when the witness testifies in the present trial. At that time, he is on the stand and can explain an earlier position and be cross-examined as to both.

The requirement that the statement be under oath also appears unnecessary. Notwithstanding the absence of an oath contemporaneous with the statement, the witness, when on the stand, qualifying or denying the prior statement, is under oath. In any event, of all the many recognized exceptions to the hearsay rule, only one (former testimony) requires that the out-of-court statement have been made under oath. With respect to the lack of evidence of the demeanor of the witness at the time of the prior statement, it would be difficult to improve upon Judge Learned Hand's observation that when the jury decides that the truth is not what the witness says now but what he said before, they are still deciding from what they see and hear in court.[5]

The rule as submitted by the Court has positive advantages. The prior statement was made nearer in time to the events, when memory was fresher and intervening influences had not been brought into play. A realistic method is provided for dealing with the turncoat witness who changes his story on the stand.[6]

New Jersey, California, and Utah have adopted a rule similar to this one; and Nevada, New Mexico, and Wisconsin have adopted the identical federal rule.

For all of these reasons, we think the House amendment should be rejected and the rule as submitted by the Supreme Court reinstated.[7]

CONFERENCE REPORT

Rule 801 supplies some basic definitions for the rules of evidence that deal with hearsay. Rule 801(d)(1) defines certain statements as not hearsay. The Senate amendments make two changes in it.

The House bill provides that a statement is not hearsay if the declarant testifies and is subject to cross-examination concerning the statement and if the statement is inconsistent with his testimony and was given under oath subject to cross-examination and subject to the penalty of perjury at a trial or hearing or in a deposition. The Senate

---

[5] Di Carlo v. United States, 6 F.2d 364 (2d Cir. 1925).

[6] *See Comment*, CAL. EVID. CODE § 1235; MCCORMICK, EVIDENCE § 38 (2d ed. 1972).

[7] It would appear that some of the opposition to this rule is based on a concern that a person could be convicted solely upon evidence admissible under this rule. The rule, however, is not addressed to the question of the sufficiency of evidence to send a case to the jury, but merely as to its admissibility. Factual circumstances could well arise where, if this were the sole evidence, dismissal would be appropriate.

amendment drops the requirement that the prior statement be given under oath subject to cross-examination and subject to the penalty of perjury at a trial or hearing or in a deposition.

The Conference adopts the Senate amendment with an amendment, so that the rule now requires that the prior inconsistent statement be given under oath subject to the penalty of perjury at a trial, hearing, or other proceeding, or in a deposition. The rule as adopted covers statements before a grand jury. Prior inconsistent statements may, of course, be used for impeaching the credibility of a witness. When the prior inconsistent statement is one made by a defendant in a criminal case, it is covered by Rule 801(d)(2).

<u>ADVISORY COMMITTEE'S NOTE TO RULE 801(d)(1)(B)</u>

Subdivision (d)(1)(B). Prior consistent statements traditionally have been admissible to rebut charges of recent fabrication or improper influence or motive but not as substantive evidence. Under the rule they are substantive evidence. The prior statement is consistent with the testimony given on the stand, and, if the opposite party wishes to open the door for its admission in evidence, no sound reason is apparent why it should not be received generally.

<u>ADVISORY COMMITTEE'S NOTE TO 2014 AMENDMENT TO RULE 801(d)(1)(B)</u>

Rule 801(d)(1)(B), as originally adopted, provided for substantive use of certain prior consistent statements of a witness subject to cross-examination. As the Advisory Committee noted, "[t]he prior statement is consistent with the testimony given on the stand, and, if the opposite party wishes to open the door for its admission in evidence, no sound reason is apparent why it should not be received generally."

Though the original Rule 801(d)(1)(B) provided for substantive use of certain prior consistent statements, the scope of that rule was limited. The rule covered only those consistent statements that were offered to rebut charges of recent fabrication or improper motive or influence. The rule did not, for example, provide for substantive admissibility of consistent statements that are probative to explain what otherwise appears to be an inconsistency in the witness's testimony. Nor did it cover consistent statements that would be probative to rebut a charge of faulty memory. Thus, the rule left many prior consistent statements potentially admissible only for the limited purpose of rehabilitating a witness's credibility. The original rule also led to some conflict in the cases; some courts distinguished between substantive and rehabilitative use for prior consistent statements, while others appeared to hold that prior consistent statements must be admissible under Rule 801(d)(1)(B) or not at all.

The amendment retains the requirement set forth in *Tome v. United States*, 513 U.S. 150 (1995): that under Rule 801(d)(1)(B), a consistent statement offered to rebut a charge of recent fabrication or improper influence or motive must have been made before the alleged fabrication or improper inference or motive arose. The intent of the amendment is to extend substantive effect to consistent statements that rebut other attacks on a witness — such as the charges of inconsistency or faulty memory.

The amendment does not change the traditional and well-accepted limits on bringing prior consistent statements before the factfinder for credibility purposes. It does not allow impermissible bolstering of a witness. As before, prior consistent statements under the amendment may be brought before the factfinder only if they properly rehabilitate a witness whose credibility has been attacked. As before, to be admissible for rehabilitation, a prior consistent statement must satisfy the strictures of Rule 403. As before, the trial court has ample discretion to exclude prior consistent statements that are cumulative accounts of an event. The amendment does not make any consistent statement admissible that was not admissible previously—the only difference is that prior consistent statements otherwise admissible for rehabilitation are now admissible substantively as well.

EDITOR'S NOTE TO 2014 AMENDMENT TO RULE 801(d)(1)(B)

An earlier version of the 2014 amendment to Rule 801(d)(1)(B), discussed in the casebook at pages 463 to 465, had cast doubt on the continued viability of the rule of *Tome v. United States*, 513 U.S. 150 (1995) (CB page 454). In *Tome* the Supreme Court had held that Rule 801(d)(1)(B) "permits the introduction of a declarant's consistent out-of-court statements to rebut a charge of recent fabrication or improper influence or motive only when those statements were made before the charged recent fabrication or improper influence or motive." *Id.* at 167 (CB page 461). After the casebook went to press late in 2012, the proposed amendment underwent "a slight modification that the advisory committee believes would preserve the *Tome* pre-motive rule as to consistent statements offered to rebut a charge of bad motive, while properly expanding substantive admissibility to statements offered to rehabilitate on other grounds . . . ." (*Report of the Standing Committee* (June 2013), at 30.) This "slight modification" is subtle but consequential. The advisory committee struck the original proposed language of amended Rule 801(d)(1)(B)(ii), which would have made admissible any past consistent statement that "otherwise rehabilitates the declarant's credibility as a witness." In its place the committee substituted the language that now appears in the rule, authorizing admission of those past consistent statements offered "to rehabilitate the declarant's credibility as a witness *when attacked on another ground*" (emphasis added)—that is, a ground other than recent fabrication or improper influence or motive, referenced in Rule 801(d)(1)(B)(i). The *Tome* rule continues to apply to statements offered under Rule 801(d)(1)(B)(i).

[This space is intentionally blank.]

[This space is intentionally blank.]

ADVISORY COMMITTEE'S NOTE TO RULE 801(d)(1)(C)–(d)(2)

Subdivision (d)(1)(C). The admission of evidence of identification finds substantial support, although it falls beyond a doubt in the category of prior out-of-court statements. Illustrative are *People v. Gould*, 54 Cal. 2d 621 (1960); *Judy v. State*, 218 Md. 168 (1958); *State v. Simmons*, 63 Wash. 2d 17 (1963); California Evidence Code § 1238; New Jersey Evidence Rule 63(1)(c) (repealed and replaced by New Jersey Rule of Evidence 803(a)(3) (1993)); New York Code of Criminal Procedure § 393-b (repealed and replaced by New York Criminal Procedure Law § 60.25, .30 (1970)). Further cases are found in 4 WIGMORE § 1130. The basis is the generally unsatisfactory and inconclusive nature of courtroom identifications as compared with those made at an earlier time under less suggestive conditions. The Supreme Court considered the admissibility of evidence of prior identification in *Gilbert v. California*, 388 U.S. 263 (1967). Exclusion of lineup identification was held to be required because the accused did not then have the assistance of counsel. Significantly, the Court carefully refrained from placing its decision on the ground that testimony as to the making of a prior out-of-court identification ("That's the man") violated either the hearsay rule or the right of confrontation because not made under oath, subject to immediate cross-examination, in the presence of the trier. Instead the Court observed:

> There is a split among the states concerning the admissibility of prior extra-judicial identifications, as independent evidence of identity, both by the witness and third parties present at the prior identification. *See* 71 A.L.R.2d 449. It has been held that the prior identification is hearsay, and, when admitted through the testimony of the identifier, is merely a prior consistent statement. The recent trend, however, is to admit the prior identification under the exception that admits as substantive evidence a prior communication by a witness who is available for cross-examination at the trial. *See* 5 A.L.R.2d Later Case Service 1225–28. . . .

388 U.S. at 272 n.3.

Subdivision (d)(2). *Admissions.* Admissions by a party-opponent are excluded from the category of hearsay on the theory that their admissibility in evidence is the result of the adversary system rather than satisfaction of the conditions of the hearsay rule. Strahorn, *A Reconsideration of the Hearsay Rule and Admissions*, 85 U. PA. L. REV. 484, 564 (1937); MORGAN, BASIC PROBLEMS OF EVIDENCE 265 (1962); 4 WIGMORE § 1048. No guarantee of trustworthiness is required in the case of an admission. The freedom which admissions have enjoyed from technical demands of searching for an assurance of trustworthiness in some against-interest circumstance, and from the restrictive influences of the opinion rule and the rule requiring firsthand knowledge, when taken with the apparently prevalent satisfaction with the results, calls for generous treatment of this avenue to admissibility.

The rule specifies five categories of statements for which the responsibility of a party is considered sufficient to justify reception in evidence against him:

(A) A party's own statement is the classic example of an admission. If he has a representative capacity and the statement is offered against him in that capacity, no inquiry whether he was acting in the representative capacity in making the statement is required; the statement need only be relevant to representative affairs. To the same effect is California Evidence Code § 1220. *Cf.* UNIF. R. EVID. 63(7) (requiring a statement to be made in a representative capacity to be admissible against a party in a representative capacity).

(B) Under established principles an admission may be made by adopting or acquiescing in the statement of another. While knowledge of contents would ordinarily be essential, this is not inevitably so: "X is a reliable person and knows what he is talking about." *See* McCORMICK § 246, at 527 n.15. Adoption or acquiescence may be manifested in any appropriate manner. When silence is relied upon, the theory is that the person would, under the circumstances, protest the statement made in his presence, if untrue. The decision in each case calls for an evaluation in terms of probable human behavior. In civil cases, the results have generally been satisfactory. In criminal cases, however, troublesome questions have been raised by decisions holding that failure to deny is an admission: the inference is a fairly weak one, to begin with; silence may be motivated by advice of counsel or realization that "anything you say may be used against you"; unusual opportunity is afforded to manufacture evidence; and encroachment upon the privilege against self-incrimination seems inescapably to be involved. However, recent decisions of the Supreme Court relating to custodial interrogation and the right to counsel appear to resolve these difficulties. Hence the rule contains no special provisions concerning failure to deny in criminal cases.

(C) No authority is required for the general proposition that a statement authorized by a party to be made should have the status of an admission by the party. However, the question arises whether only statements to third persons should be so regarded, to the exclusion of statements by the agent to the principal. The rule is phrased broadly so as to encompass both. While it may be argued that the agent authorized to make statements to his principal does not speak for him, MORGAN, BASIC PROBLEMS OF EVIDENCE 273 (1962), communication to an outsider has not generally been thought to be an essential characteristic of an admission. Thus a party's books or records are usable against him, without regard to any intent to disclose to third persons. 5 WIGMORE § 1557; *see also* McCORMICK § 78, at 159–61; *accord* N.J. EVID. R. 63(8)(a) (repealed and replaced by N.J. R. EVID. 803(b)(2), (3) (1993)). Compare Uniform Rule of Evidence 63(8)(a) and California Evidence Code § 1222, which limit status as an admission in this regard to statements authorized by the party to be made "for" him, which is perhaps an ambiguous limitation to statements to third persons. Falknor, *Vicarious Admissions and the Uniform Rules*, 14 VAND. L. REV. 855, 860–61 (1961).

(D) The tradition has been to test the admissibility of statements by agents, as admissions, by applying the usual test of agency. Was the admission made by the agent acting in the scope of his employment? Since few principals employ agents for the purpose of making damaging statements, the usual result was exclusion of the statement. Dissatisfaction with this loss of valuable and helpful evidence has been increasing. A substantial trend favors admitting statements related to a matter within the scope of the agency or employment. Grayson v. Williams, 256 F.2d 61 (10th Cir. 1958); Koninklijke Luchtvaart Maatschappij N.V. KLM Royal Dutch Airlines v. Tuller, 292 F.2d 775, 784 (D.C. Cir. 1961); Martin v. Savage Truck Line, Inc., 121 F. Supp. 417 (D.D.C. 1954), and numerous state court decisions collected in 4 WIGMORE 66–73 (Supp. 1964), with comments by the editor that the statements should have been excluded as not within scope of agency. For the traditional view see *Northern Oil Co. v. Socony Mobil Oil Co.*, 347 F.2d 81, 85 (2d Cir. 1965) and cases cited therein. Similar provisions are found in Uniform Rule 63(9)(a), Kansas Statutes Annotated § 60-460(i)(1), and New Jersey Evidence Rule 63(9)(a) (repealed and replaced by New Jersey Rule of Evidence 803(b)(4) (1993)).

(E) The limitation upon the admissibility of statements of coconspirators to those made "during the course and in furtherance of the conspiracy" is in the accepted pattern. While the broadened view of agency taken in item [(D)] might suggest wider admissibility of statements of coconspirators, the agency theory of conspiracy is at best a fiction and ought not to serve as a basis for admissibility beyond that already established. *See* Levie, *Hearsay and Conspiracy*, 52 MICH. L. REV. 1159 (1954); Comment, 25 U. CHI. L. REV. 530 (1958). The rule is consistent with the position of the Supreme Court in denying admissibility to statements made after the objectives of the conspiracy have either failed or been achieved. Krulewitch v. United States, 336 U.S. 440 (1949); Wong Sun v. United States, 371 U.S. 471, 490 (1963). For similarly limited provisions see California Evidence Code § 1223 and New Jersey Evidence Rule 63(9)(b) (repealed and replaced by N.J. R. EVID. 803(b)(5) (1993)). *Cf.* UNIF. R. EVID. 63(9)(b).

REPORT OF THE SENATE COMMITTEE ON THE JUDICIARY

The House approved the long-accepted rule that "a statement by a coconspirator of a party during the course and in furtherance of the conspiracy" is not hearsay as it was submitted by the Supreme Court. While the rule refers to a coconspirator, it is this Committee's understanding that the rule is meant to carry forward the universally accepted doctrine that a joint venturer is considered as a coconspirator for the purposes of this rule even though no conspiracy has been charged. United States v. Rinaldi, 393 F.2d 97, 99 (2d Cir.), *cert. denied*, 393 U.S. 913 (1968); United States v. Spencer, 415 F.2d 1301, 1304 (7th Cir. 1969).

Rule 801(d)(2) has been amended in order to respond to three issues raised by *Bourjaily v. United States*, 483 U.S. 171 (1987). First, the amendment codifies the holding in *Bourjaily* by stating expressly that a court shall consider the contents of a coconspirator's statement in determining "the existence of the conspiracy and the participation therein of the declarant and the party against whom the statement is offered." According to *Bourjaily*, Rule 104(a) requires these preliminary questions to be established by a preponderance of the evidence.

Second, the amendment resolves an issue on which the Court had reserved decision. It provides that the contents of the declarant's statement do not alone suffice to establish a conspiracy in which the declarant and the defendant participated. The court must consider in addition the circumstances surrounding the statement, such as the identity of the speaker, the context in which the statement was made, or evidence corroborating the contents of the statement in making its determination as to each preliminary question. This amendment is in accordance with existing practice. Every court of appeals that has resolved this issue requires some evidence in addition to the contents of the statement. *See, e.g.*, United States v. Beckham, 968 F.2d 47, 51 (D.C. Cir. 1992); United States v. Sepulveda, 15 F.3d 1161, 1181–82 (1st Cir. 1993), *cert. denied*, 512 U.S. 1223 (1994); United States v. Daly, 842 F.2d 1380, 1386 (2d Cir.), *cert. denied*, 488 U.S. 821 (1988); United States v. Clark, 18 F.3d 1337, 1341–42 (6th Cir.), *cert. denied*, 513 U.S. 852 (1994); United States v. Zambrana, 841 F.2d 1320, 1344–45 (7th Cir. 1988); United States v. Silverman, 861 F.2d 571, 577 (9th Cir. 1988); United States v. Gordon, 844 F.2d 1397, 1402 (9th Cir. 1988); United States v. Hernandez, 829 F.2d 988, 993 (10th Cir. 1987), *cert. denied*, 485 U.S. 1013 (1988); United States v. Byrom, 910 F.2d 725, 736 (11th Cir. 1990).

Third, the amendment extends the reasoning of *Bourjaily* to statements offered under subdivisions (C) and (D) of Rule 801(d)(2). In *Bourjaily*, the Court rejected treating foundational facts pursuant to the law of agency in favor of an evidentiary approach governed by Rule 104(a). The Advisory Committee believes it appropriate to treat analogously preliminary questions relating to the declarant's authority under subdivision (C), and the agency or employment relationship and scope thereof under subdivision (D).

Statements falling under the hearsay exclusion provided by Rule 801(d)(2) are no longer referred to as "admissions" in the title to the subdivision. The term "admissions" is confusing because not all statements covered by the exclusion are admissions in the colloquial sense—a statement can be within the exclusion even if it "admitted" nothing and was not against the party's interest when made. The term "admissions" also raises confusion in comparison with the Rule 804(b)(3) exception for declarations against interest. No change in application of the exclusion is intended.

Rule 802.   THE RULE AGAINST HEARSAY

Hearsay is not admissible unless any of the following provides otherwise:

- a federal statute;

- these rules; or

- other rules prescribed by the Supreme Court.

(Enacted Jan. 2, 1975; as restyled Apr. 26, 2011, eff. Dec. 1, 2011)

NOTE BY FEDERAL JUDICIAL CENTER

The rule enacted by the Congress is the rule prescribed by the Supreme Court, amended by substituting "prescribed" in place of "adopted" and by inserting the phrase "pursuant to statutory authority."

ADVISORY COMMITTEE'S NOTE

The provision excepting from the operation of the rule hearsay which is made admissible by other rules adopted by the Supreme Court or by Act of Congress continues the admissibility thereunder of hearsay which would not qualify under these Evidence Rules. The following examples illustrate the working of the exception:

Federal Rules of Civil Procedure

Rule [4(*l*)(1)]:   proof of service by affidavit.

Rule 32:   admissibility of depositions.

Rule [43(c)]:   affidavits when motion based on facts not appearing of record.

Rule 56:   affidavits in summary judgment proceedings.

Rule 65(b):   showing by affidavit for temporary restraining order.

Federal Rules of Criminal Procedure

Rule 4(a):   affidavits to show grounds for issuing warrants.

Rule [47]:   affidavits to determine issues of fact in connection with motions.

Acts of Congress

10 U.S.C. § 7730:   affidavits of unavailable witnesses in actions for damages caused by vessel in naval service, or towage or salvage of same, when taking of testimony or bringing of action delayed or stayed on security grounds.

29 U.S.C. § 161(4):   affidavit as proof of service in NLRB proceedings.

38 U.S.C. § [8506]:   affidavit as proof of posting notice of sale of unclaimed property by Veterans Administration.

Rule 803.   EXCEPTIONS TO THE RULE AGAINST HEARSAY— REGARDLESS OF WHETHER THE DECLARANT IS AVAILABLE AS A WITNESS

The following are not excluded by the rule against hearsay, regardless of whether the declarant is available as a witness:

(1) *Present Sense Impression.* A statement describing or explaining an event or condition, made while or immediately after the declarant perceived it.

(2) *Excited Utterance.* A statement relating to a startling event or condition, made while the declarant was under the stress of excitement that it caused.

(3) *Then-Existing Mental, Emotional, or Physical Condition.* A statement of the declarant's then-existing state of mind (such as motive, intent, or plan) or emotional, sensory, or physical condition (such as mental feeling, pain, or bodily health), but not including a statement of memory or belief to prove the fact remembered or believed unless it relates to the validity or terms of the declarant's will.

(4) *Statement Made for Medical Diagnosis or Treatment.* A statement that:

    (A) is made for—and is reasonably pertinent to—medical diagnosis or treatment; and

    (B) describes medical history; past or present symptoms or sensations; their inception; or their general cause.

(5) *Recorded Recollection.* A record that:

    (A) is on a matter the witness once knew about but now cannot recall well enough to testify fully and accurately;

    (B) was made or adopted by the witness when the matter was fresh in the witness's memory; and

    (C) accurately reflects the witness's knowledge.

If admitted, the record may be read into evidence but may be received as an exhibit only if offered by an adverse party.

(6) *Records of a Regularly Conducted Activity.* A record of an act, event, condition, opinion, or diagnosis if:

(A) the record was made at or near the time by—or from information transmitted by—someone with knowledge;

(B) the record was kept in the course of a regularly conducted activity of a business, organization, occupation, or calling, whether or not for profit;

(C) making the record was a regular practice of that activity;

(D) all these conditions are shown by the testimony of the custodian or another qualified witness, or by a certification that complies with Rule 902(11) or (12) or with a statute permitting certification; and

(E) the opponent does not show that the source of information or the method or circumstances of preparation indicate a lack of trustworthiness.

(7) *Absence of a Record of a Regularly Conducted Activity.* Evidence that a matter is not included in a record described in paragraph (6) if:

(A) the evidence is admitted to prove that the matter did not occur or exist;

(B) a record was regularly kept for a matter of that kind; and

(C) the opponent does not show that the possible source of the information or other circumstances indicate a lack of trustworthiness.

(8) *Public Records.* A record or statement of a public office if:

    (A) it sets out:

        (i) the office's activities;

        (ii) a matter observed while under a legal duty to report, but not including, in a criminal case, a matter observed by law-enforcement personnel; or

        (iii) in a civil case or against the government in a criminal case, factual findings from a legally authorized investigation; and

    (B) the opponent does not show that the source of information or other circumstances indicate a lack of trustworthiness.

(9) *Public Records of Vital Statistics.* A record of a birth, death, or marriage, if reported to a public office in accordance with a legal duty.

(10) *Absence of a Public Record.* Testimony—or a certification under Rule 902—that a diligent search failed to disclose a public record or statement if:

    (A) the testimony or certification is admitted to prove that

        (i) the record or statement does not exist; or

        (ii) a matter did not occur or exist, if a public office regularly kept a record or statement for a matter of that kind; and

    (B) in a criminal case, a prosecutor who intends to offer a certification provides written notice of that intent at least 14 days before trial, and the defendant does not object in writing within 7 days of receiving the notice— unless the court sets a different time for the notice or objection.

(11) *Records of Religious Organizations Concerning Personal or Family History.* A statement of birth, legitimacy, ancestry, marriage, divorce, death, relationship by blood or marriage, or similar facts of personal or family history, contained in a regularly kept record of a religious organization.

(12) *Certificates of Marriage, Baptism, and Similar Ceremonies.* A statement of fact contained in a certificate:

> **(A)** made by a person who is authorized by a religious organization or by law to perform the act certified;

> **(B)** attesting that the person performed a marriage or similar ceremony or administered a sacrament; and

> **(C)** purporting to have been issued at the time of the act or within a reasonable time after it.

(13) *Family Records.* A statement of fact about personal or family history contained in a family record, such as a Bible, genealogy, chart, engraving on a ring, inscription on a portrait, or engraving on an urn or burial marker.

(14) *Records of Documents That Affect an Interest in Property.* The record of a document that purports to establish or affect an interest in property if:

> **(A)** the record is admitted to prove the content of the original recorded document, along with its signing and its delivery by each person who purports to have signed it;

> **(B)** the record is kept in a public office; and

> **(C)** a statute authorizes recording documents of that kind in that office.

(15) *Statements in Documents That Affect an Interest in Property.* A statement contained in a document that purports to establish or affect an interest in property if the matter stated was relevant to the document's purpose—unless later dealings with the property are inconsistent with the truth of the statement or the purport of the document.

(16) *Statements in Ancient Documents.* A statement in a document that was prepared before January 1, 1998, and whose authenticity is established.

(17) *Market Reports and Similar Commercial Publications.* Market quotations, lists, directories, or other compilations that are generally relied on by the public or by persons in particular occupations.

(18) *Statements in Learned Treatises, Periodicals, or Pamphlets.* A statement contained in a treatise, periodical, or pamphlet if:

> **(A)** the statement is called to the attention of an expert witness on cross-examination or relied on by the expert on direct examination; and

> **(B)** the publication is established as a reliable authority by the expert's admission or testimony, by another expert's testimony, or by judicial notice.

If admitted, the statement may be read into evidence but not received as an exhibit.

(19) *Reputation Concerning Personal or Family History.* A reputation among a person's family by blood, adoption, or marriage—or among a person's associates or in the community—concerning the person's birth, adoption, legitimacy, ancestry, marriage, divorce, death, relationship by blood, adoption, or marriage, or similar facts of personal or family history.

(20) *Reputation Concerning Boundaries or General History.* A reputation in a community—arising before the controversy—concerning boundaries of land in the community or customs that affect the land, or concerning general historical events important to that community, state, or nation.

(21) *Reputation Concerning Character.* A reputation among a person's associates or in the community concerning the person's character.

(22) *Judgment of a Previous Conviction.* Evidence of a final judgment of conviction if:

(A) the judgment was entered after a trial or guilty plea, but not a nolo contendere plea;

(B) the conviction was for a crime punishable by death or by imprisonment for more than a year;

(C) the evidence is admitted to prove any fact essential to the judgment; and

(D) when offered by the prosecutor in a criminal case for a purpose other than impeachment, the judgment was against the defendant.

The pendency of an appeal may be shown but does not affect admissibility.

(23) *Judgments Involving Personal, Family, or General History, or a Boundary.* A judgment that is admitted to prove a matter of personal, family, or general history, or boundaries, if the matter:

(A) was essential to the judgment; and

(B) could be proved by evidence of reputation.

(24) [*Other Exceptions.*] [Transferred to Rule 807.]

(Enacted Jan. 2, 1975; as amended Dec. 12, 1975; Mar. 2, 1987, eff. Oct. 1, 1987; April 11, 1997, eff. Dec. 1, 1997; Apr. 17, 2000, eff. Dec. 1, 2000; as restyled Apr. 26, 2011, eff. Dec. 1, 2011; as amended Dec. 1, 2014; Dec. 1, 2017.)

<u>NOTE BY FEDERAL JUDICIAL CENTER</u>[8]

The rule enacted by the Congress retains the twenty-four exceptions set forth in the rule prescribed by the Supreme Court. Three of the exceptions, numbered (6), (8), and (24) have been amended in respects that may fairly be described as substantial.

---

[8] [Few of the wording changes detailed in this note by the Federal Judicial Center survived unscathed the 2011 restyling of the Federal Rules.—GF]

Others, numbered (5), (7), (14), and (16), have been amended in lesser ways. The remaining seventeen are unchanged. The amendments are, in numerical order, as follows.

Exception (5) as prescribed by the Supreme Court was amended by inserting after "made" the phrase "or adopted by the witness."

Exception (6) as prescribed by the Supreme Court was amended by substituting the phrase, "if kept in the course of a regularly conducted business activity, and if it was the regular practice of that business activity to make the memorandum, report, record, or data compilation, all," in place of "all in the course of a regularly conducted activity"; by substituting "source" in place of "sources"; by substituting the phrase, "the method or circumstances of preparation," in place of "other circumstances"; and by adding the second sentence.

Exception (7) as prescribed by the Supreme Court was amended by substituting the phrase, "kept in accordance with the provisions of paragraph (6)," in place of "of a regularly conducted activity." The exception prescribed by the Supreme Court included a comma after "memoranda," while the congressional enactment does not.

Exception (8) as prescribed by the Supreme Court was amended by inserting in item [(A)(ii)] after "law" the phrase, "as to which matters there was a duty to report, excluding, however, in criminal cases matters observed by police officers and other law enforcement personnel," and by substituting in item [(A)(iii)] the phrase "civil actions and proceedings," in place of "civil cases."

Exception (14) as prescribed by the Supreme Court was amended by substituting "authorizes" in place of "authorized."

Exception (16) as prescribed by the Supreme Court was amended by substituting the phrase, "the authenticity of which," in place of "whose authenticity."

Exception (24) as prescribed by the Supreme Court was amended by substituting "equivalent" in place of "comparable," and adding all that appears after "trustworthiness" in the exception as enacted by the Congress.

ADVISORY COMMITTEE'S NOTE TO RULE 803(1)–(3)

The exceptions are phrased in terms of nonapplication of the hearsay rule, rather than in positive terms of admissibility, in order to repel any implication that other possible grounds for exclusion are eliminated from consideration.

The present rule proceeds upon the theory that under appropriate circumstances a hearsay statement may possess circumstantial guarantees of trustworthiness sufficient to justify nonproduction of the declarant in person at the trial even though he may be available. The theory finds vast support in the many exceptions to the hearsay rule developed by the common law in which unavailability of the declarant is not a relevant factor. The present rule is a synthesis of them, with revision where modern developments and conditions are believed to make that course appropriate.

In a hearsay situation, the declarant is, of course, a witness, and neither this rule nor Rule 804 dispenses with the requirement of first-hand knowledge. It may appear from his statement or be inferable from circumstances. *See* Rule 602.

Exceptions (1) and (2). In considerable measure these two examples overlap, though based on somewhat different theories. The most significant practical difference will lie in the time lapse allowable between event and statement.

The underlying theory of exception (1) is that substantial contemporaneity of event and statement negative the likelihood of deliberate or conscious misrepresentation. Moreover, if the witness is the declarant, he may be examined on the statement. If the witness is not the declarant, he may be examined as to the circumstances as an aid in evaluating the statement. MORGAN, BASIC PROBLEMS OF EVIDENCE 340–41 (1962).

The theory of exception (2) is simply that circumstances may produce a condition of excitement which temporarily stills the capacity of reflection and produces utterances free of conscious fabrication. 6 WIGMORE § 1747, at 135. Spontaneity is the key factor in each instance, though arrived at by somewhat different routes. Both are needed in order to avoid needless niggling.

While the theory of exception (2) has been criticized on the ground that excitement impairs accuracy of observation as well as eliminating conscious fabrication, Hutchins & Slesinger, *Some Observations on the Law of Evidence: Spontaneous Exclamations*, 28 COLUM. L. REV. 432 (1928), it finds support in cases without number. *See* cases in 6 WIGMORE § 1750; Annotation, 53 A.L.R.2d 1245 (statements as to cause of or responsibility for motor vehicle accident); Annotation, 4 A.L.R.3d 149 (accusatory statements by homicide victims). Since unexciting events are less likely to evoke comment, decisions involving exception (1) are far less numerous. Illustrative are *Tampa Electric Co. v. Getrost*, 151 Fla. 558 (1942);

Houston Oxygen Co. v. Davis, 139 Tex. 1 (1942); and cases cited in McCORMICK § 273, at 585 n.4.

With respect to the *time element*, exception (1) recognizes that in many, if not most, instances precise contemporaneity is not possible, and hence a slight lapse is allowable. Under exception (2) the standard of measurement is the duration of the state of excitement. "How long can excitement prevail? Obviously there are no pat answers and the character of the transaction or event will largely determine the significance of the time factor." Slough, *Spontaneous Statements and State of Mind*, 46 IOWA L. REV. 224, 243 (1961); McCORMICK § 272, at 580.

Participation by the declarant is not required: a non-participant may be moved to describe what he perceives, and one may be startled by an event in which he is not an actor. Slough, *supra*; McCORMICK, *supra*; 6 WIGMORE § 1755; Annotation, 78 A.L.R.2d 300.

Whether *proof of the startling event* may be made by the statement itself is largely an academic question, since in most cases there is present at least circumstantial evidence that something of a startling nature must have occurred. For cases in which the evidence consists of the condition of the declarant (injuries, state of shock), see *Travellers' Insurance Co. v. Mosley*, 75 U.S. (8 Wall.) 397 (1869); *Wheeler v. United States*, 211 F.2d 19 (D.C. Cir. 1953), *cert. denied*, 347 U.S. 1019 (1954); *Wetherbee v. Safety Casualty Co.*, 219 F.2d 274 (5th Cir. 1955); *Lampe v. United States*, 229 F.2d 43 (D.C. Cir. 1956). Nevertheless, on occasion the only evidence may be the content of the statement itself, and rulings that it may be sufficient are described as "increasing," Slough, *supra*, at 246, and as the "prevailing practice," McCORMICK § 272, at 579. Illustrative are *Armour & Co. v. Industrial Commission*, 78 Colo. 569 (1926); *Young v. Stewart*, 191 N.C. 297 (1926). Moreover, under Rule 104(a) the judge is not limited by the hearsay rule in passing upon preliminary questions of fact.

Proof of declarant's perception by his statement presents similar considerations when declarant is identified. People v. Poland, 22 Ill.2d 175 (1961). However, when declarant is an unidentified bystander, the cases indicate hesitancy in upholding the statement alone as sufficient, Garrett v. Howden, 73 N.M. 307 (1963); Beck v. Dye, 200 Wash. 1 (1939), a result which would under appropriate circumstances be consistent with the rule.

Permissible *subject matter* of the statement is limited under exception (1) to description or explanation of the event or condition, the assumption being that spontaneity, in the absence of a startling event, may extend no farther. In exception (2), however, the statement need only "relate" to the startling event or condition, thus affording a broader scope of subject matter coverage. 6 WIGMORE §§ 1750, 1754; *see* Sanitary Grocery Co. v. Snead, 90 F.2d 374 (D.C. Cir. 1937) (slip-and-fall case sustaining admissibility of clerk's statement, "That has been on the floor for a couple of hours"); Murphy Auto Parts Co. v. Ball, 249 F.2d 508 (D.C. Cir. 1957) (upholding admission, on issue of driver's agency, of his statement that he had to call on a customer and was in a hurry to get home); Quick, *Hearsay, Excitement, Necessity and the Uniform Rules: A Reappraisal of Rule 63(4)*, 6 WAYNE L. REV. 204, 206–09 (1960).

Similar provisions are found in Uniform Rule 63(4)(a) and (b); California Evidence Code § 1240 (as to exception (2) only); Kansas Statutes Annotated § 60-460(d)(1) and (2); New Jersey Evidence Rule 63(4) (repealed and replaced by New Jersey Rule of Evidence 803(c)(1)–(2) (1993)).

Exception (3) is essentially a specialized application of exception (1), presented separately to enhance its usefulness and accessibility. *See* MCCORMICK §§ 265, 268.

The exclusion of "statements of memory or belief to prove the fact remembered or believed" is necessary to avoid the virtual destruction of the hearsay rule which would otherwise result from allowing state of mind, provable by a hearsay statement, to serve as the basis for an inference of the happening of the event which produced the state of mind. Shepard v. United States, 290 U.S. 96 (1933); Maguire, *The Hillmon Case—Thirty-Three Years After*, 38 HARV. L. REV. 709, 719–31 (1925); Hinton, *States of Mind and the Hearsay Rule*, 1 U. CHI. L. REV. 394, 421–23 (1934). The rule of *Mutual Life Insurance Co. v. Hillmon*, 145 U.S. 285 (1892), allowing evidence of intention as tending to prove the doing of the act intended, is, of course, left undisturbed.

The carving out, from the exclusion mentioned in the preceding paragraph, of declarations relating to the execution, revocation, identification, or terms of declarant's will represents an ad hoc judgment which finds ample reinforcement in the decisions, resting on practical grounds of necessity and expediency rather than logic. MCCORMICK § 271, at 577–78; Annotation, 34 A.L.R.2d 588, 62 A.L.R.2d 855. A similar recognition of the need for and practical value of this kind of evidence is found in California Evidence Code § 1260.

REPORT OF THE HOUSE COMMITTEE ON THE JUDICIARY

Rule 803(3) was approved in the form submitted by the Court to Congress. However, the Committee intends that the rule be construed to limit the doctrine of *Mutual Life Insurance Co. v. Hillmon*, 145 U.S. 285, 295–300 (1892), so as to render statements of intent by a declarant admissible only to prove his future conduct, not the future conduct of another person.

ADVISORY COMMITTEE'S NOTE TO RULE 803(4)

Exception (4). Even those few jurisdictions which have shied away from generally admitting statements of present condition have allowed them if made to a physician for purposes of diagnosis and treatment in view of the patient's strong motivation to be truthful. MCCORMICK § 266, at 563. The same guarantee of trustworthiness extends to statements of past conditions and medical history, made for purposes of diagnosis or treatment. It also extends to statements as to causation, reasonably pertinent to the same purposes, in accord with the current trend. Shell Oil Co. v. Indus. Comm'n, 2 Ill.2d 590 (1954); MCCORMICK § 266, at 564; N.J. EVID. R. 63(12)(c) (repealed and replaced by N.J. R. EVID. 803(c)(4) (1993)). Statements as to fault would not ordinarily qualify under this latter language. Thus a patient's statement that he was struck by an automobile would qualify but not his statement that the car was driven through a red light. Under the exception the statement need not have been made to a physician. Statements to hospital attendants, ambulance drivers, or even members of the family might be included.

Conventional doctrine has excluded from the hearsay exception, as not within its guarantee of truthfulness, statements to a physician consulted only for the purpose of enabling him to testify. While these statements were not admissible as substantive evidence, the expert was allowed to state the basis of his opinion, including statements of this kind. The distinction thus called for was one most unlikely to be made by juries. The rule accordingly rejects the limitation. This position is consistent with the provision of Rule 703 that the facts on which expert testimony is based need not be admissible in evidence if of a kind ordinarily relied upon by experts in the field.

REPORT OF THE HOUSE COMMITTEE ON THE JUDICIARY

After giving particular attention to the question of physical examination made solely to enable a physician to testify, the Committee approved Rule 803(4) as submitted to Congress, with the understanding that it is not intended in any way to adversely affect present privilege rules or those subsequently adopted.

Report of the Senate Committee on the Judiciary

The House approved this rule as it was submitted by the Supreme Court "with the understanding that it is not intended in any way to adversely affect present privilege rules." We also approve this rule, and we would point out with respect to the question of its relation to privileges, it must be read in conjunction with Rule 35 of the Federal Rules of Civil Procedure which provides that whenever the physical or mental condition of a party (plaintiff or defendant) is in controversy, the court may require him to submit to an examination by a physician. It is these examinations which will normally be admitted under this exception.

Advisory Committee's Note to Rule 803(5)

Exception (5). A hearsay exception for recorded recollection is generally recognized and has been described as having "long been favored by the federal and practically all the state courts that have had occasion to decide the question." United States v. Kelly, 349 F.2d 720, 770 (2d Cir. 1965) (citing numerous cases and sustaining the exception against a claimed denial of the right of confrontation). Many additional cases are cited in Annotation, 82 A.L.R.2d 473, 520. The guarantee of trustworthiness is found in the reliability inherent in a record made while events were still fresh in mind and accurately reflecting them. Owens v. State, 67 Md. 307, 316 (1887).

The principal controversy attending the exception has centered, not upon the propriety of the exception itself, but upon the question whether a preliminary requirement of impaired memory on the part of the witness should be imposed. The authorities are divided. If regard be had only to the accuracy of the evidence, admittedly impairment of the memory of the witness adds nothing to it and should not be required. McCormick § 277, at 593; 3 Wigmore § 738, at 76; Jordan v. People, 151 Colo. 133 (1962), *cert. denied*, 373 U.S. 944 (1963); Hall v. State, 223 Md. 158 (1960); State v. Bindhammer, 44 N.J. 372 (1965). Nevertheless, the absence of the requirement, it is believed, would encourage the use of statements carefully prepared for purposes of litigation under the supervision of attorneys, investigators, or claim adjusters. Hence the example includes a requirement that the witness not have "sufficient recollection to enable him to testify fully and accurately." To the same effect are California Evidence Code § 1237 and New Jersey Evidence Rule 63(1)(b) (repealed and replaced by New Jersey Rule of Evidence 803(c)(5) (1993)), and this has been the position of the federal courts. Vicksburg & Meridian R.R. Co. v. O'Brien, 119 U.S.

99 (1886); Ahern v. Webb, 268 F.2d 45 (10th Cir. 1959); *see also* NLRB v. Hudson Pulp & Paper Corp., 273 F.2d 660, 665 (5th Cir. 1960); NLRB v. Fed. Dairy Co., 297 F.2d 487 (1st Cir. 1962). *But cf.* United States v. Adams, 385 F.2d 548 (2d Cir. 1967).

No attempt is made in the exception to spell out the method of establishing the initial knowledge or the contemporaneity and accuracy of the record, leaving them to be dealt with as the circumstances of the particular case might indicate. Multiple person involvement in the process of observing and recording, as in *Rathbun v. Brancatella*, 93 N.J.L. 222 (1919), is entirely consistent with the exception.

Locating the exception at this place in the scheme of the rules is a matter of choice. There were two other possibilities. The first was to regard the statement as one of the group of prior statements of a testifying witness which are excluded entirely from the category of hearsay by Rule 801(d)(1). That category, however, requires that declarant be "subject to cross-examination," as to which the impaired memory aspect of the exception raises doubts. The other possibility was to include the exception among those covered by Rule 804. Since unavailability is required by that rule and lack of memory is listed as a species of unavailability by the definition of the term in Rule 804(a)(3), that treatment at first impression would seem appropriate. The fact is, however, that the unavailability requirement of the exception is of a limited and peculiar nature. Accordingly, the exception is located at this point rather than in the context of a rule where unavailability is conceived of more broadly.

REPORT OF THE HOUSE COMMITTEE ON THE JUDICIARY

Rule 803(5) as submitted by the Court permitted the reading into evidence of a memorandum or record concerning a matter about which a witness once had knowledge but now has insufficient recollection to enable him to testify accurately and fully, "shown to have been made when the matter was fresh in his memory and to reflect that knowledge correctly." The Committee amended this rule to add the words "or adopted by the witness" after the phrase "shown to have been made," a treatment consistent with the definition of "statement" in the Jencks Act, 18 U.S.C. § 3500. Moreover, it is the Committee's understanding that a memorandum or report, although barred under this rule, would nonetheless be admissible if it came within another hearsay exception. This last stated principle is deemed applicable to all the hearsay rules.

FEDERAL RULES OF EVIDENCE

224

Rule 803(5) as submitted by the Court permitted the reading into evidence of a memorandum or record concerning a matter about which a witness once had knowledge but now has insufficient recollection to enable him to testify accurately or fully, "shown to have been made when the matter was fresh in his memory and to reflect that knowledge correctly." The House amended the rule to add the words "or adopted by the witness" after the phrase "shown to have been made," language parallel to the Jencks Act.

The Committee accepts the House amendment with the understanding and belief that it was not intended to narrow the scope of applicability of the rule. In fact, we understand it to clarify the rule's applicability to a memorandum adopted by the witness as well as one made by him. While the rule as submitted by the Court was silent on the question of who made the memorandum, we view the House amendment as a helpful clarification, noting, however, that the Advisory Committee's Note to this rule suggests that the important thing is the accuracy of the memorandum rather than who made it.

The Committee does not view the House amendment as precluding admissibility in situations in which multiple participants were involved.

When the verifying witness has not prepared the report, but merely examined it and found it accurate, he has adopted the report, and it is therefore admissible. The rule should also be interpreted to cover other situations involving multiple participants, e.g., employer dictating to secretary, secretary making memorandum at direction of employer, or information being passed along a chain of persons, as in *Curtis v. Bradley*.[9]

The Committee also accepts the understanding of the House that a memorandum or report, although barred under this rule, would nonetheless be admissible if it came within another hearsay exception. We consider this principle to be applicable to all the hearsay rules.

<u>ADVISORY COMMITTEE'S NOTE TO RULE 803(6)</u>

Exception (6) represents an area which has received much attention from those seeking to improve the law of evidence. The

---

[9] 65 Conn. 99 (1894); *see also* Rathbun v. Brancatella, 93 N.J.L. 222 (1919); MCCORMICK ON EVIDENCE § 303 (2d ed. 1972).

Commonwealth Fund Act was the result of a study completed in 1927 by a distinguished committee under the chairmanship of Professor Morgan. MORGAN ET AL., THE LAW OF EVIDENCE: SOME PROPOSALS FOR ITS REFORM 63 (1927). With changes too minor to mention, it was adopted by Congress in 1936 as the rule for federal courts. 28 U.S.C. § 1732. A number of states took similar action. The Commissioners on Uniform State Laws in 1936 promulgated the Uniform Business Records as Evidence Act, 9A U.L.A. 506, which has acquired a substantial following in the states. Model Code Rule 514 and Uniform Rule 63(13) also deal with the subject. Difference of varying degrees of importance exist among these various treatments.

These reform efforts were largely within the context of business and commercial records, as the kind usually encountered, and concentrated considerable attention upon relaxing the requirement of producing as witnesses, or accounting for the nonproduction of, all participants in the process of gathering, transmitting, and recording information which the common law had evolved as a burdensome and crippling aspect of using records of this type. In their areas of primary emphasis on witnesses to be called and the general admissibility of ordinary business and commercial records, the Commonwealth Fund Act and the Uniform Act appear to have worked well. The exception seeks to preserve their advantages.

On the subject of what witnesses must be called, the Commonwealth Fund Act eliminated the common law requirement of calling or accounting for all participants by failing to mention it. United States v. Mortimer, 118 F.2d 266 (2d Cir. 1941); La Porte v. United States, 300 F.2d 878 (9th Cir. 1962); MCCORMICK § 290, at 608. Model Code Rule 514 and Uniform Rule 63(13) did likewise. The Uniform Act, however, abolished the common law requirement in express terms, providing that the requisite foundation testimony might be furnished by "the custodian or other qualified witness." UNIFORM BUSINESS RECORDS AS EVIDENCE ACT § 2; 9A U.L.A. 506. The exception follows the Uniform Act in this respect.

The element of unusual reliability of business records is said variously to be supplied by systematic checking, by regularity and continuity which produce habits of precision, by actual experience of business in relying upon them, or by a duty to make an accurate record as part of a continuing job or occupation. MCCORMICK §§ 281, 286–287; Laughlin, *Business Entries and the Like*, 46 IOWA L. REV. 276 (1961). The model statutes and rules have sought to capture these factors and to extend their impact by employing the phrase "regular course of business," in conjunction with a definition of "business" far broader than its ordinarily accepted meaning. The result is a tendency unduly to emphasize a requirement of routineness and repetitiveness and an insistence that other types of records be squeezed into the fact patterns which give rise to traditional business records. . . .

Amplification of the kinds of activities producing admissible records has given rise to problems which conventional business records by their nature avoid. They are problems of the source of the recorded information, of entries in opinion form, of motivation, and of involvement as participant in the matters recorded.

Sources of information presented no substantial problem with ordinary business records. All participants, including the observer or participant furnishing the information to be recorded, were acting routinely, under a duty of accuracy, with employer reliance on the result, or in short "in the regular course of business." If, however, the supplier of the information does not act in the regular course, an essential link is broken; the assurance of accuracy does not extend to the information itself, and the fact that it may be recorded with scrupulous accuracy is of no avail. An illustration is the police report incorporating information obtained from a bystander: the officer qualifies as acting in the regular course but the informant does not. The leading case, *Johnson v. Lutz*, 253 N.Y. 124 (1930), held that a report thus prepared was inadmissible. Most of the authorities have agreed with the decision. Gencarella v. Fyfe, 171 F.2d 419 (1st Cir. 1948); Gordon v. Robinson, 210 F.2d 192 (3d Cir. 1954); Standard Oil Co. v. Moore, 251 F.2d 188, 214 (9th Cir. 1957), *cert. denied*, 356 U.S. 975 (1958); Yates v. Bair Transp., Inc., 249 F. Supp. 681 (S.D.N.Y. 1965); Annotation, 69 A.L.R.2d 1148; *cf.* Hawkins v. Gorea Motor Express, Inc., 360 F.2d 933 (2d Cir. 1966). *Contra*, 5 WIGMORE § 1530a, at 391 n.1. The point is not dealt with specifically in the Commonwealth Fund Act, the Uniform Act, or Uniform Rule 63(13). However, Model Code Rule 514 contains the requirement "that it was the regular course of that business for one with personal knowledge . . . to make such a memorandum or record or to transmit information thereof to be included in such a memorandum or record." The rule follows this lead in requiring an informant with knowledge acting in the course of the regularly conducted activity.

Entries in the form of opinions were not encountered in traditional business records in view of the purely factual nature of the items recorded, but they are now commonly encountered with respect to medical diagnoses, prognoses, and test results, as well as occasionally in other areas. The Commonwealth Fund Act provided only for records of an "act, transaction, occurrence, or event," while the Uniform Act, Model Code Rule 514, and Uniform Rule 63(13) merely added the ambiguous term "condition." The limited phrasing of the Commonwealth Fund Act, 28 U.S.C. § 1732, may account for the reluctance of some federal decisions to admit diagnostic entries. N.Y. Life Ins. Co. v. Taylor, 147 F.2d 297 (D.C. Cir. 1944); Lyles v. United States, 254 F.2d 725 (D.C. Cir. 1957), *cert. denied*, 356 U.S. 961 (1958); England v. United States, 174 F.2d 466 (5th Cir. 1949); Skogen v. Dow Chem. Co., 375 F.2d 692 (8th Cir. 1967). Other federal decisions, however, experienced no difficulty in freely admitting diagnostic entries. Reed v. Order of United Commercial Travelers of Am., 123 F.2d 252 (2d Cir. 1941); Buckminster's Estate v. Comm'r of Internal Revenue, 147 F.2d 331 (2d Cir. 1944); Medina v. Erickson, 226 F.2d 475 (9th Cir. 1955); Thomas v. Hogan, 308 F.2d 355 (4th Cir. 1962); Glawe v. Rulon, 284 F.2d 495 (8th Cir. 1960). In the state courts, the trend favors admissibility. Borucki v. MacKenzie Bros. Co., 125 Conn. 92 (1938); Allen v. St. Louis Pub. Serv. Co., 365 Mo. 677 (1956); People v. Kohlmeyer, 284 N.Y. 366 (1940); Weis v. Weis, 147 Ohio St. 416 (1947). In order to make clear its adherence to the latter position, the rule specifically includes both diagnoses and opinions, in addition to acts, events, and conditions, as proper subjects of admissible entries.

Problems of the motivation of the informant have been a source of difficulty and disagreement. In *Palmer v. Hoffman*, 318 U.S. 109 (1943), exclusion of an accident report made by the since deceased engineer, offered by defendant railroad trustees in a grade crossing collision case, was upheld. The report was not "in the regular course of business," not a record of the systematic conduct of the business as a business, said the Court. The report was prepared for use in litigating, not railroading. While the opinion mentions the motivation of the engineer only obliquely, the emphasis on records of routine operations is significant only by virtue of impact on motivation to be accurate. Absence of routineness raises lack of motivation to be accurate. The opinion of the Court of Appeals had gone beyond mere lack of motive to be accurate: the engineer's statement was "dripping with motivations to misrepresent." Hoffman v. Palmer, 129 F.2d 976, 991 (2d Cir. 1942). The direct introduction of motivation is a disturbing factor, since absence of motive to misrepresent has not traditionally been a requirement of the rule; that records might be self-serving has not been a ground for exclusion. Laughlin, *Business Records and the Like*, 46 IOWA L. REV. 276, 285 (1961). As Judge Clark said in his dissent, "I submit that there is hardly a grocer's account book which could not be excluded on that basis." 129 F.2d at 1002. A physician's evaluation report of a personal injury litigant would appear to be in the routine of his business. If the report is offered by the party at whose instance it was made, however, it has been held inadmissible, Yates v. Bair Transp., Inc., 249 F. Supp. 681 (S.D.N.Y. 1965), otherwise if offered by the opposite party, Korte v. N.Y., New Haven &

Hartford R.R. Co., 191 F.2d 86 (2d Cir.), *cert. denied*, 342 U.S. 868 (1951).

The decisions hinge on motivation and which party is entitled to be concerned about it. Professor McCormick believed that the doctor's report or the accident report were sufficiently routine to justify admissibility. MCCORMICK § 287, at 604. Yet hesitation must be experienced in admitting everything which is observed and recorded in the course of a regularly conducted activity. Efforts to set a limit are illustrated by *Hartzog v. United States*, 217 F.2d 706 (4th Cir. 1954) (error to admit worksheets made by since deceased deputy collector in preparation for the instant income tax evasion prosecution), and *United States v. Ware*, 247 F.2d 698 (7th Cir. 1957) (error to admit narcotics agents' records of purchases). See also exception (8), *infra*, as to the public record aspects of records of this nature. Some decisions have been satisfied as to motivation of an accident report if made pursuant to statutory duty, United States v. N.Y. Foreign Trade Zone Operators, Inc., 304 F.2d 792 (2d Cir. 1962); Taylor v. Balt. & Ohio R.R. Co., 344 F.2d 281 (2d Cir. 1965), since the report was oriented in a direction other than the litigation which ensued. *Cf.* Matthews v. United States, 217 F.2d 409 (5th Cir. 1954). The formulation of specific terms which would assure satisfactory results in all cases is not possible. Consequently the rule proceeds from the base that records made in the course of a regularly conducted activity will be taken as admissible but subject to authority to exclude if "the sources of information or other circumstances indicate lack of trustworthiness."

Occasional decisions have reached for enhanced accuracy by requiring involvement as a participant in matters reported. Clainos v. United States, 163 F.2d 593 (D.C. Cir. 1947) (error to admit police records of convictions); Standard Oil Co. v. Moore, 251 F.2d 188 (9th Cir. 1957) (error to admit employees' records of observed business practices of others), *cert. denied*, 356 U.S. 975 (1958). The rule includes no requirement of this nature. Wholly acceptable records may involve matters merely observed, e.g., the weather.

The form which the "record" may assume under the rule is described broadly as a "memorandum, report, record, or data compilation, in any form." The expression "data compilation" is used as broadly descriptive of any means of storing information other than the conventional words and figures in written or documentary form. It includes, but is by no means limited to, electronic computer storage. The term is borrowed from revised Rule 34(a) of the Rules of Civil Procedure.

REPORT OF THE HOUSE COMMITTEE ON THE JUDICIARY

Rule 803(6) as submitted by the Court permitted a record made "in the course of a regularly conducted activity" to be admissible in certain circumstances. The Committee believed there were insufficient guarantees of reliability in records made in the course of activities falling outside the scope of "business" activities as that term is broadly defined in 28 U.S.C. § 1732. Moreover, the Committee concluded that the additional requirement of section 1732 that it must have been the regular practice of a business to make the record is a necessary further assurance of its trustworthiness. The Committee accordingly amended the rule to incorporate these limitations.

REPORT OF THE SENATE COMMITTEE ON THE JUDICIARY

Rule 803(6) as submitted by the Supreme Court permitted a record made in the course of a regularly conducted activity to be admissible in certain circumstances. This rule constituted a broadening of the traditional business records hearsay exception which has been long advocated by scholars and judges active in the law of evidence.

The House felt there were insufficient guarantees of reliability of records not within a broadly defined business records exception. We disagree. Even under the House definition of "business" including profession, occupation, and "calling of every kind," the records of many regularly conducted activities will, or may be, excluded from evidence. Under the principle of *ejusdem generis*, the intent of "calling of every kind" would seem to be related to work-related endeavors—e.g., butcher, baker, artist, etc.

Thus, it appears that the records of many institutions or groups might not be admissible under the House amendments. For example, schools, churches, and hospitals will not normally be considered businesses within the definition. Yet, these are groups which keep financial and other records on a regular basis in a manner similar to business enterprises. We believe these records are of equivalent trustworthiness and should be admitted into evidence.

Three states, which have recently codified their evidence rules, have adopted the Supreme Court version of Rule 803(6), providing for admission of memoranda of a "regularly conducted activity."

None adopted the words "business activity" used in the House amendment.[10]

Therefore, the Committee deleted the words "business" as it appears before the word "activity." The last sentence then is unnecessary and was also deleted.

It is the understanding of the Committee that the use of the phrase "person with knowledge" is not intended to imply that the party seeking to introduce the memorandum, report, record, or data compilation must be able to produce, or even identify, the specific individual upon whose first-hand knowledge the memorandum, report, record, or data compilation was based. A sufficient foundation for the introduction of such evidence will be laid if the party seeking to introduce the evidence is able to show that it was the regular practice of the activity to base such memorandums, reports, records, or data compilations upon a transmission from a person with knowledge, e.g., in the case of the content of a shipment of goods, upon a report from the company's receiving agent or in the case of a computer printout, upon a report from the company's computer programmer or one who has knowledge of the particular record system. In short, the scope of the phrase "person with knowledge" is meant to be coterminous with the custodian of the evidence or other qualified witness. The Committee believes this represents the desired rule in light of the complex nature of modern business organizations.

CONFERENCE REPORT

The House bill provides in subsection (6) that records of a regularly conducted "business" activity qualify for admission into evidence as an exception to the hearsay rule. "Business" is defined as including "business, profession, occupation and calling of every kind." The Senate amendment drops the requirement that the records be those of a "business" activity and eliminates the definition of "business." The Senate amendment provides that records are admissible if they are records of a regularly conducted "activity."

The Conference adopts the House provision that the records must be those of a regularly conducted "business" activity. The Conferees changed the definition of "business" contained in the House provision in order to make it clear that the records of institutions and associations like schools, churches, and hospitals are admissible under this provision. The records of public schools

---

[10] See NEV. REV. STAT. § 51.135; N.M. STAT. ANN. § 20-4-803(6) (Supp. 1973) (current version at N.M. R. EVID. 11-803(F)); WIS. STAT. ANN. § 908.03(6) (West Supp. 1973).

and hospitals are also covered by Rule 803(8), which deals with public records and reports.

ADVISORY COMMITTEE'S NOTE TO 2000 AMENDMENT TO RULE 803(6)

The amendment provides that the foundation requirements of Rule 803(6) can be satisfied under certain circumstances without the expense and inconvenience of producing time-consuming foundation witnesses. Under current law, courts have generally required foundation witnesses to testify. *See, e.g.*, Tongil Co. v. Vessel Hyundai Innovator, 968 F.2d 999 (9th Cir. 1992) (reversing a judgment based on business records where a qualified person filed an affidavit but did not testify). Protections are provided by the authentication requirements of Rule 902(11) for domestic records, Rule 902(12) for foreign records in civil cases, and 18 U.S.C. § 3505 for foreign records in criminal cases.

ADVISORY COMMITTEE'S NOTE TO 2014 AMENDMENT TO RULE 803(6)(E)

The rule has been amended to clarify that if the proponent has established the stated requirements of the exception—regular business with regularly kept record, source with personal knowledge, record made timely, and foundation testimony or certification—then the burden is on the opponent to show that the source of information or the method or circumstances of preparation indicate a lack of trustworthiness. While most courts have imposed that burden on the opponent, some have not. It is appropriate to impose this burden on the opponent, as the basic admissibility requirements are sufficient to establish a presumption that the record is reliable.

The opponent, in meeting its burden, is not necessarily required to introduce affirmative evidence of untrustworthiness. For example, the opponent might argue that a record was prepared in anticipation of litigation and is favorable to the preparing party without needing to introduce evidence on the point. A determination of untrustworthiness necessarily depends on the circumstances.

[This page is intentionally blank.]

[This space is intentionally blank.]

<u>ADVISORY COMMITTEE'S NOTE TO RULE 803(7)</u>

Exception (7). Failure of a record to mention a matter which would ordinarily be mentioned is satisfactory evidence of its nonexistence. *Comment,* UNIF. R. EVID. 63(14). While probably not hearsay as defined in Rule 801, *supra,* decisions may be found which class the evidence not only as hearsay but also as not within any exception. In order to set the question at rest in favor of admissibility, it is specifically treated here. McCORMICK § 289, at 609; MORGAN, BASIC PROBLEMS OF EVIDENCE 314 (1962); 5 WIGMORE § 1531; UNIF. R. EVID. 63(14); CAL. EVID. CODE § 1272; KAN. STAT. ANN. § 60-460(n); N.J. EVID. R. 63(14) (repealed and replaced by N.J. R. EVID. 803(c)(7) (1993)).

<u>REPORT OF THE HOUSE COMMITTEE ON THE JUDICIARY</u>

Rule 803(7) as submitted by the Court concerned the *absence* of entry in the records of a "regularly conducted activity." The Committee amended this rule to conform with its action with respect to Rule 803(6).

<u>ADVISORY COMMITTEE'S NOTE TO 2014 AMENDMENT TO RULE 803(7)(C)</u>

The rule has been amended to clarify that if the proponent has established the stated requirements of the exception—set forth in Rule 803(6)—then the burden is on the opponent to show that the possible source of the information or other circumstances indicate a lack of trustworthiness. The amendment maintains consistency with the proposed amendment to the trustworthiness clause of Rule 803(6).[*]

---

[*] [For a fuller explanation of this amendment, please see the Advisory Committee's Note to the 2014 Amendment to Rule 803(6)(E) at page 232 above.—GF]

[This page is intentionally blank.]

[This space is intentionally blank.]

ADVISORY COMMITTEE'S NOTE TO RULE 803(8)

Exception (8). Public records are a recognized hearsay exception at common law and have been the subject of statutes without number. MCCORMICK § 291. See, for example, 28 U.S.C. § 1733, the relative narrowness of which is illustrated by its nonapplicability to nonfederal public agencies, thus necessitating resort to the less appropriate business record exception to the hearsay rule. Kay v. United States, 255 F.2d 476 (4th Cir. 1958). The rule makes no distinction between federal and nonfederal offices and agencies.

Justification for the exception is the assumption that a public official will perform his duty properly and the unlikelihood that he will remember details independently of the record. Wong Wing Foo v. McGrath, 196 F.2d 120 (9th Cir. 1952); *see also* Chesapeake & Del. Canal Co. v. United States, 250 U.S. 123 (1919). As to items [(A)(i)] and [(A)(ii)], further support is found in the reliability factors underlying records of regularly conducted activities generally. *See* exception (6), *supra*.

(A) Cases illustrating the admissibility of records of the office's or agency's own activities are numerous. Chesapeake & Del. Canal Co. v. United States, 250 U.S. 123 (1919) (Treasury records of miscellaneous receipts and disbursements); Howard v. Perrin, 200 U.S. 71 (1906) (General Land Office records); Ballew v. United States, 160 U.S. 187 (1895) (Pension Office records).

(B) Cases sustaining admissibility of records of matters observed are also numerous. United States v. Van Hook, 284 F.2d 489 (7th Cir. 1960) (letter from induction officer to District Attorney, pursuant to army regulations, stating fact and circumstances of refusal to be inducted), *remanded for resentencing*, 365 U.S. 609 (1961); T'Kach v. United States, 242 F.2d 937 (5th Cir. 1957) (affidavit of White House personnel officer that search of records showed no employment of accused, charged with fraudulently representing himself as an envoy of the President); Minnehaha County v. Kelley, 150 F.2d 356 (8th Cir. 1945) (Weather Bureau records of rainfall); United States v. Meyer, 113 F.2d 387 (7th Cir.) (map prepared by government engineer from information furnished by men working under his supervision), *cert. denied*, 311 U.S. 706 (1940).

(C) The more controversial area of public records is that of the so-called "evaluative" report. The disagreement among the decisions has been due in part, no doubt, to the variety of situations encountered, as well as to differences in principle. Sustaining admissibility are such cases as *United States v. Dumas*, 149 U.S. 278 (1893) (statement of account certified by Postmaster General in action against postmaster); *McCarty v. United States*, 185 F.2d 520 (5th Cir. 1950) (Certificate of Settlement of General Accounting Office showing indebtedness and letter from Army official stating Government had performed, in action on contract to purchase and remove waste food from Army camp), *reh'g denied*, 187 F.2d 234 (1951),; *Moran v. Pittsburgh–Des Moines Steel Co.*, 183 F.2d 467 (3d Cir. 1950) (report of Bureau of Mines as to cause of gas tank explosion); *In re W.*, 164 F. Supp. 659 (E.D. Pa. 1958) (report by Immigration and Naturalization Service investigator that petitioner was known in community as wife of man to whom she was not married). To the opposite effect and denying admissibility are *Franklin v. Skelly Oil Co.*, 141 F.2d 568 (10th Cir. 1944) (state fire marshal's report of cause of gas explosion); *Lomax Transportation Co. v. United States*, 183 F.2d 331 (9th Cir. 1950) (Certificate of Settlement from General Accounting Office in action for naval supplies lost in warehouse fire); *Yung Jin Teung v. Dulles*, 229 F.2d 244 (2d Cir. 1956) ("Status Reports" offered to justify delay in processing passport applications). . . . Various kinds of evaluative reports are admissible under federal statutes: 7 U.S.C. § 78 (findings of Secretary of Agriculture prima facie evidence of true grade of grain); 7 U.S.C. § 210(f) (findings of Secretary of Agriculture prima facie evidence in action for damages against stockyard owner); 7 U.S.C. § 292 (order by Secretary of Agriculture prima facie evidence in judicial enforcement proceedings against producers association monopoly); 7 U.S.C. § 1622(h) (Department of Agriculture inspection certificates of products shipped in interstate commerce prima facie evidence); 8 U.S.C. § 1440(c) (separation of alien from military service on conditions other than honorable provable by certificate from department in proceedings to revoke citizenship); 18 U.S.C. § 4245 (certificate of Director of Prisons that convicted person has been examined and found probably incompetent at time of trial prima facie evidence in court hearing on competency); 42 U.S.C. § 269(b) (bill of health by appropriate official prima facie evidence of vessel's sanitary history and condition and compliance with regulations); 46 U.S.C. § [11104] (certificate of consul presumptive evidence of refusal of master to transport destitute seamen to United States). While these statutory exceptions to the hearsay rule are left undisturbed, Rule 802, the willingness of

Congress to recognize a substantial measure of admissibility for evaluative reports is a helpful guide.

Factors which may be of assistance in passing upon the admissibility of evaluative reports include: (1) the timeliness of the investigation, McCormick, *Can the Courts Make Wider Use of Reports of Official Investigations?*, 42 IOWA L. REV. 363 (1957); (2) the special skill or experience of the official, *id.*, (3) whether a hearing was held and the level at which conducted, Franklin v. Skelly Oil Co., 141 F.2d 568 (10th Cir. 1944); (4) possible motivation problems suggested by *Palmer v. Hoffman*, 318 U.S. 109 (1943). Others no doubt could be added.

The formulation of an approach which would give appropriate weight to all possible factors in every situation is an obvious impossibility. Hence the rule, as in exception (6), assumes admissibility in the first instance but with ample provision for escape if sufficient negative factors are present. In one respect, however, the rule with respect to evaluative reports under item [(A)(iii)] is very specific: they are admissible only in civil cases and against the government in criminal cases in view of the almost certain collision with confrontation rights which would result from their use against the accused in a criminal case.

REPORT OF THE HOUSE COMMITTEE ON THE JUDICIARY

The Committee approved Rule 803(8) without substantive change from the form in which it was submitted by the Court. The Committee intends that the phrase "factual findings" be strictly construed and that evaluations or opinions contained in public reports shall not be admissible under this rule.

HOUSE OF REPRESENTATIVES

Feb. 6, 1974, 120 Cong. Rec. 2387 (1974)

Amendment offered by Ms. Holtzman

Ms. HOLTZMAN. Mr. Chairman, I offer an amendment.

The Clerk read as follows:

> Amendment offered by Ms. Holtzman: On page 94, line 11, after the word "law" and before the comma, insert the following: "as to which matters there was a duty to report."

Ms. HOLTZMAN. Mr. Chairman, I will try to be very brief, because it is late in the day.

My amendment is offered to clarify and narrow a provision on the hearsay rule (Rule [803(8)(A)(ii)]). This rule now provides that if any Government employee in the course of his duty observes something—in fact, anything—and makes a report of that observation, that report can be entered into evidence at a trial whether criminal or civil, without the opportunity to cross-examine the author of the report.

While I respect Government employees, I think we would all concede that they are fallible, exactly like every other human. We do not provide such broach exceptions to the hearsay rule for ordinary mortals.

My amendment makes it crystal clear that random observations by a Government employee cannot be introduced as an exception to the hearsay rule and be insulated from cross-examination. My amendment would allow reports of "matters observed" by a public official only if he had a duty to report about such matters. One operating under such a duty is far more likely to observe and report accurately.

I urge adoption of this amendment in order to narrow and restrict the broad exception to the hearsay rule in the bill.

Mr. HUNGATE. Mr. Chairman, I rise in opposition to the amendment.

This is a matter that was considered in the Subcommittee, and we decided to stay with the language as presented to the House here, which states as follows:

> Records, reports, statements, or data compilations, in any form, of public offices or agencies, setting forth (A) the activities of the office or agency, or (B) matters observed pursuant to duty imposed by law. . . .

Mr. Chairman, this is where the point of disagreement occurred. We stayed with that version of the bill, and I would recommend that version to the Committee of the Whole House.

Mr. DANIELSON. Mr. Chairman, I rise in support of the amendment offered by the gentlewoman from New York (Ms. Holtzman).

I think if we leave this language in the proposed bill, we are opening the door to a host of problems, the like of which we have probably never seen in a trial court.

I think the proper approach, in order to eliminate this, is simply to adopt the gentlewoman's amendment, and eliminate this provision, simply because there is absolutely no restriction on the sort of material which could come in under the language as proposed.

I urge adoption of the gentlewoman's amendment.

Mr. DENNIS. Mr. Chairman, I rise in support of the gentlewoman's amendment.

So that the Committee will know what we are talking about here, this permits the introduction in evidence as an exception to the hearsay rule of public records and reports, statements, or data compilations in any form of matters observed pursuant to duty imposed by law. The gentlewoman would add "as to which matters there was a duty to report."

Again it is a matter of judgment, but the difference would be this: Supposing you had a divorce case and you tried to put in a report of a social worker, rather than putting the social worker in the stand; under the Committee's language anything she said in the report which would be observed by her pursuant to her general duties would be admissible. Under the amendment, only those things as to which she had some duty to make a report would be admissible.

If the law required her to observe and report certain things about a condition in the home, that could come in, but if she put in a lot of other stuff there, she could not put that in without calling her as a witness and giving the opposition a chance to cross-examine her.

On the whole I think the amendment improves the bill, and I support it.

The CHAIRMAN. The question is on the amendment offered by the gentlewoman from New York (Ms. Holtzman).

The amendment was agreed to.

Amendment offered by Mr. Dennis

Mr. DENNIS. Mr. Chairman, I offer an amendment.

The Clerk read as follows:

> Amendment offered by Mr. Dennis: On page 94, line 11 of
> the bill, after the word "law," insert the words "excluding,
> however, in criminal cases matters observed by police
> officers and other law enforcement personnel."

Mr. DENNIS. Mr. Chairman, this goes to the same subject matter as
the last amendment. It deals with official statements and reports.

What I am saying here is that in a criminal case, only, we
should not be able to put in the police report to prove your case
without calling the policeman. I think in a criminal case you ought
to have to call the policeman on the beat and give the defendant the
chance to cross examine him, rather than just reading the report
into evidence, that is the purpose of this amendment.

Ms. HOLTZMAN. Mr. Chairman, I rise in support of the
amendment.

I will be very brief again.

I commend my colleague for raising this point. Again his
purpose is to restrict the possible abuse of hearsay evidence.

I think the gentleman's amendment is very valuable and
reaffirms the right of cross-examination to the accused. It also
permits those engaged in civil trials the right of cross-examination.
Cross-examination guarantees due process of law and a fair trial.

(Ms. HOLTZMAN asked and was given permission to revise
and extend her remarks.)

Mr. SMITH of New York. Mr. Chairman, I rise in opposition to the
amendment.

Mr. Chairman, in reading this amendment it seems to me that
the effect of the gentleman's amendment is to treat police officers
and other law enforcement officers as second-class citizens, because
we have already agreed that we are going to allow in as exceptions
to the hearsay rule matters observed pursuant to duty imposed by
law. The gentleman from Indiana would exclude from that as
follows: "Excluding, however, in criminal cases, matters observed

by police officers and other law enforcement personnel." This would be so even though they were matters observed pursuant to a duty imposed by law.

I just think we are treading in an area the impact of which will be very unfortunate and the effect of which is to make police officers and law enforcement officers second-class citizens and persons less trustworthy than social workers or garbage collectors.

. . .

Mr. DENNIS. Mr. Chairman, I would like to say on that point that of course that is not my idea. I think the point is that we are dealing here with criminal cases, and in a criminal case the defendant should be confronted with the accuser to give him the chance to cross-examine. This is not any reflection on the police officer, but in a criminal case that is the type of report with which, in fact, one is going to be concerned.

. . .

Mr. JOHNSON of Colorado. Mr. Chairman, as an ex-prosecutor I cannot imagine that the gentleman would be advocating that a policeman's report could come in to help convict a man, and not have the policeman himself subject to cross-examination.

Is that what the gentleman is advocating?

Mr. SMITH of New York. That is what I am advocating in that the policeman's report, if he is not available, should be admissible when it is made pursuant to a duty imposed on that law enforcement officer by law. This is the amendment we have just adopted, and for other public officers these police reports ought to be admissible, whatever their probative value might be.

Mr. JOHNSON of Colorado. Mr. Chairman, if the gentleman will yield further, as I said, I was a prosecutor in a state court, and there were so many cases where good cross-examination indicated a lack of investigative ability on the part of the man who made the report that I became more and more convinced that good cross-examination was one of the principal elements in any criminal trial. If the officer who made the investigation is not available for cross-examination, then you cannot have a fair trial.

I cannot believe the gentleman would be saying that we should be able to convict people where the police officer's statement is not subject to cross-examination.

Mr. SMITH of New York. All I am saying to the gentleman from Colorado is that—and I will concede that the gentleman has probably had greater experience in this field than I have had—all I am saying is that it seems to me that it should be allowed for the jury to consider such a report, together with all of the other aspects of the case, if this report was made by a police officer pursuant to a duty imposed upon that police officer by law.

I will have to admit to the gentleman from Colorado that it is not the best evidence.

Mr. JOHNSON of Colorado. If the gentleman will yield still further, I will have to say that in my opinion the Supreme Court would have to ultimately declare that kind of a rule unconstitutional if we did pass it, and that the present amendment is one that would have to be passed if we are going to preserve the rights and traditions of individuals that have been in existence since 1066—I think that is when it started.

Mr. BRASCO. Mr. Chairman, I move to strike the requisite number of words.

(Mr. BRASCO asked and was given permission to revise and extend his remarks.)

Mr. BRASCO. Mr. Chairman, I would like to ask the author of the amendment, the gentleman from Indiana (Mr. Dennis) a question. I am deeply disturbed and troubled about these rules that have been brought out today.

It seems to me that many critical areas have been overlooked.

One of the basic tenets of our law is that one should be confronted by one's accuser and be able to cross-examine the accuser.

There are many, many exceptions to the hearsay rule here.

As I understand it the gentleman from New York (Mr. Smith) is advocating, in opposition to the amendment offered by the gentleman from Indiana (Mr. Dennis) that if a police officer made a report that he saw Mr. X with a gun on such and such an occasion, and then thereafter that police officer is unavailable that that statement could be used in a criminal trial against Mr. X without the defense attorney having the opportunity to cross-examine the officer with respect to his position with relation to Mr. X, the time of the day, whether he was under a light, or whether there was no light, how much time did he have in which to see the gun, and all other observations relevant to the case.

Mr. DENNIS. Mr. Chairman, I would say in answer to the question raised by the gentleman from New York (Mr. Brasco) that if the statements of the police officer in his report would, in the language of the bill, be "matters observed pursuant to a duty imposed by law, and as to which he was under a duty to make a report," and I rather think they might be, that then what the gentleman says is true, and would be true.

I am trying to remove that possibility, by saying that the rule will not apply in the case the gentleman is talking about.

Mr. BRASCO. I support the gentleman. I am just standing up talking, because I cannot believe that we would for one moment entertain any other rule. I would hope we would do it with all cases in hearsay.

. . .

Mr. HUNT. I had no intention of getting into this argument, but when the gentleman brings in the word "investigator," then I have to get in.

Mr. BRASCO. I did not say it.

Mr. HUNT. I know the gentleman from New York did not, but it was discussed. The only time I can recall in my 34 years of law enforcement that a report of an investigator was admissible in court was to test the credibility of an officer. We would never permit a report to come in unchallenged. We would never even think about bringing in a report in lieu of the officer being there to have that officer cross-examined; but reports were admitted as evidentiary fact for the purpose of testing the officer's credibility and perhaps to refresh his memory. That has always been the rule of law in the state of New Jersey, and I hope it will always remain that way— and even the federal canons.

Mr. BRASCO. I do not think that the gentleman's amendment interferes with that at all. I think what he is talking about is that the prosecution could use this to prove its case in chief with the possibility of no other evidence being presented.

Mr. HUNT. He is talking about bringing the report in lieu of an officer, and that certainly is not the case.

Mr. DENNIS. Mr. Chairman, will the gentleman yield?

Mr. BRASCO. I yield to the gentleman from Indiana.

Mr. DENNIS. I thank the gentleman for yielding. I certainly agree this amendment has nothing to do with what my friend, the gentleman from New Jersey, is talking about. This applies only to a hearsay exception, where it would be attempted to bring this report in instead of the officer to prove one's case in chief, which one could do if we do not pass this amendment; but we could still use the report to contradict him and cross-examine him.

Mr. HUNT. Certainly, but the gentleman is speaking of the best evidence available in lieu of the direct evidence.

Mr. DENNIS. I say we should bring in the man who saw it and put him on the stand.

Mr. HUNT. Certainly, the gentleman is right.

The CHAIRMAN. The question is on the amendment offered by the gentleman from Indiana (Mr. Dennis).

The amendment was agreed to.

REPORT OF THE SENATE COMMITTEE ON THE JUDICIARY

The House approved Rule 803(8), as submitted by the Supreme Court, with one substantive change. It excluded from the hearsay exception reports containing matters observed by police officers and other law enforcement personnel in criminal cases. Ostensibly, the reason for this exclusion is that observations by police officers at the scene of the crime or the apprehension of the defendant are not as reliable as observations by public officials in other cases because of the adversarial nature of the confrontation between the police and the defendant in criminal cases.

The Committee accepts the House's decision to exclude such recorded observations where the police officer is available to testify in court about his observation. However, where he is unavailable as unavailability is defined in Rule 804(a)(4) and (a)(5), the report should be admitted as the best available evidence. Accordingly, the Committee has amended Rule 803(8) to refer to the provision of [proposed] Rule 804(b)(5) [deleted], which allows the admission of such reports, records or other statements where the police officer or other law enforcement officer is unavailable because of death, then existing physical or mental illness or infirmity, or not being successfully subject to legal process.

The House Judiciary Committee report contained a statement of intent that "the phrase 'factual findings' in subdivision [(A)(iii)] be strictly construed and that evaluations or opinions contained in public reports shall not be admissible under this rule." The Committee takes strong exception to this limiting understanding of the application of the rule. We do not think it reflects an understanding of the intended operation of the rule as explained in the Advisory Committee notes to this subsection. The Advisory Committee notes on subsection [(A)(iii)] of this subdivision point out that various kinds of evaluative reports are now admissible under federal statutes. 7 U.S.C. § 78 (findings of Secretary of Agriculture prima facie evidence of true grade of grain); 42 U.S.C. § 269(b) (bill of health by appropriate official prima facie evidence of vessel's sanitary history and condition and compliance with regulations). These statutory exceptions to the hearsay rule are preserved. Rule 802. The willingness of Congress to recognize these and other such evaluative reports provides a helpful guide in determining the kind of reports which are intended to be admissible under this rule. We think the restrictive interpretation of the House overlooks the fact that while the Advisory Committee assumes admissibility in the first instance of evaluative reports, they are not admissible if, as the rule states, "the sources of information or other circumstances indicate lack of trustworthiness."

The Advisory Committee explains the factors to be considered:

> Factors which may be of assistance in passing upon the admissibility of evaluative reports include: (1) the timeliness of the investigation, McCormick, *Can the Courts Make Wider Use of Reports of Official Investigation?*, 42 IOWA L. REV. 363 (1957); (2) the special skill or experience of the official, *id.*; (3) whether a hearing was held and the level at which conducted, Franklin v. Skelly Oil Co., 141 F.2d 568 (10th Cir. 1944); (4) possible motivation problems suggested by *Palmer v. Hoffman*, 318 U.S. 109 (1943). Others no doubt could be added.

The Committee concludes that the language of the rule together with the explanation provided by the Advisory Committee furnish sufficient guidance on the admissibility of evaluative reports.

CONFERENCE REPORT

The Senate amendment adds language, not contained in the House bill, that refers to another rule that was added by the Senate in another amendment ([proposed] Rule 804(b)(5)—Criminal law enforcement records and reports [deleted]).

In view of its action on [proposed] Rule 804(b)(5) (Criminal law enforcement records and reports) [deleted], the Conference does not adopt the Senate amendment and restores the bill to the House version.

ADVISORY COMMITTEE'S NOTE TO 2014 AMENDMENT TO RULE 803(8)(B)

The rule has been amended to clarify that if the proponent has established that the record meets the stated requirements of the exception—prepared by a public office and setting out information as specified in the rule—then the burden is on the opponent to show that the source of information or other circumstances indicate a lack of trustworthiness. While most courts have imposed that burden on the opponent, some have not. Public records have justifiably carried a presumption of reliability, and it should be up to the opponent to "demonstrate why a time-tested and carefully considered presumption is not appropriate." *Ellis v. Int'l Playtex, Inc.*, 745 F.2d 292, 301 (4th Cir. 1984). The amendment maintains consistency with the proposed amendment to the trustworthiness clause of Rule 803(6).[*]

The opponent, in meeting its burden, is not necessarily required to introduce affirmative evidence of untrustworthiness. For example, the opponent might argue that a record was prepared in anticipation of litigation and is favorable to the preparing party without needing to introduce evidence on the point. A determination of untrustworthiness necessarily depends on the circumstances.

---

[*] [The Advisory Committee's Note to the 2014 Amendment to Rule 803(6)(E) appears at page 232 above.—GF]

[This page is intentionally blank.]

[This space is intentionally blank.]

ADVISORY COMMITTEE'S NOTE TO RULE 803(9)–(10)

Exception (9). Records of vital statistics are commonly the subject of particular statutes making them admissible in evidence. *See* UNIFORM VITAL STATISTICS ACT, 9C U.L.A. 350 (1957). The rule is in principle narrower than Uniform Rule 63(16) which includes reports required of persons performing functions authorized by statute, yet in practical effect the two are substantially the same. *Comment*, UNIF. R. EVID. 63(16). The exception as drafted is in the pattern of California Evidence Code § 1281.

Exception (10). The principle of proving nonoccurrence of an event by evidence of the absence of a record which would regularly be made of its occurrence, developed in exception (7) with respect to regularly conducted [business] activities, is here extended to public records of the kind mentioned in exceptions (8) and (9). 5 WIGMORE § 1633(6), at 519. Some harmless duplication no doubt exists with exception (7). For instances of federal statutes recognizing this method of proof, see 8 U.S.C. § 1284(b) (proof of absence of alien crewman's name from outgoing manifest prima facie evidence of failure to detain or deport) and 42 U.S.C. § 405(c)(3), (4)(B), (4)(C) (absence of [Department of Health, Education, and Welfare] record prima facie evidence of no wages or self-employment income).

The rule includes situations in which absence of a record may itself be the ultimate focal point of inquiry, *e.g.*, People v. Love, 310 Ill. 558 (1923) (certificate of Secretary of State admitted to show failure to file documents required by Securities Law), as well as cases where the absence of a record is offered as proof of the nonoccurrence of an event ordinarily recorded.

The refusal of the common law to allow proof by certificate of the lack of a record or entry has no apparent justification, 5 WIGMORE § 1678(7), at 752. The rule takes the opposite position, as do Uniform Rule 63(17); California Evidence Code § 1284; Kansas Statutes Annotated § [60-460(n)]; N.J. Evidence Rule 63(17) (repealed and replaced by N.J.R. Evid. 803(c)(10) (1993)). Congress has recognized certification as evidence of the lack of a record. 8 U.S.C. § 1360(d) (certificate of Attorney General or other designated officer that no record of Immigration and Naturalization Service of specified nature or entry therein is found, admissible in alien cases).

ADVISORY COMMITTEE'S NOTE TO 2013 AMENDMENT TO RULE 803(10)

Rule 803(10) has been amended in response to *Melendez-Diaz v. Massachusetts*, 557 U.S. 305 (2009). The *Melendez-Diaz* Court declared that a testimonial certificate could be admitted if the accused is given advance notice and does not timely demand the presence of the official who prepared the certificate. The amendment incorporates, with minor variations, a "notice-and-demand" procedure that was approved by the *Melendez-Diaz* Court. *See* TEX. CODE CRIM. PROC. ANN., art. 38.41.

EDITOR'S NOTE TO 2013 AMENDMENT TO RULE 803(10)

The 2013 amendment to Rule 803(10) incorporated a notice-and-demand procedure of the sort suggested by the Supreme Court in *Melendez-Diaz v. Massachusetts, supra,* and by two Justices in *Bullcoming v. New Mexico*, 131 S. Ct. 2705 (2011) (CB page 652). The Court ruled in these cases that the admission against criminal defendants of certificates reporting the results of drug or blood tests conducted by state lab analysts, in lieu of the analysts' testimony at trial, violated the defendants' Sixth Amendment right to confront the witnesses against them. At the same time the *Melendez–Diaz* Court deemed constitutional the "simplest form" of notice-and-demand statutes, which "require the prosecution to provide notice to the defendant of its intent to use an analyst's report as evidence at trial, after which the defendant is given a period of time in which he may object to the admission of the evidence absent the analyst's appearance live at trial." *Melendez-Diaz*, 557 U.S. at 325–27 & n.12; *cf. Bullcoming*, 131 S. Ct. at 2718 (CB page 652) (opinion of Ginsburg, J.) (similar).

The newly enacted subparagraph (B) of Rule 803(10) prescribes such a procedure in a very different context—when the prosecution seeks to prove by certification that a diligent search turned up no public record or statement of the sort sought. This change likely will benefit the government in illegal-reentry prosecutions, which often turn on admission of a certificate of nonexistence of record (CNR) stating that a record search revealed that the defendant had never applied for or been granted permission to reenter the United States following his removal. Some courts have deemed CNRs inadmissible under *Melendez-Diaz*. *See, e.g., United States v. Orozco–Acosta*, 607 F.3d 1156, 1161 & n.3 (9th Cir. 2010) (as amended), *cert. denied*, 131 S. Ct. 946 (2011).

[This space intentionally left blank.]

[This space intentionally left blank.]

ADVISORY COMMITTEE'S NOTE TO RULE 803(11)–(23)

Exception (11). Records of activities of religious organizations are currently recognized as admissible at least to the extent of the business records exception to the hearsay rule, 5 WIGMORE § 1523, at 371, and exception (6) would be applicable. However, both the business record doctrine and exception (6) require that the person furnishing the information be one in the business or activity. The result is such decisions as *Dailey v. Grand Lodge Brotherhood of Railroad Trainmen*, 311 Ill. 184 (1924), holding a church record admissible to prove fact, date, and place of baptism, but not age of child except that he had at least been born at the time. In view of the unlikelihood that false information would be furnished on occasions of this kind, the rule contains no requirement that the informant be in the course of the activity. *See* CAL. EVID. CODE § 1315 and *Comment*.

Exception (12). The principle of proof by certification is recognized as to public officials in exceptions (8) and (10), and with respect to authentication in Rule 902. The present exception is a duplication to the extent that it deals with a certificate by a public official, as in the case of a judge who performs a marriage ceremony. The area covered by the rule is, however, substantially larger and extends the certification procedure to clergymen and the like who perform marriages and other ceremonies or administer sacraments. Thus certificates of such matters as baptism or confirmation, as well as marriage, are included. In principle they are as acceptable evidence as certificates of public officers. *See* 5 WIGMORE § 1645, as to marriage certificates. When the person executing the certificate is not a public official, the self-authenticating character of documents purporting to emanate from public officials, *see* Rule 902, is lacking and proof is required that the person was authorized and did make the certificate. The time element, however, may safely be taken as supplied by the certificate, once authority and authenticity are established, particularly in view of the presumption that a document was executed on the date it bears.

For similar rules, some limited to certificates of marriage, with variations in foundation requirements, see Uniform Rule 63(18); California Evidence Code § 1316; Kansas Statutes Annotated § 60-460(p); New Jersey Evidence Rule 63(18) (repealed and replaced by New Jersey Rule of Evidence 803(c)(12) (1993)).

Exception (13). Records of family history kept in family Bibles have by long tradition been received in evidence. 5 WIGMORE §§ 1495–1496 (citing numerous statutes and decisions); *see also* SSA Evidence, 20 C.F.R. § [404.716], recognizing family Bible entries as proof of age in the absence of public or church records. Opinions in the area also include inscriptions on tombstones, publicly displayed pedigrees, and engravings on rings. WIGMORE, *supra*. The rule is substantially identical in coverage with California Evidence Code § 1312.

Exception (14). The recording of title documents is a purely statutory development. Under any theory of the admissibility of public records, the records would be receivable as evidence of the contents of the recorded document, else the recording process would be reduced to a nullity. When, however, the record is offered for the further purpose of proving execution and delivery, a problem of lack of first-hand knowledge by the recorder, not present as to contents, is presented. This problem is solved, seemingly in all jurisdictions, by qualifying for recording only those documents shown by a specified procedure, either acknowledgement or a form of probate, to have been executed and delivered. 5 WIGMORE §§ 1647–1651. Thus what may appear in the rule, at first glance, as endowing the record with an effect independently of local law and inviting difficulties of an *Erie* nature under *Cities Service Oil Co. v. Dunlap*, 308 U.S. 208 (1939), is not present, since the local law in fact governs under the example.

Exception (15). Dispositive documents often contain recitals of fact. Thus a deed purporting to have been executed by an attorney in fact may recite the existence of the power of attorney, or a deed may recite that the grantors are all the heirs of the last record owner. Under the rule, these recitals are exempted from the hearsay rule. The circumstances under which dispositive documents are executed and the requirement that the recital be germane to the purpose of the document are believed to be adequate guarantees of trustworthiness, particularly in view of the nonapplicability of the rule if dealings with the property have been inconsistent with the document. The age of the document is of no significance, though in practical application the document will most often be an ancient one. *See Comment*, UNIF. R. EVID 63(29).

Similar provisions are contained in Uniform Rule 63(29); California Evidence Code § 1330; Kansas Statutes Annotated § 60-460(aa); New Jersey Evidence Rule 63(29) (repealed and replaced by New Jersey Rule of Evidence 803(c)(15) (1993)).

Exception (16). Authenticating a document as ancient, essentially in the pattern of the common law, as provided in Rule 901(b)(8), leaves open as a separate question the admissibility of assertive statements contained therein as against a hearsay objection. 7 WIGMORE § 2145a. Wigmore further states that the ancient document technique of authentication is universally conceded to apply to all sorts of documents, including letters, records, contracts, maps, and certificates, in addition to title documents, citing numerous decisions. *Id.* § 2145. Since most of these items are significant evidentially only insofar as they are assertive, their admission in evidence must be as a hearsay exception. *But see* 5 *id.* § 1573, at 429, referring to recitals in ancient deeds as a "limited" hearsay exception. The former position is believed to be the correct one in reason and authority. As pointed out in MCCORMICK § 298, danger of mistake is minimized by authentication requirements, and age affords assurance that the writing antedates the present controversy. *See* Dallas County v. Commercial Union Assurance Co., 286 F.2d 388 (5th Cir. 1961) (upholding admissibility of 58-year-old newspaper story); *cf.* MORGAN, BASIC PROBLEMS OF EVIDENCE 364 (1962). *But see* MORGAN, *supra*, at 254.

For a similar provision, but with the added requirement that "the statement has since generally been acted upon as true by persons having an interest in the matter," see California Evidence Code § 1331.

ADVISORY COMMITTEE'S NOTE TO 2017 AMENDMENT TO RULE 803(16)

The ancient documents exception to the rule against hearsay has been limited to statements in documents prepared before January 1, 1998. The Committee has determined that the ancient documents exception should be limited due to the risk that it will be used as a vehicle to admit vast amounts of unreliable electronically stored information (ESI). Given the exponential development and growth of electronic information since 1998, the hearsay exception for ancient documents has now become a possible open door for large amounts of unreliable ESI, as no showing of reliability needs to be made to qualify under the exception.

The Committee is aware that in certain cases—such as cases involving latent diseases and environmental damage—parties must rely on hardcopy documents from the past. The ancient documents exception remains available for such cases for documents prepared before 1998. Going forward, it is anticipated that any need to admit old hardcopy documents produced after January 1, 1998, will decrease, because reliable ESI is likely to be available and can be offered under a reliability-based hearsay exception. Rule 803(6) may be used for many of these ESI documents, especially given its flexible standards on which witnesses might be qualified to provide an adequate foundation. And Rule 807 can be used to admit old documents upon a showing of reliability—which will often (though not always) be found by circumstances such as that the document was prepared with no litigation motive in mind, close in time to the relevant events. The limitation of the ancient documents exception is not intended to raise an inference that 20-year-old documents are, as a class, unreliable, or that they should somehow not qualify for admissibility under Rule 807. Finally, many old documents can be admitted for the non-hearsay purpose of proving notice, or as party-opponent statements.

The limitation of the ancient documents hearsay exception is not intended to have any effect on authentication of ancient documents. The possibility of authenticating an old document under Rule 901(b)(8)—or under any ground available for any other document—remains unchanged.

The Committee carefully considered, but ultimately rejected, an amendment that would preserve the ancient documents exception for hardcopy evidence only. A party will often offer hardcopy that is derived from ESI. Moreover, a good deal of old information in hardcopy has been digitized or will be so in the future. Thus, the line between ESI and hardcopy was determined to be one that could not be drawn usefully.

The Committee understands that the choice of a cutoff date has a degree of arbitrariness. But January 1, 1998, is a rational date for treating concerns about old and unreliable ESI. And the date is no more arbitrary than the 20-year cutoff date in the original rule. *See* Committee Note to Rule 901(b)(8) ("Any time period selected is bound to be arbitrary.").

Under the amendment, a document is "prepared" when the statement proffered was recorded in that document. For example, if a hardcopy document is prepared in 1995, and a party seeks to admit a scanned copy of that document, the date of preparation is 1995 even though the scan was made long after that—the subsequent scan does not alter the document. The relevant point is the date on which the information is recorded, not when the information is prepared for trial. However, if the content of the document is *itself* altered after the cutoff date, then the hearsay exception will not apply to statements that were added in the alteration.

[This space is intentionally blank.]

Exception (17). Ample authority at common law supported the admission in evidence of items falling in this category. While Wigmore's text is narrowly oriented to lists, etc., prepared for the use of a trade or profession, 6 WIGMORE § 1702, authorities are cited which include other kinds of publications, for example, newspaper market reports, telephone directories, and city directories. *Id.* §§ 1702–1706. The basis of trustworthiness is general reliance by the public or by a particular segment of it, and the motivation of the compiler to foster reliance by being accurate.

For similar provisions, see Uniform Rule 63(30); California Evidence Code § 1340; Kansas Statutes Annotated § 60-460(bb); New Jersey Evidence Rule 63(30) (repealed and replaced by New Jersey Rule of Evidence 803(c)(17) (1993)). Uniform Commercial Code § 2-724 provides for admissibility in evidence of "reports in official publications or trade journals or in newspapers or periodicals of general circulation published as the reports of such [established commodity] market."

Exception (18). The writers have generally favored the admissibility of learned treatises, McCORMICK § 296, at 621; MORGAN, BASIC PROBLEMS OF EVIDENCE 366 (1962); 6 WIGMORE § 1692, with the support of occasional decisions and rules, City of Dothan v. Hardy, 237 Ala. 603 (1939); Lewandowski v. Preferred Risk Mut. Ins. Co., 33 Wis.2d 69 (1966); UNIF. R. EVID. 63(31); KAN. STAT. ANN. § 60-460(cc), but the great weight of authority has been that learned treatises are not admissible as substantive evidence though usable in the cross-examination of experts. The foundation of the minority view is that the hearsay objection must be regarded as unimpressive when directed against treatises since a high standard of accuracy is engendered by various factors: the treatise is written primarily and impartially for professionals, subject to scrutiny and exposure for inaccuracy, with the reputation of the writer at stake. 6 WIGMORE § 1692. Sound as this position may be with respect to trustworthiness, there is, nevertheless, an additional difficulty in the likelihood that the treatise will be misunderstood and misapplied without expert assistance and supervision. This difficulty is recognized in the cases demonstrating unwillingness to sustain findings relative to disability on the basis of judicially noticed medical texts. Ross v. Gardner, 365 F.2d 554 (6th Cir. 1966); Sayers v. Gardner, 380 F.2d 940 (6th Cir. 1967); Colwell v. Gardner, 386 F.2d 56 (6th Cir. 1967); Glendenning v. Ribicoff, 213 F. Supp. 301 (W.D. Mo. 1962); Cook v. Celebrezze, 217 F. Supp. 366 (W.D. Mo. 1963); Sosna v. Celebrezze, 234 F. Supp. 289 (E.D. Pa. 1964); *see also* McDaniel v. Celebrezze, 331 F.2d 426 (4th Cir. 1964). The rule avoids the danger of misunderstanding and misapplication by limiting the use of treatises as substantive evidence to situations in which an expert is on the stand and available to explain and assist in the application of the treatise if desired. The limitation upon receiving the publication itself physically in evidence, contained in the last sentence, is designed to further this policy.

The relevance of the use of treatises on cross-examination is evident. This use of treatises has been the subject of varied views. The most restrictive position is that the witness must have stated expressly on direct his reliance upon the treatise. A slightly more liberal approach still insists upon reliance but allows it to be developed on cross-examination. Further relaxation dispenses with reliance but requires recognition as an authority by the witness, developable on cross-examination. The greatest liberality is found in decisions allowing use of the treatise on cross-examination when its status as an authority is established by any means. Annotation, 60 A.L.R.2d 77. The exception is hinged upon this last position, which is that of the Supreme Court, Reilly v. Pinkus, 338 U.S. 269 (1949), and of recent well considered state court decisions, City of

St. Petersburg v. Ferguson, 193 So. 2d 648 (Fla. App. 1966), *cert. denied*, 201 So. 2d 556 (Fla. 1967); Darling v. Charleston Mem'l Cmty. Hosp., 33 Ill.2d 326 (1965); Dabroe v. Rhodes Co., 64 Wash. 2d 431 (1964).

In *Reilly v. Pinkus*, 338 U.S. 269 (1949), the Court pointed out that testing of professional knowledge was incomplete without exploration of the witness's knowledge of and attitude toward established treatises in the field. The process works equally well in reverse and furnishes the basis of the rule.

The rule does not require that the witness rely upon or recognize the treatise as authoritative, thus avoiding the possibility that the expert may at the outset block cross-examination by refusing to concede reliance or authoritativeness. Dabroe v. Rhodes Co., 64 Wash. 2d 431 (1964). Moreover, the rule avoids the unreality of admitting evidence for the purpose of impeachment only, with an instruction to the jury not to consider it otherwise. The parallel to the treatment of prior inconsistent statements will be apparent. *See* Rules 613(b) and 801(d)(1).

Exceptions (19), (20), and (21). Trustworthiness in reputation evidence is found "when the topic is such that the facts are likely to have been inquired about and that persons having personal knowledge have disclosed facts which have thus been discussed in the community; and thus the community's conclusion, if any has been formed, is likely to be a trustworthy one." 5 WIGMORE § 1580, at 444; *see also id.* § 1583. On this common foundation, reputation as to land boundaries, customs, general history, character, and marriage have come to be regarded as admissible. The breadth of the underlying principle suggests the formulation of an equally broad exception, but tradition has in fact been much narrower and more particularized, and this is the pattern of these exceptions in the rule.

Exception (19) is concerned with matters of personal and family history. Marriage is universally conceded to be a proper subject of proof by evidence of reputation in the community. 5 WIGMORE § 1602. As to such items as legitimacy, relationship, adoption, birth, and death, the decisions are divided. *Id.* § 1605. All seem to be susceptible to being the subject of well-founded repute. The "world" in which the reputation may exist may be family, associates, or community. This world has proved capable of expanding with changing times from the single uncomplicated neighborhood, in which all activities take place, to the multiple and unrelated worlds of work, religious affiliation, and social activity, in each of which a reputation may be generated. People v. Reeves, 360 Ill. 55 (1935); State v. Axilrod, 248 Minn. 204 (1956); Mass. Stat. 1947, ch. 410, § 1, MASS. GEN. LAWS ANN. ch. 233, § 21A; 5 WIGMORE § 1616. The family has often served as the point of beginning for allowing community reputation. 5 WIGMORE § 1488. For comparable provisions see Uniform Rule 63(26), (27)(c); California Evidence Code §§ 1313, 1314; Kansas Statutes Annotated § 60-460(x), (y)(3); New Jersey Evidence Rule 63(26) (repealed and replaced by New Jersey Rule of Evidence 804(b)(4) (1993)), (27)(c) (repealed and replaced by New Jersey Rule of Evidence 803(c)(19) (1993)).

The first portion of exception (20) is based upon the general admissibility of evidence of reputation as to land boundaries and land customs, expanded in this country to include private as well as public boundaries. MCCORMICK § 299, at 625. The reputation is required to antedate the controversy, though not to be ancient. The second portion is likewise supported by authority, *id.*, and is designed to facilitate proof of events when judicial notice is not available. The historical character of the subject matter dispenses with any need that the reputation antedate the controversy with respect to which it is offered. For similar provisions see Uniform Rule 63(27)(a), (b); California Evidence Code §§ 1320–1322; Kansas Statutes Annotated § 60-460(y)–(y)(2); New Jersey Evidence Rule 63(27)(a), (b) (repealed and replaced by New Jersey Rule of Evidence 803(c)(20) (1993)).

Exception (21) recognizes the traditional acceptance of reputation evidence as a means of proving human character. MCCORMICK §§ 44, 158. The exception deals only with the hearsay aspect of this kind of evidence. Limitations upon admissibility based on other grounds will be found in Rules 404, relevancy of character evidence generally, and 608, character of witness. The exception is in effect a reiteration, in the context of hearsay, of Rule 405(a). Similar provisions are contained in Uniform Rule 63(28); California Evidence Code § 1324; Kansas Statutes Annotated § 60-460(z); New Jersey Evidence Rule 63(28) (repealed and replaced by New Jersey Rule of Evidence 803(c)(21) (1993)).

Exception (22). When the status of a former judgment is under consideration in subsequent litigation, three possibilities must be noted: (1) the former judgment is conclusive under the doctrine of res judicata, either as a bar or a collateral estoppel; or (2) it is admissible in evidence for what it is worth; or (3) it may be of no effect at all. The first situation does not involve any problem of evidence except in the way that principles of substantive law generally bear upon the relevancy and materiality of evidence. The rule does not deal with the substantive effect of the judgment as a bar or collateral estoppel. When, however, the doctrine of res judicata does not apply to make the judgment either a bar or a collateral estoppel, a choice is presented between the second and third alternatives. The rule adopts the second for judgments of criminal conviction of felony grade. This is the direction of the decisions, Annotation, 18 A.L.R.2d 1287, 1299, which manifest an increasing reluctance to reject in toto the validity of the law's factfinding processes outside the confines of res judicata and collateral estoppel. While this may leave a jury with the evidence of conviction but without means to evaluate it, as suggested by Judge Hinton, Note, 27 ILL. L. REV. 195 (1932), it seems safe to assume that the jury will give it substantial effect unless defendant offers a satisfactory explanation, a possibility not foreclosed by the provision. But see *North River Insurance Co. v. Militello*, 104 Colo. 28 (1939), in which the jury found for plaintiff on a fire policy despite the introduction of his conviction for arson. For supporting federal decisions see Clark, J., in *New York & Cuba Mail Steamship Co. v. Continental Insurance Co.*, 117 F.2d 404, 411 (2d Cir. 1941); *Connecticut Fire Insurance Co. v. Ferrara*, 277 F.2d 388 (8th Cir. 1960).

Practical considerations require exclusion of convictions of minor offenses, not because the administration of justice in its lower echelons must be inferior, but because motivation to defend at this level is often minimal or nonexistent. Cope v. Goble, 39 Cal. App. 2d 448 (1940); Jones v. Talbot, 87 Idaho 498 (1964); Warren v. Marsh, 215 Minn. 615 (1943); Annotation, 18 A.L.R.2d 1287, 1295–97; 16 BROOK. L. REV. 286 (1950); 50 COLUM. L. REV. 529 (1950); 35 CORNELL L.Q. 872 (1950). Hence the rule includes only convictions of felony grade, measured by federal standards.

Judgments of conviction based upon pleas of nolo contendere are not included. This position is consistent with the treatment of nolo pleas in Rule 410 and the authorities cited in the Advisory Committee's Note in support thereof.

While these rules do not in general purport to resolve constitutional issues, they have in general been drafted with a view to avoiding collision with constitutional principles. Consequently the exception does not include evidence of the conviction of a third person, offered against the accused in a criminal prosecution to prove any fact essential to sustain the judgment of conviction. A contrary position would seem clearly to violate the right of confrontation. Kirby v. United States, 174 U.S. 47 (1899), error to convict of possessing stolen postage stamps with the only evidence of theft being the record of conviction of the thieves. The situation is to be distinguished from cases in which conviction of another person is an element of the crime, *e.g.*, 15 U.S.C. § 902(d) (repealed 1968) (interstate shipment of firearms to a known convicted felon), and, as specifically provided, from impeachment.

For comparable provisions see Uniform Rule 63(20); California Evidence Code § 1300; Kansas Statutes Annotated § 60-460(r); New Jersey Evidence Rule 63(20) (repealed and replaced by New Jersey Rule of Evidence 803(c)(22) (1993)).

Exception (23). A hearsay exception in this area was originally justified on the ground that verdicts were evidence of reputation. As trial by jury graduated from the category of neighborhood inquests, this theory lost its validity. It was never valid as to chancery decrees. Nevertheless the rule persisted, though the judges and writers shifted ground and began saying that the judgment or decree was as good evidence as reputation. *See* City of London v. Clerke, Carth. 181, (1691) 90 Eng. Rep. 710 (K.B.); Neill v. Duke of Devonshire, [1882] 8 App. Cas. 135. The shift appears to be correct, since the process of inquiry, sifting, and scrutiny which is relied upon to render reputation reliable is present in perhaps greater measure in the process of litigation. While this might suggest a broader area of application, the affinity to reputation is strong, and [exception] (23) goes no further, not even including character.

The leading case in the United States, *Patterson v. Gaines*, 47 U.S. (6 How.) 550, 599 (1847), follows in the pattern of the English decisions, mentioning as illustrative matters thus provable: manorial rights, public rights of way, immemorial custom, disputed boundary, and pedigree. More recent recognition of the principle is found in *Grant Bros. Construction Co. v. United States*, 232 U.S. 647 (1914) (in action for penalties under Alien Contract Labor Law, decision of board of inquiry of Immigration Service admissible to prove alienage of laborers, as a matter of pedigree); *United States v. Mid-Continent Petroleum Corp.*, 67 F.2d 37 (10th Cir. 1933) (records of commission enrolling Indians admissible on pedigree); *Jung Yen Loy v. Cahill*, 81 F.2d 809 (9th Cir. 1936) (board decisions as to citizenship of plaintiff's father admissible in proceeding for declaration of citizenship). *Contra In re* Estate of Cunha, 49 Haw. 273 (1966).

EDITOR'S NOTE

As originally enacted in 1975, the Federal Rules included two catchall hearsay exceptions, one that did not require the declarant's unavailability (FRE 803(24)) and one that did (FRE 804(b)(5)). Rule 807, enacted in 1997, consolidated and displaced both rules. In deference to the original structure, I have left the legislative history of the original rules where it was, largely following FRE 803(24). Today that history bears on the interpretation of Rule 807.—GF

<u>ADVISORY COMMITTEE'S NOTE TO RULE 803(24)</u>

Exception (24). The preceding twenty-three exceptions of Rule 803 and the first [four] exceptions of Rule 804(b), *infra*, are designed to take full advantage of the accumulated wisdom and experience of the past in dealing with hearsay. It would, however, be presumptuous to assume that all possible desirable exceptions to the hearsay rule have been catalogued and to pass the hearsay rule to oncoming generations as a closed system. Exception (24) and its companion provision in Rule [804(b)(5)] are accordingly included. They do not contemplate an unfettered exercise of judicial discretion, but they do provide for treating new and presently unanticipated situations which demonstrate a trustworthiness within the spirit of the specifically stated exceptions. Within this framework, room is left for growth and development of the law of evidence in the hearsay area, consistently with the broad purposes expressed in Rule 102. *See* Dallas County v. Commercial Union Assurance Co., 286 F.2d 388 (5th Cir. 1961).

<u>REPORT OF THE SENATE COMMITTEE ON THE JUDICIARY</u>

The proposed Rules of Evidence submitted to Congress contained identical provisions in Rules 803 and 804 (which set forth the various hearsay exceptions), admitting any hearsay statement not specifically covered by any of the stated exceptions, if the hearsay statement was found to have "comparable circumstantial guarantees of trustworthiness." The House deleted these provisions (proposed Rules 803(24) and [804(b)(5)]) as injecting "too much uncertainty" into the law of evidence and impairing the ability of practitioners to prepare for trial. The House felt that Rule 102, which directs the courts to construe the Rules of Evidence so as to promote growth and development, would permit sufficient flexibility to admit hearsay evidence in appropriate cases under various factual situations that might arise.

We disagree with the total rejection of a residual hearsay exception. While we view Rule 102 as being intended to provide for a broader construction and interpretation of these rules, we feel that, without a separate residual provision, the specifically enumerated exceptions could become tortured beyond any reasonable circumstances which they were intended to include (even if broadly construed). Moreover, these exceptions, while they reflect the most typical and well recognized exceptions to the hearsay rule, may not encompass every situation in which the reliability and appropriateness of a particular piece of hearsay evidence make clear that it should be heard and considered by the trier of fact.

The Committee believes that there are certain exceptional circumstances where evidence which is found by a court to have guarantees of trustworthiness equivalent to or exceeding the guarantees reflected by the presently listed exceptions, and to have a high degree of probativeness and necessity could properly be admissible.

The case of *Dallas County v. Commercial Union Assurance Co.*, 286 F.2d 388 (5th Cir. 1961) illustrates the point. The issue in that case was whether the tower of the county courthouse collapsed because it was struck by lightning (covered by insurance) or because of structural weakness and deterioration of the structure (not covered). Investigation of the structure revealed the presence of charcoal and charred timbers. In order to show that lightning may not have been the cause of the charring, the insurer offered a copy of a local newspaper published over fifty years earlier containing an unsigned article describing a fire in the courthouse while it was under construction. The Court found that the newspaper did not qualify for admission as a business record or an ancient document and did not fit within any other recognized hearsay exception. The court concluded, however, that the article was trustworthy because it was inconceivable that a newspaper reporter in a small town would report a fire in the courthouse if none had occurred. *See also* United States v. Barbati, 284 F. Supp. 409 (E.D.N.Y. 1968).

Because exceptional cases like the *Dallas County* case may arise in the future, the Committee has decided to reinstate a residual exception for Rules 803 and 804(b).

The Committee, however, also agrees with those supporters of the House version who felt that an overly broad residual hearsay exception could emasculate the hearsay rule and the recognized exceptions or vitiate the rationale behind codification of the rules.

Therefore, the Committee has adopted a residual exception for Rules 803 and 804(b) of much narrower scope and applicability than the Supreme Court version. In order to qualify for admission, a hearsay statement not falling within one of the recognized exceptions would have to satisfy at least four conditions. First, it must have "equivalent circumstantial guarantees of trustworthiness." Second, it must be offered as evidence of a material fact. Third, the court must determine that the statement "is more probative on the point for which it is offered than any other evidence which the proponent can procure through reasonable efforts." This requirement is intended to insure that only statements which have high probative value and necessity may qualify for admission under the residual exceptions. Fourth, the court must determine that "the general purposes of these rules and the interests of justice will best be served by admission of the statement into evidence."

It is intended that the residual hearsay exceptions will be used very rarely, and only in exceptional circumstances. The Committee does not intend to establish a broad license for trial judges to admit hearsay statements that do not fall within one of the other exceptions contained in Rules 803 and 804(b). The residual exceptions are not meant to authorize major judicial revisions of the hearsay rule, including its present exceptions. Such major revisions are best accomplished by legislative action. It is intended that in any case in which evidence is sought to be admitted under these subsections, the trial judge will exercise no less care, reflection, and caution than the courts did under the common law in establishing the now-recognized exceptions to the hearsay rule.

In order to establish a well-defined jurisprudence, the special facts and circumstances which, in the court's judgment, indicate that the statement has a sufficiently high degree of trustworthiness and necessity to justify its admission should be stated on the record. It is expected that the court will give the opposing party a full and adequate opportunity to contest the admission of any statement sought to be introduced under these subsections.

CONFERENCE REPORT

The Senate amendment adds a new [exception], (24), which makes admissible a hearsay statement not specifically covered by any of the previous twenty-three [exceptions], if the statement has equivalent circumstantial guarantees of trustworthiness and if the court determines that (A) the statement is offered as evidence of a material fact; (B) the statement is more probative on the point for which it is offered than any other evidence the proponent can procure through reasonable efforts; and (C) the general purposes of these rules and the interests of justice will best be served by admission of the statement into evidence.

The House bill eliminated a similar, but broader, provision because of the conviction that such a provision injected too much uncertainty into the law of evidence regarding hearsay and impaired the ability of a litigant to prepare adequately for trial.

The Conference adopts the Senate amendment with an amendment that provides that a party intending to request the court to use a statement under this provision must notify any adverse party of this intention as well as of the particulars of the statement, including the name and address of the declarant. This notice must be given sufficiently in advance of the trial or hearing to provide any adverse party with a fair opportunity to prepare to contest the use of the statement.

ADVISORY COMMITTEE'S NOTE TO 1997 AMENDMENT TO RULE 803(24)

The contents of Rule 803(24) and Rule 804(b)(5) have been combined and transferred to a new Rule 807. This was done to facilitate additions to Rules 803 and 804. No change in meaning is intended.

Rule 804.   EXCEPTIONS TO THE RULE AGAINST HEARSAY— WHEN THE DECLARANT IS UNAVAILABLE AS A WITNESS.

(a) Criteria for Being Unavailable.   A declarant is considered to be unavailable as a witness if the declarant:

(1) is exempted from testifying about the subject matter of the declarant's statement because the court rules that a privilege applies;

(2) refuses to testify about the subject matter despite a court order to do so;

(3) testifies to not remembering the subject matter;

(4) cannot be present or testify at the trial or hearing because of death or a then-existing infirmity, physical illness, or mental illness; or

(5) is absent from the trial or hearing and the statement's proponent has not been able, by process or other reasonable means, to procure:

(A) the declarant's attendance, in the case of a hearsay exception under Rule 804(b)(1) or (6); or

(B) the declarant's attendance or testimony, in the case of a hearsay exception under Rule 804(b)(2), (3), or (4).

But this subdivision (a) does not apply if the statement's proponent procured or wrongfully caused the declarant's

---

unavailability as a witness in order to prevent the declarant from attending or testifying.

(b) The Exceptions. The following are not excluded by the rule against hearsay if the declarant is unavailable as a witness:

(1) *Former Testimony.* Testimony that:

(A) was given as a witness at a trial, hearing, or lawful deposition, whether given during the current proceeding or a different one; and

(B) is now offered against a party who had—or, in a civil case, whose predecessor in interest had—an opportunity and similar motive to develop it by direct, cross-, or redirect examination.

(2) *Statement Under the Belief of Imminent Death.* In a prosecution for homicide or in a civil case, a statement that the declarant, while believing the declarant's death to be imminent, made about its cause or circumstances.

(3) *Statement Against Interest.* A statement that:

(A) a reasonable person in the declarant's position would have made only if the person believed it to be true because, when made, it was so contrary to the declarant's proprietary or pecuniary interest or had so great a tendency to invalidate the declarant's claim against someone else or to expose the declarant to civil or criminal liability; and

(B) is supported by corroborating circumstances that clearly indicate its trustworthiness, if it is offered in a criminal case as one that tends to expose the declarant to criminal liability.

(4) *Statement of Personal or Family History.* A statement about:

    (A) the declarant's own birth, adoption, legitimacy, ancestry, marriage, divorce, relationship by blood, adoption, or marriage, or similar facts of personal or family history, even though the declarant had no way of acquiring personal knowledge about that fact; or

    (B) another person concerning any of these facts, as well as death, if the declarant was related to the person by blood, adoption, or marriage or was so intimately associated with the person's family that the declarant's information is likely to be accurate.

(5) *[Other Exceptions.]* [Transferred to Rule 807.]

(6) *Statement Offered Against a Party That Wrongfully Caused the Declarant's Unavailability.* A statement offered against a party that wrongfully caused—or acquiesced in wrongfully causing—the declarant's unavailability as a witness, and did so intending that result.

(Enacted Jan. 2, 1975; as amended Dec. 12, 1975; Mar. 2, 1987, eff. Oct. 1, 1987; Nov. 18, 1988; Apr. 11, 1997, eff. Dec. 1, 1997; Apr. 28, 2010, eff. Dec. 1, 2010; as restyled Apr. 26, 2011, eff. Dec. 1, 2011.)

<u>NOTE BY FEDERAL JUDICIAL CENTER</u>

The rule prescribed by the Supreme Court was amended by the Congress in a number of respects as follows:

Subdivision (a). Paragraphs (1) and (2) were amended by substituting "court" in place of "judge," and paragraph (5) was amended by inserting "(or in the case of a hearsay exception under subdivision (b)(2), (3), or (4), his attendance or testimony)."

Subdivision (b). Exception (1) was amended by inserting "the same or" after "course of," and by substituting the phrase "if the party against whom the testimony is now offered, or, in a civil action or proceeding, a predecessor in interest, had an opportunity and similar motive to develop the testimony by direct, cross, or redirect examination" in place of "at the instance of or against a party with an opportunity to develop the testimony by direct, cross, or redirect examination, with motive and interest similar to those of the party against whom now offered."

Exception (2) as prescribed by the Supreme Court, dealing with statements of recent perception, was deleted by the Congress.

. . . Exception (2) as enacted by the Congress is exception (3) prescribed by the Supreme Court, amended by inserting at the beginning, "In a prosecution for homicide or in a civil action or proceeding."

Exception (3) as enacted by the Congress is exception (4) prescribed by the Supreme Court, amended in the first sentence by deleting, after "another," the phrase "or to make him an object of hatred, ridicule, or disgrace," and amended in the second sentence by substituting, after "unless," the phrase, "corroborating circumstances clearly indicate the trustworthiness of the statement," in place of "corroborated."

Exception (4) as enacted by the Congress is exception (5) prescribed by the Supreme Court without change.

Exception (5) as enacted by the Congress is exception (6) prescribed by the Supreme Court, amended by substituting "equivalent" in place of "comparable" and by adding all after "trustworthiness."

<u>Advisory Committee's Note to Rule 804(a)–(a)(3)</u>

As to firsthand knowledge on the part of hearsay declarants, see the introductory portion of the Advisory Committee's Note to Rule 803.

Subdivision (a). The definition of unavailability implements the division of hearsay exceptions into two categories by Rules 803 and 804(b).

At common law the unavailability requirement was evolved in connection with particular hearsay exceptions rather than along general lines. For example, see the separate explications of unavailability in relation to former testimony, declarations against interest, and statements of pedigree, separately developed in McCormick §§ 234, 257, 297. However, no reason is apparent for making distinctions as to what satisfies unavailability for the different exceptions. The treatment in the rule is therefore uniform although differences in the range of process for witnesses between civil and criminal cases will lead to a less exacting requirement under item (5). *See* Fed. R. Civ. P. [45(b)(2)]; Fed. R. Crim. P. 17(e).

Five instances of unavailability are specified:

(1) Substantial authority supports the position that exercise of a claim of privilege by the declarant satisfies the requirement of unavailability (usually in connection with former testimony). Wyatt v. State, 35 Ala. App. 147 (1950); State v. Stewart, 85 Kan. 404 (1911); Annotation, 45 A.L.R.2d 1354; UNIF. R. EVID. 62(7)(a); CAL. EVID. CODE § 240(a)(1); KAN. STAT. ANN. § 60-459(g)(1). A ruling by the judge is required, which clearly implies that an actual claim of privilege must be made.

(2) A witness is rendered unavailable if he simply refuses to testify concerning the subject matter of his statement despite judicial pressures to do so, a position supported by similar considerations of practicality. Johnson v. People, 152 Colo. 586 (1963); People v. Pickett, 339 Mich. 294 (1954). *Contra* Pleau v. State, 255 Wis. 362 (1949).

(3) The position that a claimed lack of memory by the witness of the subject matter of his statement constitutes unavailability likewise finds support in the cases, though not without dissent. MCCORMICK § 234, at 494. If the claim is successful, the practical effect is to put the testimony beyond reach, as in the other instances. In this instance, however, it will be noted that the lack of memory must be established by the testimony of the witness himself, which clearly contemplates his production and subjection to cross-examination.

REPORT OF THE HOUSE COMMITTEE ON THE JUDICIARY

Rule 804(a)(3) was approved in the form submitted by the Court. However, the Committee intends no change in existing federal law under which the court may choose to disbelieve the declarant's testimony as to his lack of memory. *See* United States v. Insana, 423 F.2d 1165, 1169–70 (2d Cir.), *cert. denied*, 400 U.S. 841 (1970).

ADVISORY COMMITTEE'S NOTE TO RULE 804(a)(4)–(5)

(4) Death and infirmity find general recognition as grounds. MCCORMICK §§ 234, 257, 297; UNIF. R. EVID. 62(7)(c); CAL. EVID. CODE § 240(a)(3); KAN. STAT. ANN. § 60-459(g)(3); N.J. EVID. R. 62(6)(c) (repealed and replaced by N.J. R. EVID. 804(a)(4) (1993)). See also the provisions on use of depositions in Rule [32(a)(4)] of the Federal Rules of Civil Procedure and Rule [15(f)] of the Federal Rules of Criminal Procedure.

(5) Absence from the hearing coupled with inability to compel attendance by process or other reasonable means also satisfies the requirement. MCCORMICK § 234; UNIF. R. EVID. 62(7)(d), (e); CAL. EVID. CODE § 240(a)(4), (5); KAN. STAT. ANN. § 60-459(g)(4), (5); N.J. EVID. R. 62(6)(b), (d) (repealed and replaced by N.J. R. EVID. 804(a)(4) (1993)). See the discussion of procuring attendance of witnesses who are nonresidents or in custody in *Barber v. Page*, 390 U.S. 719 (1968).

If the conditions otherwise constituting unavailability result from the procurement or wrongdoing of the proponent of the statement, the requirement is not satisfied. The rule contains no requirement that an attempt be made to take the deposition of a declarant.

REPORT OF THE HOUSE COMMITTEE ON THE JUDICIARY

Rule 804(a)(5) as submitted to the Congress provided, as one type of situation in which a declarant would be deemed "unavailable," that he be "absent from the hearing and the proponent of his statement has been unable to procure his attendance by process or other reasonable means." The Committee amended the rule to insert after the word "attendance" the parenthetical expression "(or, in the case of a hearsay exception under subdivision (b)(2), (3), or (4), his attendance or testimony)." The amendment is designed primarily to require that an attempt be made to depose a witness (as well as to seek his attendance) as a precondition to the witness being deemed unavailable. The Committee, however, recognized the propriety of an exception to this additional requirement when it is the declarant's former testimony that is sought to be admitted under subdivision (b)(1).

REPORT OF THE SENATE COMMITTEE ON THE JUDICIARY

Subdivision (a) of Rule 804 as submitted by the Supreme Court defined the conditions under which a witness was considered to be unavailable. It was amended in the House.

The purpose of the amendment, according to the Report of the House Committee on the Judiciary, is "primarily to require that an attempt be made to depose a witness (as well as to seek his attendance) as a precondition to the witness being unavailable."

Under the House amendment, before a witness is declared unavailable, a party must try to depose a witness (declarant) with respect to dying declarations, declarations against interest, and declarations of pedigree. None of these situations would seem to warrant this needless, impractical, and highly restrictive complication. A good case can be made for eliminating the unavailability requirement entirely for declarations against interest cases.[11]

In dying declaration cases, the declarant will usually, though not necessarily, be deceased at the time of trial. Pedigree statements which are admittedly and necessarily based largely on word of mouth are not greatly fortified by a deposition requirement.

Depositions are expensive and time-consuming. In any event, deposition procedures are available to those who wish to resort to them. Moreover, the deposition procedures of the Civil Rules and Criminal Rules are only imperfectly adapted to implementing the amendment. No purpose is served unless the deposition, if taken, may be used in evidence. Under Civil Rule [32(a)(4)] and Criminal Rule [15(f)], a deposition, though taken, may not be admissible, and under Criminal Rule 15(a) substantial obstacles exist in the way of even taking a deposition.

For these reasons, the Committee deleted the House amendment.

The Committee understands that the rule as to unavailability, as explained by the Advisory Committee, "contains no requirement that an attempt be made to take the deposition of a declarant." In reflecting the Committee's judgment, the statement is accurate insofar as it goes. Where, however, the proponent of the statement, with knowledge of the existence of the statement, fails to confront the declarant with the statement at the taking of the deposition, then the proponent should not, in fairness, be permitted to treat the declarant as "unavailable" simply because the declarant was not amenable to process compelling his attendance at trial. The Committee does not consider it necessary to amend the rule to this effect because such a situation abuses, not conforms to, the rule. Fairness would preclude a person from introducing a hearsay statement on a particular issue if the person taking the deposition was aware of the issue at the time of the deposition but failed to depose the unavailable witness on that issue.

CONFERENCE REPORT

Subsection (a) defines the term "unavailability as a witness." The House bill provides in subsection (a)(5) that the party who desires to use the statement must be unable to procure the declarant's attendance by process or other reasonable means. In the

---

[11] UNIF. R. EVID. 63(10); KAN. STAT. ANN. 60-460(j); N.J. EVID. R. 63(10) (repealed and replaced by N.J. R. EVID. 803(c)(25) (1993)).

case of dying declarations, statements against interest, and statements of personal or family history, the House bill requires that the proponent must also be unable to procure the declarant's *testimony* (such as by deposition or interrogatories) by process or other reasonable means. The Senate amendment eliminates this latter provision.

The Conference adopts the provision contained in the House bill.

ADVISORY COMMITTEE'S NOTE TO RULE 804(b)–(b)(1)

Subdivision (b). Rule 803, *supra*, is based upon the assumption that a hearsay statement falling within one of its exceptions possesses qualities which justify the conclusion that whether the declarant is available or unavailable is not a relevant factor in determining admissibility. The instant rule proceeds upon a different theory: hearsay which admittedly is not equal in quality to testimony of the declarant on the stand may nevertheless be admitted if the declarant is unavailable and if his statement meets a specified standard. The rule expresses preferences: testimony given on the stand in person is preferred over hearsay, and hearsay, if of the specified quality, is preferred over complete loss of the evidence of the declarant. The exceptions evolved at common law with respect to declarations of unavailable declarants furnish the basis for the exceptions enumerated in the proposal. The term "unavailable" is defined in subdivision (a).

Exception (1). Former testimony does not rely upon some set of circumstances to substitute for oath and cross-examination, since both oath and opportunity to cross-examine were present in fact. The only missing one of the ideal conditions for the giving of testimony is the presence of trier and opponent ("demeanor evidence"). This is lacking with all hearsay exceptions. Hence it may be argued that former testimony is the strongest hearsay and should be included under Rule 803, *supra*. However, opportunity to observe demeanor is what in a large measure confers depth and meaning upon oath and cross-examination. Thus in cases under Rule 803 demeanor lacks the significance which it possesses with respect to testimony. In any event, the tradition, founded in experience, uniformly favors production of the witness if he is available. The exception indicates continuation of the policy. This preference for the presence of the witness is apparent also in rules and statutes on the use of depositions, which deal with substantially the same problem.

Under the exception, the testimony may be offered (1) against the party *against* whom it was previously offered or (2) against the party *by* whom it was previously offered. In each instance the question resolves itself into whether fairness allows imposing, upon the party against whom now offered, the handling of the witness on the earlier occasion. (1) If the party against whom now offered is the one *against* whom the testimony was offered previously, no unfairness is apparent in requiring him to accept his own prior conduct of cross-examination or decision not to cross-examine. Only demeanor has been lost, and that is inherent in the situation. (2) If the party against whom now offered is the one *by* whom the testimony was offered previously, a satisfactory answer becomes somewhat more difficult. One possibility is to proceed somewhat along the line of an adoptive admission, i.e., by offering the testimony proponent in effect adopts it. However, this theory savors of discarded concepts of witnesses' belonging to a party, of litigants' ability to pick and choose witnesses, and of vouching for one's own witnesses. *Cf.* MCCORMICK § 246, at 526–27; 4 WIGMORE § 1075. A more direct and acceptable approach is simply to recognize direct and redirect examination of one's own witness as the equivalent of cross-examining an opponent's witness. Falknor, *Former Testimony and the Uniform Rules: A Comment*, 38 N.Y.U. L. REV. 651 n.1 (1963); MCCORMICK § 231, at 483; *see also* 5 WIGMORE § 1389. Allowable techniques for dealing with hostile, double-crossing, forgetful, and mentally deficient witnesses leave no substance to a claim that one could not adequately develop his own witness at the former hearing. An even less appealing argument is presented when failure to develop fully was the result of a deliberate choice.

The common law did not limit the admissibility of former testimony to that given in an earlier trial of the same case, although it did require identity of issues as a means of insuring that the former handling of the witness was the equivalent of what would now be done if the opportunity were presented. Modern decisions reduce the requirement to "substantial" identity. MCCORMICK § 233. Since identity of issues is significant only in that it bears on motive and interest in developing fully the testimony of the witness, expressing the matter in the latter terms is preferable. *Id.* Testimony given at a preliminary hearing was held in *California v. Green*, 399 U.S. 149 (1970), to satisfy confrontation requirements in this respect.

As a further assurance of fairness in thrusting upon a party the prior handling of the witness, the common law also insisted upon identity of parties, deviating only to the extent of allowing substitution of successors in a narrowly construed privity. Mutuality as an aspect of identity is now generally discredited, and the requirement of identity of the offering party disappears except as it might affect motive to develop the testimony. Falknor, *supra*, at 652; MCCORMICK § 232, at 487–88. The question remains whether strict identity, or privity, should continue as a requirement with respect to the party against whom offered. . . .

REPORT OF THE HOUSE COMMITTEE ON THE JUDICIARY

Rule 804(b)(1) as submitted by the Court allowed prior testimony of an unavailable witness to be admissible if the party against whom it is offered or a person "with motive and interest similar" to his had an opportunity to examine the witness. The Committee considered that it is generally unfair to impose upon the party against whom the hearsay evidence is being offered responsibility for the manner in which the witness was previously handled by another party. The sole exception to this, in the Committee's view, is when a party's predecessor in interest in a civil action or proceeding had an opportunity and similar motive to examine the witness. The Committee amended the rule to reflect these policy determinations.

REPORT OF THE SENATE COMMITTEE FOR THE JUDICIARY

Former testimony. Rule 804(b)(1) as submitted by the Court allowed prior testimony of an unavailable witness to be admissible if the party against whom it is offered or a person "with motive and interest similar" to his had an opportunity to examine the witness.

The House amended the rule to apply only to a party's predecessor in interest. Although the Committee recognizes considerable merit to the rule submitted by the Supreme Court, a position which has been advocated by many scholars and judges, we have concluded that the difference between the two versions is not great and we accept the House amendment.

ADVISORY COMMITTEE'S NOTE TO RULE 804(b)(2)

Exception (2). The exception is the familiar dying declaration of the common law, expanded somewhat beyond its traditionally narrow limits. While the original religious justification for the exception may have lost its conviction for some persons over the years, it can scarcely be doubted that powerful psychological pressures are present. See 5 Wigmore § 1443 and the classic statement of Chief Baron Eyre in *Rex v. Woodcock*, (1789) 168 Eng. Rep. 352 (K.B.) 353, 1 Leach 500, 502.

The common law required that the statement be that of the victim, offered in a prosecution for criminal homicide. Thus declarations by victims in prosecutions for other crimes, e.g., a declaration by a rape victim who dies in childbirth, and all declarations in civil cases were outside the scope of the exception.

An occasional statute has removed these restrictions, as in Colorado Revised Statutes § [13-25-119], or has expanded the area of offenses to include abortions, 5 WIGMORE § 1432, at 224 n.4. Kansas by decision extended the exception to civil cases. Thurston v. Fritz, 91 Kan. 468 (1914). While the common law exception no doubt originated as a result of the exceptional need for the evidence in homicide cases, the theory of admissibility applies equally in civil cases. . . . The same considerations suggest abandonment of the limitation to circumstances attending the event in question, yet when the statement deals with matters other than the supposed death, its influence is believed to be sufficiently attenuated to justify the limitation. Unavailability is not limited to death. See subdivision (a) of this rule. Any problem as to declarations phrased in terms of opinion is laid at rest by Rule 701, and continuation of a requirement of first-hand knowledge is assured by Rule 602.

Comparable provisions are found in Uniform Rule 63(5); California Evidence Code § 1242; Kansas Statutes Annotated § 60-460(e); New Jersey Evidence Rule 63(5) (repealed and replaced by New Jersey Rule of Evidence 804(b)(2) (1993)).

REPORT OF THE HOUSE COMMITTEE ON THE JUDICIARY

Rule 804(b)(3) as submitted by the Court (now Rule 804(b)(2) in the bill) proposed to expand the traditional scope of the dying declaration exception (i.e., a statement of the victim in a homicide case as to the cause or circumstances of his believed imminent death) to allow such statements in all criminal and civil cases. The Committee did not consider dying declarations as among the most reliable forms of hearsay. Consequently, it amended the provision to limit their admissibility in criminal cases to homicide prosecutions, where exceptional need for the evidence is present. This is existing law. At the same time, the Committee approved the expansion to civil actions and proceedings where the stakes do not involve possible imprisonment, although noting that this could lead to forum shopping in some instances.

ADVISORY COMMITTEE'S NOTE TO RULE 804(b)(3)

Exception (3). The circumstantial guaranty of reliability for declarations against interest is the assumption that persons do not make statements which are damaging to themselves unless satisfied for good reason that they are true. Hileman v. Nw. Eng'g Co., 346 F.2d 668 (6th Cir. 1965). If the statement is that of a party offered by his opponent, it comes in as an admission, Rule [801(d)(2)], and there is no occasion to inquire whether it is against interest, this not being a condition precedent to admissibility of admissions by opponents.

The common law required that the interest declared against be pecuniary or proprietary but within this limitation demonstrated striking ingenuity in discovering an against-interest aspect. Higham v. Ridgway, (1808) 103 Eng. Rep. 717 (K.B.), 10 East 109; R v. Overseers of Birmingham, (1861) 121 Eng. Rep. 897 (Q.B.), 1 B. & S. 763; McCORMICK § 256, at 551 nn.2–3.

The exception discards the common law limitation and expands to the full logical limit. One result is to remove doubt as to the admissibility of declarations tending to establish a tort liability against the declarant or to extinguish one which might be asserted by him, in accordance with the trend of the decisions in this country. McCORMICK, § 254, at 548–49. . . . And finally, exposure to criminal liability satisfies the against-interest requirement. The refusal of the common law to concede the adequacy of a penal interest was no doubt indefensible in logic, see the dissent of Mr. Justice Holmes in *Donnelly v. United States*, 228 U.S. 243 (1913), but one senses in the decisions a distrust of evidence of confessions by third persons offered to exculpate the accused arising from suspicions of fabrication either of the fact of the making of the confession or in its contents, enhanced in either instance by the required unavailability of the declarant. Nevertheless, an increasing amount of decisional law recognizes exposure to punishment for crime as a sufficient stake. People v. Spriggs, 60 Cal. 2d 868 (1964); Sutter v. Easterly, 354 Mo. 282 (1945); Band's Refuse Removal, Inc. v. Fair Lawn Borough, 62 N.J. Super. 522 (App. Div. 1960); Newberry v. Commonwealth, 191 Va. 445 (1950); Annotation, [92 A.L.R.3d 1164]. The requirement of corroboration is included in the rule in order to effect an accommodation between these competing considerations. When the statement is offered by the accused by way of exculpation, the resulting situation is not adapted to control by rulings as to the weight of the evidence, and hence the provision is cast in terms of a requirement preliminary to admissibility. *Cf.* Rule [406]. The requirement of corroboration should be construed in such a manner as to effectuate its purpose of circumventing fabrication.

Ordinarily the third-party confession is thought of in terms of exculpating the accused, but this is by no means always or necessarily the case: it may include statements implicating him, and under the general theory of declarations against interest they would be admissible as related statements. *Douglas v. Alabama*, 380 U.S. 415 (1965), and *Bruton v. United States*, 391 U.S. 123 (1968), both involved confessions by codefendants which implicated the accused. While the confession was not actually offered in evidence in *Douglas,* the procedure followed effectively put it before the jury, which the Court ruled to be error. Whether the confession might have been admissible as a declaration against penal interest was not considered or discussed. *Bruton* assumed the inadmissibility, as against the accused, of the implicating confession of his codefendant, and centered upon the question of the effectiveness of a limiting instruction. These decisions, however, by no means require that all statements implicating another person be excluded from the category of declarations against interest. Whether a statement is in fact against interest must be determined from the circumstances of each case. Thus a statement admitting guilt and implicating another person, made while in custody, may well be motivated by a desire to curry favor with the authorities and hence fail to qualify as against interest. See the dissenting opinion of Mr. Justice White in *Bruton*. On the other hand, the same words spoken under different circumstances, e.g., to an acquaintance, would have no difficulty in qualifying. The rule does not purport to deal with questions of the right of confrontation.

The balancing of self-serving against disserving aspects of a declaration is discussed in MCCORMICK § 256.

For comparable provisions, see Uniform Rule 63(10); California Evidence Code § 1230; Kansas Statutes Annotated § 60-460(j); New Jersey Evidence Rule 63(10) (repealed and replaced by New Jersey Rule of Evidence 803(c)(25) (1993)).

<u>REPORT OF THE HOUSE COMMITTEE ON THE JUDICIARY</u>

Rule 804(b)(4) as submitted by the Court (now Rule 804(b)(3) in the bill) provided as follows:

> *Statement against interest.* A statement which was at the time of its making so far contrary to the declarant's pecuniary or proprietary interest or so far tended to subject him to civil or criminal liability or to render invalid a claim by him against another or to make him an object of hatred, ridicule, or disgrace, that a reasonable man in his position would not have made the statement unless he believed it to be true. A statement tending to exculpate the accused is not admissible unless corroborated.

The Committee determined to retain the traditional hearsay exception for statements against pecuniary or proprietary interest. However, it deemed the Court's additional references to statements tending to subject a declarant to civil liability or to render invalid a claim by him against another to be redundant as included within the scope of the reference to statements against pecuniary or proprietary interest. *See* Gichner v. Antonio Triano Tile & Marble Co., 410 F.2d 238 (D.C. Cir. 1969). Those additional references were accordingly deleted.

The Court's rule also proposed to expand the hearsay limitation from its present federal limitation to include statements subjecting the declarant to criminal liability and statements tending to make him an object of hatred, ridicule, or disgrace. The Committee eliminated the latter category from the subdivision as lacking sufficient guarantees of reliability. *See* United States v. Dovico, 380 F.2d 325, 327 nn.2 & 4 (2nd Cir.), *cert. denied*, 389 U.S. 944 (1967). As for statements against penal interest, the Committee shared the view of the Court that some such statements do possess adequate assurances of reliability and should be admissible. It believed, however, as did the Court, that statements of this type tending to exculpate the accused are more suspect and so should have their admissibility conditioned upon some further provision insuring trustworthiness. The proposal in the Court rule to add a requirement of simple corroboration was, however, deemed ineffective to accomplish this purpose since the accused's own testimony might suffice while not necessarily increasing the reliability of the hearsay statement. The Committee settled upon the language "unless corroborating circumstances clearly indicate the trustworthiness of the statement" as affording a proper standard and degree of discretion. It was contemplated that the result in such cases as *Donnelly v. United States*, 228 U.S. 243 (1913), where the circumstances plainly indicated reliability, would be changed. The Committee also added to the rule the final sentence from the 1971 Advisory Committee draft, designed to codify the doctrine of *Bruton v. United States*, 391 U.S. 123 (1968). The Committee does not intend to affect the existing exception to the *Bruton* principle where the codefendant takes the stand and is subject to cross-examination, but believed there was no need to make specific provision for this situation in the rule, since in that event the declarant would not be "unavailable."

<u>REPORT OF THE SENATE COMMITTEE ON THE JUDICIARY</u>

The rule defines those statements which are considered to be against interest and thus of sufficient trustworthiness to be admissible even though hearsay. With regard to the type of interest declared against, the version submitted by the Supreme Court included, *inter alia*, statements tending to subject a declarant to civil liability or to invalidate a claim by him against another. The House struck these provisions as redundant. In view of the conflicting case law construing pecuniary or proprietary interests narrowly so as to exclude, e.g., tort cases, this deletion could be misconstrued.

Three states which have recently codified their rules of evidence have followed the Supreme Court's version of this rule, i.e., that a statement is against interest if it tends to subject a declarant to civil liability.[12]

The Committee believes that the reference to statements tending to subject a person to civil liability constitutes a desirable clarification of the scope of the rule. Therefore, we have reinstated the Supreme Court language on this matter.

The Court rule also proposed to expand the hearsay limitation from its present federal limitation to include statements subjecting the declarant to statements tending to make him an object of hatred, ridicule, or disgrace. The House eliminated the latter category from the subdivision as lacking sufficient guarantees of reliability. Although there is considerable support for the admissibility of such statements (all three of the state rules referred to *supra* would admit such statements), we accept the deletion by the House.

The House amended this exception to add a sentence making inadmissible a statement or confession offered against the accused in a criminal case, made by a codefendant or other person implicating both himself and the accused. The sentence was added to codify the constitutional principle announced in *Bruton v. United States*, 391 U.S. 123 (1968). *Bruton* held that the admission of the extrajudicial hearsay statement of one codefendant inculpating a second codefendant violated the Confrontation Clause of the Sixth Amendment.

The Committee decided to delete this provision because the basic approach of the rules is to avoid codifying, or attempting to codify, constitutional evidentiary principles, such as the Fifth Amendment's right against self-incrimination and, here, the Sixth Amendment's right of confrontation. Codification of a constitutional principle is unnecessary and, where the principle is under development, often unwise. Furthermore, the House provision does not appear to recognize the exceptions to the *Bruton* rule, e.g., where the codefendant takes the stand and is subject to cross-examination . . . .

CONFERENCE REPORT

The Senate amendment to subsection (b)(3) provides that a statement is against interest and not excluded by the hearsay rule when the declarant is unavailable as a witness, if the statement tends to subject a person to civil or criminal liability or renders

---

[12] NEV. REV. STAT. § 51.345; N.M. STAT. § 20-4-804(4) (Supp. 1973) (current version at N.M. R. EVID. 11-804(B)(3)); WIS. STAT. ANN. § 908.045(4) (West Supp. 1973).

invalid a claim by him against another. The House bill did not refer specifically to civil liability and to rendering invalid a claim against another. The Senate amendment also deletes from the House bill the provision that subsection (b)(3) does not apply to a statement or confession, made by a codefendant or another, which implicates the accused and the person who made the statement, when that statement or confession is offered against the accused in a criminal case.

The Conference adopts the Senate amendment. The Conferees intend to include within the purview of this rule statements subjecting a person to civil liability and statements rendering claims invalid. The Conferees agree to delete the provision regarding statements by a codefendant, thereby reflecting the general approach in the Rules of Evidence to avoid attempting to codify constitutional evidentiary principles.

ADVISORY COMMITTEE'S NOTE TO 2010 AMENDMENT TO RULE 804(b)(3)

Rule 804(b)(3) has been amended to provide that the corroborating circumstances requirement applies to all declarations against penal interest offered in criminal cases. A number of courts have applied the corroborating circumstances requirement to declarations against penal interest offered by the prosecution, even though the text of the rule did not so provide. *See, e.g.,* United States v. Alvarez, 584 F.2d 694, 701 (5th Cir. 1978) ("[B]y transplanting the language governing exculpatory statements onto the analysis for admitting inculpatory hearsay, a unitary standard is derived which offers the most workable basis for applying Rule 804(b)(3)."); United States v. Shukri, 207 F.3d 412 (7th Cir. 2000) (requiring corroborating circumstances for against-penal-interest statements offered by the government). A unitary approach to declarations against penal interest assures both the prosecution and the accused that the rule will not be abused and that only reliable hearsay statements will be admitted under the exception.

All other changes to the structure and wording of the rule are intended to be stylistic only. There is no intent to change any other result in any ruling on evidence admissibility.

The amendment does not address the use of the corroborating circumstances for declarations against penal interest offered in civil cases.

In assessing whether corroborating circumstances exist, some courts have focused on the credibility of the witness who relates the hearsay statement in court. But the credibility of the witness who relates the statement is not a proper factor for the court to consider in assessing corroborating circumstances. To base admission or exclusion of a hearsay statement on the witness's credibility would usurp the jury's role of determining the credibility of testifying witnesses.

CHANGES MADE AFTER PUBLICATION AND COMMENTS

The rule, as submitted for public comment, was restyled in accordance with the style conventions of the Style Subcommittee of the Committee on Rules of Practice and Procedure. As restyled, the proposed amendment addresses the style suggestions made in public comments.

The proposed Committee note was amended to add a short discussion on applying the corroborating circumstances requirement.

SUMMARY OF PUBLIC COMMENTS

David F. Binder, Esq. (08-EV-001) favors the amendment as it will make the rule consistent with much of the case law, which has extended the corroborating circumstances requirement to declarations against interest offered by the prosecution. He suggests that the amendment clarify that the corroborating circumstances requirement applies only to hearsay offered as a declaration against penal interest under Rule 804(b)(3), and is not intended to affect admissibility under other hearsay exceptions. This suggestion was implemented in the rule as restyled after public comment.

The Federal Magistrate Judges Association (08-EV-003) is in agreement with the general principle that the prosecution, as well as the accused, must show corroborating circumstances clearly indicating trustworthiness before a declaration against penal interest may be admitted. . . .

Professor David P. Leonard (08-EV-004) favors the amendment because it is "sensible and fair to level the playing field by imposing the same restrictions on the prosecution as are imposed on the accused." . . .

The National Association of Criminal Defense Lawyers (08-EV-005) approves the extension of the corroborating circumstances requirement to declarations against penal interest offered by the prosecution. The Association recommends, however, that the corroborating circumstances requirement be deleted insofar as it applies to statements offered by the accused.

Professor Richard Friedman (08-EV-006) advocates the elimination of the corroborating circumstances requirement as applied to hearsay statements offered by an accused. Professor Friedman also suggests that the proposed amendment be changed to add language that would reject the Supreme Court's analysis in *Williamson v. United States*, 512 U.S. 594 (1994), by providing that a non-adverse statement that is part of a broader inculpatory statement would be admissible if "it appears likely that the declarant would make the statement in question only if believing it to be true." Finally, Professor Friedman suggests that the text of the rule include language providing that the credibility of the in-court witness is irrelevant to the reliability of the hearsay statement—and that if such a statement is not included in the text, it should at least be included in the Committee note. The Committee added a paragraph to the Committee note in response to Professor Friedman's suggestion.

ADVISORY COMMITTEE'S NOTE TO 2011 RESTYLING OF RULE 804(b)(3)

No style changes were made to Rule 804(b)(3), because it was already restyled in conjunction with a substantive amendment, effective December 1, 2010.

ADVISORY COMMITTEE'S NOTE TO RULE 804(b)(4)–(5)

Exception (4). The general common law requirement that a declaration in this area must have been made *ante litem motam* has been dropped, as bearing more appropriately on weight than admissibility. *See* 5 WIGMORE § 1483. Item [(A)] specifically disclaims any need of firsthand knowledge respecting declarant's own personal history. In some instances it is self-evident (marriage) and in others impossible and traditionally not required (date of birth). Item [(B)] deals with declarations concerning the history of another person. As at common law, declarant is qualified if related by blood or marriage. 5 WIGMORE § 1489. In addition, and contrary to the common law, declarant qualifies by virtue of intimate association with the family. *Id.* § 1487. The requirement sometimes encountered that when the subject of the statement is the relationship between two other persons the declarant must qualify as to both is omitted. Relationship is reciprocal. *Id.* § 1491.

For comparable provisions, see Uniform Rule 63(23)–(25); California Evidence Code §§ 1310, 1311; Kansas Statutes Annotated § 60-460(u)–(w); New Jersey Evidence Rule 63(23)–(25) (repealed and replaced by New Jersey Rule of Evidence 804(b)(4) (1993)).

Exception (5). In language and purpose, this exception is identical with Rule 803(24). See the Advisory Committee's Note to that provision.

<u>CONFERENCE REPORT</u>

The Senate amendment adds a new subsection, [(b)(5)], which makes admissible a hearsay statement not specifically covered by any of the [four] previous subsections, if the statement has equivalent circumstantial guarantees of trustworthiness and if the court determines that (A) the statement is offered as evidence of a material fact; (B) the statement is more probative on the point for which it is offered than any other evidence the proponent can procure through reasonable efforts; and (C) the general purposes of these rules and the interests of justice will best be served by admission of the statement into evidence.

The House bill eliminated a similar, but broader, provision because of the conviction that such a provision injected too much uncertainty into the law of evidence regarding hearsay and impaired the ability of a litigant to prepare adequately for trial.

The Conference adopts the Senate amendment with an amendment that renumbers this subsection and provides that a party intending to request the court to use a statement under this provision must notify any adverse party of this intention as well as of the particulars of the statement, including the name and address of the declarant. This notice must be given sufficiently in advance of the trial or hearing to provide any adverse party with a fair opportunity to prepare to contest the use of the statement.

<u>ADVISORY COMMITTEE'S NOTE TO 1997 AMENDMENT TO RULE 804(b)(5)–(6)</u>

Subdivision (b)(5). The contents of Rule 803(24) and Rule 804(b)(5) have been combined and transferred to a new Rule 807. This was done to facilitate additions to Rules 803 and 804. No change in meaning is intended.

Subdivision (b)(6). Rule 804(b)(6) has been added to provide that a party forfeits the right to object on hearsay grounds to the admission of a declarant's prior statement when the party's deliberate wrongdoing or acquiescence therein procured the unavailability of the declarant as a witness. This recognizes the need for a prophylactic rule to deal with abhorrent behavior "which strikes at the heart of the system of justice itself." United States v. Mastrangelo, 693 F.2d 269, 273 (2d Cir. 1982), *cert. denied*, 467 U.S. 1204 (1984). The wrongdoing need not consist of a criminal act. The rule applies to all parties, including the government.

Every circuit that has resolved the question has recognized the principle of forfeiture by misconduct, although the tests for determining whether there is a forfeiture have varied. *See, e.g.,* United States v. Aguiar, 975 F.2d 45, 47 (2d Cir. 1992); United States v. Potamitis, 739 F.2d 784, 789 (2d Cir.), *cert. denied,* 469 U.S. 918 (1984); Steele v. Taylor, 684 F.2d 1193, 1199 (6th Cir. 1982), *cert. denied,* 460 U.S. 1053 (1983); United States v. Balano, 618 F.2d 624, 629 (10th Cir. 1979), *cert. denied,* 449 U.S. 840 (1980); United States v. Carlson, 547 F.2d 1346, 1358–59 (8th Cir. 1976), *cert. denied,* 431 U.S. 914 (1977). The foregoing cases apply a preponderance of the evidence standard. *Contra* United States v. Thevis, 665 F.2d 616, 631 (5th Cir.) (clear and convincing standard), *cert. denied,* 459 U.S. 825 (1982). The usual Rule 104(a) preponderance of the evidence standard has been adopted in light of the behavior the new Rule 804(b)(6) seeks to discourage.

Rule 805.   HEARSAY WITHIN HEARSAY

Hearsay within hearsay is not excluded by the rule against hearsay if each part of the combined statements conforms with an exception to the rule.

(Enacted Jan. 2, 1975; as restyled Apr. 26, 2011, eff. Dec. 1, 2011.)

NOTE BY FEDERAL JUDICIAL CENTER

The rule enacted by the Congress is the rule prescribed by the Supreme Court without change.

ADVISORY COMMITTEE'S NOTE

On principle it scarcely seems open to doubt that the hearsay rule should not call for exclusion of a hearsay statement which includes a further hearsay statement when both conform to the requirements of a hearsay exception. Thus a hospital record might contain an entry of the patient's age based on information furnished by his wife. The hospital record would qualify as a regular entry except that the person who furnished the information was not acting in the routine of the business. However, her statement independently qualifies as a statement of pedigree (if she is unavailable) or as a statement made for purposes of diagnosis or treatment, and hence each link in the chain falls under sufficient assurances. Or, further to illustrate, a dying declaration may incorporate a declaration against interest by another declarant. *See* MCCORMICK § 290, at 611.

Rule 806. ATTACKING AND SUPPORTING THE DECLARANT'S CREDIBILITY

When a hearsay statement—or a statement described in Rule 801(d)(2)(C), (D), or (E)—has been admitted in evidence, the declarant's credibility may be attacked, and then supported, by any evidence that would be admissible for those purposes if the declarant had testified as a witness. The court may admit evidence of the declarant's inconsistent statement or conduct, regardless of when it occurred or whether the declarant had an opportunity to explain or deny it. If the party against whom the statement was admitted calls the declarant as a witness, the party may examine the declarant on the statement as if on cross-examination.

(Enacted Jan. 2, 1975; as amended, Mar. 2, 1987, eff. Oct. 1, 1987; Apr. 11, 1997, eff. Dec. 1, 1997; as restyled Apr. 26, 2011, eff. Dec. 1, 2011.)

<u>NOTE BY FEDERAL JUDICIAL CENTER</u>

The rule enacted by the Congress is the rule prescribed by the Supreme Court, amended by inserting the phrase "or a statement defined in Rule 801(d)(2), (C), (D), or (E)."

<u>ADVISORY COMMITTEE'S NOTE</u>

The declarant of a hearsay statement which is admitted in evidence is in effect a witness. His credibility should in fairness be subject to impeachment and support as though he had in fact testified. *See* Rules 608 and 609. There are, however, some special aspects of the impeaching of a hearsay declarant which require consideration. These special aspects center upon impeachment by inconsistent statement, arise from factual differences which exist between the use of hearsay and an actual witness and also between various kinds of hearsay, and involve the question of applying to declarants the general rule disallowing evidence of an inconsistent statement to impeach a witness unless he is afforded an opportunity to deny or explain. *See* Rule 613(b).

The principal difference between using hearsay and an actual witness is that the inconsistent statement will in the case of the witness almost inevitably of necessity in the nature of things be a *prior* statement, which it is entirely possible and feasible to call to his attention, while in the case of hearsay the inconsistent statement may well be a *subsequent* one, which practically precludes calling it to the attention of the declarant. The result of insisting upon observation of this impossible requirement in the hearsay situation is to deny the opponent, already barred from cross-examination, any benefit of this important technique of impeachment. The writers favor allowing the subsequent statement. MCCORMICK § 37, at 69; 3 WIGMORE § 1033. The cases, however, are divided. Cases allowing the impeachment include *People v. Collup*, 27 Cal. 2d 829 (1946); *People v. Rosoto*, 58 Cal. 2d 304 (1962); *Carver v. United States*, 164 U.S. 694 (1897). *Contra* Mattox v. United States, 156 U.S. 237 (1895); People v. Hines, 284 N.Y. 93 (1940). The force of *Mattox*, where the hearsay was the former testimony of a deceased witness and the denial of use of a subsequent inconsistent statement was upheld, is much diminished by *Carver*, where the hearsay was a dying declaration and denial of use of a subsequent inconsistent statement resulted in reversal. The difference in the particular brand of hearsay seems unimportant when the inconsistent statement is a *subsequent* one. True, the opponent is not totally deprived of cross-examination when the hearsay is former testimony or a deposition, but he is deprived of cross-examining on the statement or along lines suggested by it. Mr. Justice Shiras, with two justices joining him, dissented vigorously in *Mattox*.

When the impeaching statement was made prior to the hearsay statement, differences in the kinds of hearsay appear which arguably may justify differences in treatment. If the hearsay consisted of a simple statement by the witness, e.g., a dying declaration or a declaration against interest, the feasibility of affording him an opportunity to deny or explain encounters the same practical impossibility as where the statement is a subsequent one, just discussed, although here the impossibility arises from the total absence of anything resembling a hearing at which the matter could be put to him. The courts by a large majority have ruled in favor of allowing the statement to be used under these circumstances. MCCORMICK § 37, at 69; 3 WIGMORE § 1033. If, however, the hearsay consists of former testimony or a deposition, the possibility of calling the prior statement to the attention of the witness or deponent is not ruled out, since the opportunity to cross-examine was available. It might thus be concluded that with former testimony or depositions the conventional foundation should be insisted upon. Most of the cases involve depositions, and Wigmore describes them as divided. 3 WIGMORE § 1031. Deposition procedures at best are cumbersome and expensive, and to require the laying of the foundation may impose an undue burden. Under the federal practice, there is no way of knowing with certainty at the time of taking a deposition whether it is merely for discovery or will ultimately end up in evidence. With respect to both former testimony and depositions the possibility exists that knowledge of the statement might not be acquired until after the time of the cross-examination. Moreover, the expanded admissibility of former testimony and depositions under Rule 804(b)(1) calls for a correspondingly expanded approach to impeachment. The rule dispenses with the requirement in all hearsay situations, which is readily administered and best calculated to lead to fair results.

Notice should be taken that Rule 26(f) of the Federal Rules of Civil Procedure, as originally submitted by the Advisory Committee, ended with the following:

> . . . and, without having first called them to the deponent's attention, may show statements contradictory thereto made at any time by the deponent.

This language did not appear in the rule as promulgated in December, 1937. *See* 4 MOORE'S FEDERAL PRACTICE ¶¶ 26.01[9], 26.35 (2d ed. 1967). In 1951, Nebraska adopted a provision strongly resembling the one stricken from the federal rule:

> Any party may impeach any adverse deponent by self-contradiction without having laid foundation for such impeachment at the time such deposition was taken.

NEB. REV. STAT. § 25-1267.07 (repealed 1982).

For similar provisions, see Uniform Rule 65; California Evidence Code § 1202; Kansas Statutes Annotated § 60-462; New Jersey Evidence Rule 65 (repealed and replaced by New Jersey Rule of Evidence 806 (1993)).

The provision for cross-examination of a declarant upon his hearsay statement is a corollary of general principles of cross-examination. A similar provision is found in California Evidence Code § 1203.

REPORT OF THE SENATE COMMITTEE ON THE JUDICIARY

Rule [806], as passed by the House and as proposed by the Supreme Court, provides that whenever a hearsay statement is admitted, the credibility of the declarant of the statement may be attacked, and if attacked may be supported, by any evidence which would be admissible for those purposes if the declarant had testified as a witness. Rule 801 defines what is a hearsay statement. While statements by a person authorized by a party-opponent to make a statement concerning the subject, by the party-opponent's agent, or by a coconspirator of a party—see Rule 801(d)(2)(C), (D), and (E)—are traditionally defined as exceptions to the hearsay rule, Rule 801 defines such admission by a party-opponent as statements which are not hearsay. Consequently, Rule 806, by referring exclusively to the admission of hearsay statements, does not appear to allow the credibility of the declarant to be attacked when the declarant is a coconspirator, agent, or authorized spokesman. The Committee is of the view that such statements should open the declarant to attacks on his credibility. Indeed, the reason such statements are excluded from the operation of Rule 806 is likely attributable to the drafting technique used to codify the hearsay rule, viz., some statements, instead of being referred to as exceptions to the hearsay rule, are defined as statements which are not hearsay. The phrase "or a statement defined in Rule 801(d)(2)(C), (D), and (E)" is added to the rule in order to subject the declarant of such statements, like the declarant of hearsay statements, to attacks on his credibility.[13]

Conference Report

The Senate amendment permits an attack upon the credibility of the declarant of a statement if the statement is one by a person authorized by a party-opponent to make a statement concerning the subject, one by an agent of a party-opponent, or one by a coconspirator of the party-opponent, as these statements are defined in Rules 801(d)(2)(C), (D), and (E). The House bill has no such provision.

The Conference adopts the Senate amendment. The Senate amendment conforms the rule to present practice.

---

[13] The Committee considered it unnecessary to include statements contained in Rule 801(d)(2)(A) and (B)—the statement by the party-opponent himself or the statement of which he has manifested his adoption—because the credibility of the party-opponent is always subject to an attack on his credibility.

Rule 807.   RESIDUAL EXCEPTION

(a) In General.   Under the following circumstances, a hearsay statement is not excluded by the rule against hearsay even if the statement is not specifically covered by a hearsay exception in Rule 803 or 804:

(1) the statement has equivalent circumstantial guarantees of trustworthiness;

(2) it is offered as evidence of a material fact;

(3) it is more probative on the point for which it is offered than any other evidence that the proponent can obtain through reasonable efforts; and

(4) admitting it will best serve the purposes of these rules and the interests of justice.

(b) Notice.   The statement is admissible only if, before the trial or hearing, the proponent gives an adverse party reasonable notice of the intent to offer the statement and its particulars, including the declarant's name and address, so that the party has a fair opportunity to meet it.

(Enacted Apr. 11, 1997, eff. Dec. 1 1997; as restyled Apr. 26, 2011, eff. Dec. 1, 2011.)

<u>ADVISORY COMMITTEE'S NOTE TO 1997 AMENDMENT TO RULE 807</u>

The contents of Rule 803(24) and Rule 804(b)(5) have been combined and transferred to a new Rule 807. This was done to facilitate additions to Rules 803 and 804. No change in meaning is intended.[14]

---

[14] [Also see the legislative materials for Rule 803(24) at pages 260 to 263. —GF]

PROPOSED AMENDMENT TO RULE 807
(Approved by the Advisory Committee on Evidence Rules
in April 2018 and by the Standing Committee on
Rules of Practice and Procedure in June 2018;
to take effect no earlier than December 1, 2019.)

EDITOR'S NOTE

In April 2018 the Advisory Committee on Evidence Rules approved a proposed amendment to Rule 807. The amendment would clarify the rule's operation and, in the advisory committee's view, would "fix a number of problems that the courts have encountered in applying" the rule.

The biggest fix addresses the "equivalen[ce]" standard that now supplies the chief constraint on the rule's application. To qualify under the present rule, hearsay must have "equivalent circumstantial guarantees of reliability." This standard requires *at least* that residual hearsay be as reliable as the *least* reliable hearsay admitted under any of the existing hearsay exceptions. Courts have found this standard "difficult to apply," the advisory committee notes, "given the different types of guarantees of reliability, of varying strength, found among the categorical exceptions (as well as the fact that some hearsay exceptions, e.g., Rule 804(b)(6), are not based on reliability at all)."

The proposed amendment would eliminate the equivalence standard and instead require trial judges to assess whether the proffered hearsay "is supported by sufficient guarantees of trustworthiness." In weighing reliability, judges are to look beyond the "circumstantial guarantees" specified in the present rule and to consider as well any "evidence . . . corroborating the statement."

Two other proposed changes amount to mere housekeeping. The amendment would drop the present requirements that residual hearsay be "evidence of a material fact" and that its admission "best serve the . . . interests of justice." These mandates, the committee explains, are redundant of Rules 401 and 102.

But the committee left unchanged the demand that residual hearsay be "more probative on the point for which it is offered than any other evidence that the proponent can obtain through reasonable efforts"—a requirement that ensures the unusual *necessity* of hearsay admitted under the rule.

A number of proposed changes seek to clarify the nature and timing of the notice the proponent must give the adverse party before offering residual hearsay. The most notable change would compel proponents to disclose the "substance" of any statements they intend to offer under this rule. The advisory committee explains that this provision would "require a description that is sufficiently specific under the circumstances to allow the opponent a fair opportunity to meet the evidence."

A final change, made in response to public comments on the original proposed amendment, addresses a long-simmering debate on the relationship between Rule 807 and Rules 803 and 804. As first enacted in 1997, Rule 807 had applied only to "statement[s] not specifically covered by Rule 803 or 804." (See page 472 below.) This language led courts to wonder whether a statement could qualify under Rule 807 if it *almost* satisfied another hearsay exception but narrowly missed doing so. As the casebook explains at pages 582 to 585, most courts had deemed such "near misses" to be admissible if the contested statements otherwise satisfied Rule 807. A minority of courts and judges, however, had insisted that if a statement *almost* but *not quite* satisfied the conditions of, say, the business records rule, that statement should not gain admission through Rule 807. Such statements, these judges said, were "specifically *covered*" by another rule even if they weren't *admitted* by that rule.

The Evidence Rules Restyling Project seemingly settled this debate by omitting the mandate that statements offered under Rule 807 not be "specifically covered" by another hearsay exception. In its restyled form, which took effect in December 2011, Rule 807 applies "*even if* the statement is not specifically covered by a hearsay exception in Rule 803 or 804." (See page 473 below.) That language suggests it no longer matters if the contested statement is or isn't "specifically covered" by a traditional hearsay exception.

The newly proposed amendment would clarify that Rule 807 no longer requires the proponent to show that a contested statement isn't "specifically covered" by a traditional hearsay exception. Instead the rule would demand that the statement "not [be] *admissible* under a hearsay exception in Rule 803 or 804." (Emphasis added.) The change means a statement that arguably is "covered by" a specific exception in Rule 803 or 804 but fails to satisfy the terms of that exception nonetheless would be admissible under Rule 807 if "the statement is supported by sufficient guarantees of trustworthiness" and satisfies the rule's other conditions.

Beyond proposing these changes to the text of the rule, the advisory committee offered a useful reminder about the rule's operation: "In deciding whether the statement is supported by sufficient guarantees of trustworthiness, the court should not consider the credibility of [the] witness who relates the declarant's hearsay statement in court. . . . The credibility of the witness relating the statement is not a part of [the hearsay] enquiry." Because the in-court witness is under oath, with her demeanor exposed to the jury, and subject to cross-examination by opposing counsel, the jury can assess her testimonial capacities and hence her reliability.

The public-comment period for the proposed amendment closed on February 15, 2018. The Advisory Committee on Evidence Rules reviewed the comments in April 2018, made changes in response, and approved the proposed amendment. The Standing Committee on Rules of Practice and Procedure added its approval in June 2018. If the proposed amendment gains final approval from the Judicial Conference and Supreme Court and if Congress does not amend, delay, or disapprove it, the amendment will take effect no earlier than December 1, 2019.

The text of the proposed amendment and the accompanying Advisory Committee's Note appear below. Deleted text is struck through; new text is underlined.

Proposed Amendment to Rule 807

Rule 807.   RESIDUAL EXCEPTION

(a) In General. Under the following circumstances conditions, a hearsay statement is not excluded by the rule against hearsay even if the statement is not specifically covered by admissible under a hearsay exception in Rule 803 or 804:

(1) the statement has equivalent circumstantial is supported by sufficient guarantees of trustworthiness— after considering the totality of the circumstances under which it was made and evidence, if any, corroborating the statement; and

(2) it is offered as evidence of a material fact;

(3 2) it is more probative on the point for which it is offered than any other evidence that the proponent can obtain through reasonable efforts; and

(4) admitting it will best serve the purposes of these rules and the interests of justice.

FEDERAL RULES OF EVIDENCE

(b) Notice. The statement is admissible only if, ~~before the trial or hearing,~~ the proponent gives an adverse party reasonable notice of the intent to offer the statement and its particulars, including the declarant's name and address,—including its substance and the declarant's name—so that the party has a fair opportunity to meet it. <u>The notice must be provided in writing before the trial or hearing—or in any form during the trial or hearing if the court, for good cause, excuses a lack of earlier notice.</u>

<u>ADVISORY COMMITTEE'S NOTE TO PROPOSED AMENDMENT</u>

Rule 807 has been amended to fix a number of problems that the courts have encountered in applying it.

Courts have had difficulty with the requirement that the proffered hearsay carry "equivalent" circumstantial guarantees of trustworthiness. The "equivalence" standard is difficult to apply, given the different types of guarantees of reliability, of varying strength, found among the categorical exceptions (as well as the fact that some hearsay exceptions, e.g., Rule 804(b)(6), are not based on reliability at all). The "equivalence" standard" has not served to guide a court's discretion to admit hearsay, because the court is free to choose among a spectrum of exceptions for comparison. Moreover, experience has shown that some statements offered as residual hearsay cannot be compared usefully to any of the categorical exceptions and yet might well be trustworthy. Thus the requirement of an equivalence analysis has been eliminated. Under the amendment, the court should proceed directly to a determination of whether the hearsay is supported by guarantees of trustworthiness. *See* Rule 104(a). As with any hearsay statement offered under an exception, the court's threshold finding that admissibility requirements are met merely means that the jury may consider the statement and not that it must assume the statement to be true.

The amendment specifically requires the court to consider corroborating evidence in the trustworthiness enquiry. Most courts have required the consideration of corroborating evidence, though some courts have disagreed. The rule now provides for a uniform approach, and recognizes that the existence or absence of corroboration is relevant to, but not dispositive of, whether a statement should be admissible under this exception. Of course, the court must consider not only the existence of corroborating evidence but also the strength and quality of that evidence.

The amendment does not alter the case law prohibiting parties from proceeding directly to the residual exception, without considering admissibility of the hearsay under Rules 803 and 804. A court is not required to make a finding that no other hearsay exception is applicable. But the proponent cannot seek admission under Rule 807 if it is apparent that the hearsay could be admitted under another exception.

The rule in its current form applies to hearsay "not specifically covered" by a Rule 803 or 804 exception. The amendment makes the rule applicable to hearsay "not admissible under" those exceptions. This clarifies that a court assessing guarantees of trustworthiness may consider whether the statement is a "near-miss" of one of the Rule 803 or 804 exceptions. If the court employs a "near-miss" analysis it should—in addition to evaluating all relevant guarantees of trustworthiness—take into account the reasons that the hearsay misses the admissibility requirements of the standard exception.

In deciding whether the statement is supported by sufficient guarantees of trustworthiness, the court should not consider the credibility of any witness who relates the declarant's hearsay statement in court. The credibility of an in-court witness does not present a hearsay question. To base admission or exclusion of a hearsay statement on the witness's credibility would usurp the jury's role of determining the credibility of testifying witnesses. The rule provides that the focus for trustworthiness is on circumstantial guarantees surrounding the making of the statement itself, as well as any independent evidence corroborating the statement. The credibility of the witness relating the statement is not a part of either enquiry.

Of course, even if the court finds sufficient guarantees of trustworthiness, the independent requirements of the Confrontation Clause must be satisfied if the hearsay statement is offered against a defendant in a criminal case.

The Committee decided to retain the requirement that the proponent must show that the hearsay statement is more probative than any other evidence that the proponent can reasonably obtain. This necessity requirement will continue to serve to prevent the residual exception from being used as a device to erode the categorical exceptions.

The requirements that residual hearsay must be evidence of a material fact and that its admission will best serve the purposes of these rules and the interests of justice have been deleted. These requirements have proved to be superfluous in that they are already found in other rules. *See* Rules 102, 401.

The notice provision has been amended to make four changes in the operation of the rule:

- First, the amendment requires the proponent to disclose the "substance" of the statement. This term is intended to require a description that is sufficiently specific under the circumstances to allow the opponent a fair opportunity to meet the evidence. *See* Rule 103(a)(2) (requiring the party making an offer of proof to inform the court of the "substance" of the evidence).

- Second, the prior requirement that the declarant's address must be disclosed has been deleted. That requirement was nonsensical when the declarant was unavailable, and unnecessary in the many cases in which the declarant's address was known or easily obtainable. If prior disclosure of the declarant's address is critical and cannot be obtained by the opponent through other means, then the opponent can seek relief from the court.

- Third, the amendment requires that the pretrial notice be in writing—which is satisfied by notice in electronic form. *See* Rule 101(b)(6). Requiring the notice to be in writing provides certainty and reduces arguments about whether notice was actually provided.

- Finally, the pretrial notice provision has been amended to provide for a good cause exception. Most courts have applied a good cause exception under Rule 807 even though the rule in its current form does not provide for it, while some courts have read the rule as it was written. Experience under the residual exception has shown that a good cause exception is necessary in certain limited situations. For example, the proponent may not become aware of the existence of the hearsay statement until after the trial begins; or the proponent may plan to call a witness who without warning becomes unavailable during trial, and the proponent might then need to resort to residual hearsay.

The rule retains the requirement that the opponent receive notice in a way that provides a fair opportunity to meet the evidence. When notice is provided during trial after a finding of good cause, the court may need to consider protective measures, such as a continuance, to assure that the opponent is not prejudiced.

Changes Made After Publication and Comment

The provision on the relationship between the residual exception and Rules 803 and 804 was changed in two respects: 1) it was moved back from a subdivision to the preface, where it was initially; and 2) the phrase "not specifically covered" was changed to "not admissible under."

The Committee Note was revised slightly to address such matters as the "near-miss" analysis, the applicability of Rule 104(a), and the relationship of Rule 807 to the Confrontation Clause.

ARTICLE IX. AUTHENTICATION AND IDENTIFICATION

Rule 901.   AUTHENTICATING OR IDENTIFYING EVIDENCE

(a) In General. To satisfy the requirement of authenticating or identifying an item of evidence, the proponent must produce evidence sufficient to support a finding that the item is what the proponent claims it is.

(b) Examples. The following are examples only—not a complete list—of evidence that satisfies the requirement:

(1) *Testimony of a Witness with Knowledge.* Testimony that an item is what it is claimed to be.

(2) *Nonexpert Opinion About Handwriting.* A nonexpert's opinion that handwriting is genuine, based on a familiarity with it that was not acquired for the current litigation.

(3) *Comparison by an Expert Witness or the Trier of Fact.* A comparison with an authenticated specimen by an expert witness or the trier of fact.

(4) *Distinctive Characteristics and the Like.* The appearance, contents, substance, internal patterns, or other distinctive characteristics of the item, taken together with all the circumstances.

(5) *Opinion About a Voice.* An opinion identifying a person's voice—whether heard firsthand or through mechanical or electronic transmission or recording—based on hearing the voice at any time under circumstances that connect it with the alleged speaker.

(6) *Evidence About a Telephone Conversation.* For a telephone conversation, evidence that a call was made to the number assigned at the time to:

(A) a particular person, if circumstances, including self-identification, show that the person answering was the one called; or

(B) a particular business, if the call was made to a business and the call related to business reasonably transacted over the telephone.

(7) *Evidence About Public Records.* Evidence that:

(A) a document was recorded or filed in a public office as authorized by law; or

(B) a purported public record or statement is from the office where items of this kind are kept.

(8) *Evidence About Ancient Documents or Data Compilations.* For a document or data compilation, evidence that it:

(A) is in a condition that creates no suspicion about its authenticity;

(B) was in a place where, if authentic, it would likely be; and

(C) is at least 20 years old when offered.

(9) *Evidence About a Process or System.* Evidence describing a process or system and showing that it produces an accurate result.

(10) *Methods Provided by a Statute or Rule.* Any method of authentication or identification allowed by a federal statute or a rule prescribed by the Supreme Court.

(Enacted Jan. 2, 1975; as restyled Apr. 26, 2011, eff. Dec. 1, 2011.)

NOTE BY FEDERAL JUDICIAL CENTER

The rule enacted by the Congress is the rule prescribed by the Supreme Court, amended in subdivision (b)(10) by substituting "prescribed" in place of "adopted," and by adding "pursuant to statutory authority."

ADVISORY COMMITTEE'S NOTE

Subdivision (a). Authentication and identification represent a special aspect of relevancy. Michael & Adler, *Real Proof*, 5 VAND. L. REV. 344, 362 (1952); MCCORMICK §§ 179, 185; MORGAN, BASIC PROBLEMS OF EVIDENCE 378 (1962). Thus a telephone conversation may be irrelevant because on an unrelated topic or because the speaker is not identified. The latter aspect is the one here involved. Wigmore describes the need for authentication as "an inherent logical necessity." 7 WIGMORE § 2129, at 564.

This requirement of showing authenticity or identity falls in the category of relevancy dependent upon fulfillment of a condition of fact and is governed by the procedure set forth in Rule 104(b).

The common law approach to authentication of documents has been criticized as an "attitude of agnosticism," MCCORMICK, CASES ON EVIDENCE 388 n.4 (3rd ed. 1956), as one which "departs sharply from men's customs in ordinary affairs," and as presenting only a slight obstacle to the introduction of forgeries in comparison to the time and expense devoted to proving genuine writings which correctly show their origin on their face, MCCORMICK § 185, at 395–96. Today, such available procedures as requests to admit and pretrial conference afford the means of eliminating much of the need for authentication or identification. Also, significant inroads upon the traditional insistence on authentication and identification have been made by accepting as at least prima facie genuine items of the kind treated in Rule 902, *infra*. However, the need for suitable methods of proof still remains, since criminal cases pose their own obstacles to the use of preliminary procedures, unforeseen contingencies may arise, and cases of genuine controversy will still occur.

Subdivision (b). The treatment of authentication and identification draws largely upon the experience embodied in the common law and in statutes to furnish illustrative applications of the general principle set forth in subdivision (a). The examples are not intended as an exclusive enumeration of allowable methods but are meant to guide and suggest, leaving room for growth and development in this area of the law.

The examples relate for the most part to documents, with some attention given to voice communications and computer print-outs. As Wigmore noted, no special rules have been developed for authenticating chattels. WIGMORE, CODE OF EVIDENCE § 2086 (3d ed. 1942).

It should be observed that compliance with requirements of authentication or identification by no means assures admission of an item into evidence, as other bars, hearsay, for example, may remain.

Example (1) contemplates a broad spectrum ranging from testimony of a witness who was present at the signing of a document to testimony establishing narcotics as taken from an accused and accounting for custody through the period until trial, including laboratory analysis. *See* CAL. EVID. CODE § 1413 (eyewitness to signing).

Example (2) states conventional doctrine as to lay identification of handwriting, which recognizes that a sufficient familiarity with the handwriting of another person may be acquired by seeing him write, by exchanging correspondence, or by other means, to afford a basis for identifying it on subsequent occasions. MCCORMICK § 189; *see also* CAL. EVID. CODE § 1416. Testimony based upon familiarity acquired for purposes of the litigation is reserved to the expert under the example which follows.

Example (3). The history of common law restrictions upon the technique of proving or disproving the genuineness of a disputed specimen of handwriting through comparison with a genuine specimen, by either the testimony of expert witnesses or direct viewing by the triers themselves, is detailed in 7 WIGMORE §§ 1991–1994. In breaking away, the English Common Law Procedure Act, 1854, 17 and 18 Vict., c. 125, § 27, cautiously allowed expert or trier to use exemplars "proved to the satisfaction of the judge to be genuine" for purposes of comparison. The language found its way into numerous statutes in this country, e.g., California Evidence Code §§ 1417, 1418. While explainable as a measure of prudence in the process of breaking with precedent in the handwriting situation, the reservation to the judge of the question of the genuineness of exemplars and the imposition of an unusually high standard of persuasion are at variance with the general treatment of relevancy which depends upon fulfillment of a condition of fact. Rule 104(b). No similar attitude is found in other comparison situations, e.g., ballistics comparison by jury, as in *Evans v. Commonwealth*, 230 Ky. 411 (1929), or by experts, Annotation, 26 A.L.R.2d 892, and no reason appears for its continued existence in handwriting cases. Consequently example (3) sets no higher standard for handwriting specimens and treats all comparison situations alike, to be governed by Rule 104(b). This approach is consistent with 28 U.S.C. § 1731: "The admitted or proved handwriting of any person shall be admissible, for purposes of comparison, to determine genuineness of other handwriting attributed to such person."

Precedent supports the acceptance of visual comparison as sufficiently satisfying preliminary authentication requirements for admission in evidence. Brandon v. Collins, 267 F.2d 731 (2d Cir. 1959); Wausau Sulphate Fibre Co. v. Comm'r of Internal Revenue, 61 F.2d 879 (7th Cir. 1932); Desimone v. United States, 227 F.2d 864 (9th Cir. 1955).

Example (4). The characteristics of the offered item itself, considered in the light of circumstances, afford authentication techniques in great variety. Thus a document or telephone conversation may be shown to have emanated from a particular person by virtue of its disclosing knowledge of facts known peculiarly to him. Globe Automatic Sprinkler Co. v. Braniff, 89 Okla. 105 (1923); CAL. EVID. CODE § 1421. Similarly, a letter may be authenticated by content and circumstances indicating it was in reply to a duly authenticated one. MCCORMICK § 192; CAL. EVID. CODE § 1420. Language patterns may indicate authenticity or its opposite. Magnuson v. State, 187 Wis. 122 (1925); Arens & Meadow, *Psycholinguistics and the Confession Dilemma*, 56 COLUM. L. REV. 19 (1956).

Example (5). Since aural voice identification is not a subject of expert testimony, the requisite familiarity may be acquired either before or after the particular speaking which is the subject of the identification, in this respect resembling visual identification of a person rather than identification of handwriting. *Cf.* Example (2), *supra,* People v. Nichols, 378 Ill. 487 (1941); McGuire v. State, 200 Md. 601 (1952); State v. McGee, 336 Mo. 1082 (1935).

Example (6). The cases are in agreement that a mere assertion of his identity by a person talking on the telephone is not sufficient evidence of the authenticity of the conversation and that additional evidence of his identity is required. The additional evidence need not fall in any set pattern. Thus the content of his statements or the reply technique, under example (4), *supra,* or voice identification under example (5), may furnish the necessary foundation. Outgoing calls made by the witness involve additional factors bearing upon authenticity. The calling of a number assigned by the telephone company reasonably supports the assumption that the listing is correct and that the number is the one reached. If the number is that of a place of business, the mass of authority allows an ensuing conversation if it relates to business reasonably transacted over the telephone, on the theory that the maintenance of the telephone connection is an invitation to do business without further identification. Mattan v. Hoover Co., 350 Mo. 506 (1942); City of Pawhuska v. Crutchfield, 147 Okla. 4 (1930); Zurich Gen. Acc. & Liab. Ins. Co. v. Baum, 159 Va. 404 (1932). Otherwise, some additional circumstance of identification of the speaker is required. The authorities divide on the question whether the self-identifying statement of the person answering suffices. Example (6) answers in the affirmative on the assumption that usual conduct respecting telephone calls furnish adequate assurances of regularity, bearing in mind that the entire matter is open to exploration before the trier of fact. In general, see McCormick § 193; 7 Wigmore § 2155; Annotation, 71 A.L.R. 5, 105 *id.* 326.

Example (7). Public records are regularly authenticated by proof of custody, without more. McCormick § 191; 7 Wigmore §§ 2158, 2159. The example extends the principle to include data stored in computers and similar methods, of which increasing use in the public records area may be expected. *See* Cal. Evid. Code §§ 1532, 1600.

Example (8). The familiar ancient document rule of the common law is extended to include data stored electronically or by other similar means. Since the importance of appearance diminishes in this situation, the importance of custody or place where found increases correspondingly. This expansion is necessary in view of the widespread use of methods of storing data in forms other than conventional written records.

Any time period selected is bound to be arbitrary. The common law period of 30 years is here reduced to 20 years, with some shift of emphasis from the probable unavailability of witnesses to the unlikeliness of a still viable fraud after the lapse of time. The shorter period is specified in the English Evidence Act, 1938, 1 & 2 Geo. 6, c. 28, and in Or. Rev. Stat. § 41.360(34) (1963) (repealed 1981). See also the numerous statutes prescribing periods of less than 30 years in the case of recorded documents. 7 Wigmore § 2143.

The application of example (8) is not subject to any limitation to title documents or to any requirement that possession, in the case of a title document, has been consistent with the document. *See* McCormick § 190.

Example (9) is designed for situations in which the accuracy of a result is dependent upon a process or system which produces it. X rays afford a familiar instance. Among more recent developments is the computer, as to which see *Transport Indemnity Co. v. Seib,* 178

Neb. 253 (1965); *State v. Veres*, 7 Ariz. App. 117 (1968); *Merrick v. United States Rubber Co.*, 7 Ariz. App. 433 (1968); Freed, *Computer Print-Outs as Evidence*, 16 AM. JUR. PROOF FACTS 273; *Symposium, Law and Computers in the Mid-Sixties*, ALI–ABA (1966); 37 ALB. L. REV. 61 (1967). Example (9) does not, of course, foreclose taking judicial notice of the accuracy of the process or system.

Example (10). The example makes clear that methods of authentication provided by Act of Congress and by the Rules of Civil and Criminal Procedure or by Bankruptcy Rules are not intended to be superseded. Illustrative are the provisions for authentication of official records in Civil Procedure Rule 44 and Criminal Procedure Rule 27, for authentication of records of proceedings by court reporters in 28 U.S.C. § 753(b) and Civil Procedure Rule [80], and for authentication of depositions in Civil Procedure Rule 30(f).

Rule 902.   EVIDENCE THAT IS SELF-AUTHENTICATING

The following items of evidence are self-authenticating; they require no extrinsic evidence of authenticity in order to be admitted:

(1) *Domestic Public Documents That Are Sealed and Signed.* A document that bears:

(A) a seal purporting to be that of the United States; any state, district, commonwealth, territory, or insular possession of the United States; the former Panama Canal Zone; the Trust Territory of the Pacific Islands; a political subdivision of any of these entities; or a department, agency, or officer of any entity named above; and

(B) a signature purporting to be an execution or attestation.

(2) *Domestic Public Documents That Are Not Sealed but Are Signed and Certified.* A document that bears no seal if:

(A) it bears the signature of an officer or employee of an entity named in Rule 902(1)(A); and

(B) another public officer who has a seal and official duties within that same entity certifies under seal—or its equivalent—that the signer has the official capacity and that the signature is genuine.

(3) *Foreign Public Documents.* A document that purports to be signed or attested by a person who is authorized by a foreign country's law to do so. The document must be accompanied by a final certification that certifies the genuineness of the signature and official position of the signer or attester—or of any foreign official whose certificate of genuineness relates to the signature or attestation or is in a chain of certificates of genuineness relating to the signature or attestation. The certification may be made by a secretary of a United States embassy or legation; by a consul general, vice consul, or consular agent of the United States; or by a diplomatic or consular official of the foreign country assigned or accredited to the United States. If all parties have been given a reasonable opportunity to investigate the document's authenticity and accuracy, the court may, for good cause, either:

> **(A)** order that it be treated as presumptively authentic without final certification; or

> **(B)** allow it to be evidenced by an attested summary with or without final certification.

(4) *Certified Copies of Public Records.* A copy of an official record—or a copy of a document that was recorded or filed in a public office as authorized by law—if the copy is certified as correct by:

> **(A)** the custodian or another person authorized to make the certification; or

> **(B)** a certificate that complies with Rule 902(1), (2), or (3), a federal statute, or a rule prescribed by the Supreme Court.

(5) *Official Publications.* A book, pamphlet, or other publication purporting to be issued by a public authority.

(6) *Newspapers and Periodicals.* Printed material purporting to be a newspaper or periodical.

(7) *Trade Inscriptions and the Like.* An inscription, sign, tag, or label purporting to have been affixed in the course of business and indicating origin, ownership, or control.

(8) *Acknowledged Documents.* A document accompanied by a certificate of acknowledgment that is lawfully executed by a notary public or another officer who is authorized to take acknowledgments.

(9) *Commercial Paper and Related Documents.* Commercial paper, a signature on it, and related documents, to the extent allowed by general commercial law.

(10) *Presumptions Under a Federal Statute.* A signature, document, or anything else that a federal statute declares to be presumptively or prima facie genuine or authentic.

(11) *Certified Domestic Records of a Regularly Conducted Activity.* The original or a copy of a domestic record that meets the requirements of Rule 803(6)(A)–(C), as shown by a certification of the custodian or another qualified person that complies with a federal statute or a rule prescribed by the Supreme Court. Before the trial or hearing, the proponent must give an adverse party reasonable written notice of the intent to offer the record—and must make the record and certification available for inspection—so that the party has a fair opportunity to challenge them.

(12) *Certified Foreign Records of a Regularly Conducted Activity.* In a civil case, the original or a copy of a foreign record that meets the requirements of Rule 902(11), modified as follows: the certification, rather than complying with a federal statute or Supreme Court rule, must be signed in a manner that, if falsely made, would subject the maker to a criminal penalty in the country where the certification is signed. The proponent must also meet the notice requirements of Rule 902(11).

(13) *Certified Records Generated by an Electronic Process or System.* A record generated by an electronic process or system that produces an accurate result, as shown by a certification of a qualified person that complies with the certification requirements of Rule 902(11) or (12). The proponent must also meet the notice requirements of Rule 902(11).

(14) *Certified Data Copied from an Electronic Device, Storage Medium, or File.* Data copied from an electronic device, storage medium, or file, if authenticated by a process of digital identification, as shown by a certification of a qualified person that complies with the certification requirements of Rule 902(11) or (12). The proponent also must meet the notice requirements of Rule 902(11).

(Enacted Jan. 2, 1975; as amended Mar. 2, 1987, eff. Oct. 1, 1987; Apr. 25, 1998, eff. Nov. 1, 1988; Apr. 17, 2000, eff. Dec. 1, 2000; as restyled Apr. 26, 2011, eff. Dec. 1, 2011; as amended Dec. 1, 2017.)

NOTE BY FEDERAL JUDICIAL CENTER

The rule enacted by the Congress is the rule prescribed by the Supreme Court, amended as follows:

Paragraph (4) was amended by substituting "prescribed" in place of "adopted," and by adding "pursuant to statutory authority."

Paragraph (8) was amended by substituting "in the manner provided by law by" in place of "under the hand and seal of."

ADVISORY COMMITTEE'S NOTE TO RULE 902(1)–(8)

Case law and statutes have, over the years, developed a substantial body of instances in which authenticity is taken as sufficiently established for purposes of admissibility without extrinsic evidence to that effect, sometimes for reasons of policy but perhaps more often because practical considerations reduce the possibility of unauthenticity to a very small dimension. The present rule collects and incorporates these situations, in some instances expanding them to occupy a larger area which their underlying considerations justify. In no instance is the opposite party foreclosed from disputing authenticity.

Paragraph (1). The acceptance of documents bearing a public seal and signature, most often encountered in practice in the form of acknowledgments or certificates authenticating copies of public records, is actually of broad application. Whether theoretically based in whole or in part upon judicial notice, the practical underlying considerations are that forgery is a crime and detection is fairly easy and certain. 7 WIGMORE § 2161, at 638; CAL. EVID. CODE § 1452. More than fifty provisions for judicial notice of official seals are contained in the United States Code.

Paragraph (2). While statutes are found which raise a presumption of genuineness of purported official signatures in the absence of an official seal, 7 WIGMORE § 2167; CAL EVID. CODE § 1453, the greater ease of effecting a forgery under these circumstances is apparent. Hence this paragraph of the rule calls for authentication by an officer who has a seal. Notarial acts by members of the armed forces and other special situations are covered in paragraph (10).

Paragraph (3) provides a method for extending the presumption of authenticity to foreign official documents by a procedure of certification. It is derived from Rule 44(a)(2) of the Rules of Civil Procedure but is broader in applying to public documents rather than being limited to public records.

Paragraph (4). The common law and innumerable statutes have recognized the procedure of authenticating copies of public records by certificate. The certificate qualifies as a public document, receivable as authentic when in conformity with paragraph (1), (2), or (3). Rule 44(a) of the Rules of Civil Procedure and Rule 27 of the Rules of Criminal Procedure have provided authentication procedures of this nature for both domestic and foreign public records. It will be observed that the certification procedure here provided extends only to public records, reports, and recorded documents, all including data compilations, and does not apply to public documents generally. Hence documents provable when presented in original form under paragraphs (1), (2), or (3) may not be provable by certified copy under paragraph (4).

Paragraph (5). Dispensing with preliminary proof of the genuineness of purportedly official publications, most commonly encountered in connection with statutes, court reports, rules, and regulations, has been greatly enlarged by statutes and decisions. 5 WIGMORE § 1684. Paragraph (5), it will be noted, does not confer admissibility upon all official publications; it merely provides a means whereby their authenticity may be taken as established for purposes of admissibility. Rule 44(a) of the Rules of Civil Procedure has been to the same effect.

Paragraph (6). The likelihood of forgery of newspapers or periodicals is slight indeed. Hence no danger is apparent in receiving them. Establishing the authenticity of the publication may, of course, leave still open questions of authority and responsibility for items therein contained. *See* 7 WIGMORE § 2150; *cf.* 39 U.S.C. § [3005(b)] (public advertisement prima facie evidence of agency of person named, in postal fraud order proceeding); CAN. UNIF. EVID. ACT (Draft 1936) (printed copy of newspaper prima facie evidence that notices or advertisements were authorized).

Paragraph (7). Several factors justify dispensing with preliminary proof of genuineness of commercial and mercantile labels and the like. The risk of forgery is minimal. Trademark infringement involves serious penalties. Great efforts are devoted to inducing the public to buy in reliance on brand names, and substantial protection is given them. Hence the fairness of this treatment finds recognition in the cases. Curtiss Candy Co. v. Johnson, 163 Miss. 426 (1932) (Baby Ruth candy bar); Doyle v. Continental Baking Co., 262 Mass. 516 (1928) (loaf of bread); Weiner v. Mager & Throne, Inc., 3 N.Y.S.2d 918 (Mun. Ct. 1938) (same); *see also* W. VA. CODE § 47-3-5 (1966) (repealed 1996) (trade-mark on bottle prima facie evidence of ownership). *Contra,* Keegan v. Green Giant Co., 150 Me. 283 (1954); Murphy v. Campbell Soup Co., 62 F.2d 564 (1st Cir. 1933). Cattle brands have received similar acceptance in the western states. MONT. CODE ANN. § 46-606 (1947) (current version at MONT. CODE ANN. § 81-3-105); State v. Wolfley, 75 Kan. 406 (1907); Annotation, 11 L.R.A. (N.S.) 87. Inscriptions on trains and vehicles are held to be prima facie evidence of ownership or control. Pittsburgh, Ft. Wayne & Chi. Ry. Co. v. Callaghan, 157 Ill. 406 (1895); 9 WIGMORE § 2510a. See also the provision of 19 U.S.C. § 1615(2) that marks, labels, brands, or stamps indicating foreign origin are prima facie evidence of foreign origin of merchandise.

Paragraph (8). In virtually every state, acknowledged title documents are receivable in evidence without further proof. Statutes are collected in 5 WIGMORE § 1676. If this authentication suffices for documents of the importance of those affecting titles, logic scarcely permits denying this method when other kinds of documents are involved. Instances of broadly inclusive statutes are California Evidence Code § 1451 and New York Civil Practice Law and Rules 4538 (McKinney 1963).

<u>REPORT OF THE HOUSE COMMITTEE ON THE JUDICIARY</u>

Rule 902(8) as submitted by the Court referred to certificates of acknowledgment "under the hand and seal of" a notary public or other officer authorized by law to take acknowledgments. The Committee amended the rule to eliminate the requirement, believed to be inconsistent with the law in some states, that a notary public must affix a seal to a document acknowledged before him. As amended the rule merely requires that the document be executed in the manner prescribed by state law.

ADVISORY COMMITTEE'S NOTE TO RULE 902(9)

Paragraph (9). Issues of the authenticity of commercial paper in federal courts will usually arise in diversity cases, will involve an element of a cause of action or defense, and with respect to presumptions and burden of proof will be controlled by *Erie Railroad Co. v. Tompkins*, 304 U.S. 64 (1938). Rule 302, *supra*. There may, however, be questions of authenticity involving lesser segments of a case or the case may be one governed by federal common law. Clearfield Trust Co. v. United States, 318 U.S. 363 (1943); *cf.* United States v. Yazell, 382 U.S. 341 (1966). In these situations, resort to the useful authentication provisions of the Uniform Commercial Code is provided for. While the phrasing is in terms of "general commercial law," in order to avoid the potential complications inherent in borrowing local statutes, today one would have difficulty in determining the general commercial law without referring to the Code. *See* Williams v. Walker–Thomas Furniture Co., 350 F.2d 445 (D.C. Cir. 1965). Pertinent Code provisions are sections 1-202 (current version at U.C.C. § 1-307 (2011)), 3-307 (current version at U.C.C. § 3-308 (2011)), and 3-510 (current version at U.C.C. 3-505 (2011)), dealing with third-party documents, signatures on negotiable instruments, protests, and statements of dishonor.

REPORT OF THE HOUSE COMMITTEE ON THE JUDICIARY

The Committee approved Rule 902(9) as submitted by the Court. With respect to the meaning of the phrase "general commercial law," the Committee intends that the Uniform Commercial Code, which has been adopted in virtually every state, will be followed generally, but that federal commercial law will apply where federal commercial paper is involved. *See* Clearfield Trust Co. v. United States, 318 U.S. 363 (1943). Further, in those instances in which the issues are governed by *Erie Railroad Co. v. Tompkins*, 304 U.S. 64 (1938), state law will apply irrespective of whether it is the Uniform Commercial Code.

ADVISORY COMMITTEE'S NOTE TO RULE 902(10)

Paragraph (10). The paragraph continues in effect dispensations with preliminary proof of genuineness provided in various Acts of Congress. *See, e.g.,* 10 U.S.C. § 936 (signature, without seal, together with title, prima facie evidence of authenticity of acts of certain military personnel who are given notarial power); 15 U.S.C. § 77f(a) (signature on SEC registration presumed genuine); 26 U.S.C. § 6064 (signature to tax return prima facie genuine).

<u>ADVISORY COMMITTEE'S NOTE TO 2000 ADDITION OF RULES 902(11) AND (12)</u>

The amendment adds two new paragraphs to the rule on self-authentication. It sets forth a procedure by which parties can authenticate certain records of regularly conducted activity, other than through the testimony of a foundation witness. See the amendment to Rule 803(6). 18 U.S.C. § 3505 currently provides a means for certifying foreign records of regularly conducted activity in criminal cases, and this amendment is intended to establish a similar procedure for domestic records, and for foreign records offered in civil cases.

A declaration that satisfies 28 U.S.C. § 1746 would satisfy the declaration requirement of Rule 902(11), as would any comparable certification under oath.

The notice requirement in Rules 902(11) and (12) is intended to give the opponent of the evidence a full opportunity to test the adequacy of the foundation set forth in the declaration.

<u>ADVISORY COMMITTEE'S NOTE TO 2017 ADDITION OF RULE 902(13)</u>

The amendment sets forth a procedure by which parties can authenticate certain electronic evidence other than through the testimony of a foundation witness. As with the provisions on business records in Rules 902(11) and (12), the Committee has found that the expense and inconvenience of producing a witness to authenticate an item of electronic evidence are often unnecessary. It is often the case that a party goes to the expense of producing an authentication witness and then the adversary either stipulates authenticity before the witness is called or fails to challenge the authentication testimony once it is presented. The amendment provides a procedure under which the parties can determine in advance of trial whether a real challenge to authenticity will be made, and can then plan accordingly.

Nothing in the amendment is intended to limit a party from establishing authenticity of electronic evidence on any ground provided in these rules, including through judicial notice where appropriate.

A proponent establishing authenticity under this rule must present a certification containing information that would be sufficient to establish authenticity were that information provided by a witness at trial. If the certification provides information that would be insufficient to authenticate the record if the certifying person testified, then authenticity is not established under this rule. The rule specifically allows the authenticity foundation that satisfies Rule 901(b)(9) to be established by a certification rather than the testimony of a live witness.

The reference to the "certification requirements of Rule 902(11) or (12)" is only to the procedural requirements for a valid certification. There is no intent to require, or permit, a certification under this rule to prove the requirements of Rule 803(6). Rule 902(13) is solely limited to authentication, and any attempt to satisfy a hearsay exception must be made independently.

A certification under this rule can establish only that the proffered item has satisfied the admissibility requirements for authenticity. The opponent remains free to object to admissibility of the proffered item on other grounds—including hearsay, relevance, or in criminal cases the right to confrontation. For example, assume that a plaintiff in a defamation case offers what purports to be a printout of a webpage on which a defamatory statement was made. Plaintiff offers a certification under this rule in which a qualified person describes the process by which the webpage was retrieved. Even if that certification sufficiently establishes that the webpage is authentic, defendant remains free to object that the statement on the webpage was not placed there by defendant. Similarly, a certification authenticating a computer output, such as a spreadsheet, does not preclude an objection that the information produced is unreliable—the authentication establishes only that the output came from the computer.

A challenge to the authenticity of electronic evidence may require technical information about the system or process at issue, including possibly retaining a forensic technical expert; such factors will affect whether the opponent has a fair opportunity to challenge the evidence given the notice provided.

The reference to Rule 902(12) is intended to cover certifications that are made in a foreign country.

ADVISORY COMMITTEE'S NOTE TO 2017 ADDITION OF RULE 902(14)

The amendment sets forth a procedure by which parties can authenticate data copied from an electronic device, storage medium, or electronic file, other than through the testimony of a foundation witness. As with the provisions on business records in Rules 902(11) and (12), the Committee has found that the expense and inconvenience of producing an authenticating witness for this evidence are often unnecessary. It is often the case that a party goes to the expense of producing an authentication witness, and then the adversary either stipulates authenticity before the witness is called or fails to challenge the authentication testimony once it is presented. The amendment provides a procedure in which the parties can determine in advance of trial whether a real challenge to authenticity will be made, and can then plan accordingly.

Today, data copied from electronic devices, storage media, and electronic files are ordinarily authenticated by "hash value." A hash value is a number that is often represented as a sequence of characters and is produced by an algorithm based upon the digital contents of a drive, medium, or file. If the hash values for the original and copy are different, then the copy is not identical to the original. If the hash values for the original and copy are the same, it is highly improbable that the original and copy are not identical. Thus, identical hash values for the original and copy reliably attest to the fact that they are exact duplicates. This amendment allows self-authentication by a certification of a qualified person that she checked the hash value of the proffered item and that it was identical to the original. The rule is flexible enough to allow certifications through processes other than comparison of hash value, including by other reliable means of identification provided by future technology.

Nothing in the amendment is intended to limit a party from establishing authenticity of electronic evidence on any ground provided in these rules, including through judicial notice where appropriate.

A proponent establishing authenticity under this rule must present a certification containing information that would be sufficient to establish authenticity were that information provided by a witness at trial. If the certification provides information that would be insufficient to authenticate the record if the certifying person testified, then authenticity is not established under this rule.

The reference to the "certification requirements of Rule 902(11) or (12)" is only to the procedural requirements for a valid certification. There is no intent to require, or permit, a certification under this rule to prove the requirements of Rule 803(6). Rule 902(14) is solely limited to authentication, and any attempt to satisfy a hearsay exception must be made independently.

A certification under this rule can establish only that the proffered item is authentic. The opponent remains free to object to admissibility of the proffered item on other grounds—including hearsay, relevance, or in criminal cases the right to confrontation. For example, in a criminal case in which data copied from a hard drive is proffered, the defendant can still challenge hearsay found in the hard drive, and can still challenge whether the information on the hard drive was placed there by the defendant.

A challenge to the authenticity of electronic evidence may require technical information about the system or process at issue, including possibly retaining a forensic technical expert; such factors will affect whether the opponent has a fair opportunity to challenge the evidence given the notice provided.

The reference to Rule 902(12) is intended to cover certifications that are made in a foreign country.

Rule 903.   SUBSCRIBING WITNESS'S TESTIMONY

A subscribing witness's testimony is necessary to authenticate a writing only if required by the law of the jurisdiction that governs its validity.

(Enacted Jan. 2, 1975; as restyled Apr. 26, 2011, eff. Dec. 1, 2011.)

NOTE BY FEDERAL JUDICIAL CENTER

The rule enacted by the Congress is the rule prescribed by the Supreme Court without change.

ADVISORY COMMITTEE'S NOTE

The common law required that attesting witnesses be produced or accounted for. Today the requirement has generally been abolished except with respect to documents which must be attested to be valid, e.g., wills in some states. MCCORMICK § 188. UNIF. R. EVID. 71; CAL. EVID. CODE § 1411; KAN. STAT. ANN. § 60-468; N.J. EVID. R. 71 (repealed and replaced by N.J. R. EVID. 903 (1993)); N.Y. C.P.L.R. 4537.

ARTICLE X. CONTENTS OF WRITINGS, RECORDINGS, AND PHOTOGRAPHS

Rule 1001. DEFINITIONS THAT APPLY TO THIS ARTICLE

In this article:

(a) A "writing" consists of letters, words, numbers, or their equivalent set down in any form.

(b) A "recording" consists of letters, words, numbers, or their equivalent recorded in any manner.

(c) A "photograph" means a photographic image or its equivalent stored in any form.

(d) An "original" of a writing or recording means the writing or recording itself or any counterpart intended to have the same effect by the person who executed or issued it. For electronically stored information, "original" means any printout—or other output readable by sight—if it accurately reflects the information. An "original" of a photograph includes the negative or a print from it.

(e) A "duplicate" means a counterpart produced by a mechanical, photographic, chemical, electronic, or other equivalent process or technique that accurately reproduces the original.

(Enacted Jan. 2, 1975; as restyled Apr. 26, 2011, eff. Dec. 1, 2011.)

NOTE BY FEDERAL JUDICIAL CENTER

The rule enacted by the Congress is the rule prescribed by the Supreme Court, amended in [subdivision (c)] by inserting "video tapes."[1]

---

[1] [The reference to video tapes did not survive the restyling project. Compare unrestyled Rule 1001(2) with restyled Rule 1001(c) at pages 486 to 487.—GF]

<u>ADVISORY COMMITTEE'S NOTE TO RULE 1001(a)–(b)</u>

In an earlier day, when discovery and other related procedures were strictly limited, the misleading named "best evidence rule" afforded substantial guarantees against inaccuracies and fraud by its insistence upon production of original documents. The great enlargement of the scope of discovery and related procedures in recent times has measurably reduced the need for the rule. Nevertheless, important areas of usefulness persist: discovery of documents outside the jurisdiction may require substantial outlay of time and money; the unanticipated document may not practically be discoverable; criminal cases have built-in limitations on discovery. Clearly & Strong, *The Best Evidence Rule: An Evaluation in Context*, 51 IOWA L. REV. 825 (1966).

[Subdivisions (a) and (b)]. Traditionally the rule requiring the original centered upon accumulations of data and expressions affecting legal relations set forth in words and figures. This meant that the rule was one essentially related to writings. Present day techniques have expanded methods of storing data, yet the essential form which the information ultimately assumes for usable purposes is words and figures. Hence the considerations underlying the rule dictate its expansion to include computers, photographic systems, and other modern developments.

<u>REPORT OF THE HOUSE COMMITTEE ON THE JUDICIARY</u>

[Subdivision (c)]. The Committee amended this rule expressly to include "video tapes" in the definition of "photographs."[2]

<u>ADVISORY COMMITTEE'S NOTES TO RULE 1001(d)–(e)</u>

[Subdivision (d)]. In most instances, what is an original will be self-evident and further refinement will be unnecessary. However, in some instances particularized definition is required. A carbon copy of a contract executed in duplicate becomes an original, as does a sales ticket carbon copy given to a customer. While strictly speaking the original of a photograph might be thought to be only the negative, practicality and common usage require that any print from the negative be regarded as an original. Similarly, practicality and usage confer the status of original upon any computer printout. Transp. Indem. Co. v. Seib, 178 Neb. 253 (1965).

---

[2] [As I noted earlier, the reference to video tapes did not survive the restyling project. Compare unrestyled Rule 1001(2) with restyled Rule 1001(c) at pages 486 to 487.—GF]

[Subdivision (e)]. The definition describes "copies" produced by methods possessing an accuracy which virtually eliminates the possibility of error. Copies thus produced are given the status of originals in large measure by Rule 1003, *infra*. Copies subsequently produced manually, whether handwritten or typed, are not within the definition. It should be noted that what is an original for some purposes may be a duplicate for others. Thus a bank's microfilm record of checks cleared is the original as a record. However, a print offered as a copy of a check whose contents are in controversy is a duplicate. This result is substantially consistent with 28 U.S.C. § [1732]. *Cf.* 26 U.S.C. § [7513] (giving full status as originals to photographic reproductions of tax returns and other documents, made by authority of the Secretary of the Treasury), 44 U.S.C. § [2112] (giving original status to photographic copies in the National Archives).

Rule 1002.   REQUIREMENT OF THE ORIGINAL

An original writing, recording, or photograph is required in order to prove its content unless these rules or a federal statute provides otherwise.

(Enacted Jan. 2, 1975; as restyled Apr. 26, 2011, eff. Dec. 1, 2011.)

NOTE BY FEDERAL JUDICIAL CENTER

The rule enacted by the Congress is the rule prescribed by the Supreme Court without change.

ADVISORY COMMITTEE'S NOTE

The rule is the familiar one requiring production of the original of a document to prove its contents, expanded to include writings, recordings, and photographs, as defined in Rule [1001(a)–(c)], *supra*.

Application of the rule requires a resolution of the question whether contents are sought to be proved. Thus an event may be proved by nondocumentary evidence, even though a written record of it was made. If, however, the event is sought to be proved by the written record, the rule applies. For example, payment may be proved without producing the written receipt which was given. Earnings may be proved without producing books of account in which they are entered. MCCORMICK § 198; 4 WIGMORE § 1245. Nor does the rule apply to testimony that books or records have been examined and found not to contain any reference to a designated matter.

The assumption should not be made that the rule will come into operation on every occasion when use is made of a photograph in evidence. On the contrary, the rule will seldom apply to ordinary photographs. In most instances a party *wishes* to introduce the item and the question raised is the propriety of receiving it in evidence. Cases in which an offer is made of the testimony of a witness as to what he saw in a photograph or motion picture, without producing the same, are most unusual. The usual course is for a witness on the stand to identify the photograph or motion picture as a correct representation of events which he saw or of a scene with which he is familiar. In fact he adopts the picture as his testimony, or, in common parlance, uses the picture to illustrate his testimony. Under these circumstances, no effort is made to prove the contents of the picture, and the rule is inapplicable. Paradis, *The Celluloid Witness*, 37 U. COLO. L. REV. 235, 249–51 (1965).

On occasion, however, situations arise in which contents are sought to be proved. Copyright, defamation, and invasion of privacy by photograph or motion picture fall in this category. Similarly as to situations in which the picture is offered as having independent probative value, e.g., automatic photograph of bank robber. *See* People v. Doggett, 83 Cal. App. 2d 405 (1948) (photograph of defendants engaged in indecent act); Mouser & Philbin, *Photographic Evidence—Is There a Recognized Basis for Admissibility?*, 8 HASTINGS L.J. 310 (1957). The most commonly encountered of this latter group is of course, the X ray, with substantial authority calling for production of the original. Daniels v. Iowa City, 191 Iowa 811 (1921); Cellamare v. Third Ave. Transit Corp., 77 N.Y.S. 2d 91 (App. Div. 1948); Patrick & Tillman v. Matkin, 154 Okla. 232 (1932); Mendoza v. Rivera, 78 D.P.R. 599 (1955).

It should be noted, however, that Rule 703, *supra*, allows an expert to give an opinion based on matters not in evidence, and the present rule must be read as being limited accordingly in its application. Hospital records which may be admitted as business records under Rule 803(6) commonly contain reports interpreting X rays by the staff radiologist, who qualifies as an expert, and these reports need not be excluded from the records by the instant rule.

The reference to Acts of Congress is made in view of such statutory provisions as 26 U.S.C. § 7513 (photographic reproductions of tax returns and documents, made by authority of the Secretary of the Treasury, treated as originals) and 44 U.S.C. § [2112] (photographic copies in National Archives treated as originals).

Rule 1003.   ADMISSIBILITY OF DUPLICATES

A duplicate is admissible to the same extent as the original unless a genuine question is raised about the original's authenticity or the circumstances make it unfair to admit the duplicate.

(Enacted Jan. 2, 1975; as restyled Apr. 26, 2011, eff. Dec. 1, 2011.)

NOTE BY FEDERAL JUDICIAL CENTER

The rule enacted by the Congress is the rule prescribed by the Supreme Court without change.

ADVISORY COMMITTEE'S NOTE

When the only concern is with getting the words or other contents before the court with accuracy and precision, then a counterpart serves equally as well as the original, if the counterpart is the product of a method which insures accuracy and genuineness. By definition in [1001(e)], *supra*, a "duplicate" possesses this character.

Therefore, if no genuine issue exists as to authenticity and no other reason exists for requiring the original, a duplicate is admissible under the rule. This position finds support in the decisions. Myrick v. United States, 332 F.2d 279 (5th Cir. 1963) (no error in admitting photostatic copies of checks instead of original microfilm in absence of suggestion to trial judge that photostats were incorrect); Johns v. United States, 323 F.2d 421 (5th Cir. 1963) (not error to admit concededly accurate tape recording made from original wire recording); Sauget v. Johnston, 315 F.2d 816 (9th Cir. 1963) (not error to admit copy of agreement when opponent had original and did not on appeal claim any discrepancy). Other reasons for requiring the original may be present when only a part of the original is reproduced and the remainder is needed for cross-examination or may disclose matters qualifying the part offered or otherwise useful to the opposing party. United States v. Alexander, 326 F.2d 736 (4th Cir. 1964); *see also* Toho Bussan Kaisha, Ltd. v. Am. President Lines, Ltd., 265 F.2d 418 (2d Cir. 1959).

REPORT OF THE HOUSE COMMITTEE ON THE JUDICIARY

The Committee approved this rule in the form submitted by the Court, with the expectation that the courts would be liberal in deciding that a "genuine question is raised as to the authenticity of the original."

Rule 1004. ADMISSIBILITY OF OTHER EVIDENCE OF CONTENT

An original is not required and other evidence of the content of a writing, recording, or photograph is admissible if:

(a) all the originals are lost or destroyed, and not by the proponent acting in bad faith;

(b) an original cannot be obtained by any available judicial process;

(c) the party against whom the original would be offered had control of the original; was at that time put on notice, by pleadings or otherwise, that the original would be a subject of proof at the trial or hearing; and fails to produce it at the trial or hearing; or

(d) the writing, recording, or photograph is not closely related to a controlling issue.

(Enacted Jan. 2, 1975; as amended Mar. 2, 1987, eff. Oct. 1, 1987; as restyled Apr. 26, 2011, eff. Dec. 1, 2011.)

NOTE BY FEDERAL JUDICIAL CENTER

The rule enacted by the Congress is the rule prescribed by the Supreme Court without change.

ADVISORY COMMITTEE'S NOTE

Basically the rule requiring the production of the original as proof of contents has developed as a rule of preference: if failure to produce the original is satisfactorily explained, secondary evidence is admissible. The instant rule specifies the circumstances under which production of the original is excused.

The rule recognizes no "degrees" of secondary evidence. While strict logic might call for extending the principle of preference beyond simply preferring the original, the formulation of a hierarchy of preferences and a procedure for making it effective is believed to involve unwarranted complexities. Most, if not all, that would be accomplished by an extended scheme of preferences will, in any event, be achieved through the normal motivation of a party to present the most convincing evidence possible and the arguments and procedures available to his opponent if he does not. *Cf.* MCCORMICK § 207.

[Subdivision (a)]. Loss or destruction of the original, unless due to bad faith of the proponent, is a satisfactory explanation of nonproduction. MCCORMICK § 201.

REPORT OF THE HOUSE COMMITTEE ON THE JUDICIARY

The Committee approved Rule [1004(a)] in the form submitted to Congress. However, the Committee intends that loss or destruction of an original by another person at the instigation of the proponent should be considered as tantamount to loss or destruction in bad faith by the proponent himself.

ADVISORY COMMITTEE'S NOTE

[Subdivision (b)]. When the original is in the possession of a third person, inability to procure it from him by resort to process or other judicial procedure is a sufficient explanation of nonproduction. Judicial procedure includes subpoena duces tecum as an incident to the taking of a deposition in another jurisdiction. No further showing is required. *See* MCCORMICK § 202.

[Subdivision (c)]. A party who has an original in his control has no need for the protection of the rule if put on notice that proof of contents will be made. He can ward off secondary evidence by offering the original. The notice procedure here provided is not to be confused with orders to produce or other discovery procedures, as the purpose of the procedure under this rule is to afford the opposite party an opportunity to produce the original, not to compel him to do so. MCCORMICK § 203.

[Subdivision (d)]. While difficult to define with precision, situations arise in which no good purpose is served by production of the original. Examples are the newspaper in an action for the price of publishing defendant's advertisement, Foster–Holcomb Inv. Co. v. Little Rock Publ'g Co., 151 Ark. 449 (1922), and the streetcar transfer of plaintiff claiming status as a passenger, Chi. City Ry. Co. v. Carroll, 206 Ill. 318 (1903). Numerous cases are collected in MCCORMICK § 200, at 412 n.1.

Rule 1005.   COPIES OF PUBLIC RECORDS TO PROVE CONTENT

The proponent may use a copy to prove the content of an official record—or of a document that was recorded or filed in a public office as authorized by law—if these conditions are met: the record or document is otherwise admissible; and the copy is certified as correct in accordance with Rule 902(4) or is testified to be correct by a witness who has compared it with the original. If no such copy can be obtained by reasonable diligence, then the proponent may use other evidence to prove the content.

(Enacted Jan. 2, 1975; as restyled Apr. 26, 2011, eff. Dec. 1, 2011.)

NOTE BY FEDERAL JUDICIAL CENTER

The rule enacted by the Congress is the rule prescribed by the Supreme Court without change.

ADVISORY COMMITTEE'S NOTE

Public records call for somewhat different treatment. Removing them from their usual place of keeping would be attended by serious inconvenience to the public and to the custodian. As a consequence judicial decisions and statutes commonly hold that no explanation need be given for failure to produce the original of a public record. MCCORMICK § 204; 4 WIGMORE §§ 1215–1228. This blanket dispensation from producing or accounting for the original would open the door to the introduction of every kind of secondary evidence of contents of public records were it not for the preference given certified or compared copies. Recognition of degrees of secondary evidence in this situation is an appropriate quid pro quo for not applying the requirement of producing the original.

The provisions of 28 U.S.C. § 1733(b) apply only to departments or agencies of the United States. The rule, however, applies to public records generally and is comparable in scope in this respect to Rule 44(a) of the Rules of Civil Procedure.

Rule 1006. SUMMARIES TO PROVE CONTENT

The proponent may use a summary, chart, or calculation to prove the content of voluminous writings, recordings, or photographs that cannot be conveniently examined in court. The proponent must make the originals or duplicates available for examination or copying, or both, by other parties at a reasonable time and place. And the court may order the proponent to produce them in court.

(Enacted Jan. 2, 1975; as restyled Apr. 26, 2011, eff. Dec. 1, 2011.)

NOTE BY FEDERAL JUDICIAL CENTER

The rule enacted by the Congress is the rule prescribed by the Supreme Court without change.

ADVISORY COMMITTEE'S NOTE

The admission of summaries of voluminous books, records, or documents offers the only practicable means of making their contents available to judge and jury. The rule recognizes this practice, with appropriate safeguards. 4 WIGMORE § 1230.

Rule 1007. TESTIMONY OR STATEMENT OF A PARTY TO PROVE CONTENT

The proponent may prove the content of a writing, recording, or photograph by the testimony, deposition, or written statement of the party against whom the evidence is offered. The proponent need not account for the original.

(Enacted Jan. 2, 1975; as amended Mar. 2, 1987, eff. Oct. 1, 1987; as restyled Apr. 26, 2011, eff. Dec. 1, 2011.)

NOTE BY FEDERAL JUDICIAL CENTER

The rule enacted by the Congress is the rule prescribed by the Supreme Court without change.

ADVISORY COMMITTEE'S NOTE

While the parent case, *Slatterie v. Pooley*, (1840) 151 Eng. Rep. 579 (Exch.), 6 M. & W. 664, allows proof of contents by evidence of an oral admission by the party against whom offered, without accounting for nonproduction of the original, the risk of inaccuracy is substantial and the decision is at odds with the purpose of the rule giving preference to the original. *See* 4 WIGMORE § 1255. The instant rule follows Professor McCormick's suggestion of limiting this use of admissions to those made in the course of giving testimony or in writing. MCCORMICK § 208, at 424. The limitation, of course, does not call for excluding evidence of an oral admission when nonproduction of the original has been accounted for and secondary evidence generally has become admissible. Rule 1004, *supra*.

A similar provision is contained in New Jersey Evidence Rule 70(1)(h) (repealed and replaced by New Jersey Rule of Evidence 1007 (1993)).

Rule 1008. FUNCTIONS OF THE COURT AND JURY

Ordinarily, the court determines whether the proponent has fulfilled the factual conditions for admitting other evidence of the content of a writing, recording, or photograph under Rule 1004 or 1005. But in a jury trial, the jury determines—in accordance with Rule 104(b)—any issue about whether:

(a) an asserted writing, recording, or photograph ever existed;

(b) another one produced at the trial or hearing is the original; or

(c) other evidence of content accurately reflects the content.

(Enacted Jan. 2, 1975; as restyled Apr. 26, 2011, eff. Dec. 1, 2011.)

NOTE BY FEDERAL JUDICIAL CENTER

The rule enacted by the Congress is the rule prescribed by the Supreme Court, amended by substituting "court" in place of "judge," and by adding at the end of the first sentence the phrase "in accordance with the provisions of Rule 104."

ADVISORY COMMITTEE'S NOTE

Most preliminary questions of fact in connection with applying the rule preferring the original as evidence of contents are for the judge, under the general principles announced in Rule 104, *supra*. Thus, the question whether the loss of the originals has been established, or of the fulfillment of other conditions specified in Rule 1004, *supra*, is for the judge. However, questions may arise which go beyond the mere administration of the rule preferring the original and into the merits of the controversy. For example, plaintiff offers secondary evidence of the contents of an alleged contract, after first introducing evidence of loss of the original, and defendant counters with evidence that no such contract was ever executed. If the judge decides that the contract was never executed and excludes the secondary evidence, the case is at an end without ever going to the jury on a central issue. Levin, *Authentication and Content of Writings*, 10 RUTGERS L. REV. 632, 644 (1956). The latter portion of the instant rule is designed to insure treatment of these situations as raising jury questions. The decision is not one for uncontrolled discretion of the jury but is subject to the control exercised generally by the judge over jury determinations. *See* Rule 104(b), *supra*.

For similar provisions, see Uniform Rule 70(2); Kansas Statutes Annotated § 60-467(b); New Jersey Evidence Rule 70(2) (repealed 1993), (3) (repealed and replaced by New Jersey Rule of Evidence 1008 (1993)).

ARTICLE XI. MISCELLANEOUS RULES

Rule 1101.   APPLICABILITY OF THE RULES

(a) To Courts and Judges.   These rules apply to proceedings before:

- United States district courts;

- United States bankruptcy and magistrate judges;

- United States courts of appeals;

- the United States Court of Federal Claims; and

- the district courts of Guam, the Virgin Islands, and the Northern Mariana Islands.

(b) To Cases and Proceedings. These rules apply in:

- civil cases and proceedings, including bankruptcy, admiralty, and maritime cases;

- criminal cases and proceedings; and

- contempt proceedings, except those in which the court may act summarily.

(c) Rules on Privilege. The rules on privilege apply to all stages of a case or proceeding.

(d) Exceptions.   These rules—except for those on privilege—do not apply to the following:

(1) the court's determination, under Rule 104(a), on a preliminary question of fact governing admissibility;

(2) grand-jury proceedings; and

(3) miscellaneous proceedings such as:

- extradition or rendition;

- issuing an arrest warrant, criminal summons, or search warrant;

- a preliminary examination in a criminal case;

- sentencing;

- granting or revoking probation or supervised release; and

- considering whether to release on bail or otherwise.

(e) Other Statutes and Rules. A federal statute or a rule prescribed by the Supreme Court may provide for admitting or excluding evidence independently from these rules.

(Enacted Jan. 2, 1975; as amended Dec. 12, 1975; Nov. 6, 1978; Apr. 2, 1982; Mar. 2, 1987, eff. Oct. 1, 1987; Apr. 25, 1988, eff. Nov. 1, 1988; Nov. 18, 1988; Apr. 22, 1993, eff. Dec. 1, 1993; as restyled Apr. 26, 2011, eff. Dec. 1, 2011.)

NOTE BY FEDERAL JUDICIAL CENTER

The rule enacted by the Congress is the rule prescribed by the Supreme Court, amended as follows:

Subdivision (a) was amended in the first sentence by inserting "the Court of Claims" and by inserting "actions, cases, and." It was amended in the second sentence by substituting "terms" in place of "word," by inserting the phrase "and 'court,'" and by adding "commissioners of the Court of Claims."

Subdivision (b) was amended by substituting "civil actions and proceedings" in place of "civil actions," and by substituting "criminal cases and proceedings" in place of "criminal proceedings."

Subdivision (c) was amended by substituting "rule" in place of "rules" and by changing the verb to the singular.

Subdivision (d) was amended by deleting "those" after "other than" and by substituting "Rule 104" in place of "Rule 104(a)."

Subdivision (e) was amended by substituting "prescribed" in place of "adopted" and by adding "pursuant to statutory authority." The form of the statutory citations was also changed.

ADVISORY COMMITTEE'S NOTE TO RULE 1101(a)

[The Advisory Committee's Note to Rule 1101(a) addressed the various enabling acts that empowered the Supreme Court to prescribe rules of evidence for various courts. Congress mooted this discussion by enacting the Rules.]

REPORT OF THE HOUSE COMMITTEE ON THE JUDICIARY

Subdivision (a) as submitted to the Congress, in stating the courts and judges to which the Rules of Evidence apply, omitted the Court of Claims and commissioners of that court. At the request of the Court of Claims, the Committee amended the rule to include the court and its commissioners within the purview of the Rules.

ADVISORY COMMITTEE'S NOTE TO RULE 1101(b)–(e)

Subdivision (b) is a combination of the language of the enabling acts, *supra*, with respect to the kinds of proceedings in which the making of rules is authorized. It is subject to the qualifications expressed in the subdivisions which follow.

Subdivision (c), singling out the rules of privilege for special treatment, is made necessary by the limited applicability of the remaining rules.

Subdivision (d). The rule is not intended as an expression as to when due process or other constitutional provisions may require an evidentiary hearing. Paragraph (1) restates, for convenience, the provisions of the second sentence of Rule 104(a), *supra*. See Advisory Committee's Note to that rule.

(2) While some states have statutory requirements that indictments be based on "legal evidence," and there is some case law to the effect that the rules of evidence apply to grand jury proceedings, 1 WIGMORE § 4(5), the Supreme Court has not accepted this view. In *Costello v. United States*, 350 U.S. 359 (1956), the Court refused to allow an indictment to be attacked, for either constitutional or policy reasons, on the ground that only hearsay evidence was presented.

It would run counter to the whole history of the grand jury institution, in which laymen conduct their inquiries unfettered by technical rules. Neither justice nor the concept of a fair trial requires such a change.

Id. at 364. The rule as drafted does not deal with the evidence required to support an indictment.

(3) The rule exempts preliminary examinations in criminal cases. Authority as to the applicability of the rules of evidence to preliminary examinations has been meagre and conflicting. Goldstein, *The State and the Accused: Balance of Advantage in Criminal Procedure*, 69 YALE L.J. 1149, 1168 n.53 (1960); Comment, *Preliminary Hearings on Indictable Offenses in Philadelphia*, 106 U. PA. L. REV. 589, 592–93 (1958). Hearsay testimony is, however, customarily received in such examinations. Thus in a Dyer Act case, for example, an affidavit may properly be used in a preliminary examination to prove ownership of the stolen vehicle, thus saving the victim of the crime the hardship of having to travel twice to a distant district for the sole purpose of testifying as to ownership. It is believed that the extent of the applicability of the Rules of Evidence to preliminary examinations should be appropriately dealt with by the Federal Rules of Criminal Procedure which regulate those proceedings.

Extradition and rendition proceedings are governed in detail by statute. 18 U.S.C. §§ 3181–3195. They are essentially administrative in character. Traditionally the rules of evidence have not applied. 1 WIGMORE § 4(6). Extradition proceedings are [excepted] from the operation of the Rules of Criminal Procedure. FED. R. CRIM. R. [1(a)(5)(A)].

The rules of evidence have not been regarded as applicable to sentencing or probation proceedings, where great reliance is placed upon the presentence investigation and report. Rule 32(c) of the Federal Rules of Criminal Procedure requires a presentence investigation and report in every case unless the court otherwise directs. In *Williams v. New York*, 337 U.S. 241 (1949), in which the judge overruled a jury recommendation of life imprisonment and imposed a death sentence, the Court said that due process does not require confrontation or cross-examination in sentencing or passing on probation, and that the judge has broad discretion as to the sources and types of information relied upon. Compare the recommendation that the substance of all derogatory information be disclosed to the defendant, in ABA PROJECT ON MINIMUM STANDARDS FOR CRIMINAL JUSTICE, SENTENCING ALTERNATIVES AND PROCEDURES § 4.4 (Tentative Draft 1967 (Sobeloff, Chairman)). *Williams* was adhered to in *Specht v. Patterson*, 386 U.S. 605 (1967), but not extended to a proceeding under the Colorado Sex Offenders

Act, which was said to be a new charge leading in effect to punishment, more like the recidivist statutes where opportunity must be given to be heard on the habitual criminal issue.

Warrants for arrest, criminal summonses, and search warrants are issued upon complaint or affidavit showing probable cause. FED. R. CRIM. P. 4(a), [41(d)]. The nature of the proceedings makes application of the formal rules of evidence inappropriate and impracticable.

Criminal contempts are punishable summarily if the judge certifies that he saw or heard the contempt and that it was committed in the presence of the court. FED. R. CRIM. P. [42(b)]. The circumstances which preclude application of the rules of evidence in this situation are not present, however, in other cases of criminal contempt.

Proceedings with respect to release on bail or otherwise do not call for application of the rules of evidence. The governing statute specifically provides:

> Information stated in, or offered in connection with, any order entered pursuant to this section need not conform to the rules pertaining to the admissibility of evidence in a court of law.

18 U.S.C. § [3142(f)]. This provision is consistent with the type of inquiry contemplated in ABA PROJECT ON MINIMUM STANDARDS FOR CRIMINAL JUSTICE, STANDARDS RELATING TO PRETRIAL RELEASE, § 4.5(b), (c), at 16 (1968). The references to the weight of the evidence against the accused, in 18 U.S.C. § [3142(g)(2)], as a factor to be considered, clearly do not have in view evidence introduced at a hearing under the rules of evidence.

The rule does not exempt habeas corpus proceedings. The Supreme Court held in *Walker v. Johnston*, 312 U.S. 275 (1941), that the practice of disposing of matters of fact on affidavit, which prevailed in some circuits, did not "satisfy the command of the statute that the judge shall proceed 'to determine the facts of the case, by hearing the testimony and arguments.'" This view accords with the emphasis in *Townsend v. Sain*, 372 U.S. 293 (1963), upon trial-type proceedings, *id.* at 311, with demeanor evidence as a significant factor, *id.* at 322, in applications by state prisoners aggrieved by unconstitutional detentions. Hence subdivision (e) applies the Rules to habeas corpus proceedings to the extent not inconsistent with the statute.[1]

Subdivision (e). In a substantial number of special proceedings, ad hoc evaluation has resulted in the promulgation of particularized evidentiary provisions, by Act of Congress or by rule adopted by the Supreme Court. Well adapted to the particular proceedings, though not apt candidates for inclusion in a set of general rules, they are left undisturbed. Otherwise, however, the Rules of Evidence are applicable to the proceedings enumerated in the subdivision.

<u>ADVISORY COMMITTEE'S NOTE TO 1987 AMENDMENT TO RULE 1101</u>

Subdivision (a) is amended to delete the reference to the District Court for the District of the Canal Zone, which no longer exists, and to add the District Court for the Northern Mariana Islands. The United States bankruptcy judges are added to conform the subdivision with Rule 1101(b) and Bankruptcy Rule 9017.

<u>ADVISORY COMMITTEE'S NOTE TO 1993 AMENDMENT TO RULE 1101</u>

This revision is made to conform the rule to changes in terminology made by Rule 58 of the Federal Rules of Criminal Procedure and to the changes in the title of United States magistrates made by the Judicial Improvements Act of 1990.

Rule 1102.   AMENDMENTS

These rules may be amended as provided in 28 U.S.C. § 2072.

(Enacted Jan. 2, 1975; as amended Apr. 30, 1991, eff. Dec. 1, 1991; as restyled Apr. 26, 2011, eff. Dec. 1, 2011.)

<u>NOTE BY FEDERAL JUDICIAL CENTER</u>

This rule was not included among those prescribed by the Supreme Court. The rule prescribed by the Court as 1102 now appears as 1103.

---

[1] [A specific reference in the unrestyled rules to habeas corpus proceedings did not survive the restyling project.—GF]

Rule 1103.   TITLE

These rules may be cited as the Federal Rules of Evidence.

(Enacted Jan. 2, 1975; as restyled Apr. 26, 2011, eff. Dec. 1, 2011.)

NOTE BY FEDERAL JUDICIAL CENTER

The rule enacted by the Congress is the rule prescribed by the Supreme Court as Rule 1102 without change.

DELETED AND SUPERSEDED MATERIALS

EDITOR'S NOTE

Below are a number of rules submitted to Congress as potential Federal Rules of Evidence. Though approved by the Supreme Court, these rules failed to win congressional enactment.

Rule 105.   SUMMING UP AND COMMENT BY JUDGE
[Not enacted.]

After the close of evidence and arguments of counsel, the judge may fairly and impartially sum up the evidence and comment to the jury upon the weight of the evidence and the credibility of the witnesses, if he also instructs the jury that they are to determine for themselves the weight of the evidence and the credit to be given to the witnesses and that they are not bound by the judge's summation or comment.

ADVISORY COMMITTEE'S NOTE

The rule states the present rule in the federal courts. Capital Traction Co. v. Hof, 174 U.S. 1, 13–14 (1899). The judge must, of course, confine his remarks to what is disclosed by the evidence. He cannot convey to the jury his purely personal reaction to credibility or to the merits of the case; he can be neither argumentative nor an advocate. Quercia v. United States, 289 U.S. 466 (1933); Billeci v. United States, 184 F.2d 394, 402, (D.C. Cir. 1950). For further discussion see the series of articles by Wright, *The Invasion of Jury: Temperature of the War*, 27 TEMP. L.Q. 137 (1953), *Instructions to the Jury: Summary Without Comment*, 1954 WASH. U. L.Q. 177, *Adequacy of Instructions to the Jury*, 53 MICH. L. REV. 505, 813 (1955); *Comment*, MODEL CODE OF EVID. R. 8; MAGUIRE, WEINSTEIN, ET AL., CASES AND MATERIALS ON EVIDENCE 737–40 (5th ed. 1965); VANDERBILT, MINIMUM STANDARDS OF JUDICIAL ADMINISTRATION 224–29 (1949).

REPORT OF THE HOUSE COMMITTEE ON THE JUDICIARY

Rule 105 as submitted by the Supreme Court concerned the issue of summing up and comment by the judge. It provided that after the close of the evidence and the arguments of counsel, the presiding judge could fairly and impartially sum up the evidence and comment to the jury upon its weight and the credibility of the witnesses, if he also instructed the jury that it was not bound thereby and must make its own determination of those matters. The Committee recognized that the rule as submitted is consistent with long standing and current federal practice. However, the aspect of the rule dealing with the authority of a judge to comment on the weight of the evidence and the credibility of witnesses—an authority not granted to judges in most state courts—was highly controversial. After much debate the Committee determined to delete the entire rule, intending that its action be understood as reflecting no conclusion as to the merits of the proposed rule and that the subject should be left for separate consideration at another time.

<u>REPORT OF THE SENATE COMMITTEE ON THE JUDICIARY</u>

This rule as submitted by the Supreme Court permitted the judge to sum up and comment on the evidence. The House struck the rule.

The Committee accepts the House action with the understanding that the present federal practice, taken from the common law, of the trial judge's discretionary authority to comment on and summarize the evidence is left undisturbed.

Rule 301.   PRESUMPTIONS IN GENERAL
              [As prescribed by the Supreme Court.]

In all cases not otherwise provided for by Act of Congress or by these rules a presumption imposes on the party against whom it is directed the burden of proving that the nonexistence of the presumed fact is more probable than its existence.

Rule 301.   PRESUMPTIONS IN GENERAL
              [As passed by House of Representatives.]

In all civil actions and proceedings not otherwise provided for by Act of Congress or by these rules, a presumption imposes on the party against whom it is directed the burden of going forward with the evidence, and, even though met with contradicting evidence, a presumption is sufficient evidence of the fact presumed, to be considered by the trier of the facts.

ADVISORY COMMITTEE'S NOTE

This rule governs presumptions generally. See Rule 302 for presumptions controlled by state law and Rule 303 for those against an accused in a criminal case.

Presumptions governed by this rule are given the effect of placing upon the opposing party the burden of establishing the nonexistence of the presumed fact, once the party invoking the presumption establishes the basic facts giving rise to it. The same considerations of fairness, policy, and probability which dictate the allocation of the burden of the various elements of a case as between the prima facie case of a plaintiff and affirmative defenses also underlie the creation of presumptions. These considerations are not satisfied by giving a lesser effect to presumptions. Morgan & Maguire, *Looking Backward and Forward at Evidence*, 50 HARV. L. REV. 909, 913 (1937); Morgan, *Instructing the Jury upon Presumptions and Burden of Proof*, 47 HARV. L. REV. 59, 82 (1933); Cleary, *Presuming and Pleading: An Essay on Juristic Immaturity*, 12 STAN. L. REV. 5 (1959).

The so-called "bursting bubble" theory, under which a presumption vanishes upon the introduction of evidence which would support a finding of the nonexistence of the presumed fact, even though not believed, is rejected as according presumptions too "slight and evanescent" an effect. Morgan & Maguire, *supra*, at 913.

In the opinion of the Advisory Committee, no constitutional infirmity attends this view of presumptions. In *Mobile, Jackson & Kansas City Railroad Co. v. Turnipseed*, 219 U.S. 35 (1910), the Court upheld a Mississippi statute which provided that in actions against railroads proof of injury inflicted by the running of trains should be prima facie evidence of negligence by the railroad. The injury in the case had resulted from a derailment. The opinion made the points (1) that the only effect of the statute was to impose on the railroad the duty of producing some evidence to the contrary, (2) that an inference may be supplied by law if there is a rational connection between the fact proved and the fact presumed, as long as the opposite party is not precluded from presenting his evidence to the contrary, and (3) that considerations of public policy arising from the character of the business justified the application in question. Nineteen years later, in *Western & Atlantic Railroad Co. v. Henderson*, 279 U.S. 639 (1929), the Court overturned a Georgia statute making railroads liable for damages done by trains, unless the railroad made it appear that reasonable care had been used, the presumption being against the railroad. The declaration alleged the death of plaintiff's husband from a grade crossing collision, due to specified acts of negligence by defendant. The jury were instructed that proof of the injury raised a presumption of negligence; the burden shifted to the railroad to prove ordinary care; and unless it did so, they should find for plaintiff. The instruction was held erroneous in an opinion stating (1) that there was no rational connection between the mere fact of collision and negligence on the part of anyone, and (2) that the statute was different from that in *Turnipseed* in imposing a burden upon the railroad. The reader is left in a state of some confusion. Is the difference between a derailment and a grade crossing collision of no significance? Would the *Turnipseed* presumption have been bad if it had imposed a burden of persuasion on defendant, although that would in nowise have impaired its "rational connection"? If *Henderson* forbids imposing a burden of persuasion on defendants, what happens to affirmative defenses?

Two factors serve to explain *Henderson*. The first was that it was common ground that negligence was indispensable to liability. Plaintiff thought so, drafted her complaint accordingly, and relied upon the presumption. But how in logic could the same presumption establish her alternative grounds of negligence that the engineer was so blind he could not see decedent's truck and that he failed to stop after he saw it? Second, take away the basic assumption of no liability without fault, as *Turnipseed* intimated might be done ("considerations of public policy arising out of the character of the business"), and the structure of the decision in *Henderson* fails. No question of logic would have arisen if the statute had simply said: a prima facie case of liability is made by proof of injury by a train; lack of negligence is an affirmative defense, to be pleaded and proved as other affirmative defenses. The problem would be one of economic due process only. While it seems likely that the Supreme Court of 1929 would have voted that due process was denied, that result today would be unlikely. See, for example, the shift in the direction of absolute liability in the consumer cases. Prosser, *The Assault upon the Citadel (Strict Liability to the Consumer)*, 69 YALE L.J. 1099 (1960).

Any doubt as to the constitutional permissibility of a presumption imposing a burden of persuasion of the nonexistence of the presumed fact in civil cases is laid at rest by *Dick v. New York Life Insurance Co.*, 359 U.S. 437 (1959). The Court unhesitatingly applied the North Dakota rule that the presumption against suicide imposed on defendant the burden of proving that the death of insured, under an accidental death clause, was due to suicide.

"Proof of coverage and of death by gunshot wound shifts the burden to the insurer to establish that the death of the insured was due to his suicide." *Id.* at 443.

"In a case like this one, North Dakota presumes that death was accidental and places on the insurer the burden of proving that death resulted from suicide." *Id.* at 446.

The rational connection requirement survives in criminal cases, Tot v. United States, 319 U.S. 463 (1943), because the Court has been unwilling to extend into that area the greater-includes-the-lesser theory of *Ferry v. Ramsay*, 277 U.S. 88 (1928). In that case the Court sustained a Kansas statute under which bank directors were personally liable for deposits made with their assent and with knowledge of insolvency, and the fact of insolvency was prima facie evidence of assent and knowledge of insolvency. Mr. Justice Holmes pointed out that the state legislature could have made the directors personally liable to depositors in every case. Since the statute imposed a less stringent liability, "the thing to be considered is the result reached, not the possibly inartificial or clumsy way of reaching it." *Id.* at 94. Mr. Justice Sutherland dissented: though the state could have created an absolute liability, it did not purport to do so; a rational connection was necessary, but lacking, between the liability created and the prima facie evidence of it; the result might be different if the basis of the presumption were being open for business.

The Sutherland view has prevailed in criminal cases by virtue of the higher standard of notice there required. The fiction that everyone is presumed to know the law is applied to the substantive law of crimes as an alternative to complete unenforceability. But the need does not extend to criminal evidence and procedure, and the fiction does not encompass them. "Rational connection" is not fictional or artificial, and so it is reasonable to suppose that Gainey should have known that his presence at the site of an illicit still could convict him of being connected with (carrying on) the business, United States v. Gainey, 380 U.S. 63 (1965), but not that Romano should have known that his presence at a still could convict him of possessing it, United States v. Romano, 382 U.S. 136 (1965).

In his dissent in Gainey, Mr. Justice Black put it more artistically:

> It might be argued, although the court does not so argue or hold, that Congress if it wished could make presence at a still a crime in itself, and so Congress should be free to create crimes which are called "possession" and "carrying on an illegal distillery business" but which are defined in such a way that unexplained presence is sufficient and indisputable evidence in all cases to support conviction for those offenses. *See* Ferry v. Ramsey, 277 U.S. 88 (1928).

> Assuming for the sake of argument that Congress could make unexplained presence a criminal act, and ignoring also the refusal of this Court in other cases to uphold a statutory presumption on such a theory, *see* Heiner v. Donnan, 285 U.S. 312 (1932), there is no indication here that Congress intended to adopt such a misleading method of draftsmanship, nor in my judgment could the statutory provisions if so construed escape condemnation for vagueness, under the principles applied in *Lanzetta v. New Jersey*, 306 U.S. 451 (1939), and many other cases.

380 U.S. at 84 n.12.

And the majority opinion in *Romano* agreed with him:

> It may be, of course, that Congress has the power to make presence at an illegal still a punishable crime, but we find no clear indication that it intended to so exercise this power. The crime remains possession, not presence, and with all due deference to the judgment of Congress, the former may not constitutionally be inferred from the latter.

382 U.S. at 144.

The rule does not spell out the procedural aspects of its application. Questions as to when the evidence warrants submission of a presumption and what instructions are proper under varying states of fact are believed to present no particular difficulties.

REPORT OF THE HOUSE COMMITTEE ON THE JUDICIARY

Rule 301 as submitted by the Supreme Court provided that in all cases a presumption imposes on the party against whom it is directed the burden of proving that the nonexistence of the presumed fact is more probable than its existence. The Committee limited the scope of Rule 301 to "civil actions and proceedings" to effectuate its decision not to deal with the question of presumptions in criminal cases. (See note to Rule 303 in discussion of rules deleted.) With respect to the weight to be given a presumption in a civil case, the Committee agreed with the judgment implicit in the Court's version that the so-called "bursting bubble" theory of presumptions, whereby a presumption vanishes upon the appearance of any contradicting evidence by the other party, gives to presumptions too slight an effect. On the other hand, the Committee believed that the rule proposed by the Court, whereby a presumption permanently alters the burden of persuasion, no matter how much contradicting evidence is introduced—a view shared by only a few courts—lends too great a force to presumptions. Accordingly, the Committee amended the rule to adopt an intermediate position under which a presumption does not vanish upon the introduction of contradicting evidence, and does not change the burden of persuasion; instead it is merely deemed sufficient evidence of the fact presumed, to be considered by the jury or other finder of fact.

Rule 303.   PRESUMPTIONS IN CRIMINAL CASES [Not enacted.]

(a) Scope.   Except as otherwise provided by Act of Congress, in criminal cases, presumptions against the accused, recognized at common law or created by statute, including statutory provisions that certain facts are prima facie evidence of other facts or of guilt, are governed by this rule.

(b) Submission to jury.   The judge is not authorized to direct the jury to find a presumed fact against the accused. When the presumed fact establishes guilt or is an element of the offense or negatives a defense, the judge may submit the question of guilt or of the existence of the presumed fact to the jury, if, but only if, a reasonable juror on the evidence as a whole, including the evidence of the basic facts, could find guilt or the presumed fact beyond a reasonable doubt. When the presumed fact has a lesser effect, its existence may be submitted to the jury if the basic facts are supported by substantial evidence, or are otherwise established, unless the evidence as a whole negatives the existence of the presumed fact.

(c) Instructing the jury.   Whenever the existence of a presumed fact against the accused is submitted to the jury, the judge shall give an instruction that the law declares that the jury may regard the basic facts as sufficient evidence of the presumed fact but does not require it to do so. In addition, if the presumed fact establishes guilt or is an element of the offense or negatives a defense, the judge shall instruct the jury that its existence must, on all the evidence, be proved beyond a reasonable doubt.

<u>ADVISORY COMMITTEE'S NOTE</u>

Subdivision (a). This rule is based largely upon ALI MODEL PENAL CODE § 1.12(5) (Proposed Official Draft 1962) and *United States v. Gainey*, 380 U.S. 63 (1965). While the rule, unlike the Model Penal Code provision, spells out the effect of common law presumptions as well as those created by statute, cases involving the latter are no doubt of more frequent occurrence. Congress has enacted numerous provisions to lessen the burden of the prosecution, principally though not exclusively in the fields of narcotics control and taxation of liquor. Occasionally, in the pattern of the usual common law treatment of such matters as insanity, they take the form of assigning to the defense the responsibility of raising specified matters as affirmative defenses, which are not within the scope of these rules. *See Comment*, MODEL PENAL CODE § 1.13 (Tentative Draft No. 4, 1955). In other instances they assume a variety of forms which are the concern of this rule. The provision may be that proof of a specified fact (possession or presence) is sufficient to authorize conviction. 26 U.S.C. § 4704(a) (repealed 1970) (unlawful to buy or sell opium except from original stamped package—absence of stamps from package prima facie evidence of violation by person in possession); 26 U.S.C. § 4724(c) (repealed 1970) (unlawful for person who has not registered and paid special tax to possess narcotics—possession presumptive evidence of violation). Sometimes the qualification is added, "unless the defendant explains the possession [presence] to the satisfaction of the jury." 18 U.S.C. § 545 (possession of unlawfully imported goods sufficient for conviction of smuggling, unless explained); 21 U.S.C. § 174 (repealed 1970) (possession sufficient for conviction of buying or selling narcotics known to have been imported unlawfully, unless explained); *see also* 26 U.S.C. § 5601(a)(1), (a)(4), (a)(8), [(b)] (relating to distilling operations). Another somewhat different pattern makes possession evidence of a particular element of the crime. 21 U.S.C. § 176b (repealed 1970) (crime to furnish unlawfully imported heroin to juveniles—possession sufficient proof of unlawful importation, unless explained); 50 U.S.C. app. § 462(b) (unlawful to possess draft card not lawfully issued to holder, with intent to use for purposes of false identification—possession sufficient evidence of intent, unless explained); *see also* 15 U.S.C. § 902(f), (i) (repealed 1968).

Differences between the permissible operation of presumptions against the accused in criminal cases and in other situations prevent the formulation of a comprehensive definition of the term "presumption," and none is attempted. Nor do these rules purport to deal with problems of the validity of presumptions except insofar as they may be found reflected in the formulation of permissible procedures.

The presumption of innocence is outside the scope of the rule and unaffected by it.

Subdivisions (b) and (c). It is axiomatic that a verdict cannot be directed against the accused in a criminal case, 9 WIGMORE § 2495, at 312, with the corollary that the judge is without authority to direct the jury to find against the accused as to any element of the crime, MODEL PENAL CODE § 1.12(1) (Proposed Official Draft 1962). Although arguably the judge could direct the jury to find against the accused as to a lesser fact, the tradition is against it, and this rule makes no use of presumptions to remove any matters from final determination by the jury.

The only distinction made among presumptions under this rule is with respect to the measure of proof required in order to justify submission to the jury. If the effect of the presumption is to establish guilt or an element of the crime or to negative a defense, the measure of proof is the one widely accepted by the courts of appeals as the standard for measuring the sufficiency of the evidence in passing on motions for direct verdict (now judgment of acquittal); an acquittal should be directed when reasonable jurymen must have a reasonable doubt. Curley v. United States, 160 F.2d 229 (D.C. Cir.), *cert. denied*, 331 U.S. 837 (1947); United States v. Honeycutt, 311 F.2d 660 (4th Cir. 1962); Stephens v. United States, 354 F.2d 999 (5th Cir. 1956); Lambert v. United States, 261 F.2d 799 (5th Cir. 1958); United States v. Leggett, 292 F.2d 423 (6th Cir. 1961); Cape v. United States, 283 F.2d 430 (9th Cir. 1960); Cartwright v. United States, 335 F.2d 919 (10th Cir. 1964); *cf.* United States v. Gonzales Castro, 228 F.2d 807 (2d Cir. 1956); United States v. Masiello, 235 F.2d 279 (2d Cir.), *cert. denied*, 352 U.S. 882 (1956); United States v. Feinberg, 140 F.2d 592 (2d Cir. 1944). *But cf.* United States v. Arcuri, 282 F. Supp. 347 (E.D.N.Y.), *aff'd*, 405 F.2d 691 (1968), *cert. denied*, 395 U.S. 913 (1969); United States v. Melillo, 275 F. Supp. 314 (E.D.N.Y. 1967). If the presumption operates upon a lesser aspect of the case than the issue of guilt itself or an element of the crime or negativing a defense, the required measure of proof is the less stringent one of substantial evidence, consistently with the attitude usually taken with respect to particular items of evidence. 9 WIGMORE § 2497, at 324.

The treatment of presumptions in the rule is consistent with *United States v. Gainey*, 380 U.S. 63 (1965), where the matter was considered in depth. After sustaining the validity of the provision of 26 U.S.C. § [5601(b)] that presence at the site is sufficient to convict of the offense of carrying on the business of distiller without giving bond, unless the presence is explained to the satisfaction of the jury, the Court turned to procedural considerations and reached several conclusions. The power of the judge to withdraw a case from the jury for insufficiency of evidence is left unimpaired; he may submit the case on the basis of presence alone, but he is not required to do so. Nor is he precluded from rendering judgment notwithstanding the verdict. It is proper to tell the jury about the "statutory inference," if they are told it is not conclusive. The jury may still acquit, even if it finds defendant present and his presence is unexplained.[1] To avoid any implication that the statutory language relative to explanation be taken as directing attention to failure of the accused to testify, the better practice, said the Court, would be to instruct the jury that they may draw the inference unless the evidence provides a satisfactory explanation of defendant's presence, omitting any explicit reference to the statute.

The Final Report of the National Commission on Reform of Federal Criminal Laws § 103(4) and (5) (1971) contains a careful formulation of the consequences of a statutory presumption with an alternative formulation set forth in the comment thereto, and also of the effect of a prima facie case. In the criminal code there proposed, the terms "presumption" and "prima facie case" are used with precision and with reference to these meanings. In the federal criminal law as it stands today, these terms are not used with precision. Moreover, common law presumptions continue. Hence it is believed that the rule here proposed is better adapted to the present situation until such time as the Congress enacts legislation covering the subject, which the rule takes into account. If the subject of common law presumptions is not covered by legislation, the need for the rule in that regard will continue.

<u>REPORT OF THE HOUSE COMMITTEE ON THE JUDICIARY</u>

Rule 303, as submitted by the Supreme Court was directed to the issues of when, in criminal cases, a court may submit a presumption to a jury and the type of instruction it should give. The Committee deleted this rule since the subject of presumptions in criminal cases is addressed in detail in bills now pending before the Committee to revise the federal criminal code. The Committee determined to consider this question in the course of its study of these proposals.

---

[1] Compare the mandatory character of the instruction condemned in *Bollenbach v. United States*, 326 U.S. 607 (1946).

Rule 406.   HABIT; ROUTINE PRACTICE
            [Subdivision (b) not enacted.]

. . .

(b) Method of proof. Habit or routine practice may be proved by testimony in the form of an opinion or by specific instances of conduct sufficient in number to warrant a finding that the habit existed or that the practice was routine.

ADVISORY COMMITTEE'S NOTE

. . .

Subdivision (b). Permissible methods of proving habit or routine conduct include opinion and specific instances sufficient in number to warrant a finding that the habit or routine practice in fact existed. Opinion evidence must be "rationally based on the perception of the witness" and helpful, under the provisions of Rule 701. Proof by specific instances may be controlled by the overriding provisions of Rule 403 for exclusion on grounds of prejudice, confusion, misleading the jury, or waste of time. Thus the illustrations following ALI Model Code of Evidence Rule 307 suggests the possibility of admitting testimony by W that on numerous occasions he had been with X when X crossed a railroad track and that on each occasion X had first stopped and looked in both directions, but discretion to exclude offers of 10 witnesses, each testifying to a different occasion.

Similar provisions for proof by opinion or specific instances are found in Uniform Rule 50 and Kansas Statutes Annotated § 60-450. New Jersey Evidence Rule 50 (repealed and replaced by New Jersey Rule of Evidence 406(b) (1993)) provides for proof by specific instances but is silent as to opinion. The California Evidence Code is silent as to methods of proving habit, presumably proceeding on the theory that any method is relevant and all relevant evidence is admissible unless otherwise provided. *Tentative Recommendation and a Study Relating to the Uniform Rules of Evidence* (Article IV. Extrinsic Policies Affecting Admissibility), *in* CAL. LAW REV. COMM'N, REP., REC. & STUDIES 620 (1964).

REPORT OF THE HOUSE COMMITTEE ON THE JUDICIARY

[The Committee's reasons for deleting subdivision (b) are stated in the report, located in the materials following Rule 406. (RB 56.)]

RULE 501. PRIVILEGES RECOGNIZED ONLY AS PROVIDED
[Not enacted.]

Except as otherwise required by the Constitution of the United States or as provided by Act of Congress, and except as provided in these rules or in other rules adopted by the Supreme Court, no person has a privilege to:

(1) Refuse to be a witness; or

(2) Refuse to disclose any matter; or

(3) Refuse to produce any object or writing; or

(4) Prevent another from being a witness or disclosing any matter or producing any object or writing.

<u>ADVISORY COMMITTEE'S NOTE</u>

No attempt is made in these rules to incorporate the constitutional provisions which relate to the admission and exclusion of evidence, whether denominated as privileges or not. The grand design of these provisions does not readily lend itself to codification. The final reference must be the provisions themselves and the decisions construing them. Nor is formulating a rule an appropriate means of settling unresolved constitutional questions.

Similarly, privileges created by Act of Congress are not within the scope of these rules. These privileges do not assume the form of broad principles; they are the product of resolving particular problems in particular terms. Among them are included such provisions as 13 U.S.C. § 9 (generally prohibiting official disclosure of census reports and conferring a privileged status on retained copies of census reports); 42 U.S.C. § [2000e-5(b)] (making inadmissible in evidence anything said or done during Equal Employment Opportunity conciliation proceeding); 42 U.S.C. § 2240 (making required reports of incidents by nuclear facility licensees inadmissible in actions for damages); [49 U.S.C. §§ 20703, 20903] (similarly as to reports of accidents by railroads), 49 U.S.C. § [1154] (declaring [Civil Aeronautics Board] accident investigation reports inadmissible in actions for damages. The rule leaves them undisturbed).

The reference to other rules adopted by the Supreme Court makes clear that provisions relating to privilege in those rules will continue in operation. See, for example, the "work product" immunity against discovery spelled out under the Rules of Civil Procedure in *Hickman v. Taylor*, 329 U.S. 495 (1947), now formalized in revised Rule 26(b)(3) of the Rules of Civil Procedure, and the secrecy of grand jury proceedings provided by Criminal Rule 6.

With respect to privileges created by state law, these rules in some instances grant them greater status than has heretofore been the case by according them recognition in federal criminal proceedings, bankruptcy, and federal question litigation. *See* Rules 502, 510. There is, however, no provision generally adopting state-created privileges.

In federal criminal prosecutions the primacy of federal law as to both substance and procedure has been undoubted. *See, e.g.*, United States v. Krol, 374 F.2d 776 (7th Cir. 1967) (sustaining the admission in a federal prosecution of evidence obtained by electronic eavesdropping, despite a state statute declaring the use of these devices unlawful and evidence obtained therefrom inadmissible). This primacy includes matters of privilege. As stated in 4 BARRON, FEDERAL PRACTICE AND PROCEDURE § 2151, at 175 (1951):

> The determination of the question whether a matter is privileged is governed by federal decisions and the state statutes or rules of evidence have no application.

In *Funk v. United States*, 290 U.S. 371 (1933), the Court had considered the competency of a wife to testify for her husband and concluded that, absent congressional action or direction, the federal courts were to follow the common law as they saw it "in accordance with present day standards of wisdom and justice." And in *Wolfle v. United States*, 291 U.S. 7 (1934), the Court said with respect to the standard appropriate in determining a claim of privilege for an alleged confidential communication between spouses in a federal criminal prosecution:

> So our decision here, in the absence of Congressional legislation on the subject, is to be controlled by common law principles, not by local statute.

Id. at 13.

On the basis of *Funk* and *Wolfle*, the Advisory Committee on Rules of Criminal Procedure formulated Rule 26, which was adopted by the Court. The pertinent part of the rule provided:

> The . . . privileges of witnesses shall be governed, except when an Act of Congress or these rules otherwise provide,

by the principles of the common law as they may be interpreted . . . in the light of reason and experience.

As regards bankruptcy, section 21(a) of the Bankruptcy Act provides for examination of the bankrupt and his spouse concerning the acts, conduct, or property of the bankrupt. The Act limits examination of the spouse to business transacted by her or to which she is a party but provides "That the spouse may be so examined, any law of the United States or of any State to the contrary notwithstanding." 11 U.S.C. § [343]. The effect of the quoted language is clearly to override any conflicting state rule of incompetency or privilege against spousal testimony. A fair reading would also indicate an overriding of any contrary state rule of privileged confidential spousal communications. Its validity has never been questioned and seems most unlikely to be. As to other privileges, the suggestion has been made that state law applies, though with little citation of authority. 2 MOORE'S COLLIER ON BANKRUPTCY ¶ 21.13, at 297 (14th ed. 1961). This position seems to be contrary to the expression of the Court in *McCarthy v. Arndstein*, 266 U.S. 34 (1924), which speaks in the pattern of Rule 26 of the Federal Rules of Criminal Procedure:

> There is no provision [in the Bankruptcy Act] prescribing the rules by which the examination is to be governed. These are, impliedly, the general rules governing the admissibility of evidence and the competency and compellability of witnesses.

With respect to federal question litigation, the supremacy of federal law may be less clear, yet indications that state privileges are inapplicable preponderate in the circuits. *In re* Albert Lindley Lee Mem'l Hosp., 209 F.2d 122 (2d Cir. 1953), *cert. denied*, 347 U.S. 960 (1954); Colton v. United States, 306 F.2d 633 (2d Cir. 1962); Falsone v. United States, 205 F.2d 734 (5th Cir. 1953); Fraser v. United States, 145 F.2d 139 (6th Cir. 1944), *cert. denied*, 324 U.S. 849 (1945); United States v. Brunner, 200 F.2d 276 (6th Cir. 1952). *Contra* Baird v. Koerner, 279 F.2d 623 (9th Cir. 1960). Additional decisions of district courts are collected in Annotation, 95 A.L.R.2d 320, 336. While a number of the cases arise from administrative income tax investigations, they nevertheless support the broad proposition of the inapplicability of state privileges in federal proceedings.

In view of these considerations, it is apparent that, to the extent that they accord state privileges standing in federal criminal cases, bankruptcy, and federal question cases, the rules go beyond what previously has been though necessary or proper.

On the other hand, in diversity cases, or perhaps more accurately cases in which state law furnishes the rule of decision, the rules avoid giving state privileges the effect which substantial authority has thought necessary and proper. Regardless of what might once have been thought to be the command of *Erie Railroad Co. v. Tompkins*, 304 U.S. 64 (1938), as to observance of state created privileges in diversity cases, *Hanna v. Plumer*, 380 U.S. 460 (1965), is believed to locate the problem in the area of choice rather than of necessity. Wright, *Procedural Reform: Its Limitations and Its Future*, 1 GA. L. REV. 563, 572–73 (1967). *Contra* Republic Gear Co. v. Borg–Warner Corp., 381 F.2d 551, 555 n.2 (2d Cir. 1967); *see also* authorities there cited. Hence all significant policy factors need to be considered in order that the choice may be a wise one.

The arguments advanced in favor of recognizing state privileges are: a state privilege is an essential characteristic of a relationship or status created by state law and thus is substantive in the *Erie* sense; state policy ought not to be frustrated by the accident of diversity; the allowance or denial of a privilege is so likely to affect the outcome of litigation as to encourage forum selection on that basis, not a proper function of diversity jurisdiction. There are persuasive answers to these arguments.

(1) As to the question of "substance," it is true that a privilege commonly represents an aspect of a relationship created and defined by a state. For example, a confidential communications privilege is often an incident of marriage. However, in litigation involving the relationship itself, the privilege is not ordinarily one of the issues. In fact, statutes frequently make the communication privilege inapplicable in cases of divorce. MCCORMICK § 88, at 177. The same is true with respect to the attorney–client privilege when the parties to the relationship have a falling out. The reality of the matter is that privilege is called into operation, not when the relation giving rise to the privilege is being litigated, but when the litigation involves something substantively devoid of relation to the privilege. The appearance of privilege in the case is quite by accident, and its effect is to block off the tribunal from a source of information. Thus its real impact is on the method of proof in the case, and in comparison any substantive aspect appears tenuous.

(2) By most standards, criminal prosecutions are attended by more serious consequences than civil litigation, and it must be evident that the criminal area has the greatest sensitivity where privilege is concerned. Nevertheless, as previously noted, state privileges traditional have given way in federal criminal prosecutions. If a privilege is denied in the area of greatest sensitivity, it tends to become illusory as a significant aspect of the relationship out of which it arises. For example, in a state having by

statute an accountant's privilege, only the most imperceptible added force would be given the privilege by putting the accountant in a position to assure his client that, while he could not block disclosure in a federal criminal prosecution, he could do so in diversity cases as well as in state court proceedings. Thus viewed, state interest in privilege appears less substantial than at first glance might seem to be the case.

Moreover, federal interest is not lacking. It can scarcely be contended that once diversity is invoked the federal government no longer has a legitimate concern in the quality of judicial administration conducted under its aegis. The demise of conformity and the adoption of the Federal Rules of Civil Procedure stand as a witness to the contrary.

(3) A large measure of forum shopping is recognized as legitimate in the American judicial system. Subject to the limitations of jurisdiction and the relatively modest controls imposed by venue provisions and the doctrine of forum non conveniens, plaintiffs are allowed in general a free choice of forum. Diversity jurisdiction has as its basic purpose the giving of a choice, not only to plaintiffs but, in removal situations, also to defendants. In principle, the basis of the choice is the supposed need to escape from local prejudice. If the choice were tightly confined on that basis, then complete conformity to local procedure as well as substantive law would be required. This, of course, is not the case, and the choice may in fact be influenced by a wide range of factors. As Dean Ladd has pointed out, a litigant may select the federal court "because of the federal procedural rules, the liberal discovery provisions, the quality of jurors expected in the federal court, the respect held for federal judges, the control of federal judges over a trial, the summation and comment upon the weight of evidence by the judge, or the authority to grant a new trial if the judge regards the verdict against the weight of the evidence." Ladd, *Privileges*, 1969 L. & Soc. Ord. 555, 564. Present Rule 43(a) of the Civil Rules specifies a broader range of admissibility in federal than in state courts and makes no exception for diversity cases. Note should also be taken that Rule 26(b)(2) of the Rules of Civil Procedure, as revised, allows discovery to be had of liability insurance, without regard to local state law upon the subject.

When attention is directed to the practical dimensions of the problem, they are found not be great. The privileges affected are few in number. Most states provide a physician–patient privilege; the proposed rules limit the privilege to a psychotherapist–patient relationship. *See* Advisory Committee's Note to Rule 504. The area of marital privilege under the proposed rules is narrower than in most states. *See* Rule 505. Some states recognize privileges for journalists and accountants; the proposed rules do not.

Physician–patient is the most widely recognized privilege not found in the proposed rules. As a practical matter it was largely eliminated in diversity cases when Rule 35 of the Rules of Civil Procedure became effective in 1938. Under that rule, a party physically examined pursuant to court order, by requesting and obtaining a copy of the report or by taking the deposition of the examiner, waives any privilege regarding the testimony of every other person who has examined him in respect to the same condition. While waiver may be avoided by neither requesting the report nor taking the examiner's deposition, the price is one which most litigant-patients are probably not prepared to pay.

RULE 502.   REQUIRED REPORTS PRIVILEGED BY STATUTE
            [Not enacted.]

A person, corporation, association, or other organization or entity, either public or private, making a return or report required by law to be made has a privilege to refuse to disclose and to prevent any other person from disclosing the return or report, if the law requiring it to be made so provides. A public officer or agency to whom a return or report is required by law to be made has a privilege to refuse to disclose the return or report if the law requiring it to be made so provides. No privilege exists under this rule in actions involving perjury, false statements, fraud in the return or report, or other failure to comply with the law in question.

ADVISORY COMMITTEE'S NOTE

Statutes which require the making of returns or reports sometimes confer on the reporting party a privilege against disclosure, commonly coupled with a prohibition against disclosure by the officer to whom the report is made. Some of the federal statutes of this kind are mentioned in the Advisory Committee's Note to Rule 501, *supra*. *See also* the note to Rule 402, *supra*. A provision against disclosure may be included in a statute for a variety of reasons, the chief of which are probably assuring the validity of the statute against claims of self-incrimination, honoring the privilege against self-incrimination, and encouraging the furnishing of the required information by assuring privacy.

These statutes, both state and federal, may generally be assumed to embody policies of significant dimension. Rule 501 insulates the federal provisions against disturbance by these rules; the present rule reiterates a result commonly specified in federal statutes and extends its application to state statutes of similar character. Illustrations of the kinds of returns and reports contemplated by the rule appear in the cases, in which a reluctance to compel disclosure is manifested. *In re* Reid, 155 F. 933 (E.D. Mich. 1906) (assessor not compelled to produce bankrupt's property tax return in view of statute forbidding disclosure); *In re* Valecia Condensed Milk Co.*, 240 F. 310 (7th Cir. 1917) (secretary of state tax commission not compelled to produce bankrupt's income tax returns in violation of statute); Herman Bros. Pet Supply, Inc. v. NLRB, 360 F.2d 176 (6th Cir. 1966) (subpoena denied for production of reports to state employment security commission prohibited by statute, in proceeding for back wages). And see the discussion of motor vehicle accident reports in *Krizak v. W.C. Brooks & Sons, Inc.*, 320 F.2d 37, 42–43 (4th Cir. 1963). *Cf. In re* Hines, 69 F.2d 52 (2d Cir. 1934).

Rule 503. LAWYER–CLIENT PRIVILEGE [Not enacted.]

(a) Definitions. As used in this rule:

(1) A "client" is a person, public officer, or corporation, association, or other organization or entity, either public or private, who is rendered professional legal services by a lawyer, or who consults a lawyer with a view to obtaining professional legal services from him.

(2) A "lawyer" is a person authorized, or reasonably believed by the client to be authorized, to practice law in any state or nation.

(3) A "representative of the lawyer" is one employed to assist the lawyer in the rendition of professional legal services.

(4) A communication is "confidential" if not intended to be disclosed to third persons other than those to whom disclosure is in furtherance of the rendition of professional legal services to the client or those reasonably necessary for the transmission of the communication.

(b) General rule of privilege. A client has a privilege to refuse to disclose and to prevent any other person from disclosing confidential communications made for the purpose of facilitating the rendition of professional legal services to the client, (1) between himself or his representative and his lawyer or his lawyer's representative, or (2) between his lawyer and the lawyer's representative, or (3) by him or his lawyer to a lawyer representing another in a matter of common interest, or (4) between representatives of the client

or between the client and a representative of the client, or (5) between lawyers representing the client.

(c) Who may claim privilege. The privilege may be claimed by the client, his guardian or conservator, the personal representative of a deceased client, or the successor, trustee, or similar representative of a corporation, association, or other organization, whether or not in existence. The person who was the lawyer at the time of the communication may claim the privilege but only on behalf of the client. His authority to do so is presumed in the absence of evidence to the contrary.

(d) Exceptions. There is no privilege under this rule:

(1) *Furtherance of crime or fraud.* If the services of the lawyer were sought or obtained to enable or aid anyone to commit or plan to commit what the client knew or reasonably should have known to be a crime or fraud; or

(2) *Claimants through same deceased client.* As to a communication relevant to an issue between parties who claim through the same deceased client, regardless of whether the claims are by testate or intestate succession or by *inter vivos* transaction; or

(3) *Breach of duty by lawyer or client.* As to a communication relevant to an issue of breach of duty by the lawyer to his client or by the client to his lawyer; or

(4) *Document attested by lawyer.* As to a communication relevant to an issue concerning an attested document to which the lawyer is an attesting witness; or

> **(5)** *Joint Clients.* As to a communication relevant to a matter of common interest between two or more clients if the communication was made by any of them to a lawyer retained or consulted in common, when offered in an action between any of the clients.

ADVISORY COMMITTEE'S NOTE

Subdivision (a). (1) The definition of "client" includes governmental bodies, Conn. Mut. Life Ins. Co. v. Shields, 18 F.R.D. 445 (S.D.N.Y. 1955); People *ex rel.* Dep't of Pub. Works v. Glen Arms Estate, Inc., 230 Cal. App. 2d 841 (1964); Rowley v. Ferguson, 48 N.E.2d 243 (Ohio Ct. App. 1942), and corporations, Radiant Burners, Inc. v. Am. Gas Assn., 320 F.2d 314 (7th Cir. 1963). *Contra* Gardner, *A Personal Privilege for Communications of Corporate Clients — Paradox or Public Policy*, 40 U. DET. L.J. 299, 323, 376 (1963). The definition also extends the status of client to one consulting a lawyer preliminarily with a view to retaining him, even though actual employment does not result. McCORMICK § 92, at 184. The client need not be involved in litigation; the rendition of legal service or advice under any circumstances suffices. 8 WIGMORE § 2294 (McNaughton rev. 1961). The services must be professional legal services; purely business or personal matters to not qualify. McCORMICK § 92, at 184.

The rule contains no definition of "representative of the client." In the opinion of the Advisory Committee, the matter is better left to resolution by decision on a case-by-case basis. The most restricted position is the "control group" test, limiting the category to persons with authority to seek and act upon legal advice for the client. *See, e.g.,* City of Philadelphia v. Westinghouse Elec. Corp., 210 F. Supp. 483 (E.D. Pa.), *mandamus and prohibition denied sub nom.* Gen. Elec. Co. v. Kirkpatrick, 312 F.2d 742 (3d Cir. 1962), *cert. denied,* 372 U.S. 943 (1963); Garrison v. Gen. Motors Corp., 213 F. Supp. 515 (S.D. Cal. 1963); Hogan v. Zletz, 43 F.R.D. 308 (N.D. Okla. 1967), *aff'd sub nom.* Natta v. Hogan, 392 F.2d 686 (10th Cir. 1968); Day v. Ill. Power Co., 50 Ill. App. 2d 52 (1964). Broader formulations are found in other decisions. *See, e.g.,* United States v. United Shoe Mach. Corp., 89 F. Supp. 357 (D. Mass. 1950); Zenith Radio Corp. v. Radio Corp. of Am., 121 F. Supp. 792 (D. Del. 1954); Harper & Row Publishers, Inc. v. Decker, 423 F.2d 487 (7th Cir. 1970), *aff'd without opinion by equally divided court,* 400 U.S. 348, *reh'g denied,* 401 U.S. 950 (1971); D.I. Chadbourne, Inc. v. Superior Court, 60 Cal. 2d 723 (1964); *cf.* Rucker v. Wabash R.R. Co., 418 F.2d 146 (7th Cir. 1969). *See generally* Simon, *The Attorney–Client Privilege as Applied to Corporations*, 65 YALE L.J. 953, 956–66 (1956); Note, *Attorney–Client*

Privilege for Corporate Clients: The Control Group Test, 84 HARV. L. REV. 424 (1970).

The status of employees who are used in the process of communicating, as distinguished from those who are parties to the communication, is treated in paragraph (4) of subdivision (a) of the rule.

(2) A "lawyer" is a person licensed to practice law in any state or nation. There is no requirement that the licensing state or nation recognize the attorney–client privilege, thus avoiding excursions into conflict of laws questions. "Lawyer" also includes a person reasonably believed to be a lawyer. For similar provisions, see California Evidence Code § 950.

(3) The definition of "representative of the lawyer" recognizes that the lawyer may, in rendering legal services, utilize the services of assistants in addition to those employed in the process of communicating. Thus the definition includes an expert employed to assist in rendering legal advice. United States v. Kovel, 296 F.2d 918 (2d Cir. 1961) (accountant); *cf.* Himmelfarb v. United States, 175 F.2d 924 (9th Cir. 1949). It also includes an expert employed to assist in the planning and conduct of litigation, though not one employed to testify as a witness. Lalance & Grosjean Mfg. Co. v. Haberman Mfg. Co., 87 F. 563 (S.D.N.Y. 1898); *see also* revised FED. R. CIV. P. 26(b)(4). The definition does not, however, limit "representative of the lawyer" to experts. Whether his compensation is derived immediately from the lawyer or the client is not material.

(4) The requisite confidentiality of communication is defined in terms of intent. A communication made in public or meant to be relayed to outsiders or which is divulged by the client to third persons can scarcely be considered confidential. MCCORMICK § 95. The intent is inferable from the circumstances. Unless intent to disclose is apparent, the attorney–client communication is confidential. Taking or failing to take precautions may be considered as bearing on intent.

Practicality requires that some disclosure be allowed beyond the immediate circle of lawyer–client and their representatives without impairing confidentiality. Hence the definition allows disclosure to persons "to whom disclosure is in furtherance of the rendition of professional legal services to the client," contemplating those in such relation to the client as "spouse, parent, business associate, or joint client." *Comment,* CAL. EVID. CODE § 952.

Disclosure may also be made to persons "reasonably necessary for the transmission of the communication," without loss of confidentiality.

Subdivision (b) sets forth the privilege, using the previously defined terms: client, lawyer, representative of the lawyer, and confidential communication.

Substantial authority has in the past allowed the eavesdropper to testify to overheard privileged conversations and has admitted intercepted privileged letters. Today, the evolution of more sophisticated techniques of eavesdropping and interception calls for abandonment of this position. The rule accordingly adopts a policy of protection against these kinds of invasion of the privilege.

The privilege extends to communications (1) between client or his representative and lawyer or his representative, (2) between lawyer and lawyer's representative, (3) by client or his lawyer to a lawyer representing another in a matter of common interest, (4) between representatives of the client or the client and a representative of the client, and (5) between lawyers representing the client. All these communications must be specifically for the purpose of obtaining legal services for the client; otherwise the privilege does not attach.

The third type of communication occurs in the "joint defense" or "pooled information" situation, where different lawyers represent clients who have some interests in common. In *Chahoon v. Commonwealth*, 62 Va. 822 (1871), the court said that the various clients might have retained one attorney to represent all; hence everything said at a joint conference was privileged, and one of the clients could prevent another from disclosing what the other had himself said. The result seems to be incorrect in overlooking a frequent reason for retaining different attorneys by the various clients, namely actually or potentially conflicting interests in addition to the common interest which brings them together. The needs of these cases seem better to be met by allowing each client a privilege as to his own statements. Thus if all resist disclosure, none will occur. Cont'l Oil Co. v. United States, 330 F.2d 347 (9th Cir. 1964). But, if for reasons of his own, a client wishes to disclose his own statements made at the joint conference, he should be permitted to do so, and the rule is to that effect. The rule does not apply to situations where there is no common interest to be promoted by a joint consultation, and the parties meet on a purely adversary basis. Vance v. State, 190 Tenn. 521, *cert. denied*, 339 U.S. 988 (1950); *cf.* Hunydee v. United States, 355 F.2d 183 (9th Cir. 1965).

Subdivision (c). The privilege is, of course, that of the client, to be claimed by him or by his personal representative. The successor of a dissolved corporate client may claim the privilege. CAL. EVID. CODE § 953; N.J. EVID R. 26(1) (repealed and replaced by N.J. R. EVID. 504 (1993)). *Contra* UNIF. R. EVID. 26(1).

The lawyer may not claim the privilege on his own behalf. However, he may claim it on behalf of the client. It is assumed that the ethics of the profession will require him to do so except under most unusual circumstances. ABA CANONS OF PROF'L ETHICS Canon 37. His authority to make the claim is presumed unless there is evidence to the contrary, as would be the case if the client were now a party to litigation in which the question arose and were represented by other counsel. *Ex parte* Lipscomb, 111 Tex. 409 (1922).

Subdivision (d) in general incorporates well established exceptions.

(1) The privilege does not extend to advice in aid of future wrongdoing. 8 WIGMORE § 2298 (McNaughton rev. 1961). The wrongdoing need not be that of the client. The provision that the client knew or reasonably should have known of the criminal or fraudulent nature of the act is designed to protect the client who is erroneously advised that a proposed action is within the law. No preliminary finding that sufficient evidence aside from the communication has been introduced to warrant a finding that the services were sought to enable the commission of a wrong is required. *Cf.* Clark v. United States, 289 U.S. 1, 15–16 (1933); UNIF. R. EVID. 26(2)(a). While any general exploration of what transpired between attorney and client would, of course, be inappropriate it is wholly feasible, either at the discovery stage or during trial to focus the inquiry by specific questions as to avoid any broad inquiry into attorney–client communications. Numerous cases reflect this approach.

(2) Normally the privilege survives the death of the client and may be asserted by his representative. Subdivision (c), *supra.* When, however, the identity of the person who steps into the client's shoes is in issue, as in a will contest, the identity entitled to claim the privilege remains undetermined until the conclusion of litigation. The choice is thus between allowing both sides or neither to assert the privilege, with authority and reason favoring the latter view. MCCORMICK § 98; UNIF. R. EVID. 26(2)(b); CAL. EVID. CODE § 957; KAN. STAT. ANN. § 60-426(b)(2); N.J. EVID. R. 26(2)(b) (repealed and replaced by N.J. R. EVID. 504(2)(b) (1993)).

(3) The exception is required by considerations of fairness and policy when questions arise out of dealings between attorney and client as in cases of controversy over attorney's fees, claims of inadequacy, of representation, or charges of professional misconduct. MCCORMICK § 95; UNIF. R. EVID. 26(2)(c); CAL. EVID. CODE § 958; KAN. STAT. ANN. § 60-426(b)(3); N.J EVID. R. 26(2)(c) (repealed and replaced by N.J. R. EVID. 504(2)(c) (1993)).

(4) When the lawyer acts as attesting witness, the approval of the client to his so doing may safely be assumed, and waiver of the privilege as to any relevant lawyer–client communications is a proper result. MCCORMICK § 92, at 184; UNIF. R. EVID. 26(2)(d); CAL. EVID. CODE § 959; KAN. STAT. ANN. § [60-426(b)(4)].

(5) The subdivision states existing law. MCCORMICK § 95, at 192–93. For similar provisions, see Uniform Rule 26(2)(e); California Evidence Code § 962; Kansas Statutes Annotated § [60-426(b)(5)]; New Jersey Evidence Rule 26(2) (repealed and replaced by N.J. R. EVID. 504(2) (1993)). The situation with which this provision deals is to be distinguished from the case of clients with a common interest who retain different lawyers. *See* subdivision (b)(3) of this rule, *supra*.

Rule 504. PSYCHOTHERAPIST–PATIENT PRIVILEGE
[Not enacted.]

(a) Definitions.

(1) A "patient" is a person who consults or is examined or interviewed by a psychotherapist.

(2) A "psychotherapist" is (A) a person authorized to practice medicine in any state or nation, or reasonably believed by the patient so to be, while engaged in the diagnosis or treatment of a mental or emotional condition, including drug addiction, or (B) a person licensed or certified as a psychologist under the laws or any state or nation, while similarly engaged.

(3) A communication is "confidential" if not intended to be disclosed to third persons other than those present to further the interest of the patient in the consultation, examination, or interview, or persons reasonably necessary for the transmission of the communication, or persons who are participating in the diagnosis and

treatment under the direction of the psychotherapist, including members of the patient's family.

(b) General rule of privilege. A patient has a privilege to refuse to disclose and to prevent any other person from disclosing confidential communications, made for the purposes of diagnosis or treatment of his mental or emotional condition, including drug addiction, among himself, his psychotherapist, or persons who are participating in the diagnosis or treatment under the direction of the psychotherapist, including members of the patient's family.

(c) Who may claim the privilege. The privilege may be claimed by the patient, by his guardian or conservator, or by the personal representative of a deceased patient. The person who was the psychotherapist may claim the privilege but only on behalf of the patient. His authority so to do is presumed in the absence of evidence to the contrary.

(d) Exceptions.

(1) *Proceedings for hospitalization.* There is no privilege under this rule for communications relevant to an issue in proceedings to hospitalize the patient for mental illness, if the psychotherapist in the course of diagnosis or treatment has determined that the patient is in need of hospitalization.

(2) *Examination by order of judge.* If the judge orders an examination of the mental or emotional condition of the patient, communications made in the course thereof are not privileged under this rule with respect to the particular purpose for which the examination is ordered unless the judge orders otherwise.

(3) *Condition an element of claim or defense.* There is no privilege under this rule as to communications relevant to an issue of the mental or emotional condition of the patient in any proceeding in which he relies upon the condition as an element of his claim or defense, or, after the patient's death, in any proceeding in which any party relies upon the condition as an element of his claim or defense.

ADVISORY COMMITTEE'S NOTE

The rules contain no provision for a general physician–patient privilege. While many states have by statute created the privilege, the exceptions which have been found necessary in order to obtain information required by the public interest or to avoid fraud are so numerous as to leave little if any basis for the privilege. Among the exclusions from the statutory privilege, the following may be enumerated; communications not made for purposes of diagnosis and treatment; commitment and restoration proceedings; issues as to wills or otherwise between parties claiming by succession from the patient; actions on insurance policies; required reports (venereal diseases, gunshot wounds, child abuse); communications in furtherance of crime or fraud; mental or physical condition put in issue by patient (personal injury cases); malpractice actions; and some or all criminal prosecutions. California, for example, excepts cases in which the patient puts his condition in issue, all criminal proceedings, will and similar contests, malpractice cases, and disciplinary proceedings, as well as certain other situations, thus leaving virtually nothing covered by the privilege. CAL. EVID. CODE §§ 990–1007. For other illustrative statutes see Illinois Revised Statutes ch. 51, § 5.1 (1967) (repealed and replaced by 735 Illinois Compiled Statutes 5/8-802 (1982)); New York Civil Practice Law and Rules 4504; N.C. Gen. Stat. § 8-53 (1953). Moreover, the possibility of compelling gratuitous disclosure by the physician is foreclosed by his standing to raise the question of relevancy. See note on "official information" privilege following Rule 509, *infra*.

The doubts attendant upon the general physician–patient privilege are not present when the relationship is that of psychotherapist and patient. While the common law recognized no general physician–patient privilege, it had indicated a disposition to recognize a psychotherapist–patient privilege, Note, *Confidential Communications to a Psychotherapist: A New Testimonial Privilege*, 47 NW. U. L. REV. 384 (1952), when legislatures began moving into the field.

The case for the privilege is convincingly stated in GRP. FOR THE ADVANCEMENT OF PSYCHIATRY, REPORT NO. 45, at 92 (1960):

> Among physicians, the psychiatrist has a special need to maintain confidentiality. His capacity to help his patients is completely dependent upon their willingness and ability to talk freely. This makes it difficult if not impossible for him to function without being able to assure his patients of confidentiality and, indeed, privileged communication. Where there may be exceptions to this general rule ... , there is wide agreement that confidentiality is a *sine qua non*

for successful psychiatric treatment. The relationship may well be likened to that of the priest–penitent or the lawyer–client. Psychiatrists not only explore the very depths of their patients' conscious, but their unconscious feelings and attitudes as well. Therapeutic effectiveness necessitates going beyond a patient's awareness and, in order to do this, it must be possible to communicate freely. A threat to secrecy blocks successful treatment.

A much more extended exposition of the case for the privilege is made in Slovenko, *Psychiatry and a Second Look at the Medical Privilege*, 6 WAYNE L. REV. 175, 184 (1960), quoted extensively in the careful *Tentative Recommendation and Study Relating to the Uniform Rules of Evidence* (Article V. Privileges), *in* CAL. LAW REV. COMM'N, REP., REC. & STUDIES 417 (1964). The conclusion is reached that Wigmore's four conditions needed to justify the existence of a privilege are amply satisfied.

Illustrative statutes are California Evidence Code §§ 1010–1026; Georgia Code § 38-418 (Supp. 1961) (repealed and replaced by Georgia Code § 24-9-40 (1978) (repealed and replaced by Georgia Code § 24-5-501 (effective Jan. 1, 2013))); Connecticut General Statutes § [52-146d] (Supp. 1966); Illinois Revised Statutes ch. 51, § 5.2 (1967) (repealed and replaced by 740 Illinois Compiled Statutes 110/10 (1979)).

While many of the statutes simply place the communications on the same basis as those between attorney and client, 8 WIGMORE § 2286 n.23 (McNaughton rev. 1961), basic differences between the two relationships forbid resorting to attorney–client save as a helpful point of departure. Goldstein and Katz, *Psychiatrist–Patient Privilege: The GAP Proposal and the Connecticut Statute*, 36 CONN. B.J. 175, 182 (1962).

Subdivision (a). (1) The definition of patient does not include a person submitting to examination for scientific purposes. *Cf.* CAL. EVID. CODE § 1101. Attention is directed to 42 U.S.C. [241(d)], as amended by the Drug Abuse and Control Act of 1970, Pub. L. No. 91-513, authorizing the Secretary of Health, Education, and Welfare to withhold the identity of persons who are the subjects of research on the use and effect of drugs. The rule would leave this provision in full force. *See* Rule 501.

(2) The definition of psychotherapist embraces a medical doctor while engaged in the diagnosis or treatment of mental or emotional conditions, including drug addiction, in order not to exclude the general practitioner and to avoid the making of needless refined distinctions concerning what is and what is not the practice of

psychiatry. The requirement that the psychologist be in fact licensed, and not merely believed to be so, is believed to be justified by the number of persons, other than psychiatrists, purporting to render psychotherapeutic aid and the variety of their theories. CAL. LAW REV. COMM'N, *supra*, at 434–37.

The clarification of mental or emotional condition as including drug addiction is consistent with current approaches to drug abuse problems. See, for example, the definition of "drug dependent person" in 42 U.S.C. 201(q), added by the Drug Abuse Prevention and Control Act of 1970, Pub. L. No. 91-513.

(3) Confidential communication is defined in terms conformable with those of the lawyer–client privilege. Rule 503(a)(4), *supra*, with changes appropriate to the difference in circumstance.

Subdivisions (b) and (c). The lawyer–client rule is drawn upon for the phrasing of the general rule of privilege and the determination of those who may claim it. *See* Rule 503(b)–(c).

The specific inclusion of communications made for the diagnosis and treatment of drug addiction recognizes the continuing contemporary concern with rehabilitation of drug dependent persons and is designed to implement that policy by encouraging persons in need thereof to seek assistance. The provision is in harmony with Congressional actions in this area. *See* 42 U.S.C. § 260 (repealed 2000) (providing for voluntary hospitalization of addicts or persons with drug dependence problems and prohibiting use of evidence of admission or treatment in any proceeding against him); 42 U.S.C. § 3419 (repealed 2000) (providing that in voluntary or involuntary commitment of addicts the results of any hearing, examination, test, or procedure used to determine addiction shall not be used against the patient in any criminal proceeding).

Subdivision (d). The exceptions differ substantially from those of the attorney–client privilege, as a result of the basic differences in the relationships. While it has been argued convincingly that the nature of the psychotherapist–patient relationship demands complete security against legally coerced disclosure in all circumstances, Louisell, *The Psychologist in Today's Legal World: Part II*, 41 MINN. L. REV. 731, 746 (1957), the committee of psychiatrists and lawyers who drafted the Connecticut statute concluded that in three instances the need for disclosure was sufficiently great to justify the risk of possible impairment of the relationship. Goldstein & Katz, *Psychiatrist–Patient Privilege: The GAP Proposal and the*

Connecticut Statute, 36 CONN. B.J. 175 (1962). These three exceptions are incorporated in the present rule.

(1) The interests of both patient and public call for a departure from confidentiality in commitment proceedings. Since disclosure is authorized only when the psychotherapist determines that hospitalization is needed, control over disclosure is placed largely in the hands of a person in whom the patient has already manifested confidence. Hence damage to the relationship is unlikely.

(2) In a court ordered examination, the relationship is likely to be an arm's length one, though not necessarily so. In any event, an exception is necessary for the effective utilization of this important and growing procedure. The exception, it will be observed, deals with a court ordered examination rather than with a court appointed psychotherapist. Also, the exception is effective only with respect to the particular purpose for which the examination is ordered. The rule thus conforms with the provisions of 18 U.S.C. § [4241] that no statement made by the accused in the course of an examination into competency to stand trial is admissible on the issue of guilt and of 42 U.S.C. § 3420 (repealed 2000) that a physician conducting an examination in a drug addiction commitment proceeding is a competent and reliable witness.

(3) By injecting his condition into litigation, the patient must be said to waive the privilege, in fairness and to avoid abuses. Similar considerations prevail after the patient's death.

Rule 505.   HUSBAND–WIFE PRIVILEGE [Not enacted.]

(a) General rule of privilege. An accused in a criminal proceeding has a privilege to prevent his spouse from testifying against him.

(b) Who may claim the privilege. The privilege may be claimed by the accused or by the spouse on his behalf. The authority of the spouse to do so is presumed in the absence of evidence to the contrary.

(c) Exceptions. There is no privilege under this rule (1) in proceedings in which one spouse is charged with a crime against the person or property of the other or of a child of either, or with a crime against the person or property of a third person committed in the course of committing a crime against the other, or (2) as to matters occurring prior to the marriage, or (3) in proceedings in which a spouse is charged with importing an alien for prostitution or other immoral purpose in violation of 8 U.S.C. § 1328, with transporting a female in interstate commerce for immoral purposes or other offense in violation of 18 U.S.C. §§ 2421–2424, or with violation of other similar statutes.

ADVISORY COMMITTEE'S NOTE

Subdivision (a). Rules of evidence have evolved around the marriage relationship in four respects: (1) incompetency of one spouse to testify for the other; (2) privilege of one spouse not to testify against the other; (3) privilege of one spouse not to have the other testify against him; and (4) privilege against disclosure of confidential communications between spouses, sometimes extended to information learned by virtue of the existence of the relationship. Today these matters are largely governed by statutes.

With the disappearance of the disqualification of parties and interested persons, the basis for spousal incompetency no longer existed, and it, too, virtually disappeared in both civil and criminal actions. Usually reached by statute, this result was reached for federal courts by the process of decision. Funk v. United States, 290 U.S. 371 (1933). These rules contain no recognition of incompetency of one spouse to testify for the other.

While some ten jurisdictions recognize a privilege not to testify against one's spouse in a criminal case, and a much smaller number do so in civil cases, the great majority recognizes no privilege on the part of the testifying spouse, and this is the position taken by the rule. Compare *Wyatt v. United States*, 362 U.S. 525 (1960), a Mann Act prosecution in which the wife was the victim. The majority opinion held that she could not claim privilege and was compellable to testify. The holding was narrowly based: The Mann Act presupposed that the women with whom it dealt had no independent wills of their own, and this legislative judgment precluded allowing a victim-wife an option whether to testify, lest the policy of the statute be defeated. A vigorous dissent took the view that nothing in the Mann Act required departure from usual doctrine, which was conceived to be one of allowing the injured party to claim or waive privilege.

About thirty jurisdictions recognize a privilege of an accused in a criminal case to prevent his or her spouse from testifying. It is believed to represent the one aspect of marital privilege the continuation of which is warranted. In *Hawkins v. United States*, 358

U.S. 74 (1958), it was sustained. *Cf.* MCCORMICK § 66; 8 WIGMORE § 2228 (McNaughton rev. 1961): *Comment,* UNIF. R. EVID. 23(2).

The rule recognizes no privilege for confidential communications. The traditional justifications for privileges not to testify against a spouse and not to be testified against by one's spouse have been the prevention of marital dissension and the repugnancy of requiring a person to condemn or be condemned by his spouse. 8 WIGMORE §§ 2228, 2241 (McNaughton rev. 1961). These considerations bear no relevancy to marital communications. Nor can it be assumed that marital conduct will be affected by a privilege for confidential communications of whose existence the parties in all likelihood are unaware. The other communication privileges, by way of contrast, have as one party a professional person who can be expected to inform the other of the existence of the privilege. Moreover, the relationships from which those privileges arise are essentially and almost exclusively verbal in nature, quite unlike marriage. *See* Hutchins & Slesinger, *Some Observations on the Law of Evidence: Family Relations,* 13 MINN. L. REV. 675 (1929); *cf.* MCCORMICK § 90, 8 WIGMORE § 2337 (McNaughton rev. 1961).

The parties are not spouses if the marriage was a sham, Lutwak v. United States, 344 U.S. 604 (1953), or they have been divorced, Barsky v. United States, 339 F.2d 180 (9th Cir. 1964), and therefore the privilege is not applicable.

Subdivision (b). This provision is a counterpart of Rules 503(c), 504(c), and 506(c). Its purpose is to provide a procedure for preventing the taking of the spouse's testimony notably in grand jury proceedings, when the accused is absent and does not know that a situation appropriate for a claim of privilege is presented. If the privilege is not claimed by the spouse, the protection of Rule 512 is available.

Subdivision (c) contains three exceptions to the privilege against spousal testimony in criminal cases.

(1) The need of limitation upon the privilege in order to avoid grave injustice in cases of offenses against the other spouse or a child of either can scarcely be denied. 8 WIGMORE § 2239 (McNaughton rev. 1961). The rule therefore disallows any privilege against spousal testimony in these cases and in this respect is in accord with the result reached in *Wyatt v. United States,* 362 U.S. 525 (1960), a Mann Act prosecution, denying the accused the privilege of excluding his wife's testimony, since she was the woman who was transported for immoral purposes.

(2) The second exception renders the privilege inapplicable as to matters occurring prior to the marriage. This provision eliminates the possibility of suppressing testimony by marrying the witness.

(3) The third exception continues and expands established congressional policy. In prosecutions for importing aliens for immoral purposes, Congress has specifically denied the accused any privilege not to have his spouse testify against him. 8 U.S.C. § 1328. No provision of this nature is included in the Mann Act, and in *Hawkins v. United States*, 358 U.S. 74 (1958), the conclusion was reached that the common law privilege continued. Consistency requires similar results in the two situations. The rule adopts the congressional approach, as based upon a more realistic appraisal of the marriage relationship in cases of this kind, in preference to the specific result in *Hawkins*. Note the common law treatment of pimping and sexual offenses with third persons as exceptions to marital privilege. 8 WIGMORE § 2239 (McNaughton rev. 1961).

With respect to bankruptcy proceedings, the smallness of the area of spousal privilege under the rule and the general inapplicability of privileges created by state law render unnecessary any special provision for examination of the spouse of the bankrupt, such as that now contained in section 21(a) of the Bankruptcy Act. 11 U.S.C. § [343].

For recent statutes and rules dealing with husband–wife privileges, see California Evidence Code §§ 970–973, 980–987; Kansas Statutes Annotated §§ 60-423(b), 60-428; New Jersey Evidence Rules 23(2) (repealed and replaced by New Jersey Rule of Evidence 501(2) (1993)), 28 (repealed and replaced by New Jersey Rule of Evidence 509 (1993)).

Rule 506.   COMMUNICATIONS TO CLERGYMEN [Not enacted.]

(a) Definitions. As used in this rule:

(1) A "clergyman" is a minister, priest, rabbi, or other similar functionary of a religious organization, or an individual reasonably believed so to be by the person consulting him.

(2) A communication is "confidential" if made privately and not intended for further disclosure except to other persons present in furtherance of the purpose of the communication.

(b) General rule of privilege. A person has a privilege to refuse to disclose and to prevent another from disclosing a confidential communication by the person to a clergyman in his professional character as a spiritual adviser.

(c) Who may claim the privilege. The privilege may be claimed by the person, by his guardian or conservator, or by his personal representative if he is deceased. The clergyman may claim the privilege on behalf of the person. His authority so to do is presumed in the absence of evidence to the contrary.

<u>ADVISORY COMMITTEE'S NOTE</u>

The considerations which dictate the recognition of privileges generally seem strongly to favor a privilege for confidential communications to clergymen. During the period when most of the common law privileges were taking shape, no clear-cut privilege for communications between priest and penitent emerged. 8 WIGMORE § 2394 (McNaughton rev. 1961). The English political climate of the time may well furnish the explanation. In this country, however, the privilege has been recognized by statute in about two-thirds of the states and occasionally by the common law process of decision. *Id.* § 2395; Mullen v. United States, 263 F.2d 275 (D.C. Cir. 1959).

Subdivision (a). Paragraph (1) defines a clergyman as a "minister, priest, rabbi, or other similar functionary of a religious organization." The concept is necessarily broader than that inherent in the ministerial exemption for purposes of Selective Service. *See* United States v. Jackson, 369 F.2d 936 (4th Cir. 1966). However, it is not so broad as to include all self-denominated "ministers." A fair construction of the language requires that the person to whom the status is sought to be attached be regularly engaged in activities conforming at least in a general way to those of a Catholic priest, Jewish rabbi, or minister of an established Protestant denomination, though not necessarily on a full-time basis. No further specification seems possible in view of the lack of licensing and certification procedures for clergymen. However, this lack seems to have occasioned no particular difficulties in connection with the solemnization of marriages, which suggests that none may be anticipated here. For similar definitions of "clergyman" see California Evidence Code § 1030; New Jersey Evidence Rule 29 (repealed and replaced by New Jersey Rule of Evidence 511 (1993)).

The "reasonable belief" provision finds support in similar provisions for lawyer–client in Rule 503 and for psychotherapist–patient in Rule 504. A parallel is also found in the recognition of the validity of marriages performed by unauthorized persons if the parties reasonably believed them to be legally qualified. HARPER & SKOLNICK, PROBLEMS OF THE FAMILY 153 (rev. ed. 1962).

(2) The definition of "confidential" communication is consistent with the use of the term in Rule 503(a)(5) for lawyer–client and in Rule 504(a)(3) for psychotherapist–patient, suitably adapted to communications to clergymen.

Subdivision (b). The choice between a privilege narrowly restricted to doctrinally required confessions and a privilege broadly applicable to all confidential communications with a clergyman in his professional character as spiritual adviser has been exercised in favor of the latter. Many clergymen now receive training in marriage counseling and the handling of personality problems. Matters of this kind fall readily onto the realm of the spirit. The same considerations which underlie the psychotherapist–patient privilege of Rule 504 suggest a broad application of the privilege for communications to clergymen.

State statutes and rules fall in both the narrow and broad categories. A typical narrow statute proscribes disclosure of "a confession . . . made . . . in the course of discipline enjoined by the church to which he belongs." ARIZ. REV. STAT. ANN. § 12-2233 (1956); *see also* CAL. EVID. CODE § 1032; UNIF. R. EVID. 29. Illustrative of the broader privilege are statutes applying to "information communicated to him in a confidential manner, properly entrusted to him in his professional capacity, and necessary to enable him to discharge the functions of his office according to the usual course of his practice of discipline, wherein such person so communicating . . . is seeking spiritual counsel and advice," FLA. STAT. ANN. § 90.241 (1960) (repealed and replaced by FLA. STAT. ANN. § 90.505 (1976)), or to any "confidential communication properly entrusted to him in his professional capacity, and necessary and proper to enable him to discharge the functions of his office according to the usual course of practice or discipline," IOWA CODE ANN. § 622.10 (1950). *See also* ILL. REV. STAT. ch. 51, § 48.1 (1967) (repealed and replaced by 735 ILL. COMP. STAT. 5/8-803 (1982)); MINN. STAT. ANN. § [595.02(1)(c)] (1945); N.J EVID. R. 29 (repealed and replaced by N.J. R. EVID. 511 (1993)).

Under the privilege as phrased, the communicating person is entitled to prevent disclosure not only by himself but also by the clergyman and by eavesdroppers. For discussion see Advisory Committee's note under lawyer–client privilege, Rule 503(b).

The nature of what may reasonably be considered spiritual advice makes it unnecessary to include in the rule a specific exception for communications in furtherance of crime or fraud, as in Rule 503(d)(1).

Subdivision (c) makes clear that the privilege belongs to the communicating person. However, a prima facie authority on the part of the clergyman to claim the privilege on behalf of the person is recognized. The discipline of the particular church and the discreetness of the clergyman are believed to constitute sufficient safeguards for the absent communicating person. See Advisory Committee's note to the similar provision with respect to attorney–client in Rule 503(c).

Rule 507.   POLITICAL VOTE [Not enacted.]

Every person has a privilege to refuse to disclose the tenor of his vote at a political election conducted by secret ballot unless the vote was cast illegally.

ADVISORY COMMITTEE'S NOTE

Secrecy in voting is an essential aspect of effective democratic government, insuring free exercise of the franchise and fairness in elections. Secrecy after the ballot has been cast is as essential as secrecy in the act of voting. Nutting, *Freedom of Silence: Constitutional Protection Against Governmental Intrusion in Political Affairs*, 47 MICH. L. REV. 181, 191 (1948). Consequently a privilege has long been recognized on the part of a voter to decline to disclose how he voted. Required disclosure would be the exercise of a "kind of inquisitorial power highly injurious to the suffrages of a free people, as well as tending to create cabals and disturbances between contending parties in popular elections." Johnston v. Charleston, 1 S.C.L. (1 Bay) 441, 442 (1795).

The exception for illegally cast votes is a common one under both statutes and case law. Nutting, *supra*, at 192; 8 WIGMORE § 2241, at 163 (McNaughton rev. 1961). The policy considerations which underlie the privilege are not applicable to the illegal voter. However, nothing in the exception purports to foreclose an illegal voter from invoking the privilege against self-incrimination under appropriate circumstances.

For similar provisions, see Uniform Rule 31; California Evidence Code § 1050; Kansas Statutes Annotated § 60-431; New

Jersey Evidence Rule 31 (repealed and replaced by New Jersey Rule of Evidence 513 (1993)).

Rule 508.   TRADE SECRETS [Not enacted.]

A person has a privilege, which may be claimed by him or his agent or employee, to refuse to disclose and to prevent other persons from disclosing a trade secret owned by him, if the allowance of the privilege will not tend to conceal fraud or otherwise work injustice. When disclosure is directed, the judge shall take such protective measure as the interests of the holder of the privilege and of the parties and the furtherance of justice may require.

ADVISORY COMMITTEE'S NOTE

While sometimes said not to be a true privilege, a qualified right to protection against disclosure of trade secrets has found ample recognition, and, indeed, a denial of it would be difficult to defend. 8 WIGMORE § 2212(3) (McNaughton rev. 1961); *see also* 4 MOORE'S FEDERAL PRACTICE ¶¶ 30.12, 34.15 (2d ed. 1963 & Supp. 1965) *and* 2A BARRON & HOLTZOFF, FEDERAL PRACTICE AND PROCEDURE § 715.1 (Wright ed., 1961). Congressional policy is reflected in the Securities Exchange Act of 1934, 15 U.S.C. § 78x, and the Public Utility Holding Company Act of 1933, [42 U.S.C. § 16453], which deny the Securities and Exchange Commission authority to require the disclosure of trade secrets or processes in applications and reports. *See also* FED. R. CIV. P. [26(c)(1)(G)], as revised, mentioned further hereinafter.

Illustrative cases raising trade secret problems are: *E.I. Du Pont de Nemours Powder Co. v. Masland*, 244 U.S. 100 (1917) (suit to enjoin former employee from using plaintiff's secret processes, countered by defense that many of the processes were well know to the trade); *Segal Lock & Hardware Co. v. FTC*, 143 F.2d 935 (2d Cir. 1944) (question whether expert locksmiths employed by FTC should be required to disclose methods used by them in picking petitioner's "pick-proof" locks); *Dobson v. Graham*, 49 F. 17 (E.D. Pa. 1889) (patent infringement suit in which plaintiff sought to elicit from former employees now in the hire of defendant the respects in which defendant's machinery differed from plaintiff's patented machinery); *Putney v. Du Bois Co.*, 240 Mo. App. 1075 (1950) (action for injuries allegedly sustained from using defendant's secret formula dishwashing compound). *See* 8 WIGMORE § 2212(3) (McNaughton rev. 1961); Annotation, 17 A.L.R.2d 383; 49 MICH. L.

REV. 133 (1950). The need for accommodation between protecting trade secrets, on the one hand, and eliciting facts required for full and fair presentation of a case, on other hand, is apparent. Whether disclosure should be required depends upon a weighing of the competing interests involved against the background of the total situation, including consideration of such factors as the dangers of abuse, good faith, adequacy of protective measures, and the availability of other means of proof.

The cases furnish examples of the bringing of judicial ingenuity to bear upon the problem of evolving protective measures which achieve a degree of control over disclosure. Perhaps the most common is simply to take testimony in camera. Annotation, 62 A.L.R.2d 509. Other possibilities include making disclosure to opposing counsel but not to his client, E.I. Du Pont de Nemours Powder Co. v. Masland, 244 U.S. 100 (1917); making disclosure only to the judge (hearing examiner), Segal Lock & Hardware Co. v. FTC, 143 F.2d 935 (2d Cir. 1944); and placing those present under oath not to make disclosure, Paul v. Sinnott, 217 F. Supp. 84 (W.D. Pa. 1963).

Rule 26(c) of the Rules of Civil Procedure, as revised, provides that the judge may make "any order which justice requires to protect a party of person from annoyance, embarrassment, oppression, or undue burden or expense, including one or more of the following: . . . (7) that a trade secret of other confidential research, development, or commercial information not be disclosed or be disclosed only in a designated way . . . ." While the instant evidence rule extends this underlying policy into the trial, the difference in circumstances between discovery stage and trial may well be such as to require a different ruling at the trial.

For other rules recognizing privilege for trade secrets, see Uniform Rule 32; California Evidence Code § 1060; Kansas Statutes Annotated § 60-432; New Jersey Evidence Rule 32 (repealed and replaced by New Jersey Rule of Evidence 514 (1993)).

Rule 509.   SECRETS   OF   STATE   AND   OTHER   OFFICIAL INFORMATION [Not enacted.]

(a) Definitions.

(1) *Secret   of   State*.   A "secret   of   state"   is   a governmental secret relating to the national defense or the international relations of the United States.

(2) *Official information.* "Official information" is information within the custody or control of a department or agency of the government the disclosure of which is shown to be contrary to the public interest and which consists of: (A) intragovernmental opinions or recommendations submitted for consideration in the performance of decisional or policymaking functions, or (B) subject to the provisions of 18 U.S.C. § 3500, investigatory files compiled for law enforcement purposes and not otherwise available, or (C) information within the custody or control of a governmental department of agency whether initiated within the department or agency or acquired by it in its exercise of its official responsibilities and not otherwise available to the public pursuant to 5 U.S.C. § 552.

(b) General rule of privilege. The government has a privilege to refuse to give evidence and to prevent any person from giving evidence upon a showing of reasonable likelihood of danger that the evidence will disclose a secret of state or official information, as defined in this rule.

(c) Procedures. The privilege for secrets of state may be claimed only by the chief officer of the government agency or department administering the subject matter which the secret information sought concerns, but the privilege for official information may be asserted by any attorney representing the government. The required showing may be made in whole or in part in the form of a written statement. The judge may hear the matter in chambers, but all counsel are entitled to inspect the claim and showing and to be heard thereon, except that, in the case of secrets of state, the judge upon motion of the government, may permit the government to make the required showing in the above form *in camera*. If the judge sustains the privilege upon a showing *in camera*, the entire text of the government's statements shall be sealed and preserved in the court's records in the event of appeal. In the case of privilege claimed for official information the court may require examination *in camera* of the information itself. The judge may take any protective measure which the interests of the government and the furtherance of justice require.

(d) Notice to government. If the circumstances of the case indicate a substantial possibility that a claim of privilege would be appropriate but has not been made because of oversight or lack of knowledge, the judge shall give or cause notice to be given to the officer entitled to claim the privilege and shall stay further proceedings a reasonable time to afford opportunity to assert a claim of privilege.

(e) Effect of sustaining claim. If a claim of privilege is sustained in a proceeding to which the government is a party and it appears that another party is thereby deprived of material evidence, the judge shall make any further orders which the interests of justice require, including striking the testimony of a witness, declaring a mistrial, finding against the government upon an issue as to which the evidence is relevant, or dismissing the action.

ADVISORY COMMITTEE'S NOTE

Subdivision (a). (1) The rule embodies the privilege protecting military and state secrets described as "well established in the law of evidence," United States v. Reynolds, 345 U.S. 1, 6 (1953), and as one "the existence of which has never been doubted," 8 WIGMORE § 2378, at 794 (McNaughton rev. 1961).

The use of the term "national defense," without attempt at further elucidation, finds support in the similar usage in statutory provisions relating to the crimes of gathering, transmitting, or losing defense information, and gathering or delivering defense information to aid a foreign government. 18 U.S.C. §§ 793, 794; *see also* 5 U.S.C. § [552]; 50 U.S.C. App. § [2152(14)]. In determining whether military or sate secrets are involved, due regard will, of course, be given to classification pursuant to executive order.

(2) The rule also recognizes a privilege for specified types of official information and in this respect is designed primarily to resolve questions of the availability to litigants of data in the files of governmental departments and agencies. In view of the lesser danger to the public interest than in cases of military and state secrets, the official information privilege is subject to a generally overriding requirement that disclosure would be contrary to the public interest. It is applicable to three categories of information.

(A) Int[ra]governmental opinions or recommendations submitted for consideration in the performance of decisional or policy making functions. The policy basis of this aspect of the privilege is found in the desirability of encouraging candor in the exchange of views within the government. Kaiser Aluminum & Chem. Corp. v. United States, 157 F. Supp. 939 (Ct. Cl. 1958); Davis v. Braswell Motor Freight Lines, Inc., 363 F.2d 600 (5th Cir. 1966); Ackerly v. Ley, 420 F.2d 1336 (D.C. Cir. 1969). A privilege of this character is consistent with the Freedom of Information Act, 5 U.S.C. § 552(b)(5), and with the standing of the agency to raise questions of relevancy, though not a party, recognized in such decisions as *Boeing Airplane Co. v. Coggeshall*, 280 F.2d 654, 659 (D.C. Cir. 1960) (Renegotiation Board) and *Freeman v. Seligson*, 405 F.2d 1326, 1334 (D.C. Cir. 1968) (Secretary of Agriculture).

(B) Investigatory files compiled for law enforcement purposes. This category is expressly made subject to the provisions of the Jencks Act, 18 U.S.C. § 3500, which insulates prior statements or reports of government witnesses in criminal cases against subpoena, discovery, or inspection until the witness has testified on direct examination at the trial but then entitles the defense to its production. Rarely will documents of this nature be relevant until the author has testified and thus place his credibility in issue. Further protection against discovery of government files in criminal cases is found in Criminal Procedure Rule [16(a)]. The breadth of discovery in civil cases, however, goes beyond ordinary bounds of relevancy and raises problems calling for the exercise of judicial control, and in making provision for it the rule implements the Freedom of Information Act, 15 U.S.C. § 552(b)(7).

(C) Information exempted from disclosure under the Freedom of Information Act, 5 U.S.C. § 552. In 1958 the old "housekeeping" statute which had been relied upon as a foundation for departmental regulations curtailing disclosure was amended by adding a provision that it did not authorize withholding information from the public. In 1966 the Congress enacted the Freedom of Information Act for the purpose of making information in the files of departments and agencies, subject to certain specified exceptions, available to the mass media and to the public generally. 5 U.S.C. § 552. These enactments are significant expressions of congressional policy. The exceptions in the Act are not framed in terms of evidentiary privilege, thus recognizing by clear implication that the needs of litigants may stand on somewhat different footing from those of the public generally. Nevertheless, the exceptions are based on values obviously entitled to weighty consideration in formulating rules of evidentiary privilege. In some instances in these rules, exceptions in the Act have been made the subject of specific privileges, e.g., military and state secrets in the present rule and trade secrets in Rule 508. The purpose of the present provision is to incorporate the remaining exceptions of the Act into qualified privilege here created, thus subjecting disclosure of the information to judicial determination with respect to the effect of disclosure on the public interest. This approach appears to afford a satisfactory resolution of the problems which may arise.

Subdivision (b). The rule vests the privileges in the government where they properly belong rather than a party or witness. *See* United States v. Reynolds, 345 U.S. 1, 7 (1953). The showing required as a condition precedent to claiming the privilege represents a compromise between complete judicial control and accepting as final the decision of a departmental officer. *See* Machin v. Zuckert, 316 F.2d 336 (D.C. Cir. 1963) (rejecting in part a claim of privilege by the Secretary of the Air Force and ordering the furnishing of information for use in private litigation). This approach is consistent with *Reynolds*.

Subdivision (c). In requiring the claim of privilege for state secrets to be made by the chief departmental officer, the rule again follows *Reynolds*, insuring consideration by a high-level officer. This provision is justified by the lesser participation by the judge in cases of state secrets. The full participation by the judge in official information cases, on the contrary, warrants allowing the claim of privilege to be made by a government attorney.

Subdivision (d) spells out and emphasizes a power and responsibility on the part of the trial judge. An analogous provision is found in the requirement that the court certify to the Attorney General when the constitutionality of an Act of Congress is in question in an action to which the government is not a party. 28 U.S.C. § 2403.

Subdivision (e). If privilege is successfully claimed by the government in litigation to which it is not a party, the effect is simply to make the evidence unavailable, as though a witness had died or claimed the privilege against self-incrimination, and no specification of the consequences is necessary. The rule therefore deals only with the effect of a successful claim of privilege by the government in proceedings to which it is a party. Reference to other types of cases serves to illustrate the variety of situations which may arise and the impossibility of evolving a single formula to be applied automatically to all of them. The privileged materials may be the statement of government witness, as under the Jencks [Act], which provides that, if the government elects not to produce the statement, the judge is to strike the testimony of the witness, or that he may declare a mistrial if the interests of justice so require. 18 U.S.C. § 3500(d). Or the privileged materials may disclose a possible basis for applying pressure upon witnesses. United States v. Beekman, 155 F.2d 580 (2d Cir. 1946). Or they may bear directly upon a substantive element of a criminal case, requiring dismissal in the event of a successful claim of privilege. United States v.

Andolschek, 142 F.2d 503 (2d Cir. 1944); *see also* United States v. Reynolds, 345 U.S. 1 (1953). Or they may relate to an element of a plaintiff's claim against the government, with the decisions indicating unwillingness to allow the government's claim of privilege for secrets of state to be used as an offensive weapon against it. United States v. Reynolds, 345 U.S. 1 (1953); Republic of China v. Nat'l Union Fire Ins. Co., 142 F. Supp. 551 (D. Md. 1956).

Rule 510.   IDENTITY OF INFORMER [Not enacted.]

(a) **Rule of privilege**. The government or a state or subdivision thereof has a privilege to refuse to disclose the identity of a person who has furnished information relating to or assisting in an investigation of a possible violation of law to a law enforcement officer or member of a legislative committee or its staff conducting an investigation.

(b) **Who may claim**. The privilege may be claimed by an appropriate representative of the government, regardless of whether the information was furnished to an officer of the government or of a state or subdivision thereof. The privilege may be claimed by an appropriate representative of a state or subdivision if the information was furnished to an officer thereof, except that in criminal cases the privilege shall not be allowed if the government objects.

(c) **Exceptions**.

(1) *Voluntary disclosure; informer a witness.* No privilege exists under this rule if the identity of the informer or his interest in the subject matter of his communication has been disclosed to those who would have cause to resent the communication by a holder of the privilege or by the informer's own action, or if the informer appears as a witness for the government.

(2) *Testimony on merits.* If it appears from the evidence in the case or from other showing by a party that an informer may be able to give testimony necessary to a fair determination of the issue of guilt or innocence in a criminal case or of a material issue on the merits in a civil case to which the government is a party, and the government invokes the privilege, the judge shall give the government an opportunity to show *in camera* facts

relevant to determining whether the informer can, in fact, supply that testimony. The showing will ordinarily be in the form of affidavits, but the judge may direct that testimony be taken if he finds that the matter cannot be resolved satisfactorily upon the affidavit. If the judge finds that there is a reasonable probability that the informer can give the testimony, and the government elects not to disclose his identity, the judge on motion of the defendant in a criminal case shall dismiss the charges to which the testimony would relate, and the judge may do so on his own motion. In civil cases, he may make any order that justice requires. Evidence submitted to the judge shall be sealed and preserved to be made available to the appellate court in the event of an appeal, and the contents shall not otherwise be revealed without consent of the government. All counsel and parties shall be permitted to be present at every stage of proceedings under this subdivision except a showing *in camera*, at which no counsel of party shall be permitted to be present.

(3) *Legality of obtaining evidence.* If the information from an informer is relied upon to establish the legality of the means by which evidence was obtained and the judge is not satisfied that the information was received from an informer reasonably believed to be reliable or credible, he may require the identity of the informer to be disclosed. The judge shall, on request of the government, direct that the disclosure be made *in camera*. All counsel and parties concerned with the issue of legality shall be permitted to be present at every stage of proceedings under this subdivision except a disclosure *in camera*, at which no counsel or party shall be permitted to be present. If disclosure of the identity of the informer is made *in camera*, the record thereof shall be sealed and preserved to be made available to the appellate court in the event of an appeal, and the contents shall not otherwise be revealed without consent of the government.

ADVISORY COMMITTEE'S NOTE

The rule recognizes the use of informers as an important aspect of law enforcement, whether the informer is a citizen who steps forward with information or a paid undercover agent. In either event, the basic importance of anonymity in the effective use of informers is apparent, Bocchicchio v. Curtis Publ'g Co., 203 F. Supp. 403 (E.D. Pa. 1962), and the privilege of withholding their identity was well established at common law. Roviaro v. United States, 353 U.S. 53, 59 (1957); McCormick § 148; 8 Wigmore § 2374 (McNaughton rev. 1961).

Subdivision (a). The public interest in law enforcement requires that the privilege be that of the government, state, or political subdivision, rather than that of the witness. The rule blankets in as an informer anyone who tells a law enforcement officer about a violation of law without regard to whether the officer is one charged with enforcing the particular law. The rule also applies to disclosures to legislative investigating committees and their staffs, and is sufficiently broad to include continuing investigations.

Although the tradition of protecting the identity of informers has evolved in an essentially criminal setting, noncriminal law enforcement situations involved possibilities of reprisal against informers fall within the purview of the considerations out of which the privilege originated. In *Mitchell v. Roma*, 265 F.2d 633 (3d Cir. 1959), the privilege was given effect with respect to persons informing as to violations of the Fair Labor Standards Act, and in *Wirtz v. Continental Finance & Loan Co.*, 326 F.2d 561 (5th Cir. 1964), a similar case, the privilege was recognized, although the basis of the decision was lack of relevancy to the issues in the case.

Only identity is privileged; communications are not included except to the extent that disclosure would operate also to disclose the informer's identity. The common law was to the same effect. 8 Wigmore § 2374, at 765 (McNaughton rev. 1961); *see also* Roviaro v. United States, 353 U.S. 53, 60 (1957); Bowman Dairy Co. v. United States, 341 U.S. 214, 221 (1951).

The rule does not deal with the question whether pre-sentence reports made under Criminal Procedure Rule [32(d)] should be made available to an accused.

Subdivision (b). Normally the "appropriate representative" to make the claim will be counsel. However, it is possible that disclosure of the informer's identity will be sought in proceedings to which the government, state, or subdivision, as the case may be, is not a party. Under these circumstances effective implementation of the privilege requires that other representatives be considered "appropriate." See, for example, *Bocchicchio v. Curtis Publishing Co.*, 203 F. Supp 403 (E.D. Pa. 1962), a civil action for libel, in which a local police officer not represented by counsel successfully claimed the informer privilege.

The privilege may be claimed by a state or subdivision of a state if the information was given to its officer, except that in criminal cases it may not be allowed if the government objects.

Subdivision (c) deals with situations in which the informer privilege either does not apply or is curtailed.

(1) If the identity of the informer is disclosed, nothing further is to be gained form efforts to suppress it. Disclosure may be direct, or the same practical effect may result from action revealing the informer's interest in the subject matter. See, for example, *Westinghouse Electric Corp. v. City of Burlington*, 351 F.2d 762 (D.C. Cir. 1965),, which held that the filing of civil antitrust actions destroyed as to plaintiffs the informer privilege claimed by the Attorney General with respect to complaints of criminal antitrust violations. While allowing the privilege in effect to be waived by one not its holder, i.e., the informer himself, is something of a novelty in the law of privilege, if the informer chooses to reveal his identity, further efforts to suppress it are scarcely feasible.

The exception is limited to disclosure to "those who would have cause to resent the communication," in the language of *Roviaro v. United States*, 353 U.S. 53, 60 (1957), since disclosure otherwise, e.g., to another law enforcing agency, is not calculated to undercut the objects of the privilege.

If the informer becomes a witness for the government, the interests of justice in disclosing his status as a source of bias or possible support are believed to outweigh any remnant of interest in non-disclosure which then remains. See *Harris v. United States*, 371 F.2d 365 (9th Cir. 1967), in which the trial judge permitted detailed inquiry into the relationship between the witness and the government. *Cf.* AG v. Briant, (1846) 153 Eng. Rep. 808 (Exch.); 15 M. & W. 169. The purpose of the limitation to witnesses for the government is to avoid the possibility of calling persons as witnesses as a means of discovery whether they are informers.

(2) The informer privilege, it was held by the leading case, may not be used in a criminal prosecution to suppress the identity of a witness when the public interest in protecting the flow of information is outweighed by the individual's right to prepare his defense. Roviaro v. United States, 353 U.S. 53 (1957). The rule extends this balancing to include civil as well as criminal cases and phrases it in terms of "a reasonable probability that the informer may be able to give testimony necessary to a fair determination of the issue of guilt or innocence in a criminal case or of a material issue on the merits in a civil case." Once the privilege is invoked a procedure is provided for determining whether the informer can in

fact supply testimony of such nature as to require disclosure of his identity, thus avoiding a "judicial guessing game" on the question. United States v. Day, 384 F.2d 464, 470 (3d Cir. 1967). An investigation in camera is calculated to accommodate the conflicting interests involved. The rule also spells out specifically the consequences of a successful claim of the privilege in a criminal case; the wider range of possibilities in civil cases demands more flexibility in treatment. *See* Advisory Committee's Note to Rule 509(e), *supra*.

(3) One of the acute conflicts between the interest of the public in non-disclosure and the avoidance of unfairness to the accused as a result of non-disclosure arises when information form an informer is relied upon to legitimate a search and seizure by furnishing probable cause for a warrant for arrest or search. McCray v. Illinois, 386 U.S. 300, *reh'g denied*, 386 U.S. 1042 (1967). A hearing *in camera* provides an accommodation of these conflicting interests. United States v. Jackson, 384 F.2d 825 (3d Cir. 1967). The limited disclosure to the judge avoids any significant impairment of secrecy, while affording the accused a substantial measure of protection against arbitrary police action. The procedure is consistent with *McCray* and the decisions there discussed.

Rule 511.   WAIVER OF PRIVILEGE BY VOLUNTARY DISCLOSURE [Not enacted.]

A person upon whom these rules confer a privilege against disclosure of the confidential matter or communication waives the privilege if he or his predecessor while holder of the privilege voluntarily discloses or consents to disclosure of any significant part of the matter or communication. This rule does not apply if the disclosure is itself a privileged communication.

ADVISORY COMMITTEE'S NOTE

The central purpose of most privileges is the promotion of some interest or relationship by endowing it with a supporting secrecy or confidentiality. It is evident that the privilege should terminate when the holder by his own act destroys this confidentiality. MCCORMICK §§ 87, 97, 106; 8 WIGMORE §§ 2242, 2327–2329, 2374, 2389–2390 (McNaughton rev. 1961).

The rule is designed to be read with a view to what it is that the particular privilege protects. For example, the lawyer–client privilege covers only communications, and the fact that a client has discussed a matter with his lawyer does not insulate the client against disclosure of the subject matter discussed, although he is privileged not to disclose the discussion itself. *See* MCCORMICK § 93. The waiver here provided for is similarly restricted. Therefore a client, merely by disclosing a subject which he had discussed with his attorney, would not waive the applicable privilege; he would have to make disclosure of the communication itself in order to effect a waiver.

By traditional doctrine, waiver is the intentional relinquishment of a known right. Johnson v. Zerbst, 304 U.S. 458, 464 (1938). However, in the confidential privilege situations, once confidentiality is destroyed through voluntary disclosure, no subsequent claim of privilege can restore it, and knowledge or lack of knowledge of the existence of the privilege appears to be irrelevant. CAL. EVID. CODE § 912; 8 WIGMORE § 2327 (McNaughton rev. 1961).

Rule 512.   PRIVILEGED   MATTER   DISCLOSED   UNDER COMPULSION   OR   WITHOUT   OPPORTUNITY   TO CLAIM PRIVILEGE [Not enacted.]

Evidence of a statement or other disclosure of privileged matter is not admissible against the holder of the privilege if the disclosure was (a) compelled erroneously or (b) made without opportunity to claim the privilege.

ADVISORY COMMITTEE'S NOTE

Ordinarily a privilege is invoked in order to forestall disclosure. However, under some circumstances consideration must be given to the status and effect of a disclosure already made. Rule 511, immediately preceding, gives voluntary disclosure the effect of a waiver, while the present rule covers the effect of disclosure made under compulsion or without opportunity to claim the privilege.

Confidentiality, once destroyed, is not susceptible of restoration, yet some measure of repair can be accomplished by preventing use of the evidence against the holder of the privilege. The remedy of exclusion is therefore made available when the earlier disclosure was compelled erroneously or without opportunity to claim the privilege.

With respect to erroneously compelled disclosure, the argument may be made that the holder should be required in the first instance to assert the privilege, stand his ground, refuse to answer, perhaps incur a judgment of contempt, and exhaust all legal recourse, in order to sustain his privilege. *See* Fraser v. United States, 145 F.2d 139 (6th Cir. 1944), *cert. denied*, 324 U.S. 849 (1945); United States v. Johnson, 76 F. Supp. 538 (M.D. Pa.), *aff'd*, 165 F.2d 42 (3rd Cir. 1947), *cert. denied*, 332 U.S. 852, *reh'g denied*, 333 U.S. 834 (1948). However, this exacts of the holder greater fortitude in the face of authority than ordinary individuals are likely to possess, and assumes unrealistically that a judicial remedy is always available. In self-incrimination cases, the writers agree that erroneously compelled disclosures are inadmissible in a subsequent criminal prosecution of the holder, MAGUIRE, EVIDENCE OF GUILT 66 (1959); MCCORMICK § 127; 8 WIGMORE § 2270 (McNaughton rev. 1961), and the principle is equally sound when applied to other privileges. The modest departure from usual principles of res judicata which occurs when the compulsion is judicial is justified by the advantage of having one simple rule, assuring at least one opportunity for judicial supervision in every case.

The second circumstance stated as a basis for exclusion is disclosure made without opportunity to the holder to assert his privilege. Illustrative possibilities are disclosure by an eavesdropper, by a person used in the transmission of a privileged communication, by a family member participating in psychotherapy, or privileged data improperly made available from a computer bank.

Rule 513.   COMMENT UPON OR INFERENCE FROM CLAIM OF PRIVILEGE; INSTRUCTION [Not enacted.]

(a) Comment or inference not permitted. The claim of a privilege, whether in the present proceeding or upon a prior occasion, is not a proper subject of comment by judge or counsel. No inference may be drawn therefrom.

(b) Claiming privilege without knowledge of jury. In jury cases, proceedings shall be conducted, to the extent practicable, so as to facilitate the making of claims of privilege without the knowledge of the jury.

(c) Jury instruction. Upon request, any party against whom the jury might draw an adverse inference from a claim of privilege is entitled to an instruction that no inference may be drawn therefrom.

ADVISORY COMMITTEE'S NOTE

Subdivision (a). In *Griffin v. California*, 380 U.S. 609, 614 (1965), the Court pointed out that allowing comment upon the claim of a privilege "cuts down on the privilege by making its assertion costly." Consequently it was held that comment upon the election of the accused not to take the stand infringed upon his privilege against self-incrimination so substantially as to constitute a constitutional violation. While the privileges governed by these rules are not constitutionally based, they are nevertheless founded upon important policies and are entitled to maximum effect. Hence the present subdivision forbids comment upon the exercise of a privilege, in accordance with the weight of authority. Courtney v. United States, 390 F.2d 521 (9th Cir. 1968); 8 WIGMORE §§ 2243, 2322, 2386; Barnhart, *Privilege in the Uniform Rules of Evidence*, 24 OHIO ST. L.J. 131, 137–38 (1963); *cf.* MCCORMICK § 80.

Subdivision (b). The value of a privilege may be greatly depreciated by means other than expressly commenting to a jury upon the fact that it was exercised. Thus, the calling of a witness in the presence of the jury and subsequently excusing him after a side-bar conference may effectively convey to the jury the fact that a privilege has been claimed, even though the actual claim has not been made in their hearing. Whether a privilege will be claimed is usually ascertainable in advance and the handling of the entire matter outside the presence of the jury is feasible. Destruction of the privilege by innuendo can and should be avoided. Tallo v. United States, 344 F.2d 467 (1st Cir. 1965); United States v. Tomaiolo, 249 F.2d 683 (2d Cir. 1957); San Fratello v. United States, 343 F.2d 711 (5th Cir. 1965); Courtney v. United States, 390 F.2d 521 (9th Cir. 1968); 6 WIGMORE § 1808, at 275–76; 6 UCLA L. REV. 455 (1959). This position is in accord with the general agreement of the authorities than an accused cannot be forced to make his election not to testify in the presence of the jury. 8 WIGMORE § 2268, at 407 (McNaughton rev. 1961).

Unanticipated situations are, of course, bound to arise, and much must be left to the discretion of the judge and the professional responsibility of counsel.

Subdivision (c). Opinions will differ as to the effectiveness of a jury instruction not to draw an adverse inference from the making of a claim of privilege. *See* Bruton v. United States, 391 U.S. 123 (1968). Whether an instruction shall be given is left to the sound judgment of counsel for the party against whom the adverse inference may be drawn. The instruction is a matter of right, if requested. This is the result reached in *Bruno v. United States*, 308 U.S. 287 (1939), holding that an accused in entitled to an instruction under the statute (now 18 U.S.C. § 3481) providing that his failure to testify creates no presumption against him.

The right to the instruction is not impaired by the fact that the claim of privilege is by a witness, rather than by a party, provided an adverse inference against the party may result.

Rule 804. HEARSAY EXCEPTIONS: DECLARANT UNAVAILABLE [Subdivision (b)(2) not enacted.]

. . .

(b) Hearsay Exceptions. The following are not excluded by the hearsay rule if the declarant is unavailable as a witness:

. . .

(2) *Statement of recent perception.* A statement not in response to the instigation of a person engaged in investigating, litigating, or settling a claim, which narrates, describes, or explains an event or condition recently perceived by the declarant, made in good faith, not in contemplation of pending or anticipated litigation in which he was interested, and while his recollection was clear.

NOTE BY THE FEDERAL JUDICIAL CENTER

Hearsay exception (b)(2) is set forth above as prescribed by the Supreme Court. It was not included in the rules enacted by the Congress but is reproduced here for such value as it may have for purposes of interpretation.

ADVISORY COMMITTEE'S NOTE

Exception (2). The rule finds support in several directions. The well known Massachusetts Act of 1898 allows in evidence the declaration of any deceased person made in good faith before the commencement of the action and upon personal knowledge. MASS. GEN. LAWS ch. 233, § 65. To the same effect is Rhode Island General Laws § 9-19-11 (repealed and replaced by Rhode Island Rule of Evidence 804(c) (effective Oct. 1, 1987)). Under other statutes, a decedent's statement is admissible on behalf of his estate in actions against it, to offset the presumed inequality resulting from allowing a surviving opponent to testify. CAL. EVID. CODE § 1261; CONN.

GEN. STAT. § 52-172; and statutes collected in 5 WIGMORE § 1576; *see also* VA. CODE § 8-286 (repealed and replaced by VA. CODE ANN. § 8.01-397 (1977)), allowing statements made when capable by a party now incapable of testifying.

In 1938 the Committee on Improvements in the Law of Evidence of the American Bar Association recommended adoption of a statute similar to that of Massachusetts but with the concept of unavailability expanded to include, in addition to death, cases of insanity or inability to produce a witness or take his deposition. 63 A.B.A. Reports 570, 584, 600 (1938). The same year saw enactment of the English Evidence Act of 1938, allowing written statements made on personal knowledge, if declarant is deceased or otherwise unavailable or if the court is satisfied that undue delay or expense would otherwise be caused, unless declarant was an interested person in pending or anticipated relevant proceedings. Evidence Act, 1938, 1 & 2 Geo. 6, c. 28 (Eng.); CROSS ON EVIDENCE 482 (3d ed. 1967).

The Model Code Rule 503(a) provided broadly for admission of any hearsay declaration of an unavailable declarant. No circumstantial guarantees of trustworthiness were required. Debate upon the floor of the American Law Institute did not seriously question the propriety of the rule but centered upon what should constitute unavailability. 18 A.L.I. Proceedings 90–134 (1941).

The Uniform Rules draftsman took a less advanced position, more in the pattern of the Massachusetts statute, and invoked several assurances of accuracy: recency of perception, clarity of recollection, good faith, and antecedence to the commencement of the action. UNIF. R. EVID. 63(4)(c).

Opposition developed to the Uniform Rule because of its countenancing of the use of statements carefully prepared under the tutelage of lawyers, claim adjusters, or investigators with a view to pending or prospective litigation. *Tentative Recommendation and a Study Relating to the Uniform Rules of Evidence* (Article VIII. Hearsay Evidence), *in* CAL. LAW REV. COMM'N, REP., REC. & STUDIES 318 (1962); Quick, *Excitement, Necessity and the Uniform Rules: A Reappraisal of Rule 63(4)*, 6 WAYNE L. REV. 204, 219–24 (1960). To meet this objection, the rule excludes statements made at the instigation of a person engaged in investigating, litigating, or settling a claim. It also incorporates as safeguards the good faith and clarity of recollection required by the Uniform Rule and the exclusion of a statement by a person interested in the litigation provided by the English act.

With respect to the question whether the introduction of a statement under this exception against the accused in a criminal case would violate his right of confrontation, reference is made to the last paragraph of the Advisory Committee's Note under exception (1), *supra*.

REPORT OF THE HOUSE COMMITTEE ON THE JUDICIARY

Rule 804(b)(2), a hearsay exception submitted by the Court, titled "Statement of recent perception," read as follows:

A statement not in response to the instigation of a person engaged in investigating, litigating, or settling a claim, which narrates, describes, or explains an event or condition recently perceived by the declarant, made in good faith, not in contemplation of pending or anticipated litigation in which he was interested, and while his recollection was clear.

The Committee eliminated this rule as creating a new and unwarranted hearsay exception of great potential breadth. The Committee did not believe that statements of the type referred to bore sufficient guarantees of trustworthiness to justify admissibility.

EVIDENCE RULES RESTYLING PROJECT

In 2011, after several years of revision and review, a subcommittee of the Judicial Conference's Evidence Advisory Committee completed a front-to-back restyling of the Federal Rules of Evidence. The effort was part of a larger project to apply uniform conventions of style and usage across all of the federal rules. The rules of appellate, criminal, and civil procedure already had been restyled.

The restyled evidence rules appeared for public comment in August 2009. After changes prompted by practitioners and academics, they won approval from the Judicial Conference of the United States in September 2010 and then from the Supreme Court, which transmitted the rules to Congress in April 2011. As Congress did not intervene, the restyled rules became law on December 1, 2011.

The restyled rules now appear in boxes in the main body of this rulebook. They also appear below, side by side with the older rules they displaced. The old rules appear on the left and the restyled rules, in shaded boxes, on the right.

Restyling Principles

As its name suggests, the restyling project aimed to improve style, not alter substance. After each of the refashioned rules the Advisory Committee appended a standard note, varying only slightly from rule to rule, to emphasize that goal:

Committee Note

The language of Rule [###] has been amended as part of the general restyling of the Evidence Rules to make them more easily understood and to make style and terminology consistent throughout the rules. These changes are intended to be stylistic only. There is no intent to change any result in any ruling on evidence admissibility.

In reprinting the restyled rules, I have omitted this standard note, but have retained the balance of the Advisory Committee's notes issued with the restyled rules, which address issues peculiar to one or a few rules.

I have retained as well, at pages 2 to 4 above, the long note appended to Restyled Rule 101, which sets out the principles that guided the restyling. Paragraph 5 of this note emphasizes the Drafting Committee's intention to make "No Substantive Change" and establishes strict standards to avoid any such change. The note mentions the role of Professor Joseph Kimble, the Committee's drafting consultant and the restyled rules' chief author. Professor Kimble's basic restyling practices overlap with the general norms of good English prose: Active constructions displace passive; short sentences displace long; affirmatives displace double negatives; plain English displaces lawyerly circumlocutions.

The Restyling Committee tailored other conventions to the Federal Rules of Evidence. A new definitional section in Rule 101 deems "case" to mean "action or proceeding" and "record" to include "memorandum, report, or data compilation." As explained in the notes to Rules 701, 703, 704, and 705, "opinions" includes "inferences." The Committee's note to restyled Rule 101 lists several such conventions.

Noteworthy Clarifications

Many of the Restyling Committee's changes have enhanced clarity. Hence "must" displaces "shall" to signify commands. The defendant is always the "defendant," never the "accused." And bulleted lists or lettered subsections displace big clumps of text.

The breakdown into bite-sized units has made many long rules more navigable. The restyled versions of Rules 606(b), 609(a), 609(d), and 807 are far clearer than their current form. But even short and seemingly simple rules can gain clarity. Consider Rule 401, which used to say:

"Relevant evidence" means evidence having any tendency to make the existence of any fact that is of consequence to the determination of the action more probable or less probable than it would be without the evidence.

Now compare the restyled version:

Evidence is relevant if:

(a) it has any tendency to make a fact more or less probable than it would be without the evidence; and

(b) the fact is of consequence in determining the action.

The new structure highlights the discrete elements of probativeness and materiality that merge in the rule's definition of relevance. (The casebook discusses this feature of Rule 401 at pages 22 to 24.)

Other changes proposed by the Restyling Committee seek to clarify the original intent of the rules' drafters:

- Rule 405(a) originally provided, "On cross-examination, inquiry is allowable into relevant specific instances of conduct." As the casebook notes at pages 271 to 272, the rule neglected to specify *on cross-examination of whom?* The restyled rule supplies an answer: "On cross-examination *of the character witness . . . .*" (Emphasis added.)

- Rule 407 originally did not say whether the phrase "if controverted" applies only to feasibility or also to ownership and control. (See the casebook at page 113.) The restyled rule provides: "But the court may admit this evidence for another purpose, such as impeachment or—if disputed—proving ownership, control, or the feasibility of precautionary measures."

- And Rule 801(d)(2) used to bear the title "Admission by party–opponent" although the rule applied to *all* statements by a party–opponent, even those that *admitted* nothing. (See casebook pages 408 to 409.) The restyled rule instead is titled, "An Opposing Party's Statement."

As proposed, the restyled rules largely succeed in avoiding substantive changes. Indeed errors fall more often on the conservative side, leaving ambiguity where clarity seemed in reach. Hence Rule 405(a) still claims to apply "[w]hen evidence of a person's character or character trait is admissible," though the rule clearly does not apply to character evidence admitted under Rules 413, 414, 415, or 609. And "prejudice" (or "prejudicial") continues to appear without the essential modifier "unfair" (or "unfairly") in Rules 609 and 703 and in the title of Rule 403.

Here and there my own editor's notes mention possible substantive changes or sources of confusion. Quibbles aside, the restyled rules are clearer, cleaner, more accessible, and more elegantly rendered than the rules they displaced.

—GF

ARTICLE I
GENERAL PROVISIONS

Rule 101.   SCOPE

These rules govern proceedings in the courts of the United States and before the United States bankruptcy judges and United States magistrate judges, to the extent and with the exceptions stated in rule 1101.

Rule 102.   PURPOSE AND CONSTRUCTION

These rules shall be construed to secure fairness in administration, elimination of unjustifiable expense and delay, and promotion of growth and development of the law of evidence to the end that the truth may be ascertained and proceedings justly determined.

ARTICLE I
GENERAL PROVISIONS

Rule 101.   SCOPE; DEFINITIONS

(a) Scope. These rules apply to proceedings in United States courts. The specific courts and proceedings to which the rules apply, along with exceptions, are set out in Rule 1101.

(b) Definitions. In these rules:

(1) "civil case" means a civil action or proceeding;

(2) "criminal case" includes a criminal proceeding;

(3) "public office" includes a public agency;

(4) "record" includes a memorandum, report, or data compilation;

(5) a "rule prescribed by the Supreme Court" means a rule adopted by the Supreme Court under statutory authority; and

(6) a reference to any kind of written material or any other medium includes electronically stored information.

Rule 102.   PURPOSE

These rules should be construed so as to administer every proceeding fairly, eliminate unjustifiable expense and delay, and promote the development of evidence law, to the end of ascertaining the truth and securing a just determination.

Rule 103. RULINGS ON EVIDENCE

(a) Effect of erroneous ruling. Error may not be predicated upon a ruling which admits or excludes evidence unless a substantial right of the party is affected, and

(1) Objection. In case the ruling is one admitting evidence, a timely objection or motion to strike appears of record, stating the specific ground of objection, if the specific ground was not apparent from the context; or

(2) Offer of proof. In case the ruling is one excluding evidence, the substance of the evidence was made known to the court by offer or was apparent from the context within which questions were asked.

Once the court makes a definitive ruling on the record admitting or excluding evidence, either at or before trial, a party need not renew an objection or offer of proof to preserve a claim of error for appeal.

(b) Record of offer and ruling. The court may add any other or further statement which shows the character of the evidence, the form in which it was offered, the objection made, and the ruling thereon. It may direct the making of an offer in question and answer form.

(c) Hearing of jury. In jury cases, proceedings shall be conducted, to the extent practicable, so as to prevent inadmissible evidence from being suggested to the jury by any means, such as making statements or offers of proof or asking questions in the hearing of the jury.

(d) Plain error. Nothing in this rule precludes taking notice of plain errors affecting substantial rights although they were not brought to the attention of the court.

Rule 103.   RULINGS ON EVIDENCE

(a) **Preserving a Claim of Error.** A party may claim error in a ruling to admit or exclude evidence only if the error affects a substantial right of the party and:

    (1) if the ruling admits evidence, a party, on the record:

        (A) timely objects or moves to strike; and

        (B) states the specific ground, unless it was apparent from the context; or

    (2) if the ruling excludes evidence, a party informs the court of its substance by an offer of proof, unless the substance was apparent from the context.

(b) **Not Needing to Renew an Objection or Offer of Proof.** Once the court rules definitively on the record—either before or at trial—a party need not renew an objection or offer of proof to preserve a claim of error for appeal.

(c) **Court's Statement About the Ruling; Directing an Offer of Proof.** The court may make any statement about the character or form of the evidence, the objection made, and the ruling. The court may direct that an offer of proof be made in question-and-answer form.

(d) **Preventing the Jury from Hearing Inadmissible Evidence.** To the extent practicable, the court must conduct a jury trial so that inadmissible evidence is not suggested to the jury by any means.

(e) **Taking Notice of Plain Error.** A court may take notice of a plain error affecting a substantial right, even if the claim of error was not properly preserved.

Rule 104.   PRELIMINARY QUESTIONS

(a) Questions of admissibility generally.   Preliminary questions concerning the qualification of a person to be a witness, the existence of a privilege, or the admissibility of evidence shall be determined by the court, subject to the provisions of subdivision (b). In making its determination it is not bound by the rules of evidence except those with respect to privileges.

(b) Relevancy conditioned on fact.   When the relevancy of evidence depends upon the fulfillment of a condition of fact, the court shall admit it upon, or subject to, the introduction of evidence sufficient to support a finding of the fulfillment of the condition.

(c) Hearing of jury.   Hearings on the admissibility of confessions shall in all cases be conducted out of the hearing of the jury. Hearings on other preliminary matters shall be so conducted when the interests of justice require, or when an accused is a witness and so requests.

(d) Testimony by accused.   The accused does not, by testifying upon a preliminary matter, become subject to cross-examination as to other issues in the case.

(e) Weight and credibility.   This rule does not limit the right of a party to introduce before the jury evidence relevant to weight or credibility.

Rule 105.   LIMITED ADMISSIBILITY

When evidence which is admissible as to one party or for one purpose but not admissible as to another party or for another purpose is admitted, the court, upon request, shall restrict the evidence to its proper scope and instruct the jury accordingly.

Rule 104.   PRELIMINARY QUESTIONS

(a) In General. The court must decide any preliminary question about whether a witness is qualified, a privilege exists, or evidence is admissible. In so deciding, the court is not bound by evidence rules, except those on privilege.

(b) Relevance That Depends on a Fact. When the relevance of evidence depends on whether a fact exists, proof must be introduced sufficient to support a finding that the fact does exist. The court may admit the proposed evidence on the condition that the proof be introduced later.

(c) Conducting a Hearing So That the Jury Cannot Hear It. The court must conduct any hearing on a preliminary question so that the jury cannot hear it if:

    (1) the hearing involves the admissibility of a confession;

    (2) a defendant in a criminal case is a witness and so requests; or

    (3) justice so requires.

(d) Cross-Examining a Defendant in a Criminal Case. By testifying on a preliminary question, a defendant in a criminal case does not become subject to cross-examination on other issues in the case.

(e) Evidence Relevant to Weight and Credibility. This rule does not limit a party's right to introduce before the jury evidence that is relevant to the weight or credibility of other evidence.

Rule 105.   LIMITING EVIDENCE THAT IS NOT ADMISSIBLE AGAINST OTHER PARTIES OR FOR OTHER PURPOSES

If the court admits evidence that is admissible against a party or for a purpose—but not against another party or for another purpose—the court, on timely request, must restrict the evidence to its proper scope and instruct the jury accordingly.

Rule 106. REMAINDER OF OR RELATED WRITINGS OR RECORDED STATEMENTS

When a writing or recorded statement or part thereof is introduced by a party, an adverse party may require the introduction at that time of any other part or any other writing or recorded statement which ought in fairness to be considered contemporaneously with it.

Rule 106. REMAINDER OF OR RELATED WRITINGS OR RECORDED STATEMENTS

If a party introduces all or part of a writing or recorded statement, an adverse party may require the introduction, at that time, of any other part—or any other writing or recorded statement—that in fairness ought to be considered at the same time.

ARTICLE II
JUDICIAL NOTICE

Rule 201.   JUDICIAL NOTICE OF ADJUDICATIVE FACTS

(a) Scope of rule. This rule governs only judicial notice of adjudicative facts.

(b) Kinds of facts. A judicially noticed fact must be one not subject to reasonable dispute in that it is either (1) generally known within the territorial jurisdiction of the trial court or (2) capable of accurate and ready determination by resort to sources whose accuracy cannot reasonably be questioned.

(c) When discretionary. A court may take judicial notice, whether requested or not.

(d) When mandatory. A court shall take judicial notice if requested by a party and supplied with the necessary information.

(e) Opportunity to be heard. A party is entitled upon timely request to an opportunity to be heard as to the propriety of taking judicial notice and the tenor of the matter noticed. In the absence of prior notification, the request may be made after judicial notice has been taken.

(f) Time of taking notice. Judicial notice may be taken at any stage of the proceeding.

(g) Instructing jury. In a civil action or proceeding, the court shall instruct the jury to accept as conclusive any fact judicially noticed. In a criminal case, the court shall instruct the jury that it may, but is not required to, accept as conclusive any fact judicially noticed.

ARTICLE II
JUDICIAL NOTICE

Rule 201.   JUDICIAL NOTICE OF ADJUDICATIVE FACTS

(a) Scope. This rule governs judicial notice of an adjudicative fact only, not a legislative fact.

(b) Kinds of Facts That May Be Judicially Noticed. The court may judicially notice a fact that is not subject to reasonable dispute because it:

    (1) is generally known within the trial court's territorial jurisdiction; or

    (2) can be accurately and readily determined from sources whose accuracy cannot reasonably be questioned.

(c) Taking Notice. The court:

    (1) may take judicial notice on its own; or

    (2) must take judicial notice if a party requests it and the court is supplied with the necessary information.

(d) Timing. The court may take judicial notice at any stage of the proceeding.

(e) Opportunity to Be Heard. On timely request, a party is entitled to be heard on the propriety of taking judicial notice and the nature of the fact to be noticed. If the court takes judicial notice before notifying a party, the party, on request, is still entitled to be heard.

(f) Instructing the Jury. In a civil case, the court must instruct the jury to accept the noticed fact as conclusive. In a criminal case, the court must instruct the jury that it may or may not accept the noticed fact as conclusive.

ARTICLE III
PRESUMPTIONS IN CIVIL ACTIONS AND PROCEEDINGS

Rule 301.   PRESUMPTIONS IN GENERAL IN CIVIL ACTIONS AND PROCEEDINGS

In all civil actions and proceedings not otherwise provided for by Act of Congress or by these rules, a presumption imposes on the party against whom it is directed the burden of going forward with evidence to rebut or meet the presumption, but does not shift to such party the burden of proof in the sense of the risk of nonpersuasion, which remains throughout the trial upon the party on whom it was originally cast.

Rule 302.   APPLICABILITY OF STATE LAW IN CIVIL ACTIONS AND PROCEEDINGS

In civil actions and proceedings, the effect of a presumption respecting a fact which is an element of a claim or defense as to which State law supplies the rule of decision is determined in accordance with State law.

ARTICLE III
PRESUMPTIONS IN CIVIL CASES

Rule 301.   PRESUMPTIONS IN CIVIL CASES GENERALLY

In a civil case, unless a federal statute or these rules provide otherwise, the party against whom a presumption is directed has the burden of producing evidence to rebut the presumption. But this rule does not shift the burden of persuasion, which remains on the party who had it originally.

Rule 302.   APPLYING STATE LAW TO PRESUMPTIONS IN CIVIL CASES

In a civil case, state law governs the effect of a presumption regarding a claim or defense for which state law supplies the rule of decision.

ARTICLE IV
RELEVANCY AND ITS LIMITS

Rule 401. DEFINITION OF "RELEVANT EVIDENCE"

"Relevant evidence" means evidence having any tendency to make the existence of any fact that is of consequence to the determination of the action more probable or less probable than it would be without the evidence.

Rule 402. RELEVANT EVIDENCE GENERALLY ADMISSIBLE; IRRELEVANT EVIDENCE INADMISSIBLE

All relevant evidence is admissible, except as otherwise provided by the Constitution of the United States, by Act of Congress, by these rules, or by other rules prescribed by the Supreme Court pursuant to statutory authority. Evidence which is not relevant is not admissible.

Rule 403. EXCLUSION OF RELEVANT EVIDENCE ON GROUNDS OF PREJUDICE, CONFUSION, OR WASTE OF TIME

Although relevant, evidence may be excluded if its probative value is substantially outweighed by the danger of unfair prejudice, confusion of the issues, or misleading the jury, or by considerations of undue delay, waste of time, or needless presentation of cumulative evidence.

ARTICLE IV
RELEVANCE AND ITS LIMITS

Rule 401.   TEST FOR RELEVANT EVIDENCE

Evidence is relevant if:

(a) it has any tendency to make a fact more or less probable than it would be without the evidence; and

(b) the fact is of consequence in determining the action.

Rule 402.   GENERAL ADMISSIBILITY OF RELEVANT EVIDENCE

Relevant evidence is admissible unless any of the following provides otherwise:

- the United States Constitution;

- a federal statute;

- these rules; or

- other rules prescribed by the Supreme Court.

Irrelevant evidence is not admissible.

Rule 403.   EXCLUDING RELEVANT EVIDENCE FOR PREJUDICE, CONFUSION, WASTE OF TIME, OR OTHER REASONS

The court may exclude relevant evidence if its probative value is substantially outweighed by a danger of one or more of the following: unfair prejudice, confusing the issues, misleading the jury, undue delay, wasting time, or needlessly presenting cumulative evidence.

Rule 404. CHARACTER EVIDENCE NOT ADMISSIBLE TO PROVE CONDUCT; EXCEPTIONS; OTHER CRIMES

(a) Character evidence generally. Evidence of a person's character or a trait of character is not admissible for the purpose of proving action in conformity therewith on a particular occasion, except:

(1) Character of accused. In a criminal case, evidence of a pertinent trait of character offered by an accused, or by the prosecution to rebut the same, or if evidence of a trait of character of the alleged victim of the crime is offered by an accused and admitted under Rule 404(a)(2), evidence of the same trait of character of the accused offered by the prosecution;

(2) Character of alleged victim. In a criminal case, and subject to the limitations imposed by Rule 412, evidence of a pertinent trait of character of the alleged victim of the crime offered by an accused, or by the prosecution to rebut the same, or evidence of a character trait of peacefulness of the alleged victim offered by the prosecution in a homicide case to rebut evidence that the alleged victim was the first aggressor;

(3) Character of witness. Evidence of the character of a witness, as provided in Rules 607, 608, and 609.

(b) Other crimes, wrongs, or acts. Evidence of other crimes, wrongs, or acts is not admissible to prove the character of a person in order to show action in conformity therewith. It may, however, be admissible for other purposes, such as proof of motive, opportunity, intent, preparation, plan, knowledge, identity, or absence of mistake or accident, provided that upon request by the accused, the prosecution in a criminal case shall provide reasonable notice in advance of trial, or during trial if the court excuses pretrial notice on good cause shown, of the general nature of any such evidence it intends to introduce at trial.

Rule 404.   CHARACTER EVIDENCE; CRIMES OR OTHER ACTS

(a) Character Evidence.

(1) *Prohibited Uses.* Evidence of a person's character or character trait is not admissible to prove that on a particular occasion the person acted in accordance with the character or trait.

(2) *Exceptions for a Defendant or Victim in a Criminal Case.* The following exceptions apply in a criminal case:

(A) a defendant may offer evidence of the defendant's pertinent trait, and if the evidence is admitted, the prosecutor may offer evidence to rebut it;

(B) subject to the limitations in Rule 412, a defendant may offer evidence of an alleged victim's pertinent trait, and if the evidence is admitted, the prosecutor may:

(i) offer evidence to rebut it; and

(ii) offer evidence of the defendant's same trait; and

(C) in a homicide case, the prosecutor may offer evidence of the alleged victim's trait of peacefulness to rebut evidence that the victim was the first aggressor.

(3) *Exceptions for a Witness.* Evidence of a witness's character may be admitted under Rules 607, 608, and 609.

(b) Crimes, Wrongs, or Other Acts.

(1) *Prohibited Uses.* Evidence of a crime, wrong, or other act is not admissible to prove a person's character in order to show that on a particular occasion the person acted in accordance with the character.

(2) *Permitted Uses; Notice in a Criminal Case.* This evidence may be admissible for another purpose, such as proving motive, opportunity, intent, preparation, plan,

Rule 405.   METHODS OF PROVING CHARACTER

(a) Reputation or opinion. In all cases in which evidence of character or a trait of character of a person is admissible, proof may be made by testimony as to reputation or by testimony in the form of an opinion. On cross-examination, inquiry is allowable into relevant specific instances of conduct.

(b) Specific instances of conduct. In cases in which character or a trait of character of a person is an essential element of a charge, claim, or defense, proof may also be made of specific instances of that person's conduct.

knowledge, identity, absence of mistake, or lack of accident. On request by a defendant in a criminal case, the prosecutor must:

>   **(A)** provide reasonable notice of the general nature of any such evidence that the prosecutor intends to offer at trial; and

>   **(B)** do so before trial—or during trial if the court, for good cause, excuses lack of pretrial notice.

Rule 405.   METHODS OF PROVING CHARACTER

(a) By Reputation or Opinion.   When evidence of a person's character or character trait is admissible, it may be proved by testimony about the person's reputation or by testimony in the form of an opinion. On cross-examination of the character witness, the court may allow an inquiry into relevant specific instances of the person's conduct.

(b) By Specific Instances of Conduct.   When a person's character or character trait is an essential element of a charge, claim, or defense, the character or trait may also be proved by relevant specific instances of the person's conduct.

Editor's Note

Note the useful clarification in Rule 405(a) that cross-examination is permitted *of the character witness*. Hence if the defendant presents a witness to testify about the defendant's peaceful reputation, the prosecutor may cross-examine the character witness about past (violent) instances of the defendant's conduct. *See* Michelson v. United States, 335 U.S. 469 (1948) (CB 234). This rule does not, however, permit cross-examination *of the defendant* concerning past instances of conduct unless the defendant makes herself a character witness. See the discussion of this point at pages 271 to 272 of the casebook.—GF

Rule 406.   HABIT; ROUTINE PRACTICE

Evidence of the habit of a person or of the routine practice of an organization, whether corroborated or not and regardless of the presence of eyewitnesses, is relevant to prove that the conduct of the person or organization on a particular occasion was in conformity with the habit or routine practice.

Rule 407.   SUBSEQUENT REMEDIAL MEASURES

When, after an injury or harm allegedly caused by an event, measures are taken that, if taken previously, would have made the injury or harm less likely to occur, evidence of the subsequent measures is not admissible to prove negligence, culpable conduct, a defect in a product, a defect in a product's design, or a need for a warning or instruction. This rule does not require the exclusion of evidence of subsequent measures when offered for another purpose, such as proving ownership, control, or feasibility of precautionary measures, if controverted, or impeachment.

Rule 406.   HABIT; ROUTINE PRACTICE

Evidence of a person's habit or an organization's routine practice may be admitted to prove that on a particular occasion the person or organization acted in accordance with the habit or routine practice. The court may admit this evidence regardless of whether it is corroborated or whether there was an eyewitness.

Rule 407.   SUBSEQUENT REMEDIAL MEASURES

When measures are taken that would have made an earlier injury or harm less likely to occur, evidence of the subsequent measures is not admissible to prove:

- negligence;

- culpable conduct;

- a defect in a product or its design; or

- a need for a warning or instruction.

But the court may admit this evidence for another purpose, such as impeachment or—if disputed—proving ownership, control, or the feasibility of precautionary measures.

Editor's Note

The restyled rule makes it clear that before a party may prove ownership, control, *or* feasibility, the opposing party must dispute the point. The unrestyled rule arguably demanded controversion only for proof of feasibility. On this point see page 113 of the casebook, which cites Mueller & Kirkpatrick's now vindicated view.—GF

Rule 408.   COMPROMISE AND OFFERS TO COMPROMISE

(a) Prohibited uses. Evidence of the following is not admissible on behalf of any party, when offered to prove liability for, invalidity of, or amount of a claim that was disputed as to validity or amount, or to impeach through a prior inconsistent statement or contradiction:

(1) furnishing or offering or promising to furnish—or accepting or offering or promising to accept—a valuable consideration in compromising or attempting to compromise the claim; and

(2) conduct or statements made in compromise negotiations regarding the claim, except when offered in a criminal case and the negotiations related to a claim by a public office or agency in the exercise of regulatory, investigative, or enforcement authority.

(b) Permitted uses. This rule does not require exclusion if the evidence is offered for purposes not prohibited by subdivision (a). Examples of permissible purposes include proving a witness's bias or prejudice; negating a contention of undue delay; and proving an effort to obstruct a criminal investigation or prosecution.

Rule 409.   PAYMENT OF MEDICAL AND SIMILAR EXPENSES

Evidence of furnishing or offering or promising to pay medical, hospital, or similar expenses occasioned by an injury is not admissible to prove liability for the injury.

Rule 408.   COMPROMISE OFFERS AND NEGOTIATIONS

(a) Prohibited Uses. Evidence of the following is not admissible—on behalf of any party—either to prove or disprove the validity or amount of a disputed claim or to impeach by a prior inconsistent statement or a contradiction:

(1) furnishing, promising, or offering—or accepting, promising to accept, or offering to accept—a valuable consideration in compromising or attempting to compromise the claim; and

(2) conduct or a statement made during compromise negotiations about the claim—except when offered in a criminal case and when the negotiations related to a claim by a public office in the exercise of its regulatory, investigative, or enforcement authority.

(b) Exceptions. The court may admit this evidence for another purpose, such as proving a witness's bias or prejudice, negating a contention of undue delay, or proving an effort to obstruct a criminal investigation or prosecution.

Rule 409.   OFFERS TO PAY MEDICAL AND SIMILAR EXPENSES

Evidence of furnishing, promising to pay, or offering to pay medical, hospital, or similar expenses resulting from an injury is not admissible to prove liability for the injury.

Rule 410.   INADMISSIBILITY OF PLEAS, OFFERS OF PLEAS, PLEA DISCUSSIONS, AND RELATED STATEMENTS

Except as otherwise provided in this rule, evidence of the following is not, in any civil or criminal proceeding, admissible against the defendant who made the plea or was a participant in the plea discussions:

(1) a plea of guilty which was later withdrawn;

(2) a plea of nolo contendere;

(3) any statement made in the course of any proceedings under Rule 11 of the Federal Rules of Criminal Procedure or comparable state procedure regarding either of the foregoing pleas; or

(4) any statement made in the course of plea discussions with an attorney for the prosecuting authority which do not result in a plea of guilty or which result in a plea of guilty later withdrawn.

However, such a statement is admissible (i) in any proceeding wherein another statement made in the course of the same plea or plea discussions has been introduced and the statement ought in fairness be considered contemporaneously with it, or (ii) in a criminal proceeding for perjury or false statement if the statement was made by the defendant under oath, on the record and in the presence of counsel.

Rule 411.   LIABILITY INSURANCE

Evidence that a person was or was not insured against liability is not admissible upon the issue whether the person acted negligently or otherwise wrongfully. This rule does not require the exclusion of evidence of insurance against liability when offered for another purpose, such as proof of agency, ownership, or control, or bias or prejudice of a witness.

Rule 410. PLEAS, PLEA DISCUSSIONS, AND RELATED STATEMENTS

(a) Prohibited Uses. In a civil or criminal case, evidence of the following is not admissible against the defendant who made the plea or participated in the plea discussions:

(1) a guilty plea that was later withdrawn;

(2) a nolo contendere plea;

(3) a statement made during a proceeding on either of those pleas under Federal Rule of Criminal Procedure 11 or a comparable state procedure; or

(4) a statement made during plea discussions with an attorney for the prosecuting authority if the discussions did not result in a guilty plea or they resulted in a later-withdrawn guilty plea.

(b) Exceptions. The court may admit a statement described in Rule 410(a)(3) or (4):

(1) in any proceeding in which another statement made during the same plea or plea discussions has been introduced, if in fairness the statements ought to be considered together; or

(2) in a criminal proceeding for perjury or false statement, if the defendant made the statement under oath, on the record, and with counsel present.

Rule 411. LIABILITY INSURANCE

Evidence that a person was or was not insured against liability is not admissible to prove whether the person acted negligently or otherwise wrongfully. But the court may admit this evidence for another purpose, such as proving a witness's bias or prejudice or proving agency, ownership, or control.

Rule 412. SEX OFFENSE CASES; RELEVANCE OF ALLEGED VICTIM'S PAST SEXUAL BEHAVIOR OR ALLEGED SEXUAL PREDISPOSITION

(a) Evidence generally inadmissible. The following evidence is not admissible in any civil or criminal proceeding involving alleged sexual misconduct except as provided in subdivisions (b) and (c):

(1) Evidence offered to prove that any alleged victim engaged in other sexual behavior.

(2) Evidence offered to prove any alleged victim's sexual predisposition.

(b) Exceptions.

(1) In a criminal case, the following evidence is admissible, if otherwise admissible under these rules:

(A) evidence of specific instances of sexual behavior by the alleged victim offered to prove that a person other than the accused was the source of semen, injury or other physical evidence;

(B) evidence of specific instances of sexual behavior by the alleged victim with respect to the person accused of the sexual misconduct offered by the accused to prove consent or by the prosecution; and

(C) evidence the exclusion of which would violate the constitutional rights of the defendant.

(2) In a civil case, evidence offered to prove the sexual behavior or sexual predisposition of any alleged victim is admissible if it is otherwise admissible under these rules and its probative value substantially outweighs the danger of harm to any victim and of unfair prejudice to any party. Evidence of an alleged victim's reputation is admissible only if it has been placed in controversy by the alleged victim.

Rule 412.   SEX-OFFENSE   CASES: THE   VICTIM'S   SEXUAL BEHAVIOR OR PREDISPOSITION

(a) Prohibited Uses. The following evidence is not admissible in a civil or criminal proceeding involving alleged sexual misconduct:

(1) evidence offered to prove that a victim engaged in other sexual behavior; or

(2) evidence offered to prove a victim's sexual predisposition.

(b) Exceptions.

(1) *Criminal Cases.* The court may admit the following evidence in a criminal case:

(A) evidence of specific instances of a victim's sexual behavior, if offered to prove that someone other than the defendant was the source of semen, injury, or other physical evidence;

(B) evidence of specific instances of a victim's sexual behavior with respect to the person accused of the sexual misconduct, if offered by the defendant to prove consent or if offered by the prosecutor; and

(C) evidence whose exclusion would violate the defendant's constitutional rights.

(2) Civil Cases. In a civil case, the court may admit evidence offered to prove a victim's sexual behavior or sexual predisposition if its probative value substantially outweighs the danger of harm to any victim and of unfair prejudice to any party. The court may admit evidence of a victim's reputation only if the victim has placed it in controversy.

(c) Procedure To Determine Admissibility.

(1) A party intending to offer evidence under subdivision (b) must—

(A) file a written motion at least 14 days before trial specifically describing the evidence and stating the purpose for which it is offered unless the court, for good cause requires a different time for filing or permits filing during trial; and

(B) serve the motion on all parties and notify the alleged victim or, when appropriate, the alleged victim's guardian or representative.

(2) Before admitting evidence under this rule the court must conduct a hearing in camera and afford the victim and parties a right to attend and be heard. The motion, related papers and the record of the hearing must be sealed and remain under seal unless the court orders otherwise.

(c) Procedure to Determine Admissibility.

(1) *Motion.* If a party intends to offer evidence under Rule 412(b), the party must:

(A) file a motion that specifically describes the evidence and states the purpose for which it is to be offered;

(B) do so at least 14 days before trial unless the court, for good cause, sets a different time;

(C) serve the motion on all parties; and

(D) notify the victim or, when appropriate, the victim's guardian or representative.

(2) *Hearing.* Before admitting evidence under this rule, the court must conduct an in camera hearing and give the victim and parties a right to attend and be heard. Unless the court orders otherwise, the motion, related materials, and the record of the hearing must be and remain sealed.

(d) Definition of "Victim." In this rule, "victim" includes an alleged victim.

Rule 413.   EVIDENCE OF SIMILAR CRIMES IN SEXUAL ASSAULT CASES

(a) In a criminal case in which the defendant is accused of an offense of sexual assault, evidence of the defendant's commission of another offense or offenses of sexual assault is admissible, and may be considered for its bearing on any matter to which it is relevant.

(b) In a case in which the Government intends to offer evidence under this rule, the attorney for the Government shall disclose the evidence to the defendant, including statements of witnesses or a summary of the substance of any testimony that is expected to be offered, at least fifteen days before the scheduled date of trial or at such later time as the court may allow for good cause.

(c) This rule shall not be construed to limit the admission or consideration of evidence under any other rule.

(d) For purposes of this rule and Rule 415, "offense of sexual assault" means a crime under Federal law or the law of a State (as defined in section 513 of title 18, United States Code) that involved—

(1) any conduct proscribed by chapter 109A of title 18, United States Code;

(2) contact, without consent, between any part of the defendant's body or an object and the genitals or anus of another person;

(3) contact, without consent, between the genitals or anus of the defendant and any part of another person's body;

(4) deriving sexual pleasure or gratification from the infliction of death, bodily injury, or physical pain on another person; or

(5) an attempt or conspiracy to engage in conduct described in paragraphs (1)-(4).

Rule 413.   SIMILAR CRIMES IN SEXUAL-ASSAULT CASES

(a) Permitted Uses. In a criminal case in which a defendant is accused of a sexual assault, the court may admit evidence that the defendant committed any other sexual assault. The evidence may be considered on any matter to which it is relevant.

(b) Disclosure to the Defendant. If the prosecutor intends to offer this evidence, the prosecutor must disclose it to the defendant, including witnesses' statements or a summary of the expected testimony. The prosecutor must do so at least 15 days before trial or at a later time that the court allows for good cause.

(c) Effect on Other Rules. This rule does not limit the admission or consideration of evidence under any other rule.

(d) Definition of "Sexual Assault." In this rule and Rule 415, "sexual assault" means a crime under federal law or under state law (as "state" is defined in 18 U.S.C. § 513) involving:

(1) any conduct prohibited by 18 U.S.C. chapter 109A;

(2) contact, without consent, between any part of the defendant's body—or an object—and another person's genitals or anus;

(3) contact, without consent, between the defendant's genitals or anus and any part of another person's body;

(4) deriving sexual pleasure or gratification from inflicting death, bodily injury, or physical pain on another person; or

(5) an attempt or conspiracy to engage in conduct described in subparagraphs (1)–(4).

Rule 414.   EVIDENCE OF SIMILAR CRIMES IN CHILD MOLESTATION CASES

(a) In a criminal case in which the defendant is accused of an offense of child molestation, evidence of the defendant's commission of another offense or offenses of child molestation is admissible, and may be considered for its bearing on any matter to which it is relevant.

(b) In a case in which the Government intends to offer evidence under this rule, the attorney for the Government shall disclose the evidence to the defendant, including statements of witnesses or a summary of the substance of any testimony that is expected to be offered, at least fifteen days before the scheduled date of trial or at such later time as the court may allow for good cause.

(c) This rule shall not be construed to limit the admission or consideration of evidence under any other rule.

(d) For purposes of this rule and Rule 415, "child" means a person below the age of fourteen, and "offense of child molestation" means a crime under Federal law or the law of a State (as defined in section 513 of title 18, United States Code) that involved—

(1) any conduct proscribed by chapter 109A of title 18, United States Code, that was committed in relation to a child;

(2) any conduct proscribed by chapter 110 of title 18, United States Code;

(3) contact between any part of the defendant's body or an object and the genitals or anus of a child;

(4) contact between the genitals or anus of the defendant and any part of the body of a child;

(5) deriving sexual pleasure or gratification from the infliction of death, bodily injury, or physical pain on a child; or

(6) an attempt or conspiracy to engage in conduct described in paragraphs (1)-(5).

Rule 414.   SIMILAR CRIMES IN CHILD-MOLESTATION CASES

(a) Permitted Uses. In a criminal case in which a defendant is accused of child molestation, the court may admit evidence that the defendant committed any other child molestation. The evidence may be considered on any matter to which it is relevant.

(b) Disclosure to the Defendant. If the prosecutor intends to offer this evidence, the prosecutor must disclose it to the defendant, including witnesses' statements or a summary of the expected testimony. The prosecutor must do so at least 15 days before trial or at a later time that the court allows for good cause.

(c) Effect on Other Rules. This rule does not limit the admission or consideration of evidence under any other rule.

(d) Definition of "Child" and "Child Molestation." In this rule and Rule 415:

(1) "child" means a person below the age of 14; and

(2) "child molestation" means a crime under federal law or under state law (as "state" is defined in 18 U.S.C. § 513) involving:

(A) any conduct prohibited by 18 U.S.C. chapter 109A and committed with a child;

(B) any conduct prohibited by 18 U.S.C. chapter 110;

(C) contact between any part of the defendant's body—or an object—and a child's genitals or anus;

(D) contact between the defendant's genitals or anus and any part of a child's body;

(E) deriving sexual pleasure or gratification from inflicting death, bodily injury, or physical pain on a child; or

(F) an attempt or conspiracy to engage in conduct described in subparagraphs (A)–(E).

Rule 415.   EVIDENCE OF SIMILAR ACTS IN CIVIL CASES CONCERNING SEXUAL ASSAULT OR CHILD MOLESTATION

(a) In a civil case in which a claim for damages or other relief is predicated on a party's alleged commission of conduct constituting an offense of sexual assault or child molestation, evidence of that party's commission of another offense or offenses of sexual assault or child molestation is admissible and may be considered as provided in Rule 413 and Rule 414 of these rules.

(b) A party who intends to offer evidence under this Rule shall disclose the evidence to the party against whom it will be offered, including statements of witnesses or a summary of the substance of any testimony that is expected to be offered, at least fifteen days before the scheduled date of trial or at such later time as the court may allow for good cause.

(c) This rule shall not be construed to limit the admission or consideration of evidence under any other rule.

Rule 415. SIMILAR ACTS IN CIVIL CASES INVOLVING SEXUAL ASSAULT OR CHILD MOLESTATION

(a) Permitted Uses. In a civil case involving a claim for relief based on a party's alleged sexual assault or child molestation, the court may admit evidence that the party committed any other sexual assault or child molestation. The evidence may be considered as provided in Rules 413 and 414.

(b) Disclosure to the Opponent. If a party intends to offer this evidence, the party must disclose it to the party against whom it will be offered, including witnesses' statements or a summary of the expected testimony. The party must do so at least 15 days before trial or at a later time that the court allows for good cause.

(c) Effect on Other Rules. This rule does not limit the admission or consideration of evidence under any other rule.

Editor's Note

As originally enacted, Rules 413, 414, and 415 had provided that specific-act evidence of the sort specified in each rule "is admissible." (RB 408, 410, 412.) This unqualified language had prompted some courts and commentators to question whether the trial judge retained the usual discretion to exclude under Rule 403 unfairly prejudicial or confusing or time-wasting evidence. Those federal courts that engaged the question uniformly ruled that despite the seeming permissiveness of the words, "is admissible," evidence offered under Rules 413, 414, and 415 was subject to Rule 403.

As restyled in 2011, Rules 413, 414, and 415 state that "the court may admit" evidence of the sort specified in each rule, suggesting the trial judge retains discretion to exclude the evidence under Rule 403. (RB 409, 411, 413.) The language change also suggests the continued operation of Rule 701 barring improper opinion evidence, Rule 802 barring hearsay, and other exclusionary rules.

Although the change from "is admissible" to "the court may admit" merely confirmed the consensus view of the courts that other exclusionary rules continued to apply, the change arguably was substantive and not merely stylistic, as it eliminated a former ambiguity in the rules. I discuss this point at somewhat more length in the casebook at pages 231 to 232 and 584 to 585.

ARTICLE V
PRIVILEGES

Rule 501.   GENERAL RULE

Except as otherwise required by the Constitution of the United States or provided by Act of Congress or in rules prescribed by the Supreme Court pursuant to statutory authority, the privilege of a witness, person, government, State, or political subdivision thereof shall be governed by the principles of the common law as they may be interpreted by the courts of the United States in the light of reason and experience. However, in civil actions and proceedings, with respect to an element of a claim or defense as to which State law supplies the rule of decision, the privilege of a witness, person, government, State, or political subdivision thereof shall be determined in accordance with State law.

ARTICLE V
PRIVILEGES

Rule 501.   PRIVILEGE IN GENERAL

The common law—as interpreted by United States courts in the light of reason and experience—governs a claim of privilege unless any of the following provides otherwise:

- the United States Constitution;

- a federal statute; or

- rules prescribed by the Supreme Court.

But in a civil case, state law governs privilege regarding a claim or defense for which state law supplies the rule of decision.

Rule 502. ATTORNEY–CLIENT PRIVILEGE AND WORK PRODUCT; LIMITATIONS ON WAIVER

The following provisions apply, in the circumstances set out, to disclosure of a communication or information covered by the attorney–client privilege or work-product protection.

(a) Disclosure made in a Federal proceeding or to a Federal office or agency; scope of a waiver. When the disclosure is made in a Federal proceeding or to a Federal office or agency and waives the attorney–client privilege or work-product protection, the waiver extends to an undisclosed communication or information in a Federal or State proceeding only if:

(1) the waiver is intentional;

(2) the disclosed and undisclosed communications or information concern the same subject matter; and

(3) they ought in fairness to be considered together.

(b) Inadvertent disclosure. When made in a Federal proceeding or to a Federal office or agency, the disclosure does not operate as a waiver in a Federal or State proceeding if:

(1) the disclosure is inadvertent;

(2) the holder of the privilege or protection took reasonable steps to prevent disclosure; and

(3) the holder promptly took reasonable steps to rectify the error, including (if applicable) following Federal Rule of Civil Procedure 26(b)(5)(B).

(c) Disclosure made in a State proceeding. When the disclosure is made in a State proceeding and is not the subject of a State-court order concerning waiver, the disclosure does not operate as a waiver in a Federal proceeding if the disclosure:

(1) would not be a waiver under this rule if it had been made in a Federal proceeding; or

Rule 502. ATTORNEY–CLIENT PRIVILEGE AND WORK PRODUCT; LIMITATIONS ON WAIVER

The following provisions apply, in the circumstances set out, to disclosure of a communication or information covered by the attorney–client privilege or work-product protection.

(a) Disclosure Made in a Federal Proceeding or to a Federal Office or Agency; Scope of a Waiver. When the disclosure is made in a federal proceeding or to a federal office or agency and waives the attorney–client privilege or work-product protection, the waiver extends to an undisclosed communication or information in a federal or state proceeding only if:

   (1) the waiver is intentional;

   (2) the disclosed and undisclosed communications or information concern the same subject matter; and

   (3) they ought in fairness to be considered together.

(b) Inadvertent Disclosure. When made in a federal proceeding or to a federal office or agency, the disclosure does not operate as a waiver in a federal or state proceeding if:

   (1) the disclosure is inadvertent;

   (2) the holder of the privilege or protection took reasonable steps to prevent disclosure; and

   (3) the holder promptly took reasonable steps to rectify the error, including (if applicable) following Federal Rule of Civil Procedure 26(b)(5)(B).

(c) Disclosure Made in a State Proceeding. When the disclosure is made in a state proceeding and is not the subject of a state-court order concerning waiver, the disclosure does not operate as a waiver in a federal proceeding if the disclosure:

   (1) would not be a waiver under this rule if it had been made in a federal proceeding; or

(2) is not a waiver under the law of the State where the disclosure occurred.

(d) Controlling effect of a court order. A Federal court may order that the privilege or protection is not waived by disclosure connected with the litigation pending before the court—in which event the disclosure is also not a waiver in any other Federal or State proceeding.

(e) Controlling effect of a party agreement. An agreement on the effect of disclosure in a Federal proceeding is binding only on the parties to the agreement, unless it is incorporated into a court order.

(f) Controlling effect of this rule. Notwithstanding Rules 101 and 1101, this rule applies to State proceedings and to Federal court-annexed and Federal court-mandated arbitration proceedings, in the circumstances set out in the rule. And notwithstanding Rule 501, this rule applies even if State law provides the rule of decision.

(g) Definitions. In this rule:

(1) "attorney–client privilege" means the protection that applicable law provides for confidential attorney–client communications; and

(2) "work-product protection" means the protection that applicable law provides for tangible material (or its intangible equivalent) prepared in anticipation of litigation or for trial.

(2) is not a waiver under the law of the state where the disclosure occurred.

(d) Controlling Effect of a Court Order. A federal court may order that the privilege or protection is not waived by disclosure connected with the litigation pending before the court—in which event the disclosure is also not a waiver in any other federal or state proceeding.

(e) Controlling Effect of a Party Agreement. An agreement on the effect of disclosure in a federal proceeding is binding only on the parties to the agreement, unless it is incorporated into a court order.

(f) Controlling Effect of this Rule. Notwithstanding Rules 101 and 1101, this rule applies to state proceedings and to federal court-annexed and federal court-mandated arbitration proceedings, in the circumstances set out in the rule. And notwithstanding Rule 501, this rule applies even if state law provides the rule of decision.

(g) Definitions. In this rule:

(1) "attorney–client privilege" means the protection that applicable law provides for confidential attorney–client communications; and

(2) "work-product protection" means the protection that applicable law provides for tangible material (or its intangible equivalent) prepared in anticipation of litigation or for trial.

ARTICLE VI
WITNESSES

Rule 601.   GENERAL RULE OF COMPETENCY

Every person is competent to be a witness except as otherwise provided in these rules. However, in civil actions and proceedings, with respect to an element of a claim or defense as to which State law supplies the rule of decision, the competency of a witness shall be determined in accordance with State law.

Rule 602.   LACK OF PERSONAL KNOWLEDGE

A witness may not testify to a matter unless evidence is introduced sufficient to support a finding that the witness has personal knowledge of the matter. Evidence to prove personal knowledge may, but need not, consist of the witness' own testimony. This rule is subject to the provisions of rule 703, relating to opinion testimony by expert witnesses

Rule 603.   OATH OR AFFIRMATION

Before testifying, every witness shall be required to declare that the witness will testify truthfully, by oath or affirmation administered in a form calculated to awaken the witness' conscience and impress the witness' mind with the duty to do so.

Rule 604.   INTERPRETERS

An interpreter is subject to the provisions of these rules relating to qualification as an expert and the administration of an oath or affirmation to make a true translation.

Rule 605.   COMPETENCY OF JUDGE AS WITNESS

The judge presiding at the trial may not testify in that trial as a witness. No objection need be made in order to preserve the point.

ARTICLE VI
WITNESSES

Rule 601.   COMPETENCY TO TESTIFY IN GENERAL

Every person is competent to be a witness unless these rules provide otherwise. But in a civil case, state law governs the witness's competency regarding a claim or defense for which state law supplies the rule of decision.

Rule 602.   NEED FOR PERSONAL KNOWLEDGE

A witness may testify to a matter only if evidence is introduced sufficient to support a finding that the witness has personal knowledge of the matter. Evidence to prove personal knowledge may consist of the witness's own testimony. This rule does not apply to a witness's expert testimony under Rule 703.

Rule 603.   OATH OR AFFIRMATION TO TESTIFY TRUTHFULLY

Before testifying, a witness must give an oath or affirmation to testify truthfully. It must be in a form designed to impress that duty on the witness's conscience.

Rule 604.   INTERPRETER

An interpreter must be qualified and must give an oath or affirmation to make a true translation.

Rule 605.   JUDGE'S COMPETENCY AS A WITNESS

The presiding judge may not testify as a witness at the trial. A party need not object to preserve the issue.

Rule 606.   COMPETENCY OF JUROR AS WITNESS

(a) At the trial. A member of the jury may not testify as a witness before that jury in the trial of the case in which the juror is sitting. If the juror is called so to testify, the opposing party shall be afforded an opportunity to object out of the presence of the jury.

(b) Inquiry into validity of verdict or indictment. Upon an inquiry into the validity of a verdict or indictment, a juror may not testify as to any matter or statement occurring during the course of the jury's deliberations or to the effect of anything upon that or any other juror's mind or emotions as influencing the juror to assent to or dissent from the verdict or indictment or concerning the juror's mental processes in connection therewith. But a juror may testify about (1) whether extraneous prejudicial information was improperly brought to the jury's attention, (2) whether any outside influence was improperly brought to bear upon any juror, or (3) whether there was a mistake in entering the verdict onto the verdict form. A juror's affidavit or evidence of any statement by the juror may not be received on a matter about which the juror would be precluded from testifying.

Rule 607.   WHO MAY IMPEACH

The credibility of a witness may be attacked by any party, including the party calling the witness.

Rule 606.   JUROR'S COMPETENCY AS A WITNESS

(a) **At the Trial.**   A juror may not testify as a witness before the other jurors at the trial. If a juror is called to testify, the court must give a party an opportunity to object outside the jury's presence.

(b) **During an Inquiry Into the Validity of a Verdict or Indictment.**

(1) *Prohibited Testimony or Other Evidence.*   During an inquiry into the validity of a verdict or indictment, a juror may not testify about any statement made or incident that occurred during the jury's deliberations; the effect of anything on that juror's or another juror's vote; or any juror's mental processes concerning the verdict or indictment. The court may not receive a juror's affidavit or evidence of a juror's statement on these matters.

(2) *Exceptions.*   A juror may testify about whether:

(A) extraneous prejudicial information was improperly brought to the jury's attention;

(B) an outside influence was improperly brought to bear on any juror; or

(C) a mistake was made in entering the verdict on the verdict form.

Rule 607.   WHO MAY IMPEACH A WITNESS

Any party, including the party that called the witness, may attack the witness's credibility.

Rule 608.   EVIDENCE OF CHARACTER AND CONDUCT OF WITNESS

(a) Opinion and reputation evidence of character. The credibility of a witness may be attacked or supported by evidence in the form of opinion or reputation, but subject to these limitations: (1) the evidence may refer only to character for truthfulness or untruthfulness, and (2) evidence of truthful character is admissible only after the character of the witness for truthfulness has been attacked by opinion or reputation evidence or otherwise.

(b) Specific instances of conduct. Specific instances of the conduct of a witness, for the purpose of attacking or supporting the witness' character for truthfulness, other than conviction of crime as provided in rule 609, may not be proved by extrinsic evidence. They may, however, in the discretion of the court, if probative of truthfulness or untruthfulness, be inquired into on cross-examination of the witness (1) concerning the witness' character for truthfulness or untruthfulness, or (2) concerning the character for truthfulness or untruthfulness of another witness as to which character the witness being cross-examined has testified.

The giving of testimony, whether by an accused or by any other witness, does not operate as a waiver of the accused's or the witness' privilege against self-incrimination when examined with respect to matters that relate only to character for truthfulness.

Rule 608.   A WITNESS'S CHARACTER FOR TRUTHFULNESS OR
            UNTRUTHFULNESS.

(a) Reputation or Opinion Evidence.   A witness's
credibility may be attacked or supported by testimony about
the witness's reputation for having a character for
truthfulness or untruthfulness, or by testimony in the form of
an opinion about that character. But evidence of truthful
character is admissible only after the witness's character for
truthfulness has been attacked.

(b) Specific Instances of Conduct.   Except for a criminal
conviction under Rule 609, extrinsic evidence is not
admissible to prove specific instances of a witness's conduct
in order to attack or support the witness's character for
truthfulness. But the court may, on cross-examination, allow
them to be inquired into if they are probative of the character
for truthfulness or untruthfulness of:

(1) the witness; or

(2) another witness whose character the witness being
cross-examined has testified about.

By testifying on another matter, a witness does not waive
any privilege against self-incrimination for testimony that
relates only to the witness's character for truthfulness.

Rule 609.   IMPEACHMENT BY EVIDENCE OF CONVICTION OF CRIME

(a) **General rule.**   For the purpose of attacking the character for truthfulness of a witness,

(1) evidence that a witness other than an accused has been convicted of a crime shall be admitted, subject to Rule 403, if the crime was punishable by death or imprisonment in excess of one year under the law under which the witness was convicted, and evidence that an accused has been convicted of such a crime shall be admitted if the court determines that the probative value of admitting this evidence outweighs its prejudicial effect to the accused; and

(2) evidence that any witness has been convicted of a crime shall be admitted regardless of the punishment, if it readily can be determined that establishing the elements of the crime required proof or admission of an act of dishonesty or false statement by the witness.

(b) **Time limit.** Evidence of a conviction under this rule is not admissible if a period of more than ten years has elapsed since the date of the conviction or of the release of the witness from the confinement imposed for that conviction, whichever is the later date, unless the court determines, in the interests of justice, that the probative value of the conviction supported by specific facts and circumstances substantially outweighs its prejudicial effect. However, evidence of a conviction more than 10 years old as calculated herein, is not admissible unless the proponent gives to the adverse party sufficient advance written notice of intent to use such evidence to provide the adverse party with a fair opportunity to contest the use of such evidence.

Rule 609. IMPEACHMENT BY EVIDENCE OF A CRIMINAL CONVICTION

(a) In General. The following rules apply to attacking a witness's character for truthfulness by evidence of a criminal conviction:

(1) for a crime that, in the convicting jurisdiction, was punishable by death or by imprisonment for more than one year, the evidence:

(A) must be admitted, subject to Rule 403, in a civil case or in a criminal case in which the witness is not a defendant; and

(B) must be admitted in a criminal case in which the witness is a defendant, if the probative value of the evidence outweighs its prejudicial effect to that defendant; and

(2) for any crime regardless of the punishment, the evidence must be admitted if the court can readily determine that establishing the elements of the crime required proving—or the witness's admitting—a dishonest act or false statement.

(b) Limit on Using the Evidence After 10 Years. This subdivision (b) applies if more than 10 years have passed since the witness's conviction or release from confinement for it, whichever is later. Evidence of the conviction is admissible only if:

(1) its probative value, supported by specific facts and circumstances, substantially outweighs its prejudicial effect; and

(2) the proponent gives an adverse party reasonable written notice of the intent to use it so that the party has a fair opportunity to contest its use.

(c) Effect of pardon, annulment, or certificate of rehabilitation.   Evidence of a conviction is not admissible under this rule if (1) the conviction has been the subject of a pardon, annulment, certificate of rehabilitation, or other equivalent procedure based on a finding of the rehabilitation of the person convicted, and that person has not been convicted of a subsequent crime that was punishable by death or imprisonment in excess of one year, or (2) the conviction has been the subject of a pardon, annulment, or other equivalent procedure based on a finding of innocence.

(d) Juvenile adjudications.   Evidence of juvenile adjudications is generally not admissible under this rule. The court may, however, in a criminal case allow evidence of a juvenile adjudication of a witness other than the accused if conviction of the offense would be admissible to attack the credibility of an adult and the court is satisfied that admission in evidence is necessary for a fair determination of the issue of guilt or innocence.

(e) Pendency of appeal.   The pendency of an appeal therefrom does not render evidence of a conviction inadmissible.   Evidence of the pendency of an appeal is admissible.

(c) Effect of a Pardon, Annulment, or Certificate of Rehabilitation. Evidence of a conviction is not admissible if:

(1) the conviction has been the subject of a pardon, annulment, certificate of rehabilitation, or other equivalent procedure based on a finding that the person has been rehabilitated, and the person has not been convicted of a later crime punishable by death or by imprisonment for more than one year; or

(2) the conviction has been the subject of a pardon, annulment, or other equivalent procedure based on a finding of innocence.

(d) Juvenile Adjudications. Evidence of a juvenile adjudication is admissible under this rule only if:

(1) it is offered in a criminal case;

(2) the adjudication was of a witness other than the defendant;

(3) an adult's conviction for that offense would be admissible to attack the adult's credibility; and

(4) admitting the evidence is necessary to fairly determine guilt or innocence.

(e) Pendency of an Appeal. A conviction that satisfies this rule is admissible even if an appeal is pending. Evidence of the pendency is also admissible.

Editor's Note

The substitution of "must" for "shall" in Rule 609(a)(1) is at first disconcerting. The Advisory Committee's Note to restyled Rule 101 explains:

The restyled rules minimize the use of inherently ambiguous words. For example, the word "shall" can mean "must," "may," or something else, depending on context. The potential for confusion is exacerbated by the fact the word "shall" is no longer generally used in

Rule 610.   RELIGIOUS BELIEFS OR OPINIONS

Evidence of the beliefs or opinions of a witness on matters of religion is not admissible for the purpose of showing that by reason of their nature the witness' credibility is impaired or enhanced.

spoken or clearly written English. The restyled rules replace "shall" with "must," "may," or "should," depending on which one the context and established interpretation make correct in each rule.

(*Supra* at 3.) Still, it is hard to shed the sense that "must" deprives the trial judge of a measure of discretion that "shall" had left intact. Here we can fall back on the balancing tests prescribed in Rules 609(a)(1)(A) and 609(a)(1)(B), as all such tests invest the trial judge with de facto discretion. We also can look to the advisory committee's assurance that no substantive change was intended. In particular there was no intent to change standards of admissibility:

> The Committee made special efforts to reject any purported style improvement that might result in a substantive change in the application of a rule. The Committee considered a change to be "substantive" if any of the following conditions were met:

> > *a.* Under the existing practice in any circuit, the change could lead to a different result on a question of admissibility (e.g., a change that requires a court to provide either a less or more stringent standard in evaluating the admissibility of particular evidence) . . . .

(Page 4 above.) In seeking to exclude evidence of past convictions, wise counsel will call the court's attention to the committee's note.—GF

Rule 610.   RELIGIOUS BELIEFS OR OPINIONS

Evidence of a witness's religious beliefs or opinions is not admissible to attack or support the witness's credibility.

Rule 611. MODE AND ORDER OF INTERROGATION AND PRESENTATION

(a) Control by court. The court shall exercise reasonable control over the mode and order of interrogating witnesses and presenting evidence so as to (1) make the interrogation and presentation effective for the ascertainment of the truth, (2) avoid needless consumption of time, and (3) protect witnesses from harassment or undue embarrassment.

(b) Scope of cross-examination. Cross-examination should be limited to the subject matter of the direct examination and matters affecting the credibility of the witness. The court may, in the exercise of discretion, permit inquiry into additional matters as if on direct examination.

(c) Leading questions. Leading questions should not be used on the direct examination of a witness except as may be necessary to develop the witness' testimony. Ordinarily leading questions should be permitted on cross-examination. When a party calls a hostile witness, an adverse party, or a witness identified with an adverse party, interrogation may be by leading questions.

Rule 611.   MODE AND ORDER OF EXAMINING WITNESSES AND PRESENTING EVIDENCE

(a) Control by the Court; Purposes. The court should exercise reasonable control over the mode and order of examining witnesses and presenting evidence so as to:

    (1) make those procedures effective for determining the truth;

    (2) avoid wasting time; and

    (3) protect witnesses from harassment or undue embarrassment.

(b) Scope of Cross-Examination. Cross-examination should not go beyond the subject matter of the direct examination and matters affecting the witness's credibility. The court may allow inquiry into additional matters as if on direct examination.

(c) Leading Questions. Leading questions should not be used on direct examination except as necessary to develop the witness's testimony. Ordinarily, the court should allow leading questions:

    (1) on cross-examination; and

    (2) when a party calls a hostile witness, an adverse party, or a witness identified with an adverse party.

Rule 612.   WRITING USED TO REFRESH MEMORY

Except as otherwise provided in criminal proceedings by section 3500 of title 18, United States Code, if a witness uses a writing to refresh memory for the purpose of testifying, either—

(1) while testifying, or

(2) before testifying, if the court in its discretion determines it is necessary in the interests of justice,

an adverse party is entitled to have the writing produced at the hearing, to inspect it, to cross-examine the witness thereon, and to introduce in evidence those portions which relate to the testimony of the witness. If it is claimed that the writing contains matters not related to the subject matter of the testimony the court shall examine the writing in camera, excise any portions not so related, and order delivery of the remainder to the party entitled thereto. Any portion withheld over objections shall be preserved and made available to the appellate court in the event of an appeal. If a writing is not produced or delivered pursuant to order under this rule, the court shall make any order justice requires, except that in criminal cases when the prosecution elects not to comply, the order shall be one striking the testimony or, if the court in its discretion determines that the interests of justice so require, declaring a mistrial.

Rule 612. WRITING USED TO REFRESH A WITNESS'S MEMORY

(a) Scope. This rule gives an adverse party certain options when a witness uses a writing to refresh memory:

(1) while testifying; or

(2) before testifying, if the court decides that justice requires the party to have those options.

(b) Adverse Party's Options; Deleting Unrelated Matter. Unless 18 U.S.C. § 3500 provides otherwise in a criminal case, an adverse party is entitled to have the writing produced at the hearing, to inspect it, to cross-examine the witness about it, and to introduce in evidence any portion that relates to the witness's testimony. If the producing party claims that the writing includes unrelated matter, the court must examine the writing in camera, delete any unrelated portion, and order that the rest be delivered to the adverse party. Any portion deleted over objection must be preserved for the record.

(c) Failure to Produce or Deliver the Writing. If a writing is not produced or is not delivered as ordered, the court may issue any appropriate order. But if the prosecution does not comply in a criminal case, the court must strike the witness's testimony or—if justice so requires—declare a mistrial.

Rule 613.   PRIOR STATEMENTS OF WITNESSES

(a) Examining witness concerning prior statement.   In examining a witness concerning a prior statement made by the witness, whether written or not, the statement need not be shown nor its contents disclosed to the witness at that time, but on request the same shall be shown or disclosed to opposing counsel.

(b) Extrinsic evidence of prior inconsistent statement of witness.   Extrinsic evidence of a prior inconsistent statement by a witness is not admissible unless the witness is afforded an opportunity to explain or deny the same and the opposite party is afforded an opportunity to interrogate the witness thereon, or the interests of justice otherwise require.   This provision does not apply to admissions of a party-opponent as defined in rule 801(d)(2).

Rule 614.   CALLING AND INTERROGATION OF WITNESSES BY COURT

(a) Calling by court.   The court may, on its own motion or at the suggestion of a party, call witnesses, and all parties are entitled to cross-examine witnesses thus called.

(b) Interrogation by court.   The court may interrogate witnesses, whether called by itself or by a party.

(c) Objections.   Objections to the calling of witnesses by the court or to interrogation by it may be made at the time or at the next available opportunity when the jury is not present.

Rule 613.   WITNESS'S PRIOR STATEMENT

(a) Showing or Disclosing the Statement During Examination. When examining a witness about the witness's prior statement, a party need not show it or disclose its contents to the witness. But the party must, on request, show it or disclose its contents to an adverse party's attorney.

(b) Extrinsic Evidence of a Prior Inconsistent Statement. Extrinsic evidence of a witness's prior inconsistent statement is admissible only if the witness is given an opportunity to explain or deny the statement and an adverse party is given an opportunity to examine the witness about it, or if justice so requires. This subdivision (b) does not apply to an opposing party's statement under Rule 801(d)(2).

Rule 614.   COURT'S CALLING OR EXAMINING A WITNESS

(a) Calling. The court may call a witness on its own or at a party's request. Each party is entitled to cross-examine the witness.

(b) Examining.   The court may examine a witness regardless of who calls the witness.

(c) Objections. A party may object to the court's calling or examining a witness either at that time or at the next opportunity when the jury is not present.

Rule 615.   EXCLUSION OF WITNESSES

At the request of a party the court shall order witnesses excluded so that they cannot hear the testimony of other witnesses, and it may make the order of its own motion. This rule does not authorize exclusion of (1) a party who is a natural person, or (2) an officer or employee of a party which is not a natural person designated as its representative by its attorney, or (3) a person whose presence is shown by a party to be essential to the presentation of the party's cause, or (4) a person authorized by statute to be present.

Rule 615.   EXCLUDING WITNESSES

At a party's request, the court must order witnesses excluded so that they cannot hear other witnesses' testimony. Or the court may do so on its own. But this rule does not authorize excluding:

(a) a party who is a natural person;

(b) an officer or employee of a party that is not a natural person, after being designated as the party's representative by its attorney;

(c) a person whose presence a party shows to be essential to presenting the party's claim or defense; or

(d) a person authorized by statute to be present.

ARTICLE VII
OPINIONS AND EXPERT TESTIMONY

Rule 701.   OPINION TESTIMONY BY LAY WITNESSES

If the witness is not testifying as an expert, the witness' testimony in the form of opinions or inferences is limited to those opinions or inferences which are (a) rationally based on the perception of the witness, and (b) helpful to a clear understanding of the witness' testimony or the determination of a fact in issue, and (c) not based on scientific, technical or other specialized knowledge within the scope of Rule 702.

Rule 702.   TESTIMONY BY EXPERTS

If scientific, technical, or other specialized knowledge will assist the trier of fact to understand the evidence or to determine a fact in issue, a witness qualified as an expert by knowledge, skill, experience, training, or education, may testify thereto in the form of an opinion or otherwise, if (1) the testimony is based upon sufficient facts or data, (2) the testimony is the product of reliable principles and methods, and (3) the witness has applied the principles and methods reliably to the facts of the case.

ARTICLE VII
OPINIONS AND EXPERT TESTIMONY

Rule 701.   OPINION TESTIMONY BY LAY WITNESSES

If a witness is not testifying as an expert, testimony in the form of an opinion is limited to one that is:

(a) rationally based on the witness's perception;

(b) helpful to clearly understanding the witness's testimony or to determining a fact in issue; and

(c) not based on scientific, technical, or other specialized knowledge within the scope of Rule 702.

Rule 702.   TESTIMONY BY EXPERT WITNESSES

A witness who is qualified as an expert by knowledge, skill, experience, training, or education may testify in the form of an opinion or otherwise if:

(a) the expert's scientific, technical, or other specialized knowledge will help the trier of fact to understand the evidence or to determine a fact in issue;

(b) the testimony is based on sufficient facts or data;

(c) the testimony is the product of reliable principles and methods; and

(d) the expert has reliably applied the principles and methods to the facts of the case.

Rule 703.   BASES OF OPINION TESTIMONY BY EXPERTS

The facts or data in the particular case upon which an expert bases an opinion or inference may be those perceived by or made known to the expert at or before the hearing. If of a type reasonably relied upon by experts in the particular field in forming opinions or inferences upon the subject, the facts or data need not be admissible in evidence in order for the opinion or inference to be admitted. Facts or data that are otherwise inadmissible shall not be disclosed to the jury by the proponent of the opinion or inference unless the court determines that their probative value in assisting the jury to evaluate the expert's opinion substantially outweighs their prejudicial effect.

Rule 704.   OPINION ON ULTIMATE ISSUE

(a) Except as provided in subdivision (b), testimony in the form of an opinion or inference otherwise admissible is not objectionable because it embraces an ultimate issue to be decided by the trier of fact.

(b) No expert witness testifying with respect to the mental state or condition of a defendant in a criminal case may state an opinion or inference as to whether the defendant did or did not have the mental state or condition constituting an element of the crime charged or of a defense thereto. Such ultimate issues are matters for the trier of fact alone.

Rule 705.   DISCLOSURE OF FACTS OR DATA UNDERLYING EXPERT OPINION

The expert may testify in terms of opinion or inference and give reasons therefor without first testifying to the underlying facts or data, unless the court requires otherwise. The expert may in any event be required to disclose the underlying facts or data on cross-examination.

Rule 703.   BASES OF AN EXPERT'S OPINION TESTIMONY

An expert may base an opinion on facts or data in the case that the expert has been made aware of or personally observed. If experts in the particular field would reasonably rely on those kinds of facts or data in forming an opinion on the subject, they need not be admissible for the opinion to be admitted. But if the facts or data would otherwise be inadmissible, the proponent of the opinion may disclose them to the jury only if their probative value in helping the jury evaluate the opinion substantially outweighs their prejudicial effect.

Rule 704.   OPINION ON AN ULTIMATE ISSUE

(a) In General—Not Automatically Objectionable.   An opinion is not objectionable just because it embraces an ultimate issue.

(b) Exception.   In a criminal case, an expert witness must not state an opinion about whether the defendant did or did not have a mental state or condition that constitutes an element of the crime charged or of a defense. Those matters are for the trier of fact alone.

Rule 705.   DISCLOSING THE FACTS OR DATA UNDERLYING AN EXPERT'S OPINION

Unless the court orders otherwise, an expert may state an opinion—and give the reasons for it—without first testifying to the underlying facts or data. But the expert may be required to disclose those facts or data on cross-examination.

Rule 706.   COURT APPOINTED EXPERTS

(a) **Appointment.** The court may on its own motion or on the motion of any party enter an order to show cause why expert witnesses should not be appointed, and may request the parties to submit nominations. The court may appoint any expert witnesses agreed upon by the parties, and may appoint expert witnesses of its own selection. An expert witness shall not be appointed by the court unless the witness consents to act. A witness so appointed shall be informed of the witness' duties by the court in writing, a copy of which shall be filed with the clerk, or at a conference in which the parties shall have opportunity to participate. A witness so appointed shall advise the parties of the witness' findings, if any; the witness' deposition may be taken by any party; and the witness may be called to testify by the court or any party. The witness shall be subject to cross-examination by each party, including a party calling the witness.

(b) **Compensation.**   Expert witnesses so appointed are entitled to reasonable compensation in whatever sum the court may allow. The compensation thus fixed is payable from funds which may be provided by law in criminal cases and civil actions and proceedings involving just compensation under the fifth amendment. In other civil actions and proceedings the compensation shall be paid by the parties in such proportion and at such time as the court directs, and thereafter charged in like manner as other costs.

(c) **Disclosure of appointment.**   In the exercise of its discretion, the court may authorize disclosure to the jury of the fact that the court appointed the expert witness.

(d) **Parties' experts of own selection.** Nothing in this rule limits the parties in calling expert witnesses of their own selection.

Rule 706.   COURT-APPOINTED EXPERT WITNESSES

(a) Appointment Process. On a party's motion or on its own, the court may order the parties to show cause why expert witnesses should not be appointed and may ask the parties to submit nominations. The court may appoint any expert that the parties agree on and any of its own choosing. But the court may only appoint someone who consents to act.

(b) Expert's Role. The court must inform the expert of the expert's duties. The court may do so in writing and have a copy filed with the clerk or may do so orally at a conference in which the parties have an opportunity to participate. The expert:

   (1) must advise the parties of any findings the expert makes;

   (2) may be deposed by any party;

   (3) may be called to testify by the court or any party; and

   (4) may be cross-examined by any party, including the party that called the expert.

(c) Compensation. The expert is entitled to a reasonable compensation, as set by the court. The compensation is payable as follows:

   (1) in a criminal case or in a civil case involving just compensation under the Fifth Amendment, from any funds that are provided by law; and

   (2) in any other civil case, by the parties in the proportion and at the time that the court directs—and the compensation is then charged like other costs.

(d) Disclosing the Appointment to the Jury. The court may authorize disclosure to the jury that the court appointed the expert.

(e) Parties' Choice of Their Own Experts. This rule does not limit a party in calling its own experts.

ARTICLE VIII
HEARSAY

Rule 801.   DEFINITIONS

The following definitions apply under this article:

(a) Statement. A "statement" is (1) an oral or written assertion or (2) nonverbal conduct of a person, if it is intended by the person as an assertion.

(b) Declarant. A "declarant" is a person who makes a statement.

(c) Hearsay. "Hearsay" is a statement, other than one made by the declarant while testifying at the trial or hearing, offered in evidence to prove the truth of the matter asserted.

(d) Statements which are not hearsay. A statement is not hearsay if—

    (1) Prior statement by witness. The declarant testifies at the trial or hearing and is subject to cross-examination concerning the statement, and the statement is (A) inconsistent with the declarant's testimony, and was given under oath subject to the penalty of perjury at a trial, hearing, or other proceeding, or in a deposition, or (B) consistent with the declarant's testimony and is offered to rebut an express or implied charge against the declarant of recent fabrication or improper influence or motive, or (C) one of identification of a person made after perceiving the person; or

ARTICLE VIII
HEARSAY

Rule 801. DEFINITIONS THAT APPLY TO THIS ARTICLE; EXCLUSIONS FROM HEARSAY

(a) Statement. "Statement" means a person's oral assertion, written assertion, or nonverbal conduct, if the person intended it as an assertion.

(b) Declarant. "Declarant" means the person who made the statement.

(c) Hearsay. "Hearsay" means a statement that:

(1) the declarant does not make while testifying at the current trial or hearing; and

(2) a party offers in evidence to prove the truth of the matter asserted in the statement.

(d) Statements That Are Not Hearsay. A statement that meets the following conditions is not hearsay:

(1) *A Declarant-Witness's Prior Statement.* The declarant testifies and is subject to cross-examination about a prior statement, and the statement:

(A) is inconsistent with the declarant's testimony and was given under penalty of perjury at a trial, hearing, or other proceeding or in a deposition;

(B) is consistent with the declarant's testimony and is offered:

(i) to rebut an express or implied charge that the declarant recently fabricated it or acted from a recent improper influence or motive in so testifying; or

(ii) to rehabilitate the declarant's credibility as a witness when attacked on another ground; or

(C) identifies a person as someone the declarant perceived earlier.

(2) Admission by party-opponent. The statement is offered against a party and is (A) the party's own statement, in either an individual or a representative capacity or (B) a statement of which the party has manifested an adoption or belief in its truth, or (C) a statement by a person authorized by the party to make a statement concerning the subject, or (D) a statement by the party's agent or servant concerning a matter within the scope of the agency or employment, made during the existence of the relationship, or (E) a statement by a co-conspirator of a party during the course and in furtherance of the conspiracy. The contents of the statement shall be considered but are not alone sufficient to establish the declarant's authority under subdivision (C), the agency or employment relationship and scope thereof under subdivision (D), or the existence of the conspiracy and the participation therein of the declarant and the party against whom the statement is offered under subdivision (E).

Rule 802.   HEARSAY RULE

Hearsay is not admissible except as provided by these rules or by other rules prescribed by the Supreme Court pursuant to statutory authority or by Act of Congress.

(2) *An Opposing Party's Statement.* The statement is offered against an opposing party and:

(A) was made by the party in an individual or representative capacity;

(B) is one the party manifested that it adopted or believed to be true;

(C) was made by a person whom the party authorized to make a statement on the subject;

(D) was made by the party's agent or employee on a matter within the scope of that relationship and while it existed; or

(E) was made by the party's coconspirator during and in furtherance of the conspiracy.

The statement must be considered but does not by itself establish the declarant's authority under (C); the existence or scope of the relationship under (D); or the existence of the conspiracy or participation in it under (E).

Rule 802.   THE RULE AGAINST HEARSAY

Hearsay is not admissible unless any of the following provides otherwise:

- a federal statute;

- these rules; or

- other rules prescribed by the Supreme Court.

**Rule 803.   HEARSAY   EXCEPTIONS;   AVAILABILITY   OF
            DECLARANT IMMATERIAL**

The following are not excluded by the hearsay rule, even
though the declarant is available as a witness:

(1)   Present sense impression. A statement describing
or explaining an event or condition made while the
declarant was perceiving the event or condition, or
immediately thereafter.

(2)   Excited utterance.   A statement relating to a
startling event or condition made while the declarant was
under the stress of excitement caused by the event or
condition.

**(3)   Then existing mental, emotional, or physical
condition.**   A statement of the declarant's then existing
state of mind, emotion, sensation, or physical condition
(such as intent, plan, motive, design, mental feeling, pain,
and bodily health), but not including a statement of
memory or belief to prove the fact remembered or
believed unless it relates to the execution, revocation,
identification, or terms of declarant's will.

**(4)   Statements for purposes of medical diagnosis or
treatment.**   Statements made for purposes of medical
diagnosis or treatment and describing medical history, or
past or present symptoms, pain, or sensations, or the
inception or general character of the cause or external
source thereof insofar as reasonably pertinent to diagnosis
or treatment.

Rule 803.   EXCEPTIONS TO THE RULE AGAINST HEARSAY— REGARDLESS OF WHETHER THE DECLARANT IS AVAILABLE AS A WITNESS

The following are not excluded by the rule against hearsay, regardless of whether the declarant is available as a witness:

(1) *Present Sense Impression.* A statement describing or explaining an event or condition, made while or immediately after the declarant perceived it.

(2) *Excited Utterance.* A statement relating to a startling event or condition, made while the declarant was under the stress of excitement that it caused.

(3) *Then-Existing Mental, Emotional, or Physical Condition.* A statement of the declarant's then-existing state of mind (such as motive, intent, or plan) or emotional, sensory, or physical condition (such as mental feeling, pain, or bodily health), but not including a statement of memory or belief to prove the fact remembered or believed unless it relates to the validity or terms of the declarant's will.

(4) *Statement Made for Medical Diagnosis or Treatment.* A statement that:

(A) is made for—and is reasonably pertinent to— medical diagnosis or treatment; and

(B) describes medical history; past or present symptoms or sensations; their inception; or their general cause.

(5) Recorded recollection. A memorandum or record concerning a matter about which a witness once had knowledge but now has insufficient recollection to enable the witness to testify fully and accurately, shown to have been made or adopted by the witness when the matter was fresh in the witness' memory and to reflect that knowledge correctly. If admitted, the memorandum or record may be read into evidence but may not itself be received as an exhibit unless offered by an adverse party.

(5) *Recorded Recollection.* A record that:

    (A) is on a matter the witness once knew about but now cannot recall well enough to testify fully and accurately;

    (B) was made or adopted by the witness when the matter was fresh in the witness's memory; and

    (C) accurately reflects the witness's knowledge.

If admitted, the record may be read into evidence but may be received as an exhibit only if offered by an adverse party.

Editor's Note

A subtle change in syntax makes paragraph (C) of Rule 803(5) a bit less sensible. As I believe the unrestyled rule made clear, the proponent must show that the record *when made* accurately reflected the witness's knowledge. As restyled, the rule seems to require that the record accurately reflects the witness's *present* knowledge. That requirement makes little sense, as paragraph (A) demands insufficient recall. *See* CHRISTOPHER B. MUELLER & LAIRD C. KIRKPATRICK, EVIDENCE § 8.43, at 889 (5th ed. 2012) ("Necessarily the witness has forgotten various aspects of the acts, events, or conditions he described before, and often has little memory about the statement itself.").—GF

(6) Records of regularly conducted activity. A memorandum, report, record, or data compilation, in any form, of acts, events, conditions, opinions, or diagnoses, made at or near the time by, or from information transmitted by, a person with knowledge, if kept in the course of a regularly conducted business activity, and if it was the regular practice of that business activity to make the memorandum, report, record, or data compilation, all as shown by the testimony of the custodian or other qualified witness, or by certification that complies with Rule 902(11), Rule 902(12), or a statute permitting certification, unless the source of information or the method or circumstances of preparation indicate lack of trustworthiness. The term "business" as used in this paragraph includes business, institution, association, profession, occupation, and calling of every kind, whether or not conducted for profit.

(7) Absence of entry in records kept in accordance with the provisions of paragraph (6). Evidence that a matter is not included in the memoranda, reports, records, or data compilations, in any form, kept in accordance with the provisions of paragraph (6), to prove the nonoccurrence or nonexistence of the matter, if the matter was of a kind of which a memorandum, report, record, or data compilation was regularly made and preserved, unless the sources of information or other circumstances indicate lack of trustworthiness.

(6) *Records of a Regularly Conducted Activity.* A record of an act, event, condition, opinion, or diagnosis if:

(A) the record was made at or near the time by—or from information transmitted by—someone with knowledge;

(B) the record was kept in the course of a regularly conducted activity of a business, organization, occupation, or calling, whether or not for profit;

(C) making the record was a regular practice of that activity;

(D) all these conditions are shown by the testimony of the custodian or another qualified witness, or by a certification that complies with Rule 902(11) or (12) or with a statute permitting certification; and

(E) the opponent does not show that the source of information or the method or circumstances of preparation indicate a lack of trustworthiness.

(7) *Absence of a Record of a Regularly Conducted Activity.* Evidence that a matter is not included in a record described in paragraph (6) if:

(A) the evidence is admitted to prove that the matter did not occur or exist;

(B) a record was regularly kept for a matter of that kind; and

(C) the opponent does not show that the possible source of the information or other circumstances indicate a lack of trustworthiness.

(8) Public records and reports. Records, reports, statements, or data compilations, in any form, of public offices or agencies, setting forth (A) the activities of the office or agency, or (B) matters observed pursuant to duty imposed by law as to which matters there was a duty to report, excluding, however, in criminal cases matters observed by police officers and other law enforcement personnel, or (C) in civil actions and proceedings and against the Government in criminal cases, factual findings resulting from an investigation made pursuant to authority granted by law, unless the sources of information or other circumstances indicate lack of trustworthiness.

(9) Records of vital statistics. Records or data compilations, in any form, of births, fetal deaths, deaths, or marriages, if the report thereof was made to a public office pursuant to requirements of law.

(10) Absence of public record or entry. To prove the absence of a record, report, statement, or data compilation, in any form, or the nonoccurrence or nonexistence of a matter of which a record, report, statement, or data compilation, in any form, was regularly made and preserved by a public office or agency, evidence in the form of a certification in accordance with rule 902, or testimony, that diligent search failed to disclose the record, report, statement, or data compilation, or entry.

(11) Records of religious organizations. Statements of births, marriages, divorces, deaths, legitimacy, ancestry, relationship by blood or marriage, or other similar facts of personal or family history, contained in a regularly kept record of a religious organization.

(8) Public Records. A record or statement of a public office if:

    (A) it sets out:

        (i)   the office's activities;

        (ii) a matter observed while under a legal duty to report, but not including, in a criminal case, a matter observed by law-enforcement personnel; or

        (iii) in a civil case or against the government in a criminal case, factual findings from a legally authorized investigation; and

    (B) the opponent does not show that the source of information or other circumstances indicate a lack of trustworthiness.

(9) Public Records of Vital Statistics. A record of a birth, death, or marriage, if reported to a public office in accordance with a legal duty.

(10) Absence of a Public Record.   Testimony—or a certification under Rule 902—that a diligent search failed to disclose a public record or statement if:

    (A) the testimony or certification is admitted to prove that

        (i) the record or statement does not exist; or

        (ii) a matter did not occur or exist, if a public office regularly kept a record or statement for a matter of that kind; and

    (B) in a criminal case, a prosecutor who intends to offer a certification provides written notice of that intent at least 14 days before trial, and the defendant does not object in writing within 7 days of receiving the notice—unless the court sets a different time for the notice or objection.

(11) Records of Religious Organizations Concerning Personal or Family History. A statement of birth, legitimacy, ancestry, marriage, divorce, death, relationship by blood or marriage, or similar facts of personal or family history, contained in a regularly kept record of a religious organization.

(12) Marriage, baptismal, and similar certificates. Statements of fact contained in a certificate that the maker performed a marriage or other ceremony or administered a sacrament, made by a clergyman, public official, or other person authorized by the rules or practices of a religious organization or by law to perform the act certified, and purporting to have been issued at the time of the act or within a reasonable time thereafter.

(13) Family records. Statements of fact concerning personal or family history contained in family Bibles, genealogies, charts, engravings on rings, inscriptions on family portraits, engravings on urns, crypts, or tombstones, or the like.

(14) Records of documents affecting an interest in property. The record of a document purporting to establish or affect an interest in property, as proof of the content of the original recorded document and its execution and delivery by each person by whom it purports to have been executed, if the record is a record of a public office and an applicable statute authorizes the recording of documents of that kind in that office.

(15) Statements in documents affecting an interest in property. A statement contained in a document purporting to establish or affect an interest in property if the matter stated was relevant to the purpose of the document, unless dealings with the property since the document was made have been inconsistent with the truth of the statement or the purport of the document.

(16) Statements in ancient documents. Statements in a document in existence twenty years or more the authenticity of which is established.

(17) Market reports, commercial publications. Market quotations, tabulations, lists, directories, or other published compilations, generally used and relied upon by the public or by persons in particular occupations.

(12) *Certificates of Marriage, Baptism, and Similar Ceremonies.* A statement of fact contained in a certificate:

    (A) made by a person who is authorized by a religious organization or by law to perform the act certified;

    (B) attesting that the person performed a marriage or similar ceremony or administered a sacrament; and

    (C) purporting to have been issued at the time of the act or within a reasonable time after it.

(13) *Family Records.* A statement of fact about personal or family history contained in a family record, such as a Bible, genealogy, chart, engraving on a ring, inscription on a portrait, or engraving on an urn or burial marker.

(14) *Records of Documents That Affect an Interest in Property.* The record of a document that purports to establish or affect an interest in property if:

    (A) the record is admitted to prove the content of the original recorded document, along with its signing and its delivery by each person who purports to have signed it;

    (B) the record is kept in a public office; and

    (C) a statute authorizes recording documents of that kind in that office.

(15) *Statements in Documents That Affect an Interest in Property.* A statement contained in a document that purports to establish or affect an interest in property if the matter stated was relevant to the document's purpose—unless later dealings with the property are inconsistent with the truth of the statement or the purport of the document.

(16) *Statements in Ancient Documents.* A statement in a document that was prepared before January 1, 1998, and whose authenticity is established.

(17) *Market Reports and Similar Commercial Publications.* Market quotations, lists, directories, or other compilations that are generally relied on by the public or by persons in particular occupations.

(18) Learned treatises.   To the extent called to the attention of an expert witness upon cross-examination or relied upon by the expert witness in direct examination, statements contained in published treatises, periodicals, or pamphlets on a subject of history, medicine, or other science or art, established as a reliable authority by the testimony or admission of the witness or by other expert testimony or by judicial notice. If admitted, the statements may be read into evidence but may not be received as exhibits.

(19) Reputation concerning personal or family history.   Reputation among members of a person's family by blood, adoption, or marriage, or among a person's associates, or in the community, concerning a person's birth, adoption, marriage, divorce, death, legitimacy, relationship by blood, adoption, or marriage, ancestry, or other similar fact of personal or family history.

(20) Reputation concerning boundaries or general history.   Reputation in a community, arising before the controversy, as to boundaries of or customs affecting lands in the community, and reputation as to events of general history important to the community or State or nation in which located.

(21) Reputation as to character.   Reputation of a person's character among associates or in the community.

(18) *Statements in Learned Treatises, Periodicals, or Pamphlets.* A statement contained in a treatise, periodical, or pamphlet if:

(A) the statement is called to the attention of an expert witness on cross-examination or relied on by the expert on direct examination; and

(B) the publication is established as a reliable authority by the expert's admission or testimony, by another expert's testimony, or by judicial notice.

If admitted, the statement may be read into evidence but not received as an exhibit.

(19) *Reputation Concerning Personal or Family History.* A reputation among a person's family by blood, adoption, or marriage—or among a person's associates or in the community—concerning the person's birth, adoption, legitimacy, ancestry, marriage, divorce, death, relationship by blood, adoption, or marriage, or similar facts of personal or family history.

(20) *Reputation Concerning Boundaries or General History.* A reputation in a community—arising before the controversy—concerning boundaries of land in the community or customs that affect the land, or concerning general historical events important to that community, state, or nation.

(21) *Reputation Concerning Character.* A reputation among a person's associates or in the community concerning the person's character.

(22) Judgment of previous conviction. Evidence of a final judgment, entered after a trial or upon a plea of guilty (but not upon a plea of nolo contendere), adjudging a person guilty of a crime punishable by death or imprisonment in excess of one year, to prove any fact essential to sustain the judgment, but not including, when offered by the Government in a criminal prosecution for purposes other than impeachment, judgments against persons other than the accused. The pendency of an appeal may be shown but does not affect admissibility.

(23) Judgment as to personal, family, or general history, or boundaries. Judgments as proof of matters of personal, family or general history, or boundaries, essential to the judgment, if the same would be provable by evidence of reputation.

(24) [Other exceptions] [Transferred to Rule 807]

(22) *Judgment of a Previous Conviction.* Evidence of a final judgment of conviction if:

    (A) the judgment was entered after a trial or guilty plea, but not a nolo contendere plea;

    (B) the conviction was for a crime punishable by death or by imprisonment for more than a year;

    (C) the evidence is admitted to prove any fact essential to the judgment; and

    (D) when offered by the prosecutor in a criminal case for a purpose other than impeachment, the judgment was against the defendant.

The pendency of an appeal may be shown but does not affect admissibility.

(23) *Judgments Involving Personal, Family, or General History, or a Boundary.* A judgment that is admitted to prove a matter of personal, family, or general history, or boundaries, if the matter:

    (A) was essential to the judgment; and

    (B) could be proved by evidence of reputation.

(24) *[Other Exceptions.]* [Transferred to Rule 807.]

Rule 804.   HEARSAY EXCEPTIONS; DECLARANT UNAVAILABLE

(a) Definition of unavailability.   "Unavailability as a witness" includes situations in which the declarant—

(1) is exempted by ruling of the court on the ground of privilege from testifying concerning the subject matter of the declarant's statement; or

(2) persists in refusing to testify concerning the subject matter of the declarant's statement despite an order of the court to do so; or

(3) testifies to a lack of memory of the subject matter of the declarant's statement; or

(4) is unable to be present or to testify at the hearing because of death or then existing physical or mental illness or infirmity; or

(5) is absent from the hearing and the proponent of a statement has been unable to procure the declarant's attendance (or in the case of a hearsay exception under subdivision (b)(2), (3), or (4), the declarant's attendance or testimony) by process or other reasonable means.

A declarant is not unavailable as a witness if exemption, refusal, claim of lack of memory, inability, or absence is due to the procurement or wrongdoing of the proponent of a statement for the purpose of preventing the witness from attending or testifying.

Rule 804.   EXCEPTIONS TO THE RULE AGAINST HEARSAY—WHEN THE DECLARANT IS UNAVAILABLE AS A WITNESS.

(a) Criteria for Being Unavailable.   A declarant is considered to be unavailable as a witness if the declarant:

(1) is exempted from testifying about the subject matter of the declarant's statement because the court rules that a privilege applies;

(2) refuses to testify about the subject matter despite a court order to do so;

(3) testifies to not remembering the subject matter;

(4) cannot be present or testify at the trial or hearing because of death or a then-existing infirmity, physical illness, or mental illness; or

(5) is absent from the trial or hearing and the statement's proponent has not been able, by process or other reasonable means, to procure:

(A) the declarant's attendance, in the case of a hearsay exception under Rule 804(b)(1) or (6); or

(B) the declarant's attendance or testimony, in the case of a hearsay exception under Rule 804(b)(2), (3), or (4).

But this subdivision (a) does not apply if the statement's proponent procured or wrongfully caused the declarant's unavailability as a witness in order to prevent the declarant from attending or testifying.

(b) Hearsay exceptions. The following are not excluded by the hearsay rule if the declarant is unavailable as a witness:

(1) Former testimony. Testimony given as a witness at another hearing of the same or a different proceeding, or in a deposition taken in compliance with law in the course of the same or another proceeding, if the party against whom the testimony is now offered, or, in a civil action or proceeding, a predecessor in interest, had an opportunity and similar motive to develop the testimony by direct, cross, or redirect examination.

(2) Statement under belief of impending death. In a prosecution for homicide or in a civil action or proceeding, a statement made by a declarant while believing that the declarant's death was imminent, concerning the cause or circumstances of what the declarant believed to be impending death.

(3) Statement against interest. A statement that:

(A) a reasonable person in the declarant's position would have made only if the person believed it to be true because, when made, it was so contrary to the declarant's proprietary or pecuniary interest or had so great a tendency to invalidate the declarant's claim against someone else or to expose the declarant to civil or criminal liability; and

(B) is supported by corroborating circumstances that clearly indicate its trustworthiness, if it is offered in a criminal case as one that tends to expose the declarant to criminal liability.

(b) The Exceptions. The following are not excluded by the rule against hearsay if the declarant is unavailable as a witness:

(1) *Former Testimony.* Testimony that:

(A) was given as a witness at a trial, hearing, or lawful deposition, whether given during the current proceeding or a different one; and

(B) is now offered against a party who had—or, in a civil case, whose predecessor in interest had—an opportunity and similar motive to develop it by direct, cross-, or redirect examination.

(2) *Statement Under the Belief of Imminent Death.* In a prosecution for homicide or in a civil case, a statement that the declarant, while believing the declarant's death to be imminent, made about its cause or circumstances.

(3) *Statement Against Interest.* A statement that:

(A) a reasonable person in the declarant's position would have made only if the person believed it to be true because, when made, it was so contrary to the declarant's proprietary or pecuniary interest or had so great a tendency to invalidate the declarant's claim against someone else or to expose the declarant to civil or criminal liability; and

(B) is supported by corroborating circumstances that clearly indicate its trustworthiness, if it is offered in a criminal case as one that tends to expose the declarant to criminal liability.

(4) Statement of personal or family history. (A) A statement concerning the declarant's own birth, adoption, marriage, divorce, legitimacy, relationship by blood, adoption, or marriage, ancestry, or other similar fact of personal or family history, even though declarant had no means of acquiring personal knowledge of the matter stated; or (B) a statement concerning the foregoing matters, and death also, of another person, if the declarant was related to the other by blood, adoption, or marriage or was so intimately associated with the other's family as to be likely to have accurate information concerning the matter declared.

(5) [Other exceptions] [Transferred to Rule 807]

(6) Forfeiture by wrongdoing. A statement offered against a party that has engaged or acquiesced in wrongdoing that was intended to, and did, procure the unavailability of the declarant as a witness.

(4) Statement of Personal or Family History. A statement about:

(A) the declarant's own birth, adoption, legitimacy, ancestry, marriage, divorce, relationship by blood, adoption, or marriage, or similar facts of personal or family history, even though the declarant had no way of acquiring personal knowledge about that fact; or

(B) another person concerning any of these facts, as well as death, if the declarant was related to the person by blood, adoption, or marriage or was so intimately associated with the person's family that the declarant's information is likely to be accurate.

(5) [Other Exceptions.] [Transferred to Rule 807.]

(6) Statement Offered Against a Party That Wrongfully Caused the Declarant's Unavailability. A statement offered against a party that wrongfully caused—or acquiesced in wrongfully causing—the declarant's unavailability as a witness, and did so intending that result.

Rule 805.   HEARSAY WITHIN HEARSAY

Hearsay included within hearsay is not excluded under the hearsay rule if each part of the combined statements conforms with an exception to the hearsay rule provided in these rules.

Rule 806.   ATTACKING AND SUPPORTING CREDIBILITY OF DECLARANT

When a hearsay statement, or a statement defined in Rule 801(d)(2), (C), (D), or (E), has been admitted in evidence, the credibility of the declarant may be attacked, and if attacked may be supported, by any evidence which would be admissible for those purposes if declarant had testified as a witness. Evidence of a statement or conduct by the declarant at any time, inconsistent with the declarant's hearsay statement, is not subject to any requirement that the declarant may have been afforded an opportunity to deny or explain. If the party against whom a hearsay statement has been admitted calls the declarant as a witness, the party is entitled to examine the declarant on the statement as if under cross-examination.

Rule 805.   HEARSAY WITHIN HEARSAY

Hearsay within hearsay is not excluded by the rule against hearsay if each part of the combined statements conforms with an exception to the rule.

Rule 806.   ATTACKING AND SUPPORTING THE DECLARANT'S CREDIBILITY

When a hearsay statement—or a statement described in Rule 801(d)(2)(C), (D), or (E)—has been admitted in evidence, the declarant's credibility may be attacked, and then supported, by any evidence that would be admissible for those purposes if the declarant had testified as a witness. The court may admit evidence of the declarant's inconsistent statement or conduct, regardless of when it occurred or whether the declarant had an opportunity to explain or deny it. If the party against whom the statement was admitted calls the declarant as a witness, the party may examine the declarant on the statement as if on cross-examination.

Rule 807.   RESIDUAL EXCEPTION

A statement not specifically covered by Rule 803 or 804, but having equivalent circumstantial guarantees of trustworthiness, is not excluded by the hearsay rule if the court determines that (A) the statement is offered as evidence of a material fact; (B) the statement is more probative on the point for which it is offered than any other evidence which the proponent can procure through reasonable efforts; and (C) the general purposes of these rules and the interests of justice will best be served by admission of the statement into evidence. However, a statement may not be admitted under this exception unless the proponent of it makes known to the adverse party sufficiently in advance of the trial or hearing to provide the adverse party with a fair opportunity to prepare to meet it, the proponent's intention to offer the statement and the particulars of it, including the name and address of the declarant.

Rule 807. RESIDUAL EXCEPTION

(a) In General. Under the following circumstances, a hearsay statement is not excluded by the rule against hearsay even if the statement is not specifically covered by a hearsay exception in Rule 803 or 804:

    (1) the statement has equivalent circumstantial guarantees of trustworthiness;

    (2) it is offered as evidence of a material fact;

    (3) it is more probative on the point for which it is offered than any other evidence that the proponent can obtain through reasonable efforts; and

    (4) admitting it will best serve the purposes of these rules and the interests of justice.

(b) Notice. The statement is admissible only if, before the trial or hearing, the proponent gives an adverse party reasonable notice of the intent to offer the statement and its particulars, including the declarant's name and address, so that the party has a fair opportunity to meet it.

Editor's Note

A slight word change seems to have settled the dispute among the judges in *United States v. Laster*, 258 F.3d 525 (6th Cir. 2001), discussed in the casebook at pages 582 to 584. At issue was the "near-miss" theory of the residual exception— the "'doctrine that a "near miss" under a specified exception . . . renders evidence inadmissible under [the] residual exception.'" United States v. Clarke, 2 F.3d 81, 84 (4th Cir. 1993), *quoted in Laster* (Moore, J., dissenting).

The unrestyled rule's opening, "[a] statement not specifically covered by Rule 803 or 804," arguably suggested, for example, that a business record that did not meet every precondition of Rule 803(6) but *was covered* by that rule couldn't gain admission under Rule 807. As restyled, Rule 807 welcomes any statement, *"even if* the statement is not specifically covered by a hearsay exception in Rule 803 or 804," if it meets Rule 807's other conditions.—GF

ARTICLE IX
AUTHENTICATION AND IDENTIFICATION

Rule 901. **REQUIREMENT OF AUTHENTICATION OR IDENTIFICATION**

(a) General provision. The requirement of authentication or identification as a condition precedent to admissibility is satisfied by evidence sufficient to support a finding that the matter in question is what its proponent claims.

(b) Illustrations. By way of illustration only, and not by way of limitation, the following are examples of authentication or identification conforming with the requirements of this rule:

(1) Testimony of witness with knowledge. Testimony that a matter is what it is claimed to be.

(2) Nonexpert opinion on handwriting. Nonexpert opinion as to the genuineness of handwriting, based upon familiarity not acquired for purposes of the litigation.

(3) Comparison by trier or expert witness. Comparison by the trier of fact or by expert witnesses with specimens which have been authenticated.

(4) Distinctive characteristics and the like. Appearance, contents, substance, internal patterns, or other distinctive characteristics, taken in conjunction with circumstances.

(5) Voice identification. Identification of a voice, whether heard firsthand or through mechanical or electronic transmission or recording, by opinion based upon hearing the voice at any time under circumstances connecting it with the alleged speaker.

ARTICLE IX
AUTHENTICATION AND IDENTIFICATION

Rule 901.   AUTHENTICATING OR IDENTIFYING EVIDENCE

(a) In General. To satisfy the requirement of authenticating or identifying an item of evidence, the proponent must produce evidence sufficient to support a finding that the item is what the proponent claims it is.

(b) Examples. The following are examples only—not a complete list—of evidence that satisfies the requirement:

(1) *Testimony of a Witness with Knowledge.* Testimony that an item is what it is claimed to be.

(2) *Nonexpert Opinion About Handwriting.* A nonexpert's opinion that handwriting is genuine, based on a familiarity with it that was not acquired for the current litigation.

(3) *Comparison by an Expert Witness or the Trier of Fact.* A comparison with an authenticated specimen by an expert witness or the trier of fact.

(4) *Distinctive Characteristics and the Like.* The appearance, contents, substance, internal patterns, or other distinctive characteristics of the item, taken together with all the circumstances.

(5) *Opinion About a Voice.* An opinion identifying a person's voice—whether heard firsthand or through mechanical or electronic transmission or recording—based on hearing the voice at any time under circumstances that connect it with the alleged speaker.

(6) Telephone conversations. Telephone conversations, by evidence that a call was made to the number assigned at the time by the telephone company to a particular person or business, if (A) in the case of a person, circumstances, including self-identification, show the person answering to be the one called, or (B) in the case of a business, the call was made to a place of business and the conversation related to business reasonably transacted over the telephone.

(7) Public records or reports. Evidence that a writing authorized by law to be recorded or filed and in fact recorded or filed in a public office, or a purported public record, report, statement, or data compilation, in any form, is from the public office where items of this nature are kept.

(8) Ancient documents or data compilation. Evidence that a document or data compilation, in any form, (A) is in such condition as to create no suspicion concerning its authenticity, (B) was in a place where it, if authentic, would likely be, and (C) has been in existence 20 years or more at the time it is offered.

(9) Process or system. Evidence describing a process or system used to produce a result and showing that the process or system produces an accurate result.

(10) Methods provided by statute or rule. Any method of authentication or identification provided by Act of Congress or by other rules prescribed by the Supreme Court pursuant to statutory authority.

(6) *Evidence About a Telephone Conversation.* For a telephone conversation, evidence that a call was made to the number assigned at the time to:

(A) a particular person, if circumstances, including self-identification, show that the person answering was the one called; or

(B) a particular business, if the call was made to a business and the call related to business reasonably transacted over the telephone.

(7) *Evidence About Public Records.* Evidence that:

(A) a document was recorded or filed in a public office as authorized by law; or

(B) a purported public record or statement is from the office where items of this kind are kept.

(8) *Evidence About Ancient Documents or Data Compilations.* For a document or data compilation, evidence that it:

(A) is in a condition that creates no suspicion about its authenticity;

(B) was in a place where, if authentic, it would likely be; and

(C) is at least 20 years old when offered.

(9) *Evidence About a Process or System.* Evidence describing a process or system and showing that it produces an accurate result.

(10) *Methods Provided by a Statute or Rule.* Any method of authentication or identification allowed by a federal statute or a rule prescribed by the Supreme Court.

Rule 902.   SELF-AUTHENTICATION

Extrinsic evidence of authenticity as a condition precedent to admissibility is not required with respect to the following:

(1) Domestic public documents under seal.   A document bearing a seal purporting to be that of the United States, or of any State, district, Commonwealth, territory, or insular possession thereof, or the Panama Canal Zone, or the Trust Territory of the Pacific Islands, or of a political subdivision, department, officer, or agency thereof, and a signature purporting to be an attestation or execution.

(2) Domestic public documents not under seal.   A document purporting to bear the signature in the official capacity of an officer or employee of any entity included in paragraph (1) hereof, having no seal, if a public officer having a seal and having official duties in the district or political subdivision of the officer or employee certifies under seal that the signer has the official capacity and that the signature is genuine.

Rule 902.   EVIDENCE THAT IS SELF-AUTHENTICATING

The following items of evidence are self-authenticating; they require no extrinsic evidence of authenticity in order to be admitted:

(1) *Domestic Public Documents That Are Sealed and Signed.* A document that bears:

(A) a seal purporting to be that of the United States; any state, district, commonwealth, territory, or insular possession of the United States; the former Panama Canal Zone; the Trust Territory of the Pacific Islands; a political subdivision of any of these entities; or a department, agency, or officer of any entity named above; and

(B) a signature purporting to be an execution or attestation.

(2) *Domestic Public Documents That Are Not Sealed but Are Signed and Certified.* A document that bears no seal if:

(A) it bears the signature of an officer or employee of an entity named in Rule 902(1)(A); and

(B) another public officer who has a seal and official duties within that same entity certifies under seal—or its equivalent—that the signer has the official capacity and that the signature is genuine.

(3) Foreign public documents. A document purporting to be executed or attested in an official capacity by a person authorized by the laws of a foreign country to make the execution or attestation, and accompanied by a final certification as to the genuineness of the signature and official position (A) of the executing or attesting person, or (B) of any foreign official whose certificate of genuineness of signature and official position relates to the execution or attestation or is in a chain of certificates of genuineness of signature and official position relating to the execution or attestation. A final certification may be made by a secretary of an embassy or legation, consul general, consul, vice consul, or consular agent of the United States, or a diplomatic or consular official of the foreign country assigned or accredited to the United States. If reasonable opportunity has been given to all parties to investigate the authenticity and accuracy of official documents, the court may, for good cause shown, order that they be treated as presumptively authentic without final certification or permit them to be evidenced by an attested summary with or without final certification.

(4) Certified copies of public records. A copy of an official record or report or entry therein, or of a document authorized by law to be recorded or filed and actually recorded or filed in a public office, including data compilations in any form, certified as correct by the custodian or other person authorized to make the certification, by certificate complying with paragraph (1), (2), or (3) of this rule or complying with any Act of Congress or rule prescribed by the Supreme Court pursuant to statutory authority.

(5) Official publications. Books, pamphlets, or other publications purporting to be issued by public authority.

(6) Newspapers and periodicals. Printed materials purporting to be newspapers or periodicals.

(7) Trade inscriptions and the like. Inscriptions, signs, tags, or labels purporting to have been affixed in the course of business and indicating ownership, control, or origin.

(3) *Foreign Public Documents.* A document that purports to be signed or attested by a person who is authorized by a foreign country's law to do so. The document must be accompanied by a final certification that certifies the genuineness of the signature and official position of the signer or attester—or of any foreign official whose certificate of genuineness relates to the signature or attestation or is in a chain of certificates of genuineness relating to the signature or attestation. The certification may be made by a secretary of a United States embassy or legation; by a consul general, vice consul, or consular agent of the United States; or by a diplomatic or consular official of the foreign country assigned or accredited to the United States. If all parties have been given a reasonable opportunity to investigate the document's authenticity and accuracy, the court may, for good cause, either:

    (A) order that it be treated as presumptively authentic without final certification; or

    (B) allow it to be evidenced by an attested summary with or without final certification.

(4) *Certified Copies of Public Records.* A copy of an official record—or a copy of a document that was recorded or filed in a public office as authorized by law—if the copy is certified as correct by:

    (A) the custodian or another person authorized to make the certification; or

    (B) a certificate that complies with Rule 902(1), (2), or (3), a federal statute, or a rule prescribed by the Supreme Court.

(5) *Official Publications.* A book, pamphlet, or other publication purporting to be issued by a public authority.

(6) *Newspapers and Periodicals.* Printed material purporting to be a newspaper or periodical.

(7) *Trade Inscriptions and the Like.* An inscription, sign, tag, or label purporting to have been affixed in the course of business and indicating origin, ownership, or control.

(8) Acknowledged documents. Documents accompanied by a certificate of acknowledgment executed in the manner provided by law by a notary public or other officer authorized by law to take acknowledgments.

(9) Commercial paper and related documents. Commercial paper, signatures thereon, and documents relating thereto to the extent provided by general commercial law.

(10) Presumptions under Acts of Congress. Any signature, document, or other matter declared by Act of Congress to be presumptively or prima facie genuine or authentic.

(11) Certified domestic records of regularly conducted activity. The original or a duplicate of a domestic record of regularly conducted activity that would be admissible under Rule 803(6) if accompanied by a written declaration of its custodian or other qualified person, in a manner complying with any Act of Congress or rule prescribed by the Supreme Court pursuant to statutory authority, certifying that the record—

(A) was made at or near the time of the occurrence of the matters set forth by, or from information transmitted by, a person with knowledge of those matters;

(B) was kept in the course of regularly conducted activity; and

(C) was made by the regularly conducted activity as a regular practice.

A party intending to offer a record into evidence under this paragraph must provide written notice of that intention to all adverse parties, and must make the record and declaration available for inspection sufficiently in advance of their offer into evidence to provide an adverse party with a fair opportunity to challenge them.

(8) *Acknowledged Documents.* A document accompanied by a certificate of acknowledgment that is lawfully executed by a notary public or another officer who is authorized to take acknowledgments.

(9) *Commercial Paper and Related Documents.* Commercial paper, a signature on it, and related documents, to the extent allowed by general commercial law.

(10) *Presumptions Under a Federal Statute.* A signature, document, or anything else that a federal statute declares to be presumptively or prima facie genuine or authentic.

(11) *Certified Domestic Records of a Regularly Conducted Activity.* The original or a copy of a domestic record that meets the requirements of Rule 803(6)(A)–(C), as shown by a certification of the custodian or another qualified person that complies with a federal statute or a rule prescribed by the Supreme Court. Before the trial or hearing, the proponent must give an adverse party reasonable written notice of the intent to offer the record—and must make the record and certification available for inspection—so that the party has a fair opportunity to challenge them.

(12) Certified foreign records of regularly conducted activity. In a civil case, the original or duplicate of a foreign record of regularly conducted activity that would be admissible under Rule 803(6) if accompanied by a written declaration by its custodian or other qualified person certifying that the record—

> **(A)** was made at or near the time of the occurrence of the matters set forth by, or from information transmitted by, a person with knowledge of those matters;

> **(B)** was kept in the course of the regularly conducted activity; and

> **(C)** was made by the regularly conducted activity as a regular practice.

The declaration must be signed in a manner that, if falsely made, would subject the maker to criminal penalty under the laws of the country where the declaration is signed. A party intending to offer a record into evidence under this paragraph must provide written notice of that intention to all adverse parties, and must make the record and declaration available for inspection sufficiently in advance of their offer into evidence to provide an adverse party with a fair opportunity to challenge them.

Rule 903.   SUBSCRIBING WITNESS' TESTIMONY UNNECESSARY

The testimony of a subscribing witness is not necessary to authenticate a writing unless required by the laws of the jurisdiction whose laws govern the validity of the writing.

(12) *Certified Foreign Records of a Regularly Conducted Activity.* In a civil case, the original or a copy of a foreign record that meets the requirements of Rule 902(11), modified as follows: the certification, rather than complying with a federal statute or Supreme Court rule, must be signed in a manner that, if falsely made, would subject the maker to a criminal penalty in the country where the certification is signed. The proponent must also meet the notice requirements of Rule 902(11).

(13) Certified Records Generated by an Electronic Process or System. A record generated by an electronic process or system that produces an accurate result, as shown by a certification of a qualified person that complies with the certification requirements of Rule 902(11) or (12). The proponent must also meet the notice requirements of Rule 902(11).

(14) Certified Data Copied from an Electronic Device, Storage Medium, or File. Data copied from an electronic device, storage medium, or file, if authenticated by a process of digital identification, as shown by a certification of a qualified person that complies with the certification requirements of Rule 902(11) or (12). The proponent also must meet the notice requirements of Rule 902(11).

Rule 903.   SUBSCRIBING WITNESS'S TESTIMONY

A subscribing witness's testimony is necessary to authenticate a writing only if required by the law of the jurisdiction that governs its validity.

ARTICLE X
CONTENTS OF WRITINGS, RECORDINGS, AND PHOTOGRAPHS

Rule 1001. DEFINITIONS

For purposes of this article the following definitions are applicable:

(1) Writings and recordings. "Writings" and "recordings" consist of letters, words, or numbers, or their equivalent, set down by handwriting, typewriting, printing, photostating, photographing, magnetic impulse, mechanical or electronic recording, or other form of data compilation.

(2) Photographs. "Photographs" include still photographs, X-ray films, video tapes, and motion pictures.

(3) Original. An "original" of a writing or recording is the writing or recording itself or any counterpart intended to have the same effect by a person executing or issuing it. An "original" of a photograph includes the negative or any print therefrom. If data are stored in a computer or similar device, any printout or other output readable by sight, shown to reflect the data accurately, is an "original".

(4) Duplicate. A "duplicate" is a counterpart produced by the same impression as the original, or from the same matrix, or by means of photography, including enlargements and miniatures, or by mechanical or electronic re-recording, or by chemical reproduction, or by other equivalent techniques which accurately reproduces the original.

Rule 1002. REQUIREMENT OF ORIGINAL

To prove the content of a writing, recording, or photograph, the original writing, recording, or photograph is required, except as otherwise provided in these rules or by Act of Congress.

ARTICLE X
CONTENTS OF WRITINGS, RECORDINGS, AND PHOTOGRAPHS

Rule 1001. DEFINITIONS THAT APPLY TO THIS ARTICLE

In this article:

(a) A "writing" consists of letters, words, numbers, or their equivalent set down in any form.

(b) A "recording" consists of letters, words, numbers, or their equivalent recorded in any manner.

(c) A "photograph" means a photographic image or its equivalent stored in any form.

(d) An "original" of a writing or recording means the writing or recording itself or any counterpart intended to have the same effect by the person who executed or issued it. For electronically stored information, "original" means any printout—or other output readable by sight—if it accurately reflects the information. An "original" of a photograph includes the negative or a print from it.

(e) A "duplicate" means a counterpart produced by a mechanical, photographic, chemical, electronic, or other equivalent process or technique that accurately reproduces the original.

Rule 1002. REQUIREMENT OF THE ORIGINAL

An original writing, recording, or photograph is required in order to prove its content unless these rules or a federal statute provides otherwise.

Rule 1003.　ADMISSIBILITY OF DUPLICATES

A duplicate is admissible to the same extent as an original unless (1) a genuine question is raised as to the authenticity of the original or (2) in the circumstances it would be unfair to admit the duplicate in lieu of the original.

Rule 1004.　ADMISSIBILITY OF OTHER EVIDENCE OF CONTENTS

The original is not required, and other evidence of the contents of a writing, recording, or photograph is admissible if—

(1) Originals lost or destroyed.　All originals are lost or have been destroyed, unless the proponent lost or destroyed them in bad faith; or

(2) Original not obtainable.　No original can be obtained by any available judicial process or procedure; or

(3) Original in possession of opponent.　At a time when an original was under the control of the party against whom offered, that party was put on notice, by the pleadings or otherwise, that the contents would be a subject of proof at the hearing, and that party does not produce the original at the hearing; or

(4) Collateral matters.　The writing, recording, or photograph is not closely related to a controlling issue.

Rule 1005.　PUBLIC RECORDS

The contents of an official record, or of a document authorized to be recorded or filed and actually recorded or filed, including data compilations in any form, if otherwise admissible, may be proved by copy, certified as correct in accordance with rule 902 or testified to be correct by a witness who has compared it with the original.　If a copy which complies with the foregoing cannot be obtained by the exercise of reasonable diligence, then other evidence of the contents may be given.

Rule 1003.   ADMISSIBILITY OF DUPLICATES

A duplicate is admissible to the same extent as the original unless a genuine question is raised about the original's authenticity or the circumstances make it unfair to admit the duplicate.

Rule 1004.   ADMISSIBILITY OF OTHER EVIDENCE OF CONTENT

An original is not required and other evidence of the content of a writing, recording, or photograph is admissible if:

(a) all the originals are lost or destroyed, and not by the proponent acting in bad faith;

(b) an original cannot be obtained by any available judicial process;

(c) the party against whom the original would be offered had control of the original; was at that time put on notice, by pleadings or otherwise, that the original would be a subject of proof at the trial or hearing; and fails to produce it at the trial or hearing; or

(d) the writing, recording, or photograph is not closely related to a controlling issue.

Rule 1005.   COPIES OF PUBLIC RECORDS TO PROVE CONTENT

The proponent may use a copy to prove the content of an official record—or of a document that was recorded or filed in a public office as authorized by law—if these conditions are met: the record or document is otherwise admissible; and the copy is certified as correct in accordance with Rule 902(4) or is testified to be correct by a witness who has compared it with the original. If no such copy can be obtained by reasonable diligence, then the proponent may use other evidence to prove the content.

Rule 1006. SUMMARIES

The contents of voluminous writings, recordings, or photographs which cannot conveniently be examined in court may be presented in the form of a chart, summary, or calculation. The originals, or duplicates, shall be made available for examination or copying, or both, by other parties at reasonable time and place. The court may order that they be produced in court.

Rule 1007. TESTIMONY OR WRITTEN ADMISSION OF PARTY

Contents of writings, recordings, or photographs may be proved by the testimony or deposition of the party against whom offered or by that party's written admission, without accounting for the nonproduction of the original.

Rule 1008. FUNCTIONS OF COURT AND JURY

When the admissibility of other evidence of contents of writings, recordings, or photographs under these rules depends upon the fulfillment of a condition of fact, the question whether the condition has been fulfilled is ordinarily for the court to determine in accordance with the provisions of rule 104. However, when an issue is raised (a) whether the asserted writing ever existed, or (b) whether another writing, recording, or photograph produced at the trial is the original, or (c) whether other evidence of contents correctly reflects the contents, the issue is for the trier of fact to determine as in the case of other issues of fact.

Rule 1006. SUMMARIES TO PROVE CONTENT

The proponent may use a summary, chart, or calculation to prove the content of voluminous writings, recordings, or photographs that cannot be conveniently examined in court. The proponent must make the originals or duplicates available for examination or copying, or both, by other parties at a reasonable time and place. And the court may order the proponent to produce them in court.

Rule 1007. TESTIMONY OR STATEMENT OF A PARTY TO PROVE CONTENT

The proponent may prove the content of a writing, recording, or photograph by the testimony, deposition, or written statement of the party against whom the evidence is offered. The proponent need not account for the original.

Rule 1008. FUNCTIONS OF THE COURT AND JURY

Ordinarily, the court determines whether the proponent has fulfilled the factual conditions for admitting other evidence of the content of a writing, recording, or photograph under Rule 1004 or 1005. But in a jury trial, the jury determines—in accordance with Rule 104(b)—any issue about whether:

(a) an asserted writing, recording, or photograph ever existed;

(b) another one produced at the trial or hearing is the original; or

(c) other evidence of content accurately reflects the content.

ARTICLE XI
MISCELLANEOUS RULES

Rule 1101. APPLICABILITY OF RULES

(a) **Courts and judges.** These rules apply to the United States district courts, the District Court of Guam, the District Court of the Virgin Islands, the District Court for the Northern Mariana Islands, the United States courts of appeals, the United States Claims Court, and to United States bankruptcy judges and United States magistrate judges, in the actions, cases, and proceedings and to the extent hereinafter set forth. The terms "judge" and "court" in these rules include United States bankruptcy judges and United States magistrate judges.

(b) **Proceedings generally.** These rules apply generally to civil actions and proceedings, including admiralty and maritime cases, to criminal cases and proceedings, to contempt proceedings except those in which the court may act summarily, and to proceedings and cases under title 11, United States Code.

(c) **Rule of privilege.** The rule with respect to privileges applies at all stages of all actions, cases, and proceedings.

ARTICLE XI
MISCELLANEOUS RULES

Rule 1101.   APPLICABILITY OF THE RULES

(a) To Courts and Judges.   These rules apply to proceedings before:

- United States district courts;

- United States bankruptcy and magistrate judges;

- United States courts of appeals;

- the United States Court of Federal Claims; and

- the district courts of Guam, the Virgin Islands, and the Northern Mariana Islands.

(b) To Cases and Proceedings. These rules apply in:

- civil cases and proceedings, including bankruptcy, admiralty, and maritime cases;

- criminal cases and proceedings; and

- contempt proceedings, except those in which the court may act summarily.

(c) Rules on Privilege. The rules on privilege apply to all stages of a case or proceeding.

(d) Rules inapplicable. The rules (other than with respect to privileges) do not apply in the following situations:

(1) Preliminary questions of fact. The determination of questions of fact preliminary to admissibility of evidence when the issue is to be determined by the court under rule 104.

(2) Grand jury. Proceedings before grand juries.

(3) Miscellaneous proceedings. Proceedings for extradition or rendition; preliminary examinations in criminal cases; sentencing, or granting or revoking probation; issuance of warrants for arrest, criminal summonses, and search warrants; and proceedings with respect to release on bail or otherwise.

(e) Rules applicable in part. In the following proceedings these rules apply to the extent that matters of evidence are not provided for in the statutes which govern procedure therein or in other rules prescribed by the Supreme Court pursuant to statutory authority: the trial of misdemeanors and other petty offenses before United States magistrate judges; review of agency actions when the facts are subject to trial de novo under section 706(2)(F) of title 5, United States Code; review of orders of the Secretary of Agriculture under section 2 of the Act entitled "An Act to authorize association of producers of agricultural products" approved February 18, 1922 (7 U.S.C. 292), and under sections 6 and 7(c) of the Perishable Agricultural Commodities Act, 1930 (7 U.S.C. 499f, 499g(c)); naturalization and revocation of naturalization under sections 310-318 of the Immigration and Nationality Act (8 U.S.C. 1421-1429); prize proceedings in admiralty under sections 7651-7681 of title 10, United States Code; review of orders of the Secretary of the Interior under section 2 of the Act entitled "An Act authorizing associations of producers of aquatic products" approved June 25, 1934 (15 U.S.C. 522); review of orders of petroleum control boards under section 5 of the Act entitled "An Act to regulate interstate and foreign commerce in petroleum and its products by prohibiting the shipment in such commerce of petroleum and its products produced in violation of State law, and for other purposes", approved February 22, 1935 (15 U.S.C. 715d); actions for fines, penalties, or forfeitures under part V of title IV of the Tariff Act of 1930

(d) Exceptions. These rules—except for those on privilege—do not apply to the following:

  (1) the court's determination, under Rule 104(a), on a preliminary question of fact governing admissibility;

  (2) grand-jury proceedings; and

  (3) miscellaneous proceedings such as:

  - extradition or rendition;

  - issuing an arrest warrant, criminal summons, or search warrant;

  - a preliminary examination in a criminal case;

  - sentencing;

  - granting or revoking probation or supervised release; and

  - considering whether to release on bail or otherwise.

(e) Other Statutes and Rules. A federal statute or a rule prescribed by the Supreme Court may provide for admitting or excluding evidence independently from these rules.

(19 U.S.C. 1581-1624), or under the Anti-Smuggling Act (19 U.S.C. 1701-1711); criminal libel for condemnation, exclusion of imports, or other proceedings under the Federal Food, Drug, and Cosmetic Act (21 U.S.C. 301-392); disputes between seamen under sections 4079, 4080, and 4081 of the Revised Statutes (22 U.S.C. 256-258); habeas corpus under sections 2241-2254 of title 28, United States Code; motions to vacate, set aside or correct sentence under section 2255 of title 28, United States Code; actions for penalties for refusal to transport destitute seamen under section 4578 of the Revised Statutes (46 U.S.C. 679); actions against the United States under the Act entitled "An Act authorizing suits against the United States in admiralty for damage caused by and salvage service rendered to public vessels belonging to the United States, and for other purposes", approved March 3, 1925 (46 U.S.C. 781-790), as implemented by section 7730 of title 10, United States Code.

Rule 1102.   AMENDMENTS

Amendments to the Federal Rules of Evidence may be made as provided in section 2072 of title 28 of the United States Code.

Rule 1103.   TITLE

These rules may be known and cited as the Federal Rules of Evidence.

Rule 1102.   AMENDMENTS

These rules may be amended as provided in 28 U.S.C. § 2072.

Rule 1103.   TITLE

These rules may be cited as the Federal Rules of Evidence.

(These materials replace pages 17 to 19 of the casebook.)

In the three decades since *Tanner*, the Supreme Court has returned in earnest to Rule 606(b) only twice—once to reaffirm *Tanner*'s central principles and once to carve out an important exception. Let's take up these rulings in turn.

WARGER V. SHAUERS: *Case Note*

Warger v. Shauers, 135 S. Ct. 521 (2014), called on the Justices to resolve whether Rule 606(b) "permits a party moving for a new trial based on juror dishonesty during voir dire to introduce juror testimony about statements made during deliberations that tend to show the alleged dishonesty."

The term *voir dire*—"to speak the truth"—refers to a preliminary examination at which a trial court considers the competency or potential bias of a juror or witness. At issue in *Warger* was the voir dire of prospective jurors held at the trial's start. A juror's dishonesty during voir dire, if proved, can supply grounds for a new trial. The challenging party "must first demonstrate that a juror failed to answer honestly a material question on *voir dire*, and then further show that a correct response would have provided a valid basis [to] challenge" and remove the juror. *McDonough Power Equip., Inc. v. Greenwood*, 464 U.S. 548, 556 (1984). But if evidence of a juror's dishonesty during voir dire emerges only during deliberations, Rule 606(b)(1)'s ban on juror testimony about statements or conduct during deliberations, if offered to unsettle a verdict, may frustrate proof of that dishonesty. *Warger v. Shauers* presented this difficulty.

Facts and Procedural History

The case arose out of a South Dakota highway collision between Gregory Warger's motorcycle and Randy Shauers's truck that cost Warger his left leg. Warger brought a diversity action in U.S. District Court, alleging negligence and seeking to recover for medical expenses, permanent disability, and other losses. After a jury verdict for defendant Shauers, a juror approached Warger's counsel and reported that the jury foreperson had told the other jurors during deliberations that her daughter had been at fault in a fatal car accident several years earlier. The foreperson allegedly said that had her daughter been sued, it would have "ruined her life." The juror recorded these allegations in an affidavit. But the district judge concluded that Rule 606(b) barred admission of the affidavit and denied Warger's motion for a new trial. *See Warger v. Shauers*, 721 F.3d 606, 609 (8th Cir. 2013).

On appeal Warger argued that Rule 606(b) should not bar juror testimony about the foreperson's comments in deliberations because the remarks about her daughter constituted "extraneous prejudicial information" of the sort addressed by Rule 606(b)(2)(A). The Eighth Circuit Court of Appeals disagreed. The court distinguished communications from outsiders or the media, which could constitute "extraneous prejudicial information," from the "subjective prejudices or improper motives of individual jurors." The latter are not an exceptional aberration of jury deliberations, but rather the norm. "Jurors' personal experiences do not constitute extraneous information; it is unavoidable they will bring such innate experiences into the jury room." *Id.* at 611.

Warger claimed in the alternative that juror testimony about the foreperson's comments during deliberations was admissible to show she lied during voir dire when she denied any potential bias in the lawsuit. Rule 606(b) doesn't bar such testimony, Warger argued, as the rule constrains only "inquir[ies] into the validity of a verdict or indictment," not challenges to the integrity of voir dire. *See id.* The appeals court rejected this approach too. Here it quoted the Tenth Circuit's decision in *United States v. Benally*, 546 F.3d 1230 (10th Cir. 2008): "'[A]llowing juror testimony through the backdoor of a voir dire challenge risks swallowing the rule. A broad question during voir dire could then justify the admission of any number of jury statements that would now be re-characterized as challenges to voir dire rather than challenges to the verdict.'" *Warger*, 721 F.3d at 612 (quoting *Benally*, 546 F.3d at 1236). The court therefore rejected the position of the Ninth Circuit, which had said flatly, "Statements which tend to show deceit during voir dire are not barred by [Rule 606(b)]." *Hard v. Burlington N. R.R.*, 812 F.2d 482, 485 (9th Cir. 1987).

At the Supreme Court

In his filings before the Supreme Court Warger added two claims. First he alleged that at common law the rule forbidding jurors to impeach their own verdicts did not apply when the truthfulness of a juror's responses during voir dire was at issue. Here the historical record was muddy. Though Rule 606(b) traces its lineage to early-eighteenth-century England, juror voir dire took rise on American shores. Hence American courts had struggled to decide whether the common-law forbears of Rule 606(b) had to yield when jurors' comments during deliberations showed they had lied during voir dire. The caselaw was mixed. Warger cited a handful of decisions in which courts had permitted juror testimony about comments made by a fellow juror during deliberations, when offered to invalidate a verdict based on the juror's dishonesty during voir dire. But as Warger admitted, some courts had reached the opposite conclusion. *See* Brief for Petitioner, *Warger v. Shauers*, No. 13-517 (U.S., May 27, 2014), at 28–29 & n.3. And as almost every case cited on the question predated Rule 606(b), which makes no provision for proof of juror dishonesty during voir dire, the significance of this common-law history was unclear.

Warger also argued that Rule 606(b) must yield to the constitutional guarantee of trial by an impartial jury. The Sixth Amendment expressly assures criminal defendants the right to "an impartial jury." And though "the right of trial by jury" secured by the Seventh Amendment in civil cases lacks that explicit guarantee, the Supreme Court has ruled that "[t]he American tradition of trial by jury, considered in connection with either criminal or civil proceedings, necessarily contemplates an impartial jury." *Thiel v. S. Pac. Co.*, 328 U.S. 217, 220 (1946). Because choosing an impartial jury requires effective voir dire to root out potential biases, "[t]he necessity of truthful answers by prospective jurors . . . is obvious." *McDonough*, 464 U.S. at 554. This constitutional imperative, Warger argued, overcomes Rule 606(b) when juror testimony about comments made in deliberations can expose a juror's dishonesty during voir dire.

That's especially true, he said, when those comments reveal a juror's *racial* bias. Consider the statement attributed to a deliberating juror in *United States v. Villar*, 586 F.3d 76, 78 (1st Cir. 2009), *cert. denied*, 131 S. Ct. 2167 (2011), quoted in Problem I.1 at page 17 of the casebook: "I guess we're profiling, but they cause all the trouble." Even if *this* case does not involve such ethnic profiling, Warger argued, the Supreme Court should construe Rule 606(b) to permit exposure of racist comments during deliberations and therefore of false claims of impartiality during voir dire.

The Ruling

This claim—and all of Warger's claims—proved wanting. The Supreme Court held Rule 606(b) "applies to juror testimony during a proceeding in which a party seeks to secure a new trial on the ground that a juror lied during *voir dire*." Writing for a unanimous Court, Justice Sotomayor explained that the Justices simply gave "Rule 606(b)'s terms their plain meaning."

In her rather brief opinion Justice Sotomayor made five main points:

• Rule 606(b)(1) "applies '[d]uring an inquiry into the validity of a verdict.' A postverdict motion for a new trial on the ground of *voir dire* dishonesty plainly entails 'an inquiry into the validity of [the] verdict': If a juror was dishonest during *voir dire* and an honest response would have provided a valid basis to challenge that juror for cause, the verdict must be invalidated."

• Though common-law courts reached mixed results, most courts read the common-law forbears of Rule 606(b) broadly to exclude juror testimony about jury deliberations when used to challenge juror conduct during *voir dire*. More recent Supreme Court rulings have followed this lower-court trend.

• Those cases that reached contrary results "predated Congress' enactment of Rule 606(b), and Congress was undoubtedly free to prescribe a broader version of the anti-impeachment rule than we had previously applied." And "[a]s enacted, Rule 606(b) prohibit[s] the use of *any* evidence of juror deliberations, subject only to the express exceptions for extraneous information and outside influences."

• A juror's past experiences, even if influential in the juror's assessment of the merits of the case, do not constitute "extraneous prejudicial information." FED. R. EVID. 606(b)(2)(A). Information generally "is deemed 'extraneous' if it derives from a source 'external' to the jury. 'External' matters include publicity and information related specifically to the case the jurors are meant to decide, while 'internal' matters include the general body of experiences that jurors are understood to bring with them to the jury room."

• "[A]ny claim that Rule 606(b) is unconstitutional in circumstances such as these is foreclosed by our decision in *Tanner*," where the Court "reasoned that the defendant's right to an unimpaired jury was sufficiently protected by *voir dire*, the observations of court and counsel during trial, and the potential use of 'nonjuror evidence' of misconduct. Similarly here, a party's right to an impartial jury remains protected despite Rule 606(b)'s removal of one means of ensuring that jurors are unbiased. Even if jurors lie in *voir dire* in a way that conceals bias, juror impartiality is adequately assured by the parties' ability to bring to the court's attention any evidence of bias [including juror testimony] before the verdict is rendered, and to employ nonjuror evidence even after the verdict is rendered."

Looking Ahead

In what otherwise struck the Court as an easy case, one concern gave the Justices pause. During oral argument Justice Alito posed the problem to Shauers's counsel:

What would happen in the really egregious case? The jurors are asked during voir dire, can you be fair to every—to parties regardless of race. Oh, yes, yes, we can. And then after there's a verdict, a juror comes—comes forward and says during the jury deliberations, the jurors were making all kinds of biased statements and they were clearly prejudiced. What would happen there?

Justice Kagan followed up: "[D]o you think that with respect to the kind of case that Justice Alito has in mind, a case of racial bias—and let's put it in a criminal context—that maybe it's not up to Congress, that at some point one begins to run into constitutional issues?" Transcript of Oral Argument, *Warger v. Shauers*, No. 13-517 (U.S., Oct. 8, 2014), at 29–31.

Without engaging this constitutional question, the Justices pointedly reserved it for a later decision: "There may be cases of juror bias so extreme," they wrote, "that, almost by definition, the jury trial right has been abridged. If and when such a case arises, the Court can consider whether the usual safeguards are or are not sufficient to protect the integrity of the process."

PEÑA-RODRIGUEZ V. COLORADO: *Case Note*

Sixteen months later the Justices deemed the question reserved in *Warger* ripe for decision. In April 2016 the Court granted certiorari in *Peña-Rodriguez v. Colorado*, 137 S. Ct. 855 (2017), and agreed to review one question: "May a no-impeachment rule constitutionally bar evidence of racial bias offered to prove a violation of the Sixth Amendment right to an impartial jury?" By a "no-impeachment rule," the Court meant Rule 606(b) or any state-law equivalent. These rules typically forbid jurors to testify in ways that impeach—or call in question—the validity of their verdicts. And by "racial bias," the Court later explained, it meant to include "bias . . . based on petitioner's Hispanic identity."

Facts and Procedural History

The case arose in a Colorado state court, where Miguel Angel Peña-Rodriguez was convicted of unlawful sexual contact and harassment after an alleged attack on two teenage sisters in the bathroom of his workplace. The girls separately identified Peña-Rodriguez as their assailant in a showup procedure shortly after the attack.

During pretrial voir dire, jurors affirmed they could decide the case fairly and impartially. Shortly after trial, however, two jurors approached defense counsel and alleged that a third juror, a former law-enforcement officer, had made several ethnically biased statements during deliberations, including:

• Where I "used to patrol, nine times out of ten Mexican men were guilty of being aggressive toward women and young girls."

• "'I think he did it because he's Mexican and Mexican men take whatever they want.'"

• I do "not think the alibi witness was credible because, among other things, he was 'an illegal.'"

The trial judge denied a motion for new trial, holding that Colorado's equivalent of FRE 606(b) barred inquiry into the juror's alleged bias during deliberations. Both the Colorado Court of Appeals and the Colorado Supreme Court affirmed. They held that the juror's expressions of ethnic bias did not constitute "extraneous prejudicial information" under Rule 606(b)(2)(A), a phrase the Colorado Supreme Court limited to "'legal content and specific factual information learned from outside the record and relevant to the issues in a case.'" *Peña-Rodriguez v. People*, 350 P.3d 287, 290 (Colo. 2015).

In rejecting Peña-Rodriguez's claim that he was denied his Sixth Amendment right to trial by an impartial jury, the Colorado Supreme Court stated "a simple but crucial principle: Protecting the secrecy of jury deliberations is of paramount importance in our justice system." Even in *Tanner*, where jurors faced allegations of mid-trial drug and alcohol abuse, Rule 606(b) did not yield to concerns about juror competency. "[W]e cannot discern a dividing line between different types of juror bias or misconduct," the Colorado high court wrote, "whereby one form of partiality would implicate a party's Sixth Amendment right while another would not." *Id.* at 293. And the court quoted the ruling of the Tenth Circuit in *United States v. Benally*, 546 F.3d 1230, 1240 (10th Cir. 2008), that "'[t]he safeguards that the Court relied upon for exposing the drug and alcohol use amongst jurors in *Tanner* are also available to expose racial biases . . . .'" True, the second *Tanner* protection—observation of jurors by court and counsel during trial—is unlikely to expose racial biases. But the Colorado court insisted that at least two of the *Tanner* protections help guard against racially biased decisionmaking: "Other jurors could have informed the court or counsel of [the biased juror's] statements prior to delivering the verdict, and any non-juror evidence of his bias remained admissible post-verdict."

At the Supreme Court

In March 2017 the United States Supreme Court reversed the Colorado high court and ruled "that where a juror makes a clear statement that indicates he or she relied on racial stereotypes or animus to convict a criminal defendant, the Sixth Amendment requires that the no-impeachment rule give way in order to permit the trial court to consider the evidence of the juror's statement and any resulting denial of the jury trial guarantee." *Peña-Rodriguez*, 137 S. Ct. at 869.

Writing for himself and Justices Ginsburg, Breyer, Sotomayor, and Kagan, Justice Kennedy stressed that "discrimination on the basis of race, 'odious in all aspects, is especially pernicious in the administration of justice.'" Unlike the "anomalous" forms of juror misconduct involved in the Court's earlier cases—the drug and alcohol abuse of *Tanner*, for example, or the pro-defendant bias in *Warger*—racial bias is "a familiar and recurring evil that, if left unaddressed, would risk systemic injury to the administration of justice."

Responding to Justice O'Connor's warning in *Tanner* that while juror testimony might remedy certain juror misconduct, it's "not at all clear . . . the jury system could survive such efforts to perfect it" (CB 12), Justice Kennedy wrote that "[a]n effort to address the most grave and serious statements of racial bias is not an effort to perfect the jury." It is instead an effort to advance "our legal system . . . ever closer to the promise of equal treatment under the law that is so central to a functioning democracy." If "[t]he jury is to be 'a criminal defendant's fundamental "protection of life and liberty against race or color prejudice,"'" the law cannot ignore evidence that the jury itself has been infected by such prejudice.

Justice Kennedy acknowledged the ancient common-law lineage of the no-impeachment rule. Yet for over a century and half, he said, the Supreme Court repeatedly reserved the possibility that "'cases might arise in which it would be impossible to refuse'" juror testimony "'without violating the plainest principles of justice.'" (Quoting *United States v. Reid*, 53 U.S. 361, 366 (1852); *see McDonald v. Pless*, 238 U.S. 264, 269 (1915) (similar).) Moreover, the "imperative to purge racial prejudice from the administration of justice was given new force and direction by the ratification of the Civil War Amendments," which weakened originalist arguments staked in older practices.

Justice Kennedy denied this new exception to the no-impeachment rule would trigger the calamities predicted by Justice O'Connor in *Tanner*. The *Tanner* Court had said a firm no-impeachment rule was essential to avoid these four ills (CB 12):

- *Harassed jurors:* Justice Kennedy noted that state ethics rules and local court rules can protect jurors from post-trial harassment by banning unsolicited inquiries from defense counsel and others seeking to overturn a verdict. Moreover, at least fifteen states and the District of Columbia, together with at least one federal appeals court, already "have recognized a racial-bias exception to the no-impeachment rule—some for over half a century—with no signs of an increase in juror harassment . . . ."

- *Constrained deliberations:* The experience of those seventeen jurisdictions also has shown "no signs of . . . a loss of juror willingness to engage in searching and candid deliberations."

- *Disrupted finality:* Justice Kennedy emphasized that "[n]ot every offhand comment indicating racial bias or hostility will justify setting aside the no-impeachment bar to allow further judicial inquiry." Instead the defense must show "that one or more jurors made statements exhibiting overt racial bias that cast serious doubt on the fairness and impartiality of the jury's deliberations and resulting verdict. To qualify, the statement must tend to show that racial animus was a significant motivating factor in the juror's vote to convict." And judges can help preserve the finality of their trials by using voir dire to weed out biased jurors and by instructing jurors "to review the evidence and reach a verdict in a fair and impartial way, free from bias of any kind."

- *Undermined trust:* And far from undermining "the community's trust in a system that relies on the decisions of laypeople," as Justice O'Connor had feared, "[a] constitutional rule that racial bias in the justice system must be addressed . . . is necessary to prevent a systemic loss of confidence in jury verdicts . . . ."

The Dissents

Three Justices dissented. Writing only for himself, Justice Thomas declared "that the Court's holding . . . cannot be squared with the original understanding of the Sixth or Fourteenth Amendments." At the time of the founding, he said, many states already forbade juror testimony about misconduct during deliberations. And by 1868, when the Fourteenth Amendment was ratified, the no-impeachment rule "had become firmly entrenched in American law. . . . In the absence of a definitive common-law tradition permitting impeachment by juror testimony, we have no basis to invoke a constitutional provision"—here the right to an impartial jury— "that merely 'follow[s] out the established course of the common law in all trials for crimes' to overturn Colorado's decision to preserve the no-impeachment rule." (Quoting 3 J. STORY, COMMENTARIES ON THE CONSTITUTION OF THE UNITED STATES, § 1785, at 662 (1833).)

Justice Alito, joined by Chief Justice Roberts and Justice Thomas, likewise condemned the Court's ruling as inconsistent with precedent. But he challenged more pointedly the majority's suggestion that expressions of racial bias warrant a firmer response than other misconduct in the jury room. "What the Sixth Amendment protects is the right to an 'impartial jury,'" Justice Alito wrote:

> Nothing in the text or history of the Amendment or in the inherent nature of the jury trial right suggests that the extent of the protection provided by the Amendment depends on the nature of a jury's partiality or bias. As the Colorado Supreme Court aptly put it, it is hard to "discern a dividing line between different *types* of juror bias or misconduct, whereby one form of partiality would implicate a party's Sixth Amendment right while another would not." *Peña-Rodriguez v. People*, 350 P. 3d 287, 293, 2015 CO 31 (2015).

Where can the Court stop, Justice Alito asked, once it acts to expose racial bias in the jury room? "At a minimum, cases involving bias based on any suspect classification—such as national origin or religion—would merit equal treatment. So, I think, would bias based on sex or the exercise of the First Amendment right to freedom of expression or association."

Justice Alito alleged too that the majority's ruling will foster the very ills against which the no-impeachment rule is supposed to guard. Defense counsel and other defense partisans now have reason to harass trial jurors for revelations of biased comments. Fear that an artless comment could prompt a post-trial inquiry may constrain jurors in their deliberations. And if evidence of racial bias unsettles convictions, finality will suffer.

But Justice Alito made no mention in this context of the fourth fear underlying the no-impeachment rule. Justice O'Connor had written in *Tanner* that "the community's trust in a system that relies on the decisions of laypeople would . . . be undermined by a barrage of postverdict scrutiny of juror conduct." Justice Alito did not venture to suggest that this concern for the *legitimacy* of juries' verdicts weighed against the Court's ruling in *Peña-Rodriquez*. Perhaps he shared the Court's concern that the public's faith in the fairness of our system would suffer if the system stubbornly insists on looking the other way when a juror explains his vote to convict saying, "I think he did it because he's Mexican."

TANNER, WARGER, & PEÑA-RODRIGUEZ: *Afterthoughts*

The lesson of Rule 606(b) is that within our system's formal bounds, jury verdicts undergo little after-the-fact scrutiny. Only in the realm of racial injustice must the rule's protection of the secrecy of jury deliberations yield to a defendant's Sixth Amendment right to an impartial jury. Beyond such fraught social turf, the centuries-old no-impeachment rule stands strong, a monument to our systemic faith in the wisdom of twelve common persons gathered together.

Hence the jury resolves our most heated social conflicts privately and without explanation. In 1920 Professor Edson Sunderland explained how hidden jury deliberations protect the reputation of the justice system by concealing any possible source of error. The system's need for legitimacy, Sunderland wrote, demands that "[t]he record . . . be absolutely flawless, but such a result is possible only by concealing, not by excluding mistakes." Edson R. Sunderland, *Verdicts, General and Special*, 29 YALE L.J. 253, 262 (1920). The jury's hidden decisionmaking process and its one- or two-word verdicts leave all mistakes and causes for criticism locked in the black box of the jury room. The jury's inscrutability, in Sunderland's marvelous imagery,

> covers up all the shortcomings which frail human nature is unable to eliminate from the trial of a case. . . . [C]oncrete details are swallowed up, and the eye of the law, searching

anxiously for the realization of logical perfection, is satisfied . . . . It serves as the great procedural opiate, which draws the curtain upon human errors and soothes us in the assurance that we have attained the unattainable.

Id. Rule 606(b) and its counterparts in state evidence codes act to safeguard the jury's inscrutability. In the average case they "draw[] the curtain upon human errors" and frustrate any official inquiry into the nature and propriety of the jury's deliberations.

But what does this have to do with evidence law?

Our long tradition of secret jury deliberations, as embodied today in Rule 606(b), means our justice system engages in very little quality control at the back end. Though the system provides for review of procedural errors and judicial errors of law, errors in the way juries interpret evidence are virtually undetectable, much less correctable. With so little quality control at the back end of our trial process, it may be wise to have quality control at the front end. That is, since we don't scrutinize the deliberative process, we have to scrutinize and regulate the quality of the evidence fed into that process. *See* John H. Langbein, *The Criminal Trial Before the Jury*, 45 U. CHI. L. REV. 263, 289 (1978).

There is an irony here: Because our system invests such enormous trust in jurors' decisions, we need a system of evidence rules that betrays deep mistrust of jurors' ability to cull good evidence from bad. Because we apparently do not trust jurors to cast off and disregard meaningless, misleading, and unreliable evidence, we screen out such evidence before they ever hear it. This screening process—the quality control we exercise over the information juries hear—is the realm of evidence law.

(The following materials replace a similar segment at pages 447 to 452 of the casebook.)

MIRANDA AND SILENCE

If someone says, "I hear you robbed that bank," we normally would expect an innocent person to refute the implied accusation. A defendant's silence in the face of such a charge therefore may serve as an adoptive admission of guilt. And because silence may be inconsistent with a later claim of innocence, evidence of silence also may serve to impeach.

Adoptive admissions, governed by Rule 801(d)(2)(B), are substantive evidence of guilt, admissible to prove the truth of the adopted accusation. Caselaw and commentators have identified four preconditions to deeming silence an adoption: (1) the adopted statement was heard and understood by the party against whom it is offered; (2) the party was at liberty to respond; (3) the circumstances naturally called for a response; and (4) the party failed to respond. *See Jenkins v. Anderson*, 447 U.S. 231, 248–49 (1980) (Marshall, J., dissenting). Likewise, when silence is used to *impeach*, one must ask "if it would have been natural, under the circumstances, to assert [or deny] the fact" at issue. *Id.*

Miranda warnings disrupt both lines of reasoning. If authorities have advised a suspect she need not speak and her words may be used against her, it's no longer natural to expect her to speak. Even in the face of a direct accusation, a person told she has "the right to remain silent" may choose to exercise that right rather than rebut the accusation. As the Supreme Court noted in *Doyle v. Ohio*, 426 U.S. 610, 617–18 (1976), her silence becomes "insolubly ambiguous." And because *Miranda* warnings contain an implicit assurance "that silence will carry no penalty," *id.* at 618, using her silence against her would be fundamentally unfair. Hence the *Doyle* Court held that post-*Miranda* silence may not be used to impeach a defendant who takes the stand at trial. *See id.*; *Wainwright v. Greenfield*, 474 U.S. 284, 291 (1986).

The diagram on the next page depicts the state of the law regarding the use of silence as an adoptive admission and to impeach. *Doyle* is noted in the box on the bottom right. Its holding, barring the use of post-*Miranda* silence to impeach, is perhaps the least controversial judgment in the diagram. Note that the top right box is almost blank. The Supreme Court has never ruled whether post-*Miranda* silence can serve as evidence of an adoptive admission. But both principle and precedent suggest the answer is no. As a matter of principle post-*Miranda* silence is always "insolubly ambiguous," whether used to impeach or as evidence of an adoption—and *any* use of post-*Miranda* silence violates an implicit assurance "that silence will carry no penalty." Moreover, three Supreme Court rulings have hinted that prosecutors may not use post-*Miranda* silence for any purpose.

In the first of these cases, *Harris v. New York*, 401 U.S. 222, 226 (1971), the Court held that statements obtained in violation of *Miranda* during police interrogation, though not admissible substantively against the defendant, may be used to impeach the defendant's testimony. *Harris* suggests the standards governing admission of impeachment evidence are more generous toward the prosecution than those governing evidence offered substantively. If *Doyle* bars use of post-*Miranda* silence even to *impeach*, therefore, the Court very likely would bar such silence if offered substantively to establish an adoptive admission.

The second Supreme Court ruling, *Kansas v. Ventris*, 556 U.S. 586, 593–94 (2009), considered the related issue of a defendant's confession obtained in violation of his Sixth Amendment right to counsel. The Court quoted *Harris* and other authorities in reaching the analogous result: though inadmissible in the prosecution's case-in-chief as substantive proof of his guilt, the defendant's statement could be used to impeach his claim of innocence on the stand.

And in *Wainwright v. Greenfield, supra*, the Court rejected the prosecutor's attempt to use the defendant's post-arrest, post-*Miranda* silence as substantive evidence of his sanity. The

MIRANDA AND SILENCE

	Defendant Not in Custody	Defendant in Custody / Pre-*Miranda*	Defendant in Custody / Post-*Miranda*
May Silence Be an "Adoption" under FRE 801(d)(2)(B)?	YES: *Salinas v. Texas*, 570 U.S. 178 (2013) (Supp. page 516)	?? (YES: *US v. Frazier*, 408 F.3d 1102, 1111 (8th Cir. 2005); NO: *US v. Flecha*, 539 F.2d 874, 877 (2d Cir. 1976); *US v. Velarde-Gomez*, 269 F.3d 1023, 1027–33 (9th Cir. 2001) (en banc))	NO*
May Silence Be Used to Impeach?	YES: *Jenkins v. Anderson*, 447 U.S. 231, 240 (1980)	YES: *Fletcher v. Weir*, 455 U.S. 603, 607 (1982) (CB page 444)	NO: *Doyle v. Ohio*, 426 U.S. 610, 617–18 (1976)

* See the discussion on page 513 above of *Harris v. New York*, 401 U.S. 222, 226 (1971) (holding that statements taken in violation of *Miranda*, though not admissible substantively against the defendant, may be used to impeach the defendant's testimony); *Kansas v. Ventris*, 556 U.S. 586, 593–94 (2009) (reaching a similar result on similar reasoning); and *Wainwright v. Greenfield*, 474 U.S. 284, 292 n.8 (1986) (rejecting the prosecution's attempt to use the defendant's post-arrest, post-*Miranda* silence as substantive evidence of his sanity).

prosecutor had argued at trial that the defendant's good judgment in responding to *Miranda* warnings by saying he would not answer questions without a lawyer tended to prove his sanity. *Greenfield*, 474 U.S. at 286. The Supreme Court rejected this gambit and suggested that substantive use of post-*Miranda* silence did more violence to the Constitution than use of such silence to impeach. "The constitutional violation might thus be especially egregious," the Justices wrote, "because, unlike *Doyle*, there was no risk 'that exclusion of the evidence [would] merely provide a shield for perjury.'" *Greenfield*, 474 U.S. at 292 n.8 (quoting *Doyle*, 426 U.S. at 626 (Stevens, J., dissenting)). That is, courts should be especially welcoming toward evidence offered to impeach because barring impeachment evidence "merely provide[s] a shield for perjury." If evidence of post-*Miranda* silence is not admissible *even to impeach*, it surely should not be admitted substantively.

Note that the Supreme Court has ruled against criminal defendants in the cases cited in the bottom middle and bottom left boxes in the diagram above. In the absence of *Miranda* warnings a defendant's silence *may* be used to impeach his testimony, whether or not he was in custody at the time of the silence. The leading cases are *Jenkins v. Anderson*, 447 U.S. 231 (1980), and *Fletcher v. Weir*, 455 U.S. 603 (1982), excerpted in the casebook at page 444. *Jenkins* and *Weir* embraced much the same reasoning: *Doyle* declared that *Miranda* warnings offer the implicit "'assurance that silence will carry no penalty.'" *Weir*, CB page 446 (quoting *Doyle*, 426 U.S. at 618). But absent such government action inducing the defendant's silence, courts should revert to the judgment of the common law, which "'traditionally has allowed witnesses to be impeached by their previous failure to state a fact in circumstances in which that fact naturally would have been asserted.'" *Weir*, CB page 446 (quoting *Jenkins*, 447 U.S. at 239).

One can imagine a powerful rejoinder to this reasoning: "*Miranda* has become embedded in routine police practice to the point where the warnings have become part of our national culture." *Dickerson v. United States*, 530 U.S. 428, 443 (2000). Everyone with a television knows she has "the right to remain silent." The Supreme Court therefore offered the implicit "'assurance that silence will carry no penalty'" to all Americans in 1966, when it decided *Miranda v. Arizona*, 384 U.S. 436 (1966). An officer's failure to recite *Miranda* warnings can't somehow erase popular knowledge. And this popular knowledge of the warnings means that a defendant's silence always will be "insolubly ambiguous." It always will be impossible to know whether a defendant's silence in the face of an accusation is an admission of guilt or an assertion of a broadly understood right to remain silent.

Salinas v. Texas

This argument came up short, however, in the Supreme Court's most recent foray into pre-*Miranda* silence. In *Salinas v. Texas*, 570 U.S. 178 (2013), the Justices reviewed the 1993 interrogation of Genovevo Salinas by Houston police officers in the aftermath of two shotgun killings. After an investigation suggested his possible involvement, Salinas met willingly with two officers at the stationhouse. There was no evidence police advised Salinas under *Miranda* and no claim he was then in custody. For nearly an hour he answered the officers' questions. But when asked whether a shotgun retrieved from the home he shared with his parents "would match the shells recovered at the scene of the murder," Salinas said nothing. One of the questioning officers testified Salinas "[l]ooked down at the floor, shuffled his feet, bit his bottom lip, cl[e]nched his hands in his lap, [and] began to tighten up." This was the only question Salinas failed to answer. The officers continued questioning, and Salinas resumed answering.

After his first trial ended in a hung jury, Salinas was retried and convicted. At both trials the prosecutor introduced evidence of his silence when asked about the shotgun. At the second trial, though, the prosecutor trained a harsher light on this silence. Consider this excerpt from the prosecutor's closing argument:

> The police officer testified that he wouldn't answer that question. . . . You know, if you asked somebody— there is a murder in New York City, is your gun going

to match up the murder in New York City? . . . You are going to say no. An innocent person is going to say: What are you talking about? I didn't do that. I wasn't there. He didn't respond that way. He didn't say: No, it's not going to match up. . . . What are you talking about? He wouldn't answer that question.

Petition for Certiorari, *Salinas v. Texas*, No. 12-246 (Aug. 24, 2012), at 5 (quoting trial record). Salinas did not testify at either trial.

The Supreme Court examined whether the substantive use against Salinas of his silence in a noncustodial, pre-*Miranda* interview violated his Fifth Amendment right against compelled self-incrimination. Hence this case concerns the top left box in the diagram on page 514 above. True, *Salinas* did not involve an *adoption* by silence. His interrogators asked Salinas whether his shotgun "would match the shells recovered at the scene of the murder." Because the officers made no *assertion*, there was no hearsay *statement* for Salinas to adopt. Still, the prosecutor argued at trial that the defendant's failure to protest his innocence in response to the officers' question about the shotgun suggested he must be guilty. Drawing such substantive inferences from silence and using silence as an adoptive admission raise similar questions both in logic and under the Constitution.

Unfortunately, however, the Supreme Court offered no clear resolution of the constitutional and logical questions presented by Salinas's silence. By a vote of five to four the Justices deemed the prosecutor's comments on that silence lawful. But they failed to muster five votes for any one theory of the case:

• Joined by Chief Justice Roberts and Justice Kennedy, Justice Alito argued that simple *silence* typically finds no protection under the Fifth Amendment. "[P]opular misconceptions notwithstanding," he wrote, "the Fifth Amendment . . . does not establish an unqualified 'right to remain silent.'" Rather the amendment "guarantees that no one may be 'compelled in any criminal case to be a witness against himself.'" Absent *official compulsion* to speak, therefore, the Fifth Amendment offers no assurance that a defendant's silence may not be used against him. This is not to say that *Miranda* warnings are false in stating that a suspect has "the right to remain silent." *Miranda* operates only in the context of custodial police interrogation, and the *Miranda* Court declared that "in-custody interrogation . . . contains *inherently compelling* pressures." *Miranda*, 384 U.S. at 467 (emphasis added).

But absent custody, Justice Alito wrote, standing silent in the face of police questioning is insufficient to invoke the right against compelled self-incrimination. After all, unexplained silence also may mean the suspect "is trying to think of a good lie, . . . is embarrassed, or . . . is protecting someone else." Hence a suspect who wishes to claim the Fifth Amendment's protection and shield his silence from negative inferences at trial must "expressly invoke the privilege against self-incrimination in response to the officer's question." And "[a] witness does not expressly invoke the privilege by standing mute."

• Justice Thomas, together with Justice Scalia, construed the Fifth Amendment's protective zone even more narrowly. Concurring only in the plurality's judgment, Justice Thomas wrote that "Salinas' claim would fail *even if* he had invoked the privilege because the prosecutor's comments regarding his precustodial silence did not compel him to give self-incriminating testimony." (Emphasis added.) Justice Thomas did not say what kind of force *would* constitute the sort of compulsion against which the amendment protects. To decide this case it was enough to say that "[a] defendant is not 'compelled . . . to be a witness against himself' simply because a jury has been told that it may draw an adverse inference from his silence."

• Joined in dissent by Justices Ginsburg, Sotomayor, and Kagan, Justice Breyer took to task both the plurality and the concurrence. Confronting Justice Alito's insistence on an express invocation of the Fifth Amendment privilege, Justice Breyer rolled out a raft of cases in which the Court had overlooked defendants' failure to invoke expressly the privilege's protection. In several such cases the "circumstances" of the defendant's silence had made his reliance on the privilege clear even absent an express claim. In other cases an express claim of the privilege *itself* would have incriminated the defendant. Turning next to Justice Thomas's argument that a prosecutor's comments on a defendant's silence do not compel the defendant to speak, Justice Breyer maintained that "'it is impermissible to penalize an individual for exercising his Fifth Amendment privilege.'" Hence the "'prosecution may not . . . use at trial *the fact that he stood mute* or claimed his privilege in the face of accusation.'" (Quoting *Miranda* v. *Arizona*, 384 U. S. 436, 468 n. 37 (1966) (emphasis added by Justice Breyer).)

Justice Breyer also addressed the inferences that mere silence supports in a post-*Miranda* world: "This Court has recognized repeatedly that many, indeed most, Americans are aware that they have a constitutional right not to incriminate themselves by answering questions posed by the police during an interrogation conducted in order to figure out the perpetrator of a crime. *See Dickerson* v. *United States*, 530 U.S. 428, 443 (2000)." *Miranda*'s absorption into popular culture, together with the context of Salinas's interrogation—"the nature of the surroundings, the switch of topic, the particular question—all suggested that the right we have and generally *know* we have was at issue at the critical moment here." Salinas's unexplained silence in the face of accusatory police questioning therefore should be deemed an implied claim of his Fifth Amendment privilege, not an admission he had nothing exculpatory to say.

As I noted earlier, however, this argument failed to carry the day. And the upshot of the Court's splintered decision in *Salinas* is that a suspect who wishes to shield her noncustodial, pre-*Miranda* silence from a prosecutor's negative inferences at trial must "expressly invoke" her Fifth Amendment privilege against compelled self-incrimination. To do so, Justice Alito wrote, "'no ritualistic formula is necessary.'" Precisely what *is* necessary the Justices did not say. No doubt a suspect may invoke her privilege by stating, "I plead the Fifth." Perhaps saying simply, "I refuse to answer," will suffice. All we know for sure is that "standing mute" will not do.

The Open Box

Our remaining questions concern those cases that fall in the top middle box of the diagram on page 514 above. At issue here is the prosecution's use for substantive purposes of a defendant's custodial silence in absence of *Miranda* warnings. Many such cases will pose no difficulty. When police officers *question* a custodial suspect before advising her under *Miranda*, the prosecution may use any resulting statement only to impeach the defendant should she take the stand, but not as substantive evidence of guilt. These are the fundamental holdings of *Miranda v. Arizona*, 384 U.S. at 476–77, and *Harris v. New York*, 401 U.S. at 226. Prosecutors in these circumstances also may not use a suspect's *silence* as substantive evidence of guilt. "[I]t is impermissible to penalize an individual for exercising his Fifth Amendment privilege when he is under police custodial interrogation," the *Miranda* Court wrote. "The prosecution may not, therefore, use at trial the fact that he *stood mute* or claimed his privilege in the face of accusation." *Miranda*, 384 U.S. at 468 n.37 (emphasis added).

Cases in the top middle box present difficulty only when a prosecutor seeks to use a defendant's custodial, pre-*Miranda* silence *outside* the context of police questioning to establish an adoptive admission. Here lower courts stand divided. The Second and Ninth Circuits have ruled that post-arrest, pre-*Miranda* silence may not be used as an adoptive admission. In *United States v. Flecha*, 539 F.2d 874, 877 (2d Cir. 1976), the case on which Problem 7.18 (CB page 444) is based, several men were arrested on suspicion of smuggling drugs. After their arrest but before *Miranda* warnings were given, one of the men said, apparently to his codefendant, Flecha, "Why so much excitement? If we are caught we are caught." Flecha was standing near enough to have heard this statement, but said nothing to deny his involvement. In ruling that the statement should not have been admitted against Flecha as an adoptive admission, the Second Circuit reasoned that even in the absence of *Miranda* warnings, those under arrest might know that it's best to stay mum when the law is at hand. Likewise, the Ninth Circuit held in *United States v. Velarde-Gomez*, 269 F.3d 1023, 1027–33 (9th Cir. 2001) (en banc), that admission of the defendant's silence in the face of post-arrest, pre-*Miranda* accusations of criminal conduct violated the Fifth Amendment. But in *United States v. Frazier*, 408 F.3d 1102, 1109–11 (8th Cir. 2005), *cert. denied*, 546 U.S. 1151 (2006), the Eighth Circuit approved substantive use of such silence. That case began with a roadside search of the defendant's rental truck. When officers told the defendant he was under arrest on drug charges, he said nothing. At trial the prosecutor argued that the defendant's silence betrayed his lack of surprise at the discovery of drugs hidden in the truck—and proved he knowingly possessed the drugs.[*]

With lower courts divided, the ultimate status of post-arrest, pre-*Miranda* silence is in doubt. On the one hand, the tenor and reasoning of *Jenkins* and *Weir* point to the substantive admissibility of such silence. Recall that those cases distinguished *Doyle v. Ohio* on the grounds that *Miranda* warnings offer an implicit "'assurance that silence will carry no penalty.'" *Weir*, CB page 446 (quoting *Doyle*, 426 U.S. at 618). Absent *Miranda* warnings, the *Jenkins* and *Weir* Courts held, silence typically is admissible to disprove facts that naturally would have been claimed if true. The Justices who ruled against Genovevo Salinas seem likely to approve evidence of silence in this context. Again Justice Alito could lead the Chief Justice in declaring that absent an express claim of the privilege against compelled self-incrimination, a defendant's silence readily supports the inference that he had nothing good to say for himself. And again Justice Thomas could argue that a prosecutor's comment on a defendant's silence is not the sort of compulsion to speak against which the Fifth Amendment protects. But Justice Thomas now will hold that ground alone, without Justice Scalia by his side. And Justice Kennedy no longer will sign on with Justice Alito.

---

[*] For a critique of *Frazier* see Frank R. Herrmann & Brownlow M. Speer, *Standing Mute at Arrest as Evidence of Guilt: The "Right to Silence" Under Attack*, 35 AM. J. CRIM L. 1, 16–21 (2007).

Against these three votes, Justice Breyer again could lead Justices Ginsburg, Sotomayor, and Kagan in noting that "most[] Americans are aware that they have a constitutional right not to incriminate themselves." Indeed he could argue that whatever doubt Americans might have about their rights when speaking with police officers *out* of custody, they are keenly aware that their rights ripen in some way on arrest. An arrestee's silence, even in absence of police interrogation, therefore should be deemed an invocation of her right against compelled self-incrimination.

With the Justices thus split, much turns on Justice Scalia's successor, Neil M. Gorsuch, and on Justice Kennedy's eventual replacement. As it seems Justice Gorsuch has not encountered this question or similar questions in the past, he would be ruling in this realm for the first time.

(These materials follow page 692 of the casebook.)

OHIO V. CLARK: *Case Note*

In June 2015 the Supreme Court at last addressed the long-festering matter of child victim testimony in abuse prosecutions. With startling unanimity the Justices ruled that very young children almost never speak with the sort of prosecutorial intent that would render their words testimonial. The result represents a triumph of clarity in the often-muddy realm of Confrontation Clause caselaw. But for those defendants who face charges of abuse supported by a small child's confused or inarticulate hearsay, *Ohio v. Clark*, 135 S. Ct. 2173 (2015), delivered a troubling defeat.

The Facts[1]

Defendant Darius Clark, known as "Dee," lived in Cleveland with his girlfriend, T.T., and her two children—L.P., a boy not quite three and a half, and A.T., a twenty-two-month-old girl.[2] T.T. claimed Clark often sent her to Washington, D.C., to work as a prostitute. When T.T. went on one such trip on March 16, 2010, she left her children in Clark's care.

The next day Clark dropped L.P. at a local Head Start preschool. Seeing blood in the boy's eye, an assistant teacher, Ramona Whitley, asked, "What happened?" "I fell," the boy

---

[1] I have drawn these facts from the opinions of the United States Supreme Court, the Ohio Supreme Court, and the Ohio Court of Appeals. *See Ohio v. Clark*, 135 S. Ct. 2173 (2015); *State v. Clark*, 137 Ohio St. 3d 346 (2013); *State v. Clark*, 2011-Ohio-6623 (Ohio Ct. App. 2011).

[2] Justice Alito's majority opinion for the Supreme Court puts the boy's age at three years and the girl's at 18 months. But the children's birthdates, as noted by the Ohio Court of Appeals, suggest these figures are at least imprecise. L.P. was born on Sept. 26, 2006, and his sister on May 17, 2008. Their injuries were discovered on March 17 and 18, 2010. *See State v. Clark*, 2011-Ohio-6623, at ¶¶2, 3.

answered. When Whitley pressed him—"How did you fall and hurt your face?"—he repeated, "I fell down." Whitley looked at the boy more closely and saw "[r]ed marks, like whips of some sort," on his face. Concerned, she took L.P. to see the class's lead teacher, Debra Jones.

Jones noted the boy's bloodstained eye and some "redness" around his neck. "Whoa, what happened?" she asked. "Who did this? What happened to you?" L.P. "seemed kind of bewildered," Jones later testified. "He said something like Dee, Dee." The boy "almost looked uncertain, but he said, Dee." Unsure if the boy understood her questions, Jones pressed him: "Is he big or little?" L.P. answered, "Dee is big."

Jones took L.P. to the office of her supervisor, who raised the boy's shirt and saw red marks on his body. The supervisor directed Whitley to call 696-KIDS, a state-run hotline for reporting suspected child abuse. This call complied with Ohio's mandatory-reporting law, which requires teachers, daycare workers, doctors, and others to report suspected cases of child abuse or neglect to either a public child services agency or a peace officer. Such reports must be made "forthwith" and must include any "information that might be helpful in establishing the cause of the injury." Failure to make a mandated report can trigger civil and criminal liability. OHIO REV. CODE §§ 2151.421(A)(1), (C), (M); 2151.99(C).

The next day a social worker found L.P. and his younger sister at Clark's mother's home and took them to a hospital. A doctor saw bruises and abrasions on L.P.'s body consistent with having been struck by a linear object. A.T.'s injuries included burn marks, two black eyes, a swollen hand, and hairline sores suggesting braids had been ripped from her head. Facing repeated questioning by two social workers, a police detective, and his maternal grandmother and great aunt, L.P. consistently blamed Clark for the children's injuries.

Procedural History

A grand jury indicted Clark on five counts of felonious assault and two counts each of child endangerment and domestic violence. After a pretrial competency hearing at which L.P. took the stand, the trial judge declared the boy, then four years old, incompetent to testify. Ohio Rule of Evidence 601(A) declares, "Every person is competent to be a witness except . . . children under ten years of age, who appear incapable of receiving just impressions of the facts and transactions respecting which they are examined, or of relating them truly." When asked at the hearing about his birthday, his sister's age, and the adults with whom he'd lived, L.P. answered first one way, then another. The trial court ruled, "He will not be able to testify as a witness."

Yet the trial court rejected Clark's motion in limine to exclude L.P.'s various out-of-court statements naming "Dee" as his attacker. Ohio Rule of Evidence 807(A) creates a hearsay exception for statements of a child under twelve describing sexual or physical abuse if the child's testimony is not "reasonably available," there is "independent proof" of the sexual or violent act, and the trial court finds "particularized guarantees of trustworthiness" of the child's out-of-court statements. Applying this rule, the trial judge admitted all seven of L.P.'s hearsay allegations—those spoken to Whitley, Jones, two social workers, a police detective, and L.P.'s grandmother and great aunt. The trial jury convicted Clark on all but one count of felonious assault, and the court imposed prison sentences totaling twenty-eight years.

The Ohio Court of Appeals reversed. Of most significance here, the court deemed testimonial L.P.'s hearsay statements to his preschool teachers. The court emphasized Whitley's and Jones's status as mandatory reporters: "[W]e find that the primary purpose of Jones and Whitley questioning L.P. was to report potential child abuse to law enforcement. Both teachers testified that their obligation to report is mandatory. . . . Therefore, we conclude that L.P.'s statements to Whitley and Jones were testimonial and improperly admitted at defendant's trial." *State v. Clark,* 2011-Ohio-6623, ¶35 (Ohio Ct. App. 2011).

Though the appeals court also held that admission of L.P.'s statements to the social workers and police detective violated Clark's confrontation right, the state appealed only the ruling regarding the preschool teachers. On this score the Ohio Supreme Court affirmed by a four-to-three vote. The majority followed the Court of Appeals in stressing the teachers' status as mandatory reporters: "At the time Jones questioned L.P., she acted as an agent of the state for purposes of law enforcement because at a minimum, teachers act in at least a dual capacity, fulfilling their obligations both as instructors and also as state agents to report suspected child abuse . . . ." Having deemed schoolteachers, if mandatory reporters, to be "state agents," the Ohio high court deployed the primary-purpose test developed in *Davis v. Washington* and *Hammon v. Indiana,* 547 U.S. 813 (2006), and applied in *Michigan v. Bryant,* 562 U.S. 344 (2011) (CB 627), to govern the admissibility of statements made during police interrogations. "Because the circumstances objectively indicate that no ongoing emergency existed and that the primary purpose of the questioning was to establish or prove past events potentially relevant to a later prosecution," the court reasoned, "the statement L.P. made to his preschool teacher is testimonial in nature, and its admission into evidence violated Clark's right to confront witnesses under the Sixth Amendment to the United States Constitution." *State v. Clark,* 137 Ohio St. 3d 346, 347 (2013).

Three dissenting justices, led by the court's chief, cast Whitley's and Jones's concerns in a different light. "[T]he teachers questioned L.P. about his injuries to protect L.P. and possibly other students from additional injury, and to maintain a secure and orderly classroom in which learning could take place. No objective witness could reasonably believe that the interviews served a prosecutorial purpose rather than a protective one." *Id.* at 356 (O'Connor, C.J., dissenting).

At the Supreme Court

In a resounding setback for criminal defendants charged with child abuse, the United States Supreme Court slapped down the reasoning and ruling of the Ohio high court. All nine Justices reached this result, albeit by three somewhat different routes.

Writing for six members of the Court, Justice Alito concluded that "neither the child nor his teachers had the primary purpose of assisting in Clark's prosecution." That was true despite the teachers' obligations under Ohio's mandatory-reporting law. L.P. spoke "in the context of an ongoing emergency involving suspected child abuse," Alito wrote. His preschool teachers rightly wondered if it was safe to send the boy home with Clark and therefore needed to know the cause of his injuries. "[T]heir questions and L.P.'s answers were primarily aimed at identifying and ending the threat," not at "gather[ing] evidence for Clark's prosecution." Their conversation was moreover "informal and spontaneous," factors the Court has identified in *Bryant* and elsewhere as indicating out-of-court statements are nontestimonial. That the teachers were mandatory reporters under Ohio law mattered little because "[l]ike all good teachers, they undoubtedly would have acted with the same purpose whether or not they had a state-law duty to report abuse."

In the course of reaching this arguably predictable result, Justice Alito dropped some unexpected and noteworthy comments. It is familiar doctrine, he said, that the Confrontation Clause extends no protection against admission of nontestimonial statements. "But that does not mean that the Confrontation Clause bars every statement that satisfies the 'primary purpose' test. The Court has recognized that the Confrontation Clause does not prohibit the introduction of out-of-court statements that would have been admissible in a criminal case at the time of the founding." Here Justice Alito referred to the forfeiture doctrine elaborated in *Giles v. California*, 554 U.S. 353 (2008) (CB 619), and the admission of dying declarations, reserved for later decision in *Crawford v. Washington*, 541 U.S. 36, 56 n.6 (2004) (CB 602). But Alito's next sentence seemed to open a far wider gap in Confrontation Clause protection than these narrow exceptions to the *Crawford* framework might suggest: "Thus, the primary purpose test is a necessary, but not always sufficient, condition for the exclusion of out-of-court statements under the Confrontation Clause."

Justice Alito added that *Clark* presents the Court with a "question we have repeatedly reserved: whether statements to persons other than law enforcement officers are subject to the Confrontation Clause." The Court "decline[d] to adopt a categorical rule," but advised that "[s]tatements made to someone who is not principally charged with uncovering and prosecuting criminal behavior are significantly less likely to be testimonial than statements given to law enforcement officers." What is more, "[s]tatements by very young children will rarely, if ever, implicate the Confrontation Clause," for "it is extremely unlikely that a 3-year-old child . . . would intend his statements to be a substitute for trial testimony." Here Justice Alito perhaps spoke too strongly. It's likely a videotaped interview of a young child by a police detective, commissioned by prosecutors as "an out-of-court substitute for trial testimony" should the child prove unable to testify at trial, would strike many judges and Justices as testimonial evidence. *Bryant*, 562 U.S. at 358 (CB 630).

The Concurrences

Joined by Justice Ginsburg, Justice Scalia concurred only in the Court's judgment. There is no need to ask whether the teachers' reporting obligation rendered them the effective equivalents of investigating officers, Justice Scalia wrote, because the child's statements would have been nontestimonial even if made to police officers in a similar setting. The child's "primary purpose here was certainly not to invoke the coercive machinery of the State against Clark. His age refutes the notion that he is capable of forming such a purpose."

Having reached this simple conclusion, Justice Scalia took pains to reject Justice Alito's suggestion that satisfying the primary-purpose test is not always a sufficient condition for excluding testimonial out-of-court statements under the Confrontation Clause: "[T]he primary-purpose test sorts out, among the many people who interact with the police informally, *who is acting as a witness and who is not*. Those who fall into the former category bear testimony, and are therefore acting as 'witnesses,' subject to the right of confrontation. There are no other mysterious requirements that the Court declines to name."

Also concurring only in the judgment, Justice Thomas hewed to his longstanding understanding of the solemn and highly formalized nature of testimonial statements. Addressing statements to private persons, such as L.P.'s teachers, Justice Thomas advocated "the same test . . . that I have employed for statements to agents of law enforcement, assessing whether those statements bear sufficient indicia of solemnity to qualify as testimonial." L.P.'s words were not sufficiently solemn, he said. "They were neither contained in formalized testimonial materials nor obtained as the result of a formalized dialogue initiated by police."

Though all three opinions were brief and wrestled with rather narrow questions, *Clark* offers cause for both debate and consternation. That is true along three dimensions.

Defining Testimonial Statements

In recent cases, Justice Alito wrote, the Court has "labored to flesh out what it means for a statement to be 'testimonial.'" The Court advanced toward that goal in *Clark*, yet still fell short of setting out a single, all-purpose definition of a testimonial statement. Helpfully Justice Alito invoked the now-familiar primary-purpose test: "Because neither the child nor his teachers had the primary purpose of assisting in Clark's prosecution, the child's statements do not implicate the Confrontation Clause and therefore were admissible at trial." In embracing the primary-purpose test in a setting at least one step removed from a police interrogation, the Court hinted but did not decide that the test may apply more generally. Nor did the Court decide whether the test should turn on the perspective of the declarant, the interrogator, or both. By concluding that neither L.P. nor his teachers aimed primarily to aid the prosecution, the Court neatly ducked this long-lingering question.

For their part Justices Scalia and Ginsburg retreated from their bold insistence in *Michigan v. Bryant* that "[t]he declarant's intent is what counts." (CB pages 639, 642.) Writing in *Clark* for himself and Justice Ginsburg, Justice Scalia declared that "L.P.'s primary purpose here was certainly not to invoke the coercive machinery of the State against Clark." Then he added, "Nor did the teachers have the primary purpose of establishing facts for later prosecution. Instead, they sought to ensure that they did not deliver an abused child back into imminent harm." At no point did Justice Scalia say whose perspective, whether child's or teachers', should predominate.

Justice Thomas, meanwhile, remained resolute. His notion of the realm of testimonial hearsay hardly has wavered since he first announced in *White v. Illinois* in 1992 that "the Confrontation Clause is implicated by [out-of-court] statements only insofar as they are contained in formalized testimonial materials, such as affidavits, depositions, prior testimony, or confessions." (CB page 593.)

No member of the Court embraced Clark's attempt to focus the primary-purpose test on "whether *a jury* would view the statement as the equivalent of in-court testimony. [Emphasis added.] The logic of this argument," Justice Alito reasoned, "would lead to the conclusion that virtually all out-of-court statements offered by the prosecution are testimonial." Because the prosecution would not offer statements that did not tend to prove the defendant's guilt, the jury could view all hearsay statements presented by the state "as a substitute for in-court testimony."

Assessing *Crawford's* Impact on Criminal Defendants

In the casebook at pages 689 to 692 I ask whether *Crawford* and its kin have helped or hurt criminal defendants. After *Clark* it seems clear that defendants in child abuse prosecutions will fare a good deal worse under *Crawford* than under the old regime of *Ohio v. Roberts*, 448 U.S. 56 (1980).

Roberts made the hearsay accusations of absent declarants admissible against the accused if those accusations bore adequate "indicia of reliability." (CB page 590.) "Reliability can be inferred without more," the Court wrote, "in a case where the evidence falls within a firmly rooted hearsay exception." Hence a child's excited accusation, made within minutes or hours of an attack, might have been admitted under *Roberts* despite the child's absence from trial—and so too a child's statement to a doctor or nurse made for purposes of medical treatment.

When a child's out-of-court statement did not fall within a firmly rooted exception, the *Roberts* doctrine deemed the hearsay "presumptively unreliable and inadmissible for Confrontation Clause purposes" unless supported by "particularized guarantees of trustworthiness." (*Idaho v. Wright*, CB 590.) This branch of the *Roberts* framework figured prominently in child abuse prosecutions. As children commonly delayed reporting abuse until any excitement or medical need had passed, their statements often gained admission at trial only through a residual exception or a specially enacted hearsay exception for statements of child victims similar to Ohio Rule of Evidence 807(A). (*See* page 525 above.) Residual exceptions, as the Supreme Court ruled in *Idaho v. Wright* (CB pages 590–91), are not firmly rooted, nor are child-victim hearsay exceptions, which first emerged in the United States in 1982.

When assessing whether a child victim's statements bore particularized guarantees of trustworthiness, the *Wright* Court proved hard to satisfy. The Justices found no such guarantees where a two-and-a-half-year-old girl leveled her accusation in response to a doctor's brashly leading questions: "Does daddy touch you with his pee-pee? Do you touch his pee-pee?" The Court deemed the child's statements wrongly admitted and reversed the defendant's abuse conviction.

Whorton v. Bockting seemed to consign to history any such constitutional review of the reliability of challenged hearsay. Boldly, even proudly, the Justices unanimously declared that "*Crawford* eliminat[ed] Confrontation Clause protection against the admission of unreliable out-of-court nontestimonial statements." (CB 618.) Yet in recent years, as I've noted in the casebook at pages 671 to 674, five Justices have embraced a statement's reliability as one touchstone of its constitutional admissibility.

Perhaps catching these Justices' hints, Clark's counsel strived to persuade the Court of the unreliability of L.P.'s claim that "Dee" inflicted the abuse revealed by the boy's injuries. Here Clark attacked on four fronts:

- First he hinted openly that it was L.P.'s mother, T.T., and not Clark, who beat the two children. She had beaten her *other* children, Clark alleged, and had beaten L.P. and A.T. in the past. In one incident T.T. had whipped L.P. with her purse strap. Though T.T. was in Washington engaging in prostitution when the children's injuries were discovered, L.P. and A.T. had been in her care the previous afternoon and evening. When told of the children's injuries, T.T. remained in Washington and did not return to Cleveland until extradited five months later. Brief for Respondent, *Ohio v. Clark*, No. 13-1352 (Jan. 7, 2015), at 8–9, 14.

- Clark alleged that the questions posed to L.P. by Whitley, Jones, and others were both leading and ambiguous. "When L.P.'s teacher first asked him 'Who did this,' she also simultaneously asked 'did he get a spanking?' . . . Instead of asking open-ended questions seeking clarification, . . . the teacher followed-up with strongly suggestive reinforcement: 'What did you say? Dee? Dee did this?' . . . Teacher Jones acknowledged that she never specified what she was asking about." *Id.* at 46.

- Facing such poorly crafted questions, L.P. responded with understandable confusion. Witnesses said he "looked uncertain" and "bewildered." He answered "something like Dee, Dee," but the teachers felt unsure if he understood their questions. And even if L.P. had said clearly that Dee abused him, Clark argued, "it is unclear whether he was talking only about his face or whether his allegation included the injuries later found on his chest and torso." *Id.*

- Finally Clark stressed the trial judge's determination that L.P. was incompetent to testify. "The Ohio Supreme Court has never explained how a child incapable at the time of trial of receiving and relaying accurate information or understanding the duty to tell the truth could previously have made accusatory statements having 'particularized guarantees of trustworthiness' such that cross-examination would be futile." *Id.* at 6–7 (quoting OHIO R. EVID. 807(A)(1)).

These arguments found an audience before the Supreme Court. At oral argument several Justices voiced concern about L.P.'s reliability in pegging "Dee" as his attacker. Justice Kagan posed the problem plainly:

This is a statement that's going . . . to have great consequence . . . . It's going to function as the most relevant kind of testimony imaginable: it's an accusation. In a case like this, there are two potential parties that could be accused. Essentially, this is fingering one of them, and it's being done by a three-year-old. And—and the question of whether that's a particularly reliable way to choose between which of these two potential people did it is like a little bit scary.

Having stated the point bluntly, Justice Kagan threw up her hands: "all of what I said seems to be—or most of what I said at least—seems to me kind of irrelevant to the question that we ask under the primary-purpose test. And what do we do with that lack of fit?" Transcript of Oral Argument, *Ohio v. Clark*, No. 13-1352 (U.S., Mar. 2, 2015), at 40–41.

Sharing Justice Kagan's concern, Justice Kennedy asked the state's counsel, "Suppose you prevail," and the Court deems L.P.'s statements to have been nontestimonial. "Isn't there still a question as to whether or not this is hearsay that is so unreliable that it violates the Confrontation Clause . . . and/or the Due Process Clause and we remand for that?" *Id.* at 7. And Justice Sotomayor pressed Clark's counsel: "But . . . you haven't raised a Due Process argument. . . . [Y]ou're fighting the unreliability here, but you're not raising the right challenge." *Id.* at 50.

Yet by the time the Justices issued their opinions, any concern about the potential unreliability of L.P.'s accusation had fallen from the case. None of the three opinions pondered the issue, and none explored possible due process arguments for excluding unreliable hearsay.

Instead all three opinions suggested that the statements of *young* children—children too young to appreciate the role their words may play in future prosecutions—face no constitutional obstacle to admissibility. That is true even if the statements bear clear signs of unreliability; even if the declarants never face cross-examination; and even if the declarants are deemed incompetent to testify because they "appear incapable of receiving just impressions of the facts and transactions respecting which they are examined, or of relating them truly." OHIO R. EVID. 601(A).

Perhaps in some future case the Justices will restore under the Due Process Clauses of the Fifth and Fourteenth Amendments some of the screening for unreliability that the *Crawford* Court condemned under the Confrontation Clause. Perhaps too the Court will rule in some future case that children of a particular age—say, five or six or seven—are presumptively capable of understanding the prosecutorial role their words could play. For now, however, the upshot of *Clark* is this: in the fraught realm of child abuse prosecutions the words of children too young to anticipate their prosecutorial use and too young to perceive events accurately or relate them truly may be received without cross-examination or constitutional scrutiny. Though Justice Scalia referred in *Clark* to the reign of *Ohio v. Roberts* as a "halcyon era for prosecutors," it's defendants who came up losers in *Clark*.

Surveying the Future of the Crawford Doctrine

On a quick read *Clark* suggests that the future of the *Crawford* doctrine is bright. All nine Justices accepted that the critical question before the Court was the one framed by *Crawford*: whether L.P.'s statements to his preschool teachers were testimonial. All nine deemed L.P.'s words nontestimonial and therefore, in accord with such rulings as *Davis* and *Bockting*, concluded that the Ohio Supreme Court had erred in holding that their admission against Clark had violated his confrontation right. And eight Justices agreed that the primary-purpose test of *Davis*, *Hammon*, and *Bryant* supplied the proper measure of the testimonial nature of L.P.'s words. Justice Thomas's disagreement on this front is familiar and longstanding and hardly disturbed the seeming harmony that otherwise prevailed among the Justices.

Meanwhile, a conflict that had been brewing among the Justices seemed to cool, as Justices Scalia and Ginsburg backed away from their insistence in *Michigan v. Bryant* that "[t]he declarant's intent is what counts." (CB pages 639, 642.) Justice Scalia's opinion in *Clark*, like Justice Alito's, concluded that because neither L.P. *nor* his teachers acted primarily to advance a future prosecution, the child's statements were nontestimonial. And *not one* Justice invoked the arguable unreliability of L.P.'s statements as grounds to exclude them under the Confrontation Clause. That is, there was no rearguard effort to revive the reliability-focused framework of *Ohio v. Roberts*.

Yet despite this seeming harmony, Justice Scalia's opinion brimmed with annoyance at Justice Alito. Spying in Alito's majority opinion an "aggressive hostility to precedent that it purports to be applying," Scalia pointedly concurred only in the judgment. Yet Alito's offending words seem harmless enough. In the course of a cookie-cutter recap of the Court's confrontation caselaw, Justice Alito reviewed the *Roberts* rule of reliability. "In *Crawford* v. *Washington*," he continued, "we adopted a different approach."

This innocuous line touched a nerve. "[W]hen else," Justice Scalia demanded, "has the categorical overruling, the thorough repudiation, of an earlier line of cases been described as nothing more than 'adopt[ing] a different approach'—as though *Crawford* is only a matter of . . . preference, and the old, pre-*Crawford* 'approach' remains available?" Pointing a finger at Justice Alito, Scalia charged: "The author unabashedly displays his hostility to *Crawford* and its progeny, perhaps aggravated by inability to muster the votes to overrule them."

Here we learn two things: The Justices apparently have vetted the question of overruling *Crawford*. And only three Justices—Scalia, Thomas, and Ginsburg—bothered to distance themselves from an opinion Justice Scalia called "unabashedly . . . hostil[e]" to *Crawford*. Perhaps these facts predict that one day soon the Justices may overhaul or even overrule *Crawford*.

But if *Crawford* stands on shaky ground, it somehow has held that same sandy turf ever since four Justices cleaved from the pro-*Crawford* ruling in *Melendez-Diaz v. Massachusetts* in 2009. (*See* CB pages 617, 646.) And after *Ohio v. Clark* it is not at all clear what would replace *Crawford* if it falls. L.P.'s statements cried out for scrutiny on grounds of their unreliability. It seems quite unlikely they could have survived the *Roberts* regime's demand for "particularized guarantees of trustworthiness." But in *Clark* all nine Justices deemed those statements properly admitted without devoting so much as a footnote to the question of their reliability. So it is hard to say where the *Crawford* doctrine could go from here.